THE MYSTICISM OF THE PASSION
IN ST. PAUL OF THE CROSS

MARTIN BIALAS

The Mysticism of the Passion in St. Paul of the Cross

(1694–1775)

An Investigation of Passioncentrism in the
Spiritual Doctrine of the Founder of the
Passionist Congregation

With an Introductory Word by
Professor Jürgen Moltmann

IGNATIUS PRESS   SAN FRANCISCO

Adapted from the German original:
Das Leiden Christi beim hl. Paul vom Kreuz
1694–1775
© 1978 Paul Pattloch Verlag
Aschaffenburg, Germany

Cover design by Roxanne Mei Lum
Cover art by Christopher J. Pelicano

© 1990 Ignatius Press, San Francisco
ISBN 0–89870–295–5
Library of Congress catalogue number 90–81768
Printed in the United States of America

This book is dedicated
in deep gratitude
to my fellow religious and former superior
Father Andreas Schmidbauer.

CONTENTS

FOREWORD

This book is based on research accepted by the Catholic Faculty of Theology of Regensburg University as a dissertation in the summer semester of the year 1977. In order that it be published in German it was slightly modified in some places, and some additional revisions were made for the English edition.

I express my gratitude especially to my professors J. Cardinal Ratzinger and the late J. B. Auer, who supervised this work by means of gentle and treasured advice in 1977–78, the year of its first publication in German.

I would also like to express my gratitude to my fellow religious and to my former superior, Fr. Andreas Schmidbauer, C.P., who permitted this study.

I thank, too, all who have cooperated in preparing this text for its publication in English. I especially thank Peter Gregory Anastasis for his translation of this work into English; Rev. Eugene Selzer, S.T.D., for his translation of difficult German passages; Rev. Philip C. Fischer, S.J., for his translation of Latin passages; Rev. Thomas F. O'Meara, O.P., and Rev. Thomas McGonigle, O.P., for their translation of key Taulerian concepts; Rev. Silvan Rouse, C.P., for his translation of difficult Italian passages; Sr. Mary Frances Lavin, C.P., for her editorial work; Sr. Mary Veronica Loring, C.P., for proofreading; and all the Passionist Nuns of Ellisville, Missouri, for their support, especially Mothers Mary Joseph Geisler, C.P., and Marie Thérèse Merlet, C.P., who permitted this translation and persevered in seeing it through to its conclusion.

Schwarzenfeld, Germany
Passionist Monastery
June 18, 1990

Rev. Martin Bialas, C.P.

INTRODUCTORY WORD

It is a great joy for me as an Evangelical theologian to be writing the Introduction for a book written by a Catholic theologian. This is a good omen about the status of ecumenism, even though such a collaboration is no longer an unusual occurrence in Germany today. Theological collaboration has replaced older controversy, and this has become a "given" for our generation. What is important about this book by Fr. Martin, however, is its subject matter: the mysticism of the passion of Christ in St. Paul of the Cross. I admit with pleasure that a new ecumenical dimension was opened for me when, in October 1973, I was invited to participate in an International Congress on *La Sapienza della Croce Oggi* (the wisdom of the cross today) organized by the Passionist Order in Rome. The lectures, discussions, life in the monastery, and writings of the founder of this Congregation all showed me how deeply ecumenical community is engraved in the heart of Christian piety and in the core of Christian belief in the Crucified; this ecumenical longing has always been and will ever remain, despite all our divisions and misunderstandings.

"The nearer we come to the cross, the nearer we come to one another"; the Church lives by this truth, and in this truth the Church is already one. That is why we need nothing so urgently as the "wisdom of the cross". In order to learn this, it is profitable to listen to the voices of the great theologians of the cross. St. Paul of the Cross is one of these. Unfortunately he is unknown in Germany, especially in the Evangelical Church. Notwithstanding, he does have something to say. What he does say concerning Christ's passion as "the wonder of divine love" is something that speaks through the centuries, since it is the liberating and redeeming truth of God and of man. We must express our gratitude to Fr. Martin, because he is the man who has presented this first comprehensive and scientific monograph about St. Paul of the Cross. We must thank him, too, that—like the founder of the Passionists—he writes in simple language and with a good style. Historians and theologians are not the only ones who will benefit from this book. Whosoever ponders the passion of Christ will read this monograph with benefit.

The seventeenth century marked not only the beginning of the age of "confessional absolutism", fierce religious wars, and baroque orthodoxies but

13

also marked the beginning of the age of the enlightenment—and of mysticism. The significance of the mysticism movements at that time has often been overlooked. Nevertheless, they cut right across the confessional lines of the churches and captured the attention of the educated as well as of the masses. They were ecumenical, and they were popular. Both elements are important in this context.

To begin his study of St. Paul of the Cross, the author first directs our attention to the spiritual and religious climate of eighteenth-century Italy. He begins with a study of Jansenism and quietism, the French writings of Madame Guyon and Bishop Fénelon's well-known defense of her. He notes the deep influence of the Spanish mysticism of Teresa of Jesus and John of the Cross upon St. Paul of the Cross and shows that, underlying the influence of both contemporary French and Spanish mysticism, there appeared again and again the impact of Tauler, with his exceedingly influential sermons.

Let us take only one of Paul's (1694–1775) contemporaries, namely, the lower Rhineland mystic and writer Gerhard Tersteegen (1697–1769), in whom we find the exact same influences: The quietistic mysticism of Madame Guyon and the writer Bernières-Louvigny, knowledge of Carmelite mysticism, and, in the background, Tauler's influence. Although Tersteegen was Reformed, we find many similarities in both men's lives. For example, Tersteegen did not part with the institutional Church but participated by way of soul-searching, writing letters, and composing hymns dealing with the interiorization of faith. Tersteegen, also like Paul, longed for a community but was not able to find it in the parishes of his Reformed Church. Since there was no Evangelical monastic order in his time, he founded *Pilgerhüte* (Pilgrim's Refuge) and strengthened other Christian associations like *Stillen im Lande* (The Silent in the Country) and *Gottesfreunde* (Friends of God) in the lower Rhineland. His piety and his theology of mystical experience leaped over confessional lines and overcame Protestant orthodoxy. His hymns may be found even today in both Evangelical and Catholic hymnals.

If someone were to compare Paul of the Cross and Gerhard Tersteegen from a theological point of view, he would detect, as a matter of course, differences between their ideas of and feelings toward the ecclesial positions of their Churches. What would be found would be a son of the Evangelical-Reformed tradition and a son of the Roman Catholic one. Moreover, he would remark that each of these two sons recognized this and found nothing false therein. Nevertheless, mystical experience led both of them to a more profound dimension of the Christian Faith, one that went beyond any specific limitation or qualification. Furthermore, the language they used to make this mystical experience intelligible for others went beyond confessional divisions existent even prior to the Reformation, and each represented a link in the uninterrupted tradition of the mystical theology of the Middle Ages. Both

spoke of becoming crucified in spirit "with Christ", and thereby of the necessity of being wholly "emptied". Both expressed the feeling of being absorbed in the "ocean" of God's love. Both returned to the certainty of a "divine nativity". Both, from that stage on, saw that everything is "in God" and "God is in everything". Both experienced God's filiation. This mystical experience effected a common state of being in the innermost depths of their souls, a state they described in an almost identical term: *sonship*.

Also paralleling the life of Paul of the Cross is that of another Evangelical contemporary, Nikolas Graf von Zinzendorf (1700–1760), who was responsible for the renewal of the *Herrnhuter Brüdergemeinde* of the *Brüder-Unität* (Unity of Brethren) and founder of the Moravian churches. It was this community that revived young Luther's theology of the cross, which radically opposed the naturalistic theology and atheism of the Renaissance. It is worthwhile mentioning here that Luther's theology of the cross was rooted in Tauler's thinking, as Luther's footnotes indicate. It was due to Zinzendorf that Protestantism was penetrated with this mysticism of suffering, unheard of until then: The cross and the gestalt of the Tortured One with his stigmata are a revelation of God's love. The author rightly refers to Graf's thirty-four homilies so similar to the saint's own meditations on the passion and to the "Litany of the Wounds". With the same dedication with which Paul of the Cross devoted himself entirely to popular missions, Zinzendorf devoted himself to the rediscovery of the voluntary fellowship of Church viewed as a single community, that is, as a base ecclesial community, as it is called today. Both of these men suffered by reason of the separation of Christ's one Church and could not accept the division. Why not? Because both of them had experienced, recognized, and believed in the deep unity of Church as a logical consequence of Christ's suffering and death.

What strikes us when we compare Paul of the Cross, Gerhard Tersteegen, and Graf Zinzendorf are the following:

1. A profound experience of faith, a mystical experience, which goes beyond traditional and collective determinations of faith.
2. An active turning to the people that is the fundamental experience of Church, which goes beyond ritual and institutional determinants of ecclesiastical life.
3. A profound immersion in Christ's passion and death, that is, the experience of the cross, which goes beyond dogmatic sentences of Christology and soteriology.

The mystical experience, the fundamental experience, and the experience of the cross all possess the same unity. And, in this unity, the Crucified One constitutes the center: whoever recognizes him recognizes the abyss of God's love, so full of sorrows; whoever recognizes him will recognize that people

for whom he suffered and died. The mysticism of the cross does not belong to an elite; it leads rather to a solidarity with abandoned people. Being close to the people does not necessarily mean populist when it flows out of the pain of Christ and is a participation in and communion with his passion.

The author has rightly referred, in many places, to the present-day importance of this mysticism of the passion and of the theology of the cross. I too believe that the "theme of the cross" represents the main theme of our time. This eighteenth-century charismatic of the cross can help us remain centered on what is essential from the standpoint of ecumenism, ethics, or theology. He does this in at least three respects.

1. *Ecumenism under the sign of the cross.* The unity of the Church represents basically a desideratum having no root in political or ecclesiastical calculation. Nor is it, in the final analysis, a desideratum arising from favorable circumstances. Naturally today, the divided world needs a common Christian avowal of the one God of peace, and woe to the Church if she has supported divisions and obstinacy in the face of this clear mission. Naturally, confessional disunity will always be inexplicable, especially for Christians from the so-called confessionally mixed countries. This is not the first time external need makes requisite the unity of Christendom within the framework of a Church in which we all may believe. The true unity of the Church becomes manifest wherein her true origin also lies, namely, in Christ's submission to a death on the cross for the atonement of the world. Christ's agony and death represent the birth pangs of the Church, who, learning of this atonement with God, places herself at the disposal of a service dedicated to the atonement of the world. The messianic people have been born from the passion of the Messiah. In other words, what always keeps the Church alive and assures her community is the Church's fundamental mystery, the redeeming death of Christ on the cross. The more profoundly the various Churches and Christian communities understand this mystery of the cross, the better will they also understand the mystery of community within the framework of the one Church of Christ. The wisdom of the Church and of her leadership can and may be, in the question of ecumenism, none other than the "wisdom of the cross", however "insane" this may appear to current thinking. Upon the Crucified One lies the promise of the resurrection and of the kingdom; and this has application for the whole inhabited earth, for all those small and great anxieties and perturbations against which this promise contends: *Ave Crux—unica Spes* (Hail, O cross, our only hope)!

2. *The imitation of the cross today.* For many Christians, in numerous countries of the world, to follow the cross today means to experience "dying with Christ"; and this is not dying from a spiritual or mystical point of view but a bodily martyrdom consisting of calumny, persecution, arrest, condemnation, and death. Our century is again a century of persecution against Christians, a

century of martyrs. Christians who until now have not experienced this persecution still must have the fact clear in their own minds: Christian faith means the imitation of Christ—to take up and bear his cross and to give their lives for him.

The "imitation of Christ" is a theme that has been neglected in the Protestant church, whether state or independent, since the time of the Reformation. Since the so-called enthusiasts had developed the belief and ethic of an imitation of Christ, orthodox Protestants suppressed it. Often, too, a state ethic or a state religion was imposed instead. Against the background of Hitler's Reich the "imitation of Christ" was rediscovered and, together with it, the relevance of the Sermon on the Mount from a practical and theological point of view. This was done above all by Dietrich Bonhoeffer. Since then, too, the imitation of Christ in the Catholic Churches of Europe is no longer a duty solely for those in monastic orders, in consequence of which ordinary churchgoers thought themselves free of the radical demands of Christ.

Mysticism and martyrdom again draw very close together. "Mystical death" and "divine rebirth" begin to be not only spiritual but also political experiences. The many existing parallels between mysticism and martyrdom offer us food for thought. In what kind of cell did John of the Cross experience the "dark night of the soul"? It was, after all, a jail cell and not a monastic cell. Furthermore, what does a monastic cell have in common with a jail cell? Poverty, solitude, suffering, temptation, death . . . and all these have been experienced by many a Christian in many a prison. The blessing-bestowing presence of the resurrected Christ, who lives in us and with us, is experienced in the actual fellowship of his suffering in jails and in torture chambers. The focal point of the mystical experience of the passion of our Lord, and of the presence of the Spirit of the Risen One, is today, for many men, the dungeon where they have been thrown on account of their positive confession and opposition to evil. Is not this martyrdom the serious outgrowth of that mysticism? Conversely, must not mystical spirituality give advice and preparation for just such a political contingency? The mystical experience of God may actually become a bridge between the cross on Golgotha and corporeal martyrdom. To practice the silence, the solitude, the prayer, the resignation in the desert of emptiness, and lastly mystical death—all these belong necessarily to the imitation of Christ. From these experiences many people are even able to say: the more profound the mystical absorption, the more free the political resistance. More than that, the more otherworldly the experience of God, the more down to earth and unselfish the imitation of Christ through love.

3. *The theology of the cross.* Last but not least we must set the cross in the center of an ecumenical theology. The cross in itself is not only a characteristically Christian symbol but also the measure of Christian theology. All the statements about Christian theology, and about God, man, and the world,

may be considered only in the perspective of the crucified Christ, since otherwise they are refuted by his death on the cross. What this means for the Christian doctrine of salvation is always presented in new outline in the history of Christian theology. What this means for the *Christian doctrine of God* has not yet been exhaustively thought through. From the theology of the cross there follows the doctrine of the Trinity. Does a doctrine about God's passion and suffering also follow from this? Today, we find a striking convergence among Catholic and Evangelical theologians, who embrace the mystery of the Trinity and of the cross.

From the theology of the cross there results also an *anthropology* of sinful, ill, imprisoned, poor, and oppressed man; of man in his reality revealed by Christ on the cross: *ecce homo!* But what sort of anthropology has the courage to start with this displaced reality, since it is a disdained, human one? More than anywhere else, this tendency of an *anthropologia crucis* is especially preeminent in the "theology of liberation". In the long run, there results from the theology of the cross the model of Christian hope toward a future of divine glory and human freedom. However, what sort of *eschatology* has hitherto taken truly seriously the fact that "the Lamb who was slain" is the very one to whom the kingdom of divine glory and the kingdom of freedom both belong?

All lines of Christian theology converge as in a focus in the Crucified One, and from out of the Crucified One everything here is baptized in the bright light of redemption. The closer a theology locates its center to the cross, the more all encompassing will be its circumference in society, history, and nature.

We may truly aver that Fr. Martin Bialas' work *The Mysticism of the Passion of Christ in St. Paul of the Cross* is an important and helpful contribution for understanding the "word of the cross", how it is enacted in the history of the founder of the Passionist Congregation, and also how it teaches us today the manner in which we are to listen, understand, think about, and live the cross.

Jürgen Moltmann

PREFACE

This book serves as an introduction to the spiritual and theological thinking of St. Paul of the Cross, founder of a religious Order, pastor, and spiritual teacher, who placed the suffering and crucified Lord at the center of his life. Theologically, his thinking was dominated less by the forcefulness of concepts than by his own existential encounter with God. This fact assumes importance when considering the source and originality of his teaching. Well worth discovery, too, is the inner logic of his thought, which this book by its method tries to render more systematic.

To appreciate the spiritual and religious thinking of this historically concrete personality, the reader needs to know something of the factors that influenced his life and development. Part One is devoted to this purpose. First, it sketches in a few strokes the life and work of the founder of the Passionist Congregation. Then, it describes the source material which he himself wrote. Next, it examines his era and its surroundings in greater detail, giving more emphasis to the environs in which the founder worked.

Because Paul's theological background was based mostly on his extensive reading of the classical authors of Christian spirituality, it is both interesting and important to examine their impact upon his writings. In this analysis, the most difficult question to answer is: In what way did the thinking of John Tauler influence the spiritual and religious thought of our saint? The answer focuses chiefly on those aspects of Tauler's work which had a specific and permanent effect on Paul of the Cross.

While Part One has as its subject the personality of St. Paul of the Cross and his reliance on theological Tradition, Part Two deals with the passioncentrism of his spiritual doctrine. To study this, it was necessary to identify characteristic features of Paul's spiritual and theological thought and then to put into bold relief his main charism: meditation upon the suffering and crucified Lord and preaching him to all. More specifically, a twofold approach was used: examination of the centrality occupied by contemplation of *Christus crucifixus* in the life and work of this "saint of the cross" and identification of the essential characteristics of his passion mysticism, apparent most of all in his writings. To summarize these briefly: the passion of our Lord is seen princi-

pally as an expression of God's love for all people, and to participate in this passion is to suffer and die with Jesus, which above all means to accept and bear all unavoidable, innocent suffering or sorrow as the cross of Christ.

Closely related to the idea of entering into or participating in the passion and death of Jesus is the concept of mystical death. In two of his letters, St. Paul of the Cross refers to having written a manuscript on this topic.[1] For two hundred years this document was considered lost. Then, in June of 1976, a copy was thought to have been found in the Passionist nuns' monastery in Bilbao, Spain.[2] As a result of this discovery, a discussion of the text was included in the original German edition of this book. Since then, however, I have had serious doubts about whether or not the document found is truly a copy of a manuscript composed by the saint.[3] Consequently, I have included in this edition a paper delivered by me in Zaragoza, Spain, in 1980. Its thesis is that St. Paul of the Cross is not the author of the treatise on mystical death.

The last chapter of the book deals with the place of the resurrection of Jesus

---

[1] "Ecco o mia figliuola in Gesù Cristo, che s'avvincina il tempo dell'anniversario della di lei morte mistica, fatta nella santa solenne professione l'anno scorso e di cui io fui testimonio ed ebbi la sorte di celebrarne la sacra funzione .... Vorrei che lei leggesse spesso quella direzione della morte mistica, che io le mandai in quel libbricciolo manoscritto, che so che molto le gioverà." / "Behold, oh my child in Jesus Christ, the anniversary of your mystical death is approaching, of that death by which you had died when you made [your] holy, solemn profession last year, to which I myself was a witness and [one] so happy to celebrate that sacred occasion [with you]. . . . I would like you to read frequently those directives on mystical death which I sent you in the form of a booklet written in my own hand, since I know you will benefit from them a lot" (L 3:610, Sept. 10, 1762, to Sr. Maria Magdalen of the Seven Sorrows, a Carmelite of Vetralla).

The second reads, "Gode sentire che il noviziato vada bene e tutt'il resto. Le compiego la "Morte Mistica" che le promisi, ma bisogna farla copiare ben corretta, rivoltando il genere e termine femminile in mascolino, e il nome di Monastero in Ritiro." / "I have heard with delight that the Novitiate and all the rest go well. I am sending you 'Mystical Death' which I had promised you. It must be carefully transcribed with attention to change it and its endings from feminine to masculine gender and to replace the word 'monastery' [a term then indicative of a nuns' convent] to 'retreat' " (L 3:442, May 17, 1765, to Fr. Peter of St. John, a fellow Passionist).

[2] The text itself uses feminine endings, and in it the word *monastery* is used instead of the word *cloister*. The publication begins and ends with the same words that were used to describe and record it in that part of the process that dealt with the saint's manuscript on mystical death.

Published by Passionist Fr. Paulino Alonso Blanco, the complete title of the twenty-four-page edition is "San Paolo della Croce, Morte Mistica ovvero Olocausto del Puro Spirito di un'Anima Religiosa".

[3] See M. Bialas, "¿Quién es el autor de la 'Muerte Mistica'?" (100 *Años de Historia Pasionista* [BO–CE 3], Zaragoza, 1980, pp. 513–24. See below, p. 246–58, for its English translation. Also see the response of A. M. Artola in *La Muerte Mistica* (Deusto, Spain: Universidad de Deusto, 1986, esp. pp. 95–168). While this part of Fr. Artola's work addresses my doubts, it does not resolve them.

in the spiritual teaching of Paul of the Cross. His stress on Jesus' passion and death may give rise to the supposition that his conceptualization of the paschal mystery is skewed with too little consideration being given to the resurrection. For this reason a separate chapter is devoted to Paul's implicit resurrection theology.

This attempt to clarify the saint's belief concerning the resurrection, as presented in his writings, appears compulsory for the following reasons: The passion and death of Jesus Christ is not an endpoint or goal in itself but only a step to his resurrection and glorification. Representing as it does a united whole, the paschal mystery must be considered both from the standpoint of crucifixion and resurrection if a complete view of it is to be obtained. To what degree a full view of Christ's passion is found in the theology of St. Paul of the Cross is examined in the last chapter. This is a disputable question, unclarified in any preexisting theological treatise on the life of the founder of the Passionist Congregation.

Of interest is the method used in the present study. This is especially important when considering Part Two, which is devoted to the saint's focus upon Christ's passion. Primary sources[4] for this analysis were his spiritual diary, the Rule of the Congregation, and approximately two thousand letters written, for the most part, for the purpose of spiritual direction. Although these sources contain an abundance of material on the theological thinking of this charismatic of the cross, it was necessary to distill from this large sea of source material the principles and passioncentric formulations of his doctrine.[5] Furthermore, in my search for the inner consistency of Paul's doctrine, I have always considered myself bound by the sources. Close attention was also paid so as not to err in terms of systematizing his doctrine arbitrarily, a mistake easily made when dealing with such a mosaic work. This is one reason why the saint's own nomenclature has been used for headings and subheadings.

The following considerations are of some import too when discussing the methodology of this research. The main object of this study, the saint's doctrine, is not to be presented primarily as a result of a solely rational analysis arrived at, for the most part, in an abstract and objective way as if it were a pure chemical distillate. Rather, the method used is an attempt to impart to others the saint's own subjective, existential experience of God, which he himself used to bring others to a deep encounter with God. His purpose in writing and communicating with others compels us, therefore, to consider his statements not only in terms of their thought content but also in terms of their contemplative meaning and to penetrate this meaning to its depths. Only in

---

[4] The most important secondary sources are the protocols of the beatification and sanctification processes of St. Paul of the Cross. Records of testimonies of 121 individuals fill over 11,600 folio pages written on both sides.

[5] Conclusions reached are the result of data collection, classification, and analysis.

such a manner is it possible to grasp the profundity of his thought. The difficulty, however, in fully understanding a spiritual teacher and a mystic and in interpreting him authentically becomes increasingly clear.

The aim of this study is to explain, with the greatest possible authenticity, the personality of St. Paul of the Cross and his passioncentric doctrine.[6] In this way, too, I hope to draw attention to a great saint and charismatic all too little known in the English-speaking world, a founder of a Congregation, a spiritual teacher considered among "the most important teachers of the eighteenth century"[7] by any serious student of spiritual and religious literature, and a man referred to as "the greatest mystic in eighteenth-century Italy".[8]

During the course of this five-year study, the question of the relationship between reflection upon and experience of faith *within* theology arose again and again. An analysis of this question and the insights attained are presented in the Excursus.

It was considered appropriate that this investigation be approached with neither the psychological distance of a problem solver nor with the appealing indifference of an objective observer. In fact, my respect and esteem for this master of the inner life grew as my familiarity with the richness of his spirituality deepened and my awareness of the profoundly religious dimensions of his writings increased.

Because this work has for its object the deeply intimate, spiritual, and religious thinking of a saint, of a man who lived and thought within a framework of intense union with Christ, it is understandable, even necessary, that theological reflection (on his thought) be carried out within the context of a lived Faith. I have, therefore, allowed myself to be guided by two basic concerns:

1. To do an academically and theologically sound investigation which satisfies the requirements of scientific criticism;
2. To allow for the introduction of my own personal convictions regarding matters of faith.

The rationale for the latter is that it is permissible for a theologian to interject his own convictions in the act of theologizing since they are those of an

[6] In order to preserve the original meaning and profundity of his thought, the saint's own words are often used in the presentation of his definitions.

[7] J. De Guibert writes, "S. Paul de la Croix y apparaît, en effet, à côté de S. Alphonse de Liguori, au premier rang des maîtres de la vie spirituelle, en ce dix-huitième siècle . . . " / "Indeed, beside St. Alphonsus Liguori, St. Paul of the Cross appeared in the first rank of the masters of the spiritual life of the eighteenth century . . . " ("Le journal de retraite de Saint Paul de la Croix", *RAM* 6 [1925]: 26–48, here 26f).

[8] M. Viller remarks in great astonishment, " . . . c'est manifestement le plus grand mystique et le plus grand spirituel italien du XVIIIe siècle . . . " ("La volonté de Dieu dans les lettres de Saint Paul de la Croix" (*RAM* 27 (1951): 132–74, here 134).

authority in the field. To state this even more strongly, there are times when they ought to be expressed.

In this research the reader is introduced to the mystery of *Christus patiens et crucifixus* (the suffering and crucified Christ) and, by means of the theology and spirituality of the founder of the Passionists, is strengthened in faith in the Crucified and Risen One and in conforming the self to him.

Finally (and perhaps this is an exaggerated claim), my intention was to adhere to the primary objective of St. Paul of the Cross: to keep before the eyes of all the figure of Christ. To preach the "word of the cross" was the basic reason that impelled Paul to found the Passionist Congregation, a monastic community whose members take a fourth and special vow to reflect upon and to preach the crucified Christ. The fulfillment of this vow was for this author, as a spiritual son of St. Paul of the Cross, the strongest reason for conducting this research.

PART ONE

The Personality of St. Paul of the Cross and His Reliance on Theological Tradition

CHAPTER I

Introductory Research

Theological tradition may be viewed as bipolar. Besides an abstract, argumentative theology learned in school, there is a practical and implicit theology which does not consist so much in the definition of abstract notions as in the fulfillment realized in the lives of deeply spiritual persons.[1] Each of these poles, independent in itself, has an important function in the healthy development of theological thought. If theology is not to remain self-contentedly estranged from life but rather to retain a historically concrete relevance, then of necessity it must be open to the acceptance of impulses which, at times acting as correctives, emanate from the theological tools employed by great Christian personalities.

We find such a theology implicit in the existential and perfected Christianity of St. Paul of the Cross (1694–1775), in whom we find some quite extraordinary characteristics. The source from which his thoughts and actions flow and from which his energy is derived is contemplation of the suffering Christ. Implicit in his theology of the passion are powerful elements of a speculative-mystical and an affective-spiritual theology, with his original contribution being the balance he achieves between these two polar positions.[2]

Hans Urs von Balthasar characterizes this aspect of St. Paul of the Cross' theology as "the most surprising example of a true fusion" of these two trends in theology.[3] Although not a scientifically educated theologian capable of enriching theology by thoughtful treatises or epoch-making statements, Paul nevertheless expresses himself in such a way in his spiritual diary[4] and in his

[1] See H. U. von Balthasar, *Mysterium Paschale*.

[2] These two elements, so powerfully present in the spirituality of St. Paul of the Cross, are rooted, on the one hand, in the writings of Tauler and St. John of the Cross and, on the other hand, in the writings of St. Teresa of Jesus and St. Francis de Sales.

[3] "Mysterium Paschale", 156, n. 6.

[4] E. Zoffoli, *Diario Spirituale di S. Paolo della Croce*. The German translation is *Das geistliche Tagebuch des heiligen Paul vom Kreuz* by Martin Bialas with Preface by J. Ratzinger (Aschaffenburg, 1976). The English translation of the diary used in this text was translated by

letters[5] that the same might be said of his work as K. Rahner said of the *Spiritual Exercises* of St. Ignatius: "There is a pious literature which antecedes theological reflection which is more original than the latter, [and] which is wiser and more experienced than the school of wisdom. . . . "[6]

It is being admitted more and more that theology has no reason for operating solely on the basis of pure theological reflection with methods limited to those of logic and argumentation. Rather, drawing on the experience of theological debate, there is an existentially engaged theological method based on the observation that narration rather than argumentation is the predominant literary form of the Gospels. Thus, the phrase *narrative theology* has been coined.[7] Characteristic of this theology are narratives that are lively, direct, concrete, and drawn from experience. These are precisely the characteristics that distinguish the implicit theology of St. Paul of the Cross.[8] Before giving our attention to the spiritual and theological writings of Paul of the Cross, however, it seems both necessary and appropriate to describe the life and work of this great mystic and founder of the Passionist Congregation.

THE LIFE AND WORK OF ST. PAUL OF THE CROSS

Paul Francis Danei, to be known later as Paul of the Cross, was born in northern Italy in the town of Ovada, situated about 50 km (31 mi.) northwest of Genoa.[9] Although his father belonged to an old and noble family of Alessandria,[10] over the course of years the family had been reduced to poverty.

Silvan Rouse with a preface by Stanislaus Breton. It is published in Fr. Jude Mead, *St. Paul of the Cross: A Source/Workbook for Paulacrucian Studies* (New Rochelle, N.Y.: Don Bosco Publications, 1983), 20–52.

[5] About two thousand letters have been collected and published in *Lettere di S. Paolo della Croce* by Fr. Amedeo of the Mother of the Good Shepherd (4 vols., Rome, 1924).

[6] In F. Wulf, ed., *Ignatius von Loyola*, 346.

[7] The phrase appeared in H. Weinrich, "Narrative Theologie", 329–34, and J. B. Metz, "Kleine Apologie des Erzählens", 334–41.

[8] We shall speak about this in more detail in several places later on.

[9] The actual birthplace and home of the father, Luke Danei, was Castellazzo, 10 km (6.25 mi.) south of Alessandria. In 1683, the father moved to Ovada for business purposes and remained there until 1701. In 1717 or 1718, after many changes of residence, he returned with his entire family to Castellazzo, where his own parents lived. See *Annali della Congregazione* (henceforth referred to as *Annali*), by Fr. John Mary of St. Ignatius, (28, n. 9; p. 29, n. 13. Also see vol. 1 of E. Zoffoli, *S. Paolo della Croce, Storia Critica* (henceforth referred to as *Storia Critica*), 70–155.

[10] The nobility of the Danei family can be officially traced back to the year 1393. Count Nicola Canefri, a friend and benefactor of St. Paul of the Cross, compiled the genealogical tree of the saint's family (*Storia Critica* 1: 56–69).

Hardship was no stranger to the Danei household. Both birth and death were major events in this trial-tried family. Paul was the second oldest of sixteen children, of whom eleven died in infancy.[11] Although the Daneis owned a small tobacco and dry-goods store, affairs connected with the business compelled the family to move frequently. As a result, Paul attended school very irregularly.[12]

Of great importance in Paul's spiritual growth and development was the personality of his mother, whose deep and lively faith had overcome so many difficulties. There was nothing remarkable about his younger years, however, other than the fact that Paul's childhood was spent in the midst of a truly Christian family and that he was open to the influence of his parents and the religious education they provided.[13]

It was not until 1713 that Paul faced the first great decision of his life. Impressed with a sermon by a priest or perhaps just by a private conversation with him, Paul was moved by a spirit of compunction and repentance. He made a general confession and resolved to make a radical surrender of

[11] The firstborn child, a daughter born in 1693, died after three days. Thus Paul Francis, born in January of 1694, became the eldest child of the family.

[12] The only detail we possess is that he attended the school of the Carmelite Fathers in Cremolino and, later on, another school in Genoa. See "The Acts of the Process of Sanctification: The Informative Process of Alessandria" (POA), testimony of Paul's sister, Teresa Danei. The protocols of the informative process were published in *I Processi di Beatificazione e Canonizzazione di S. Paolo della Croce* (keyword: *Processi*), vol. 2, by Fr. Gaetano dell' Addolorata. If the depositions quoted are available in published form, then the volume and page number of the text are given after the keyword *Processi*, as exemplified in the following footnote.

[13] It is appropriate to point to two events from the childhood of St. Paul of the Cross that at first seem unimportant, even trivial, but actually have a great effect upon his later life. It is known that his mother would read to her ten children the lives of the ancient Christian monks and hermits (POV, 106v., testimony of Fr. John Mary; *Processi* 1:31). These stories greatly impressed little Paul, and he, together with his younger brother, John Baptist, tried to imitate the lives of these men (*Storia Critica* 1:104). This childhood experience may very well have been the source of Paul's later motivation to live as a hermit for a few years. At the same time, tradition tells us that the mother's devotion to the crucified Christ played an important role in the way she reared her children. It was this "devotion" that the children tried to apply in their own fashion whenever they had pains or when she herself had to demand something unpleasant of them. At such times, she would put a cross into their hands, saying, "Behold, my children! How much Jesus Christ suffered!" (POO, 269v., testimony of the priest Salvatore di Gennaro; *Processi* 2:234; *Storia Critica* 1:104). The image of the crucifix left a deep impression in the psyche of the children. When we find in the later life of St. Paul of the Cross that the passion of Christ is at the center of his thought, we cannot help but recall the education provided by his mother. Of course, this is not the only or the complete explanation of the passioncentrism found in the life of the founder of the Passionists. Still, today one knows, from the results of depth psychology, what a great importance early childhood experiences have in the later life of a person.

his life to God.[14] He subsequently called this event his conversion to penitence.[15]

Some years later Pope Clement XI called for a crusade against the Turks.[16] Since Paul desired to die a martyr, he assumed the crusade was his call from God, and he enlisted as a volunteer. After a while (a few months, perhaps spent in barracks and camps), Paul came to the conclusion that this was not the proper way to serve God.[17] In the year 1716, he returned to his parents' home, where he spent the next four years energetically helping his father in business.

1. On the Way to Becoming the Founder of a Congregation

At this point, we are entering that period in the life of St. Paul of the Cross in which the history of his vocation as founder of a Congregation takes shape. Because there are original documents preserved[18] in which Paul himself speaks of the progression in his vocation to establish a monastic order, we are not forced to deal with vague conjectures and inferences made from secondary sources. Paul's vocation matured in four stages. Initially, he felt called to retire into solitude... to wear a poor, black tunic... to live in extreme poverty... to lead a life of penance.[19] In other words, he felt called to live as a hermit.

The second stage of Paul's vocation consisted of an inspiration to "gather companions who would live together and work to strengthen souls in the fear

[14] The testimony of Fr. John Mary states, "... all'udire un discorso familiare del parroco, sentissi talmente commosso e compunto, che risolvette di darsi ad una vita santa e perfetta." / "... after listening to a familiar sermon of his parish priest, he was so moved and filled with compunction that he resolved to begin to live a holy and perfect life" (POV, 107v.; Processi 1:32).

[15] See Lettere di San Paolo della Croce, published by Fr. Amedeo of the Mother of the Good Shepherd, 4:217, or, in abbreviated form, L 4:217, Dec. 1720, to Bishop Gattinara: "... due anni circa dopo che il mio amantissimo Iddio m'ha convertito a penitenza, passando ... " / "... as about two years have passed since my so beloved God converted me to penitence ... "

[16] See L. Freihern v. Pastor, Geschichte der Päpste, 15:81–84, 89–91.

[17] In the beatification processes, Paul's sister Teresa gives us the following account of his decision to leave the army: "Ma per una ispirazione avuta da lui in una chiesa, in cui si faceva l'orazione delle quarant'ore nel giovedì grasso, se n'è venuto via." / "He would not have changed his mind but for an inspiration received by him in a church, where forty hours' devotion was being conducted on Holy Thursday" (POA, 115v.; Processi 2:25).

[18] This history of his vocation is described in the Preface to the Congregation's Rule written by Paul of the Cross (L 4:217–20, Dec. 1720, to Bishop Gattinara).

[19] "... di ritirarmi in solitudine... di portare una povera tonica nera... viviere con altissima povertà... fare vita penitente" (L 4:217, Dec. 1720, to Bishop Gattinara).

of God".[20] In his own words, Paul admitted he did not pay any attention to this call at the beginning. After a series of repeated inner lights, however, God strengthened in Paul "the desire and interior impulse to gather companions and, with the approval of Mother Church, to found a Congregation with the name 'the Poor of Jesus' ".[21]

The third stage was considered to have been reached from the moment Paul arrived at the inner certainty that he was called by God to found a religious community. Only when the specific and extraordinary mission of the new Congregation was made clear to him was the fourth and last stage of Paul's vocation reached. More will be said later about this stage.

As early as 1715 (a date deduced from assertions made in quoted material), Paul had a firm desire to retire as a hermit. Upon his return from military service, however, he remained with his family for several more years because of his parents' appeal for his assistance. Decisive in the life of Paul as hermit and as founder of the Passionist Congregation was the date November 22, 1720. On that day, he bid farewell to his family and received from the hands of his former confessor and spiritual director Bishop Gattinara of Alessandria the garb of a hermit, which became the black tunic of his Congregation.[22]

Paul spent the next six weeks, from November 23, 1720, to January 1, 1721, living under the poorest of conditions in a small storage cell adjacent to the sacristy of the church of St. Charles in Castellazzo. These weeks served as a preparatory retreat for his life as hermit and founder. Told by Bishop Gattinara to record his feelings and inner experiences which occurred during this time, Paul of the Cross (as he later came to be known)[23] did so. An authentic transcript of this spiritual diary[24] has been preserved and is most revealing. For example, in an entry of the first day Paul encapsulated the basic principle underlying his entire spirituality: to be crucified with Christ.[25]

---

[20] "... che mi venne un altra ispirazione di radunare compagni per stare poi unito assieme per promuovere nelle anime il santo timore di Dio" (as above, L 4:218).

[21] "... mi ha dato Iddio maggior desiderio ed impulso di congregare compagni, e con la permissione di santa madre Chiesa fondare una Congregazione intitolata: I poveri di Gesù ... " (L 4:219f.).

[22] See Annali, 34f.; POV, 131v.–132v., testimony of Fr. John Mary; Processi 1:42. This episode may be considered the birth of the Passionist Congregation, since by now Paul had very decidedly planned to obey the call he had received from God.

[23] He spoke of this title in a letter (L 2:92, July 29, 1746, to Fr. Fulgentius).

[24] The spiritual diary was published several times. We refer especially to the critical edition, Diario Spirituale, with its Introduction and Commentary by E. Zoffoli. Its German edition, Das geistliche Tagebuch des heiligen Paul vom Kreuz, with Preface by J. Ratzinger, was translated by Martin Bialas. The English translation used here was translated by Silvan Rouse with a preface by Stanislaus Breton. It is published in Fr. Jude Mead, St. Paul of the Cross: A Source/Workbook for Paulacrucian Studies. All three sources will be cited in each footnote that pertains to the diary. As an example, see n. 25 below.

[25] At the end of this entry it is written, "Non desidero saper altro, ne gustar alcuna

During this forty-day retreat, St. Paul of the Cross wrote the Rule of the new monastic community whose members were to be called the Poor of Jesus. The original manuscript, according to his own statement, was written in an amazingly short time of five days (December 2–7, 1720).[26] Unfortunately, it has not been preserved for us. At the conclusion of these days spent in prayer, penance, and fasting, Paul wanted to leave for Rome to obtain papal approbation of this Rule. Bishop Gattinara, however, thought that the time was not yet ripe and succeeded in dissuading the young founder.

In the following months, Paul lived as a hermit in the vicinity of Castellazzo, where he taught catechism to children, preached at Masses on Sundays, and even conducted a mission for the people at the request of his bishop.[27]

In September 1721, Paul journeyed to Rome to obtain papal approval of the Rule for his new Congregation. In this he met with great disillusionment, being chased away by the Quirinal's vigilant guards, who did not spare the use of rough words.[28] After that encounter, an audience with the pope was scarcely to be considered.

Upon his return to Castellazzo, Paul accepted his first recruit, his brother John Baptist, who too received the black habit of the Congregation from the hands of Bishop Gattinara and was thus clothed as a hermit (today we could say as a Passionist). Until the end of his life in 1765, John Baptist would remain his brother's most faithful companion.

During the three years that followed, the two brothers tried to make the Congregation's Rule the norm regulating their lives. According to the Rule, members of the "Poor of Jesus" had the duty not only to strive for personal sanctification but also to engage in active work for the good of their neighbor.[29] The Danei brothers did this by going out from the hermitage where they lived to help with such pastoral activities as teaching catechism and preaching in neighboring parishes.

---

consolazione, solo che desidero d'esser crocifisso con Gesù." / "I do not desire to know anything else, or to taste any consolation. I desire only to be crucified with Jesus" (*Diario Spirituale*, 53; *Tagebuch*, 57; Rouse, 29). Paul's biblical reference is Gal 2:19.

[26] In a comment on the Rule contained in an authentic transcript (L 4:221), Paul writes, " . . . scrivevo tanto presto, come vi fosse stato in cattedra uno a dettarmi, mi sentivo venir le parole dal cuore." / " . . . I wrote as quickly as if someone were dictating to me; I felt the words coming from my heart."

[27] POV, 134v.–136v., testimony of Fr. John Mary; *Processi* 1:44f.; *Annali*, 37f.

[28] Fr. John Mary testified to the following during the informative process at Vetralla: " . . . e richiese udienza dal papa Innocenzo decimo terzo, die santa memoria, ad uno de' palatini, quale gli rispose bruscamente, dicendo: 'Sapete quanti birbi capitano tutto dì? Andate, andate!' " / " . . . and he asked a palatine guard to be admitted for an audience with Pope Innocent XIII, of holy memory; but the former refused him abruptly, saying, 'Do you know how many rogues come here day after day? Clear out! Clear out!' " (POV, 137v.; *Processi* 1:45).

[29] See *Regulae et Constitutiones*, 2.

Still preoccupied about the need for papal approbation of the Rule, Paul, this time accompanied by his brother, set out again for Rome. Despite his desire for written authorization, Paul only obtained Pope Benedict's verbal approval to gather companions.[30] By now Paul had become convinced that, if the Rule were ever to receive full approbation, it would be necessary for him to remain in Rome, where he could find friends and benefactors capable of negotiating requirements of approbation with the Holy See. He therefore welcomed the invitation of Cardinal Corradini to care for invalids in the newly built Hospital of St. Gallicano, where Paul confronted human suffering in a dramatic way.[31]

Besides assigning them to nurse the ill, the hospital director, Don Emilio Lami,[32] also charged the brothers with the spiritual care of both patients and staff. This they accomplished with such satisfaction that Don Emilio encouraged them both to study for the priesthood. After a short period of instruction in pastoral theology at a Franciscan college at St. Bartholomew's on the isle of Tiber, they were ordained to the priesthood by Pope Benedict XIII in St. Peter's Basilica on June 7, 1727.[33]

The two Danei brothers enjoyed religious freedom at the hospital. They wore their black habits, and, insofar as possible, they ordered their day in conformity with the Rule of the Poor of Jesus. Still, it was not the kind of life to which Paul felt called. Having found influential friends who were willing to press for the approval of the Congregation's Rule at the Holy See, Paul decided it would be best to leave the matter of approbation in their hands and for him to leave both the hospital and Rome.[34]

[30] When the pope consecrated an altar in the Church of St. Mary in Domnica (also called Navicella), Paul with the help of Cardinal Corradini took advantage of the opportunity to present his concern to the pontiff.

[31] Cardinal Corradini ordered the construction of a hospital for the treatment of persons with skin diseases. To assure its future, he also established a religious community whose members bound themselves to look after the medical and spiritual needs of the patients. The Danei brothers entered this community and took vows according to the Rule of this new society. But they had a special intention, which the cardinal granted them, of forming their lives according to the Rule of the "Poor of Jesus".

[32] Emilio Lami was both a priest and physician, a dermatologist who specialized in the treatment of certain skin diseases and who developed a new and highly successful treatment method (*Storia Critica* 1:331–35).

[33] Because of the paucity of sources, it is difficult to draw definite conclusions about the themes, duration, or depth of their studies. All that is known is that a Franciscan priest, Fr. Dominic, a professor of morals who taught for a time at the Missionary College and who belonged to its monastery, was their teacher.

[34] Cardinal Corradini obtained the necessary dispensation from the vows from the Roman Penitentiary.

2. Establishment of the Congregation

Quite a few years earlier, the two Danei brothers had withdrawn to a hermitage on Mount Argentario, a promontory situated on the coast about 150 km (93 mi.) northwest of Rome. They loved the site, its seclusion and picturesque beauty; now they decided to reestablish themselves there, only this time in a different hermitage. Thus, this mountain in Tuscany became the home of the first Passionist community.

Within a short period of time, however, it became apparent that the tiny hermitage did not offer sufficient space to accommodate all who wanted to live the spirit of St. Paul of the Cross. They decided to build the Congregation's first church and monastery, and, overcoming immense difficulties, they attained their goal. The church and cloister were consecrated in 1737.[35]

Still awaiting solution was the problem most basic to the new Congregation: approbation of its Rule. After examination by a commission of cardinals and the inclusion of some modifications, it was approved by Pope Benedict XIV on May 15, 1741,[36] more than twenty years after its original formulation.

Henceforth, the name of the new religious Congregation was *Congregatio Sanctissimae Crucis et Passionis Domini Nostri Iesu Christi* (Congregation of the Most Holy Cross and Passion of Our Lord Jesus Christ). Even this Congregation's name indicated its distinctiveness and special mission: Its members were to contemplate and preach the cross and passion of our Lord Jesus Christ. It is at this time that Paul arrived at the fourth and last stage in the maturation of his vocation. Above all, it consisted in his charism, his special grace: to make known, through contemplation and preaching, the passion and death of Jesus to a sinful world.

This charism of the founder was institutionalized in the form of a special vow noted in the oldest preserved transcript of the Rule in a chapter entitled "On the Fulfillment of the Vow of Promoting Devotion to the Passion and Death of Our Lord Jesus Christ, among Believers".[37] Paul's extraordinary vocation was to increase in all an awareness of the suffering of Christ. This vocation remains to this day the mission of his Congregation in the Church and world. Because of this, each Passionist makes, over and above the three

---

[35] See Martin Bialas, *Im Zeichen des Kreuzes, Leben und Werk des heiligen Paul vom Kreuz, des Gründers des Passionisten*, 38–41.

[36] A number of Rules would be approved during Paul's lifetime. In 1746, the same pope issued (his approbation in the form of) a brief. In 1769, Clement XIV gave his approval in the bull *Supremi apostolatus*. Finally, on Sept. 15, 1775, some weeks before the founder's death, Pope Pius VI issued a new bull, *Praeclara virtutum exempla*, in which he explicitly confirmed the Passionist Congregation as an institution of the Roman Catholic Church.

[37] See *Regulae et Constitutiones*, 56, col. 1.

traditional vows of chastity, poverty, and obedience, a fourth vow to preach Christ Crucified in a special way.[38]

St. Paul of the Cross desired that his new Congregation be exempt, that is, that it be directly under pontifical rather than local episcopal authority. He further wanted its members to make solemn rather than simple vows. Notwithstanding his desires, the 1741 approbation put the new Congregation under episcopal authority,[39] and its members were permitted simple vows only.

Not content with this solution, St. Paul of the Cross again petitioned for the privileges of exemption and solemn vows. Five years later, in 1746, the Rule was again approved in a brief[40] issued by Benedict XIV in which Passionists were no longer placed under episcopal authority, the new Congregation having been granted its desired status of exemption.[41] The privilege of making solemn vows, however, was not granted.

Since the newly built monastery on Mount Argentario could no longer accommodate all who wanted to enter, the Passionists began building two

[38] In all probability the fourth vow was not a constituent part of the original Rule. There are three arguments in favor of this supposition:
1. The letter to Bishop Gattinara of Dec. 1720, which we have already quoted many times and which serves as an introduction to the original Rule (no longer preserved), does not make any reference to a fourth vow, even though the importance of meditating on the passion of our Lord Jesus Christ is mentioned repeatedly.
2. In the same letter, the founder calls the new Congregation "I poveri di Gesù" (the Poor of Jesus) and not the Congregation of the Passion of Our Lord Jesus Christ.
3. Some notes of Troia's Bishop Cavalieri, dated 1725 and therefore written after the original manuscript of the Rule have been preserved. These mention the "oblighi principali della Congregazione" (main obligations of the Congregation) and explicitly cite only three vows ("tre voti"). See *Regulae et Constitutiones*, 151–54.

[39] In Chapter 2 of the Rule, the following is written: "Le case, o siano Ritiri di questa Congregazione, dovranno esser soggetto immediatamente in tutto e per tutto al Vescovo nella di cui diocesi sarà fondata la Casa, or sia Ritiro, ed al Superiore della medesima Congregazione." / "The houses, better said the retreats of this Congregation, must be immediately subject, in all and for all, to the authority of the bishop in whose diocese the house or retreat is built and to the authority of the superior of the same Congregation" (*Regulae et Constitutiones*, 4, col. 2).

[40] Since 1741, St. Paul of the Cross had been trying to obtain a brief approving the Rule. Nevertheless, the members of the commission expressed their opinion as follows: " . . . posse approbari praevio Rescripto Sanctitatis suae, non autem praeviis Litteris in forma Brevis, cum haec Congregatio recens sit, et paucos habeat Clericos, qui eidem Congregationi adscripti sint . . . " / " . . . [the commission] can approve the previous rescript of His Holiness but [it cannot issue] a letter in the form of a brief because the Congregation is new and has only a few clerics enrolled in it . . . " (*Acta Congregationis* 11 (1931): 257).

[41] Chapter 2 of this edition states, "Domus nostrae . . . subiecta erunt Episcopo, vel Ordinario in iis dumtaxat quae ad culturam animarum Episcopo commissarum pertinebunt, *in reliquis censebuntur exempta.*" / "Our houses . . . will be subject to the bishop, but they will render to him an account of pastoral care only; *as to the rest they are exempt*" (*Regulae et Constitutiones*, 4, col. 3).

new monasteries.[42] Organizational growth was needed too. With the issuance of his brief approving the Congregation's Rule in April 1746, Pope Benedict XIV named St. Paul of the Cross the first superior general. Shortly after, Paul summoned the first General Chapter, whose members elected him superior general and entrusted him with primary responsibility for the future of the whole Congregation.

All new foundations face difficulties, and it was not long before conflicts occurred for Paul of the Cross. Mendicant monks in nearby monasteries felt their rights to solicit funds for their own upkeep jeopardized by the new monastery. By 1748, their complaint reached Rome.[43] Because the aim of the attack was to prevent the establishment of new foundations, Paul of the Cross felt compelled to defend himself and his Congregation before the authorities. He was not lacking in support. Many bishops and priests had observed the endeavors of the Passionists and supported them. Then, too, Pope Benedict XIV displayed much goodwill to the new Congregation. In April 1750, the dispute was settled by a commission of cardinals, who issued a document allowing Passionists to resume the work of establishing new foundations. Although the pope himself approved this document,[44] the attacks still did not end.

That the founder considered these attacks to be a serious threat is obvious even in subsequent years. In his letters he frequently alluded to this problem. For example, he wrote to a friend, "My distress is great, and it grows greater and greater, that now, in my old age, it will all collapse and go up in smoke."[45] Just how in the midst of such difficulties his mysticism of the cross and passion was a source of strength for him is evident from the following passage: "Pray for me, because I am in a terrible abyss of tempests with water

[42] On Mar. 6, 1744, the Monastery of the Holy Angel in Vetralla, some kilometers to the south of Viterbo, was obtained; and on Mar. 8, 1744, the Retreat of St. Eutizio at Soriano, to the east of Viterbo, was consecrated (Fr. John Mary, "Storia delle Fondazioni", *Bollettino* 4 [1923]: 272–77, 309–13, 333–38).

[43] Chapter 14 of the 1736 edition of the Rule states, "L'Ill.mo, e R.mo Ordinario della diocesi, dove sarà fondata la Congregazione, farà la carità di eleggere in ogni luogo della sua diocesi qualche servo di Dio che riceva l'elemosine dai Benefattori con raccomandarci alle loro carità, acciò al tempo del grano, vino, olio faccino quell'elemosine alla Congregazione che S.D.M. li spirerà ... " / "The most Illustrious and Right Reverend, the ordinary of the diocese where the Congregation is established, will be so kind as to choose, from within his diocese, a servant of God to receive the alms of benefactors whose charity is implored, so that alms may be given to the Congregation at the wheat, wine, and oil seasons ... " (*Regulae et Constitutiones*, 46, col. 1).

[44] See *Storia Critica* 1:840–77.

[45] " ... che i miei bisogni sono sempre più estremi e vado pensando, che nella mia vecchiaia vedrò tutto per terra ed ogni cosa andata in fumo ... " (L 1:718, June 13, 1760, to Thomas Fossi).

up to my neck, but I remain fastened to the safety plank, the holy cross, and I hope not to be wrecked."[46]

Despite the immense problems associated with the new foundations, St. Paul of the Cross succeeded in establishing five new monasteries prior to 1760. Fortunately, he did not lack men who wanted to lead lives in accordance with his spirit and the Rule he conceived.

3. Spiritual Director and Lay Missionary

St. Paul of the Cross was not only the founder of the Passionists; he was also a fervent spiritual director and lay missionary. At the age of twenty-six and as yet neither cleric nor priest, he felt called to an aposolate of leading people to a conversion of mind and heart. In his spiritual diary of December 1720, he records his "continual desire for the conversion of all sinners".[47]

This same apostolic thrust is also contained in the Rule. In the first chapter of the Rule of 1736 it is specified that one of the essential aims of the Congregation is to work for the salvation of others.[48] The founder saw in lay missions a form of ministry especially suited to this purpose.[49] In fact, the 1741 papal rescript approving the Rule for the first time designated missions as the sole purpose (*finis unicus*) of the Congregation.[50] Therefore, it is understand-

[46] "Preghi per me che sono in un abisso di tempeste coll'acqua fino alla gola, ma sto ancora attaccato alla tavola della Santa Croce, e spero non farò naufragio" (L 1:462, July 30, 1739, to Sr. M. Cherubina Bresciani).

[47] "Non mi si parte il continuo desiderio della conversione di tutti i Peccatori ... " / "The continual desire for the conversion of all sinners does not leave me ... " (*Diario Spirituale,* 71; *Tagebuch,* 87; Rouse, 34).

[48] In the 1736 edition we read, "E siccome uno dei fini principali di questa minima Congregazione consiste non solamente nell' esser indefessi nella santa orazione per loro stessi affine d'attendere alla santa unione con Dio, ma anche stradarvi i nostri prossimi, ammaestrandoli col modo più facile che si potrà in sì angelico esercizio ... " / "Since one of the essential aims of this least Congregation consists not merely in being indefatigable in holy prayer so that we may attain holy union with God but also in putting our fellow creatures on the right path by instructing them in this angelic exercise in the simplest way ... " (*Regulae et Constitutiones,* 2, col. 1).

[49] There were three reasons for this:
  1. The primary purpose of lay missions at that time was to effect a conversion of heart in those attending. This corresponded with St. Paul of the Cross' own view, the conversion of sinners being the primary purpose of his apostolate.
  2. Lay missions provided good opportunities to preach to the faithful, above all, to preach Christ Crucified.
  3. Since lay missions were of limited duration, it was possible for the priests to remain in their retreats for extended periods of time and therefore to live a life of contemplation as prescribed by the Rule.

[50] " ... quod Clerici huius Congregationis, quorum finis unicus est peragendi sacras Missiones, debeant specialiter Missiones facere, et Clericos ad praedictum effectum mittere

able why this ministry took first place in the activities of Paul of the Cross.

During the course of his life, Paul conducted approximately 180 missions[51] in over thirty dioceses in Italy.[52] The method he used was essentially that which was customary at that time. Besides the usual subject matter (sacraments, sin, death, judgment, heaven, and hell), Paul placed special emphasis on meditation on the passion of our Lord Jesus Christ, which, as prescribed in the 1736 Rule, was given each evening of the mission.[53] These meditations compensated for the severity of the sermons on the last judgment and hell, which were overly emphasized in those days.[54]

St. Paul of the Cross stressed the point that after every mission each priest must return to the monastery to recollect himself in "solitude, prayer, and fasting".[55] For him, the monastic qualities of solitude, silence, and prayer formed the essential substructure of the Congregation and its apostolate. He presents this idea very clearly in a letter written to a priest desirous of becoming a Passionist. "Our Congregation", he states, "is built on this foundation. If it were destroyed, the whole edifice would collapse, and we would be severed from that special mission given this Congregation by

---

per Locos, Oppida, et Rura in ahere minus salubri, Insulis et Regionibus incultis posita, et in quibus aliae domus Missionariorum non reperiunter, ut ita sit provisum Christifidelibus ibidem commorantibus, et Sacris Missionibus destitutis, semper tamen de consensu Ordinariorum..." / "... therefore the clerics of this Congregation, whose sole purpose is to conduct holy missions, should specialize in giving them, and clerics should be sent to preach in [various] sites, towns, and villages, except for islands and regions in sparsely populated areas that are not conducive to health unless no other missionaries are to be found; in this way they provide for Christ's faithful and for those deprived of holy missions, all always being done with the approval of the ordinaries..." (*Acta Congregationis* 11 (1931): 256).

[51] A complete and detailed listing of all the works of St. Paul of the Cross is contained in *Storia Critica* 3:1224–1419.

[52] In the year 1738, Paul of the Cross, named "apostolic missionary" by pontifical indult, was allowed to hold lay missions in all the dioceses of Italy. Paul remarked in a letter addressed to the marchioness of Pozzo, "... tanto più che giusto ora, mentre sono stato in Roma, ho ottenuto l'Indulto Apostolico per fare le Missioni in Italia." / "... all the more just now, during my stay in Rome, I have obtained an apostolic indult to hold missions in Italy" (L 1:51).

[53] Chapter 18, dealing with the fulfillment of the fourth vow, stipulates, "Li Fratelli sacerdoti che saranno abili per la santa predicazione dovranno nelle sante Missioni meditare a viva voce alli popoli la SS.ma Passione di Gesù Cristo, e ciò lo faranno avanti o dopo la predica della Missione..." / "During holy missions, the brethren priests who are skilled in preaching should meditate, aloud before the people, on the most holy passion of Jesus either before or after the mission sermon..." (*Regulae et Constitutiones,* 57f., col. 1).

[54] See E. Henau, "Riflessioni sulla predicazione di S. Paolo della Croce".

[55] To Canon Felix Pagliari of Frascati, Paul wrote, "Su tal riflesso le nostre sante Regole ci obbligano che dopo le missioni, esercizi spirituali ecc. ci ritiriamo subito nei Ritiri di nostra solitudine, per raccogliere lo spirito 'in oratione et ieiunio'." / "After the conclusion of missions, spiritual exercises, etc., we are compelled by our holy Rule to return immediately [to the] solitude [of our] retreats to recollect ourselves 'in prayer and fasting'" (L 3:418, Feb. 13, 1768).

God."[56] The founder himself very cleverly negotiated his time to allow for the dual activities of action and contemplation. He went on missionary journeys three times a year (in spring, autumn, and winter) and spent the remaining time in the monastery.[57]

Paul of the Cross and his brother John Baptist jointly led several missions. While Paul took charge of preaching, lectures, and meditations, his brother was busy conducting spiritual exercises for priests and religious.

A deep friendship existed between the two brothers.[58] For decades, John Baptist was Paul's confessor and spiritual director. When John Baptist died in August 1765, these tasks fell to Fr. John Mary, who was also the Congregation's first historian and author of the *Annali della Congregazione,* a historic work in which he described the establishment and growth of the Passionists from 1720 to 1795.[59]

4. *A Painful but Fruitful Evening of Life*

Given the abundance of suffering that was in store for him, Paul's title *of the Cross* seems particularly well chosen. Over and above spiritual sufferings,[60] which accompanied the establishment of his Congregation, serious illness often threatened his life. On several occasions he was thought to be on his deathbed. On one such occasion during the summer of 1767, he was so ill everyone thought he would die. He himself, thinking the same, prepared for death and received the anointing of the sick.[61] The illness passed, however, and he regained his strength. For Paul, these occasions of spiritual and physical suffering were opportunities to enter existentially into the mysticism of the cross and passion.[62]

[56] "Su tale fondamento è posta la nostra Congregazione; e se si getta a terra questo, è totalmente rovinato l'edifizio, perchè fuori affatto della vocazione che Dio ne ha data" (L 3:418, Feb. 13, 1768).

[57] More often than not, such a journey would take five to eight weeks. That is why many conducted missions, one after another, before returning to the retreat.

[58] Since the brothers very often worked together in apostolic endeavors, it is no wonder that John Baptist was frequently called Paul of the Cross' "shadow" (see *Storia Critica* 1:254).

[59] These *Annals,* written in Italian, were first published in 1967 with Introduction and Commentary by Fr. Gaetano (see below, pp. 60–63 of this book).

[60] From 1746 on, Paul served as the father general and therefore had the responsibility for the future of the Congregation. In his letters he would many times take his friends into his confidence and voice his inner distress to them.

[61] Paul was at death's door again in Sept. 1770 and in Jan. and July 1771.

[62] St. Paul of the Cross saw occasions of unavoidable suffering as good opportunities to participate in the passion of Jesus. See below, Chap. IV. Also see Martin Bialas, "Leiden als Gnade in der Passionsmystik des Paul vom Kreuz". In English, see Martin Bialas, "Human Suffering as Grace in the Thought of St. Paul of the Cross".

For more than twenty years, St. Paul of the Cross fought for the establishment of a monastery in Rome. Finally, in the autumn of 1766, a friend and benefactor gave him the title of a house located near the famous church of St. John Lateran. To meet the housing requirements of a monastic community, renovations were made. In January 1767, a small community of Passionists moved into this new retreat named "Hospice of the Crucified". While establishing this retreat, Paul came to know Cardinal Antonio Ganganelli,[63] who became a strong supporter of the Congregation and an intimate friend of the saint.

Two years later, on May 19, 1769, Cardinal Ganganelli was elected pope.[64] Within two or three days, the newly elected Pope Clement XIV received the congratulations of the founder in a private audience.[65] Wanting the saint to remain near him, Clement XIV invited Paul to remain in Rome. Not being able to refuse the pope's request, Paul established himself in the Hospice of the Crucified instead of returning to Vetralla, where he had been staying.

As pontiff, Clement XIV used his authority in favor of the Congregation. On November 15, 1769, he approved its Rule by a papal brief. A few days later he issued the papal bull *"Supremi apostolatus"*, giving the new Congregation numerous privileges like those of the older orders. Moreover, the Congregation was explicitly acknowledged as an official ecclesiastical institution.[66]

St. Paul of the Cross now devoted himself to the fulfillment of another important goal, the foundation of a monastery of Passionist nuns who, living a strictly enclosed contemplative life, were to support the apostolic work of the priests by their lives of prayer and sacrifice. His long-delayed desire became a reality when on May 3, 1771, eleven nuns entered the newly built monastery[67] at Corneto (Tarquinia), their Rule

[63] Fr. John Mary reported in the *Annals* that when Paul lived in Rome he met with the cardinal, for the first time, on Nov. 12, 1766, to discuss the soon-to-be-established Hospice of the Crucified. He wrote, "Visitò altresì, in questa congiuntura, il card. Ganganelli, per la prima volta, e contrassero subito stretissima famigliarità ... " / "At this point he also visited Cardinal Ganganelli, for the first time, and they immediately became very close friends ... " (*Annali*, 230).

[64] In 1766 and 1767 the saint foretold that the cardinal would become pope. Several witnesses attested to this fact during the sanctification processes. See *Storia Critica* I:1247f.; *Annali*, 230, n. 22; POV, 223v.–224v., testimony of Fr. John Mary (*Processi* I:89f.).

[65] How friendly the newly elected pope was with the founder is obvious from the fact that the pontiff would send the coach of the pontifical court to bring Paul to the Quirinal.

[66] The contents of this document may be found in *Storia Critica* I:1268–70.

[67] A decisive contribution for the foundation of the Passionist nuns was given by intimate friends of St. Paul of the Cross, the family Costantini of Corneto (today Tarquinia). They sold a part of their estate so that the monastery and church might be built.

having received prior approbation by the Holy See.[68]

While still a cardinal, Pope Clement XIV had on several occasions visited the founder at the Hospice of the Crucified. He was therefore aware of its cramped living conditions. As a result, he wanted to provide the Passionists with better lodging in Rome. Soon an occasion presented itself. The monastery of SS. John and Paul, situated on the Coelian Hill, one of the seven hills of ancient Rome, became free.[69] Wanting to assure the future of the new Passionist Congregation, the pope gave Paul the monastery, its church, and adjoining gardens. On December 9, 1773, the holy founder and a number of his brethren moved into the large monastery. From then on, this retreat became the center of the Passionist Congregation, the Generalate itself being established there.[70]

Half a year later the monastery of SS. John and Paul received a most honored guest. On June 26, 1774, the titular feast of the church and monastery, the pontiff came to pay a visit to the old and ailing founder of the Congregation.[71] This, however, was not the only time Paul of the Cross was to receive a papal visit. Nineteen days after his election, Pope Pius VI, successor of Clement XIV, attended forty hours' devotion in the basilica of SS. John and Paul and afterward visited Paul in his sickroom and talked with him at length.[72]

At the sixth General Chapter of the Passionists, held from May 15–20, 1775, Paul of the Cross, despite his failing health, was reelected general.[73] Within a few weeks it became apparent that his health had deteriorated to the point that death was imminent. On October 18, 1775, Paul, recognizing his approaching death, requested the last sacraments, after which his long life devoted to the

[68] After a second verification, the Rule was approved by a pontifical rescript on Sept. 3, 1770 (see Father Gaétan du S. Nom de Marie, *S. Paul de la Croix et la Fondation des Religieuses Passionistes; Regole e Constituzione delle Religiose della SS. Croce e Passione di Gesù Cristo* [Rome, 1927]).

[69] In the beginning, Pope Clement XIV had thought of giving the Passionists the Jesuit novitiate along with the Church of St. Andrew, both of which had become available as a result of the suppression of the Society. Nevertheless, one of the cardinals, a member of the commission dealing with the suppression, proposed that Paul of the Cross exchange the above-mentioned church for the Monastery of SS. John and Paul, once the home of the Vincentians. The pontiff assented to this. However, this proposal necessitated a long series of difficult negotiations with the Vincentians. Finally, on Dec. 7, 1773, the Vincentians moved to St. Andrew's, and on Dec. 9 the Passionists entered SS. John and Paul (Fr. John Mary, "Storia delle Fondazioni", *Bollettino* 7, [1926]: 108–15; *Storia Critica* 1:1438–64).

[70] There the Generalate has remained until the present day.

[71] See *Annali*, 294f.

[72] See POV, 215v.–216r., testimony of Fr. John Mary (*Processi* 1:85f.).

[73] See *Annali*, 297–300.

crucified Christ came to an end.[74] At his death, the Congregation numbered two hundred members living in twelve retreats.

DESCRIPTION OF SOURCE MATERIAL

1. *The Spiritual Diary*

This is the oldest preserved document of St. Paul of the Cross, written at the behest of his former confessor and spiritual director Msgr. M. Gattinara, bishop of Alessandria. In it the saint recorded his interior lights and insights that occurred during a retreat in a cell near the sacristy of the church of St. Charles in Castellazzo between the dates of November 23, 1720, and January 1, 1721.[75]

Although the original manuscript was unfortunately not preserved, a reliable handwritten copy of the diary is kept in the Passionist archives in Rome.[76] Published in 1867 for the first time,[77] it has since been republished[78] and translated into other languages. Worth mentioning are the Italian editions of Fr. Stanislao, which included a detailed commentary and appeared in Torino in 1926;[79] E. Zoffoli's critical edition of

[74] POV, 263v.–265v., testimony of Fr. John Mary (*Processi* 1:110).
Preparations for the process of beatification were begun fourteen months after his death with Pope Pius VI himself urging the priests to prepare the process (*Annali*, 312). On May 1, 1853, Paul of the Cross was beatified by Pope Pius IX, and on June 29, 1867, the same pope declared him a saint. His feast is celebrated each year on Oct. 19.

[75] See above pp. 30–33 of this text.

[76] "Archivium Generale Congregationis Passionis" (AGCP).

[77] By 1867, 166 of the founder's letters had been published in Rome by Benedict Guerra in a work entitled *Lettere scelte di S. Paolo della Croce, Fondatore della Congregazione dei Passionisti, agli Ecclesiastici.* The founder's spiritual diary was included in this selection. See *Storia Critica* I, chap. 17; *Diario Spirituale*, 28, n. 40. Also see Stanislao dell'Addolorata, *Diario di S. Paolo della Croce* (2d ed.), 3.

[78] In 1924, four volumes of letters were published in Rome by the Passionist Father Amedeo of the Mother of Good Shepherd. These contained Paul's spiritual diary and 1,884 letters written by him and preserved in the archives of the Passionist Generalate. Most were original manuscripts.
The publication of the spiritual diary of Paul of the Cross has had a far-reaching impact. The first volume of the above-mentioned collection of letters places it right at the beginning—the first and oldest letter and the most important document of the earlier years of the founder.

[79] The 1926 version is, in fact, a summary of earlier material published by Fr. Stanislao in the periodical *Bollettino della Congregazione* (Rome). The earlier references follow:
1920: 54–60, 80–82, 257–61, 283–86, 320–27
1921: 41–50, 71–78, 112–21, 136–46, 183–91, 237–44, 272–78

1964,[80] with its German translation of 1976; and three English translations.[81]

Since, on the one hand, the diary is one of the most important sources providing insight into the doctrine of St. Paul of the Cross and since, on the other hand, its original text has not been preserved, it is necessary to relate something about the copy's origin and reliability.

Paul turned the original manuscript over to Bishop Gattinara, who in turn left it in the possession of Canon Sardi, a young friend of the saint.[82] Two or three weeks prior to Paul's death, the Passionists asked Sardi to send the diary and other writings of the founder to Rome. In a letter dated October 14, 1775,[83] Sardi replied that he hesitated to send the desired documents to Rome for fear they be lost in the mail (the documents included not only the diary but also many letters written by the saint to Bishop Gattinara and to Sardi himself).[84]

Some time after the founder's death, Fr. John Mary of St. Ignatius again asked Sardi to send Paul of the Cross' writings to Rome. Sardi first deliberated with his friends, the earl of Canefri and Fr. John Baptist Stortiglioni, a Capuchin exprovincial. After both had read the request, Fr. Stortiglioni decided to send the diary along with four or five letters of the saint (addressed to Bishop Gattinara) to the Capuchin Fr. Cherubino da Voghera, who was

---

1922: 17–25, 88–92, 108–16

[80] Based as they both were on the 1867 edition, neither the 1924 edition, in which the diary was published along with Paul's other letters, nor the 1926 edition, in which the diary was published separately with a commentary included, were historically reliable editions. Basing his work on the most reliable of manuscripts, Enrico Zoffoli issued a critical edition of the diary in 1964. This text includes a review in which variants are recorded and footnotes to and explanations of the text are provided.

[81] M. Bialas, *Das geistliche Tagebuch des heiligen Paul vom Kreuz*. The English translation of the spiritual diary used in this text was that of Fr. Silvan Rouse with Preface by Fr. Stanislaus Breton. It is included in the text compiled by Fr. Jude Mead, *St. Paul of the Cross: A Source/Workbook for Paulacrucian Studies*.

[82] In a written statement made at the 1777 proceedings dealing with the saint's writings (see CIC canons 2024–48), Sardi states, "Cioè è vero, che io ho avuto e tenuto presso di me per molti anni uno scritto statomi dato e consegnato dall'or fu Monsignore Francesco Gattinara già vescovo di q.ta Città, e poi Arcivescovo di Torino, mentre io era tra i suoi famigliari, e me le ho dato a titolo di regallo . . . " / "It is true, indeed, that I had and kept near me, for some years, a manuscript given and consigned to me by Msgr. Francis Gattinara, then bishop of this town and later archbishop of Torino. As one of his friends, he gave me the manuscript as a present . . ." (*Diario Spirituale*, 24).

[83] This letter, preserved in AGCP, was published by Enrico Zoffoli in his critical edition of the spiritual diary (*Diario Spirituale*, 18–20; *Tagebuch*, 49–52).

[84] About this, Sardi writes, " . . . non giudico ben fatto di mandargli ora à Roma non tanto p. non far un troppo grosso convoglio, quanto p. non . . . dargli à qualche disgrazia." / " . . . I do not consider it prudent to send it to Rome at present since it is not only too big a parcel [to mail but also] for fear it may be lost" (*Diario Spirituale*, 19).

preaching in the cathedral at Todi.[85] Fr. Cherubino was to deliver the papers to the Passionist bishop of Todi, Thomas Struzzieri, who was then to take the documents to Rome on his next occasion to travel there.

Fr. Cherubino, however, never received the documents. Inquiries and investigations at the post offices of Alessandria, Bologna, Narni, and Todi were to no avail. The original manuscript of Paul's spiritual diary and some of his letters had been lost en route.

Fortunately, Canon Sardi was a very prudent man, and he himself had made a handwritten copy of these important papers. In a written statement, confirmed by oath,[86] Sardi testified that the respective copy was written "in his own hand" letter by letter in conformity with the original, except for superfluous errors made in the course of transcription.[87] Later this copy became the property of the Passionist Generalate in Rome, where it is preserved today.

2. The Rule of the Order

The original 1720 *text.* The original text of the Rule composed by St. Paul of the Cross during December 2–7, 1720, during the time of his retreat in Castellazzo,[88] has not been preserved in its entirety. Only its Introduction,

[85] Also preserved is a written statement in which Fr. Stortiglioni writes, " . . . mi hai poi esso Sig.r Can.co fatto tenere il d.o scritto, il quale ho io letto con somma mia soddisfazione, indi l'ho chiuso in una mia lettera diretta al P. Cherubino Maria da Voghera n.ro Capuccino . . . , allora attuale Predicatore Quaresimale nella Cattedrale di Todi, per indi consegnarlo a Monsignor Vescovo di quella stessa Città . . . " / " . . . then the canon asked me to keep the said manuscript, which I read with the greatest satisfaction. Later I put it in an envelope addressed to the Capuchin Fr. Cherubim Mary da Voghera . . . at that time Lenten preacher in the Cathedral of Todi; he was to give it to the bishop of the same town . . . " (*Diario Spirituale,* 25).

[86] This statement was made by Canon Sardi in late Oct. 1777 in the presence of the vicar general of Alessandria. It is printed in the *Diario Spirituale,* 23–25.

[87] The reliability of the copy is evident from the following excerpt taken from Sardi's deposition: "Però io posso assicurare ch'era in tutto e per tutto concorde, ed uniforme a quello, che mi è qui stato esibito, trascritto da me dallo stesso originale di mia propria mano e carattere, come ho riconosciuto previa attenta lettura, e ricognizione, che ne ho quivi fatta, seppura forse nel trascriverlo non avessi io fatto qualche sbaglio, il quale però penso e dico, che non potrà essere se non picciolo e leggiero, e non di sostanza, perchè avendolo scritto solamente ad uso, e per piacer mio, e senza credermi allora, che dovesse servire all'effetto presente, non posso dire d'avervi usata tutta l'attenzione necessaria." / "Nevertheless, I can assure you it is all in accord with and identical to that manuscript given to me. [It was] copied by me from the original, in my own hand and script, as I stated previously. I also state I did not make any modifications except possibly for some errors [of transcription] which, I think and affirm, cannot be but small and without import or substance since they occurred because I was writing for my own use and pleasure only, not taking [therefore] necessary precautions" (*Diario Spirituale,* 24).

[88] For more details, see above pp. 30–33 of this text and *Storia Critica* 1:187–92.

Epilogue, and a few lines of the text have been handed down to us[89] along with the story that tells why. In the beginning of February 1775, Paul of the Cross made a customary canonical visit to the Passionist Monastery of the Presentation on Mount Argentario. At that time he commanded that all papers written by him and preserved in the monastery be burned. The rector, however, asked one of the priests to copy quickly a part of the manuscript containing the original Rule.[90] It is this copy only that has been preserved, containing the Introduction, Epilogue, and a fragment of the Rule.[91] Initially kept in the archives of the bishop of Alessandria, it was later brought to Mount Argentario, where it was preserved as a true jewel along with the other writings of the saint.[92]

St. Paul of the Cross wrote the Rule for his own community without ever having seen a Rule of any other religious order,[93] his experience being limited to familiarity with the statutes of a confraternity he directed in his native town of Castellazzo.[94] Neither did he have any precise idea of the rights of the Church or of a Congregation.

It is understandable, therefore, that Bishop Cavalieri of the diocese of Troia, in which Paul spent some time, added notes and supplements to the founder's text.[95] These additions pertained mostly to ecclesiastical law. Although the bishop himself belonged to a religious order called the *Pii Operarii* (Pious Workers),[96] it cannot be concluded that the Rule and Constitutions of the Pious Workers exerted an important influence upon those of the Passionists. In fact, there were but a few places where the one text corresponded significantly with the other.[97]

Importantly, the 1720 text did not contain the fourth vow requiring mem-

[89] This is a reference to the previously quoted letter to Bishop Gattinara of Dec. 1720 (L 4:217–20).

[90] See POR, 2427v., testimony of Bro. Bartholomew.

[91] In the informative processes of Vetralla, Fr. John Mary of St. Ignatius quoted the entire wording of this fragment from memory. See POV, 122v.–128r.; *Processi* 1:38–40.

[92] *Storia Critica* I, chap. 15.

[93] Fr. Giorgini makes the following observation in his analysis of the original manuscript of the Rule: "At experientia de Religiosorum vita communitaria carebat (nullam enim Religiosorum Regulam legerat, ut ipse dicit) . . . " / "He was lacking in experience about life in a religious community (he had not read even a single rule of religious life, as he himself states) . . . " (*Regulae et Constitutiones*, 13f.).

[94] M. Bialas, *Im Zeichen des Kreuzes*, 15.

[95] These notes were published in *Regulae et Constitutiones*, 151–54. Some were also published in H. Van Laer, *Saint Paul de la Croix et le Saint-Siège*, 143f.

[96] The Congregation of the Pii Operarii (Pious Workers) represent a worldwide order of priests who devote themselves, in an extraordinary way, to preaching and to giving lay missions. Their founder was Carlo Caraffa (1561–1633). See *Lexikon für Theologie und Kirche*, 2d ed., 2:935; *New Catholic Encyclopedia* 3 (1967), 98 (keywords: Caraffa, Carlo II, Ven.).

[97] Fr. Giorgini juxtaposes areas of similarity and agreement between the two texts in *Regulae et Constitutiones*, 14, n. 25.

bers of the Congregation to contemplate the passion of our Lord Jesus Christ and to preach it above all.[98]

The Codex Altieri *text* (1736). This is the oldest preserved text of the Passionist Rule. Its full title is *"Regole e Costituzioni da osservarsi dalla Congregazione dei minimi Chierici scalzi sotto l'invocazione della Santa Croce di Gesù Cristo, e della sua Passione"* (Rules and constitutions to be observed in the Congregation of the Least Discalced Clerics concerning the invocation of the holy cross of Jesus Christ, and of his passion).[99]

Although it is now stored in the archives of the Passionist Generalate in Rome,[100] it had, until recently, been kept in the library of the family Altieri (hence its name *"Codex Altieri"*). It is included in the critical edition of the various texts of the Rule published by Fr. Giorgini.[101] Written in 1736 by St. Paul of the Cross, it was sent to Cardinal Altieri in Rome. Except for the notes incorporated by Bishop Cavalieri and Paul's own modifications added in 1730 to lessen the severity of the manner of life, it is essentially the same text as that written in 1720.[102]

The 1741 *text.* The text *"Regole e Costituzioni da osservarsi dalla Congregazione dei minimi Chierici Regolari scalzi sotto l'invocazione della Santa Croce e Passione di Gesù Cristo"* (Rules and constitutions to be observed in the Congregation of the Least Discalced Regular Clerics concerning the invocation of the holy cross and passion of Jesus Christ) was approved by Benedict XIV in a papal rescript after it had first been confirmed by a commission appointed by the Holy See.[103] The rescript itself was written in such a way that, although the Rule had been approved, the Congregation was not as yet recognized as an ecclesiastical institution.[104] Also, the new Congregation still did not have the right of exemption, its members being subordinate to the ordinary in the locality of their monastery. Neither could its members make solemn vows, a right which St. Paul of the Cross had so wanted and struggled to obtain.

The 1746 *text.* Because of the Congregation's spread, as evidenced by its new foundations, St. Paul of the Cross decided to apply again to the Holy See for approbation of the Rule by papal brief. In December 1744, the pope convoked a commission which consisted of three cardinals who were asked to

[98] See n. 38 in this chapter.

[99] *Regulae et Constitutiones,* 15, and *Storia Critica* 1:15.

[100] The manuscript consists of thirty pages (size 29 × 20 cm), written on both sides. It was not written by the founder himself but by a copyist of the vicar general of Orbetello (*Regulae et Constitutiones,* 15–18).

[101] The modified passages are organized in the form of an appendix and published in Fr. Giorgini's edition of the Rule. The first column consists of the entire text of the 1736 Rule. Cols. 2–6 contain versions of the Rules of 1741, 1746, 1769, 1775, and 1930.

[102] *Regulae et Constitutiones,* 16.

[103] See Van Laer, 26–35.

[104] *Regulae et Constitutiones,* 20.

review the Order's Rule. Their study completed, the cardinals gave an affirmative response in March 1746.[105] On April 18, Benedict XIV issued the brief entitled *"Ad pastoralis dignitatis fastigium"*. Thus, the Rule and Constitutions were once more approved.

The text, translated into Latin,[106] was entitled *"Regulae et Constitutiones observandae a clericis discalceatis Passionis Domini Nostri Iesu Christi"* (Rules and constitutions to be observed by the Discalced Clerics of the passion of our Lord Jesus Christ). Although many clarifications and additions were introduced into the text,[107] its content presented very few basic differences from the 1741 version.[108]

The 1760 text. On June 6, 1760, at the beginning of the pontificate of Clement XIII, St. Paul of the Cross again tried to obtain the privilege of solemn vows for his Congregation. The commission called to approve the Rule and to respond to Paul's request decided that the severity of life demanded by the Rule and constitutions militated against making solemn vows.[109] The vote of November 23, 1760, by the members of this commission called for the addition of five supplementary stipulations to the text of the Rule.[110] On November 25, 1760, Pope Clement XIII issued a rescript that confirmed the 1746 version along with the outcome of the vote by the commission of cardinals. Although the original

---

[105] This approval is published in *Regulae et Constitutiones,* 157.

[106] Commenting on the translations, Giorgini states, "Versio latina Regulae ab Auditore cardinalis Albani genere dicendi severo et gravi perfecta, ipsi Regulae quamdam addidit venustatem. Interpres enim non verbum pro verbo sed ex sensu eleganti sermone expressit . . . " / "The disciplined and authoritative style of the translation, made by one of Cardinal Albani's students, is perfect and adds elegance to the Rule itself. The interpretation is not word by word; rather the translator expresses [its meaning] superbly."

[107] Changes were made in the following chapters: Chapter 10: De electione et munere magistri novitiorum (Concerning the election and office of master of novices); Chapter 22: De faciendis a fratribus laicis (Concerning the duties of lay brothers); Chapter 24: De studio litterarum (Concerning literary studies); Chapter 32: De electione praesidum Congregationis (Concerning the election of the ruling body of the Congregation); Chapter 33: De Superioribus domorum particularium eorumque regimine (Concerning superiors of individual houses and their governance). See Fr. Giorgini's work *Regulae et Constitutiones.*

[108] In his introduction to the various versions of the Rule, Giorgini mentions an Italian edition dating from the period 1744–46 (*Regulae et Constitutiones,* 23).

[109] Discussing the 1760 text, Giorgini wrote, "Haec Cardinalium deliberatio non convenit cum Pauli mente; insuper eodem tempore plerique Congregationis sodalium, Cardinales rogaverunt ut non ligarentur votis solemnibus; qua de causa die vigesimo tertio mensis novembris 1760 Cardinalium Consilium decrevit: 'Nihil innovetur pro nunc quoad emissionem votorum solemnium.'" / "This decision of the cardinals was not in accord with the mind of Paul; at the same time, however, many members of the Congregation had requested that solemn vows not be approved. For that reason, the cardinals decreed on Nov. 23, 1760, 'Nothing can be changed with respect to solemn vows'" (*Regulae et Constitutiones,* 24).

[110] These additions refer to the jurisdiction of the rector and instructions for the conduct of lay missions (*Regulae et Constitutiones,* 24).

papal rescript and the cardinals' vote have not been preserved, there is a document in the archives[111] entitled "An authentic transcript of our Rule, which had already been approved by Pope Benedict XIV himself, in the year 1746, with additions provided by an extraordinary commission and again approved by Clement XIII by pontifical rescript of November 23, 1760."[112]

The 1769 text. The founder of the Passionists saw God's providence at work in the election of his intimate friend Cardinal L. Ganganelli as Pope Clement XIV.[113] As pontiff, Clement became a resolute protector of the Congregation. In May of 1769, only ten days after assuming the pontifical throne, he received Paul in a private audience. On that occasion, Paul handed the new pope a petition in which he presented his still unfulfilled desires for the Congregation, although by now he no longer asked for the special privilege of solemn vows.[114]

Clement XIV received the petition favorably and sent it to the Curia for an examination and ecclesiastical opinion of its contents. About forty days later,[115] two examiners, having completed their work, handed the pope their "consultative vote".[116] The pontiff gave his approval and ordered that a brief be prepared along with a bull by which the Rule of the Congregation was to be officially confirmed. These drafts were then sent to the founder for his approval. These pontifical documents are of great importance because they definitely demonstrate the protection afforded St. Paul of the Cross and his Congregation by Clement XIV. All requests made in Paul's petition were fulfilled.[117]

On November 15, 1769, the apostolic brief *"Salvatoris et Domini Nostri"* was signed.[118] The Rule of the Congregation received solemn approba-

---

[111] AGCP, sec. 2, B.IIa.

[112] On the basis of several documents stored in AGCP, it is evident that the papal rescript was signed not on Nov. 23 but on Nov. 25, 1760 (Van Laer, 125, n. 43; *Regulae et Constitutiones*, 24).

"Copia autentica delle nostre Regole già approvate da Benedetto XIV nel 1746, poi conformate con nuove addizioni d'una Congregazione speciale da Clemente XIII con suo rescritto pontificio ai 23 novembre 1760." The text of this copy was not recorded in the synopsis of the Rule. The above-mentioned additions made by the papal commission were added as footnotes in the corresponding sections of the 1769 edition.

[113] Vincent Strambi tells us in his biography of St. Paul of the Cross that, on several occasions, the founder had foretold the election of Cardinal Ganganelli as pope (Strambi, *Vita*, 145f.; in English see Strambi, *The Life of the Blessed Paul of the Cross*, 1:269, 3:130f.).

[114] The founder fully understood the Holy See's practice and the politics underlying it of not granting the privilege of solemn vows to any newly established Congregation. Nevertheless, he requested both an exemption to this policy and the right of "ius mendicandi", i.e., the right to collect alms (*Storia Critica* 1:1265–67).

[115] Strambi, *Vita*, 146. In English, Strambi, *Life*, 1:271.

[116] See *Regulae et Constitutiones*, App. 9, 174f.

[117] See n. 114 above and *Regulae et Constitutiones*, 26.

[118] This is published in the *Acta Congregationes* 12 (1934): 312–15.

tion,[119] and complete authority to present and interpret this Rule in a clear way was given to the General Chapter.[120] Thus all of St. Paul of the Cross' efforts in seeking papal approbation of his Congregation over the course of forty-eight years were crowned with success. On November 16, Pope Clement XIV issued the bull *"Supremi apostolatus",*[121] which gave official approval of the Passionist Congregation as a pontifical institute having simple vows. The text of this Rule, as approved in the brief and in the bull, has been published in a critical work by Fr. Giorgini.[122]

The 1775 text. The original of this text, preserved in the archives of the Generalate,[123] was first published by the vice general Fr. John Baptist of St. Vincent Ferreri in 1776; it is divided into thirty-eight chapters.[124] Not completely satisfied with the 1769 edition, St. Paul of the Cross undertook a revision of the text, adding more exact definitions and changes.[125] In this work, he was spurred on by a desire of conceiving "lasting rules to be put into practice by the strong and weak alike".[126]

---

[119] It says there, among other things, " . . . praeinserta Statuta, Regulas, sive Constitutiones una cum omnibus additionibus et declarationibus praedictis auctoritate Apostolica, tenore praesentium confirmamus et approbamus, illisque inviolabilis Apostolicae firmitatis robur adiicimus . . . " / " . . . by this present document we confirm and approve by [our] apostolic authority the previously mentioned statutes, rules, and/or constitutions together with all the aforementioned additions and declarations, and we add the authority of [our] apostolic inviolability . . . " (*Acta Congregationes* 12 [1934]: 314).

[120] "Volumus autem, ut in Generalibus Comitiis dumtaxat Regulae ipsae et Constitutiones huiusmodi interpretari, ac declarari possint, ita tamen, ut si quae in eis immutanda, resecanda, et addenda, experientia suadente, videantur, de his ad Apostolicam hanc Sanctam Sedem referendum decernatur" / "We intend, moreover, that, at least in general chapters, rules and constitutions of this kind can be interpreted and clarified—with this proviso, however, that if experience suggests that anything needs to be changed, deleted, or added, a decision be made to refer these matters to this Holy Apostolic See" (ibid.).

[121] The text is written on a large pergament (93 × 78 cm), containing 71 lines and bearing the signature of Cardinal Negroni, Msgr. Manassei, and L. Eugenio (*Storia Critica* 1:1268). The text was published in *Bullarii Romani continuatio* (Rome, 1841), 4:66–72. See *Regulae et Constitutiones,* 24, n. 120.

[122] The text has been published in the fourth column of Fr. Giorgini's synopsis.

[123] AGCP, sec. 4 A8, A9.

[124] *Regulae et Constitutiones,* 24.

[125] During the course of the apostolic process in Rome, one of the nine canonization processes of St. Paul of the Cross, Fr. Joseph Hyacinth related the following: " . . . il quale mi ordinò di portarmi ogni giorno da lui per leggergli uno, o più Capitoli delle Regole, non potendo per le sue gravi ed abituali infermità ciò fare per sè stesso" / " . . . who asked me to read to him, every day, one or more chapters from the Rule, since he was not able to do so himself by reason of his serious and chronic infirmities" (PAR, 1763v., published in *Bollettino* 10 [1929]: 76).

[126] " . . . non avendo altro in mira, se non che le Regole, nella maniera che si sarebbero riformate, dovessero essere permanenti, e da potersi osservare non meno dai robusti che dai deboli." / " . . . having nothing else on his mind but the Rules and how they might be

Discussed and approved by the participants of the General Chapter of May 15–20, 1775 (held in the church of SS. John and Paul),[127] this modified form of the Rule was again submitted to the Holy See by St. Paul of the Cross for its approval. On September 15, 1775, Pope Pius VI issued the bull *"Praeclara virtutum exempla"*, which recognized the modified Rule in an official way.[128] The 1775 text is preserved for its historical and inspirational value in the latest edition of the Congregation's Rule.[129]

3. *Letters of St. Paul of the Cross*

Undoubtedly, the preserved letters of Paul of the Cross constitute a source of data superior to all other sources and are most helpful in reconstructing an exact and authentic picture of his doctrine. The approximately two thousand letters contain such a quantity of detail that, put together, they are like a mosaic revealing the characteristic features and principles of his thought.[130] Nevertheless, these letters represent only a part of those written by the founder during his long life. Using the saint's own statement that he customarily wrote twenty-four or even thirty letters a week,[131] we can easily assume that he may have written at least ten thousand letters in his lifetime.[132]

---

adapted so as to be observed not only by those with strong natures but also by the weak" (ibid.).

[127] See F. Giorgini, *Decreti e Raccomandazioni dei Capitoli Generali della Congregazione della SS. Croce e Passione di N.S.G.C.*, 7–9, 15f.

[128] Arch. Vat. Segr. Brevi, vol. 4366, 313v.–319v.; *Bullarii Romani continuatio*, 5:155–58 (see *Regulae et Constitutiones*, 28, n. 135).

[129] This text, "Regulae et Consitutiones Congregationis Clericorum Excalceatorum SS.mae Crucis et Passionis Domini Nostri Iesu Christi", is presented in the fifth column of the synopsis of the Rule.

[130] 1,855 letters in a four-volume edition were compiled by Fr. Amedeo in Rome in 1924. His edition, however, did not use authentic hand-written sources, but relied upon letters published in an 1867 edition. Later, eighty-five additional letters were discovered. These appeared in the Italian publication *Bollettino*. Year and page references are given below:

1926: 147–53, 205–18, 244–49, 266–74, 302–4
1927: 13–19, 172–80, 291–308, 323–25, 356–64
1928: 39–48, 90–96, 135–55, 167–76, 207–9

[131] "Ogni settimana ordinariamente sono 20, 24 ed anche 30 lettere che ricevo, e rispondo a tutte da me." / "Ordinarily, I receive twenty, twenty-four, and even thirty letters a week, and I answer all of them myself" (L 2:201, July 17, 1749, to Fr. Fulgentius of Jesus; also see L 2:205 and L 2:805, among others).

[132] All preserved letters were written during a fifty-five-year interval (1720–75). Using some simple arithmetic, we can estimate the total number of letters written during this time period. If we use Paul's own words and assume he wrote an average of 20 letters per week for each week of the 55 years, we arrive at a total of 50,000 letters, or about 1,000 letters per year. Using a more realistic average of 3.5 letters per week, which would allow for weeks or months in which writing was limited by illness or other factors, we arrive at an estimate of

Fortunately, the vast majority of his letters which are preserved are originals, written by Paul himself.[133]

That only a relatively small proportion of letters have been preserved may be explained in part by the founder's instructions to his correspondents to burn his letters.[134] Consider, for example, Rosa Calabresi, who had in her keeping more than five hundred letters written to her by Paul over an eight-year period. During a time of severe illness, she personally burned all of them upon an order of the saint, who feared they might be read by others.[135] Similar instructions were given to others.[136]

Given the numerous works accomplished by the saint, his apostolic involvement and the tasks associated with founding a Congregation, it is easy to understand why he often used night hours for his correspondence.[137] From hints dropped in his letters, it is also apparent that Paul, being pressed for time,

---

10,000 letters written in the fifty-five-year period, or about 180 letters per year.

[133] Fr. Amedeo indicates at the end of each letter included in his 1924 edition whether the letter conforms with an original or with a copy. He uses the following four categories: (1) conforme all'originale (conforms to the original), (2) conforme a copia autenticata (conforms to an authenticated copy), (3) conforme a copia antica o antichissima (conforms to a very old or ancient copy), and (4) conforme a copia (conforms to a copy). These four categories give us a frame of reference regarding the authenticity of his sources. See Fr. Amedeo's preface to L 1:16.

[134] To Sr. Colomba Gertrude Gandolfi, he wrote, "Quando ha lette le mie lettere le bruci, che non meritano d'essere conservate." / "After reading my letters, please burn them all, because they do not deserve to be preserved" (L 2:515, Feb. 28, 1764; also see L 1:176, 250).

[135] "In una malattia mortale che ebbi, mi fu insinuato di bruciare quelle lettere che mi ritrovavo, se non avevo piacere che se ne sapesse il contenuto. Mi piacque l'insinuazione, perchè concernevano affari di mia conscienza, e perciò ordinai che si bruciassero tutte le lettere che avevo ricevute dal p. Paolo, onde presentemente non ho veruna delle medesime da esibire." / "During a very serious illness that I had, it was suggested to me to burn the letters I still had in my possession, so that they not be read or their contents become known. I liked that suggestion since the letters contained matters of conscience, and so I ordered that all letters received from Father Paul be burned" (POR, 1967v., testimony of Rosa Calabresi; quoted in *Storia Critica* 2:213, n. 26).

[136] See Preface to Fr. Amedeo's four-volume edition: L 1:13; also see *Storia Critica* 2:214f.

[137] The following is from a fragment of a letter written by Paul: "Lo sa Dio come sto, che questa notte ho avuto da lambiccare la testa, e scritto non poco ... " / "Only God knows how I troubled my head last night, writing not a little ... " (L 1:225, undated letter to Agnes Grazi; also see L 2:476 and L 1:333).

often wrote in a hurry.[138] In many cases even the quality of his penmanship betrays this haste.[139] Not infrequently, writing so many letters imposed a hardship upon him, especially during times of poor health, which was the case more often than not.[140]

Those with whom Paul corresponded belonged to various social strata and held a variety of positions. For instance, among his correspondents are found an equal number of popes, cardinals, and influential figures in society and politics along with people in ordinary walks of life, e.g., mothers and fathers of families and young men and women. The greater part of his letters, however, are addressed to priests and religious,[141] among whom the brothers and sisters of his Congregation occupy first place. It is amazing to see the founder's intuitive grasp of the concrete and respective situations posed by each of his correspondents.

Two categories of letters can be distinguished on the basis of content, i.e., those concerned with the management and spread of the Congregation and those written for the purpose of spiritual direction. Undoubtedly, the establishment of twelve monasteries, the number of missions conducted by Paul during his lifetime, and the repeated papal approbations of the Rule necessitated innumerable letters. Nevertheless, the majority of the preserved letters are those written for the purpose of providing guidance and spiritual direction.[142] These latter are of two types: those containing pithy bits of

---

[138] He frequently begins his letters in the following manner: "Questa mattina ho ricevuto una sua lettera, alla quale rispondo in fretta, perchè il latore vuol partire." / "This morning I received a letter from you, and I am answering in a hurry since the carrier is about to leave" (L 2:17, Aug. 26, 1738, to Don B. Cianchini). In several letters, mostly shorter ones, he apologizes for his haste in the close of the letter: " . . . e lasciandola nel Costato SSmo. di Gesù, con profondo rispetto di stima ed ossequio mi riprotesto in fretta e di partenza." / " . . . and entrusting you to the Most Holy Side of Jesus Christ, with deep respect for your regard [and] in deference to you, I apologize for ending this letter in a rush, but it must be mailed" (L 2:356, Oct. 1, 1751 to F. Zelli; also see L 1:115 and L 3:677, among others).

[139] Storia Critica 2:222, and Henau, De Passiemystiek, 25.

[140] " . . . e ben vedo che le mie occupazioni sono superiori alle mie forze naturali, e se Dio non mi dà gran forza, poco la durerò; questo benedetto tavolino mi abbatte molto." / " . . . and I well see that my occupations are beyond my natural powers and, were God not empowering me, I would last but a short time; this writing desk, albeit blest, burdens me a lot" (L 2:283, Sept. 5, 1743, to Canon P. Cerruti; also see L 1:448, Oct. 10, 1736, to Sr. Ch. Bresciani).

[141] The reason may be that persons, regardless of their status in society, sought the founder for his consultation and guidance in their spiritual needs.

[142] Except for the following, few letters addressed to the same correspondent have been preserved. The exceptions are:
  1. Thomas Fossi (later known as Fr. Thomas of Jesus and Mary, after his entrance into the Passionist Congregation), 172 letters (L 1:533–820)
  2. Agnes Grazi, 165 letters (L 1:96–353)
  3. Fr. Fulgentius of Jesus, 59 letters (L 2:68–206)
  4. Sr. Colomba Gertrude Gandolfi, 53 letters (L 2:439–523)

information or advice; and those of much greater length which, for the most part, deal with situations involving the religious or mystical life of the correspondent. It is not unusual for such letters to extend to three, four, or five printed pages.

It is noteworthy that the salutations of Paul's letters connoted not just acquaintanceship but deep friendship.[143] Too, it was not uncommon for him to speak quite openly about his spiritual life, both his cares and troubles and his joys and consolations.[144] Obviously the founder had a pronounced need to open himself to others.[145]

This readiness to communicate his interior life effected a sense of trust in everyone directed by Paul, the result being wholehearted submission to his direction and disclosure of even the smallest stirrings of conscience.[146] These friendships and relationships rooted in trust were for Paul not ends in themselves but rather means by which he served those he directed and drew them more closely to God.[147]

Since the greater part of the preserved letters are those written for the purpose of spiritual direction, we can easily reformulate Paul's thinking on

[143] To Agnes Grazi, he writes, "Ecco con quanta confidenza in Dio si dilata il mio spirito col suo; ma e non è forse dovere che il povero Padre qualche volta faccia qualche sfogo di carità con i suoi figliuoli? Amiamo Dio, facciamoci piccoli assai, che Dio ci farà grandi." / "Behold with what great confidence in God my spirit expands with yours. Yet is it not fitting that your poor father at times give vent to some overflow of charity with his children? Let us love God, let us make ourselves the least, so that God will make us great" (L 1:195, Aug. 29, 1737; also see L 2:290, Aug. 10, 1741).

[144] L 1:156, Oct. 3, 1736, and L 1:252, June 15, 1740, to Agnes Grazi, and L 1:610, Dec. 6, 1751, to Thomas Fossi.

[145] During the canonization process, Fr. Hyacinth, a fellow religious and confidant of the founder, expressed this quality in the following way: "Aveva il cuore in mano." / "He had [his] heart in [his] hand" (par 1731v., as quoted in Storia Critica 2:277).

[146] In many letters, the founder discusses matters of conscience.

[147] In all letters, where a friendly and trusting tone can be detected, it is immediately obvious that the saint is by no means trying to draw others to himself. On the contrary, he seems to make use of friendship and trust for the correspondent's own spiritual and religious progress.

When speaking of the "friendships" of St. Paul of the Cross, the following needs to be said. Certainly the laws of human sympathy and antipathy played a part in the formation of these trusting relationships. When women were involved, it is also possible that some of the attractions (not recognized by the saint) had their origin in the difference between the sexes. I am of the opinion, however, that such attractions do not speak at all against the integrity of his person, because a saint too—better said, a saint especially—must represent first of all a human person in a perfect way. Holiness is not opposed to true humanness, nor does it hinder its development. Rather, holiness completes humanness in all its fullness. It develops and perfects the human person according to the pattern of being given him by the Creator. Put in another way, humanness and holiness do not oppose each other in a mutually exclusive way but enhance each other in a reciprocal and complementary way.

different aspects of the spiritual life.[148] Because of the amount of detailed information contained in the letters, it is also possible to identify characteristic features of his own personality. In fact, because the founder's letters are so distinctly colored by his own personal thoughts and feelings, they may be considered a reflection of his personality. Although from a literary standpoint there is nothing extraordinary in these letters,[149] they represent the single most important source of information on his thought.

4. Sermons and Meditations

Seventy-three sermons and fourteen meditations on Christ's passion given by St. Paul of the Cross have been preserved. Of these, all but the last nine sermons were transcribed by the founder himself. They are bound in two volumes[150] and preserved in the archives of the Passionist Order. Age plus frequent usage have left them in a bad state.[151]

Apart from the original transcriptions,[152] there is also a very good and legible copy of the entire set of sermons and meditations in the Passionist archives in Rome.[153] Between the years 1925 and 1929, thirty-two sermons and five meditations on Christ's passion were published in the *"Bollettino della Congregazione"*.[154]

Although the content of Paul's letters reveal his originality, his sermons and meditations are, for the most part, material of a different kind. He himself judiciously admitted in his letters that his sermons were copied from other

[148] The spiritual thought of the saint, as revealed mostly in his letters, will be presented in Part Two of this study.

[149] *Storia Critica* 2:221f.

[150] Vol. 1 contains 316 pages; vol. 2 has 198.

[151] While it is true that individual pages have been restored in recent years, there are still many places where writing is faint and letters can hardly be deciphered.

[152] Although the originals were not dated, it is highly probable they were written by the founder in his earlier years, perhaps prior to his ordination as priest (June 7, 1727). It seems certain he took these materials with him on his frequent missionary journeys, hence their bad state (see *Storia Critica* 3:982f.).

[153] These transcriptions, with still legible handwriting, have been compiled in a 700-page tome. Attached to the bottom of the first sheet is another piece of paper containing a statement by the archivist, Fr. Ignatius of St. Teresa, in which he states that the manuscript contains many errors indicative of the transcriber's poor mastery of Latin and Italian (AGCP).

[154] The dates of these are:

    1925: 5–14, 69–71, 180–83, 218–28, 277–84, 307–13, 375–78
    1926: 29–31, 115–22, 137–40, 166–68, 195–99, 232–43, 260–65, 295–301, 363–66
    1927: 20–23, 40–49, 70–73, 168–72, 200–202, 260–72
    1928: 230–40, 268–78, 293–95, 328–30, 354–62
    1929: 10–13, 54–56, 90–93, 139–48, 196–202, 328–32, 363–65

sources.[155] Since many witnesses have testified that the founder was an extraordinarily gifted orator and preacher,[156] we conclude that these sermons were not memorized or read but functioned as background and reference material for his own original deliveries.[157]

It is nearly impossible to determine all the authors or texts used by the saint. In one of his letters, he states he borrowed greatly from *Svegliarino Cristiano*.[158] This is an Italian translation[159] of a work entitled *Sermonarium*, a kind of anthology of sermons published by the bishop of Cadiz (Spain), Msgr. José de Barcia y Zambrana. A comparison of the sermons of St. Paul of the Cross with the above-mentioned text[160] reveals that some of the sermons were transcribed in their entirety. In others, whole fragments were omitted, and not infrequently the succession of treated points was modified.[161]

The subject matter of the homilies dealt with the "four last things", that is, death, judgment, hell, and heaven.[162] These themes were the foundation stones of lay missions in the eighteenth century, the primary purpose being to effect a conversion, i.e., to motivate a person to receive the sacrament of

[155] See E. Henau, "Riflessioni sulla predicazione di S. Paolo della Croce", 512.

[156] *Storia Critica* 3:1014–31.

[157] The fact that St. Paul of the Cross appealed to other authors may be justified in that he possessed no formal or systematic education in theology. Also, we may presume he copied the sermons during the early years of his apostolate. Had he written them in his later years, they surely would have reflected more of his own experience as a preacher.

[158] In a letter, he writes, "Alcuni sermoni che io ho scritto, li ho preso da libri, specialmente dallo *Svegliarino cristiano.*" / "Certain homilies written by me have been taken from other books, especially [the book] *Svegliarino cristiano*" (Henau, "Riflessioni", 512, n. 455).

[159] The exact title reads *Svegliarino cristiano di discorsi dottrinali sopra particolari assunti, disposto acciocchè il peccatore ritorni al suo dovere e vinca il pericoloso letargo delle sue colpe, animandosi alla penitenza, con applicazioni all'Avvento e Quadragesima.* The founder's copy, which is a second edition printed in Milan in 1719, may be found in the Passionist Monastery of the Presentation on Monte Argentario (*Storia Critica* 3:983f.).

[160] We have compared it with a Spanish work translated into German by Marcos Fridl entitled *Christ-eyfriger Seelen-Wecker oder lehrreiche Predigten . . .* This translation consists of six volumes printed by the publishing house J. C. Bencard in Augsburg-Dillingen in 1715–20.

[161] For example, take the homily entitled "Nobilità dell'anima" (*Bollettino* 6 [1925]: 218–28). This is a word-by-word transcription of a work by Barcia y Zambrana (*Christ-eyfriger Seelen-Wecker* I, ser. 2, 87–102). Nevertheless, Paul used only one-third of the text for his sermon. The sermon entitled "Orribile vista delle circostanze del peccato nel momento della morte e del giudizio" (*Bollettino* 7 [1926]: 166–68) is also a word-by-word copy taken from the above-mentioned collection of sermons. (See *Christ-eyfriger Seelen-Wecker* I, ser. 22, 407f.). This practice, however, does not mean he had neither a theological principle nor a purpose in mind when selecting sermons. Most likely, his selection of sermons was determined by practical necessity, fitting a specific sermon to a specific occasion.

[162] The number of sermons within each category of the four last things follows: death (7), last judgment (4), hell (7), and heaven (2). Of the four sermons on the last judgment, two were on the particular judgment and two on the general. (See the summary presented in the volume containing manuscripts of the sermons in AGCP.)

penance.[163] Therefore, sermons impressed upon listeners the seriousness of their situation in a most dramatic way.[164] Viewed from today's theology, it is terrible and bewildering to see the degree to which fear dominated the content of these sermons.[165]

There is no original composition by St. Paul of the Cross among his fourteen meditations on the passion.[166] What attracts our attention, in these as well as in the sermons, however, are the numerous, mostly Latin, quotations.[167] These include quotations from Scripture and from a wide variety of other works, such as those by Justin, Augustine, Bonaventure, Bernard of Clairvaux, Anselm of Canterbury, and others. Aside from what might be considered the works of the Church Fathers, Vincent Ferreri is often cited, and many other citations are taken from the spiritually edifying literature of Paul's time. A considerable portion of the meditations are devoted to the revelations of St. Bridget, which, next to sacred Scripture, were quoted most frequently.[168]

Organizationally, these meditations on the passion consisted of separate fragments of the evangelists' accounts of the passion. Each fragment is surrounded by rich scenery and often a lot of fantasy. First and foremost, the purpose of the meditation was to arouse the listener's compassion and then—at the point where personal sin is seen as the cause of Jesus' suffering—to effect a strong loathing for the listener's own sins.[169]

What we have already said about the function of the written sermons is also applicable to the written meditations: They were intended to stimulate ideas and to serve as points of reference. In favor of this opinion is the fact that all the preserved meditations are relatively short compositions and, if read in a

---

[163] C. Giorgini, *La Maremma Toscana nel Settecento*, 220f; Henau, "Riflessioni", 509f.; *Storia Critica* 3:928ff.

[164] Sin was a main theme presented in lay missions. No less than eight of the saint's sermons dealt with this topic.

[165] The rationale was that fear would provoke an abhorrence of sin. In Paul's homilies on hell, the "place" of hell was described in words meant to provoke trembling. Seven sermons of this nature are among those preserved.

[166] It is difficult to determine the exact sources used by the founder. Paul himself gives us no hint. It is certain, however, that the writings belong to the Christian literature of that time, upon which the founder happened more or less by chance.

[167] Besides the diversification of style and sometimes of expression, these citations and references to recognized authors are demonstrative proof that St. Paul of the Cross used reference material for the composition of his contemplations on the suffering of our Lord Jesus Christ.

[168] Sections of St. Bridget's revelations are quoted in Latin when the quotation is an exact word-for-word citation.

[169] The predominance of the sin motif as explanation of the suffering of Jesus is another indication these meditations were not of the saint's own composition. In the thinking of St. Paul of the Cross, God's love for us more than our sin is the real reason for our Lord's passion. This is evident in many sections of his letters (see Part Two of this book).

preaching style, would scarcely last more than fifteen minutes. We know from the testimony of witnesses, however, that the saint's oral meditations on the passion lasted much longer.[170] Furthermore, it is highly improbable that the founder, while speaking on Christ's passion, the main theme of his own life, did not use his own ideas too.

In summary, it can be concluded that the sermons and meditations, although written in the founder's own hand, differ in content from his letters. Only very limited and narrow conjectures, therefore, about the theological thought of the saint can be based on them.[171]

5. Depositions of Witnesses during Beatification and Canonization Processes

Having discussed what may be considered "direct sources" of information, that is, material written by the saint himself, we shall now deal with "indirect sources" of information, that is, with the testimony of people who knew St. Paul of the Cross personally and bore witness to their knowledge of him after his death. The processes for the founder's beatification and canonization provided the opportunity for giving this testimony.[172] With the encouragement of Pope Pius VI, these proceedings began in January 1777, just fifteen months after Paul's death.[173]

Taken into consideration here are the Italian transcriptions of depositions given by 121 witnesses called in six informative processes and three apostolic ones. This testimony fills twenty-two volumes and over 11,600 pages written on both sides. All depositions are preserved in the archives of the Passionist Congregation.[174]

[170] *Storia Critica* 3:1086.

[171] Surely we could draw some conclusions about Paul's theology on the basis of selections he borrowed from others. However, these conclusions would always remain to a great degree hypothetical and uncertain.

[172] A detailed description of these processes is contained in the first volume of E. Zoffoli's critical biography of Paul of the Cross. In this text, the author provides us with the dates and locations of the processes and then draws our attention to the 121 witnesses. Over and above background information on the witnesses as persons, he also describes the relationship of each with the founder. Zoffoli obtained this information from the depositions of the witnesses. In fact, a question about the witness' relationship with the saint was a constituent part of the list of questions witnesses were required to answer (*Storia Critica* 1:24–64).

[173] In the *Annali della Congregazione*, Fr. John Mary writes, "Facendo premura il sommo pontefice Pio VI, felicemente regnante, che del p. Paolo s'incominciassero i processi per via ordinaria ... " / "At the urging of the Holy Father Pius VI, happily reigning, the processes regarding Father Paul were to begin in the usual way ... " (*Annali*, 312).

[174] Here we are concerned with a certified manuscript called "transumptum" requested by the Congregation of Rites in conformity with the law (CIC, c. 2054). This manuscript was designated as a "copia publica" (*Processi* 1:10). The original "transumptum" was submitted to the Congregation of Rites for verification, but by order of Emperor Napoleon I, it and

Because Paul of the Cross engaged in apostolic activity in several locations in Italy, it was necessary to hold the processes in more than one diocese. As a result, between the years 1777 and 1780, informative processes were simultaneously held in six different sites: Rome, Corneto-Tarquinia,[175] Gaeta, Alessandria, Vetralla, and Orbetello.[176] Apostolic proceedings (following procedures outlined in canons 2087–97) took place in Rome, Viterbo, and Corneto-Tarquinia between the years 1792 and 1804.[177]

Of all the testimony taken during these nine canonical processes, only a third has been published to date,[178] but further publications are expected. Without a doubt these documents represent an almost inexhaustible fount of detail and information on the life of the founder. At the same time, it is necessary to deal with this testimony in a very objective manner and with critical distance.[179]

Such reservations regarding the claim of historical authenticity of the testimony of witnesses seem fully justified on the following grounds. Using the date of the testimony as the reference point, facts and related events in most cases occurred many years, sometimes many decades, earlier. We can conclude, therefore, that the exactness and reliability of the depositions depended solely on the recall of the witnesses.[180] Moreover, there was a proportionate

---

other documents of the secret archives of the Vatican were transferred to the archives of the French state located in the Louvre in Paris in 1810 (*Processi* 1:10, n. 38).

[175] Today's town of Tarquinia was called Corneto during the time of Paul of the Cross.

[176] The exact duration of the different informative processes and the number of witnesses are as follows:

Rome (POR), 1/11/1777–7/19/1779, 20 witnesses
Alessandria (POA), 7/4/1777–10/13/1777, 9 witnesses
Gaeta (POG), 6/16/1777–3/27/1778, 9 witnesses
Vetralla (POV), 2/5/1778–3/6/1779, 23 witnesses
Orbetello (POO), 3/24/1778–2/19/1779, 17 witnesses
Corneto-Tarquinia (POC), 4/21/1777–1/16/1778, 24 witnesses

[177] The dates of the first and last sessions of the three apostolic processes and the number of witnesses at each site follow:

Rome (PAR), 5/23/1792–12/3/1803, 16 witnesses
Corneto-Tarquinia (PAC), 10/11/1794–3/21/1803, 11 witnesses
Viterbo (PAV), 10/1794–8/8/1804, 14 witnesses

[178] Published to date are the informative processes of Vetralla (*Processi* 1) and those of Alessandria, Gaeta, Orbetello, and Corneto-Tarquinia (*Processi* 2) in *I Processi di Beatificazione e Canonizzazione di S. Paolo della Croce, Fondatore dei Passionisti e delle Claustrali Passioniste,* by Fr. Gaetano dell'Addolorata, vol. 1 (1969) and vol. 2 (1973).

[179] In my opinion, testimony regarding St. Paul of the Cross was too uncritically accepted in many of the investigations. The reader will be alerted to such situations in the appropriate spots.

[180] Most depositions give the impression that witnesses recall related happenings quite well. Nevertheless, we need to remember what psychology teaches us about the inner laws of the process of recollecting. During recollection, there is no way in which the "reproducing"

number of witnesses whose ability to make distinctions and report events in an objectively factual manner was limited.

Also to be taken into account is the fact that the ground rules which governed the informative (as opposed to the apostolic) processes were not designed to maximize reliability in the reporting of historical events. For example, canon 2050[181] indicated it was not necessary to have detailed certainty about a person's virtues, miracles, or martyrdom. It sufficed that the person had an enduring reputation for such and that it came about spontaneously and in an upright manner. With the looseness inherent in this type of goal setting, it is understandable that witnesses, with the best intentions in the world and in good faith, could give less-than-accurate information about the occurrence of past events. Even though an oath was required of them, it was hardly an inherent obstacle to the way in which they, without burdening their consciences, bore testimony to the reputation of the saint as "a servant of God".[182]

Depositions taken during apostolic processes, in contrast, were to include actual proof of virtues and miracles, even in an isolated case, and proof of martyrdom and its cause.[183] In point of fact, however, the length of time between the fact attested to and its occurrence was so long (more often than not several decades) that it was almost impossible to achieve the immediacy needed to ensure historical reliability of oral testimony.

Despite the presence of variables which tended to reduce confidence in the reliability of some testimony, there were a great number of historically reliable depositions. This reliability was a function of the qualifications of the witness as a discerner of truth and error and of the closeness of his contact with the founder. For example, the depositions of Fr. John Mary[184] are

---

memory reproduces lived material unchanged. Recollection is not a computer process that retrieves stored information and prints it out without any modification.

[181] Canon 2050 §2: "Non est necesse ut constet in specie de virtutibus, martyrio, miraculis, sed sufficit ut probetur fama in genere, spontanea, non arte aut diligentia humana procurata, orta ab honestis et gravibus personis, continua, in dies acta et vigens in praesenti apud maiorem partem populi." / "It is not necessary that there be detailed certainty about someone's virtues, martyrdom, or miracles, but it suffices that his or her reputation in general be shown not to have been procured by human scheme or efforts but to have arisen spontaneously among upright and earnest people and to have continued and flourished up to the present among a sizable number of people."

[182] It is necessary to take into consideration here what was said in n. 180 above.

[183] Canon 2087: " . . . ad instruendum processum apostolicum tum super fama sanctitatis, miraculorum aut martyrii, tum super virtutibus et miraculis in specie vel super martyrio eiusdemque causa". / " . . . in order to initiate the apostolic process, on the one hand, as regards someone's reputation for sanctity, miracles, or martyrdom and [/or], on the other hand, as regards his or her virtues and miracles in detail or his or her martyrdom and the reason for it".

[184] See above, pp. 39 and below pp. 60–63.

regarded as highly reliable. As Paul's confessor and spiritual director, he knew the saint very well. As author of several works describing the origin and growth of the Congregation, Fr. John Mary was also well acquainted with events and their dates and times.[185]

It is apparent from the words and phrases used in many of the depositions that events and facts were reported in an exaggerated manner.[186] At least partially, this tendency may be attributed to the spirit of the age. It is well known that those of the baroque period employed, with great enjoyment, an emphatic and grandiloquent style. Also, some depositions unmistakably indicate witness' bias in relating only the marvelous and extraordinary.[187]

6. The Annals of Fr. John Mary

Among the many indirect sources of information on the life and activity of St. Paul of the Cross, the *Annals* of Fr. John Mary are especially important because of their high degree of historical reliability.[188] These *Annals* record the history of the establishment and growth of the Congregation between the years 1720 and 1795 [189] and portray the personality of the founder in a special

[185] Special import is also due to the testimony of Rosa Calabresi given during the informative process in Rome. Rosa had corresponded with Paul for ten years prior to visiting Rome during the Holy Year of 1775. The first personal encounter of these two people, so favored with mystical graces, occurred on Apr. 22 of that year. Over the next two months, they met almost daily in the sacristy of the Basilica of SS. John and Paul. During these conferences, the founder (eighty-one years old at the time) revealed to Rosa many details about his religious and spiritual life. As a result, she knew as no one else the interior life of this venerable saint. Although her testimony was treated with some scepticism and reserve during the processes, it has since been found to be historically reliable (see POR, 2008v.; PAR, 2243v., testimony of Rosa Calabresi; *Storia Critica* I, chap. 31; 3:301–14; also see Gioacchino de Sanctis, *Rosa Calabresi, discepola e confidente di S. Paolo della Croce* [Badia di Ceccano, 1956]).

[186] For example, " . . . mi ha asserito che nelle meditazioni, che dava il P. Paolo, s'eccitava una commozione, ed un pianto universale con gemiti e singulti, che non sa esprimerli." / " . . . it has been told to me that, during meditations given by Fr. Paul, much commotion and lament was raised [among the people] with moans and sighs that belie description": POV, 1389v. (*Processi* 1:632), testimony of Fr. Joseph Mary of the Crucified. Similarly, POV, 632v. (*Processi* 1:283), testimony of Bro. Vittorio; POR 240v., testimony of G. Suscioli; and many others.

[187] Occurrences labeled "miraculous" were frequently cited in the life and activities of Paul of the Cross. If such events were critically or realistically analyzed, however, it would have been evident that they could have been explained by purely natural causes.

[188] The complete title of the *Annals* is *Annali della Congregazione della SS.ma Croce e Passione di N.S.G.C.*

[189] The original, written by hand, may be found in the archives of the Passionist Generalate in Rome (sec. A, V–I, 3). The pages are bound in two volumes. Vol. 1 (188 pages) contains events from the years 1720–82, and vol. 2 (84 pages), from the years 1783–95.

way. This all the more so because the author was less interested in detailing the contemporary setting and interrelationships which influenced the founding of the Congregation than in motivating readers, especially Passionists, to an imitation of their founder-saint.[190]

Despite their purported purpose and the author's moralizing for the edification of his readers, the *Annals*, taken as a whole, possess a high degree of historical reliability in the recording of facts described therein. This is primarily due to the author's strong lifelong interest in history. Besides these *Annals*, Fr. John Mary composed other historically inspired works such as a history of the establishment of the monasteries,[191] five voluminous biographies,[192] twenty-nine shorter ones,[193] and obituaries on more than seventy members of the Congregation who died during 1745–90. On the basis of the opinion of some specialists in history,[194] it is reasonable to

[190] The author identifies his purpose in the Introduction of this book in the following way: "Ad effetto adunque che ad ognuno degli alunni di questa povera Congregazione si renda palese il principio, ed i progressi della medesima, e con ciò si animi a conservarne fedelmente, ed ad osservarne esattamente le leggi, imitando i suoi santi fondatori, ed i suoi più conspicui fratelli, ci sforzeremo, in questi Annali, di accenare scarsamente ciò che di più rimarchevole è stato operato dai nostri padri fondatori e loro fedeli seguaci . . . " / "[These *Annals* are written] for the purpose of tangibly presenting to each disciple of this poor Congregation the [history of] the establishment and development of the Order and thus motivate him to keep the Rule faithfully and to observe it exactly, imitating the saintly founders and our most illustrious brethren. Let us strive ourselves in these *Annals* to render in a few words what was most remarkable and what was achieved by our founding fathers and their faithful disciples . . . " (*Annali*, 26).

[191] The complete title of this work is *Libro nel quale si narrano le fondazioni della Congregazione dei Chierici Scalzi della SS. Croce e Passione di Gesù Cristo, fatto dal P. Paolo della Croce ancor vivente e dopo la di lui gloriosa morte dagli altri suoi successori nella carica di Prepositi Generali*. The original, written by hand, consists of 198 pages. It is preserved in AGCP in Rome. The entire work was published in the periodical *Bollettino della Congregazione* from 1922 to 1926, as cited below:

1922: 337–46
1923: 147–53, 178–85, 215–18, 241–47
1924: 106–15, 175–84, 209–17, 239–49, 276–84, 313–15, 340–47
1925: 41–47, 72–85, 183–91, 232–44, 313–17, 341–49
1926: 74–88

[192] These biographies are the stories of the lives of St. Paul of the Cross' four companions who took part in the establishment of the Congregation (Fr. John Baptist, Paul's blood brother; Fr. Fulgentius of Jesus; Fr. Mark Aurelius of the Most Holy Sacrament; and Bishop Thomas Struzzieri) and of the nun (Mother Mary Crucified).

[193] All subjects were members of the Congregation: fifteen priests, ten clerical students, and four lay brothers.

[194] Two specialists have expressed their complete confidence in the historical reliability of the entries in the *Annals*: Fr. F. Antonelli, referent of the historical department of the Congregation of Rites (see *Annali*, 8), and Fr. Vincent Monachino, dean of the faculty of ecclesiastical history of the Pontifical University of Rome (*Annali*, 10).

assume that the author of the *Annals* was thoroughly familiar with historical method.

Two factors which greatly aided Fr. John Mary's work were his phenomenal memory[195] and his familiarity with St. Paul of the Cross. For the composition of his historical works, however, Fr. John Mary relied less on memory, although he possessed an excellent one, than on the prompt recording of events which he had either observed or in which he participated. He then cited these detailed notes to support his statements in the *Annals*.[196] Because Fr. John Mary was Paul's intimate friend and for ten years his confessor and spiritual director, and because there were numerous opportunities for the type of discussions in which John Mary could obtain an in-depth view of Paul's personality, the statements John Mary makes regarding deeds or motives of the saint may be preceded by the word *authoritative*.[197]

After having considered the person of the author, so important for a correct evaluation of the *Annals,* it is now time to consider more details about the source itself. Although the handwritten original is anonymous, the author is beyond all doubt Fr. John Mary.[198] Furthermore, it appears that, in his reports on the years 1720–75, the author expresses himself quite laconically, while he treats the years 1775–95 in a less concise and more rambling style.

Taxonomically, the archival data are categorized chronologically. Small paragraphs are written under each year's heading. Each paragraph is numbered, bears a heading, and contains a few sentences.[199] Facts are recorded, one after another—more or less independently—in the manner of a chronicle. Hardly any attempt is made to interpret individual events or to evaluate them.

The *Annals'* mark of distinction is that they provide a multiplicity of detail on the personality of the founder and the establishment of his Congregation. Furthermore, the details are firsthand reports of an author who—at least from time to time—lived in the same community with the saint and was himself a participant in the foundation of the Congregation.

In 1967, the *Annals* were published in their entirety by Fr. Gaetano, who,

[195] Testimony given by Fr. John Mary during the beatification processes evoked the following statement from the general counselor of the faith: "Oh disertum hominem et acris ingenii, ac memoriae pene incredibilis ... !" / "Oh eloquent man of keen intelligence and almost incredible memory ... !" (*Annali,* 7).

[196] The author himself affirms that the notes he had taken were jotted down in a hurry (PAR, 559v.).

[197] After the death of his brother, Fr. John Baptist, in Aug. 1765, St. Paul of the Cross chose Fr. John Mary as his confessor and spiritual director.

[198] There are good grounds for stating this, namely, (1) he is cited as its author in contemporary documents, (2) numerous statements in the *Annals* unequivocally indicate his authorship, and (3) most of the manuscript is written in his own hand.

[199] The complete work contains 1,235 paragraphs.

not content with merely editing the work, wrote several notes which clarified related facts and which, at times, sharpened the focus on the events and added a certain quality of completeness to them.[200]

[200] These have been published in the periodical *Acta Congregationis SS. Crucis et Passionis D.N.I.C.* in the issues of Oct. 1962 through Dec. 1967.

This critical analysis is most valuable. It contains references to literature and verifications of quotations from other sources. Also, in respective places, it cites quotations from the letters of St. Paul of the Cross.

CHAPTER II

Background and Basis of the Spiritual-Theological Thought of St. Paul of the Cross

Every person is unique, distinguishable from other persons and characterized by idiosyncrasies. This does not mean, however, that an individual remains isolated in this uniqueness, like an island soaring above the main. Birth situates a person in an absolutely fixed point within the space-time system of our world. Therefore, if someone wants to understand the life and activity of a person, then he must take into consideration the actual epoch and concrete setting in which that person lived. It is as if space and time represent the two banks bounding the river of human life from its beginning to its end. These banks, of necessity, influence each person's life.

Nevertheless, the person is not first and foremost or in any exclusive way the product of environment. Each has his own acting space, can actuate his liberty, and, up to a certain degree, decide the course of his own life. Every person possesses, therefore, a basic potential[1] of pursuing his own values, aspirations, and goal-directed activities—and in this way becomes true to himself.

For these reasons the epoch in which St. Paul of the Cross lived and the surroundings in which he acted are described in great detail in this chapter.[2] Also examined are the nature and kind of influences discernible in his spiritual-theological thought.[3]

---

[1] At the same time, there is no doubt that the probability of realizing this potential may be diminished (and considerably, too) in concrete cases as a result of a variety of causes, e.g., disease, external oppression, etc.

[2] See below, pp. 66–96.

[3] Since St. Paul of the Cross acquired his storehouse of knowledge in the fields of theology and spirituality not by means of study in a college or university but as an autodidact, or self-taught student, he depended upon extensive reading of the great spiritual masters and writers of Christian tradition. For this reason especially, it is both informative and important to determine which authors were his preferred ones and what sort of influence they exerted upon his spiritual and theological thought. This aspect of the analysis of Paul's thinking is discussed beginning on p. 96.

SPIRITUAL AND RELIGIOUS CLIMATE OF EIGHTEENTH–CENTURY ITALY: QUIETISM AND JANSENISM

When describing forces acting upon the history of a certain time period, it is important not to restrict the investigation to the spectacular events of the great and mighty personalities of the age. To do so results in a perception limited to a thin stratum of actors playing on history's stage. Rather, the historian must focus attention, before all else, on the broad strata of the anonymous but enduring people.[4] For example, in eighteenth-century Europe, despite the fact that the Church had lost her past influence in the sphere of politics and her former leadership in the development of the European spirit, people were still living the Christian tradition.[5] To study this period, therefore, it is necessary to examine not just political history[6] but also the history of Christian tradition and spirituality.[7] This is all the more important because our "actor", St. Paul of the Cross, was a man of the people, living with and among the people and, moreover, one who made "being a Christian" the decisive norm of his life.

I. Quietism

Although the origin and rise of Jansenism antedate quietism, the latter will be discussed first. This is because quietism had its roots in Italy, more specifically in Rome. Thus, by virtue of its geographical proximity alone, it had an impact upon the time and space in which Paul lived. As both a religious and a mystical movement, quietism, by virtue of its thematic proximity, also had an impact upon the spiritual and theological atmosphere in which the saint lived.

According to its traditional conceptualization and etymology, quietism may be defined as a theory which holds that "for the soul to find God and reach perfect contemplation, it should remain in a state of total passivity, thus

[4] O. Köhler and W. Müller in H. Jedin, ed., *Handbuch der Kirchengeschichte,* 5:v (Introduction).

[5] See n. 4 above.

[6] Political events are discussed beginning on p. 80.

[7] Historical descriptions of the epoch of absolutism and enlightenment generally present a distorted picture since they put in bold relief only those aspects that "already heralded modern society while impulses of conservation and preservation and religious creativity in art and music were given little notice . . ." This distortion is "made more acute by the fact that the history of the Church from this period, all too often, is treated within the framework of political history while the history of Christian spirituality, both in Catholicism and Protestantism, is neglected" (O. Köhler and W. Müller, in H. Jedin, *Handbuch der Kirchengeschichte,* 5:vi:).

permitting God to act. Any exertion on the soul's part is not only superfluous but also noxious and, even more than that, is considered to be a sign of the culpability of the individual."[8]

In the history of mysticism, there have always existed trends lacking proper balance in their overemphasis on the passive element as the main principle of the spiritual life. Consequently, they have been condemned as heretical by ecclesiastical authorities. As examples, we only need mention the "Alumbrados" of Spain or the "Guérinets" of France.[9] Although it is possible to present the basic influences leading to and the forerunners of quietism, what is essential in our consideration is a series of events occasioned by a Spanish priest, Miguel de Molinos, in Rome.

Upon his arrival in Rome in 1664, Molinos joined a movement called *Scuola di Cristo*.[10] Shortly thereafter, he gained popularity as a spiritual director. Bishop Piermatteo Petrucci and Cardinal Benedetto Odescalchi (after the year 1676, Pope Innocent XI) were his great protectors.

Molinos' book *Guía espiritual* appeared in 1675.[11] It soon became widely known and was translated into several languages. Its theses, strongly influenced by the thinking of the Rhineland, Flemish, and Spanish mystics, taught

---

[8] L. Cognet, in *Lexikon für Theologie und Kirche,* 2d ed., article on quietism 8, cols. 939–41, here col. 939. In some of the condemned sentences of Molinos we read, "Velle operari active, est Deum offendere, qui vult esse [ipse] solus agens: et ideo opus est, seipsum in Deo totum [et] totaliter derelinquere et postea permanere velut corpus exanime." / "To want to act in an active way is to offend God himself, who wants to be [only he himself] the sole agent; it is, therefore, necessary to abandon oneself entirely and totally to him, remaining thereafter as a body without a soul" (sent. 2; Henry Denzinger and Adolf Schönmetzer, *Enchiridion symbolorum* [33d edition] [Barcelona, Herder, 1965], 2202). It is further written, "Activitas naturalis est gratiae inimica, impeditque Dei operationes et veram perfectionem; quia Deus operari vult in nobis sine nobis." / "Natural activity is injurious since it hinders God's action and true perfection, because God wants to act in us but without us" (sent. 4; Denzinger and Schönmetzer, 2204).

[9] Also see L. Cognet, *Lexikon.* For other references see E. Beyreuther in *Die Religion in Geschichte und Gegenwart* (Tübingen, 3d ed.), article on quietism, 5, cols. 736–38. A more detailed presentation of the history of quietism may be found in the book by H. Heppe: *Geschichte der quietistischen Mystik in der katholischen Kirche.* In the first chapter of this book, Heppe investigates quietistic trends before the appearance of Miguel de Molinos (1–110). Also see M. Petrocchi, *Il Quietismo Italiano del Seicento,* especially the second chapter, entitled "Il primo quietismo Italiano", 21–58. Finally, see R. A. Knox, *Christliches Schwärmertum.*

[10] E. Zoffoli speaks of a brotherhood Molinos joined: " . . . si era iscritto ad una Confraternità de movimento, detta 'Scuola di Cristo', trovando in Italia un ambiente piuttosto adatto alla diffusione delle sue idee." / " . . . he entered a confraternity called 'School of Christ' and found in it, in Italy, an environment rather suitable to his ideas." (*Storia Critica* 3:29).

[11] In H. Heppe's opinion, the book was published for the first time in Italian. The exact title is *Guida spirituale, che disinvolge l'anima e la conduce per l'interior camino all'acquisto della perfetta contemplazione e del ricco tesoro della pace interiore,* by Dr. Miguel de Molinos (see Heppe, 112f.).

that an attitude of passivity must be adopted by anyone seeking to reach the stage of *contemplatio acquisita* (acquired contemplation).[12] On the whole, the book may be characterized as harmless.

Molinos also wrote a great number of letters for purposes of spiritual direction. The content of these letters and his "controversial manner of life" (including grave moral perversions) led to his arrest in 1685.[13] Although Pope Innocent XI intervened immediately in his favor,[14] he permitted the opening of the formal judicial process that ended in 1687 with Molinos being sentenced to life imprisonment.[15] The document *"Caelestis Pastor"* condemned sixty-eight sentences taken from his letters and from his "defense papers presented to the Inquisition".[16]

As a result of Molinos' condemnation, a deep scepticism toward all mystical writings began to spread throughout Italy. Several books, which up until then were held in high esteem, were put on the Index.[17] An investigation was also carried out against Cardinal Petrucci.[18] He made a retraction in the presence of the pope, however, and thus preserved his rights as cardinal. He died holding the official position of bishop of Jesi.[19]

---

[12] B. Schneider, in *Handbuch der Kirchengeschichte* 5:141.

[13] The Roman Inquisition uncovered approximately 12,000 letters of Molinos.

[14] In the preceding year, 1686, Innocent XI had appointed to the College of Cardinals Bishop Petrucci, who, with Molinos, shared the same ideas.

[15] He died in the Roman prison of the Inquisition in 1696.

[16] See Denzinger and Schönmetzer, 2201–68.

B. Schneider, in *Handbuch der Kirchengeschichte* 5:141. Not one of the condemned sentences containing the worst errors of quietism springs from the writing of *Guía espiritual*. In general, it is rather difficult to determine in what measure Molinos really spread some of the ideas that made for questioning the correctness of his belief. That is why L. Cognet states, "The present state of research does not as yet permit us to determine with exactitude the real measure of his guilt" (*Lexikon* 8, col. 940).

[17] See L. Cognet, *Lexikon*. The climate occasioned by the condemnation was such that authors, e.g., Tauler, Suso, Teresa of Avila, and John of the Cross, who until then had been accepted by theologians and ecclesiastical authorities, were treated with scepticism and suspicion for fear of aiding and abetting quietistic errors. See A. M. Walz, "Tauler im italienischen Sprachraum", 371–95, esp. 377–80.

[18] This investigation resulted in the Indexing of eight of his writings (see Heppe, 135–44, 281f; M. Petrocchi, *Il Quietismo*, 58–89). Among these eight writings was a work having as its subject matter Tauler's spiritual doctrine. It was entitled *Ponti d'interna e christiana perfettione del Venerabil Servo di Dio F. Giovanni Taulero* . . . (Geneva, 1682), cited in A. M. Walz, 380, n. 23.

[19] Also in need of mentioning are the brothers Leoni, who too were jailed in the prison of the Inquisition for their quietistic errors. They were sentenced on Sept. 4, 1687, the day after Molinos' condemnation (see Heppe, 271). They were accused of having spread doctrines considered by the Inquisition to be *temerariae, scandalosae, erroneae,* and *haereticales* (temerarious, scandalous, erroneous, and heretical). See J. De Guibert, *Documenta ecclesiastica christianae perfectionis,* 288–93.

About ten years later in France, the writings of J. M. Guyon occasioned a new quarrel over the "errors of quietism".[20] The major disputants in this case were Bishop Fénelon and Bishop Bossuet. While Fénelon defended the orthodoxy of Madame Guyon,[21] Bossuet vehemently rejected it. The latter, winning his case against Fénelon in a defamatory way,[22] succeeded in forcing King Louis XIV to threaten and intimidate Pope Innocent XII.[23] The resulting papal brief, *"Cum dies"*, ended the unfortunate quarrel: twenty-three sentences from Fénelon's "Maximes des Saints" were condemned. Fénelon yielded immediately and without mental reservation. Regrettably, this condemation led to a quasi-complete disappearance of all French literature in the field of mystical theology until the nineteenth century.[24]

Because of the strong antimystical sentiment, which had spread throughout Italy as a result of the condemnation of quietism and which persisted well into the first half of the eighteenth century,[25] it is astonishing that Paul of the Cross, by age twenty-seven, had already read the classics in spiritual-mystical literature.[26] This predilection for and eagerness to read and meditate upon writings of the mystics remained with him throughout his life.[27]

Since at that time it was forbidden to discuss the leanings of quietism, the saint did not openly express his opinion of the quarrel.[28] He was surely well informed, however, about the quietistic problem. It is known that he was

---

[20] A detailed presentation of Madame Guyon's case may be read in Heppe, 145–242, 283–443, 449–89. Also see R. A. Knox, *Christliches Schwärmertum*, 289–319.

[21] This he did in his work "Explication des Maximes des Saints", which appeared in Feb. 1697.

[22] In June 1698 he published the writing "Relation sur le quiétisme", a "terrible pamphlet of a defamatory kind, ridiculing Madame Guyon and Fénelon" (L. Cognet, in *Lexikon* 8, col. 940).

[23] Ibid.

[24] Ibid., col. 941.

[25] See A. M. Walz, "Tauler im italienischen Sprachraum", 377–80.

[26] The entries in his spiritual diary from Nov. 23, 1720, to Jan. 1, 1721, represent evident proof of this, since we can discern in them the influence (even leading at several points to similar formulations of content) of SS. Francis de Sales, Teresa of Jesus, and John of the Cross (see M. Bialas, *Tagebuch*, esp. commentary to the diary).

[27] John Tauler became the saint's preferred author after 1748. This will be discussed in greater detail below, beginning on p. 123.

[28] St. Paul of the Cross certainly had sufficient education to give a well-balanced opinion. Yet in his modesty and humility, he felt neither called nor competent to give a clarification, even on a question concerning the theology of spirituality. Taking into account the saint's extensive reading of the great spiritual writers of Christian tradition, it is obvious that he was not misled either by quietistic partialities or by the general mistrust of mystical literature that ensued. Rather, he continued unswervingly on his way, since he knew it to be the right one. Undoubtedly, these observations speak to us of a strong personality built upon a close relationship with God and upon his own intellectual understanding.

acquainted with the works of Paul Segneri the Elder,[29] the person who first observed errors in the writings of Molinos and who, in opposing them, became the "first foe of quietism".[30] The silence of our saint, therefore, might be said to signal not just moderation and reserve but even "much understanding and esteem" for the message of the "quietistic authors".[31] The balance evident in his judgments and in his cautions against quietistic partialities, however, reflected a keen ability to reason and discern the proper spiritual-mystical path in life.[32] Moreover, the great mystics whose works he read continually were *autores probati* (proven authors) whose writings gave Paul a solid basis for distinguishing the genuine and balanced from the prejudiced and exaggerated.

Were someone to so desire, he could certainly find in Paul's letters some sentences which sound one-sided and which, detached from the general train of his thought, could be interpreted as quietistic.[33] At the same time, there are two basic elements in Paul's spiritual life that are patently visible and that defend him against a charge of overemphasizing the passive element of contemplation in a quietistic manner. The first is the saint's unremitting effort to encourage all under his direction to a more intense practice of virtue.[34] The second is the saint's demand, repeated over and over again, that meditation

[29] Enrico Zoffoli refers to this observation in vol. 2 of his critical biography of St. Paul of the Cross: "In refettorio si compiaceva di leggere la classica opera di A. Rodriguez; quando poi si passava al *Cristiano istruito* di P. Segneri (1624–1694), restava impressionatissimo dalla descrizione dell'inferno." / "In the refectory, he liked to read the classical work of A. Rodriguez; later, when he came upon the book *Cristiano Istruito* of P. Segneri (1624–94), he remained impressed a good deal by its description of hell" (*Storia Critica* 2:83). Zoffoli bases his comments on the testimony of Fr. Hyacinth during the apostolic process in Rome (PAR, 1781r.).

[30] See Heppe, 135. In 1680, Segneri wrote the book *Concordia tra la fatica e la quiete nell'Orazione,* in which he objected to Molinos' one-sided doctrine without mentioning his name (see Heppe, 133–35). Also see Petrocchi, *Il Quietismo,* 92–97; B. Schneider, *Lexikon* 9, col. 596, article entitled "Paolo Segneri, the Elder"; and J. De Guibert, *Documenta ecclesiastica,* 523f.).

[31] Heppe, 135.

[32] It has not been possible to determine if St. Paul of the Cross has specifically read Segneri's work, cited above in n. 30. All known sources, however, indicate Paul was acquainted with the writings of Segneri, who belonged to the known and approved authors of seventeenth-century spiritual and ascetical literature. Moreover, in terms of their fame as missionaries, Segneri was second only to St. Vincent de Paul. Finally, it was Segneri who, by his methodology, gave the lay mission its classical form (see V. Schurr, in *Lexikon* 10, cols. 856–60, article entitled "Volksmission"). It is understandable, therefore, that Paul of the Cross would have had a special interest in Segneri's works.

[33] In his work *Introduzione alla Spiritulità di S. Paolo della Croce, Morte Mistica e Divina Natività* C. Brovetto reached the same conclusions concerning St. Paul of the Cross and quietism (36f.); his final conclusion was that St. Paul of the Cross' stance was antiquietistic.

[34] See below, pp. 143–44 and 173–84.

begin with the humanity of Christ, especially of Christ in his passion, in order to attain vision in faith and profound contemplative prayer.[35]

To summarize: If we want to interpret Paul's spiritual-theological thought in a correct way, then we must take into consideration the quietistic movement, even though Paul himself was not directly involved in the argument. That is why we conclude with the following quotation from M. Petrocchi: "The mystical theology of St. Paul of the Cross . . . might not be explained without studying the preceding quietistic dispute that impassioned seventeenth-century Italy."[36]

2. Jansenism

While arguments surrounding quietism influenced Christian spirituality, formulations of the questions proposed by Jansenism (at least in its origin) concerned Christian dogmatics, namely, Augustinian teaching on grace.[37] The Jansenist movement, however, was very complex.[38] Although active in the Catholic countries of Europe for more than a hundred years, its development differed in each.[39]

By the second half of the sixteenth century, Pope Pius V had condemned eighty sentences in the writings of Michael Baius, a teacher of theology at the Louvain. All sentences condemned in the papal bull *"Ex omnibus*

[35] Also see below pp. 212–16.

[36] "La teologia mistica di San Paolo della Croce . . . non si spiegherebbe senza la precedente ontata quietista che appassionò il Seicento italiano." / "The mystical theology of St. Paul of the Cross . . . might not be explained without [the study of] the preceding quietistic dispute, which impassioned seventeenth-century Italy" (Massimo Petrocchi, *Il Quietismo*, 130).

[37] In posttridentine theology, the dispute over grace played an important role. It is worthwhile mentioning here the differences between Dominican and Jesuit theologians. The Jesuit Molina, in his book entitled *Liberi arbitrii cum gratiae donis . . . concordia* (1588), put emphasis on the human will, while the Dominican Bañez, with his "gratia efficax" and "praedeterminatio physica", placed more emphasis on the work of divine grace. The brief "Congregatio de auxiliis gratiae" of Pope Clement VIII did not give any definitive solution to this dispute (see P. Honigsheim, in *Die Religion in Geschichte und Gegenwart* [3d ed.] 3, col. 532, article on Jansenism; F. Stegmüller, in *Lexikon* 4, cols. 1002–7, on the dispute about grace).

[38] Besides the teaching on grace, there were other problems that arose from its moral rigorism and applied ecclesiology (Episcopalism, Febronianism, Josephinism, and Gallicanism), which all led to the "dispute over Jansenism". See L. Willaert, in *Lexikon* 5, cols. 865–69, in the article "Jansenism, Jansenists, and the dispute over Jansenism".

[39] Over and above all other considerations, E. Zoffoli underscores the antimystical character of Jansenism and characterizes this movement by an appropriate formulation: " . . . esso nacque in Belgio, si maturò in Francia e si diffuse in Europa con nefaste consequenze per la Chiesa e il Papato." / " . . . it was born in Belgium, matured in France, and spread throughout Europe with unfortunate consequences for the Church and papacy" (*Storia Critica* 3:32f.).

afflictionibus" concerned the author's doctrine on the person and grace.[40]

Some years later, Cornelius Jansenius (1585–1638) composed his main work, *Augustinus . . .*, in which he dealt first and foremost with the teaching on grace of this Father of the Church. This work, published in the Louvain two years after the author's death,[41] touched off the "dispute over Jansenism" which lasted more than one hundred years. In 1642, Pope Urban VIII, in his bull *"In eminenti"*, and in 1653, Pope Innocent X, in his bull *"Cum occasione"*,[42] condemned numerous sentences implicitly or explicitly contained in Jansenius' book.

As a result of the pontifical condemnation of Baius and Jansenius, Jansenists allied themselves with the "opponents of Roman centralism".[43] In the years that followed, many political disputes led to a "politicization" of Jansenism. As a consequence, this movement began making more and more its own requests formulated by Episcopalism and Gallicanism.

In regard to the latter, the influence of the French theologian Pasquier Quesnel (1634–1719) is very important. His essential work, an edition of the complete works of Leo the Great, was published in Paris in 1675 and put on the Index in 1676 because of its commentary, which was replete with Gallican ideas. Another of his books, *Reflexions morales sur les Evangiles,* also caused conflict with ecclesiastical authorities. Pope Clement XI in 1713, in the bull *"Unigenitus"*, condemned 101 sentences from among the book's theses, which were similar in content to the errors made by Baius and Jansenius.[44]

The dispute over Jansenism did not remain confined to the domain of eccclesiology and theology but extended itself into the areas of morality and asceticism. Events linked to the French Cistercian abbey of Port-Royal occasioned one of the dispute's more dramatic conflicts. The abbess of the convent was Mère Angélique Arnauld,[45] who at one time had had St. Francis de Sales as

[40] See Denzinger and Schönmetzer, 1901–80.

[41] About Jansen as a person, L. Willaert writes, "Jansen's submission to ecclesiastical ministry, formulated in his last will, is beyond any doubt. He was esteemed and respected by everybody, a pious and exemplary priest and bishop full of zeal for reform . . . " (*Lexikon* 5, col. 870, in the article "Cornelius Jansen, the Younger").

[42] See Denzinger and Schönmetzer, 2001–7. The errors of Jansenism were again condemned by Pope Alexander VIII in 1690. Also see Denzinger and Schönmetzer, 2301–32.

[43] See L. Willaert's article on Jansen, *Lexikon* 5, col. 865.

[44] Denzinger and Schönmetzer, 2400–2501.

[45] Living in Paris during the second half of the sixteenth century, the Arnauld family played a prominent part in the history of French Jansenism. Besides Mère Angélique, three other brothers were connected with the Jansenist dispute. A friend of Duvergier, Robert (1588–1674) retired as a "Solitaire" to Port-Royal, where six of his daughters had already entered. Although he did not share all the rigorism of Port-Royal, Henry (1597–1692), as bishop of Angers, was also associated with Jansenism. The Jansenists venerated him as a saint on the basis of his conduct, but he was also praised and esteemed within the ecclesiastical circles of Rome. Antoine (1612–94), called "Le Grand", was the most important personage in

spiritual director. When Duvergier de Hauranne (Abbé Saint-Cyran)[46] became her confessor, she and the other nuns were introduced to a series of Jansenistic principles with which to govern their lives. On the one hand, they submitted to rigorous penitential exercises; but, on the other hand, they omitted the reception of Holy Eucharist.[47] Within a short period of time, the cloister at Port-Royal became the spiritual center of French Jansenism[48] and, for many years, the center about which the quarrels over Jansenism were fought. The abbey's influence, however, terminated abruptly in the year 1711. At the behest of King Louis XIV, Port-Royal was completely destroyed.[49]

Among those embroiled in the arguments surrounding Port-Royal was Blaise Pascal, who intervened on the side of rigorous morals. His involvement occurred in the following manner. In January of 1656, Pascal visited his sister, Jacqueline, who was a nun in the abbey of Port-Royal. This visit occurred shortly after Antoine Arnauld, the youngest brother of the abbess, had become involved in a violent argument at the Sorbonne.[50] Upon Pascal's arrival, Jacqueline convinced him to write a polemic supporting the arguments of Antoine. Pascal complied with the request and intervened in the quarrel by writing the world famous *Lettres à un Provincial,* in which he posited laxity in morals on the part of the Jesuits.[51] As an immediate result

French Jansenism after Duvergier's death. We shall speak more of Antoine. See J. Oswald, in *Lexikon* 1, col. 889f. (keyword: Arnauld).

[46] Duvergier (1581–1643) was a very good friend of Jansen. In 1635, he became the confessor and spiritual director of several nuns and of the "Solitaires" of Port-Royal. He and Mère Angélique were the spiritual leaders of the cloister (see L. Cognet, *Handbuch der Kirchengeschichte* 5:36–41).

[47] See *Storia Critica* 3:33f. Also see ibid., 53–57.

[48] One way in which it exerted a great influence was by means of its hermits or so-called Solitaires, i.e., Jansenists who retired there, lived a life of meditation and prayer, and became active in Jansenistic change. Such men included R. Arnauld, A. and I. Le Maistre, P. Nicole, and Blaise Pascal. See St. Skalweit, in *Lexikon* 8, col. 629f. (keyword: Port-Royal).

[49] See L. Cognet, *Handbuch der Kirchengeschichte* 5:55–62. Also see K. Bihlmeyer and H. Tüchle, *Kirchengeschichte* 3:239–44.

[50] Arnauld's writings were the underlying basis for the quarrel. In 1643, he published a work entitled "De la fréquente communion", in which he came out against a too frequent reception of Communion. This position created quite a sensation. In 1649, he published another called "Considerations", again addressed to the Sorbonne. In it he tried to justify himself. In 1653, although Pope Innocent X had rejected five of Jansenius' sentences, Antoine, in his work "Lettres à un duc et pair", defended the Jansenist distinction between *quaestio iuris* and *quaestio facti.* (*Quaestio iuris:* The Church is infallible when speaking on a matter of faith. *Quaestio facti:* The Church is not infallible in her judgment of theologians as to whether or not they correctly or incorrectly presented a doctrine.) In the same year, 1656, Arnauld and sixty other doctors were expelled from the Sorbonne because of their insubordination (see Bihlmeyer and Tüchle, 241; J. Oswald, in *Lexikon* 1, col. 890).

[51] Pascal painted a distorted picture of "Jesuit morals" in this work, which, because of the

and from henceforward, Jansenism, in any of its forms, bore an anti-Jesuit character.[52]

The Jansenism that influenced eighteenth-century Italy was inspired to a great extent by the ideas developed by the bishop of Trier, J. N. von Hontheim, in his book *De statu ecclesiae*. In this voluminous work, Hontheim, using the pseudonym Justinus Febronius,[53] advanced the idea of restraining papal rights in favor of the episcopacy and promoted the need for reunification in faith.[54]

While Kaiser Joseph II, who reigned from 1765 to 1790, was "reforming" the Church within the German empire in conformity with principles of enlightenment and making it into a state-church system, his younger brother, Peter Leopold, the grand duke of Tuscany, during the same interval was following in his older brother's footsteps.[55] With respect to zeal for reform, Peter Leopold was in no way inferior to his brother from Vienna. Although there were many things in need of change in Tuscany,[56] the way in which the grand duke executed his reforms indicated that he drew his inspiration from the ideas of Gallicanism and Febronianism. As a result, what characterized Italian Jansenism, especially with regard to the reforming work of Grand

---

magic of his incomparable style, resulted in a long-lasting damage to them. "By identifying laxity with the Jesuits, Pascal so discredited the Society of Jesus that it was incapable of ridding itself of [the charge]" (L. Cognet, as cited in n. 49).

[52] This charge had such a long-lasting effect because it was grounded on opinions not limited by local conditions or fluctuations of time. Basically, the accusation was grounded in two fundamentally different viewpoints on the nature of the human person and grace. Jesuit theology (as compared with Augustinian) was based on a more positive view of the person, and, therefore, gave greater importance to free will. In contrast, Jansenism pleaded for a strong Augustinianism anthropologically and in terms of the nature of grace. The outcome for the Jansenists was an unsound rigorism in morals and, for the Jesuits, a more generous ethical judgment of human activity and casuistic morals. Another reason for the Jansenists' anti-Jesuit stance was grounded in the Jesuits' loyalty to the pope and his office—this loyalty being a function of Ignatian spirituality. The representatives of Jansenism—because of the frequent regulations and judgments that issued from the competent Roman tribunals—took an opposing stance with regard to the papacy and the Magisterium and joined themselves to those forces that fought against "Roman centralization".

[53] Nuntius Oddi deserves the credit for identifying the author of the work as Von Hontheim, who admitted his authorship only after a series of obstinate denials (see H. Raab, in *Lexikon* 5, col. 479f.; keyword: Hontheim).

[54] *De statu ecclesiae* was placed on the Index in 1764. Although Von Hontheim retracted his position, he moderated this retraction in later years in his work "J. Febronii: Commentarius in suam retractationem" (see H. Raab, as cited in n. 53 above).

[55] After the demise of the Medici family in 1737, the grand duchy of Tuscany was ruled by the princes of the Lothringen-Habsburg house (see Bihlmeyer and Tüchle 3:215).

[56] Full details will be given subsequently. Also, refer to the study *La Maremma Toscana*, by C. Giorgini.

Duke Peter Leopold, was not so much the Augustinian doctrine on grace as it was the idea of the development of a national Church as envisioned by Quesnel and von Hontheim. While Jansenism in Italian Tuscany had only a limited theological impact,[57] its practical influence was considerable due to the political power of Peter Leopold, whose influence lasted for at least twenty-five years and who was the leader of this particular religious-political movement.

There were, of course, reforms initiated by the grand duke that were thoroughly positive in nature, such as equalization of prebends, redirection of donations in favor of poor priests, making obligatory stable residence for priests, distribution of Holy Communion during Holy Mass, establishment of a minimum age of twenty-four years for priestly ordination, etc.[58] However, he instituted all these changes without consulting authorities in Rome.[59] Over and above this, he tried to obtain the independence of bishops from the pope and Rome. He forbade appeals to Rome since (1) "the infallibility of the Church reposed in the totality of faithful and not in the papacy", and (2) "the jurisdiction of the bishops comes from Jesus himself".[60] These Gallican articles were taken to be sentences of faith.[61]

Peter Leopold had as an advisor in ecclesiastical affairs the bishop of Prato and Pistoia, Scipione de' Ricci, a fanatic adherent of Jansenism and Febronianism and a staunch supporter of the reforms. To show how strongly embedded was the idea of a national Church, the grand duke and his "spiritual advisor" ordered an arbitrary translation of the missals and a reform of the breviary. Moreover, orders that tended to pauperize rather than destroy religious life were given and executed by force. Missions and spiritual exercises along with devotions to the Heart of Jesus were forbidden. Numerous monasteries were closed, twenty-five hundred religious were driven from them, and a number of oratories were profaned.[62]

During a diocesan synod chaired by Bishop Ricci in Pistoia in September of 1786, a number of diocesan clergy officially adopted the thinking of Quesnel

[57] L. Willaert, in *Lexikon* 5, col. 869, in the article "Cornelius Jansen, the Younger".

[58] See W. Müller, in *Handbuch der Kirchengeschichte* 5:584.

[59] See C. Giorgini, *La Maremma Toscana*, esp. the section "L'opera di Leopoldo in materia ecclesiastica", 255–61. (The problems that ensue for faith and the Church when the state assumes as its own matters of ecclesiastical importance were recently researched in the case of Spain. Also see the circumspect and valuable study of Laurentino Novoa, *Religionsfreiheit in Spanien. Geschichte — Problematik — Zukunftsperspektiven.*)

[60] From W. Müller, *Handbuch der Kirchengeschichte* 5:585.

[61] Ibid.

[62] A detailed and lively description of these "negative reforms" is presented in Pastor's book *Geschichte der Päpste*, in which he elaborates upon negative ways of acting and resistance of people (see 16:93–114).

and von Hontheim on a national Church.[63] These synod documents were published immediately and circulated throughout the world.[64] Nonetheless, only two bishops of Tuscany would later adopt the synod statements. The overwhelming majority rejected these and other similar statements on the occasion of the national synod in Florence in 1787.

These unilateral and forced reforms came to a sudden end, however. In 1790, the grand duke of Tuscany relinquished his duchy when he, now as Emperor Leopold II (1790–92), succeeded his brother in Vienna. In 1791, Ricci was forced to resign his bishopric because of the great resistance he encountered on the part of the people and because of the decision of the Chapter of Pistoia and Prato, whose members declared themselves against him.[65] In 1794, the bull "Auctorem fidei" condemned eighty-five statements from the 1786 synod of Pistoia.[66]

Other regions in Italy also had influential people who were Jansenists or who had strong Jansenist leanings. For example, there existed in Rome a Jansenist circle about Monsignor Botarri, prefect of the Vatican Library; and to this group belonged the nephew of Pope Clement XII, Cardinal Neri-Corsini. In the kingdom of Naples, A. Serrao, the bishop of Potenza, adopted Jansenist teachings, and in Pavia the movement was represented by Abbots Peter Tamburini and Joseph Zola.[67]

E. Zoffoli appropriately describes the spiritual-religious climate of the second half of the eighteenth-century in Italy in the following way:

> The sky that had always shone with a merry and lively optimism for the pious people of Italy was now dark. God was again and again presented as a Judge and not as a Father. . . . The masters of the spiritual life took more care to keep people from receiving Holy Eucharist than in directing them to [receive] well and in a dignified manner. People were convinced that the renunciation of Holy Communion—on the grounds of being wholly penitent— was most pleasing to God.[68]

[63] The number of participants totaled 234, including 171 pastors and 13 members of religious orders. Participants in the deliberations included some who belonged to neither the diocese of Pistoia nor that of Tuscany. Among these were three Josephist theologians from Pavia, including Tamburini. Known for his Jansenist convictions, he was named promoter of the synod and became, as Ricci observed in his memoirs, the soul of this undertaking against the "old machine of papal monarchy" (Pastor, Geschichte der Päpste, 16:104).

[64] See W. Müller, Handbuch der Kirchengeschichte, 5:585.

[65] See Pastor, Geschichte der Päpste, 16:109f.

[66] See Denzinger and Schönmetzer, 2600–2700.

[67] See Storia Critica 3:36. Other works on Italian Jansenism also need to be mentioned: A. C. Jemolo, Il Giansenismo in Italia prima della Revoluzione (Bari, 1928); E. Dammig, Il movimento giansenista a Roma nella seconda metà del sec. XVIII (Città del Vaticano, 1945); J. Orcibal, Nuove ricerche storiche sul giansenismo (Rome, 1954).

[68] "Il cielo delle anime, che in Italia era stato sempre luminoso del più sano ottimismo, si rannuvolò: Dio era presentato più come giudice che come padre. . . . I maestri di spirito eran

If anyone were to ask how St. Paul of the Cross opposed the Jansenist movement, we would only be able to answer indirectly, taking into consideration the whole train of his thought. Although the term *Jansenism* does not appear in any of the sources handed down to us, we must not draw the conclusion that the saint was unaware of the quarrels surrounding it. Indeed, with all his apostolic activity, he would have inevitably encountered some of the effects of this complex movement. This is especially so because many of his missions and spiritual exercises were conducted in the region of Tuscany.[69]

What has already been said about his attitude toward quietism is also valuable in regard to his attitude toward Jansenism: He deliberately avoided such theological conflicts and condemnations because he felt he had no call to argue such issues. There were, however, some distinguishing anti-Jansenist features in his thought and in the conceptualization of his faith.

To begin with were his incessant attempts to encourage those he directed to receive the sacraments more frequently, especially Holy Communion.[70] It is

---

più solleciti di privare le anime dei sacramenti che di prepararle a ben riceverli, convinti che astenersi della Comunione per far penitenza riusciva più gradito a Dio." / "The sky of the soul, which in Italy had always shone with pure optimism became cloudy: God was presented as a judge rather than as a father. . . . The masters of the spiritual life, being convinced that to refrain from Holy Communion as a penance was more agreeable to God [than to receive], were more occupied with depriving people of the sacraments than in preparing them to receive the sacraments in a dignified manner (*Storia Critica* 3:36f.).

[69] Refer to the table listing apostolic activities of the founder in *Storia Critica* 3:1393–1406.

[70] To this end, let us look at some passages from his letters. To Anna Maria Calcagnini he wrote, "In quanto alla santa comunione vorrei la faceste ogni mattina, senza lasciarla mai, e pregatene chi vi confessa, anche in nome mio, ed ivi bevete nel fonte della santità le acque vive dell'eterna vita." / "As concerns Holy Communion, I would like you to receive it every morning without interruption and to confess your sins, and thus you will drink from the spring of holiness, the living waters of eternal life" (L 3:809, June 1, 1768).

To the priest D. Giovanni Lucattini, he gave the following advice: "Lucia potrebbe accostarsi al Confessore uno o due volte la settimana, ma la SS.ma Comunione la faccia ogni mattina sulla coscienza mia. Già sanno il decreto della Sacra Congregazione del Concilio ecc., che lascia ai confessori la cura in ordine alla SS.ma Comunione quotidiana come quelli che vedono l'interno, per lo svelamento che gli vien fatto dalle anime ecc." / "Lucy may go to confession once or twice a week, but as concerns Holy Communion let her receive it every morning with my dispensation. You already know the decree of the Holy Council, etc., which gave to the confessors the right to permit daily reception of Holy Communion, as they are those who see into the interior through the disclosures of [their penitents]" (L 2:814, Aug. 17, 1751). Paul refers here to the decree of Innocent XI, "Cum ad aures", of Feb. 12, 1769. See Denzinger-Schönmetzer, 2090–95.

In another letter of Mar. 5, 1770, to an abbess of a Capuchin monastery in S. Fiora, he wrote, "Godo nel Signore di sentire che abbiano introdotto la SS.ma Comunione quotidiana, e le accerto che io lo desiderai fin da quando fui costì. Ne sia benedetto e ringraziato il Signore. Si accertino dunque che è volontà di Dio che la continuino, e tengano per perduto quel giorno che la lascieranno senza legitima causa." / "I rejoice in God upon hearing that

known too that after his ordination the saint himself received Holy Eucharist daily.[71] To this we must add his devotion to the Heart of Jesus, which was an essential part of his passion mysticism,[72] his recognition and esteem for the hierarchy, and his sincere and deep appreciation for the Society of Jesus.[73]

Holy Communion has been introduced every day, and I assure you that this was my desire even before it happened. Let us bless and thank the Lord for this. Be assured this is God's will and continue (daily reception) forever, considering it a lost day in which this good habit is abandoned without a legitimate reason" (*Bollettino* 8 (1927): 178f.). Many more citations could have been used. See *Storia Critica* 2:1494–1503; S. L. Pompilio, *L'Esperienza mistica della Passione in San Paolo della Croce*, 101f.

[71] During the informative processes of Vetralla, the saint's confessor, Father John Mary, declared the following: "... si pose sotto di un altro direttore quale, conoscendo la sua virtù, lo faceva communicare ogni giorno. Ed esso, per tenersi nascosto agl'occhi degl' uomini, andavasi a communicare un giorno in una chiesa, ed un giorno in un altra." / "... he went to another spiritual director, who, being acquainted with his virtues, permitted him to receive Holy Communion daily. To remain unnoticed by the people, he received Communion in one church on one day and in another church on the next" (POV, 113r.; *Processi* 1:34).

[72] In the letters of St. Paul of the Cross, we often come across references to the Heart of Jesus. For him, this means—first and foremost—the Heart of Jesus Crucified ("Il Cuore di Gesù Crocifisso"). We must add here that adoration of the Heart of Jesus found in our founder is not identical in all its points with that form of adoration originating in the visions of St. Margaret Mary Alacoque. It has been established, however, that Paul had learned of the events of Paray-le-Monial, and this knowledge was a vital stimulus for him (*Storia Critica* 2:1184–86, 1449–64).

[73] In an extant letter written by Paul on Sept. 22, 1767, i.e., six years after suppression of the Jesuits, to the Jesuit priest Luigi Reali, who was assisting in a series of lectures being given in Rome at the time, we can see how much the saint suffered because of the suppression: "Riguardo poi all'estreme afflizioni, alle quali soggiace cotesta inclita Compagnia di Gesù, s'assicuri pure che anco io ne sono molto a parte, ed al solo pensarvi non posso a meno di non gemere e lagrimare, vedendo angustiati in simil guisa tanti poveri innocenti Religiosi, e nel tempo stesso trionfare il demonio, diminuita la maggior gloria di Dio e tante anime perdute per mancanza di quell'aiuto spirituale che dai medesimi Padri gli era somministrato in tutte le parti del mondo, e su tal riflesso non manco per parte mia di farne continuamente specialissime orazioni, sperando che dopo varie tempeste quel Dio che 'mortificat et vivificat', sarà per fare risorgere a suo tempo con maggior splendore la Compagnia suddetta; e questo è stato sempre ed è il mio sentimento." / "I look at the extreme afflictions suffered by the illustrious Society of Jesus, and I assure you I am not insensible to them too; when I think only of this I cannot refrain from sighing and weeping, seeing so many religious persecuted in such a way and, at the same time, seeing the devil triumphant, God's greater glory diminished, and so many souls lost on account of the absence of spiritual help provided by the Jesuit fathers all over the world. In making such reflections, I do not forget to pray always in a special way that, after so many tempests, God, who *mortificat et vivificat*, will know how to raise up again, at the opportune moment, the Society of Jesus to greater splendor. This is now and has always been my feeling" (L 4:21).

The author G. C. Cordara (1704–85) is incorrect, therefore, when he implies in the epilogue of his autobiography that the Passionist founder, a close friend of Pope Clement

Moreover, his imagery of God, in which the attributes of goodness, love, and benevolence predominate, was far removed from the Jansenistic conception of God.[74] At the same time, the saint desired those things Jansenists tried to obtain in an incorrect or one-sided manner, such as improved education for priests, stricter discipline in cloisters, and less laxity and probabilism among secular clergy;[75] furthermore, he stressed the practice of virtue and self-control.

It should also be mentioned that Paul of the Cross possessed a susceptibility to one of the points raised by Jansenism. It has been handed down to us that in different periods of his life, he was haunted by morbid thoughts which tempted him to think his election and salvation were doubtful.[76] One of the witnesses in the sanctification processes states, " . . . that, because of this [tendency], he trusted still more in divine mercy just as a child has trust in a mother's arms".[77]

In conclusion, we can say that St. Paul of the Cross, who lived in Italy at a time in which Jansenism was active, did not remain untouched by this complex movement but responded to its challenge in a Catholic way.

XIV, encouraged the pope to suppress the Society of Jesus. This autobiography is published in part in J. Döllinger's *Beiträge zur politischen, kirchlichen und Cultur-Geschichte*, 3:3–74. As cited in *Storia Critica* 1:1412, Cordara himself states the pope and Paul were talking privately, with no others present—*solus et inobservatus exegit.* Consequently, Cordara's position is "pure suspicion", as Pastor writes in his *Geschichte der Päpste* 16:2, para. 334, n. 8). See P. Gaetano dell'Addolorata, C.P., "S. Paolo della Croce e la soppressione della Compagnia di Gesù", 13:102–12. Also see *Storia Critica* 1:1407–14.

[74] See Bialas, *Tagebuch,* especially the part "How the saint thinks of God and man . . . ", 31–34.

[75] In the archives of the Passionist Generalate in Rome, there is preserved a record of a conversation between St. Paul of the Cross and Canon D. Joseph Suscioli, which took place sometime between 1740 and 1750. This conversation expressed the deep concern of the saint regarding the negative influence on the faithful resulting from the clergy's excessive probabilism and laxity in manners (*Storia Critica* 1:1422f.).

[76] During the informative processes in Orbetello, a witness gave testimony that Paul, at the age of twenty-five, contended with great temptations regarding predestination. Full of inner doubts, he anxiously asked his spiritual director, at that time Monsignor Gattinara, "Ah, Monsignore, chi sa se mi salverò?" / "Ah, Monsignor, who knows if I shall be saved?" The bishop answered, "Qui bona egerunt ibunt in vitam aeternam, qui vero mala, in ignem aeternum: haec est fides catholica." / "Those who have done good will enter into eternal life, those who have done evil into eternal fire: this is the Catholic Faith." These words of his director of conscience were sufficient to destroy his doubts. See POO, 345v. (*Processi* 2:264), testimony of Fr. Joseph Andrew.

[77] " . . . che confidava perciò assai più nella divina misericordia di quello che fosse stato un bambino nelle braccia della sua madre" (POR, 248v.), testimony of Canon D. Joseph Suscioli.

ACTUAL ENVIRONMENT IN THE
LIFE OF ST. PAUL OF THE CROSS:
THE TUSCAN MAREMMA[78] OF
BAROQUE EIGHTEENTH—CENTURY ITALY

If we are to understand and interpret correctly Paul's doctrine and activity, we need to consider the population and environment in which he lived and worked. For the first twenty-eight years of his life, the saint lived in the northern Piedmont region of Italy. He grew to adulthood, therefore, in what is called central Italy. After this, he and his brother John Baptist lived for a few years in the diocese of Gaeta (about 100 km [62 mi.] south of Rome) and Troia-Foggia in southern Italy. It was during this interval that, through the influence of friends in Rome, he obtained initial approbation of his Rule. In the fall of 1727, Paul moved to Mount Argentario (about 150 km [93 mi.] northwest of Rome), where he established the first Passionist monastery. During the next forty-five years, the founder devoted himself with dedication and zeal to the fulfillment of two primary objectives: establishment of new monasteries and apostolic work.

A review of missions and spiritual exercises conducted by Paul of the Cross during these years[79] reveals that most were given in the pontifical state of Tuscany. During the first fifteen years of this time period, he considered the vicinity near Monte Argentario to be the preferred "region for missions". For this reason, it is important for us to become familiar with this area and the living conditions of its people.

Fortunately, there is a historical monograph on eighteenth-century living conditions of people from this part of Tuscany, called the *Maremma* because of its bad climate and numerous swamps.[80] This work, by Candeloro Giorgini, is entitled *La Maremma Toscana nel Settecento: Aspetti sociali e religiosi*.[81] Its conclusions are used in subsequent pages whenever the special situation of this region or information on the social stratification of its people are discussed.

[78] The word *Maremma* is Italian. It is derived from the word *mare*, which means sea. By it is understood the swampy coastal area of central Italy. See *Der Große Duden*, vol. 1, *Rechtschreibung*, Mannheim (1973): 447.

[79] Refer to the table illustrating the apostolic works of St. Paul of the Cross in *Storia Critica* 3:1393–1406.

[80] Etymologically, the Italian word *Maremma* simply means a thick, swampy region extending along a seashore (F. Palazzi, *Novissimo Dizionario della Lingua Italiana*, 679). Nevertheless, this word is used in Italy, more often than not, as a proper noun referring to the marshy region of central Italy.

[81] This work was published in Edizioni "ECO", S. Gabriele (Teramo, 1968). As a dissertation, it was accepted by the faculty of ecclesiastical history of the Pontifical University (Gregoriana). The author belongs to the Passionist Congregation.

1. *The Structure of the Region and Its Population*

The Tuscan *Maremma* in the time of St. Paul of the Cross had a population of thirty-three thousand people within three dioceses.[82] It covered an area of almost five thousand sq. km (a size slightly smaller than the 5,328 sq. km. that comprise the state of Delaware). Although the region was primarily agricultural, numerous swamps limited the amount of land available for farming and constrained productivity. The economic situation of the people was one of utter misery.[83]

A variety of reasons accounted for the region's poor economy: improper tillage, high rents paid to landlords, no free trade of agricultural products, ceilings on prices, high local taxes, bad harvests, natural catastrophes, and devastation following military operations of 1700–1714 (War of Spanish Succession) and 1733–38 (War of Polish Succession).[84]

Poor roads limited communication between isolated villages and hamlets.[85] As a result, people preferred to live in towns and villages. Among village inhabitants there existed a kind of apolitical parochial mentality. Almost all were illiterate.[86] There were, however, teachers and professors in the more important towns, whose pupils were, for the most part, clerical students,[87] and some young men of the aristocracy and better-situated families.

An unfavorable climate, intense heat in the plain during summer, and poor food and hygiene[88] all contributed to the heavy toll taken by pulmonary tuberculosis and typhoid fever. Many fell prey to malaria, carried by the mosquito all too readily bred in the marshes. The mean age of the population

---

[82] These three dioceses and their populations follow: Sovana, 15,600; Massa Maritima, 6,300; and Grosseto, 8,500. Porto S. Stefano and Orbetello, with a population totaling 2,800, came under the jurisdiction of the Abbey *Tre Fontane* in Rome. These two cities did not belong to the grand duchy of Tuscany but to the *Stato dei Presidi*.

[83] See C. Giorgini, *La Maremma Toscana*, "Introduction", xiii.

[84] See C. Giorgini's overview of the geographical, historial and economic situation of the eighteenth-century Maremma as cited in ibid., 3–11.

[85] Most villages had less than 500 inhabitants. In only five towns did the population exceed 1,000.

[86] Giorgini remarks, "La popolazione maremmana nella quasi totalità era analfabeta." / "The population of the Maremma was almost completely illiterate" (*La Maremma Toscana*, 22).

[87] These clerics included not only mature and young men but also young boys and teenagers, who were considered to belong to the clerical state by virtue of their tonsure. Even those who were older received only a scanty education, about which more will be discussed later.

[88] It was still the general custom in 1767 to shelter domestic animals, e.g., sheep, steers, and swine, in the people's own homes, which contained few and poorly separated rooms (Giorgini, *La Maremma Toscana*, 19).

was nineteen years.[89] Women accounted for the majority of older adults, since exposure to and death from malaria was much greater among men.

The *forestieri* lived under deplorable and miserable conditions. These were itinerant workers from neighboring regions who migrated to the Maremma to work as temporary farm hands during the summer months, a time of labor shortage. Giorgini states, "Driven by misery and tempted by high wages, they emigrated there, although they knew they would either die there or return as victims of a perilous bite in their veins."[90] Still, they came in droves to gain money in this region. From May through September, in many parts of the Maremma there were more forestieri than native inhabitants.[91]

Yet these "guest workers" were, more often than not, unwelcome guests. Their "bad manners" were met with scepticism and ill will. Local animosity and poor roads between the villages and cultivated fields effected the isolation of the forestieri in camps or colonies of sorts, outside village limits and near their places of work. Most lodging consisted of primitive huts containing straw mattresses or the like for sleep. Meals were served in the fields.

The amount of misery becomes more apparent when we consider that in the event of illness there was no one even to care for the patient, let alone to obtain medical help. Under such conditions, serious illness, mostly malaria, was followed by certain death, with the age of workers dying under these circumstances ranging from twenty-five to thirty-five years.[92] It goes almost without saying that mortality rates among migrants were much higher than among the native adult population in that area.[93]

Without a doubt, the great influx of summer laborers into the Maremma (about fifteen thousand migrant workers as compared with a total population of thirty-three thousand year-round inhabitants) brought with them additional social problems. Despite this, the regents of Tuscany did nothing until the middle of the eighteenth century to help develop agriculture in the swamplands and support free trade. It was not until the reign of Grand Duke

---

[89] Very few men reached the age of fifty or sixty years. For example, in 1767, of eighty inhabitants of the hamlet Caldana, only four were older than fifty years. In the region of the plain of Grosseto only five percent of the inhabitants were sixty years or older (ibid., 25).

[90] See ibid., 29.

[91] See ibid., 33, Table 7.

[92] See ibid., 31–32, Table 7.

[93] Sources of information on the social strata of that time also reveal grave abuse in the burial of the dead. After dying in misery and poverty far from their own families and homeland, without medical or spiritual assistance, they were often buried hurriedly in a field or near a path, or their corpses were carried into the forest and covered with a heap of stones. That such was not an infrequent occurrence is apparent from the fact that in many places various Christian confraternities cited burial of the dead as one of their duties in addition to attending to ill workers (ibid., 32ff.).

Peter Leopold that a program was worked out to reclaim swamps, establish free trade of agricultural produce, and fix rents at uniform rates.[94]

2. The Clergy

Focusing our attention on the clergy living in this area, we find that they, like the aristocracy, were endowed with numerous privileges. This had a negative effect in that the clerical state thereby attracted those who aspired to ecclesiastical positions because of the privileged life it offered rather than for the sake of Christ and his Church.

The requirements for entrance into the clerical state seem strange and comical to us: minimum age of seven years, reception of baptism and confirmation, knowledge of the *rudimenti della fede* (rudiments of the Faith),[95] attendance at a school in which the candidate had already begun to learn reading, and written certification by a competent priest. If a young man (better said, male child) fulfilled these requirements, he was tested by a bishop or representative and, if approved, admitted to the clerical state. At this point, he was allowed to wear clerical garb and not infrequently was tonsured within a short period of time. As soon as he became a cleric, he began to enjoy the privileges of this state and, in most cases, received what was very important for many a family—a benefice and appointment to the canonry.[96]

There was no standardized program for the education of clerics in any of the three dioceses of the Maremma. Only in 1725 were vague requirements about the intellectual formation of candidates to the priesthood developed by the *Concilio Romano*. These guidelines stipulated that the study of Latin had to have begun and the contents of Bellarmine's small catechism mastered before minor orders were conferred. Before ordination to the priesthood, candidates were to have mastered the contents of the *Catechismus Romanus*. It was further prescribed that they possess knowledge of the diocesan synods and liturgical rubrics and that they participate in the resolution of cases in moral theology.[97] This was the sum total of education and knowledge required of a cleric who

[94] Ibid., 42f. The economic and financial reforms carried out under Grand Duke Peter Leopold are treated in great detail in H. Büchi, "Finanzen und Finanzpolitik Toskanas im Zeitalter der Aufklärung (1737–1790).

[95] These memorized rudiments of the Faith consisted of the Our Father, Hail Mary, Salve Regina, and Credo. In addition, the Ten Commandments; commandments of the Church, capital sins, and theological and moral virtues; and the acts of faith, hope, love, and contrition were required learning (Giorgini, *La Maremma Toscana,* 78, n. 2).

[96] It was not unusual that people other than priests were members of the canonry, as documented by Giorgini, ibid., 79, n. 4.

[97] CIC, c. 131.

desired ordination. There is no cause for wonder, therefore, as to why bishops often complained of the ignorance of their priests.[98]

The above-mentioned Council of Rome also stipulated that a candidate for ordination had to spend "a semester" in a seminary. There was no long-lasting seminary, however, among the dioceses in the Maremma during the entire eighteenth century.[99] Although there were pastors eager to establish one, all attempts eventually failed due to costs involved.[100] Lack of cooperation among bishops prevented the establishment of an interdiocesan seminary.

How did the clerics acquire a theological education without a seminary or a school of theology? According to C. Giorgini, the candidate usually acquired this theological knowledge from the Roman catechism and the Council of Trent. In Msgr. Della Ciaia's seminary, students learned, besides Latin, how to listen to confessions, administer sacraments, and handle Church laws. They attended catechism classes each day and heard lectures on the resolution of cases involving moral problems. This completed the theological formation of future priests.[101] It was the exception rather than rule to have a professor of moral theology or philosophy available in a diocese.

During the eighteenth century, there were many priests in the Maremma and throughout all of Tuscany and Italy.[102] In fact, there was a diocesan priest

[98] Take, for example, the following candid statement made in 1731 by Monsignor Ciani, bishop of Massa, one of the four dioceses of the Maremma. He states, "Da ciò che ho detto non pensino che la nominata isola [Elba] e la diocesi siano privi di ecclesiastici, chè anzi questi abbondano, ma non valgano quasi nulla poiché essendo privi di ogni scienza ed educazione non possono apportare alcun aiuto ed appena sono capaci di celebrare la Messa ed è impossibile affidare loro uffici più alti." / "From what I have said, you must not think that the island mentioned [Elba] and the dioceses are deprived of clergy. On the contrary, there are many, but they are practically worthless because they have no scientific [background] or education. They are unable to help, scarcely capable of celebrating Mass, and it is impossible to trust them with higher positions" (Giorgini, La Maremma Toscana, 81).

[99] Bishop Ciani goes on to state in the same account, "Perciò quando urge la necessità di esaminare qualcuno per le confessioni o per i concorsi mi trovo tra le angustie non sapendo cosa fare, poiché non si può rimproverarli non essendo colpevoli, mancando nei paesi i maestri e in diocesi il seminario." / "When it comes to the question of examining someone for faculties to hear confessions or for other positions, I am in a great dilemma. I do not know what to do. I cannot rebuke them because they are not guilty; [the guilt lies] in the lack of teachers, and in that there is no seminary to serve the dioceses (ibid.)."

[100] In 1702, Monsignor Della Ciaia founded a seminary in Sovana. Later, in 1705, it was moved to the bishop's residence in Pitigliana. In 1704, Bishop Falconetti opened a school to educate his clergymen in the diocese of Grosseto. Both seminaries were closed in 1717, bringing these resources to an end. In 1772, Bishop Vannucci opened a seminary in the diocese of Massa and prepared twenty-five to thirty students. It was closed, however, by reason of an order given by the grand duke in 1791 (see ibid., 86–91).

[101] Ibid., 81f.

In 1769, in Orbetello there were 2,000 inhabitants, twenty-seven priests, and eleven clerics. At least twenty-four Masses were celebrated daily (ibid., 96f.).

[102] This is demonstrated by means of the following data: Of a total population of 15

for every hundred inhabitants. In most parishes, which usually numbered from four hundred to six hundred faithful, one priest was entrusted with responsibility for their spiritual welfare. Normally, however, two or three other priests were attached to the same church.[103] They had no pastoral responsibilities but celebrated daily Mass to fulfill the obligations benefices made incumbent upon them. The many donations received for "perpetual" Masses necessitated the celebration of many Masses each day.[104]

Because of their worldly lives, priests who were not responsible for pastoral care often created problems for their bishops. Although bishops frequently lamented such problems encountered during visitations,[105] there was little change. These priests, not being obliged to provide pastoral care, made little effort to do so. Because of inadequate instruction, many were incapable of preaching, hearing confessions, or administering sacraments (and certainly were not delegated to do so). "Nevertheless," writes Giorgini,

> these ecclesiastics after all were not any worse than their colleagues in other parts of Italy and Europe. . . . They were protagonists and victims of the social and ecclesiastical system we have described, and in which

---

million, 310,000 were members of the clerical, priestly, or religious state. In 1758, the population of the grand duchy of Tuscany was 924,625. Of these, there were 8,336 priests, 3,509 clerics, 5,501 monks, and 9,400 nuns. Thus, of the total number of 924,625 people, there were 26,908 persons who were either clerics, priests, or religious. Data on comparable numbers of priests and clerics per population for the dioceses of the Maremma, i.e., Sovana, Grosseto, and Massa, during the eighteenth century are also available (ibid., 93–7, 278).

[103] In many locations, especially where there was a canonry, there may have been stationed as many as twenty to thirty priests. Only about one-third, however, were responsible for pastoral care (ibid., 96f.).

[104] C. Giorgini writes, "L'insistenza del Concilio Romano del 1725 nel raccomandare ai vescovi che ordinassero, 'per quanto fosse possibile, solo coloro che riconoscevano instruiti almeno in teologia morale', tradisce una situazione generale." / "The insistence of the Council of Rome (1725) upon the recommendation that bishops ordain 'to the greatest extent possible only those instructed, as a minimum, in moral theology', revealed the general situation" (ibid., 84).

[105] Msgr. Selvi visited the Grosseto diocese in the years 1796–97 and, in his report, attacked those priests and clerics who waste their time by doing nothing. He writes, " . . . che passavano la maggior parte del tempo nelle piazze, nei café, ed in altre botteghe, a marcire nell'ozio, e nel gioco, ed in prendersi la pessima occupazione d'instituire un'Academia di maledicenza, che distrugge il massimo precetto su di cui si basa la nostra S. Religione, cioè la Carità, e rende al tempo stesso odioso, e vituperevole il nostro Ministero." / " . . . those who are spending the greatest part of their time in markets, cafes, and other public houses, rotting away by idleness, gambling, and participating in that worst of all occupations instituted by the academy of slandering, thereby destroying the supreme precept on which our doctrine is based, namely, that of charity, and even now rendering our ministry odious and dishonorable" (ibid., 108).

the rulers, both ecclesiastical and civil, lacked the courage, and perhaps even the possibility, to confront the system and reform it.[106]

The bishops were deeply aware of the problems raised by these hosts of priests so lacking in education and with no obligation for pastoral care. Still, "they augmented the number of priests, not so much for pastoral purposes but for the purpose of celebrating innumerable Masses, obliged by large donations".[107]

Bishops too were not without fault. Because of the unhealthy climate that prevailed in the Maremma during the summer months, they left their dioceses for four to six months each year. This exacted a toll upon the diocese and, among other things, led to estrangement between bishops and clergy.

There were far fewer religious order clergy than diocesan, the ratio being one to three. Although monasteries had many privileges, religious life in a monastery still did not possess the same advantages that were available to diocesan clergy. This explains the fewer number of religious clergy.[108]

Because of the inhospitable climate, monasteries in the Maremma were not infrequently designated as places of punishment for religious of various orders. It is understandable, therefore, why abuses, which occasioned complaints of competent bishops, occurred in some of these monasteries.[109] Except in isolated cases, however, the religious Rule was faithfully observed. Also, religious order priests assisted diocesan priests in neighboring parishes in many ways[110]

[106] Questi ecclesiastici in fondo non erano molto più difettosi dei loro colleghi di altre regioni d'Italia e d'Europa. . . . Essi erano attori e vittime del sistema sociale ed ecclesiastico già descritto e che i dirigenti sia ecclesiastici che civili non ebbero il coraggio e forse neanche la possibilità, di affrontare e di rinnovare." / "These ecclesiastics after all were not any worse than their colleagues in other parts of Italy and Europe. . . . They were protagonists and victims of the social and ecclesiastical system we have described and in which the rulers, both ecclesiastical and civil, lacked the courage and perhaps even the possibility to confront the system and reform it" (ibid., 135).

[107] "I vescovi a loro volta aumentavano i sacerdoti non tanto per la cura pastorale, quanto per la celebrazione delle innumerevoli Messe ordinate dai fondatori dei legati pii" (ibid., 96).

[108] Ibid., 140f.

[109] In 1746, Monsignor Franci, the bishop of Grosseto, wrote, "È difficile che in questi piccoli conventi situati in una regione di aria tanto perniciosa, non sorgano scandali e liti poiché in essi sono posti di famiglia i religiosi in pena di qualche delitto commesso, e che quindi non vi vengono spontaneamente e per di più sono sprovvisti di quella scienca e costumi ecclesiastici convenienti . . . " / "It is difficult not to give scandal and be contentious in these small monasteries situated in a region with such an unhealthy climate, since they house those of the religious family brought here for the punishment of some offense committed. They do not come voluntarily, and more than that they are deprived of the comfort of ecclesiastical study and customs . . . " (ibid., 141).

[110] It should be noted here that the first Passionist monastery was built by Paul on Monte Argentario, and in 1769 a second was built not far away from the first. At that time, twenty-eight Passionists were housed in the two monasteries. The priests conducted lay missions and gave spiritual exercises, especially in the neighboring towns and villages.

and, in general, had a better intellectual and religious-spiritual formation than diocesan clergy.

3. *The Religious Condition of the Population*

Since it is extremely important to understand the religious condition of the people during this time, we now focus attention on this point. Because 95% of the population were illiterate, word of mouth was the only way to convey religious instruction to the masses. There were two main ways to accomplish this: by means of sermons delivered at Mass[111] and catechism classes conducted on Sunday and holy day afternoons.[112] However, when it is realized that many parish priests either frequently omitted sermons[113] or read a fragment from a religious book,[114] and that parents told many a child to care for cattle or perform other chores on Sunday afternoons, it is easy to grasp the extent of the people's ignorance of religion and the spiritual life.[115] Also, as already

[111] At that time it was customary that, after the sermon during Mass, the parish priest pray, together with his parishioners, those prayers that belonged to the rudiments of the Faith (see n. 95 above). In this way, the people learned the prayers by heart and permanently retained them in their memories. Sometimes, the priest would add a short explanation of the prayers. This way of instruction was called "insegnamento della dottrina", i.e., teaching of doctrine, being somewhat different from "spiegazione del catechismo", or explanation of the catechism (Giorgini, *La Maremma Toscana,* 112f.).

[112] The basic text for teaching catechism was Bellarmine's *Little Catechism.* It was the custom to ring the bell of the parish church or to allow some of the children to run through the streets ringing bells and inviting parents to send their children to catechism classes (ibid., 113). It has been handed down to us that Paul of the Cross, when living with his brother in the hermitage of the Annunciation on Monte Argentario (from the spring to the fall of 1722), would go to Port-Ercole (a small town at the base of Monte Argentario) and teach "Christ's doctrine" despite rain, frost, or heat. Adults, too, came to listen to him. (See POO, 272r., testimony given by the priest S. di Gennaro, in *Processi* 2:235; Bialas, *Im Zeichen des Kreuzes,* 26.)

[113] In 1736, a priest from Orbetello, a town in the immediate vicinity of the monastery on Monte Argentario and in which the administrative personnel of the "Stato dei Presidi" resided, omitted his Sunday sermons for several months due to "severe rheumatic pains necessitating rest". Since repeated warnings by competent ecclesiastical superiors failed to effect the desired results, Fr. Anthony Danei, a brother of St. Paul of the Cross and assigned to the missionary apostolate of Monte Argentario, was sent to help the priest (see Giorgini, *La Maremma Toscana,* 112).

[114] Numerous bishops explicitly granted their priests this alternative "per aiutare coloro che non erano capaci di predicare" / "to help those incapable of preaching" (ibid., 112).

[115] This degree of ignorance was not limited to the population of the Tuscan Maremma but was characteristic of the whole of Italy. The issue was addressed by Pope Benedict XIII at the Council of Rome in 1725. He writes, "Noi pensiamo a queste ed altre cose dolorose, cioè che i ragazzi da istruirsi nella dottrina cristiana non abitano tutti nelle città e nei paesi, anzi non pochi vivono nella campagna addetti alla custodia degli animali, cosicché dopo ricevuto il Battesimo vivono senza educazione spirituale, e non sanno nemmeno se esista lo Spirito Santo; inoltre negli stessi paesi si incontrano adulti che ignorano anche i principali misteri

pointed out, priests themselves all too frequently had only a scanty knowledge of theology. Nevertheless, the people attended Holy Mass frequently and participated enthusiastically in processions and other religious celebrations. Often they followed their own initiatives: festivals were prepared, triduums and novenas were conducted, and entire families came together to pray the Rosary.[116] For the most part, local Christian confraternities organized these activities.

An embarrassing problem developed in that there were too many Church feast days.[117] Since, on these days, work was prohibited, people did not know what to do with their time. This resulted in men spending most of their time in public houses drinking wine and playing cards; women left many domestic chores undone. Consequently, toward the end of the eighteenth century, the Church began to reduce the number of feasts.

The people loved to hold processions.[118] For example, the "mysteries of

---

della nostra fede, quali quelli della Trinità e dell'Incarnazione e ciò che è più lamentabile si vergognano di andare a scuola per impararli. Cercando quindi in qualche modo di procurare la loro eterna salute, comandiamo strettamente ai parroci che durante la Messa, dopo l'omelia, a voce alta e facendo rispondere il popolo, insegnino a poco a poco in lingua volgare, cantando, almeno le seguenti cose: segno della croce, misteri della Trinità e dell'Incarnazione, il simbolo degli apostoli, la preghiera del Signore, il saluto angelico, il decalogo, i precetti della Chiesa, i sette sacramenti e l'atto di contrizione. Questa stessa cosa si faccia, sotto pena della sospensione dalla celebrazione della Messa ad arbitrio del vescovo, anche negli oratorii, capelle e chiese rurali, dove si celebra la Messa." / "We have thought of these and other painful things, namely, that those needing to be instructed in Christian doctrine do not all live in towns or villages; rather, quite a few are living in the plains, obliged to care for animals, under such conditions that, after having received baptism, they are forced to live with no spiritual education and do not even know about the existence of the Holy Spirit. Furthermore, in the same areas, there are adults who are ignorant of the main mysteries of our Faith, such as the Trinity and Incarnation; and, what is more lamentable, they are ashamed to go to school to learn about them. Consequently, in an attempt to find a means by which it is possible for them to procure eternal salvation, we strictly bid priests, after the homily during Holy Mass, to use a loud voice and to ask the people to respond so that they may learn, little by little, through the vernacular and through song at least the following: the sign of the cross, the mysteries of the Trinity and Incarnation, the Apostles' Creed, the Lord's Prayer, the Hail Mary, the Ten Commandments, the precepts of the Church, the seven sacraments, and the act of contrition. This same [instruction] must also be carried out in oratories, chapels, and rural churches, wherever Holy Mass is celebrated, under the authority of the bishop and under pain of suspension [of faculties] for celebrating Holy Mass" (ibid., 164).

[116] The clergy considered these activities of the laymen as a welcome opportunity to obtain a supplementary income. Such practice resulted in the people's belief that no priestly service could be obtained "without paying for it" (ibid., 165).

[117] The number of official and special feasts numbered almost ninety for the entire year.

[118] In almost all places of the Maremma, just like in other regions of Italy, two processions were held each month—one in honor of our Lady of the Rosary and the other in honor of the Most Holy Eucharist (Giorgini, La Maremma Toscana, 169).

Jesus' life" were dramatized in Corpus Christi Day processions with a great part of the local population actively participating. Such celebrations, added a certain quality of folklore to the great feasts of the Church.

Repentance was the theme of processions held during Lent and Holy Week. Public self-flagellations performed by all members of the confraternities were a constituent part of these processions. Not until the end of the eighteenth century did these nocturnal "scourging processions" come to be forbidden by local bishops, as these things always led to excess.

Sacraments were received infrequently. It was customary for men to go to confession and receive Holy Communion once a year during Eastertide.[119] Members of confraternities repeated this process during the year at the time of major feasts. Eucharistic adoration, however, was one of the people's steadfast devotions. Near the tabernacle, a picture or statue of the crucified Christ was often placed to remind people of the relationship between the Eucharist and the passion of our Lord Jesus Christ.

The poverty and misery experienced by the people evoked special devotions to the suffering Christ. These devotions took several forms. There were first of all the "solemn Fridays", which were all Fridays in March, for it was thought that Jesus' death occurred on a Friday in that month. Therefore, the passion of Christ was recalled especially on those days.

Processions of repentance were also used to recall his passion. Many taking part would carry heavy crosses on their shoulders, hang chains and ropes about their necks, and on their heads wear crowns of thorns. Their self-flagellation, mentioned previously, was intended to be a reminder of Jesus' scourging as well as penance for their own sins.[120]

The stations of the cross were the most enduring expression of devotion to the passion of Jesus, however. After Clement XII in 1731 and Benedict XIV ten years later permitted all churches to erect the way of the cross (with indulgences granted to those who prayed them), this form of devotion quickly became popular. Leonard of Port Maurice, especially, worked very hard to establish this devotion,[121] with St. Paul of the Cross and the Passionists contributing to its spread. After the stations were said, a time was often set aside for contemplation on the passion.

Not to be underestimated in the contributions they made to the religious life of the people were the various confraternities. They were operative in all

---

[119] Bishops and parish priests were very careful that all members of a parish fulfilled their Easter duty. In order to have proof thereof, a slip of paper was given to each penitent in the confessional. It contained the name of the church and the respective year. These slips of paper were collected at the reception of Holy Communion (ibid., 186f.).

[120] See F. Dressler, in *Lexikon* 4, col. 610 (keyword: Geissler oder Flagellanten).

[121] See C. Pohlmann, *Kanzel und Ritiro: Der Volksmissionar Leonhard von Porto Maurizio,* 146–50, 179–87.

parishes, and even the smallest parish had at least one. Members gathered together in the parish church or in a special room called an oratory for common prayer and services.

Some confraternities were dedicated to the performance of charitable services. For example, members would distribute alms to prisoners and bury the dead.[122] Others provided porters for small hospitals or established houses to shelter and care for people.[123] During the course of the eighteenth century, their structure fell into decline and even ruin; but even though reform in both organization and praxis was needed, they remained a strong component of the religious and social life of the people.[124] When, therefore, in 1785, Grand Duke Peter Leopold decreed that all confraternities be abolished and their goods and oratories nationalized, the effect worked to the disadvantage of the people.

Since confraternities were democratically structured, this decree denied the people their only opportunity to participate in a democracy. Members had been able in council or through a parliament to make decisions about the activities they would undertake in common. Confraternities had also given people opportunities to develop leadership and administrative skills and to experience organization. After 1785, however, all this was denied them, and no substitutes were provided.

Missions also exerted an important influence upon the spiritual life of the people of Tuscany in the whole of eighteenth-century Italy. With their classical form inherited from St. Vincent de Paul (1581–1660) and Paul Segneri the Elder (1624–94),[125] these popular missions aimed to "shake people out of their spiritual lethargy by reminding them of their origin and the eternal life to be bestowed upon them after their judgment before God".[126]

This objective explains the fear motive that penetrated mission sermons, especially those dealing with sin, death, judgment, and hell.[127] The specific goal of these missions was considered attained if all participants went to

---

[122] See n. 93 above.

[123] There were no government-maintained hospices in the Maremma until the middle of the eighteenth century. The care of poor invalids was almost exclusively incumbent upon religious houses (see Giorgini, *La Maremma Toscana*, 70–73).

[124] There were still many confraternities in the dioceses of the Maremma around the year 1750: 88 in Sovana, 32 in Grosseto, 20 in Massa, and 6 in the town of Orbetello and in Porto S. Stefano (ibid., 207).

[125] See V. Schurr, in *Lexikon* 10, cols. 858–60, article on popular missions.

[126] " . . . di scuotere dal torpore spirituale mediante il ricordo dell'origine e del fine dell'uomo e della vita futura che lo attende dopo il giudizio definitivo di Dio" (Giorgini, *La Maremma Toscana*, 220).

[127] See E. Henau, "Riflessioni", 508–16.

confession and then received Holy Communion.[128] Still, these missions did contribute to strengthening the faith of the people. Besides the main sermons, an instruction emphasizing catechetical themes was given each day.[129]

Since all members of a parish or diocese were asked to participate in a mission, and since the great majority did so, missions also possessed a social importance. Representatives of the aristocracy and of the common people, rich and poor, influential, handicapped, and neglected all congregated together, came into contact with one another, participated in the same mission, and heard the same sermons and lectures. Thus, missions contained within themselves a possibility, albeit a limited one, of helping to break down the historical obstacles and barriers that existed between the various social classes, because all were in common professing the same Faith.

In summary, two characteristic features of the Tuscan Maremma capsulize all that has been said: great poverty of the people and engrained ignorance of the clergy.

4. St. Paul of the Cross and His "Poor Italians"

What did St. Paul of the Cross think of the problems of the Maremma? Because of the many missions and spiritual exercises which he gave in the area, he was directly in touch with the people and clergy and knew their burning problems. He frequently spoke of such in his letters. To Cardinal Altieri, in whose jurisdiction the first Passionist monastery was founded Paul wrote of the "poor, forsaken Maremma"[130] and, by means of a new monastery, wanted to be of greater help to them.[131] How much the saint suffered with the people is obvious in another letter to the cardinal in which

---

[128] Missionaries frequently reported on the number of hosts distributed during popular missions. Of the missionaries, the Vincentians, founded by St. Vincent de Paul, kept more written records of their missions in the Maremma of the eighteenth century than did any other religious group. St. Paul of the Cross and his companions did not keep written records of their work (see Giorgini, *La Maremma Toscana,* 220–52).

[129] Surely the interval of time between two separate missions held in any one place was quite long. Nevertheless, we know that St. Paul of the Cross held three missions in Orbetello between 1731 and 1735 and three in Pitigliano between 1731 and 1736 (see *Storia Critica* 3:1393–97). If, however, we take into account the great ignorance in religious matters prevalent at the time, we may look upon these popular missions as "intensive courses in matters of Faith".

[130] " . . . queste povere abbandonate maremma . . . " / " . . . this poor, abandoned Maremma" (L 1:363, July 5, 1737).

[131] " . . . abilitarsi vieppiù per poter giovare ai poveri prossimi, e massime di queste miserabili maremma abbandonate" / " . . . to have greater ability to help these poorest of the poor of this miserable, forsaken 'Maremma' " (L 1:360, on the occasion of the Feast of Corpus Christi, 1737).

he discussed the apostolic work carried out in the Maremma by those living at the monastery on Mount Argentario. He stated, "The great poverty reigning in this land has impressed us deeply; if His Eminence knew this poverty well, he would not be able to keep from weeping inconsolable tears."[132]

Throughout his life, Paul also manifested an abiding concern for the clergy. In 1732, he wrote, "God knows the great needs of this region, the need for good instruction of priests, and other very great needs."[133] That such statements were based on his own experience is illustrated in a letter in which he disclosed the following thoughts to his friend and patron Mgsr. G. Oldo, bishop of Terracina:

> The experience I had of having spent so many years giving missions in the impoverished Maremma of Tuscany and also the few I spent in the regions of the ecclesiastical states has allowed me to assess tangibly the extreme needs of the ecclesiastics, which are not infrequently greater than those of the laity—*servantis servandi* [serving the servants]—Oh God, how often have I wanted to weep.[134]

The saint did not content himself with deploring the spiritual and religious needs that he encountered among both laity and clergy. Rather, he wanted to do something that would alleviate these needs. His plan was to build a house on Mount Argentario in which spiritual exercises could be conducted apart from the monastery. To Msgr. Gattinara's successor,[135] the bishop of his native diocese of Alessandria, he wrote,

> Besides this, a new house in which spiritual exercises may be given will be built, not just for the clerics and priests of the neighboring dioceses (almost all of which are exposed to the unhealthy air of the Maremma) but also for the laity, who, at opportune times, could retire [to this house] for spiritual exercises.[136]

---

[132] " ... ci hanno particolarmente mosso i bisogni grandi di questi paesi, che, se V. E. li sapesse ben a fondo, non potrebbe non piangerli a lagrime inconsolabili" (L 1:366, July 25, 1737).

[133] " ... lui sa i bisogni grandi di queste parti, la necessità che v'è della cultura degli Ecclesiastici e altri grandissimi bisogni" (L 1:359, Apr. 9, 1732, to Cardinal Altieri).

[134] "L'esperenza però che ho di tanti anni di missione fatta nelle povere maremme di Toscana e qualche poco ancora in quelle dello Stato ecclesiastico, m'ha fatto toccare con mano gli estremi bisogni che spesso si trovano per i poveri ecclesiastici, non di rado più bisognosi dei secolari (servatis servandis).—O Dio, quanto vorrei piangere!" (L 2:687, Mar. 25, 1749).

[135] Bishop Gatinara took over the administration of the diocese of Turin in 1726.

[136] "Oltre di questo si farà una casa d'esercizi, non solo per gli ecclesiastici delle diocesi circonvicine [che quasi tutte in queste maremme di cattiva aria, sono senza Seminario], ma altresì per i secolari, che a'suoi tempi vorranno ritirarsi a fare i santi esercizi" (L 1:378, Mar. 31, 1732).

Unfortunately, he was not able to put this plan into effect. Despite this, St. Paul of the Cross, through the many lay missions and spiritual exercises he conducted throughout his life, made a significant contribution to religious instruction of laity and clergy of the Maremma.

As founder, the sphere of his activity and his zealous and indefatigable apostolic works were not limited to the Tuscan Maremma. He also had the opportunity to come to know large portions of central Italy, and his correspondence gave him a clear picture of the situation from northern to southern Italy. Throughout his life, he continued corresponding with friends from his own Piedmont area of northern Italy, and he would even sign his letters the "Lombard".[137] He corresponded with friends and benefactors in southern Italy too. Furthermore, he often had opportunities to speak with educated and influential people in the Church and with public authorities.

Paul could not fail to notice, therefore, that the spirit and ideals of the Enlightenment had deeply affected Italy. In letters he often referred to his "poor Italians". To his friend Msgr. Count Garagni, who was a great protector of the Passionist Congregation at the Holy See, he wrote, "We are in very calamitous times due to piety having grown so cold and libertinage having increased so much that, if God does not provide, I don't know what will happen."[138] In another passage, he lamented, "As for me, I have reason to fear that the sins and libertinage of our poor Italians will provoke the wrath of Almighty God."[139]

It must not be inferred from such statements, however, that the saint's perception of his age was unequivocally pessimistic or that it had a depressing or paralyzing effect on his activity. These words must be purely and simply understood as a serious warning of a current danger, a warning motivated by a deep regard for his people and a genuine love of his country.[140] On the basis of the many lay missions he had conducted, he knew well that people were good, that they came in great numbers to hear his preaching of the passion, and that they wanted to hear what he had to say. So many false notions and so much ignorance of religious matters were caused less by bad will on the part

[137] See *Storia Critica* 2:514–17.

[138] "Siamo in tempi troppo calamitosi, che la pietà si è raffreddata al sommo ed è cresciuto tanto il libertinaggio, che se Dio non provvede, non so che sarà" (L 2:231, June 19, 1743). Also see A. Huerga, "San Pablo de la Cruz, un místico insigne en la época de la Ilustración", 331–51.

[139] "Io però ho fondamento di temere che i peccati e il libertinaggio della nostra povera Italia, abbia molto provocato l'iracondia dell'Altissimo . . . " (L 3:127, May 7, 1761, to Canon Sardi).

[140] Although the nation Italy was not as yet viewed as a political entity in itself, a national identity or bonding was kept alive, above all, by Dante's language, which was spoken in many regions of the country although in different dialects. Also, a common cultural heritage was kept alive in the people by an idea of common origin.

of individuals than by the unfortunate structuring of ecclesiastical, social, and political systems of the day.

5. A Child of His Time?

It is undoubtedly true that the great majority of the anonymous masses of the eighteenth century lived, by and large, in the Christian tradition.[141] Of course, the person who belonged to the baroque age had his own way of expressing traditional Christian concepts. It must be stated, however, that in the liturgy of the baroque period and in the piety of the people, forces of continuity and preservation were highly esteemed.[142]

The baroque period had inherited from the Gothic popular forms of expressing devotion to the passion and to the sorrows of Mary and, from the crusading Romanesque period, devotion to the cross and holy sepulchre. These forms were passed on in their entirety and, on the whole, emphasized even more. Everything was "baroque"—louder, livelier, brighter, more splendid, and more enthusiastic.[143]

Exaggeration or overproduction, so characteristic of this age, found expression in lay missions. During sermons, preachers availed themselves of any and all means of presenting content in concrete and vivid ways so as to make the greatest possible impact and impression.[144] Perhaps the best examples of successful popular missionaries using these techniques were Paul Segneri the Elder and Leonard of Port Maurice. Paul of the Cross, of course, has not entered into history in class with these men, but still he is, with Alphonsus of Liguori, one of the most important evangelizers of the eighteenth century.

[141] See H. Jedin, O. Köhler, and W. Müller, in *Handbuch der Kirchengeschichte* 5:v (of the Introduction).

[142] See G. Schreiber, "Der Barock und das Tridentinum", 386.

[143] Schreiber, 387.

[144] When delivering their sermons, preachers used not only rhetorical and artistic devices but also illustrative materials. It is known that Leonard of Port Maurice would place a skull on his pulpit, especially when preaching about death. Appeal to repentance was heightened by the self-flagellation performed openly by the preacher at his pulpit when the sermon dealt with sin and repentance (and this was the subject matter of most sermons held during the lay missions of that day, hence the phrase *prediche de terrore*). C. Pohlmann, therefore, writes of Leonard, "His favorite instrument was a discipline, i.e., a scourge. Thus the scourge is no longer just a symbol but the very reality of repentance and expiation" (Pohlmann, 100). It was, moreover, customary in preaching missions to carry into the pulpit a huge crucifix so constructed that the arms of the corpus could be moved. A complete description of mission sermons of the baroque era and their cultural and contemporary significance may be found in Pohlmann, 49–126.

St. Paul of the Cross also used self-flagellation during his sermons, as customary during the lay missions of that time, to evoke remorse and return to virtue in the hearts of his hearers. See POG, 386r.–386v. (*Processi* 2:139); POC, 129v. (*Processi* 2:425), and in other places.

These missionaries not only employed the spoken word and such means as enabled the spoken word to exercise greater effect on its hearers but also gave people opportunity to participate in an active way. This was especially so during the evening penitential processions, in which great numbers of people took part. This active participation promoted a sense of personal involvement. Among the missionaries of this age, Leonard of Port Maurice was especially effective in accommodating his style to the needs of popular piety. C. Pohlmann remarks,

> Leonard allows all religious needs to be fully addressed during a mission. The picture of the Madonna turns the church into a place of pilgrimage. The pilgrims work themselves up in penitential and Marian processions. The "dead Christ" as it is carried along becomes a captivating center of attention in the sacred drama. Personal involvement is intensified in the dramatic process of carrying a cross, in self-flagellation and in laying hold of crowns of thorns, skulls, and chains as people let themselves be led along by impulses of repentance and humility.[145]

Undoubtedly, superficiality was a danger concealed in such extravagant participation in popular manifestations of devotion. After several years of experience as a missionary, this effect became quite obvious to Paul,[146] who, from about the year 1742, forbade penitential processions during his lay missions.[147]

Although, for the most part, Paul's missions adhered to the format of the day, a special evening meditation on the passion was his own innovation.[148]

---

[145] Pohlmann, 131.

[146] During the informative processes for the beatification of Paul of the Cross, many witnesses gave testimony to the fact that during the lay missions of 1731–36, Paul of the Cross would lead solemn penitential processions carrying a heavy wooden cross on his shoulders. See POG, 385v.–386r. (*Processi* 2:138), testimony of Joseph Rocchi; POG, 340r.–341v. (*Processi* 2:122f.), testimony of Juliana Tullini; Strambi, *Vita.*

[147] In a letter written by the saint in Pieve, during one of his missions, he speaks of "processioni di penitenza . . . di notte" (nighttime penitential processions). See L 2:56. However, according to a statement by Fr. G. Suscioli, who was himself a participant in a mission, it had been some time since the saint had become aware of the inappropriateness of these processions because they did not bring about the desired effect, namely, the conversion and repentance of sinners (see POR, 221r.).

[148] Sr. Angela Teresa related the method St. Paul of the Cross used in his lay missions: "Stante che in Ronciglione ogni tre anni devono farsi le missioni, ho avuto l'occasione di sentirne molte: e dei padri capuccini, e de' gesuiti, e dei signori delle missioni, e dei minori osservanti riformati e del padre Paolo, ma il metodo di questo, tanto a mio giudizio, quanto al giudizio ancora degl'altri miei paesani, era stimato più a proposito e prudenziale." / "Owing to the fact that in Ronciglione [the Sister's birthplace] missions were held once every three years, I had the opportunity to listen to many of them—those of the Capuchin Fathers, the Jesuits, the Vincentians, the Friars Minor of the Reformed Observance, and Fr. Paul. In my judgment and in the judgment of my people, his were considered more to the point and more prudent" (POC, 320r.–320v. in *Processi* 2:503).

Because he considered it of such prime importance, he even included this practice in the Rule of 1736. He wrote,

> Our brethren who are priests and who have the talent for holy preaching should give an oral meditation on the most holy passion of our Lord Jesus Christ during their missions for the people, and they should give it either before or after the mission sermon. . . . [149]

These contemplations on the sufferings of Jesus, in which the primary theme was the love of God for all people, compensated for the *prediche di terrore* (fear sermons), in which the main subject matter consisted of frightening descriptions of divine justice, God's severity, and the torments of hell that would be suffered for sin committed.[150]

In conclusion, it can be said that St. Paul of the Cross was essentially a "child of his time", who was quite familiar with the needs and problems of the people he served and for whose salvation he labored. While not ignoring and, in fact, to a great extent complying with the devotional sensitivities of the people, he was also aware of his educative responsibilities and developed his own initiatives. In brief, he followed his own way, once cognizant that prior methods were not effective in achieving his objectives.

PAUL OF THE CROSS AS AUTODIDACT

As previously mentioned, St. Paul of the Cross did not have much opportunity for formal education during his childhood and adolescence.[151] God, however, "had given him talent and an open mind, and, had he studied, he would have made certain progress". This is what his fellow Passionist Fr. John Mary, who knew the founder very well, stated at the apostolic process in Rome.[152]

Information we do have on Paul's educational background is scanty. We can assume he had begun the study of Latin when taught by the Carmelite Fathers in Cremolino.[153] It has also been handed down to us that he attended school

---

[149] "Li Fratelli sacerdoti che sarranno abili per la santa predicazione dovranno nelle sante Missioni meditare a viva voce alli popoli la SS.ma Passione di Gesù Cristo, e ciò lo faranno avanti, o dopo la predica della Missione" (*Regulae et Constitutiones,* 56 and 58, col. 1).

[150] See Henau, "Riflessioni", n. 129.

[151] See Chap. I, n. 12.

[152] "Iddio gli aveva dato talento ed apertura di mente, e se avesse proseguito gli studi, avrebbe forse fatto dei progressi . . . " (PAR, 331r., testimony of Fr. John Mary).

[153] The Daneis lived in Cremolino from 1701–9 in a parish completely cared for by Carmelite Fathers. Paul was taught by them but we know nothing for sure about the depth or duration of his instruction. At that time, however, the study of Latin was one of the primary objectives of education.

in Genoa about the year 1710. These pieces of information are so vague, however, that it is not possible to give any precise information about the duration of his instruction or about the schools he attended.[154]

Even if St. Paul of the Cross did not have years of formal education, he did have a variety of opportunities for increasing his knowledge and rounding off his spiritual and intellectual development. From the early years of his youth, he regularly consulted a priest as confessor and spiritual director. Certainly these contacts, including those in Castellazzo, where he was a frequent guest in a Capuchin monastery, gave him means of increasing his store of knowledge and of exposing him to instruction.

Paul's lively interest in spiritual matters and his intellectual giftedness were the reasons that, despite his sporadic involvement in schools, he attained a relatively high degree of knowledge and education. He especially tried to extend the horizons of his thought by reading, and he particularly liked the works of great mystics and masters of spirituality.

Entries in his spiritual diary, written at age twenty-seven, make it quite plain he had read the writings of John of the Cross, Teresa of Avila, and Francis de Sales.[155] Moreover, these entries indicate the saint not only had a well-founded knowledge and rich experience in the spiritual life but also possessed, to a high degree, a capability of describing mystical experience and occurrences. Undoubtedly, familiarity with the major texts of the spiritual life had contributed to the development of this capability.

We cannot say for sure which theological and scientific works St. Paul of the Cross read and studied, since the extant sources make no such reference. That he read and studied theological works, however, is mentioned several times.[156] Certainly the opportunity to read was there even when he lived

---

Teresa Danei, the saint's sister, declared the following about Paul's experience in school: "Nostro padre l'ha mandato a scuola nel luogo di Cremolino del Monferrato; e mi ricordo ch'esso nostro padre contava che il di lui maestro diceva non saper più cosa insegnarli, perchè ne sapeva già quanto lui." / "Our father sent him to a school in Cremolino del Monteferrato. I remember our father telling us Paul's schoolmaster did not know what else to teach him, because Paul already knew more than he": POA, 126v. (Processi 2:29). See Storia Critica 2:112; Bollettino 9 (1928): 116–20, in which are printed some documents containing information about the saint's childhood and youth.

[154] In Zoffoli's opinion, the school was either an archepiscopal seminary for children or a boarding school of the Order (see Storia Critica 2:120).

[155] See Bialas, Tagebuch. Included with the diary are multiple footnotes presenting parallel phrases found in the writings of these well-known authors. These footnotes are found on pp. 56–136 of Tagebuch, a term used to refer to the German translation of Paul's spiritual diary.

[156] In the report of the apostolic visit made by a delegation of the bishops of Pitigliano in 1729 to the hermitage of St. Anthony, where St. Paul of the Cross lived in community with some companions, the following is recorded: "...et in eodem cubiculo retinent libros morales, S. Scripturae et Spirituales..." / "...and in the same cubicle they keep books of moral theology, Bibles, and spiritual reading material..." (see Storia Critica 1:376, n. 12;

with his own family in Castellazzo (1718–20), since the theological library of Don Cristoforo, who lived in the same town, was available to him.

That Paul had a good spiritual and theological foundation must have been apparent to others, too. Cardinal Corradini judged it adequate for ordination to the priesthood, the only stipulation being that Paul and his brother John Baptist take some courses in pastoral theology at the Friars Minor monastery of St. Bartholomew on the island of Tiber. The duration of these courses was probably no longer than a few weeks or months.[157]

Paul of the Cross was not one to consider his education complete upon ordination. Those who knew him well unanimously declared he was naturally diligent and "constantly" studying.[158] He also greatly desired that members of his Congregation not neglect their own continuing theological and spiritual education. In fact, the oldest edition of the Rule specified that clerics and priests devote three to four hours to study each day.[159]

While not forgetting to give thanks to God, who had granted him some talent and capability, Paul of the Cross would refer to himself as a poor *ignorantello*.[160] To Don Cerruti,[161] his former confessor, spiritual director, and close friend, Paul wrote,

> His Divine Majesty, who chooses "the foolish and the weak" [1 Cor 1:27], has, in his mercy, given me, like one gives alms, some ability (but I confide this to your heart only and in confidence). He has given me light to prepare sermons, spiritual conferences, etc. He has given me some knowledge of moral theology so that I can absolve sin. Moreover, he has with certainty given me a dedication to study and its pursuit.[162]

2:79–86; *Regulae et Constitutiones,* 155f.

[157] His professor was Father Dominic Mary, O.F.M. See Chap. I, n. 33 of this book.

[158] The priest Luigi Pennachioni, who often visited the saint in his St. Anthony hermitage and who wanted to join him, stated, " . . . ed il giorno l'ho veduto di continuo studiare." / " . . . and I saw him studying continually by day" (POO, 579r., in *Processi* 2:362).

[159] The Rule of the Order (1736 and 1741 editions) contains a whole chapter (Chapter 25) in which time for studying is defined: one and one-half hours each morning (during the summer, two hours) are reserved for studying and two hours each afternoon (see *Regulae et Constitutiones,* 78–80, cols. 1, 2).

[160] " . . . questi dotti vanno a fondo, e non sono come me che sono un povero ignorantello." / " . . . these men of learning go to what is fundamental, and they are not like me, a poor 'ignorantello' " (L 1:274, Aug. 26, 1741, to Agnes Grazi).

[161] Canon Cerruti was the saint's spiritual director prior to Bishop Gattinara.

[162] " . . . il gran Dio della Maestà, che 'infirma et stulta mundi eligit' [1 Cor 1:27], si è degnato farmi l'elemosina di qualche abilità [ciò lo dico al suo cuore per sua regola], avendomi dato lume di aggiustarmi prediche, istruzioni ecc., come pure nella Morale per confessare essendomi però impiegato altresì in qualche studio, quale ho procurato continuare quanto'ho potuto" (L 2:275, Aug. 2, 1741).

Although motivated by a strong desire to deepen his knowledge and spirituality, Paul did not let such study become an end in itself. Rather, it stood in the service of (and, for Paul, was a necessary basis of) his priestly and pastoral ministry.

Constant reading of spiritual and mystical works and his own personal experience gave Paul an inner assuredness when it came to answering questions concerning the interior life. In a letter to Agnes Grazi, a woman directed by Paul for the last thirteen years of her life and who, in her own interior encounters with God, had penetrated the depths of mysticism, a question arose concerning discernment of spirits. Paul reassured her, saying, "Believe me, I know all about these things, for I have made many little studies of them for the glory of God."[163] Time and time again, he appealed in his letters to works he had "read", without any further indication of book or author.[164]

Besides being familiar with the classics of Christian spirituality, Paul was at least acquainted with the Church Fathers and theologians. In his letters, references were made to Augustine,[165] John Chrysostom,[166] Bernard of

[163] "Mi creda che queste cose le so, e che ho fatto qualche piccolo studio per la gloria di Dio" (L 1:100, Aug. 2, 1733).

[164] For example, L 1:423, July 7, 1741, to F. A. Appiani: "Io ho letto gran cose sopra cio . . . " / "I have read great things thereof . . . " In L 3:157, July 23, 1757, to Fr. John Mary of St. Ignatius: "Io ho letto qualche cosa, specialmente in uno che è il principe de' mistici." / I have read something, especially in [the writings of] one who is the prince of mystics" (Paul is most likely referring to John of the Cross). In L 3:12, Feb. 9, 1762, to Generoso Petrarca: "So bene, per quel poco che ho letto . . . " / "I know this well taking into account what little I have learned."

[165] In L 1:401, June 26, 1736, to F. A. Appiani, Paul wrote, "S. Agostino si lamentava con dire: O bellezza tanto antica e tanto nuova, ti andavo cercando fuori di me, e ti avevo in me." / "St. Augustine cried out, saying: 'O beauty so ancient and so new; I looked for you outside of me, and I had you within.'" Paul obviously is referring here to that famous passage in Chapter 27 of Book 10 of *The Confessions*: "Too late have I loved you, O beauty so ancient and so new, too late have I loved you! Behold, you were within me, while I was outside . . . " In German, see J. Bernhart, *Bekenntnisse* (Munich, 1966, 3d ed.), 546. In English, see the translation by John K. Ryan, *The Confessions of St. Augustine*, 254. The form and content of Paul's quotation indicate he cited it from memory. Similar citations are found in L 1:44, Jan. 3, 1729, to Marchioness D. M. della Scala del Pozzo; L 1:805, Oct. 8, 1772, to Thomas Fossi; L 3:340, July 5, 1755, to a superior of the Congregation.

[166] L 3:717, Jan. 12, 1765, to Fr. Anthony of St. Teresa: "Se lei vuole ricever dono di orazione, stia in silenzio. 'Silentium, quod lutum exhibet figulo; idem ipse exhibe Conditori tuo. 'È massima di S. Giovanni Crisostomo, tutta d'oro." / "If you want to receive the gift of prayer, remain in silence.' It is a maxim of St. John Chrysostom, and a golden one." Also see L 3:743, Dec. 12, 1765, in which Paul quotes the same passage to a new priest of the Congregation.

Clairvaux,[167] Thomas Aquinas,[168] and Bonaventure.[169] For the most part, brief passages from the works of these authors were selected and used to elucidate principles of the spiritual life.

Paul's favorite authors were the great spiritual teachers and writers: John of the Cross, Teresa of Avila, Francis de Sales, and John Tauler. He was familiar with contemporary authors, too, as indicated by the books found in his room at the time of his death. Although these particular works may not have had any significant influence on his thought, they have been preserved in the Passionist Generalate in Rome.[170]What books and authors did exert a lasting influence on his thinking and doctrine, however, is the subject matter of this section. The analysis, made on the basis of existing documents, is presented below.

[167] See L 3:741, Nov. 23, 1765, to an unknown person, and L 1:401, June 26, 1736, to F. A. Appiani.

[168] He speaks of St. Thomas in a letter in which he discusses the virtue of humility (L 1:804f., Oct. 8, 1772, to Thomas Fossi).

[169] The founder recommended that the master of novices, Fr. Peter of St. John, read a certain small book by St. Bonaventure that Paul called "un tesoro di tutte le perfezioni" / "a treasury of all perfections" (L 3:438, Oct. 24, 1764; L 3:166, Sept. 27, 1758, to Fr. John Mary of St. Ignatius).

[170] These books have been placed under glass in the room where the saint died. The chamber itself, being situated near the entrance to SS. John and Paul, was transformed into a chapel.

Besides prayer books, there were the following seven:

1. Amedeo di Castrovillari, O.F.M., *Il zelo apostolico nelle sante missioni, in cui se propone quanto puol' occorrere, e bisognare ad un sagro Operaio nel suo Ministero,* tomo secondo, Rome, 1720.

2. Arcangelo Arcangeli, S.J., *Esercizio devoto da praticarsi ne' nove giorni, o nove mercoledì precedenti alla festa di S. Francesca Romana...,* Rome, 1765. (There is a handwritten dedication on the first page of this book: "Maria Agnese Le manda questo libro e prega V. R. à raccomandarla al Sig. Iddio per molti suoi bisogni spirituali." / "Mary Agnes sends you this book and prays that Your Reverence commend her to God for her many spiritual needs.")

3. P. Paolo Maria Ardizzoni, O.M.D., *Meditatazioni della vita e Passione di nostro Signor Gesù Cristo,* Bologna, 1713.

4. P. Paolo di Barry, S.J., *L'arte d'imparare a ben morire...,* Milan, 1764.

5. P. Giovanni Crasset, S.J., *La manna del deserto per le persone in ritiramento, colle considerazioni sopra le principali azioni del Cristiano,* Venezia, 1641.

6. P. Giovanni Crasset, S.J., *Brevi meditazioni sopra i novissimi per ciascun giorno del mese con piccol'aggiunta,* Rome, 1752.

7. Joseph Sangermans, *Viator christianus in patriam tendens per motus anagogicos,* Rome, 1719.

This list of books is presented in *Storia Critica* 2:87f.

1. *Scripture as a Primary Source*

The saintly founder of the Passionists read many books of theology and spirituality during his long life. While the Bible was never the only book for him, it was the "book of books", which he read assiduously and upon which he meditated. He likened Scripture to a most profound and pure source of life, as if it were, as described in Revelation, a spring giving rise to "rivers of living water". For Paul, Scripture was a "fountain" from which he drank "living water" to quench the burning thirst of his longing for God.

There are many depositions in the protocols of the beatification processes that testify to the fact that St. Paul of the Cross spent a good part of each day reading Scripture.[171] To indicate the high esteem he showed for the word of God, he always read it with his head uncovered;[172] and, it was said, he always kept a Bible with him.[173]

We need not depend on just the testimony of others, however. Paul himself called the Bible the *Libro dei lumi* (book of light).[174] For him, Scripture represented the highest authority in deciding whether a certain opinion agreed or disagreed with Christian belief. He made this point quite clearly in the following quote from a letter to Fr. Thomas Fossi, written by Paul at an advanced age:

> "The spirit blows where he wills, whither he comes, or whither he goes, we know not"—spoke Jesus Christ [Jn 3:8]. Equally and similarly I speak to you, Father. About these worries and troubles you are talking about, I want you to know that St. Teresa and other saints had their spirit tested by many, among whom were the most educated. Some agreed with them, and others didn't. Now, how should we behave ourselves when we have approval on the one hand and disapproval on the other? Should we worry about it? We know holy Scripture and [we know that] theologians, moralists, mystics, dogmatic theologians, and apologists, after having studied [a case], approve

---

[171] "Se la passava buona parte del giorno colla lezzione della Sagra Scrittura" POV, 149r. (*Processi* 1:51), testimony of Fr. John Mary. Also see POV, 66v. (*Processi* 1:13); POV, 392v. (*Processi* 1:140); POR, 1159r. In connection with the entire paragraph in the text above, read L. Díez Merino, "La Biblia en el magisterio de San Pablo de la Cruz", 475–503.

[172] Fr. Hyacinth remarks, "Allorquando era applicato a questa lettura, lo faceva con tale venerazione e rispetto, come se fosse applicato all'orazione, tenendo il capo scoperto del tutto..." / "Whenever he applied himself to this reading, he did it with as much veneration and respect as if he were praying, uncovering his head completely..." (PAR, 1780r.).

[173] The Passionist lay brother Francis-Louis stated the following in his testimony at the informative process in Rome: "... non lasciava ... di leggere continuamente la S. Scrittura, quale continuamente teneva presso di sé." / "... he read sacred Scripture continually, always having a copy at hand" (POR, 1159r.).

[174] See L 4:79, Oct. 25, 1768, to Joseph Strambi.

or disapprove of spirits depending upon whether they agree or disagree with what God has chosen to reveal and manifest in holy Scripture.[175]

Paul does not just speak *about* Scripture; he frequently quotes from it. There are references to the Old and New Testaments in hundreds of letters, and they stand out because he cites the Latin text even though he does not cite chapter and verse. It is readily apparent that many times he is quoting from memory, as evidenced by the many inaccuracies in the passages he quotes. Sometimes he omits words or even sentences. At other times, to clarify a point, he inserts his own words or modifies tenses, changes word order, or substitutes synonymous phrases for the original ones.[176] Rather than being inaccuracies and modifications that falsify meaning, these errors or alterations are like those encountered when almost anyone quotes from memory.

Paul must have been well versed in Scripture to have cited it so frequently. Furthermore, he did not limit himself to a few sections of the Bible but quoted passages from almost all the books of the Old and New Testaments.[177] The number and conformity of the passages quoted convincingly demonstrate that the saint read and meditated upon the books of the Old and New Testaments all his life.[178]

The manner in which the texts are used should not be judged by the standards of today's exegesis. Often, there are "verbal reminiscences" that

---

[175] " 'Spiritus ubi vult spirat, et nescis unde venit, aut quo vadat'; disse Gesù Cristo. Così io dirò a V.R. In quanto alle angustie e soffocamento che V.R. dice, vorrei un poco sapere. Quando S. Teresa viveva, ed altri Santi e Sante, ed il loro spirito, anche da uomini dottissimi, era da chi approvato, da chi disapprovato, come si diportassero in tali approvazioni o disapprovazioni, se per questo si angustiavano, o . . . ? Noi abbiamo la Sagra Scrittura, da cui tutti i teologi ed i moralisti e mistici e dogmatici e polemici ecc. hanno ricavato le loro opere ed hanno approvato o disapprovato gli spiriti secondo che, o accordavano o disaccordavano da quanto Iddio si è degnato rivelare e manifestare nella Sagra Scrittura" (L 1:819, Sept. 1, 1773).

[176] An example is the above-quoted passage from the gospel of John (3:8). The exact text of the Vulgate edition follows: "Spiritus ubi vult spirat; et vocem eius audis, sed nescis unde veniat, aut quo vadat." / "The wind blows where it will. You hear the sound it makes, but you do not know where it comes from, or where it goes." St. Paul of the Cross' version, i.e., "Spiritus ubi vult spirat, et nescis unde venit, aut quo vadat", was simplified.

[177] In the approximately 2,000 letters of St. Paul of the Cross, the Bible is cited more than 500 times. Of these quotations, approximately 200 are from the Old Testament and 300 from the New. Zoffoli presents a complete listing of biblical quotes in his second volume of his critical biography. See *Storia Critica* 2:97–110 and 115–21, respectively.

[178] As related by witnesses in the beatification processes, it was not uncommon for the founder to evoke astonishment and admiration on the part of other clerics and priests and from among his companions. (See POR, 1056v., testimony of the lay brother Francis-Louis, and POR, 222r., testimony of Fr. Joseph Suscioli.)

explain the use of a particular passage. The scriptural citations are understood in their "literal content" while, nevertheless, the larger context in which they are found is for the most part respected. In other words, the greater context within which the citation is placed needs to be considered first.

It is readily apparent that St. Paul of the Cross refers more frequently to some biblical writings than to others. For example, he refers to the psalms sixty-four times. The reason for this seeming preference may lie in his familiarity with them. He prayed the psalms daily in the liturgy of the hours.[179]

Using as an indicator of his preferences the frequency with which he referred to the various New Testament writings, Paul's favorites were the Gospel of St. Matthew (an account accorded a somewhat more privileged position in former times), that of the evangelist John, and the Pauline Letters.[180] These last two preferences may be explained in that they are so congruent with the basic principles underlying Paul's own thought, namely, God's infinite love for all as represented in the writings of St. John (Jn 20:2) and our redemption by Christ Crucified, a belief central to the preaching and theology of the apostle of the Gentiles.

The affinity between Paul of the Cross and the apostle Paul seems to have been grounded in more than a belief system, as important as that is. There exists in the writings of each a burning love for Christ Crucified and the mysticism of the passion. Their letters provide lasting evidence of this. There is also in each an untiring effort to announce to the world λόγος τοῦ σταυροῦ (the liberating power of the cross). Finally, there is their determined, but more than that, ethical-ascetical striving, not for some self-willed asceticism but for an asceticism rooted in the wonderful plenitude of Christ's πνεῦμα (Spirit) and χάρις (grace).

Throughout his life, Paul of the Cross retained a special reverence for this apostle and tried "to imitate him in all things".[181] The extent to which he succeeded is evidenced in the words of Pope Clement XIV, who called Paul Danei *un*

---

[179] The Rule of the Congregation composed by Paul of the Cross specifies that the breviary is to be said in common like a prayer spoken in chorus, even though Passionists, as members of a "Congregation", are not so obliged by ecclesiastical law. (See *Regulae et Constitutiones*, 68–73.) This communal recitation of the divine office effected the memorization of many biblical texts, especially the psalms.

[180] The frequencies are St. Matthew, 38; St. John, 41; the Pauline Letters, 131. Of the latter, the letter to the Romans and the two letters to the Corinthians account for 47 citations.

[181] His companion, Bro. Francis-Louis, declared at the informative process of Rome, "Per lui nutrisse una divozione particularissima ... perché procurasse d'imitarlo in tutto e per tutto." / "He had a special devotion to him [Paul the Apostle] ... because he attempted to imitate him in all and for all" (POR, 1034r., as quoted in *Storia Critica* 2:113).

S. Paolo dei nostri tempi (a St. Paul of our own time).[182] To conclude, we need but affirm that sacred Scripture was the source most frequently read by the founder of the Passionists, and it shaped, in a most intensive way, his theological doctrine.

2. *Influence of the Writers of Classical Spirituality upon St. Paul of the Cross*

Paul of the Cross considered the spiritual direction of those entrusted to him to be a great duty, one he conscientiously discharged throughout his life. Although his own interior experience of God was undoubtedly the best basis for helping others in their journey to God, he was not content to rely solely on his own powers of discernment. He continually widened his intellectual horizons by reading in the field of Christian spirituality.

As sources point out, the saint read the writings of some authors with predilection. Besides Tauler, about whom we will later speak, these authors were masters of spiritual literature: St. Francis de Sales, St. Teresa of Jesus, and St. John of the Cross. In declaring all three to be Doctors of the Church, the Church openly expressed its conviction that they are "proven authors".[183] By means of their spirituality, Paul himself grew in theological knowledge. The imprint of each upon his thinking and writing is discussed in the following pages.

St. Francis de Sales (1567–1622). It has been handed down to us that as early as 1718–20 Paul was already conversant with the doctrine of the great bishop of Geneva.[184] This familiarity with Salesian thought manifested itself in Paul's spiritual diary, written between November 23, 1720, and January 1, 1721.[185] In it, Paul used concepts and phrases that paralleled expressions of Francis de Sales.

---

[182] " . . . sembrandomi nella persona del P. Paolo di sentire un S. Paolo Apostolo, chiamandolo anche 'un S. Paolo dei nostri tempi' la santa memoria di Clemente XIV." / " . . . it seems to me that I sensed in the person of Fr. Paul another Apostle Paul, and even Clement XIV, of holy memory, called him 'a St. Paul of our own time' " (POR, 779r., testimony of Bro. Francis-Louis).

[183] St. Francis de Sales was declared a Doctor of the Church in 1877, St. John of the Cross in 1926, and St. Teresa of Jesus in 1970.

[184] The Franciscan Father Francis Anthony Capriata as a child lived in Castellazzo and was a very good friend of Paul Danei, who at the time still lived with his own family in the same town. During the informative process of Alessandria, Fr. Francis declared, " . . . ed io fra gli altri, che riconosco a lui la mia risoluzione di rendermi capuccino, e che ho ricevuto da lui le istruzioni dell'orazione mentale per tutte le vie purgativa, illuminativa ed unitiva, nelle quali ho presente che mostrava servirsi molto, anzi in tutto delle dottrine di San Francesco di Sales, che possedeva mirabilmente." / " . . . and I am one among others whom I know owe to him [Paul] my resolution to become a Capuchin, and who received from him instruction in mental prayer for the purgative, illuminative, and unitive ways. In this, it appears that Paul preferred and greatly relied upon St. Francis de Sales' doctrine, which he comprehended wonderfully" (POA, 202v.–203r., in *Processi* 1:50).

[185] Compare above history of this time period with the text beginning above on p. 30.

For example, in meditating upon the lack of comfort in the life of Jesus, Paul was led to an inner experience of the intermingling of love and sorrow. He stated, " . . . in my own poor soul, there was a mingling of sorrow and love . . . " (*si frammischiava nella poverissima anima mia il dolore e amore . . .*).[186] St. Francis de Sales wrote clearly of this intermingling in his treatise *On the Love of God*.[187]

When talking of God, St. Paul of the Cross frequently used the notions of *Sommo Bene* (Sovereign Good), *amato bene* (well beloved), *infinito amore* (infinite love), and *infinita misericordia* (infinite mercy).[188] St. Francis de Sales used the same appellatives in his writings.

In a diary entry of November 29, 1720, Paul clarified the function of the will during prayer by likening it to that of an infant nursing at its mother's breast.[189] St. Francis de Sales used the same imagery in two places in Book 6 of *On the Love of God*.[190] When speaking of the soul, the founder divided its functions into memory, intellect, and will, formulations similar to those of Francis de Sales.[191] When describing his spiritual states, Paul used such phrases as *melting away*[192] and *loving attention*,[193] phrases used previously by Francis de Sales.[194]

In his spiritual diary, Paul did not quote verbatim any text from the writings of Francis de Sales or mention his name. Formulations of thought

---

[186] Entry of Dec. 28, 1720 (*Diario Spirituale*, 82; *Tagebuch*, 104, n. 82; Rouse, 37).

[187] In Bk. 5, Chap. 5, of *On the Love of God*, the heading reads, "Concerning the Condolence and Complacence of Love in Our Lord's Passion". In the first few sentences of this chapter, it is written, "How can a devout soul seeing this abyss of weariness and distress in the divine lover be without a sorrow both holy and loving?" (See F. Reisinger, *Werke des hl. Franz von Sales* 3:247f. In English, see St. Francis de Sales, *On the Love of God*, John K. Ryan, trans. and ed. [New York: Image Books, 1963, 1st ed.], 1:246).

[188] "Sommo bene" (sovereign good) on Nov. 27 and 30, Dec. 10–13, 15–18, 21, 23, and 26; "amato bene" (well beloved) on Dec. 23; "infinita amore" (infinite love) on Dec. 4, 24, and 26; and "infinita misericordia" (infinite mercy) on Dec. 7 and 26.

[189] *Diario Spirituale*, 60; *Tagebuch*, 66f.; Rouse, 30.

[190] Chaps. 9 and 10. This imagery is also found in seven other places in St. Francis' treatise *On the Love of God*. St. Teresa of Jesus also uses this image in Chap. 31 of *Way of Perfection*. An analysis of Paul's text demonstrates, however, that he had in his own mind's eye the descriptions provided by St. Francis de Sales.

[191] See *Diario Spirituale*, 60; *Tagebuch*, 66f.; or Rouse, 30. Also see Bk. 6, Chap. 10, of Ryan, *On the Love of God* (1:294).

[192] Entry of Dec. 8, 1720, states, " . . . perché l'anima non può più parlare e sente a liquefarsi . . . " (*Diario Spirituale*, 67; *Tagebuch*, 79; Rouse, 32).

[193] Entry of Dec. 23, 1720, states, " . . . perché perde un pò di attenzione amorosa . . . " (*Diario Spirituale*, 78; *Tagebuch*, 98; Rouse, 36).

[194] In Bk. 6, Chap. 12, of *On the Love of God*, St. Francis de Sales speaks of melting away and of the outpouring of the soul into God (Reisinger 3:304–7; Ryan, *On the Love of God*, 1:299–302). In Chap. 6 of the same book, he says that to contemplate is "to look with loving attention at the truth of God's beauty and goodness" (Reisinger 3:290; Ryan, *On the Love of God*, 1:285).

and parallel expressions, however, clearly demonstrate that Paul of the Cross "had been brought up in the school of the sweet bishop of Geneva, whose writings he eagerly studied and read in his first years of religious life".[195] As a result of his study, the founder incorporated into his own thinking many of Francis de Sales' ideas and concepts, which later came to light in entries in Paul's diary.

Since the diary is the oldest source of information on Paulacrucian thought, and since it contains so many entries with Salesian overtones, it can be stated that St. Francis de Sales was a favorite author of the saint and substantially influenced the Passionist founder, even in his early years before 1720.[196] Paul's interest in Salesian thinking did not wane in his later years. In a letter to Nicolina Martinez de Gaeta, written six years after the retreat at Castellazzo, he asked to borrow for a time both volumes of On the Love of God.[197] A few days later, he wrote saying he had received the books.[198]

Other letters indicate that, throughout his life, Paul's own spiritual-theological thinking included ideas taken from the writings of St. Francis de Sales. This indebtedness may be shown in Paul's use of similar examples and analogies, developed originally by Francis to clarify teachings.[199] More often than not using even the same context as that used by St. Francis, Paul draws upon the same comparisons and metaphors in his letters to others.[200] This point is developed at some length in the following paragraphs.

For instance, to exemplify union with God, St. Francis de Sales uses, in his treatise On the Love of God, the metaphor of a drop of water that falls into the ocean. To Jesus, in a lover's colloquy, Francis exclaims, "Plunge this drop of

---

[195] " . . . che si era formato alla scuola del dolce Vescovo di Ginevra, i cui scritti ricercò e lesse avidamente nei primi anni di vita religiosa" (L 1:viii, in Preface).

[196] Storia Critica 2:123.

[197] This woman was the mother of Rev. Don Emanuele Martinez, who, as a cleric, often visited the brothers Paul and John Baptist Danei when they were living in the hermitage "della Civita" near Gaeta (L 1:60, n. 1).

L 1:64, May 26, 1726: " . . . la supplico a farci la carità imprestarci i due tomi che trattano del ssmo. amore di Dio di S. Francesco di Sales, che fra un mese o poco più le restituiremo . . . " / " . . . I beseech you to be so kind as to let me borrow the two volumes of St. Francis de Sales that treat of the most holy love of God. I will return them in a month or less . . . "

[198] L 1:65, June 3, 1726. This information was also reported by Don Emanuele Martinez during the informative process of Gaeta (see POG, 269v.–270r., in Processi 2:102).

[199] In his essay "The Theology of St. Francis de Sales" J. Martin states (p. 80), "In many cases, the saint is striving to avoid dry definitions by giving concrete images of the experience. Rather than presenting a series of arguments in due form, he builds into his discourse an inner structure and rhetorical fabric that—by means of the basic information presented, conclusions drawn, examples given, analogies or explanations elaborated upon, and by digressions [appropriately] inserted—presents a clear discussion . . . "

[200] In the treatise On the Love of God more than 120 different metaphors and comparisons are used (see Reisinger 4:393–95).

spirit which you have given me into the sea of your goodness from which it comes."[201] The Passionist founder uses the same metaphor in a letter written to Marianna Girelli in 1766. In it, he transforms this metaphor into a little allegory in which he anthropomorphizes the little drop of water,[202] making it, full of yearning, say, "I desire to plunge into the sea." What is most interesting is the fact that in the moral of this allegory, Paul quotes almost verbatim from Francis' exhortation to Theotimus. Paul writes, "Let, therefore, this drop of spirit, that God has given you, sink into its origin which is God [*lasciate che codesta goccia di spirito che Dio vi ha data, si perda nella sua origine che è Dio*].[203]

In Chapter 2 of Book 6 of *On the Love of God*, St. Francis de Sales speaks about contemplation, giving the example of a bee that flies from flower to flower looking for honey.[204] We find the same example[205] in a letter written by St. Paul of the Cross in 1729 to the Marchioness Marianna del Pozzo. In Chapter 11 of the same Book 6, Francis explains to Theotimus that the soul, which goes to God and wants to remain there, has to practice "self-abnegation".[206] Francis explains this by using the analogy of a statue in a niche.[207] Paul of the Cross repeats this imagery.[208]

[201] Bk. 7, Chap. 3 (Reisinger 4:44; Ryan, *On the Love of God* 2:24).

[202] St. Francis de Sales uses the literary tool of personification in his examples, too. See Bk. 6, Chap. 11, of *On the Love of God* (Reisinger 3:302; Ryan, *On the Love of God* 1:298–99).

[203] With his usage of parables evidencing the intuitive understanding of which he was capable, Paul writes, "Farò una parabola, giacchè anche il nostro Divin Maestro parlava con parabole. Io per esempio, mi trovo alla spiaggia del mare, tengo una goccia d'acqua: Oh, povera picciola goccia, dove vorresti essere? Sentite la risposta. Al mare, al mare! dice essa. Ed io che fo? Suoto il dito e lascio cadere quella povera picciola goccia nel mare. Or dimando io: Vi è questa goccia nel mare, è vero? Certamente vi è; ma trovala, se ti dà l'animo. È abissata in quel gran mare suo centro. Oh, se potesse parlare, che direbbe? Fate la conseguenza, signora Marianna, ed applicate la parabola.—Perdete di vista e cielo e terra e mare e arena ed ogni cosa creata, e lasciate che codesta goccia di spirito che Dio vi ha data, sa perda nella sua origine che è Dio . . ." / " 'Oh, poor tiny droplet, where would you like to be?' Now, listen to its answer: 'Into the sea, into the sea', it replied. As for me, what do I do? I shake my finger and let fall that poor tiny droplet into the sea. Now, I ask, 'The droplet is now in the sea, isn't it?' Certainly it is there, but try to find it—if you have the courage. It is sunk into the center of that great sea. Oh, if it could speak, what would it say? Signora Marianna, draw the moral and put the parable into practice. Forget the sky and the earth and the sands and every created thing and permit the droplet of spirit God has given you to lose itself in its source, which is God" (L 3:748, Mar. 11, 1766).

[204] Bk. 6, Chap. 2 (Reisinger 3:278; Ryan, *On the Love of God* 1:272).

[205] L 1:44, Jan. 3, 1729: " . . . tutta raccolta in Dio come un'ape sopra al fiore e succhi il miele del S. Amore in un divoto silenzio . . ." / " . . . be completely recollected in God like a bee hovering over a flower and drinking the honey of divine love in divine silence . . . "

[206] Bk. 6, Chap. 11, is entitled "Continuation of the Discussion of the Different Degrees of Holy Quiet, and Concerning an Excellent Form of Self-Denial Sometimes Practiced in It" (Reisinger 3:300; Ryan, *On the Love of God* 1:296–99).

[207] Reisinger 3:302f.; Ryan, *On the Love of God* 1:298.

[208] L 2:301, Jan. 1, 1765, to Mother Mary Crucified Costantini.

As mentioned previously, Paul frequently alludes to the quotation from Augustine's *Confessions* (Book 10, Chapter 27).[209] Francis de Sales also employs this quotation in his treatise *On the Love of God* (Book 1, Chapter 12).[210] Paul, therefore, may have become acquainted with this citation from the work of St. Francis de Sales.

In a letter of 1743, which is of importance in the development of his spiritual teaching, St. Paul of the Cross defines love as being a "unifying power" (*l'amore è virtù unitiva*).[211] Although this same definition may be found in Book 7 of *On the Love of God,*[212] Francis was, at this point, citing Dionysius the Areopagite.[213]

Paul also discusses different levels or strata of spirit or soul. He speaks of an "inferior part of the soul" (*parte inferiore dello spirito*) and of a "supreme part of the soul" (*la suprema parte dell'anima*). This supreme part, which he often refers to as sanctuary, interior temple, or inner chamber (*santuario, tempio interiore, gabinetto interiore*), represents the place "where faith, hope, and love exert their principal functions" (*dove fanno le loro principali funzioni la fede, la speranza e la carità*).[214] In the doctrine of Francis de Sales, the supreme point or apex of the soul is the special abode of faith, hope, and

[209] L 1:44, Jan. 3, 1729, to the Marchioness Marianna del Pozzo; and L 1:401, June 26, 1736, to Francis Anthony Appiani.

[210] Reisinger 3:82f.; Ryan, *On the Love of God* 1:85.

[211] L 2:440, July 10, 1743, to Sr. C. Gertrude Gandolfi; and, supplementary to this, L 3:804, Mar. 10, 1767, to A. M. Calcagnini.

[212] Reisinger 4:34f.; Ryan, *On the Love of God* 2:16.

[213] The common designation "Pseudo-Dionysius" is not used here to avoid ascribing to this great thinker an epithet that carries with it a disparaging connotation. See Hans Urs von Balthasar, *Herrlichkeit,* 1: 147–51.

This definition is taken from "De Divinis Nominibus" 4:15. It states: » ενωτικὴν τινα καὶ συγκρατικὴν εννοήσωμεν δύναμιν . . . ‹ (*Patrologia graeca* 3:714 and referenced in *Storia Critica* 2:129).

[214] L 1:538, Oct. 10, 1736, to Thomas Fossi. The entire fragment reads as follows: "È buono esercitarsi in essa operando con la suprema parte dello spirito, che è il vero santuario dell'anima, dove fanno le lore principali funzioni la fede, la speranza e la carità; pertanto lei fa bene a non curarsi di verun contento, e massime quando ridonda molto nella parte inferiore, parte che è tutta animalesca, ma contentarsi solamente di gustare Dio con la suprema parte dell'anima, in viva e pura fede, giacchè il giusto [come sta scritto] vive di fede [Rom 1:17]; e così con questa attenzione amorosa a Dio in pura fede, ne nasce quel riposo d'amore in Dio, in cui la volontà s'abissa tutta nel Somme Bene." / "It is good to practice this [prayer] in the higher part of the spirit, which is the true sanctuary of the soul, where faith, hope, and charity exercise their main functions. Meanwhile you do well to pay no heed to any kind of satisfaction, more especially if it reacts in the lower part, the part that is purely natural. Be satisfied instead to enjoy God in the higher part in pure and living faith, for [it is written] the just man lives by faith [Rom 1:17]. Hence from this loving attentiveness to God in pure faith there springs that loving repose in God in which the will is completely engulfed in the Supreme Good" (as translated by Edmund Burke, Roger Mercurio, and Silvan Rouse in *Words from the Heart,* 123).

love.[215] In using this notion, both Francis and Paul borrow from medieval mysticism.[216]

This series of parallels could be extended to make even more apparent the influence of St. Francis de Sales upon the writing of St. Paul of the Cross. What seems astonishing is that Paul, who depends so heavily upon Francis, so seldom mentions him. In an attempt to explain this observation, two suppositions are advanced. Because of his frequent reading of and familiarity with Francis' main work, *On the Love of God,* Paul made his own, in the true sense of the work, many Salesian concepts. He may not have been aware, therefore, that he was speaking another's words. Another possibility is that Paul had only one very practical aim in writing, namely, the spiritual direction of others. It is likely that he simply felt no need to document sources.

Before concluding this section, it should be noted there is one place where Paul refers to his esteem for St. Francis de Sales and cites him. In a letter written in 1767, the founder speaks, among other things, of the difficulty of finding a good and experienced spiritual director. Then, he makes reference to a similar point made in Book I of *Introduction to the Devout Life.*[217] In it, Francis de Sales is giving advice to Philothea on choosing a spiritual guide. He refers her to the words of "Avila" (meaning John of Avila), who stated, " 'For this end, choose one among a thousand.' " St. Francis himself then expands on the thought, stating, "I say, 'Choose one among ten thousand.' For there are fewer suitable than can be imagined who are capable of this office."[218]

---

[215] *On the Love of God,* 1:12 (Reisinger 3:84; Ryan, *On the Love of God* 1:85).

[216] In his study *Das Seelenleben in der Gottesliebe nach dem "Theotimus" des hl. Franz von Sales,* 224f., n. 245), F. Rotter remarks, "Thus, his [St. Francis de Sales'] teaching on the supreme part of the soul is a medieval heirloom. In order to establish the validity of this much disputed notion, he revives the teaching on the levels of perfection, a traditional doctrine in Augustinian-Franciscan mysticism [Augustine, Hugo and Richard of St. Victor, Bonaventure]. With regard to its content, this notion is rooted in the phrase *acies mentis* used especially by Augustine and Richard of St. Victor, and in the concept of a superior reason originating from Ludolf of Saxony and St. Teresa. Finally, this teaching of St. Francis de Sales is similar to the teaching of the German mystics on the ground of the soul or [on] its divine spark existing in its inner stratum—of course, without proof of external lines of linkage."

[217] Paul's letter actually states, "Santa Teresa dice che fra mille, appena si troverà un vero Direttore di spirito, esperto del cammino della santa orazione e di tutta la condotta spirituale." / "St. Teresa says that, among one thousand men, there will scarcely be one true spiritual director, skillful in the path of holy prayer and in the totality of spiritual conduct" (L 3:804, Mar. 10, 1767, to Anna Maria Calcagnini). Here, Paul confuses Teresa of Avila with John of Avila, as the referenced quotation in "Introduction to the Devout Life" unequivocally shows. Yet, this "reputed" citation indicates the vividness with which Paul remembers the text of St. Francis de Sales. Paul's letter goes on to state, " . . . e San Francesco di Sales dice che fra diecimila, appena se ne troverà uno. Oh, quanto è difficile l'intendere e il saper parlare delle cose interiori!" (St. Francis de Sales says that hardly one can be found among ten thousand. Oh, how difficult it is to understand and to know how to express interior things!) (L 3:804).

[218] Reisinger 1:40. Also see Francis de Sales, *Introduction to the Devout Life,* John Ryan, trans. and ed., 43.

To conclude, the following points may be stressed. The author who had the most decisive influence upon the thinking of Paul of the Cross and one whose works Paul read throughout his life was St. Francis de Sales. Hence, it is he who is designated here as Paul's favorite author. Of Francis' works, the founder favored *On the Love of God.* This treatise fascinated him, the reason being that the infinite love of God was, for Paul, the fundamental principle and end point of his spiritual life. Some of his contemporaries knew of the affinity between him and St. Francis de Sales, and it was to the "mild bishop of Geneva" that they mostly compared Paul.[219]

St. Teresa of Jesus (Teresa de Cepeda y Ahumada, 1515–1582). Because of his contact with the Carmelite priests in their school in Cremolina,[220] Paul had the opportunity to come into contact with Carmelite spirituality even as a child. During that time, one or more of the Carmelites would have introduced him to the writings of that popular saint-mystic, Teresa of Jesus (known more commonly as Teresa of Avila). It was she who became, second only to St. Francis de Sales, another of Paul's favorite authors.

This conclusion is based on more than mere conjecture. Historical data make it clear that Teresa's writings influenced the spiritual doctrine of Paul of the Cross. Some examples follow.[221]

On December 3, 1720, Paul included in his spiritual diary an explicit quotation from the *Autobiography* of this Doctor of the Church. After relating that day's sorrows and fears, he wrote, "However, my soul embraces them because it knows that this is God's will, and that these are the joys of Jesus. I feel like saying with St. Teresa, 'To suffer or to die'."[222]

This was the first time St. Paul of the Cross introduced a direct quotation in his diary and gave the author's name. Obviously, this famous saying of Teresa[223] moved him deeply. Consequently, he himself ascribed to suffering an important role in the "way of perfection".

Although Paul does not refer directly to St. Teresa in any other entries, he does use several expressions that substantially parallel her own, especially those that delve into the meaning and appreciation of suffering. For example,

[219] See PAR, 1168v., statement of Fr. Joseph of St. Mary.

[220] It is not known how long Paul was under the tutelage of the Carmelite Fathers. He lived with his family in Cremolina, however, from 1701 to 1709 (*Storia Critica* 1:110–17).

[221] Specific, individual examples are the most suitable way of illustrating or historically proving direct influence.

[222] "E pur l'anima le abbraccia, perchè sa che è volontà di Dio, e che sono le gioie di Gesù; mi viene da dire con Santa Teresa: O patire, o morire" (*Diario Spirituale,* 63; *Tagebuch,* 72; Rouse, 31).

[223] In Chap. 40 of her *Autobiography,* Teresa writes, "I sometimes say to him with my whole will, 'To die, Lord, or to suffer! I ask nothing else of thee for myself but this' " (Alkofer 1:420). In English, this and all subsequent references to the *Autobiography* are taken from Peers, *Autobiography* (quotation here, 395).

in a letter in which St. Teresa discusses the suffering she endures, she states, "I realize better every day what grace our Lord has shown me in enabling me to understand the blessings of suffering . . . "[224] On December 21, 1720, St. Paul of the Cross wrote the following in his spiritual diary: "I would like to be able to say that everyone would experience this great grace, which God, in his mercy, grants when he sends suffering to us, and especially when the suffering is devoid of consolation."[225] Furthermore, both saints speak of sufferings as "joys"[226] and "tokens of God's love".[227] Both, too, find that their esteem of the value of suffering effects an inner "longing" for it,[228] and from this longing

---

[224] Letter of May 11, 1575, to Don Alvaro de Mendoza. In German, see Alkofer 3:180. In English, see *The Letters of St. Teresa,* translated from Spanish and annotated by the Benedictines of Stanbrook, 1:191–92.

[225] "Vorrei poter dire che tutto il mondo sentisse la grande grazia che Dio per sua pietà fa, quando manda da patire, e massime quando il patire è senza conforto" (*Diario Spirituale,* 75; *Tagebuch,* 94; Rouse, 35).

[226] The entry of Nov. 26 reads, " . . . so che dico al mio Gesù che le sue croci sono le gioie del mio cuore" / " . . . I know that I tell my Jesus that his crosses are the joys of my heart" (*Diario Spirituale,* 57; *Tagebuch,* 62; Rouse, 29). In a letter to Doña Agnes Nieto, Teresa says, "The time will come when you will prize your trials more than all the joys of your past life . . . nothing will delight us more than suffering, nor could we have a safer sign that we are serving God truly" (Alkofer 3:113; Benedictines of Stanbrook 4:69).

[227] In an entry of Nov. 27, 1720, St. Paul of the Cross refers to cold, snow, and ice as being sweet to him, so great was his desire to suffer. He longed for them and, in his own words, "saying to my beloved Jesus, 'Your afflictions, dear God, are the pledges of your love'" (*Diario Spirituale,* 57; *Tagebuch,* 63; Rouse, 30). In a letter of Nov. 7, 1571, to Doña Luisa de la Cerda, St. Teresa of Jesus writes, "Evidently you are one of those whom he destines to reign with him and whom he dearly loves, since he makes you 'drink of the chalice' by means of your many illnesses" (Alkofer 3:93; Benedictines of Stanbrook 1:88–89).

[228] In his spiritual diary, Paul talks of his longing for suffering on two occasions. On Nov. 27, he states, "At that moment, so great was my joy in and desire for suffering that the cold, the snow, and the ice seemed delightful to me, and I desired them with great fervor . . . " On Dec. 21, he writes, " . . . I beg for my Crucified Jesus not to deliver me from it. On the contrary, I desire them in order to suffer . . . " (*Diario Spirituale,* 57 and 74, respectively; *Tagebuch,* 63 and 92; Rouse, 30 and 34–35).

In a letter of Dec. 30, 1575, to Mother Mary Baptist, prioress of the convent in Valladolid, St. Teresa describes the grief she endures because of her reform of the cloisters. She brings up the point that disciplinary action may be taken against her in the form of a transfer to provoke her to great torment. She continues, "I understand . . . they think it will pain me keenly, yet I am so glad of it that I fear it will never come to pass" (Alkofer 3:224; Benedictines of Stanbrook 1:235).

In her *Book of the Foundations,* she tells the story of one of her coreligious, Beatrice of the Incarnation. Teresa writes that Beatrice's desire to suffer was not easily satisfied. The saint continues, " . . . thus, on a festival of the cross, after she [Beatrice] had listened to a sermon, this desire increased so much that she flung herself on her bed in a flood of tears, and when they asked her what was the matter, she begged them to pray to God that he would give her many trials and she would then be happy" (Alkofer 2:97; and Peers, *Book of the Foundations,* Chap. 12, 3:59).

springs the cry "either to suffer or to die", a cry which St. Paul of the Cross makes his own.

In the diary entry of December 21, Paul writes that Jesus, "during all his holy life, did nothing else but suffer".[229] Although at first glance this assertion may sound exaggerated, it is important to remember the emphasis Paul places on the strong relationship between suffering and love.[230] St. Teresa also uses similar formulations in her *Autobiography*[231] and letters.[232]

On the basis of these verbal similarities and areas of corresponding content, it is apparent that the founder of the Passionists had already become acquainted with the works of St. Teresa by the time he wrote his spiritual diary. Especially striking is his reliance on the doctrine of the "teacher of Avila" in terms of the role of suffering in the "way of perfection". This reliance on Teresa may be explained by a profound compatibility in the thinking of these two saints.

Their spiritualities were rooted in common ground: the suffering and crucifixion of Jesus. For example, one of the reasons given by Teresa for entering the Carmelite Order was the suffering of Christ,[233] and later on it was the "suffering Christ" who called her to conversion.[234] "To be crucified with Jesus" (*essere crocifisso con Gesù*) was the starting point of Paul's thinking and the goal or end point of his acting.[235] This common rootedness makes it

---

[229] " . . . il quale in tutta la sua ss. vita non ha fatto altro che patire" (*Diario Spirituale*, 75; *Tagebuch*, 94; Rouse, 35).

[230] See *Tagebuch*, 94f., n. 70. Also see Bialas, "Leiden als Gnade", 434f. In English, see M. Bialas, "Human Suffering as Grace in the Thought of Paul of the Cross" (*The Passionist*, no. 3 [1976]: 98–121, here 106f.).

[231] In Chap. 22, Teresa states that true poverty of spirit consists "in seeking, not comfort or pleasure in prayer (for it has already abandoned earthly comforts and pleasures), but consolation [by means of] trials for the love of him who suffered trials all his life long . . . " (Alkofer 1:211; Peers, *Autobiography*, 215).

[232] In a letter to Doña Juana de Ahumada, Teresa states, "May our Lord be praised, for he came to earth for nothing but to suffer . . . " (Alkofer 4:336; Benedictines of Stanbrook 4:117).

[233] W. Herbstrith, *Teresa von Avila—Die erste Kirchenlehrerin*, 65. A comparable text in English makes the same point. See Marcelle Auclair, *Teresa of Avila*, 36.

[234] In Chap. 9 of her *Autobiography*, St. Teresa narrates how a picture of an "Ecce Homo" was for her a stimulus that motivated her inner conversion. She writes, "It represented Christ sorely wounded; and so conducive was it to devotion that when I looked at it I was deeply moved to see him thus, so well did it picture what he suffered for us. So great was my distress when I thought how ill I had repaid him for those wounds that I felt as if my heart were breaking. . . . I believe I told him then that I would not rise from that spot until he had granted me what I was beseeching of him. And I feel sure that this did me good, for from that time onward I began to improve" (Herbstrith, 93f.; Peers, *Autobiography*, 115).

[235] In the first entry in his diary, Paul writes, "Io so che per misericordia del nostro caro Dio, non desidero saper altro, ne gustar alcuna consolazione, solo che desidero d'esser crocifisso con Gesù." / "Through the mercy of our good God, I know that I do not desire to

possible to apply to the doctrine of St. Paul of the Cross the words W. Herbstrith[236] applied to the doctrine of St. Teresa. He stated, "This doctrine, therefore, is convincing, because it takes as its starting point the humanity of Jesus and his crucifixion for others."

Teresian influence is apparent not only in Paul's entries in his spiritual diary but also in his letters, where he mentions her no less than forty times.[237] Although this in itself is sufficient reason to say the Passionist founder remained bound to the teachings of this Spanish mystic all his life, it is proper to support this supposition with appropriate references.

In Chapter 11 of her *Autobiography*, St. Teresa presents a simile to help elucidate four stages of prayer.[238] She presents the well-known example of different states of prayer being like different ways in which a garden is watered. In a letter to a fellow religious, Fr. Bartholomew, Paul uses Teresa's simile, but in a simplified form, and he explicitly names her as its author.[239] Years later, he again uses her simile when writing to a Sister of his Congregation.[240] This time, however, he does not give a citation.

Teresa frequently compares the soul to a garden. For example, in Chapter 14, she states, " . . . it used to give me great delight to think of my soul as a garden and of the Lord as walking in it".[241] Apparently, Paul has the same

know anything else, nor to taste any consolation. I desire only to be crucified with Jesus" (*Diario Spirituale*, 53; *Tagebuch*, 57; Rouse, 20).

[236] Herbstrith, 67.

[237] J. Mead, *Priestly Spirituality According to the Doctrine of St. Paul of the Cross*, 93.

[238] Alkofer 1:108–11; Peers, *Autobiography*, 125f.

[239] In this letter, St. Paul of the Cross states, " . . . ed in quanto all'orazione, senta di grazia una parabola di S. Teresa: L'ortolano cavando l'acqua dai pozzi, per adacquar l'orto, conviene che usi non poca fatica; ma quando viene la pioggia del cielo cessa la fatica e se ne sta su la porta della capanna, compiacendosi dell'acqua che irriga l'orto, con maggiore ubertà di quello che esso faceva cavandola dal pozzo, e sta quieto e si rallegra." / " . . . with regard to prayer, be so kind as to listen to one of St. Teresa's parables: The gardener, who draws water from wells to water his orchard, suffers no little fatigue; but, when the rain pours down from the sky, his fatigue ends. He stays at the door of his cottage, enjoying the rain that irrigates his orchard and that brings with it more fertility than that taken from the well; thus, he remains there quiet and happy" (L 3:347, Dec. 24, 1767).

[240] "Per farle capire qualche cosa delle grazie che lei riceve presentemente dal Signore, si figuri che lei prima con la meditazione era come una giardiniera che cercava e portava acqua ad una pianta; ora con l'orazione in cui la Divina Bontà l'ha posta, è come la giardiniera la quale senza sua fatica o con poca fatica manda dalla fontana l'acqua alla pianta oppure come quando piove che si bagna ed inzuppa bel bello e meglio la pianta." / "To understand something of the grace you are now receiving from the Lord, consider that before, with your meditation, you were like a gardener drawing and bringing water to a plant. Now, with the prayer the Divine Goodness has granted you, you are like a gardener, who with little or no fatigue, brings water from a fountain to the plant or [who just watches] as rain bathes and thoroughly soaks the plant in water" (L 4:188, Apr. 27, 1775).

[241] Alkofer 1:137; Peers, *Autobiography*, 152.

simile in mind in the following excerpt from a letter to Agnes Grazi: "... Jesus will walk in the little garden of your heart."[242]

In a letter of 1760 to the priest Don Anthony Lucattini, Paul tells of an epidemic responsible for the death of three of his coreligious in one of the Passionist monasteries. Next he speaks of Lucy Burlini's[243] request sent by way of her confessor, Fr. Lucattini, to Paul. She asks St. Paul of the Cross to send her a Father. The saint responds to this request saying,

> When I can, I will send her one; but, for the moment, I have nobody suffering from the same disease as Lucy—and only those suffering the same understand the sacrosanct language. If I am talking nonsense, patience! It seems to me St. Teresa uses the same vocabulary.[244]

Undoubtedly, the experienced director is referring to Lucy's problem not as a physical disease but as a state resulting from her unappeasable longing for God's love. Here Paul seems to be referring to Chapter 20 in Teresa's *Autobiography*, in which she refers to her own state as if it were a disease and to anyone undergoing such a difficulty capable of being comforted only by another who has "passed through the same torment".[245]

Another factor in Paul's life that encouraged him to delve deeply into Teresian spirituality was his relationship with the Carmelite nuns of Vetralla.[246] During the course of his life, he conducted spiritual exercises for them on seven different occasions.[247] He was also a spiritual advisor and friend of the Carmelite Sister Maria Angela Colomba, who was paralyzed for more than thirty years.[248] It is reasonable to suppose, therefore, that the saint,

---

[242] "Gesù passegerà nel giardinetto del suo cuore ... " / "Jesus will walk in the little garden of your heart ... " (L 1:228, Mar. 7, 1739, to Agnes Grazi).

[243] Lucy Burlini was unmarried and supported herself by weaving in her parents' home. She lived an exemplary life like "Christ in the world" and was blessed with the gift of prayer. Because she could neither read nor write, St. Paul of the Cross, her spiritual director for years, corresponded with her through her confessor, Don A. Lucattini (*Storia Critica* 3:216–40).

[244] "Se potrò lo manderò, ma non ho in pronto soggetto che sia infermo dell'infermità di Lucia; e solo quelli che patiscono tale infermità, intendono il sacrosanto linguaggio. Se ho detto uno sproposito, pazienza; anche S. Teresa si serve, mi pare, di tal vocabolo" (L 2:830, Jan. 11, 1760).

[245] Alkofer 1:154; Peers, *Autobiography*, Chap. 20, 195.

[246] See *Storia Critica* 3:262–82, "Il Carmelo de Vetralla".

[247] POV, 308v. (*Processi* 1:196, testimony of Sr. Maria Angela di Gesù): "... e col medemo ho trattato in occasione che, circa sette volte, è venuto a dettare gl'esercizi spirituali in questo venerabile monastero ... " / "... and in this manner he came whenever he had the opportunity—about seven times—to conduct spiritual exercises [for us] in this venerable monastery ... " (also see *Annali*, 216).

[248] How much Paul appreciated Sister Colomba is obvious in the letters in which he speaks of her. See L 3:85, June 24, 1751, to the Dominican Father Mugnani, and L 3:90, June 27, 1751, to the prioress of this Carmelite cloister.

in order to prepare himself for both tasks, engrossed himself in Carmelite teaching.

Another important similarity between the teaching of St. Teresa and St. Paul of the Cross is their emphasis on never abandoning prayer centered on Jesus. To Thomas Fossi, Paul writes,

> It's true that this memory of the sacred passion of Jesus Christ and the imitation of his holy virtues should never be left aside—even after having attained a great degree of recollection and having reached a very high degree of prayer. The passion still remains the door through which the soul enters into union with God, to profound recollection and true contemplation.[249]

For Teresa, too, contemplation of Jesus' humanity, especially in his passion, is never to be left behind, even if the summit of contemplation is reached. She writes, "I have seen clearly that it is by this door that we must enter if we wish his Sovereign Majesty to show us great secrets."[250] In the *Interior Castle,* this Doctor of the Church expressly disapproves of the opinion that maintains that, after having reached a certain stage of prayer, a person may meditate alone upon the Godhead, leaving behind the humanity of Christ. She warns her sisters not to give any credence to people holding such false opinions.[251]

In all the periods of the life of St. Paul of the Cross we encounter a mysticism steeped in the mystery of suffering, a mysticism which in many ways is identical to the great St. Teresa's mysticism of the passion. This parallel thought is especially obvious when the question in point is a matter of discerning the nature of the suffering and its value. It recurs not only in his spiritual diary but also in his many letters, in which suffering is frequently referred to as "gift of God",[252]

---

[249] "Vero è che tal memoria della Passione SSma. di Gesù Cristo con l'imitazione delle sue sante virtù non si deve lasciare, abbenchè vi fosse il più profondo raccoglimento ed alto dono d'orazione, anzi questa è la porta che conduce l'anima all'intima unione con Dio, all'interiore raccoglimento ed alla sublime contemplazione" (L 1:582, July 5, 1749, to Thomas Fossi).

[250] Alkofer 1:208, in *Leben,* Chap. 22; Peers, *Autobiography,* Chap. 22, 213.

[251] See Seelenburg, 6, *Wohnung,* Chap. 7, nos. 5–7; Alkofer 5:165–67, here 165; Peers, *Interior Castle,* Chap. 7, 2:304.

[252] "I patimenti sono i più preziosi regali che il nostro buon Dio soglia compartire alle anime sue dilette..." / "Sufferings are the most precious gifts our Good God wants to give to his beloved" (L 2:30, June 20, 1760, to Maria Venturi Grazi). Paul writes in a similar fashion to Mother Mary Crucified in a letter dated Jan. 1, 1765 (L 2:300). In a letter to Luiz de Cepeda, Saint Teresa writes, "This obviously proves you are a true servant of God, since sufferings are the most precious gift God can give on this earth" (Alkofer 3:625).

"treasure",[253] "joy",[254] and "great grace".[255]

In a letter written to Sr. Colomba Gandolfi in July of 1743, Paul takes up Teresa's previously quoted statement and elaborates upon it. He writes, "Indeed, when the cross of our dear Jesus has planted its roots more deeply into your heart, then you will rejoice, 'to suffer and not die', or [better], 'to suffer or die', or better [still], 'neither to suffer nor die but only to turn perfectly to the will of God'."[256] The nature of Paul's elaboration indicates he does not parrot classical statements made by Teresa. Rather, he incorporates her thoughts in keeping with his own empirical world, bringing them into conformity with his own thinking and experience. This is not to deny, however, the considerable influence the doctrine of the great Teresa had on his own thought.

St. John of the Cross (Juan de Yepes y Alvarez, 1542–1591). Among Paul's favorite authors, St. John of the Cross, the co-reformer of the Carmelite Order, ranked third. It may be that Paul became aware of St. John of the Cross through the writings of St. Teresa, who mentioned him frequently. Exactly when or how Paul was introduced to the writings of John is unknown, however.

Paul first refers to the works of this saint in a letter to Agnes Grazi written in 1736.[257] In it, he quotes the fifth stanza taken from the Prologue to the *Dark Night of the Soul.* After citing Romans 1:17, "The just man lives by faith", Paul exclaims, "Oh night, obscure night: night more desirable than the dawn:

---

[253] "Ringrazio Dio che le fa parte del gran tesoro della Santa Croce, dei disprezzi . . . " / "I thank God that he has given you part of the great treasure of the Holy Cross, of contempt, etc." (L 1:118, Oct. 28, 1734, to Agnes Grazi; also see L 1:216, 2:104, 3:656, and others). St. Teresa writes in a similar fashion in a letter of Nov. 7, 1571, to Doña Luisa de Cerda (Alkofer 3:95; Benedictines of Stanbrook 1:89).

[254] "Le tue croci, caro Dio, sono le gioie del mio cuore." / "Your crosses, dear God, are the joys of my heart" (L 1:24, Feb. 6, 1721, to Sister Teresa Pontas; also see L 1:570, 3:363, and others). St. Teresa expresses herself similarly (Alkofer 3:113; also see n. 226 above).

[255] " . . . essendo sempre una gran grazia che Dio ci fa, quando ci dà da patire." / " . . . being as it is always a grace when God lets us suffer". (L 3:719, Mar. 12, 1765, to a religious woman whose name is unknown; also L 1:685, 3:366, 3:629, and others. In the *Letters of St. Teresa,* see Alkofer 3:180 or Benedictines of Stanbrook 1:191.)

See Bialas, "Leiden als Gnade". Also see "Il dolore umano come grazia in san Paolo della Croce", (*La Sapienza della Croce Oggi* 2:53–67). In English, see Bialas, "Human Suffering", 98–121.

[256] "Credo che la Croce del nostro dolce Gesù avrà poste più profonde radici nel vostro cuore e che cantarete: 'Pati et non mori', o pure: 'aut pati aut mori', o pure ancor meglio: 'nec pati, nec mori', ma solamente la totale trasformazione nel Divin Beneplacito" (L 2:440, July 10, 1743, to Sr. Colomba Gandolfi).

[257] Even though the first direct reference to St. John of the Cross in the writings of St. Paul of the Cross does not occur until 1736, we cannot necessarily conclude that Paul became aware of the works of this Spanish mystic only at that time. Neither may we conclude that Paul was unaware of these works at the time he wrote his spiritual diary even though he does not directly quote or refer to John of the Cross. Indeed, given his interest in spiritual-mystical literature, it is likely that, even in his youth, Paul knew of the writings of John of the Cross.

night who canst unite the Lover with the beloved; transform the beloved into the Lover."[258] Although Paul attributes these words to "a great saint", he does not give a more specific reference. He states, "Thus sang a great saint, and he called the night a holy prayer in faith; he called the night more brilliant than the rising sun."[259] Almost twenty years later, Paul cites the same passage in a letter to Sr. Colomba Gertrude Gandolfi.[260]

In counseling a religious on how to behave with regard to visions, revelations, and locutions, Paul of the Cross specifically cites the teaching of St. John of the Cross. The founder writes,

> I will tell you the doctrine of St. John of the Cross, a great master of the spiritual life. He teaches us to reject visions, revelations, and locutions, especially if they are frequent, so as to free one's self from any deception (in the event such might be the case). For, says the saint, if they are from God, even if they are rejected, their effect and impression are so good and holy they will always remain. On the other hand, if they have been caused by the enemy, then the person, in rejecting them, frees himself from deceit.[261]

It should be noted that more than any other master of Christian spirituality, St. John of the Cross emphasizes in all of his writings the need to take an

---

[258] See L 1:137, Apr. 26, 1736, to Agnes Grazi. The actual quote from the *Dark Night of the Soul* follows:
Oh, night that guided me,
Oh, night more lovely than the dawn,
Oh, night that joined Beloved with lover,
Lover transformed in the Beloved!
In German, see Fr. Aloysius of the Immaculate Conception and Fr. Ambrose of St. Teresa, *Des Heiligen Johannes vom Kreuz: Sämtliche Werke*, 2:2. In English, see Peers, *The Complete Works of St. John of the Cross*, translated from the critical edition of Fr. Silverio de Santa Teresa, C.D., 1:348.

[259] This stanza in "Songs of the Soul" reads:
O night that led'st me thus!
O night more winsome than the rising sun!
O night that madest us,
Lover and lov'd, as one,
Lover transform'd in lov'd,
love's journey done!
(Peers, *Complete Works* 2:441).

[260] L 2:471, Feb. 3, 1755.

[261] "... Io le dico una dottrina di S. Giovanni della Croce, gran Maestro di spirito, il quale insegna che le visioni, rivelazioni, locuzioni, massime quando sono frequenti, devonsi sempre scacciare, per liberarsi dall'inganno se mai vi fosse, poichè (dice il santo), se sono di Dio, benchè si scaccino, tanto il loro buon effetto e l'impressione divina, sempre lo lasciano nello spirito, e se tali cose sono del nemico, col discacciarle, l'anima si libera dall'inganno" (L 3:540, Sept. 25, 1758, to Sr. Magdalen of St. Joseph).

extremely critical attitude, even a negative one, when confronted with extraordinary experiences in the spiritual life.[262]

The founder's appreciation for the work of this Spanish mystical doctor
(*doctor mysticus*) is apparent in a letter written in 1757 to Fr. John Mary,
spiritual director of novices. In it, Paul calls John of the Cross the prince of
mystics (*il principe dei mistici*).[263]

Despite the fact that St. John of the Cross was not raised to the rank of
Doctor of the Church until 1926, he was referred to as Doctor by Paul in
1773. Although the name John of the Cross was not explicitly mentioned in
this particular reference, the context indicates the title "doctor" unmistakably
referred to this Spanish mystic.[264]

Besides direct references, there are also several formulations of thought in
the letters of St. Paul of the Cross that find their origin in the thinking of John
of the Cross. For example, in his great lyric *Living Flame of Love,* John of the
Cross makes use of imagery rooted in Spanish mythology.[265] When speaking
of deaths of those who die of love, John states they "die amid the delectable
encounters and impulses of love, like the swan, which sings most sweetly
when it is about to die . . . "[266] Paul uses the same simile in a letter written in
1759: "How beautiful were one to die in naked suffering on the cross of Jesus
Christ, while singing like a swan in purity of heart, 'Fiat voluntas tua!' "[267]

The symbolic language that John of the Cross used to express union of the
soul with God—in the dark night, in nightly silence, and in midnight darkness—
appealed to our founder. This imagery played a large role in the thought of St.

[262] See especially Bks. 2 and 3 of *Ascent of Mount Carmel.*

[263] In this letter, Paul speaks especially of the meaning of suffering for the person striving
for union with God. He states, "Io ho letto qualche cosa, specialmente in uno che è il principe
de' mistici; è vero che ordinariamente si passano tali purghe: 'alius sic, alius autem sic'." / "I
have read of some things especially in [the writings of] one who is a prince of mystics; it is
true that ordinarily there are such purgations: 'alius sic, alius autem sic' " (L 3:157, July 23,
1757).

[264] This letter refers again to the question of how to handle extraordinary inner lights and
revelations. The founder states, "In quanto poi all'abbondanza dei lumi, che lei riceve, che
alcuni hanno qualche connessione con la rivelazione, quando sono molti e frequenti, ci è
sospetto d'inganno. Onde è consiglio di un Santo Dottore Mistico di discacciarli sempre, o
buoni o falsi che siano." / "With respect to the abundance of lights you receive, some of them
linked perhaps with revelations—when they are many and frequent, there is suspicion of
deceit. Hence follows the advice of a saintly mystical doctor to expel them always, whether
they be either true or false" (L 1:808, Jan. 26, 1773, to Thomas Fossi).

[265] In his study of St. John of the Cross entitled *Herrlichkeit,* Hans Urs von Balthasar
discusses the literary beauty of the writings of this mystic. In his summary evaluation, he
states his opinion that this saint achieved the status of Doctor of the Church by virtue more
of his poetry than of his prose (von Balthasar, *Herrlichkeit* 2:531).

[266] Frs. Aloysius and Ambrose 3:31; Peers, *Complete Works* 3:35, 135.

[267] " . . . che bel morire sarabbe in un nudo penare su la Croce di Gesù Cristo, cantando
come un cigno in puro spirito: 'Fiat voluntas tua!' " (L 1:706, July 31, 1759, to Thomas Fossi).

John of the Cross and manifested itself in several of his writings, e.g., Chapter 24 of *Dark Night of the Soul,* where he quotes from the book of Wisdom (18:14–15): "For when peaceful stillness compassed everything and the night in its swift course was half-spent, your all-powerful word from heaven's royal throne bounded down."[268] Paul used this same reference when speaking of the "darkness of midnight", during which occurs mystical divine nativity.[269] In this passage, the influence of both John of the Cross and Tauler is seen.

In several other places in his letters, Paul draws upon imagery found in the writing of John of the Cross. In a letter of 1736, the founder writes, "Above all, I am very pleased God has taken from you consolations and sweets which are for children. Now eat solid food. Abraham, the great father of our Faith, ordered neither banquet nor feast at the birth of his long-desired Isaac but gave a great feast when Isaac was weaned."[270] A comparison of this passage with the text in the *Dark Night* shows Paul's dependence upon the thought of John of the Cross.[271]

---

[268] The exact quotation states:

> As soon as these two houses of the soul have together become tranquilized and strengthened, with all their inmates—namely, the faculties and desire—and have put these inmates to sleep and made them to be silent with respect to all things, both above and below, this divine wisdom immediately unites itself with the soul by making a new bond of loving possession, and there is fulfilled that which is written in the book of Wisdom, in these words: 'Dum quietum silentium teneret omnia et nox in suo cursu medium iter haberet, omnipotens sermo tuus de coelo a regalibus sedibus prosilivit' (Wis 18:14f.).

(Frs. Aloysius and Ambrose 2:180; Bk. 2, Chap. 24, *Dark Night of the Soul;* Peers, *Complete Works* 1:484).

[269] In a letter to the Passionist Father Aurelius of the Blessed Sacrament, Paul writes, "E molto godo nel Signore che ella si ritrovi nel buio della mezzanotte, come in cifra par mi dica nel gratissimo suo foglio, poichè in tal tempo seguì il gran prodigio di carità della Nascita temporale del Divin Verbo Umanato: 'Dum medium silentium teneret omnia et nox in suo cursu medium iter haberet, omnipotens sermo tuus', etc. [Wis 18:14f.]—Così appunto succede nella Mistica Divina Natività, cioè, nella mezzanotte più oscura della fede ecc." / "It is a great joy for the Lord to meet the soul in the darkness of night half spent, for it seems to me [midnight] is the cipher of his most delightful page [of history]. It was at such a time that the great miracle of love, the birth of the divine incarnate Word took place in time. 'For when peaceful stillness compassed everything and the night in its swift course was half-spent, your all-powerful word, etc.' [Wis 18:14–15]. The mystical divine nativity takes place in just the same way—in the most obscure midnight of faith, etc." (L 4:24, Dec. 22, 1767).

[270] "Sopra tutto godo assai che Dio l'abbia spogliato delle consolazioni e di quei zuccherini da fanciulli. Ora si mangiano cibi sodi [see Heb 5:12].—Abramo, gran Padre della nostra fede, non fece banchetto e gran festa quando nacque il tanto desiderato Isacco, ma fece far festa quando si slatto [see Gen 21:8]." (See letter of Aug. 14, 1736, to F. A. Appiani, published in *Bollettino* 9 [1928]: 44.)

[271] In Bk. 1 Chap. 12, of *Dark Night,* it is written, "...even as Abraham made a great feast when he weaned his son Isaac, even so is there joy in heaven because God is now taking

In his spiritual diary, St. Paul of the Cross capsulizes his thinking on the Gospel value of humility in an entry on November 30, 1720.[272] This concept, i.e., he who humbles himself shall be exalted (Lk 14:11), continues to occupy a central place in the doctrine of our saint.[273] In a letter written to Don G. A. Lucattini, who was directed by Paul for more than fifteen years, the saint speaks of the effects of contemplation. He urges the priest, who is pious and eager for spiritual direction, to "look not at the gifts bestowed in prayer but only to contemplate the Sovereign Giver" of these gifts. He then continues:

> Jacob saw a ladder, etc., with angels ascending and descending [Gen 28:12]. This is a symbol of the contemplative who ascends to God by contemplation, descends with knowledge of his own nothingness, and then ascends again, with heart determined to mount step by step [Ps 84:6]. All of this is an interior work of faith.[274]

Although some of the oldest literature in the field of Christian spirituality uses the image of Jacob's ladder to describe the effects of contemplation, it is clear from the striking similarity of contexts that, in writing this letter, Paul was inspired by the work of John of the Cross, who in the *Dark Night* spends an entire chapter explaining how hidden contemplation is like a ladder.[275] By it, a person ascends to God and loses the self therein.[276] Having experienced such exaltation, the person descends, as it were, to experience again humiliation and annihilation. Humbled thus, he becomes ready to ascend again.

A comparison of the doctrines of these two mystics reveals other obvious correlations.[277] For example, St. John of the Cross stresses interior detachment

---

this soul from its swaddling clothes, . . . and likewise taking from it the milk of the breast and the soft and sweet food proper to children, and making it eat bread with crust . . . " (Frs. Aloysius and Ambrose 2:51; Peers, *Complete Works* 1:384).

[272] In this entry of Nov. 30, 1720 (*Diario Spirituale*, 61f.; *Tagebuch*, 69f; Rouse, 31), becoming humble and then being raised up is placed within the context of the primordial event of the angels' fall from heaven, recorded in Scripture and in former Jewish and early Christian literature (J. Michl, in *Lexikon* 6 col. 394; keyword: Michael).

[273] In several of his letters, Paul stresses, again and again, that the person is answerable for his own humbling of self, better said, self-annihilation. The person is, therefore, first of all obliged to reject all disordered self-love. Only then is he readied to "become raised" by God. See below, pp. 162–69.

[274] " . . . non si specchi nei doni, che riceve in orazione, ma nel Sovrano Donatore. Giacobbe 'vidit scalam' ecc. 'et Angelos ascendentes et descendentes' figura dell'anima contemplativa che ascende a Dio con la contemplazione e discende nella cognizione del suo orribil nulla, e poi di nuove ascende: 'ascensione in corde suo disposuit'. Sono tutti lavori interiori di fede . . . " (L 2:811, July 20, 1751).

[275] Bk. II, Chap. 18, is entitled "Explains How This Secret Wisdom Is Likewise a Ladder" (Frs. Aloysius and Ambrose 2:148–50; Peers, *Complete Works* 1:460–63).

[276] Frs. Aloysius and Ambrose 2:149f.; Peers, *Complete Works* 1:463.

[277] See P. E. Llamas, "San Pablo de la Cruz y San Juan de la Cruz: En busca de las fuentes de su doctrina mística", 581–607.

from all consolations and all creatures as indispensable conditions for attaining to union with God.[278] In this context, St. Paul of the Cross often refers to *spogliarsi* (to strip or divest one's self) and *annichilare* (to become as nothing). These purgations are mandatory if a person is to rid himself of all that is not of God, since any bond becomes a burden, an obstacle blocking the soul on its way to union with God. To reiterate, self-emptying and entering into one's own nothingness are not goals or end points in themselves but means of attaining greater union with God.

A prominent place is given to the cross and passion in this way of union with God. In Chapter 7 of Book 2 of the *Ascent,* which, according to Hans Urs von Balthasar,[279] is the programmatic chapter of John of the Cross' classic work, an appeal is made to Jesus' words "If any man will follow my road, let him deny himself and take up his cross and follow me" (Mk 8:34–35).[280] In elaborating upon this passage, the Spanish mystic shows how any person, striving for union with God, must walk this path: the way of self-emptying and annihilation of self. In fact, it is in this negation of self that union with God consists: "In a living death of the cross, both as to sense and as to spirit".[281]

This is also the way indicated by St. Paul of the Cross for those who long for union with God in love. The person must allow himself to be "stripped of all consolation" and to "remain with Jesus on the cross. . . . This is the short way . . . to live most purely in the Uncreated and Immense Good."[282]

This dying to self should not be understood as "merely a completely negative annihilation of the self, but as a means of liberating a person's own nothingness of being in order to reach the plenitude of life".[283] Neither should it be understood as an asceticism in which suffering is valued for its own sake, since, according to John of the Cross, no suffering, no spiritual or bodily pain, effects union with God. Rather, it is the love that accepts and accompanies suffering that gives birth to union. Finally, only suffering that conforms to the

---

[278] See Bk. 2, Chap. 7, of *Ascent of Mount Carmel* (Frs. Aloysius and Ambrose 1:97–105; Peers, *Complete Works,* Chap. 7, 1:87–93).

[279] See von Balthasar, *Herrlichkeit,* p. 521, n. 271.

[280] In Frs. Aloysius' and Ambrose's German text and in Peers' translation, see Chap. 7.

[281] "And when he comes to be reduced to nothing, which will be the greatest extreme of humility, spiritual union will be wrought between the soul and God, which in this life is the greatest and the highest state attainable. This consists not, then, in refreshment and in consolations and spiritual feelings but in a living death of the Cross, both as to sense and as to spirit—that is, both inwardly and outwardly" (Frs. Aloysius and Ambrose 1:104; Peers, *Complete Works* 1:92–93).

[282] In a letter to Agnes Grazi of June 29, 1736, Paul wrote, "Godo, che Dio vi spogli d'ogni contento . . . Oh, quanto è buono lo stare in Croce con Gesù . . . Questa è la via corta . . . per vivere purissimamente nell'Increato ed Immenso Bene" (L 1:139).

[283] P. Varga, "Schöpfung in Christus nach Johannes vom Kreuz", 21:58.

will of Christ is to be desired, since suffering without Christ "is devoid of meaning".[284]

John of the Cross' basic principle that union with God consists of a "living death of the cross", however, is stressed by Paul of the Cross from the outset. His own programmatic formulation, "to be crucified with Christ", appears in the first entry of his spiritual diary: "I desire to know nothing else nor to taste any consolation; my sole desire is to be crucified with Christ."[285]

Later, more will be said in greater detail about the close relationship between suffering and love in the teaching of St. Paul of the Cross.[286] Only one characteristic feature of his teaching need be mentioned here, that is, his repeated reference to God as an "infinite sea of charity" (*infinito mare della carità*), with the most obvious manifestation of this love being Christ's passion. Indeed, Paul states, "From the sea of divine charity proceeds that sea of the most holy passion of our Lord Jesus Christ, both seas being, in reality, one."[287]

For St. John of the Cross, also, Christ's cross disclosed to the world the love of God. This conceptualization of divine love occasioned P. Vargas' remark that for John, the passion of Christ and love had the same meaning.[288] Hans Urs von Balthasar made a similar observation. Taking into consideration the importance of Jesus Crucified in the doctrine of John of the Cross, he stated, "The valid image of God in this world is the image of Crucified Love. Nothing else. All the greatness of the *Canticle* is explained and justified only as a disclosure of the 'treasure hidden' in this image."[289]

Any consideration of the ways in which John of the Cross influenced Paul of the Cross must take into consideration the former's pronounced rootedness in faith. His decisive and consequent reduction of everything (all experience, all reality) to the striving of the soul to achieve its goal of union with God through faith—which so singularly characterizes his doctrine—profoundly influenced the mysticism of the founder of the Passionists.

In several letters, written for the purpose of spiritual direction, Paul draws his correspondent's attention to the fact that, no matter what degree of prayer has been attained, he can only journey onward toward the goal of union with God "in faith". Often, he qualifies the caliber of faith needed, calling it pure faith (*in fede pura*) or purest faith (*in fede purissima*).[290] He also speaks frequently of darkness or the night of faith (*buio, notte della fede*), and it is not by

---

[284] Ibid.

[285] *Diario Spirituale*, 53; *Tagebuch*, 57; Rouse, 29.

[286] See below, pp. 200–202, of this book.

[287] " ... mare della divina carità, da cui ne procede questo mare della Passione Santissima di Gesù Cristo, che sono due mari in uno ... " (L 2:717, July 4, 1748, to Lucy Burlini).

[288] See Varga, 59, n. 290.

[289] See von Balthasar, *Herrlichkeit*, 523f.

[290] See L 1:275 and 742, 2:717, 3:149. In his letters, St. Paul of the Cross also frequently wrote of faith being closely linked with love. See L 1:491; 2:721; 3:398, 812, and 820.

chance that he memorized the fifth stanza of the *Dark Night* and referred to it in two of his letters, as mentioned previously. In addition, Paul includes a little poem (or one stanza perhaps of a longer poem which has not been preserved) in which he speaks of dark faith as the sure guide of holy love.[291]

Like St. John of the Cross, Paul too attempted to commit his doctrine to longer verse. He composed a poem entitled "A Little Song Appropriate for Your Direction", which he included in a letter to Agnes Grazi. It consists of twenty-nine stanzas,[292] with the first stanza manifesting quite clearly that, for Paul, faith represented the only valid way by which a person attains to union with God. He writes,

> In the obscurity of faith,
> The soul that believes in God,
> Always entirely in every place,
> Consumes itself in that great fire.[293]

On the basis of these examples and of the similarities that exist in the basic doctrines of these two saints "of the cross", it can be concluded that St. Paul of the Cross had the benefit of a fine education in St. John of the Cross' school of mystical theology.

TAULER'S INFLUENCE UPON ST. PAUL OF THE CROSS

In addition to the influence of St. Francis de Sales, St. Teresa of Jesus, and St. John of the Cross, John Tauler (1300–1361), the renowned German master of the spiritual life, also had a lasting impact upon the spiritual-theological

---

[291] In a letter written in 1741 to Mother Mary Crucified, Paul writes the following six-line poem:

La fede oscura,	Oh dark faith
Guida sicura,	sure guide
Del Santo Amor!	of holy love!
Oh qual dolcezza,	How sweet
La sua certezza,	is the certitude
Mi reca al cuor!	you give to my heart!

It is unlikely this poem (L 2:289) was written by Paul himself. On July 9, 1768, he again included it in one of his letters, this time introducing it as having been written by a devout soul "così cantava un'anima devota" (L 4:49, to the Sisters of the Cloister "Corpus Domini", also named "Ginnasi" after its founder, Cardinal Dominic Ginnasi, as indicated in L 4:47, n. 1). The poem is also quoted in a letter of Aug. 4, 1740, to Agnes Grazi (L 1:259). Part of it appears in another letter of Mar. 13, 1764 (L 3:387).

[292] This poem was included in a letter written by Paul to Agnes Grazi on Sept. 5, 1740. Its title in Italian is "Canzonetta appropriata all' S. Direzione" (L 1:260f.).

[293] Ibid.

thought of Paul of the Cross.[294] How much Paul valued and admired this Rhineland mystic is obvious from the following words of St. Vincent Strambi, a contemporary of the founder of the Passionist Congregation and his first biographer:

> An exceedingly great delight took hold of him when reading of the pious John Tauler, into whose "ground" he delved with great insight and more and more deeply. He spoke quite often of what he had read, and, when he spoke, he did so with much inner involvement. Just mentioning the name of Tauler would cause his countenance to become illuminated and his eyes to fill with tears of joy and great appreciation. . . . He also exhorted others to make their own the sublime teaching of this author in order to arrive at union with God.[295]

Others who knew St. Paul of the Cross very well, especially the brethren with whom he lived and worked, were also aware of his affection for the Rhineland's *Doctor Illuminatus*. Witnesses at the beatification and sanctification processes frequently touched upon this subject. For instance, during the informative process of Rome, Fr. Joseph of St. Mary related the following: "On a certain occasion, when I was rector, he addressed me with these very words, 'My dear Father Rector, today is the time to apply Tauler's fundamental principle, that is, inner solitude, and to persevere thus in the repose of love, *in sinu Dei* [in the bosom of God] . . . ' "[296] During the protocol of the process of Orbetello, another member of his community related, "He often inculcated [a love for] interior recollection in me and in other religious, saying, 'When the spirit penetrates the ground of Tauler . . . oh, how many things does it

---

[294] Tauler's influence upon St. Paul of the Cross has often been the object of research, with investigators being primarily interested in finding parallels between and similar formulations of thought in the writings of the two. They have been less interested in pointing out the independence of the founder's thought. See R. Coccalotto, "L'influsso di Taulero nella vita e nella dottrina di S. Paolo della Croce", 136–45, 287–309; A. Walz, "Tauler im italienischen Sprachraum", 371–95, esp. 382–87. Also see A. Walz, "Influencia Tauleriana en S. Pablo de la Cruz", 397–408; *Storia Critica* 2:160–208. (Among his many contributions, Zoffoli analyzes the notion *fondo*, as used by St. Paul of the Cross in his letters. This analysis, entitled "Nel fondo del Taulero", is found on 199–208.) Finally, see S. Breton, *La Mystique de la Passion*, in which Tauler's influence upon the founder was stressed most of all (perhaps too strongly).

[295] "Si compiaceva sommamente della lettura del piissimo Giovanni Taulero, nel di cui fondo egli penetrava con gran lume; onde ne discorreva poi spesso, e ne parlava con tanto gusto, che nominando solamente Taulero s'infiammava nel viso, e piangeva con pianto misto di allegrezza, e divozione . . . Esortava ancora gli altri di approfittarsi delle sublimi dottrine, che insegna quell'Autore per introdursi all'unione con Dio" (Strambi, *Vita*, 300).

[296] "In una certa occasione si espresse con me, che allora ero rettore, in questi precisi termini: 'Amatissimo Padre Rettore, ora è tempo di stare nel fondo di Taulero, voglio dire in solitudine interna, e prendere riposo d'amore in sinu Dei' . . . " (POR, 1518r.).

understand! But such things may not be put into words!' "[297] To his confessor Paul confided that, during a time of inner turmoil and suffering, he tried to find encouragement and confidence in spiritual reading. He stated,

> My inner state is so gloomy and dark, so confused with fears and grief, that I find no book capable of giving me confidence or putting me at peace. Now I am reading the mystical treatise of Tauler. There I find something but not everything . . . "[298]

As these examples attest, Paul's companions were well aware of his enthusiasm for and the intensity with which he penetrated more and more deeply the spiritual doctrine of the great German mystic.

Without exaggeration, one can say that the "founder of the Passionists may be considered one of Tauler's most faithful admirers and one of the most persistent propagators of his spiritual doctrine" in the Italian language.[299] Paul's decisive support for Tauler's doctrine and his unswerving conviction of Tauler's orthodoxy are of even greater importance when one recalls that this Rhineland master was discredited several times in connection with the quarrels surrounding quietism. For example, in the sixteenth century, the Capuchins of the order's Belgian province were forbidden to read or keep Tauler's writings *sub poena excommunicationis latae sententiae* (under pain of excommunication).[300] At the same time, this teacher of Alsace was considered by the Society of Jesus as "an inappropriate or even disapproved" author. At the end of the seventeenth century, Tauler's writings were again discredited and placed on the Index due to a work written by Cardinal Petrucci. In it, the author had referred to Tauler's teaching.[301]

How did Tauler's writing appear in Italy? After several printings in German (Middle High German),[302] a Carthusian monk, Laurentius Surius, who belonged to an important Carthusian monastery in Cologne, translated its text into Latin. In 1548, this edition appeared in Cologne.[303] Later, it ran into several printings.

---

[297] "Inculcava spesso il raccoglimento interno, sí a me che a tutti l'altri religiosi, e soleva dire: 'Un'anima, quando è entrata nel fondo del Taulero . . . oh, quante cose intende, ma non si sa spiegare'" (POO, 217r. [*Processi* 2:214f.], testimony of Fr. Ludovico of the Heart of Jesus).

[298] "La mia condotta interna è sí oscura e sí tenebrosa e sí intrecciata dai timori ed avvelimenti, che non trovo in verun libro da potermi sollevare, né che sia abile a quietarmi. Leggo il trattato mistico del Taulero: qui ci trovo qualche cosa, ma non tutto . . . " (POV, 883v. [*Processi* 1:399]).

[299] Walz, "Tauler im italienischen Sprachraum" (see n. 294 above), 382.

[300] Ibid., 378.

[301] Ibid., 377–80. Also see above, pp. 66–71.

[302] Prior printings in German were those of Leipzig (1498), Basel (1521), and Cologne (1543). See G. Hofmann, "Literaturgeschichtliche Grundlagen zur Tauler-Forschung", 474.

[303] L. Surius translated the 1543 edition printed in Cologne. See Hofmann, "Grundlagen",

475.

Surius' work, however, contained writings that were incorrectly attributed to Tauler. Surius himself added two of these.[304] Several other sermons not penned by Tauler but ascribed to him were contained in the basic German text of 1543 edited by Peter Canisius and translated into Latin by Surius.[305]

Since this Latin edition contained so many pseudo-Taulerian writings, it is referred to in specialized literature as "Surius-Tauler" or "Surius-paraphrase". Nevertheless, it was this Latin edition that was widely read. Furthermore, all editions contained sermons and treatises considered to be "truly belonging to Tauler". Only at the beginning of the twentieth century did specialists set about screening and comparing the pretended texts of Tauler with other preserved manuscripts in order to publish critical editions of his writings.[306] Only eighty sermons from Surius-Tauler are now considered to have been composed by Tauler himself.

Now let us consider further the manner by which Tauler's spiritual doctrine spread to Italy. Parts of Surius-Tauler had already appeared in the Italian language in the sixteenth century.[307] At the end of the seventeenth century the complete Surius-paraphrase was published. Two editions of this Latin work were printed in Macerata. Although the first edition appeared without a year of publication being given, it is assumed to have been printed sometime between 1668 and 1671.[308] The second edition was printed in

[304] These are "De X caecitatibus et XIV amoris radicibus" and "Exercitia D. T. piissima super vitam et passionen Christi." Again, see Hofmann, "Grundlagen", 475.

[305] Of 151 sermons edited by Peter Canisius, about seventy are no longer considered to have been written by Tauler. The treatise *Divinae institutiones* is a work in which Canisius brought together ideas of Eckhart, Suso, and Ruysbroeck. See Walz, "Tauler im italienischen Sprachraum", 373, and Hofmann, "Grundlagen", 474.

[306] In 1910, Ferdinand Vetter edited a critical text (in Middle High German) of Tauler's writings. Entitled *Die Predigten Taulers,* it appeared in the collection *Deutsche Texte des Mittelalters,* vol. II, edited by the German Academy of Sciences. In 1968, a new but unchanged edition was printed by Weidmann (Dublin and Zurich). In the following annotations, this edition is noted by the keyword Vetter.

In the years 1924–1929, a critical edition of Tauler's works, edited by A. L. Corin, appeared in Paris. It contained two extended manuscripts from the Bibliothèque de la Faculté de Philosophie et Lettres de l'Université de Liège (fasc. 33, 42) in Vienna: *Sermons de Tauler et autres écrits mystiques: I Le codex Vindobonensis 2744. II. Le Codex Vindobonensis 2739.* (cited in Hofmann, "Grundlagen", 478).

In 1961, G. Hofmann edited the Middle High German text of Vetter's work and translated it into modern German. He also included the Viennese manuscripts. This text is noted by the keyword Hofmann.

[307] A. Walz ("Tauler im italienischen Sprachraum", 374) mentions two Italian editions appearing in Florence in the second half of the sixteenth century.

[308] This time interval may be determined with precision. The issue was edited by the Capuchin friar Boniface da Frosinone, who was the provincial of the Roman province of the Capuchins from 1668 to 1671. See *Storia Critica* 2:165.

1697.[309] Both Macerata editions were unchanged printings of the Surius translation, just as it appeared in Cologne in 1548.

It is known that St. Paul of the Cross used the first of the Macerata editions, the one bearing no year of publication. Considered a precious relic, this copy has been preserved to this day in Vetralla's monastery of St. Angelo, where the saint often stayed during his life.[310] It is not known, however, nor have we been able to discover on the basis of the sources available to us, on what occasion Paul obtained the book. When, therefore, did the Passionist founder learn to appreciate and love the spiritual teaching of this *Doctor Illuminatus* of the Rhineland? To answer this question, it is necessary to rely upon circumstantial evidence and to base our conclusions on that evidence.

1. *The Beginning of Tauler's Influence*

Supplementary evidence permits the supposition that even before 1720 St. Paul of the Cross had become acquainted with the spirituality of John Tauler. It has been handed down to us that Paul, while living in Genoa between the years 1709 and 1714, quite often met with Giovanna Battista Solimani,[311]

---

[309] Hofmann, "Grundlagen", 477.

[310] Another copy of this edition is preserved in the Passionist Generalate in Rome. It is likely that the saint used this copy during the time he lived at SS. John and Paul, from 1773 until the end of his life. It is preserved in the "Bibliotheca Commissionis Historicae C.P." The exact title is *D. Joannis Thauleri—clarissimi ac illuminati theologi, ordinis praedicat. Sermones de tempore et de Sanctis totius anni, plane piissimi: reliquaque eius pietati ac devotioni maxime inservientia. Opera Omnia, a R. F. Laurentio Surio Carthusiano in Latinum Sermonem translata, postremo recognita, et nunc iterum diligentissime recusa (Quorum Catalogum post Praefationem invenies). Coloniae et denuo Maceratae, ex tipographia Jacobi Philippi Pannelli. DD. Superiorum permissu.* There is also an Italian text entitled *La vita ed institutioni del sublime ed illuminato Teologo Giovanni Taulero. Tradotte nuovamente de Latina in Lingua Toscana, dal R. P. Serafino Razzi dell'Ordine de'Frati Predicatori. Con Licenza e Privilegio. In Fiorenza, per Filippo Ciunti. 1590.* Perhaps St. Paul of the Cross used this edition also.

[311] In his work *Una Mistica del secolo XVIII* (Genoa [1960]: 58), G. Musso writes, "Tra le molte persone che per vari motivi erano soliti visitare la Serva di Dio, vi fu un Chierico di nome Paolo, figlio di Luca Danieri e di Anna Maria Massari. Questo piissimo giovane, nativo di Ovada era venuto a Genova e, trovandosi in condizioni economiche assai disagiate, aveva trovato alloggio per carità, in casa del Marchese Paolo Gerolamo Pallavicini. Avendo comprendo che la Serva di Dio era veramente illuminata di luce soprannaturale, il giovane veniva sovente a visitarla per discutere problemi spirituali e per aver consigli." / "Among the many people who would habitually visit the servant of God [Giovanna Battista Solimani] was a cleric [named] Paul, the son of Luke Danei and Anna Maria Massari. This very pious youth, who, having arrived in Genoa and being in rather uncomfortable financial straits, found lodging in the home of Marquis Paolo Gerolamo Pallavicini. After learning that this servant of God Giovanna was truly enlightened by supernatural light, the youth often went to visit her and to discuss spiritual matters [with her] or to seek her advice" (*Storia Critica* 2:167, n. 30).

a pious and gifted woman well acquainted with Tauler's doctrine. Indeed, in a later period of his life, the founder took as confessor and spiritual director Giovanna's long-standing director, the Capuchin priest Fr. Colombo da Genoa. Like the Capuchin provincial Fr. Boniface da Frosinone, who published the first edition of Surius-Tauler printed in Macerata,[312] Fr. Colombo was a great admirer of Tauler and may have drawn the saint's attention to the German mystic.

Over and above these more or less vague reference points in the saint's life, an analysis of the content of his letters permits us to fix a date on the approximate time period in Paul's life when his own doctrine became more strongly influenced by Taulerian thought. The notions of "ground" (*il fondo*) and "divine rebirth" (*la divina rinascita*) appear for the first time in the letters of our saint in the year 1748. Of course, this does not necessarily mean that Paul had not read Surius-Tauler *before* this date. It would be logical to assume that, had he done so, the founder would have appreciated Tauler's greatness even then (and, from that point on, would have quite naturally recommended him to others).[313]

We find in the letters of Paul not only the notions of "ground" and "divine nativity", which occupied a central place in Tauler's teaching, but also other content paralleling Tauler's thought. Although this in itself does not prove any direct influence, it is obvious from formulations used that the saint knew well and borrowed from the Surius-Tauler text.

In a letter dated 1751, the founder affirms that during prayer the Holy Spirit would have to come and manifest his presence to that person. For this to happen, however, some conditions must be met. Paul writes, "The conditions which best prepare a person for such a 'heavenly' prayer are the following: *vera abstractio, perfecta nuditas, interioris hominis inhabitatio et unitas* [true detachment, perfect nakedness of spirit, interiority, and harmony with the inner self]."[314] "This means", Paul goes on to state, "to free one's self completely from all that is not of God . . . to remain divested of everything coming from the senses. . . and to remain in inner solitude, totally immersed in the Infinite Good . . . "[315]

---

[312] See n. 308 above.

[313] Supporting this supposition is the following information: During the informative process of Vetralla, the priest Don Giuseppe Sisti remarked that the works of St. John of the Cross had been recommended to him by the saint in the years 1746–47: "Ed egli mi disse che mi servissi dell'opere mistiche di San Giovanni della Croce . . . " / "He told me to read the mystical works of St. John of the Cross . . . " (POV, 43v.; *Processi* 1:4). If, at this time, the saint had already "discovered" Tauler, he would certainly have made some mention of him, just as he did after 1748 (*Storia Critica* 2:168f.).

[314] "Le disposizioni per questa sopraceleste orazione, le più prossime sono le seguenti: 'Vera abstractio, perfecta nuditas, interioris hominis inhabitatio et unitas' " (L 2:808, May 25, 1751, to Don G. A. Lucattini).

[315] "Altissima astrazione da tutto ciò che non è Dio, perfetto spogliamento di tutto il sensibile . . . e starsene in solitudine interiore, immerso tutto nell'Infinito Bene . . . " (ibid.).

It is significant that the saint introduces these three "preliminary dispositions" (*disposizioni*) in Latin. Customarily, he writes in Latin only when quoting from Scripture. The conclusion is evident: We have here a sentence taken from the Latin edition of Surius-paraphrase. The First Sermon of Pentecost states,

Enim vero proxima atque purissima ad sancti Spiritus excellentem susceptionem praeparatio in quattuor consistit, quae sine medio ad ipsam nos excellentiori modo disponunt, quae sunt haec: Vera abstractio, interna nuditas, interioris hominis inhabitatio et unitas.

[Those] who rightly comprehend this preparation, and who understand the noblest manner of receiving the Spirit, are those who cut off all things but God, who are made entirely empty, and thus attain to the interior life and divine unity.[316]

In his sermon, Tauler follows this statement with a sequential explanation of these notions, a format characteristic of his preaching.

[316] Surius-Tauler, 277 (Vetter, 97, l. 12f.; Hofmann, "Grundlagen", 161). Surius-paraphrase quotations are taken from a 1615 edition published in Cologne under the name Apud Arnoldum Quentelium. Since this edition and those of Macerata represent new but unchanged printings of the 1548 edition, the page numbers of all three editions correspond with each other. In the event the quoted text is taken from Vetter's critical edition of Tauler or to the New High German of G. Hofmann, the page number is given. With Vetter's work the line number is also provided.

A relatively small number of works in English contain sermons cited in this section on John Tauler. Among these are:

1. *Spiritual Conferences by John Tauler,* E. Colledge and Sr. M. Jane, O.P., trans. and ed. This book is a translation of selected excerpts of sermons translated from Vetter's critical edition written in German.
2. *The Sermons and Conferences of John Tauler,* Paulist Father Walter Elliott, trans. This book, a limited edition of only 500 copies, was translated from the German edition of Julius Hamburger (Frankfurt am Main, 1864). Also consulted were Sainte-Foi's French translation of 1855 (Paris) and Surius' Latin version.
3. *The Inner Way: Thirty-Six Sermons for Festivals by John Tauler,* Arthur Wollaston Hutton, M.A., rector of St. Mary-Le-Bow, trans. This is also a translation of Hamburger's work published in Frankfurt in 1826 and in Prague in 1872. Included in this small work are a number of sermons for feastdays not included in Elliott's work referenced above.

The specific Latin passage cited above, "Enim vero proxima . . . ", corresponds to Elliott's *Sermons and Conferences of John Tauler* (323). The Colledge and Jane edition is said to contain the First Sermon of Pentecost (178f.). However, its content does not correspond with the First Sermon in Elliott's edition but rather with that of the Second Sermon of Pentecost.

Paul also incorporates Latin phrases, indicative of his reliance on Surius-paraphrase, in a letter written to a young fellow religious, Fr. Bartholomew, who had been given the great grace of interior union with God. The saint explains to the priest how he is to behave when special divine favors are granted him in prayer. Paul writes,

> You are to behave in *passivo modo* [in a passive manner] in your nothingness, poverty, etc., and you are to attribute to God your respective gift: *Deus a quo bona cuncta procedunt* [to God, from whom all good proceeds], etc. Nothing in us is our own; we have nothing, can do nothing, know nothing: *nihil, nihil* [nothing, nothing]. *"Non sum, non sum"* [I am not, I am not], says the humble John the Baptist [Jn 1:20–22].[317]

A similar point regarding one's nothingness is also made in Surius-Tauler in the First Sermon of the Solemnity of the Circumcision of Our Lord. It is an exhortation on how useful and wise it is to humble one's self before God and to confess one's own powerlessness:

> *Expediret illi, ut iugiter velut extremae sortis vermiculus, divinae maiestatis pedibus provolutus, se nihil posse, nihil esse, nihil praevalere, absque fictione sentiret . . .* /This is expedient: One should feel with utmost sincerity that he can do nothing, is nothing, and has no power at all, just like the most insignificant worm, lying prostrate at the feet of the Divine Majesty.[318]

Paul not only uses Latin phrases from Surius-Tauler but also writes in the spirit of its formulations. Take, again, the notion of *passivo modo*, a favorite formulation of Surius-Tauler.[319] In the Sermon on the Assumption of Mary, this notion is developed in the following manner. God characteristically works wonders out of "nothing". Consequently, nothingness lies passive and ready to experience the act of God. If a person wants to receive God's gifts in

[317] " . . . Si ponga nel suo nichilo 'passive modo', nudo, povero ecc., attribuendo a Dio ogni bene: 'Deus a quo bona cuncta procedunt' ecc. Il nostro è il nulla, nulla avere, nulla potere, nulla sapere: nihil, nihil. 'Non sum, non sum', diceva l'umilissimo S. Giovanni Battista" (L 3:347f., Dec. 24, 1767, to P. Bartholomew of St. John).

[318] Surius-Tauler, 60; This particular passage corresponds with Elliott, 85. The translation given above, however, may be a better rendering of the passage's intent. The Sermon of the Feast of the Circumcision is not contained in the Colledge and Jane edition.

In the sermon for the Feast of the Assumption of the Blessed Virgin Mary, Tauler quotes a passage from Dionysius the Areopagite. He states, "As St. Dionysius says, 'God is not only that which you can receive of him. He is above all wisdom, above all beings, above all goodness, above all that you can receive or know of him. He is more than and higher than anything that a person's understanding can conceive; higher and yet lower, more and yet more, and far above all things.' " (In German this quotation was taken from Vetter, 204, l. 3–6. In English, see Hutton, 154. Also see Surius-Tauler, 591. The Sermon for the Assumption is not contained in the Elliott edition or the Colledge and Jane edition.)

[319] See Coccalotto, 288–92.

abundance, then such a person must acknowledge that ultimately he is "truly nothing".[320] (As shown above, Paul synthesizes this thinking when giving advice to others.)

Furthermore, just as Paul used the *non sum, non sum* (Jn 1:20) of the Baptist to call others to the practice of humility, so too did the author of the Sermon of the Fourth Sunday of Advent contained in Surius-Tauler. In it, the Baptist's answer, given in response to questions posed by the priests and levites, is interpreted (as it will later be reinterpreted by Paul) as a manifestation of deep humility worthy of imitation.[321]

Moreover, in the above-cited letter to Fr. Bartholomew, the founder further writes,

> The more one will center one's thought in God in the most profound depth of interior solitude, the more often he will celebrate the mystical divine nativity in the interior temple, then, [the more he] will, in that moment, be reborn into a Godlike, deiform, and holy life: *et fiet in te Divina Nativitas* [and the divine nativity will take place in you].[322]

This text is also strongly influenced by Taulerian thought and formulations, with "divine nativity" and its resultant "divine piety" being themes dear to the Rhineland master of the spiritual life. However, the Latin formulation *et fiet in te Divina Nativitas* turns out to be a function of the literary independence of Surius-Tauler.

When St. Paul of the Cross speaks of the necessity of interiorization, he refers with predilection to the soul as an "interior desert" (*deserto interiore*),

[320] This sermon states, "Sic nimirum ubicumque proprie et divine operaturus est, nullo ad hoc opus habet, nisi nihilo. Nihilum enim passivo modo operationis eius, quam quodlibet aliquid, capacius est . . . ut omnia ille in vos effundat dona sua: hoc ante omnia agite carissimi, hoc cum primis curate, ut in fundo vestro in veritate nihil estis" (Surius-Tauler, 591f.). This passage in Hutton (156) states, "When God chooses to work alone, he needs nothing but nothing. That which is nothing is more receptive to his works than that which is something . . . and if you desire especially, that he pour out upon you all his gifts: see to it, above all things, that in truth, in the very depths of your heart, you are nothing." (This sermon is found in neither the Elliott edition nor the Colledge and Jane edition.)

[321] "Hoc verbum 'non sum' omnes proferre recusant; et huc omne eorum tendit studium, ut illud fugiant abnegantque. . . . Sed revera si quis vel eo pertingere posset, ut cum D. Joanne hoc ipsum verbum ex animo proferret, ille compendiosiorem vicinioremque viam, quae in hac possit vita obtineri, haud dubie reperisset." / "All people refuse to make this statement: 'I am not'; and their every effort is toward evading and giving the lie to it. . . . But really, if one ever managed, with St. John [the Baptist], to make this very statement from the heart, he would undoubtedly have discovered a shorter and handier path, a path that can be taken in this life" (Surius-Tauler, 32f.).

[322] "Quanto più spesso si riconcentrerà in Dio nel più profondo della solitudine interiore, tanto più frequentemente si celebrerà nel tempio interiore la mistica Divina Natività e lei rinascerà ogni momento più a vita deifica, deiforme e santa: et fiet in te Divina Nativitas" (L 3:348, Dec. 24, 1767, to Fr. Bartholomew of St. John).

wherein one must withdraw. In a letter dated 1757, he explains this "introversion" by using the biblical example of God's appearing in the fire of a flaming bush to Moses, who was tending sheep in the desert (Ex 3:1).[323] Interpreting "sheep" and "desert" allegorically, the saint writes,

> Remain as far as possible in complete detachment from all created things, in true nakedness and poverty of spirit, in true interior solitude. Let the sheep of your spiritual faculties and emotions go *ad interiora deserti* [into the interior desert]. And, when they are lost in God, then let them be lost, because it is happiness to be lost in your source. Oh, never-ending and rich loss! Oh, holy desert, where the soul learns the science of saints, like Moses, in the deep solitude of Mount Horeb![324]

This biblical reference and its allegorical interpretation had been read by the founder of the Passionists in Surius-Tauler's Second Sermon of the Third Sunday of Advent:

> Revera omnem mundi speciem atque imaginem e corde excludere, et in interiora deserti simul cum Mose tendere, et illic una cum ipso commorari, quo oves quisque suas melius pascere, et interiores tentationes ac phantasias depellere possit, id longe optimum est. Sicut enim Mosi oves suas ad interiora solitudinis minanti, "Deus in flamma ignis de medio rubi apparuit" (Ex 3:2a): ita et hic ardentissimo amore, flammigerisque desideriis succedentur et implebitur.

> We must drive out of our hearts the world and its images and advance into the interior of the desert, to dwell there with Moses. There we can more easily guard our flocks, that is to say, free ourselves from our interior temptations and the caprices of our imagination. When Moses had led his flocks into the interior of the desert, God showed himself to him in a burning bush, which signifies that the fire of charity and holy desires shall

[323] Ex 3:1-2 states, "Moyses autem pascebat oves Iethro soceri sui sacerdotis Madian: cumque minasset gregem ad interiora deserti, venit ad montem Dei Horeb. Apparuitque ei Dominus in flamma ignis de medio rubi: et videbat quod rubus arderet, et non combureretur." / "Now Moses fed the sheep of Jethro his father-in-law, the priest of Midian; and he drove the flock to the inner parts of the desert and came to the mountain of God, Horeb. And the Lord appeared to him in a flame of fire out of the midst of a bush: and he saw that the bush was on fire and was not burnt" (from the Douay-Rheims translation of the Latin Vulgate).

[324] "Si conservi al possibile in alta astrazione da tutto il creato, in vera nudità e povertà di spirito, ed in vera solitudine interiore, lasciando andare le pecorelle delle potenze e sentimenti 'ad interiora deserti', e se si perdono in Dio, lascile perdere, poichè si perdono felicemente nella sua origine. O perdita infinitamente ricca! O sacro deserto, in cui l'anima impara la scienza dei Santi, come Mosè nella profonda solitudine del monte Oreb!" (*Bollettino* 7 [1926]: 246f., a letter of June 30, 1757, to Fr. John Mary of St. Ignatius).

fill our heart, and then it is that we can follow God whithersoever he calls us.[325]

During the informative process of Orbetello, a witness still remembered exactly how St. Paul of the Cross, when he would find himself in a state of interior desolation, used to say, *"Salve amaritudo amarissima, omnis gratiae plena"* (Hail most bitter sorrow, full of all grace).[326] Thus had the saint made his own this sentence from Surius-Tauler taken from the First Sermon of the Fifth Sunday after the celebration of the Holy Trinity. There it is written:

> Nihil sentit Dei, nullam habet notitiam Dei, et cetera omnia nihil eum afficiunt, nihilque sapiunt, estque ei velut inter duos parietes pendeat, aut (quo in proverbio dicitur) a fronte praecipitium, a tergo lupi sunt, ubi non est quo se vertat, nihil quod agat, nisi hoc tantum, ut se fessum recipiat et dicat: Salve amaritudo amarissima, omnis plena gratiae. / And while he feels not and rightly knows not God, neither does he feel at home with created things. He seems to himself penned in between two steep walls, a sword before him, a spear behind him. What shall he do? He dares not go forward; he dares not go backward. He can but sit down disconsolate and exclaim, All hail to thee, O pure and bitter pain, may God bless thee, for thou art full of graces.[327]

Taking into account quotations from the depositions of witnesses at the beatification and sanctification processes and the literal concord between texts of Surius-Tauler and the letters of Paul of the Cross (of which an even greater number may be easily cited), it is obvious that the saint read and meditated upon Tauler's sermons, extracting from them and making his own many thoughts and formulations. Although the primary attraction of the Passionist founder to the great Dominican was his strongly expressed mysticism of interiority, Paul was not unappreciative of entering into the interior prior to his "discovery of Tauler". On the contrary, it was the saint's high regard for interiorization in his own spiritual doctrine that so attracted him to the thinking of Tauler.

Although it is highly likely the founder of the Congregation came into contact with Tauler even in the early period of his life before 1720, his correspondence nevertheless indicates that his deeper discovery of Tauler did not occur until around the year 1748. By that time, Paul of the Cross had reached a mature age of fifty-four years and had accumulated extensive

[325] Surius-Tauler, 32; Elliott, 57. This sermon is missing in Vetter's and Colledge and Jane's editions.

[326] Fr. Joseph Hyacinth, who entered the Passionists in 1746, often had the opportunity of speaking with the saint. At the protocol of the ordinary process of Orbetello, he declared, "Era costume del Servo di Dio padre Paolo di replicare nelle sue gran desolazioni queste parole: 'Salve, amaritudo amarissima, omnis gratiae plena!' insegnando a noi il pratticare il medesimo . . . " (POO, 524v.; *Processi* 2:320).

[327] Surius-Tauler, 378; Elliott, 440 (Vetter, 161, ll. 23f.; Hofmann, 305). This particular passage is not included in the excerpts of this sermon contained in the Colledge and Jane text.

experience in apostolic work, having conducted many lay missions and spiritual exercises. Although strained to the utmost by "exterior actions" and
organizational planning due to his activity as founder, he had also become an
"expert on the interior life". Contributing to and evidencing this expertise
were numerous spiritual conferences, which he as a director of conscience had
had with individuals of varying social strata, and many letters written for
purposes of spiritual direction. To these experiences, which kept him in touch
with the exterior world, must be added those "interior experiences" occasioned
by his own person's coming into touch with God. The richness of these
experiences effected in him a great inner maturity, making him highly receptive to Tauler's world of thought.

Today it is known that almost all of Tauler's sermons that have been handed
down to us originated during the "age of maturity" of this great Dominican
monk.[328] He too had diverse experiences shaping his life. Weilner states, "If
we look backward from the standpoint of his later serenity, [we find Tauler]
deplores the situation of being rooted in the outside."[329] His steady and
insistent summons is to interiorization.

We may speak of St. Paul of the Cross in a similar way. Even though from
an early period in his life this "saint of the cross" considered this *introire in
seipsum* as something important, a finding apparent in his letters, he was
inspired by and had his attention drawn to the necessity of self-withdrawal
and interiorization with greater explicitness and urgency after having read
and studied the Surius-Tauler edition, and 1748 seems to have been the year
this deeper discovery took place.[330] Prior to that year, the phrases *divine
nativity* (*divina natività*) and *to be born again* (*rinascere*), certain distinctive signs
of Tauler's influence, were hardly found in Paul's letters. After 1748, they are
encountered more than sixty times.[331] On the basis of Tauler's observable

[328] See I. Weilner, *Johannes Taulers Bekehrungsweg, Die Erfahrungsgrundlagen seiner Mystik*,
74.

[329] Ibid.

[330] It may be considered astonishing that St. Paul of the Cross, who was entirely "Italian"
in his thoughts and feelings (*Storia Critica* 2:511–17), was attracted even so by Tauler's intense
appeal for "interiorization". It may be called "astonishing" since, according to P. Pourrat,
"the German mysticism of the Middle Ages is . . . completely opposed to the worldly sense of
the Romans", the reason being "the peculiarity of German piety, which concentrates itself on
the inner part of the soul and leaves it only to be raised toward God" (2:345). In English, see
Christian Spirituality, (Westminster, Md.: Newman Press, 1953), 2:228. Also see *Dictionnaire de
Théologie Catholique* 5:69, and Weilner, 72. According to this observation, one cannot
present the spiritual-theological thought of the Passionist founder as representative of a
specific "national mentality". On the basis of the same observation, it is also interesting to
note that no other teacher from the Roman cultural arena appreciated Tauler's mysticism of
"interiority" or so integrated it into his own spiritual doctrine as did St. Paul of the Cross.

[331] Costante Brovetto, in his study *Introduzione alla Spiritualità di S. Paolo della Croce,
Morte Mistica e Divina Natività*, presents an appendix that chronologically lists all texts that

impact upon Paul's spiritual-theological thought, the doctrine of the founder of the Passionists cannot be typed as representative of a specific "national mentality".

2. Modalities of Receptivity to Taulerian Thought

Undoubtedly, the teaching of the "divine nativity in the ground of the soul" belongs to the main body of Taulerian thought. Thematically, it recurs in many homilies, and it is the end point of his explanation in others.[332] In a Christmas sermon, Tauler explains the "triple birth" about which all Christians should think with "jubilation, love, and thanksgiving".[333] For Tauler, the first nativity is that in which the Father begets his Son. The second is the historical birth of Jesus born of the holy Virgin Mary. The third is "that mysterious birth which should happen, and does happen every day and every instant in holy souls, when they dispose themselves for it by deep attention and sincere love".[334] By far the greatest part of this homily is devoted to the latter birth, i.e., the divine nativity in a soul.

When we compare St. Paul of the Cross' explanation of the divine nativity to Tauler's, we discover some differences. Superficially, such disparities could be attributed to the idiom or to the emphases in the spiritual doctrine of the Passionist founder. Upon closer examination of the points in question, however, it becomes apparent that Paul, in his encounter with Tauler, had his own ideas about the "movement of the soul toward God". For example, Paul took from Tauler the principle of "divine nativity in the ground of the soul" but interpreted it in his own way. He then incorporated this interpretation in his own teaching.

Some of the differences between Taulerian and Paulacrucian emphases

---

refer literally to mystical death and divine nativity. The date of the letter, the name of the correspondent, and the volume number are also included.

[332] For example, the divine nativity, the theme of the First Sermon for Christmas, begins with the text from Isaiah, "Puer natus est nobis et filius datus est nobis" ("A child is born to us, and a son is given to us"). This text deals with the "triple birth" of our Lord. (See Elliott, 66–71; Colledge and Jane, 153–58; Vetter, 7–12; Hofmann, "Grundlagen", 13–20; Surius-Tauler, 40–44.) The Second Sermon for the Feast of Epiphany teaches "how a person who desires to find and recognize the true light must await and watch for the divine birth in his inmost soul" (Elliott, 109). For the complete sermon, see Elliott, 107–13; Vetter, 16–20; Hofmann, "Grundlagen", 27–34; Surius-Tauler, 72–77. The last part of the First Sermon of the Feast of St. John the Baptist also discusses divine nativity in the soul (Elliott, 646–53; Hutton, 82–93; Vetter, 168f.; Hofmann, "Grundlagen", 330–32; Surius-Tauler, 559f.).

[333] Elliott, 66 (Colledge and Jane, 153; Hofmann, "Grundlagen", 12; Vetter, 7; Surius-Tauler, 40).

[334] Elliott, 66 (Colledge and Jane, 153; Hofmann, "Grundlagen", 13; Vetter, 7 and 20f.; Surius-Tauler, 40).

become clearer upon examination of quotations from Paul's letters. Take, for instance, the following passage from a letter written in 1768: " . . . in this way you will succeed in remaining completely in God, lovingly attentive to him in the desert of your spirit. In this way too your soul will be reborn to a Godlike life in the Divine Word, Jesus Christ."[335] If we reflect upon these words, it is obvious that St. Paul of the Cross does not speak of a "divine nativity in the soul" but of a "rebirth of the soul in the Divine Word". It is true we find, in some letters, the formulation "divine nativity" (*divina natività*). We even find the Latin sentence *"fiat in te Divina Nativitas"* (may the divine nativity take place in you). In these instances, more often than not the saint gives a proximate explanation only. Any time he interprets this phrase, however, he virtually always speaks of it as the "rebirth of the soul in the Divine Word".[336]

At first sight, someone might be able to say this latter formulation, a habitual one for the saint, represents only another, unimportant way of formulating the same idea, or in other words the differences between the two formulations are superficial. Given more time to think through the issue, however, one may realize that the saint, for the most part, has reinterpreted "divine nativity in the ground of the soul" as "rebirth of the soul in God's Word". This reinterpretation must have a rationale.

The following considerations may be useful in explaining these different formulations of thought. Neo-Platonism was a discernible and strong influence in Tauler's thought, as it was in all the mysticism of Flanders and of the Rhineland during the Middle Ages.[337] For Tauler, the neo-Platonic teaching of emanation represented a fundamental theory. For example, in a previously cited Christmas sermon, he stated, "Thus does God dwell within himself and go forth out of himself to return again into himself. Therefore, all outgoing is for the sake of ingoing again."[338] Appealing to Augustine as an authority in

---

[335] " . . . in tal forma prosegua a starsene tutta in Dio con attenzione amorosa nel sacro deserto interiore del suo spirito. In tal forma l'anima sua rinascerà a vita deifica nel Divin Verbo, il dolce Gesù" (L 4:48, July 9, 1768, to the Sisters of the Corpus Domini Monastery).

[336] For example, in a letter to the Passionist Father Hyacinth of the Most Holy Trinity, Paul writes, "Carissimo et amatissimo, desidero che lei celebri nell'intimo dello spirito quella divina natività, che si fa nel sacro silenzio della notte della S. Fede e che rinasca nel Divin Verbo a vita deifica, 'et fiat in te divina nativitas et in omnibus tuis . . . ' " / "Most dear and beloved, I desire that you celebrate in the deepest part of your spirit that divine nativity, which takes place in the sacred silence of the night of holy faith and during which [you are] reborn in the Divine Word to a deified life, 'et fiat in te divina nativitas et in omnibus tuis' [and may the divine nativity take place in you and in all your activities]" (L 4:108, Dec. 19, 1769; similarly, L 3:348, Dec. 23, 1767, to Fr. Bartholomew; L 3:801, Dec. 15, 1767, to Cardinal Lorenzo Ganganelli [later Clement XIV]; and L 3:96, Dec. 23, 1757, to the mother superior of the Carmelite monastery in Vetralla).

[337] Weilner, 68–72.

[338] Elliott, 67 (Hofmann, "Grundlagen", 15; Vetter, 9 ll. 1f.; Surius-Tauler, 41). This particular citation is not included in its entirety in the Colledge and Jane edition.

philosophy, Tauler went on to remark, "The ineffable riches of the Divine Good are so overflowing that God cannot contain himself, and by his very nature he is forced to expend and communicate himself. 'It is God's nature to expend himself', says St. Augustine."[339] To summarize briefly: For John Tauler, the neo-Platonic theory of emanation represented the single most influence in his spiritual background (apart from New Testament references) from which he viewed the birth of God in the soul.[340]

It was a different matter for St. Paul of the Cross. Because he lacked an educational background in philosophy, he was not bound by any philosophical system. We could say, therefore, that he "bore no previous philosophical burden".[341] Whenever the saint spoke of "rebirth in the Word of God", he based his formulation on the scriptural phrase taken from 1 Peter 1:23, "Your rebirth has come, not from a destructible but from an indestructible seed, through the living and enduring Word of God".[342] For example, the saint wrote the following passage in a letter of 1769 to the nuns of the monastery *Corpus Domini* in Rome: " . . . seek God in this way and speak to him in pure and naked faith in the holy interior desert, wherein will be celebrated that mystical divine nativity by which the soul is reborn in the Divine Word."[343]

Use of the word *ground* represents another difference between the spirituality of John Tauler and of Paul of the Cross. Reasons that led to Tauler's use of the term probably lie in the distinctive characteristics of his own spiritual life. In order to gain a better understanding of his use of it, many have attempted to clarify the spectrum of meaning contained in this notion.[344] Without a doubt, the word *ground* and its intended content do give us a clue to Tauler's

---

[339] Elliott, 67 (Colledge and Jane, 154; Hofmann, "Grundlagen", 14; Vetter, 8, ll. 22f.; Surius-Tauler, 41).

[340] See D. M. Schlüter, "Philosophische Grundlagen der Lehren Johannes Taulers", 122–61.

[341] Nevertheless, by his intensive study of St. Francis de Sales' works and especially those of John of the Cross, the Passionist founder placed himself in the mainstream of mystical theology's rich tradition, a tradition in which neoplatonic forms of thinking have exerted a strong impact, primarily through the works of Dionysius the Areopagite (see Balthasar, *Herrlichkeit* 2, pt. 1:207–14).

[342] Similarly, in James 1:18, "He wills to bring us to birth with a word spoken in truth so that we may be a kind of firstfruits of his creatures"; and, in Jn 3:3, "I solemnly assure you, no one can see the reign of God unless he is begotten from above."

[343] " . . . ed in tal forma cercare e trattare con Dio in pura e nuda fede nel sacro deserto interiore, ove si celebra quella divina natività mistica, in cui l'anima rinasce nel Divin Verbo" (L 4:59, Dec. 19, 1769).

[344] See works such as H. Kunisch, *Das Wort "Grund" in der Sprache der deutschen Mystik des 14. und 15. Jahrhunderts* (Osnabrück, 1929); H. S. Denifle, *Die deutschen Mystiker des 14. Jarhunderts;* P. Wyser, "Der 'Seelengrund' in Taulers Predigten", 203–311; A. Walz, " 'Grund' und 'Gemüt' bei Tauler, Erwägungen zur geistlichen und predigerishchen Ausdrucksweise eines Rufers zur Innerlichkeit", 328–69. Finally, also see Weilner, 101–24.

thought.[345] Again and again in his sermons, he invites his audience to enter into the "ground" of one's self. This "ground" is also the place where the "divine nativity" takes place. In his First Sermon for the Feast of St. John the Baptist, Tauler states, "Oh! dear children, turn your eyes inwardly, [to the true ground] where this birth must really be born, which will cause great joy throughout Christendom."[346]

Because of Tauler's frequent reference to "ground", it is no wonder that we also find this notion of "ground" (*fondo*) in the writings of St. Paul of the Cross. Reading Surius-Tauler led him to love and appreciate the doctrine of the great German caller to interiority. At the same time, it is astonishing he does not use the word *ground* in any one of fifty-three places where he speaks of the "rebirth of the soul in the Divine Word", a notion so obviously reminiscent of Taulerian thought.[347] Of course, no definite conclusions (for example, the saint deliberately avoided this notion) may be drawn from this observation since in some letters he does use these characteristic words of Tauler. Still, the infrequency with which he uses the phrase is striking. Furthermore, whenever the founder does speak of the necessity of self-withdrawal, he continues to use the same terminology after having come into contact with Tauler as he did before. Even in those places where Paul introduces the Taulerian notion of "ground", he uses other notions that are solely characteristic of Paulacrucian thought, e.g., *santuario dell'anima, solitudine interiore, tempio dell'anima, gabinetto interiore* (sanctuary of the soul, interior solitude, temple of the soul, interior chamber), etc.[348] This observation indicates St. Paul of the Cross had already discovered his way and described it in his own terminology before he discovered Tauler's doctrine.

Until now and in the pages that follow we have been and will continue to be working in particular with examples of Paul's receptivity to Taulerian thought that throw light on the originality of the thinking of the Passionist founder. This by no means is intended to cast doubt upon his predilection and high esteem for the Rhineland mystic or to diminish the importance of Paul's literary dependence on Tauler, which has already been shown by means of many examples. The point of view we are trying to emphasize and illustrate is that our saint did indeed borrow several Taulerian ideas presented in a

---

[345] Although the notion of "ground" (fundus, $\pi v \vartheta \mu \dot{\eta} v$, $\beta \dot{\alpha} \vartheta o \varsigma$) as used in spiritual and mystical theology was not used first by Tauler, it is his favorite term when he speaks of mystical union (unio mystica). See Wyser, esp. 216–32.

[346] Hutton, 90 (Elliott, 651; Colledge and Jane, 231; Hofmann, "Grundlagen", 330; Vetter, 168, ll. 1–4; Surius-Tauler, 559).

[347] See *Storia Critica* 2:208.

[348] *Storia Critica* 2:207. In a letter to Thomas Fossi, Paul writes, "Stia in vera solitudine interiore nel fondo o essenza dello spirito, che è lo stesso che dire di stare nel tempio dell'anima." / "Keep yourself in true interior solitude, in the ground or essence of the spirit, which is the same as saying remain in the temple of your soul" (L 1:580, May 30, 1749).

Surius-Tauler edition. This does not obviate the point, however, that by the time Paul became receptive to Tauler's ideas, he had already developed and made operant his own basic notions about the "way of the soul to God".[349]

Now let us return to the most obvious theme from Paul of the Cross' letters that are reminiscent of Tauler, namely, to the phrase *rebirth of the soul in the Divine Word.* In a letter to a fellow religious, Fr. John of St. Raphael, the founder wrote,

> Pay attention to that divine inner solitude. Enter by faith and love into the innermost reaches of that sacred desert and there lose yourself totally in God. Love and be silent. Repose *in sinu Dei* [in the bosom of God] in the sacred silence of faith and love; there you will be reborn, each moment, to a new deified life in the Divine Word, Jesus Christ. Let this love impart to you its pains, which are to become your own, through the sacred impression of holy love, in naked faith, and without images.[350]

What belongs to Paul's own thought in this passage and what is characteristic of his teaching is clear: focus on the passion of Christ. In one breath he speaks of "rebirth in the Divine Word" and the "impression of the sufferings of Jesus".[351] He himself calls this way of suffering the "royal road". In the same letter quoted above, he states, "I speak to you in this way because I know that your good God guides you along this royal road."[352]

In Tauler's thinking, the cross and passion of Jesus also occupy a prominent place.[353] However, when it is a matter of a subjective cross and suffering that must be borne by an individual, then Tauler often talks of this in terms of its usefulness in attaining to correct interiorization—we are speaking of self-

[349] Previous investigations studying Tauler's influence upon Paul of the Cross looked primarily at similarities in and parallels between their thought without adequate consideration of what was original in the spiritual doctrine of the Passionist founder. In this context, however, it is worth mentioning that E. Zoffoli always pointed out that which was original to Paul (*Storia Critica* 2:160–208).

[350] "Fate gran conto, carissimo, di quella divina solitudine interiore, entrate colla fede e coll'amore nel più profondo di quel sacro deserto, ivi perdetevi tutto in Dio, amate e tacete; riposate 'in sinu Dei' in sacro silenzio di fede e d'amore, ivi rinascete ogni momento a nuova vita deifica nel Divin Verbo Cristo Gesù, e l'amore vi faccia vostre le sue pene, per impressione sacra di santo amore, in nuda fede, senza immagini" (L 3:191, Aug. 16, year unknown).

[351] In this study, the point in question is the "impression of Christ's passion on the soul" (see below, pp. 202–5).

[352] "Vi parlo così, perchè so che il vostro buon Dio vi guida per questa regia strada" (L 3:191, Aug. 16, year unknown).

[353] Weilner (76) states that, for Tauler, "The life and suffering of Jesus Christ are a 'symbol' beyond which even the most gifted friend of God cannot go. Regarding adoration of the Crucified, Tauler resembles his renowned friend, Suso, and in no way lags behind in terms of richness and profusion of expression."

withdrawal (self-composure). Tauler calls such God-caused "parting" from every created thing a "heavy cross"[354] because everyone who desires to achieve intimacy with God must reject all that is sensible and rational. In Tauler's words, this means to "leave them [sense and reason] readily behind ... and, diverting our souls from them, [to] turn quickly to God in our highest spirit".[355] By this cross (this "parting"), the person arrives at his "true ground" (or, as sometimes translated, "true source"). The Rhineland master summarizes his desire to carry this cross in the following prayer, which concludes the Second Sermon for the Feast of the Exaltation of the Cross:

> That we may be drawn with all our hearts, as he desired to draw all things after him, and that we may thus inherit the cross, that by the holy cross, we may enter into the true source, may God help us. Amen.[356]

Rather than viewing the cross as what must be borne if one is to attain to correct "introversion", the Passionist founder sees the cross to be carried as the cross of Christ. To bear this cross means, above all else, to have the opportunity of bearing it "with Christ", thus sharing in his crucifixion.[357] Since the cross and the passion of Christ are the "clearest expression of God's love", then the person who accepts and bears the cross as the cross of Christ receives a greater share of God's love and, therefore, comes to realize a greater union

---

[354] The scriptural passage cited at the beginning of the Second Sermon for the Feast of the Exaltation of the Holy Cross is, "And I, if I be lifted up from the earth, will draw all things to myself" (Jn 12:32). Included in Tauler's elaboration on this theme is the following: "Now, our dear Lord says that he 'will draw all things unto himself'. He who desires to draw things must first collect them and then draw them. This our Lord does also; he first gathers up all a person's wanderings; the dissipation of his senses, powers, words, and works; and inwardly, all his thoughts and intentions, imaginations, desires, pleasures, and understanding. Then, when all are collected, God draws the person to himself. For, first of all you must cast off all to which you cling externally and internally in your gratifications. This casting off is a weary cross, and the heavier and stronger the clinging, the heavier the cross will also be." See Hutton, 184 (Elliott, 694–95; Hofmann, "Grundlagen", 454; Vetter, 354, ll. 21–30; Surius-Tauler, 606). This sermon is not included in the Colledge and Jane edition.
[355] Elliott, 698 (Hutton, 189; Hofmann, "Grundlagen", 457f.; Vetter, 357, ll. 23–26; Surius-Tauler, 608). This sermon is not included in the Colledge and Jane edition.
[356] Hutton, 190 (Elliott, 699; Hofmann, "Grundlagen", 459; Vetter, 358, ll. 21–24; Surius-Tauler, 609). This sermon is not included in the Colledge and Jane edition.
[357] The phrase "to be crucified with Christ" (Gal 2:19) is not only Paul's fundamental principle but also his program of life. This is apparent even in his spiritual diary, where we encounter the following programmatic statement: " ... non desidero altro, nè gustare alcuna consolazione, solo che desidero d'esser crocefisso con Gesù." / " ... I know that I do not desire to know anything else or to taste any consolation. I desire only to be crucified with Jesus" (Diario Spirituale, 53; Tagebuch, 57; Rouse, 29). There are also several other places in his letters where we find references to bearing bodily or spiritual suffering as bearing the cross of Christ. See Bialas, "Leiden als Gnade", 427–41. In Italian, see Bialas, "Il dolore umano", 53–67. In English, see Bialas, "Human Suffering", 98–121.

with him. As opposed to Tauler, Paul looks upon the cross not primarily as a condition by which the person enters into the "true ground" where the soul comes to a deeper union with God but as a participation in the cross of Christ through which the self consummates interiorly a more intense becoming one with God in love.[358]

In a similar manner, Tauler also narrowly limits "passion"[359] in terms of its relationship to true interiorization. He sees suffering as useful and fruitful for the person, first and foremost, when he remains in suffering in the "ground" (of the soul), peaceful and free of all consternation.[360] Without undervaluing exterior suffering, which consists of bearing bodily pain or spiritual deprivations, Tauler also speaks of interior sufferings. "I mean", he says, "suffering from the direct act of God in our inner life. As high as God is above creatures, so is this pain greater than any that man can inflict upon us."[361] The most valuable suffering, therefore, is to permit God to work within us, because the soul can be united with God only in a passive state.[362] In conformity with Taulerian thought we arrive at beatitude,

> . . . if we but passively sit still and wait for God's action in us, giving him all room in our souls to continue and complete his blessed work. For God's is

[358] In the long run, it is not pain but love that represents the unifying virtue: "L'amore è virtù unitiva e fa sue le pene dell'Amato Bene . . . " / "Love is a unifying virtue, and it makes its own the pain of the beloved . . . " (L 1:489, Jan. 2, 1743, to Sr. M. Bresciani).

[359] Both Tauler and St. Paul of the Cross often use the notions of "cross" and "suffering" synonymously. For purposes of clarity, however, we will keep the notions distinct.

[360] In the First Sermon for the Twelfth Sunday after Trinity, Tauler quotes St. Gregory saying, "What is your bearing in sudden storms of adversity; when beset with difficulties all unforeseen? If you shall rest quiet in these visitations, your soul resting in peace, without any outburst of impatience, with no fault of word or act or even motion, then without doubt you love God truly." See Elliott, 496 (Hofmann, "Grundlagen", 380; Vetter, 192, l. 33, to 193, l. 3. This sermon is not contained in Surius-Tauler or the Colledge and Jane edition.

[361] See the First Sermon for the Feast of All Saints entitled "The Beatitudes" in Elliott, 723 (also see Hutton, 226; Hofmann, "Grundlagen", 552; Surius-Tauler, 628; neither Vetter nor Colledge and Jane contain this sermon in their editions).

[362] The Rhineland mystic also speaks of "enduring God" in the Sermon for the Eighth Sunday after Trinity. Referring explicitly to Dionysius the Areopagite, he states, "The disciples of Dionysius once asked him how it happened that Timothy surpassed them all so greatly in holiness, although they did all the good works that he did. Their master answered, 'Timothy is a man who permits God to work within him.' This takes place in a living faith in God, which is unspeakably above all the works that by outward act a [person] can do. But to follow this method what is needed before all else is to sink down into a deep self-renunciation, by which one never sees [one's] self in God's work but sees God alone, leaves [one's] self wholly to God to work his way in him, reserving only what is really one's own, namely, his nothingness" (Elliott, 470–71 [Vetter, 190, ll. 10–14; Hofmann, "Grundlagen", 353; Surius-Tauler, 408; the Colledge and Jane edition does not contain this sermon]; also see C. Pleuser, "Die Benennungen und der Begriff des Leides bei J. Tauler", esp. 70–73).

most pure act, and the soul, on the contrary, in this supernatural relation to him, is purely passive.[363]

We can assert, therefore, that for Tauler suffering and the cross are primarily viewed in connection with correct self-withdrawal and interiorization.

St. Paul of the Cross sees and explains suffering from the starting point of the passion of Jesus. Suffering provides the person with an opportunity to suffer "with Jesus". The specific value that suffering hides within itself for the person in quest of God lies in this "participation in Jesus' passion". This concept of participation is a fundamental principle that continuously charac-terizes the spiritual doctrine of the saint.[364] When it is a question of evaluating and explaining suffering, therefore, the criterion Paul uses is not so much the degree of interiorization but the intensity of union with Jesus in love.

It also needs to be stressed that in the thinking of the founder of the Passionists, as in Taulerian thought, a central place is occupied by a desire for self-withdrawal and interiorization. At the same time, the saint constantly points to Christ Crucified and calls for participation in his suffering. This twofold aspect of the doctrine of our mystic, i.e., that of both introversion and the passion, is presented clearly in advice given in a letter written by him. After having discussed "rebirth in the Divine Word, Jesus Christ", he continues,

> Remain in the interior part of your self, shutting the doors of your senses to all creatures. Remain in your nothingness and let this horrible nothingness of yours lose itself in the never-ending infinite that is God. Make the most holy sufferings of the Bridegroom your own and enter that sacred, interior desert clad in festive garments. Do you know in what manner? I want to say you are to be clad with Jesus and completely imbued with the [sufferings] of his pas-sion. And, this must be accomplished in pure faith, without any images . . . [365]

Tauler's sermons obviously indicate that he was, from a spiritual point of view, a pupil of Meister Eckhart.[366] Both belong to the same "school", and, one can ascertain, both shared a high degree of interest in philosophical

---

[363] Elliott, 723 (Hutton, 227; Hofmann, "Grundlagen", 553; Surius-Tauler, 628; this sermon, the First Sermon for the Feast of All Saints, is missing from the Vetter and Colledge and Jane editions).

[364] See Breton, *La Mystique.* Also see below, Chap. IV.

[365] "Stia dentro di sè, serri la porta de' suoi sensi in faccia a tutte le creature, stia nel suo niente e lasci perdere questo suo orribil nulla nell'infinito tutto, che è Dio. Si faccia sue le Pene SSme. dello Sposo e se n'entri in quel sacro deserto interiore, sempre vestita da festa; sapete come? Voglio dire vestita di Gesù e tutta penetrata dalle sue pene. Tutto ciò si fa in pura fede, senza immagini . . . " (L 3:483, Nov. 5 [year unknown], to Sr. Maria Innocenza).

[366] It is disputed whether or not Tauler had "personally known Meister Eckhart and listened to his lectures". Regardless, his sermons prove undoubtedly that Tauler knew Eckhart's world of ideas very well. "Tauler could have procured Eckhart's writings either in Strassburg or in Cologne in 1339" (H. C. Scheeben, "Zur Biographie Johann Taulers", 22).

categories of thought and theological conviction.[367] Nevertheless, their respective purposes are different. Eckhart is striving (one might even say passionately striving) "to describe and explain the things of faith in a purely philosophical manner".[368] In contrast, Tauler does not waste his time in philosophical speculations but interests himself in pastoral care. Although he preaches to Dominican nuns, he does not teach them any deeply grounded insight regarding the complex intricacy of the soul. Rather, he desires to lead them into interior union with God. While Eckhart's thought moves with predilection in the realm of metaphysics, a strong ethical-moral and ascetical-religious interest dominates Tauler's. Understandable, then, is Tauler's basic intention of encouraging his audience to put greater effort into the practice of virtue.

Like Tauler, St. Paul of the Cross was also led chiefly by his desire to be of help in guiding people onward in their way to God and to a greater practice of virtue. In regard to this basic aim, both teachers of the spiritual life were absolutely alike. The Passionist founder was neither a philosopher nor a specialist in theology but a director of conscience, a practitioner of the spiritual life, a mystic.

When we try to answer the question of how great a role the practice of virtue played in Tauler's spiritual doctrine, we find a certain "relativizing of the path of virtue". He distinguishes between the "exterior path", which leads to the practice of virtue, and the "interior path", which leads to immersion in the "ground" of the soul. Of the two, the former, although it can lead to bliss, is the way of beginners and the longer one. The latter is the shorter and better path, and it leads to much greater bliss. In a sermon, Tauler states,

> The active and outward life is in external devout practices and good works, according to God's guidance and the suggestion of God's friends. This is especially seen in the practice of virtue, such as humility, meekness, silence, self-denial. The other is far above this, namely, our entering into our soul's innermost depths in search of God, according to his own words, "Lo, the kingdom of God is within you" [Lk 17:21].[369]

Of course, Tauler does not reject the path that leads to God through the practice of virtue, but he recommends as best the path of introversion, of self-withdrawal into one's "ground", as the shortest and most promising one.

We do not find this "teaching of two paths" in the writings of St. Paul of the Cross. For him, the path of virtue has no substitute. The more profoundly one encounters God in one's innermost self, the more strongly the individ-

[367] This idea is presented very clearly in Denifle, Chap. 18, n. 351, in which the author provides us with a "proper hermeneutics of mystical language".
[368] Weilner, 95.
[369] See the Third Sermon for the Third Sunday of Trinity. Elliott, 418–19 (Colledge and Jane, 76; Hofmann, "Grundlagen", 273f.; Vetter, 143, l. 30, to 144, l. 4; Surius-Tauler, 359).

ual will be united with God in love, and therefore the more skilled he will
become in the practice of virtue. For Paul, "practice of the holy virtues is the
criterion of spiritual progress".[370] Thus, exercise of virtue and plunging
into one's interior are not two alternatives for him but correlates bound to
each other.

This correlative relationship between introversion and the practice of virtue
manifests itself most clearly when the saint describes "his way" of union
with God, a way leading to contemplation of the passion of Jesus. In a
letter written in 1749 to Thomas Fossi, Paul states,

> It's true that this memory of the sacred passion of Jesus Christ and the
> imitation of his holy virtues should never be left aside—even after you have
> attained a great degree of recollection and have reached a very high degree
> of prayer, the passion still remains the door through which the soul enters
> into union with God, to deep recollection, and to true contemplation.[371]

An important fruit of contemplating the suffering of the Lord is that it
enables the person to practice virtue in a much improved way. Interiority and
the practice of virtue, therefore, exert a mutual action upon each other. In a
letter written in 1751 to Lucy Burlini, Paul adapts the Taulerian motif of
rebirth in God. He writes,

> And if, in this solitude in which you are reborn to a new deiform life, that is
> [to a] holy life, the Divine Spouse brings you to fish in the sea of his passion,
> then fish, daughter, and let yourself be penetrated completely by love and
> sorrow and make the sufferings of Jesus your own. In this vast sea of the
> sacred passion, fish for the pearls of all the virtues of Jesus. This divine
> fishing trip in the sorrows of the Son of God is accomplished in pure faith,
> without leaving solitude or interior silence. Jesus will teach you everything
> if you are humble and dead to all.[372]

In his treatise on Tauler, I. Weilner establishes that the Rhineland mystic

[370] For instance, in a letter to Sr. Maria Cherubina Bresciani, Paul writes, "Sappia, mia
figliuola, che il profitto spirituale non si misura con le dolcezze, ma coll'esercizio delle sante
virtù ... " / "It is worth knowing, my daughter, that spiritual profit is not measured by
sweets, but by the practice of holy virtue ... " (L 1:460, July 30, 1739).

[371] "Vero è che tal memoria della Passione SSma. di Gesù Cristo con l'imitazione delle sue
sante virtù non si deve lasciare; abbenchè vi fosse il più profondo raccoglimento ed alto dono
d'orazione, anzi questa è la porta che conduce l'anima all'intima unione con Dio, all'interiore
raccoglimento ed alla più sublime contemplazione" (L 1:582, July 5, 1749).

[372] "E se in tal solitudine, è rinata a nuova vita deifica, che vuol dire vita santa, lo Sposo
Divino vi porta a pescare nel mare della SSma. sua Passione; pescate pure, figliuola, lasciatevi
penetrare tutta dall'amore e dal dolore, e fatevi vostre le pene di Gesù.—In questo gran mare
della SSma. Passione, pescherete le perle di tutte le virtù di Gesù Cristo. Questa divina pesca
nel gran mare delle pene del Figliuolo di Dio si fa pure senza partirsi dalla solitudine e dal
silenzio interiore. Gesù v'insegnerà tutto, se sarete ben umile e morta a tutto" (L 2:725, Aug.
17, 1751).

mainly uses notions and imagery expressive of the dimension of depth when describing a person's primitive religious experience. While St. Thomas Aquinas and Meister Eckhart "try to elucidate especially the ontological structure of our relationship with God", giving preference to the high pole (*scintilla animae*, or spark of the soul),[373] Tauler's "ground" motif undoubtedly demonstrates that, in his thought, the inner pole occupies a principal position. This focus on the dimension of depth may be attributed (as Weilner notes) to an "ethical" impulse, which guides him.[374]

When we investigate in detail the notions and metaphors used by Paul of the Cross to describe the soul, we ascertain that he too gave preference to the inner pole, to the dimension of depth. His repeated use of several images points to this conclusion. For example, he often referred to the soul under such names as *deserto interiore, gabinetto interno, solitudine profonda, romitorio, santuario intimo,* and *tempio interiore* (interior desert, inner chamber, profound solitude, hermitage, intimate sanctuary, and interior temple); and, after 1748, he introduced the Taulerian notion of "ground" (*il fondo*) in his letters. Another characteristic feature of the spiritual doctrine of these two "masters of the interior life" was their continuous and urgent demand for self-withdrawal for interiorization.

An analysis of the terminology and imagery used in Paulacrucian spirituality, however, reveals an additional emphasis on the dimension of width and on its immeasurability. Paul's most loved and often used metaphor to describe God is "sea". To give it added strength, he often adds the adjectives *infinite* and *immense.* Thus, he speaks of *mare infinito* (infinite sea) or *mare immenso* (immense sea).[375]

In summarizing Tauler's influence upon St. Paul of the Cross, we conclude that Tauler was an author whose works were intensively read and meditated upon by Paul in the later period of his life. This finding is apparent in his letters and in the testimony of witnesses at the beatification and sanctification processes. What drew Paul to the Dominican monk from Strasbourg was, first and foremost, the latter's mysticism of interiority. The concepts of "divine nativity" and "the ground of the soul" spoken of in Paul's letters are undoubtedly reminiscent of Tauler. The manner in which Paul takes and modifies these ideas and inserts them into his own teaching, however, indicates he does not "copy" Tauler without thinking. On the contrary, by the time Paul discovered Tauler, he had already achieved a high degree of originality in his own spiritual and theological thought.

Since the saint had the possibility of coming into contact with Tauler's

---

[373] Weilner, 100.

[374] This impulse may be described as a desire to lead the person to an inner "friendship" with God (ibid.).

[375] The metaphor "sea" and its import will be discussed in other sections of this study.

world of ideas only through the medium of Surius' Latin translation, we really find only reminiscences of Tauler in Paul's teaching, and (because of Paul's dependence upon Surius) it is also possible to discover similarities to and parallels between the saint's teaching and other Rhineland and Flemish authors.[376]

[376] Recently it has been argued that St. Paul of the Cross was also strongly influenced by Henry Suso (see Giovanna della Croce, *Enrico Suso, La sua vita, la sua fortuna in Italia*, 160–68). Some parallels in content are presented as evidence. Nevertheless, the agreements between and similarities in content are insufficient to establish direct influence or dependence. Had Paul read Suso's works with the same intensity as he had read Tauler (as claimed by the above-mentioned author), then it would not have remained unknown to those who were close to the saint over a long period of time. Yet nothing is mentioned referring to this point in the beatification and sanctification processes. The supposed influence of Henry Suso (in the current state of research on St. Paul of the Cross) is a hypothesis only. Not one of the parallels presented demonstrates that Suso's writings provided *literary* inspiration for Paul. Real agreements may be explained in other ways:
  1. For both the Passionist founder and for Suso, the passion and death of Christ were basic themes. It is, therefore, possible and even more strongly probable that some parallels are to be found in their sayings.
  2. Similar formulations of content may be attributed to Paul's familiarity with Surius-Tauler.
  3. Because Paul was widely read in the field of ascetical-mystical literature, he may have come into contact with Suso's world of ideas in this way too.
It may be true, however, that the founder had read Suso's works. Nonetheless, Henry Suso was not one of the saint's favorite authors, as was, for instance, John Tauler. In this matter, see I. Colosio, O.P., "A proposito di una recente opera sul B. Enrico Suso", 167–83, esp. 171f., where it is written, "Se S. Paolo mai lo cita e non vi accenna, è segno che non lo conosceva o per lo meno non era tra le sue fonti principali" (172). "If St. Paul of the Cross ever does cite him [Suso] but does not so indicate, [then] this is a sign [Paul] was not familiar with [Suso] or, at least, that he was not one of [Paul's] main sources" (172). We consider this opinion to be judicious and in correspondence with actual circumstances. In order to adopt another opinion, more convincing arguments than those that have already been introduced in the above-mentioned work need to be brought forward.

PART TWO

The Passion of Our Lord Jesus Christ
as the Main Focus of
Paulacrucian Spiritual-Theological Thought

The primary goal of Part One was to present those factors active in the formation of the Passionist founder's personality as a whole and in the development of his spiritual and theological thought. Consequently, it only occasionally examined the passioncentrism of his doctrine. Part Two focuses exclusively on the founder's spiritual teaching with an emphasis on its passioncentrism, which is examined in its depth and entirety. When dealing with this subject matter, it is important not to forget the content covered in Part One. In other words, whenever the importance of the passion of Christ in the theology of Paul of the Cross is studied or discussed or whenever his implicit theology is treated thematically, the background of his spiritual doctrine and those factors which influenced him must be kept in mind.

Because St. Paul of the Cross was not a specialist in theology, who thought and wrote about God in a distant and "objective" way, but rather a mystic and spiritual teacher who spoke largely from the experience of his own encounter with God, it is mandatory to ponder the saint's statements[1] not just rationally but also meditatively to grasp their dimension in depth. For the same reason, it is not enough to analyze his spiritual and theological thought with some kind of "theo-logic".[2] One must try to approach it with the comprehensive view of a "theo-logia", which is not limited to cold reasoning but rather allows sufficient room for the personal-existential dimension.

[1] Refer to the Excursus in this text. See especially subsection 2, "Theology and Experience".
[2] The term *theo-logic* is meant to convey an objective and philosophical discourse on God, in which the legitimate interest of the science of theology is represented in a conscious way (see G. Ebeling [*Die Religion in Geschiehte und Gegenwart* 6, cols. 754f.; keyword: theology]).

CHAPTER III

The Passioncentrism of the Spiritual Doctrine of St. Paul of the Cross

In all ages there have been people who have directed all their energy toward the fulfillment of a single mission and whose lives have been dominated by a single thought. St. Paul of the Cross, the founder of the Passionists, was one of these. Like a red thread woven into a cloth, the leitmotif running through Paul's entire life was to meditate upon Christ Crucified and to announce him to all.

More than nineteen hundred years earlier another had adopted the same maxim as the basic principle of his life. This was none other than the Apostle Paul, who wrote in his First Letter to the Corinthians, "I determined that while I was with you I would speak of nothing but Jesus Christ and him crucified" (I Cor 2:2). For Paul of the Cross, this life program was not a matter taken up after long and difficult reflection. It was, rather, a special charism imparted to him by God. Throughout his life he considered this gift a duty which carried with it great responsibility.[1] Before studying his life's "focus", however, we should present the essential features of his spiritual doctrine.

PRINCIPLES OF HIS SPIRITUAL LIFE

Although the principles that governed Paul's life were not committed to writing in any kind of treatise in a thematic or systematic way,[2] they were committed to writing in his spiritual diary and in numerous letters. The former, written by him when he was not quite twenty-seven years old, and the

---

[1] See Bialas, *Im Zeichen des Kreuzes,* 71.

[2] The only thematically organized writing, which may have been composed by Paul of the Cross, is the treatise *Mystical Death* given to a Carmelite nun on the occasion of her clothing or profession. (See below, p. 246–58, in which I dispute Paul's authorship of the treatise and pp. 258–69 for the treatise itself.)

latter, written for the purpose of spiritual direction, allow us to uncover the "guiding principles" of his spiritual and theological thought.[3] Using these resource materials, we can study and speak of his "spiritual life". In order to present the content in this section in a manner that preserves the originality and profundity of his thought, we consistently try to let the saint speak for himself by using his own formulations.

1. *Submission to the Divine Will* (Rassegnazione alla Divina Volontà)

The idea of the will of God played a predominant role in Paul's life, even in the early phase of his interior pursuits. Entries in his spiritual diary testify eloquently to this fact. These notes, which (to use the words of J. Ratzinger) manifest quite well "the melancholy, fears, and temptations specific to one consecrated solely to God",[4] speak more often than not of God's will. In fact, Paul considered the several interior and exterior sufferings borne by him during his forty-day retreat (Nov. 23, 1720–Jan. 1, 1721) precisely as sufferings "sent by the will of God". It was, therefore, with this attitude of surrender and with a spirit of "prayer, solitude, and penance" that Paul prepared himself for his mission as founder of the Passionist Congregation.

As the entries make clear, this basic conviction or belief in the will of God was for the saint a fountain of joy and strength. In notes from the third day of his retreat, he stated, "But this contentment is not felt, since at this time there is distress of a particular kind. It is [rather] a certain contentment that the most holy will of our good God is being done."[5] In the entry of December 21, in which he described his temptations and inner struggles more fully, he concluded by saying that to endure such is pleasing to God "because the soul becomes indifferent to such an extent that it no longer considers whether it is in pain or in joy. It remains attached only to the most holy will of her beloved Spouse, Jesus . . . "[6] Since there is nothing in this statement indicating an

---

[3] Lest I "estrange" the originality of Paul's spiritual-theological concepts by unjustified systematization, I have attempted to derive fundamental concepts from the inner logic of his own letters and spiritual diary. To achieve this I have used titles that are the saint's own formulations. Undoubtedly, it would be possible to identify other concepts characteristic of his spirituality. However, the principles that are put forth in this chapter seem to express more adequately and to place in bold relief the theological-spiritual thought of the saint in its totality and specificity.

[4] See *Tagebuch,* 5 (Introduction).

[5] "Ma questa contentezza non si sente, perchè in questo tempo vi è del travaglio, e particolare; è una certa contentezza che sia fatta la Volontà santissima del nostro caro Dio" (*Diario Spirituale,* 55; *Tagebuch,* 59; Rouse, 29).

[6] "Perchè l'anima viene ad essere indifferente a segno che non pensa più nè a patire, nè a godere; solo che sta fissa alla volontà ssma. del suo diletto sposo Gesù . . . " (*Diario Spirituale,* 75; *Tagebuch,* 94; Rouse, 35).

"exaltation of the human will", it is obvious that the indifference mentioned by Paul was not a function of stoical ataraxia but resulted from the effort of conforming his will to the divine.

Imperturbable confidence in God. St. Paul of the Cross' ultimate goal in life was the fulfillment of God's will. Undergirding this goal was an imperturbable confidence in God. Paul was firmly convinced of the fact that God always desires the best for the human person, and this Father-God is pure goodness and mercy. In his diary, Paul frequently praised and thanked God for his infinite goodness, mercy, and love.[7] This faith in God's infinite love and benevolence did not vanish in the face of temptations and suffering. Despite inner struggles and spiritual and bodily pain, Paul never departed from a strong faith and a firm conviction that he was always in the protective and salvific hands of God. For example, in the entry of December 21, 1720, he stated, "I also know that God holds the soul in his arms, but the soul is not aware of it. Hence it seems to be utterly abandoned and in great misery."[8] This knowledge of being in God's custody gave Paul strength, and, as a result, he did not lose his peace of heart. Other entries in his diary speak of this effect.[9]

At this point, a critical question may be raised: Is there not contained in such resignation to the will of God, who gives—or at least permits—temptations and sufferings, a certain kind of blind fatalism? One may reply that the cause or motive underlying this resignation is not an obtuse surrender before an inexorable facticity but a positive belief in a beneficent and protecting God who acts essentially (and in the last analysis exclusively and solely) from the abyss of his love for each person. The relationship between God and St. Paul of the Cross is always to be viewed, therefore, from the standpoint of this reciprocal and sweeping movement of personal love. An example drawn from interpersonal relationships will help us to understand this better. Whenever two or more persons are united by bonds of deep and unselfish love, then all their actions and manifestations of their state of being together are to be seen and interpreted on the basis of this unifying force of love. The hermeneutical key to this "logic of love" is the inviolable confidence in the other's goodness.

---

[7] Paul speaks of God's mercy (*misericordia di Dio*) in the entries of Nov. 23 and 27 and in those of Dec. 7, 26, and 28. He praises the "infinite love of God" (*infinito amore di Dio*) in the notes of Dec. 4, 24, and 26, 1720.

[8] "Intendo anche che Dio la tiene in braccio, ma non se ne accorge, e da questo ne viene, che si pare in un grand'abbandonamento, e in gran miseria..." (*Diario Spirituale*, 74; *Tagebuch*, 91f.; Rouse, 34).

[9] The following entries in his diary exemplify this. On Nov. 26, he states, "...questa malinconia non leva la pace del cuore..." / "...this melancoly does not take away peace of heart..." On Dec. 6, "...molestato da pensieri, ma in pace." / "...I was...bothered by thoughts, but in peace." And, in his entry of Dec. 15-18, "...perturbato da scropuli, ma bensì in pace con Dio." / "...disturbed by scruples, but rather [my heart] was at peace with God."

Trust in the infinite goodness and love of God and surrender to his divine will represented fundamental elements that characterized not only the Passionist founder's entries in his diary but also his whole epistolary, that is, the whole of his letters written during more than fifty-five years. In these, the saint frequently inspired courage in his correspondents and tried to reinforce their confidence in God. For example, in a letter written in 1728, Paul stated, "Be not afraid, but put all your trust in God. I give you good news that the Divine Mercy has great riches and holy lights prepared for your soul."[10] Before leaving his native Castellazzo to answer his call to establish a Congregation, Paul wrote a long letter to his brothers and sisters. In it, he stated,

> Please love this dear Father with a most ardent love, and have the strongest and, at the same time, a most reverent confidence in him. Above all, sacrifice to his most holy love all your actions, all your words, all your efforts, cares, pains, and tears.[11]

The great importance the founder attached to surrender to the divine will may be seen in the following quotation taken from a letter written to the Marchioness Marianna della Scala del Pozzo, with whom he corresponded in the "early period of his life" (1721–38).[12] He wrote, "The greatest perfection of a soul consists in a true abandonment of one's entire self into the hands of the greatest Good. This abandonment embraces a perfect resignation to the divine will in all the events which befall it."[13] The phrase *in all the events* is understood to mean those occurrences that are beyond the control of an individual. When, however, there is a question of the "events" falling within the realm of human freedom of decision, then what God desires may no

---

[10] "Non si spaventi però e molto confidi in Dio, le dò questa buona nuova che la Divina Misericordia ha preparato gran ricchezze e santi lumi per la sua anima" (L 1:41, Nov. 11, 1728, to Marchioness Marianna della Scala del Pozzo).

[11] "Amate questo caro Padre con un ardentissimo amore, abbiategli tenerissima ma reverentissima confidenza: insomma tutte le vostre azioni, tutte le vostre parole, sospiri, pene, travagli e lacrime siano tutte sacrificate al suo SS. Amore" (L 1:53, Feb. 21, 1722).

[12] Since the oldest preserved documents of St. Paul of the Cross date from 1720 only, we can call the period from 1720 to 1740 his "early period"—"early" from a relative point of view in that his correspondence continues until 1775. Paul's thinking *before* 1720 or, in other words, *before* age twenty-six is practically unknown. Even in the beatification and sanctification processes, no exact declarations were made in this respect.

[13] "La maggior perfezione d'un'anima consiste in un vero abbandonamento di tuttta se stessa nelle mani del sommo Bene. Questo abbandonamento abbracia una perfetta rassegnazione alla Divina Volontà in tutti gli eventi, che ci accadano" (L 1:49, Oct. 4, 1734). In L 1:286, June 21, 1742, to Agnes Grazi, we find this unequivocal affirmation: "La santità consiste in essere totalmente unito alla volontà di Dio." / "Holiness consists in being completely united with God's will."

longer be clearly discernible.[14] In such situations, it is necessary to ask for advice in order to be able to know the divine will.[15] The founder was nevertheless convinced that God "pours forth his celestial light needed to know his most holy will" upon anyone who seriously asks for it.[16]

How the founder himself concretely discerned God's will may be made clearer by taking an example from his own life: the history of his own call to found the Passionist Congregation. Paul, at the age of twenty, experienced a desire to retire into solitude.[17] Yet, at that time, he did not follow this desire because he recognized something else to be God's will for him. He described this as follows: "Since I was needed to support my parents and to show my love by serving them, I could not satisfy that desire [of withdrawal into solitude], but I kept it always in my heart."[18] Only later on, when his parents no longer had need of him, did he leave home to

[14] The saint himself had experienced such an inner uncertainty. In the Preface to the Rule of the Order, written in Dec. 1720 and given to Bishop Gattinara, he stated, "Io non sapevo ciò che Dio volesse da me, e per questo non pensavo ad altro, solo che . . ." / "I did not know what God wanted of me, so for this reason I did not think of anything further, but . . ." (L 4:218).

[15] A consultation with a confessor or spiritual director may also be envisioned. In keeping with this thinking, Paul writes in the Preface to the Rule, " . . . fuorichè la conferiva col Rdo. mio P. Direttore." / " . . . besides this I will confer with my spiritual director" (L 4:218).

[16] " . . . infonderà loro il lume celeste per conoscere la ssma. sua volontà" / " . . . he will impart to them heavenly light in order to know his will" (L 2:804, Aug. 2, 1749, to a religious Sister). At times, Paul experienced strong inner certitude about what the will of God was for him. For instance, in 1721, he wrote the following to his spiritual director, Bishop Gattinara: "Tanto mi confido nel mio Crocefisso Signore, che sono più che certo, che tutto riescerà. Dio mi ha dato l'ispirazione e segno certissimo che Dio vuole. Di chi devo temere? Mi parerebbe peccare d'infedeltà se di ciò dubitassi." / "So much do I trust in my crucified Lord that I am more than certain everything will turn out well. God has given me the inspiration and an absolutely certain sign of what he wills. Why should I fear?" (L 1:22, Mar. 11, 1721). The saint was speaking here of his intention to go to Rome to obtain papal approval of the Congregation's Rule. In the autumn of the same year he put his plan into action. His mission, however, ended in dazzling failure. He was rejected and, with severe words, turned away by the first Quirinal guard he met. It is obvious, therefore, that sometimes even "failure" must be considered to be God's will. Surely, the saint was beginning to learn, even at the start of his activity as founder, how much he would have to suffer for the name of God (see Acts 9:16).

[17] Paul writes in the Preface, "mi sentii mosso il cuore al desiderio di quella solitudine." / "I felt my heart moved by the desire of that solitude" (L 4:217).

[18] "Ma siccome ero impiegato nell'officio di carità per l'assistenza ai parenti, non potei mai affetuarlo, solo che sempre lo tenevo nel cuore" (L 4:217). In telling of the history of his vocation, he states, "Ma siccome non potevo seguire la santa ispirazione per la necessaria assistenza alla casa, cioè a mio padre e madre e fratelli, tenevo la sopradetta vocazione sempre coperta nel cuore . . ." / "However, as I was unable to follow this inspiration because my help was needed at home, that is, by my father, mother, and brothers, I always kept this vocation hidden in my heart . . ." (L 4:218).

follow his call. In the meantime, seven years had passed. He was then twenty-seven years old.

Example of Jesus Christ. If we look more closely at this basic principle of "surrendering to God's will", which plays such an important part in the spiritual teaching of the Passionist founder,[19] and if we want to fix or locate its placement in that teaching, then we need to emphasize its relationship to Paul's total Christ mysticism. For example, the saint frequently linked the necessity of surrendering to the divine will to the example of Jesus, whose "food" it was to do the "will of his Father" (Jn 4:34). As early as 1734,[20] Paul wrote to the Marchioness del Pozzo, "Jesus Christ said to his apostles that his food was to do the will of the eternal Father. Oh, that one were able to plumb well the depths of this divine language."[21] In another letter to Sr. Maria Cherubina Bresciani,[22] the saint spoke thematically of the fulfillment of God's will in the following way:

> This is a very important point. Great perfection is found in resigning yourself in all things to the divine will; an even greater perfection is to live abandoned, with complete indifference to the divine good pleasure. Still, the pinnacle of perfection is to nourish yourself on the divine will in a spirit of pure faith and love. Oh, sweet Jesus, what a great thing you taught us in your life, by word and deed. Remember, this most loving Savior said to his disciples that his food was to do the will of his eternal Father. *"Meus cibus est ut faciam voluntatem eius, qui misit me, et ut perficiam opus eius"* [Jn 4:34].[23]

As indicated in the above quotation, the founder distinguished three different degrees of fulfilling God's will. He spoke of "resignation to the divine

[19] M. Viller affirms, " . . . sans doute parce que la doctrine de la volonté de Dieu apparaît saillante dans sa pensée, comme une pièce centrale qui explique et commande tout." / " . . . without a doubt, because the doctrine of the will of God was predominant in his thought as a centerpiece that explains and commands all" (see "La volonté de Dieu dans les lettres de S. Paul de la Croix", 133.

[20] We do not find any references to this verse from the Gospel of St. John in his spiritual diary.

[21] "Gesù Cristo disse a'suoi Apostoli, che il suo cibo era il fare la volontà dell'Eterno Padre. Oh chi intendesse bene a fondo questo divino linguaggio!" (L 1:49, Oct. 4, 1734).

[22] This Sister Maria Cherubina belonged to the Monastery of the cloistered Franciscan nuns of Piombino. In the year 1733, the saint gave these Sisters their yearly spiritual exercises. The most striking fruit of these exercises was the "conversion" of the above-mentioned Sister, who had previously led a rather lukewarm and superficial life in the Order. The saint was, for more than twenty-eight years, her spiritual director and advisor. Forty-six letters written to her by Paul of the Cross have been handed down to us (see L 1:436–526).

[23] "Gran punto è questo: è gran perfezione il rassegnarsi in tutto al divino volere; maggior perfezione è il vivere abbandonata, con grande indifferenza, nel Divin Beneplacito; massima, altissima perfezione è il cibarsi in puro spirito di fede e d'amore della Divina Volontà. Oh, dolce Gesù, che gran cosa ci avete insegnato con parole ed opere di eterna vita! Si ricordi che quest'amabil Salvatore disse ai suio diletti Discepoli che il suo cibo era di far la volontà dell'Eterno suo Padre. 'Meus cibus est ut faciam voluntatem eius qui misit me et ut perficiam opus eius' " (L 1:491, Dec. 18, 1743).

will" (il rassegnarsi al divino volere), "living abandoned to the divine good pleasure" (il vivere abbandonato nel Divin Beneplacito), and, in its highest form, "to have as food the divine will in a pure spirit of faith and of love" (il cibarsi in puro spirito di fede e d'amore della Divina Volontà). The first degree is that of "resignation". At this stage, the person tries to recognize and accept the will of God in the concrete, unalterable circumstances of daily life. To do so is difficult for the individual: he must, from one occasion to the next, repeat the act of resignation in such a way that, at this level of fulfilling God's will, he is playing a kind of one-character play.

By the time a person reaches the second degree, he has developed a sort of "ease" in fulfilling the divine will. Consciousness of doing so has developed into an inner attitude of "living" in God's will. Added to this is a stronger desire to do what God wants. The individual likes to surrender himself to God, to be lost in God. The Italian word abbandonato connotes this manner of surrendering, this losing of one's self in God.[24]

"To live in God's will" may also be examined from another point of view. In a letter written in 1729 to the Marchioness del Pozzo (in the early period of the saint's life), Paul spoke of God's abiding presence within the person. He advised the marchioness to pray as did St. Augustine: "Oh, my God, I went searching for you outside of myself, and I had you within, within myself!"[25] In the same letter, Paul invited her "to abandon [herself] completely to God's holy will" and "to bury all anxiety, worry, etc. in the dear will of God".[26] So if God is present to the person, then the person will be in relationship with God and eager to live according to his will.

The third and highest degree of fulfilling God's will consists of living in the manner of Christ, who considered his Father's will as food. We are, however, not able to do this with the same immediacy as Christ but only in a "pure spirit of faith and love" (in puro spirito di fede e di amore).[27] In describing this degree, two characteristic features of the spirituality of Paul of the Cross are present: his intense Christ-centeredness and his emphasis on faith and love.

---

[24] See Palazzi, 2. In his letters, St. Paul of the Cross frequently uses the notions of abbandonare and abbandonamento. Only once, however, does he use this term in his spiritual diary; and when he does so, he uses it to connote a negative state. The entry of Dec. 21 states, "Intendo anche che Dio la tiene in braccio, mà non se accorge, e da questo ne viene, si pare in un grand'abbandonamento ..." / "I also know that God holds the soul in his arms, but she is not aware of it. Hence she seems to be utterly abandoned and in great misery ..." (Diario Spirituale, 74; Tagebuch, 91f.; Rouse, 34).

[25] "Diciamo con S. Agostino: 'O mio Dio, vi andavo cercando fuori di me e vi avevo in me, dentro di me.'" This quotation from St. Augustine's Confessions, Bk. 10, Chap. 27, appears in Paul's letter of Jan. 3, 1729, to Marchioness della Scala del Pozzo (L 1:44).

[26] "... s'abbandoni tutta nella sua SS. Volontà ... seppelisca tutte le afflizioni, travagli ecc. nella cara Volontà di Dio ..." (L 1:45).

[27] See L 1:491.

This reference to the example of Jesus, who identified his Father's will as food (Jn 4:34), and the requirement of doing just that "in faith" represent recurring themes which we find more often than not whenever the saint encouraged another to live a life of surrender to God's will. In a letter written at the age of seventy-seven years, Paul expressed himself in the following way:

Now I would like to tell you about a principle of faith which embraces the highest perfection. Jesus Christ said to his apostles one day that his food was to do the will of his eternal Father. What an important point this is. Therefore, in every event of life, in all interior and exterior worries, desolations, aridities . . . in bodily pain, in all of these find the food of the divine will . . . [28]

In an earlier letter, our mystic chose language rich in imagery to describe the relationship between submission to the divine will and faith, hope, and love:

In all things may the divine will be your food; even more, take the gentle, most holy will of God as your spouse and wed her this moment with the ring of faith in which are set the other jewels of hope and love. [29]

Besides this profound and mystical manner of viewing God's will, we also find in St. Paul of the Cross a healthy and firm realism whenever the matter under discussion is the concrete discernment of the will of God in the life of a particular individual. This realism is especially evident in 172 extant letters written by the saint to Thomas Fossi.[30] Husband and father of several children, Fossi was among those who actively and materially supported the establishment of the Congregation. After his wife's death, he himself, in the year 1768 and at the age of fifty-seven, entered the Passionists and later became a priest.

During an intimate and personal friendship of over forty years, however, our saint noted that Fossi tended to become too zealous and inconsiderate in his religious and spiritual life. For that reason, Paul tried in several letters to

[28] "Ora le dirò solamente una gran massima di fede, che abbraccia tutta le più alta perfezione: Gesù Cristo disse un giorno ai suoi Apostoli che il suo cibo era il far la volontà del suo Eterno Padre. Oh, gran punto è questo. Dunque lei, in tutti gli eventi, in tutte le angustie interne ed esterne, desolazioni, aridità . . . pene di corpo ecc., in tutti questi incontri si cibi della Divina Volontà . . . " (L 3:833, Dec. 1770, to Anna Maria Calcagnini).

[29] "Sopratutto sia il cibo suo la Divina Volontà, anzi questa dolce Volontà SS.ma del nostro Dio, se la prenda per sposa e si sposi con essa ogni momento coll'anello della fede, in cui siano incastrate le altre gioie della speranza e carità" (L 1:591, May 16, 1750, to Thomas Fossi).

[30] See L 1:533–820.

make known to Thomas God's will for him, namely, how to live as a good Christian husband and father.[31] Perhaps this intent is best illustrated in one of the letters written by Paul, who, evidencing his skill as a director of conscience, invited Fossi to live in conformity with the state in which God had placed him. In a tone combining elements of both humor and irony, Paul also cautioned Thomas "not to believe that a married man must live the life of a Capuchin—which would be an error".[32]

The will of God and suffering. Undoubtedly, the will of God is difficult to fulfill. It may be especially "problematic" in the face of events that result in suffering. St. Paul of the Cross' total submission to the will of God, however, was especially manifest in situations in which unavoidable and innocent suffering had to be endured. He saw the will of God not as an arbitrary will but as a salvific will, a will leading in the long run to the happiness and holiness of the person. This unshakable confidence in God's goodness and love represented a force that enabled him to accept and bear all kinds of pain as the will of God. An attentive search of entries in his spiritual diary reveals the calm with which he bore any bodily or spiritual suffering.[33]

Convinced that God treats the individual with love, mercy, and goodwill above all, Paul accordingly and willingly accepted those occurrences in life that caused him suffering. In fact, he was so convinced of God's goodness that sufferings effected in him a "kind of joy",[34] and he "embraced them" because

---

[31] So it is written in a letter of Aug. 9, 1738: "E necessario, che lei faccia una vita da buon cristiano accasato, e che attenda agli obblighi del suo stato, che accudisca alla sua casa.... Questa è la volontà di Dio, e lei puol farsi santo anche in mezzo ai suoi affari, quando sono diretti alla pura gloria di Dio." / "It is necessary that you live the life of a good, married Christian, who is attending to the duties of his state, who is looking after his home.... This is God's will, and you can become a saint in the middle of your occupations too, when they are directed to the pure glory of God" (L I:545). Five years later, he wrote again, " ... e che non mancherà di assistere ai suoi affari, così volendo il peso che tiene come padre di famiglia, procurando di conservar ogni pace con chi Dio le ha data per compagna, e con esser esatto nell'educare i figli nel santo timor di Dio. Di questo non ne dubito perchè è il principale suo obbligo." / " ... and do not cease to attend to your affairs, since such is your duty as father of a family, trying moreover to preserve peace with her given to you as spouse by God, and also be prompt in the education of your sons in the holy fear of God. Do not hold any doubt about these, because such is your main obligation" (L I:553, Sept. 5, 1743).

[32] "Lei viva secondo lo stato in cui Dio lo ha posto ... nè creda che un coniugato debba far vita da capuccino, che ciò sarebbe errore" (L I:597, Oct. 6, 1750).

[33] On Nov. 25, he speaks of an "inner pain". On Dec. 3, he speaks of "affliction and sadness". On Dec. 21, he describes in great detail his readiness to bear interior and exterior sufferings. On Dec. 30, he talks of his deep desolation.

[34] " ... è una certa contentezza, che sia fatta la volontà. SSma. del nostro caro Dio ... " / " ... and it is a certain contentment that the most holy will of our good God is being done ... " (*Diario Spirituale*, 55; *Tagebuch*, 59; Rouse, 29).

he "knew they represented the will of God".[35] We encounter this total confidence in the infinite goodness and love of God and its resultant submission to the divine will (especially in the acceptance of difficulties and suffering) not only in entries in his spiritual diary but also in letters dating from his early period. Furthermore, these principles remained characteristic of his theological and spiritual thought throughout his life.

In a letter written in December of 1765, the "saint of the Cross" wrote of attacks and hostilities directed against his activity in founding the Congregation. In it, we see to what degree he derived solid, interior strength from his firm conviction that, in the last analysis, the will of God will be accomplished. His confidence was so powerful that he lost neither his inner balance nor his peace of heart despite all "outer attacks". Let us allow the saint, however, to speak for himself in his own lively and picturesque language:

> In such situations I behave myself as vinedressers or gardeners do who see a storm approaching, or when it begins to rain or hail or lightening or thunder. They go and seek shelter in their huts and stay there in peace until the storm passes. That's what I want to do, with the grace of God: to remain quiet and peaceful in the shelter of God's will, under the almighty protection of the Most High, and thus to await in peace and in tranquility of heart the passage of this terrible storm of persecution by adversaries.[36]

Using the same lifelike imagery, Paul in another letter wrote,

> Just so must we behave: In the midst of such storms brought on by our sins and the sins of the world, let us remain sheltered in the golden refuge of the divine will, rejoicing and keeping festival that in all things the sublime divine good pleasure be fulfilled.[37]

---

[35] " ... pur l'anima la abbraccia, perchè sa che è volontà di Dio ... " / " ... then the soul embraces it, because it knows that this is God's will ... " (*Diario Spirituale*, 63; *Tagebuch*, 72; Rouse, 31).

[36] "Io vado pensando di fare come fa il vignaiuolo o l'ortolano, i quali quando vedono imminente il temporale ed incomincia cadere pioggia e grandine, fulmini e tuoni, se ne fuggono alla capanna ed ivi stanno in pace sedendo sino che passi la tempesta. Così io desidero di fare, e voglio farlo colla Divina Grazia, di starmene quieto e tranquillo sotto la capanna della Divina Volontà ed onnipotente protezione dell'Altissimo, aspettando in pace e tranquillità di cuore che passi il temporale tempestoso della persecuzione degli avversari" (L 2:413, Dec. 31, 1765, to G. F. Sancez).

[37] " ... così noi, in mezzo a tante tempeste, che ci minacciano i nostri ed i peccati del mondo, stiamocene ritirati nell'aurea capanna della Divina Volontà, compiacendoci e facendo festa che si adempia in tutto il sovrano Divin Beneplacito ecc" (L 3:753, May 24, 1768, to Marianna Girelli).

From the above, it is obvious the founder considered the misfortunes which befall an individual to be the consequences of sin, and in the background of this conviction stood (even if not exclusively) the idea of expiation.[38]

Certainly St. Paul of the Cross knew that the sinister actions of the evil one, the *diabolos,* can bring suffering into the world over and above the sins of people. When, however, it was a matter of urging an individual to accept unavoidable and "innocent" suffering, then Paul's firm confidence in the goodness and benevolence of God became a profound power source undergirding his conviction. In other words, Paul was convinced that God the Father will "direct" all things to work out best for his sons and daughters if they but always keep him and his will before their eyes in all they do. This basic conviction of the saint was clearly expressed in a letter written by him at the age of seventy-nine. Quoting St. Catherine of Siena,[39] he wrote,

> ... whoever seeks nothing else than to please God, nor wills anything else than God's will ... and lets God think and take care of one's troubles, be sure that, just as God told St. Catherine of Siena, if one thinks of pleasing God, then God will think of that person.[40]

In his spiritual diary, the saint, as already mentioned, spoke most frequently of the will of God when it was a matter of experiencing suffering.[41] On December 3, 1720, he spoke of being distressed by "anguish or affliction", at which point he quoted the celebrated dictum of St. Teresa of Avila: "To suffer or to die". He wanted to suffer, or better said he "embraced" these sufferings since, as he himself affirmed, " ... it is God's will".[42] Paul again cited the

[38] See Basilio de S. Pablo, "La contemplación reparadora en San Pablo de la Cruz", 449–65.

[39] The founder probably read these words of St. Catherine in the writings of St. Francis de Sales. In his treatise *On the Love of God,* Francis writes, " ... God will always will in sufficient measure all you could will for yourself without putting yourself in trouble. ... Let his willing always be sufficient for you since it is always the best. Thus it was that he ordered his beloved St. Catherine of Siena, for he said to her, 'Think in me, and I will think for you.'" (See Bl. Raymond of Capua, *Vita S. Catherinae Senenis,* Par. I, c. 2., as quoted in German in Reisinger 4:161, and, in English, Ryan, *On the Love of God* 2, Bk. 9, Chap. 15, 136.)

[40] " ... chi non cerca che di dare gusto a Dio, nè vuole altro che Dio ... ne lascia la cura e pensiero a Dio stesso, sicuro che, come disse a S. Caterina da Siena, se uno pensa a dar gusto a Dio ecc., Iddio pensa a lui" (L 1:820, Sept. 1, 1773, to Thomas Fossi).

[41] See n. 33 above.

[42] The following is found in that day's entry: "Fui tutto il giorno afflitto con grandi afflizione ... e quando mi vengono questa sorta di affanni o sia afflizioni ... mi paio l'uomo più miserabile e desolato che si trovi, e pur l'anima le abbraccia, perchè sa che è volontà di Dio ... ; mi viene da dire con santa Teresa, 'O patire o morire'." / "I was afflicted all day long with great sufferings ... and when this kind of anguish or affliction comes to me ... I seem to be the most miserable and desolate man alive. However, my soul embraces them because she knows that this is God's will ... I feel like saying with St. Teresa, 'To suffer or to die'" (*Diario Spirituale,* 63; *Tagebuch,* 72; Rouse, 31).

Spanish saint in a letter written in 1743. In it, he distinguished between suffering itself, which was not the main issue, and the accomplishment of God's will, which was the main issue. He wrote,

> I believe the cross of our sweet Jesus has already planted its roots more deeply in your heart, and now you are singing, *"Pati et non mori"* [to suffer and not die], or *"aut pati aut mori"* [to either suffer or die], or better *"nec pati nec mori"* [to neither suffer nor die], but to be solely transformed by the divine good pleasure.[43]

To sum up all that concerns this basic principle, which we find strongly emphasized in the spiritual-theological thought of St. Paul of the Cross, we may assert: The call to surrender to God's will was found throughout the saint's epistolary. "God's will", however, was always closely associated with the certainty of God's love and goodness toward all people. Confidence and assurance that the person is constantly immersed in the all-embracing flow of God's love formed the soil which nourished Paul's teaching on the will of God. This divine will was to be thought of not as a blind, arbitrary will but as a salvific one that, in the long run, is always directed toward the person's well-being and holiness. This knowledge of God's loving care provides inner strength and patience during both interior and exterior suffering. The strongest basis and the reason most frequently given by Paul for confidence in God's will as a loving will was to be found in the example of Jesus Christ, who considered his "food" to be the will of God. Thus, St. Paul of the Cross' doctrine of "surrender to the divine will" had, we may affirm, a very strong christological imprint.

2. *"Nothingness" and "All"* (Niente-Tutto)

The above subtitle would seem to suggest that we will now be dealing with profound speculations about the nature of God and the human person. But this is not the case, for the founder of the Passionists was neither a theorist nor a philosopher. Indeed, he may even be said to have possessed a certain scepticism of and antipathy toward purely speculative and vacuous philosophy.[44] Acknowledging this characteristic of the founder is of importance in our understanding of the following: When Paul spoke of "nothingness" and "all", he was not primarily probing metaphysical concepts. This delimitation is important: If we keep it in mind, many statements—seemingly exaggerated or,

[43] "Credo che la Croce del nostro dolce Gesù avrà poste più profonde radici nel vostro cuore e che cantarete, 'Pati et non mori', o pure, 'aut pati aut mori', o pure ancor meglio, 'nec pati, nec mori', ma solamente la totale trasformazione nel Divin Beneplacito" (L 2:440, July 10, 1743, to Sr. Colomba Gandolfi).

[44] This does not mean the saint's theological ideas were banal or trivial. His thought, however, was not distinguished so much by its logical-intellectual acuteness as it was by its religious-mystical profundity.

more strongly put, scandalous and alienating from a philosophical point of view—lose their halo of exaggeration or exaltation.

Creation and original sin as theological background. The basic principle underlying the littleness of the human person and the greatness of God—a principle which, in the saint's mind, was of "fundamental" importance in the true sense of the word—must first and foremost be conceived as a conceptual explanation of the relationship between creature and Creator. In hindsight we may say that to accept one's creatureliness was, for Paul, to accept one's nothingness; to accept God as Creator was to accept God as all. However, if we look closely at the formulations used by Paul during the early period of his call as founder, we do not find that he himself used this specific nothing-all antithesis to describe the fact of the human person as a created being; rather, we see a progression of his thought in that direction.

Part of this progression of thought had to do with the fact that to accept one's creatureliness is humility; and it is in terms of humility—rather than in terms of the nothing-all antithesis—that Paul, more often than not, expressed the awareness of his nothingness during his early period. Because of their simplicity and originality, entries in Paul's spiritual diary give us a good insight into how he looked upon himself and, in so doing, demonstrate his deep humility, a humility that was neither artificial nor written in an awkward and fictional manner but had its source in the depths of his personality. At the same time, we may be surprised and shocked when we read his forceful and harsh self-denunciations. He referred to himself as "a great sinner",[45] as doing "nothing good",[46] an "abyss of ingratitude".[47] He declared himself to be "worse than a demon",[48] and he

---

[45] The entry from Nov. 27, 1720, ends with the following: "Mi rallegravo che il nostro grande Iddio si voglia servire di questo gran peccatore, e dall'altra parte non sapevo dove gettarmi, vedendomi tanto vile; basta: so che dico al mio caro Gesù, che tutte le creature canteranno le sue misericordie." / "I rejoiced that our great God should wish to make use of this great sinner; on the other hand, I knew not where to turn, realizing that I am so wretched. Enough! I know that I tell my beloved Jesus that all creatures shall sing his mercies" (*Diario Spirituale*, 59; *Tagebuch*, 64; Rouse, 30).

[46] In the entry dated Dec. 15–18 the following may be read: "Mi par bene che non faccia niente di buono, come è così, ma mi confido nella somma Bontà del Sommo Bene, che sia da tutti amato. Amen." / "It seems to me that I do nothing good, as is indeed true, but I entrust myself to the supreme kindness of the Sovereign Good. May he be loved by all. Amen" (*Diario Spirituale*, 71; *Tagebuch*, 87; Rouse, 33–34).

[47] The following is written on Dec. 28: "... connoscendo essere un abisso d'ingratitudine" / "... knowing that I was an abyss of ingratitude" (*Diario Spirituale*, 82; *Tagebuch*, 105; Rouse, 37).

[48] The statement that he is "worse than a demon" (essendo peggior d'un demonio) appears in the entries of Dec. 5 and 7 (*Diario Spirituale*, 65f.; *Tagebuch*, 75 and 78; and Rouse, 32).

even tried to increase his degree of abasement by calling himself a "dirty cesspool".[49]

These self-denunciations, however, were not independent or isolated sayings. Paul spoke simultaneously of God's infinite mercy and goodness[50] and considered himself to be a "miracle of God's infinite mercy".[51] Often, his discourses ended with a hymn of gratitude, laud, and praise of God.[52] This balance indicates Paul's humility was true: It was inseparable from trust and confidence in God.

Knowledge of his own weakness, ingratitude, and sinfulness did not result in pusillanimity, quitting, or frustration. On the contrary, recognition of his own "nothingness" was a happy occasion in which he took delight, as we see in the entry of January 1, 1721, the last day of his preparatory retreat: "With great confidence and delight I was telling my Jesus about my miseries without growing tired."[53]

For St. Paul of the Cross, to accept one's own "nothingness" (and he spoke of "being cast into nothingness" as early as 1726) and to submit one's self unconditionally to God's love and goodness, to "mistrust" one's self while having unlimited trust in God,[54] meant to affirm one's proper creatureliness; and, in the final analysis, affirming one's creatureliness is nothing other than the virtue of humility. It is most obvious that, in Paul's conception, humility

[49] "Ho avuto gran cognizione di me; mi pare, quando Dio mi dà quest'altissima cognizione di me, di esser peggiore di un demonio, di essere una sporchissima cloaca, come con verità è così . . . " / "I have received great self-knowledge, and when God gives me this very deep knowledge, it seems to me that I am worse than a demon, that I am a very dirty cesspool (and it is really so)" (*Diario Spirituale*, 66; *Tagebuch*, 78; Rouse, 32).

[50] See nn. 45 and 46 above.

[51] After having designated himself as an "abyss of ingratitude" in the entry of Dec. 28, he continues, "So che dico al mio Divin Salvatore, che non mi posso chiamar altro, che un miracolo delle sue infinite misericordie. Ne sia da tutti lodato e magnificato il suo Santissimo Nome. Amen." / "I know that I told my divine Savior that I could call myself nothing other than a miracle of his infinite mercy. May his Holy Name be praised and glorified by all. Amen" (*Diario Spirituale*, 82; *Tagebuch*, 106; Rouse, 37). He speaks in a similar fashion in the entry of Jan. 1, 1721 (87, 113, and 37-38, respectively).

[52] In the entry of Dec. 7 in which he calls himself a "cesspool", he also states, " . . . gli dico che con farmi tante grazie, e sì innumerabili favori risplenderanno più le sue infinite misericordie, perchè le fa al più gran peccatore; in tutto sia lodato il suo SS. Nome." / "I tell him that in giving me so many graces and such innumerable favors, he only manifests his infinite mercies all the more because he gives them to the greatest of sinners. May his most Holy Name be praised in all things" (*Diario Spirituale*, 67; *Tagebuch*, 78; Rouse, 32). He expresses himself similarly on Dec. 28 (see n. 51 above) and on Jan. 1.

[53] "Raccontavo con grande confidenza, ma senza fatica, e con gran dolcezza al mio Gesù le mie miserie . . . " (*Diario Spirituale*, 85; *Tagebuch*, 110; Rouse, 37).

[54] In L 1:62, Feb. 16, 1726, to Nicolina Pecorini Martinez, Paul writes, "Facciamo orazione, confidiamo in Dio, sconfidiamo di noi stessi e non dubitiamo che Dio sarà la nostra Via, Vita e Verità." / "Let us pray, let us trust in God, let us mistrust ourselves, and let us not doubt that God will be our way, life, and truth [Jn 14:6]."

and confidence in God were bound together intimately with the result being that genuine humility led to greater trust in God. It is also obvious that the founder saw the greatest example of Christian humility in the Person of the Redeemer, Jesus Christ. Paul wrote,

> Oh, when shall we perfectly imitate this dear Savior who "emptied himself" [Phil 2:7] . . . ah, when are we going to become like little babes clinging to the breast of the charity of Jesus, our Spouse and Helper? When shall we become so simple and childlike so as to consider it great happiness to be the least of all, cast into nothingness?[55]

Fifteen years later, in another letter to Agnes Grazi, Paul stated,

> But, return immediately and plunge [yourself] into your own nothingness to experience your own unworthiness, and from this knowledge must spring then a greater confidence in God, who does so much good . . . [56]

When St. Paul of the Cross strongly urged those who would strive for perfection to "annihilate" themselves (*annichilarsi*), this in no way represented a request to give up on self. It was, rather, an appeal to imitate "the deepest humility and annihilation of the Divine Redeemer", a humility the Son of Man "so divinely taught in all his actions".[57] Before all else, to "become nothing" for Paul meant to be humble in a radical way, according to the example of Jesus, and to place all one's trust in God.

An infinite trust in God and a deep distrust of one's self—these represented an essential quality of the antithetical mode of expressing the "allness" of God and the "nothingness" of the human person. Nevertheless, this discussion of "nothingness" and "all" cannot be grasped by everyone. Only those who live a profound interiority are able to understand the meaning of such phrases. In a letter of 1766, the saint defined his terms and spoke of the difficulty involved in understanding these things. He explained,

> In order to be holy an *N* and a *T* are necessary. Whoever possesses a more interior spirit understands the meaning [of this], but whoever has not yet entered true, profound solitude is unable to grasp its meaning. Moreover, I

[55] "Ah, quando imiteremo perfettamente questo caro Salvatore, che *exinanivit se* . . . Ah, quando saremo diventati così piccoli bambini attaccati alle mammelle della SSma. Carità di Gesù nostro caro Sposo, Padre e Tutore, e che saremo tanto semplici e piccoli che avremo per gran fortuna l'essere fatti gli ultimi di tutti, buttati nel niente . . . ?" (L 1:68, Aug. 29, 1726, to Fr. Erasmus Tuccinardi).

[56] "Ma ritorni presto a buttarsi nel suo niente a conoscere la sua indegnità, e da questa cognizione ne ha da nascere una maggior fiducia in Dio, che fa tanto bene . . . " (L 1:267, Apr. 3, 1741).

[57] " . . . con imitare fedelmente le sue altissime virtù e principalmente quella profondissima umiltà ed annichilamento che in tutte le sue santissime azioni ci ha tanto divinamente insegnato" (L 1:256, Aug. 4, 1740, to Agnes Grazi).

say, the N is you since you are a horrible nothingness! The T represents God, who is infinite *Tutto* [allness] in his essence. Therefore, let the N of your nothingness disappear into the never-ending allness that is God most high, and thus be lost completely in the abyss of the immense Divinity. Oh, what a noble work this is![58]

As previously stated, Paul of the Cross did not use the concepts of "nothingness" (*niente*) and "allness" (*tutto*) in a pure, metaphysical sense. It was not a desire to engage in philosophical speculation but rather to consider seriously those fundamental religious truths about creation and original sin that impelled him to speak of our "nothingness" and of the "allness" of God—who "in his essence" is being *par excellence*. Paul referred to this fundamental truth regarding God's essence in a letter of 1740. He wrote, "In his essence, God is he who is, 'I am who am'" (Ex 3:14). In the same letter he wrote of sin in the following way: "...whoever has sinned is worse than nothingness, because sin is a horrible nothing, worse than nothing".[59] As "nothingness", the human person has obtained his being only through the creative work of God. Without God, one would fall back again into nothingness. By saying that sin is "worse than nothingness", the founder indicated that for him "nothingness" has a moral dimension, too.[60] The reality of the sinfulness of the human person, of his own horrible nothingness, brings us now to the point of considering the role

[58] "Per essere santo vi vuole un N ed un T. Chi camminava più di dentro, indovinava il significato, ma chi non era ancor entrato in vera profonda solitudine, non sapeva indovinarne il significato; ed io soggiungo: La N sei tu che sei un orribil nulla; il T è Dio, che è l'infinito tutto per essenza. Lascia dunque sparire la N del tuo niente nell'infinito tutto, che è Dio Ottimo Massimo, ed ivi perditi tutto nell'abisso della immensa Divinità. Oh, che nobile lavoro è questo!" (L 3:747, Mar. 11, 1766, to Marianna Girelli).

[59] The entire fragment of this letter written by the founder to Sr. M. Cherubina Bresciani on Aug. 9, 1740, reads as follows: "Chi vuole trovare il vero tutto, che è Dio, bisogna buttarsi nel niente. Dio è quello che per essenza, è quello che è: *Ego sum qui sum.* Noi siamo quelli che non siamo, perchè per quanto scavaremo a fondo non troveremo altro che niente, niente; e chi ha peccato, è peggio dello stesso niente, perchè il peccato è un orribile nulla, peggio del nulla. Dio dal niente ha creato tutto il visibile e l'invisibile, ma dal peccato la sua onnipotenza non vi puol cavare niente, perchè il peccato è un orribile nulla, che s'oppone a quell'Infinito Essere d'infinita perfezione." / "Whoever wants to find the whole truth, who is God, must consider one's self as nothing. In his essence, God is he who is: *Ego sum qui sum* [I am who am]. We are they who are not, because no matter how deep we dig into the ground of our soul, we find only nothingness, nothingness. Whoever has sinned is worse than nothing, because sin is a horrible nothing. God has created all that is visible and invisible, but from sin his Omnipotence can draw nothing, because sin is a horrible nothingness opposed to the infinite Being of infinite perfection" (L 1:471).

[60] Certainly someone may object to this manner of argumentation where ontological and moral planes intersect each other. Yet these statements (see n. 59 above) show how strongly Paul's thinking was shaped by the fundamental truths of Christian faith (e.g., creation, the fall).

redemption and justification played in the spiritual-theological thought of Paul of the Cross.

Redemption and justification. Does not Paul's view of the human person as "nothing" and, even more so, as "worse than nothing" because of his sins, result in pessimism? This would be true had his thought remained fixed at this point. Paul knew, however, that God had not forsaken humankind in its sin. Rather, he destroyed the power of sin and justified us through the redemptive sacrifice of Jesus Christ. This point was made clear in the same letter in which the saint discussed the nothingness of the human person and the horrible nothingness of sin. He wrote,

> Yet, what follows is also true: This great and infinite Good, who alone can draw good from evil, creates—in the justification of the sinner—a greater work of his omnipotence than had he created a thousand worlds, more vast and beautiful than this one, since God draws the sinner—by justifying him—out of an abyss more dismal and deep than [that of] his own nothingness, [that is, out of the abyss of] sin.[61]

Creatio ex nihilo (creation from nothingness) and the original fall were the basic truths the Passionist founder relied upon when he spoke of human "nothingness". Furthermore, when he spoke of the "allness" that is God, the saint referred not to a deistic-pantheistic God but to the God "of Abraham, of Isaac, and of Jacob", a redeeming and mighty God acting upon history and humankind, a God who sacrificed his only Son for the salvation of all. The concepts, therefore, of "all" and "nothing" primarily represented "expressions of existential and committed ways of thinking" about fundamental Christian truths of creation, the fall, and redemption—truths which may be considered the basic triad of Christian Faith.

At the same time, this avowal of self-nothingness, which the saint always placed in bold relief, was not for him an end in itself.[62] This is obvious in the following letter, in which Paul described entering into the awareness of one's nothingness as a first step, a necessary premise only, in the act of casting one's own "nothingness" into the "allness of God":

> Oh, what a noble exercise it is indeed to annihilate one's self before God in pure faith without images, so that this nothingness of ours may be cast into

[61] "Vero è che quel gran Bene Infinito, che sa cavare dallo stesso male il bene, colla giustificazione però del peccatore, fa uno sforzo maggiore della sua onnipotenza, che se creasse mille mondi assai più vaghi e più belli di questo, perchè cava il peccatore (col giustificarlo) da un abisso più tetro e più profondo dello stesso nulla, che è il peccato" (L 1:472, Aug. 9, 1740, to Sr. M. Cherubina Bresciani).

[62] " . . . e lasci sparire il suo niente nel Divino Tutto . . . " / " . . . and let your nothingness disappear in the Divine All . . . " (L 1:284, June 11, 1742, to Agnes Grazi; also compare this footnote with n. 58 above).

that true "all" that is God and thus be lost in that immense sea of never-ending love . . . [63]

In other words, the human person must annihilate himself *before God,* that is, he must become aware that he is only a creature and owes all good to God. This "annihilation" is to be understood primarily as an "existential feature" of the state of creaturehood.

To complete this "dialectic" of "nothingness" and "all", there belongs, besides the doctrine of creation, a consideration of the role of the mystery of salvation as it presented itself in the theological background of the saint. As previously indicated,[64] Paul of the Cross likened the justification of the sinner to a new creation.[65] The following passage indicates the effect or outcome the saint had in mind when speaking of allowing the nothingness of the human soul to come to rest in the never-ending sea of God's love:

> . . . while the loving soul is swimming in this sea, it will be penetrated from within and without by infinite love and completely united with and transformed in Jesus Christ; more than that, by love the soul becomes one with Jesus Christ . . . [66]

Therefore, to cast one's "nothingness" into God's "all", to let this "nothingness" rest in God's "all", also means to allow the redeeming sacrifice of Christ to work efficaciously upon the self. This line of thought consequently evokes the saint's concept of salvific grace. Paul's becoming lost in God does not mean self-discouragement or self-destruction. On the contrary, it means an ultimate finding or discovery of one's true self, as the saint exclaimed in one of his letters: "Oh, happiest loss by which the soul losing all in God is truly found!"[67]

Paul used this antithetical notional pair of nothing-all not only to describe the correct relationship between the human person and God as Creator but

---

[63] "Oh, che nobile esercizio e mai questo di annichilarsi avanti a Dio in pura fede senza immagini, e poi buttare questo nostro niente in quel vero Tutto che è Dio, ed ivi perdersi in quell'immenso mare d'infinita carità . . . " (L 1:484f., June 26, 1742, to Sr. Cherubina Bresciani).

[64] See n. 61 above.

[65] See 2 Cor 5:17 and Gal 6:15.

[66] " . . . in cui nuotando l'anima amante resta penetrata di dentro e di fuori da questo amore infinito, e tutta unita e trasformata in Gesù Cristo per amore . . . " (L 1:485, June 26, 1742, to Sr. M. Cherubina Bresciani).

[67] In a letter written in 1743, Paul indicates the way to self-discovery in the following words: "Pertanto io vorrei che lei si esercitasse molto nella perfetta cognizione del suo nulla, e poi vorrei che abissasse questo suo nulla in quell'immenso Tutto, che è il nostro buon Dio. Oh, perdita felicissima, per cui l'anima perdendosi tutta in Dio resta ben trovata!" / "Therefore, I would like you to practice frequently this perfect awareness of your own nothingness, and then I would like you to plunge your nothingness into that immense all, that is our good God. Oh happiest loss, by which the soul losing all in God is truly found" (L 1:488, Jan. 2, 1743, to Sr. M. Cherubina Bresciani).

also to describe the "correct relationship of the creature to created things". In another letter of 1740, the saint wrote,

> You must lose sight of all creatures and all images of them and plunge yourself more and more into the knowledge of your true, horrible nothing-ness . . . take care to die more and more to yourself and everything created and then place this, your nothingness, in that all which is God, and there lose yourself and abase yourself in such a manner that, forgetful of yourself and of all creatures, you may have no other thought than this object of infinite perfection.[68]

It is significant that the saint, in the latter part of his life, especially after having met with the ideas of Tauler (about 1748), used the phrase *mystical death* (*morte mistica*) to describe the proper distancing of self from created things.[69]

Summing up these ideas, we may conclude: The polarity of the human person's "nothingness" and God's "all" occupied an important place in the spiritual teaching of St. Paul of the Cross. This "antithetical manner of speech", however, represented not a one-sided, philosophical conceptualiza-tion of his basic thought but rather a profound consideration and an "existential marriage" of the truths of faith regarding creation, original sin, and salvation.

3. *Mystical Death–Divine Nativity* (morte mistica–divina natività)

The symbolic expression *mystical death–divine nativity* represents another fun-damental principle which typifies and characterizes the spiritual-theological thought of St. Paul of the Cross. That this twofold notion is recognized as a "thought form" (*forma mentis*) and "key notion" of the saint's spiritual teach-ing is due primarily to the work of C. Brovetto[70] in his monograph on the founder of the Passionist Congregation. Since Tauler's notion of "divine rebirth" has already been discussed (see "Modalities of receptivity to Taulerian

---

[68] "Lei deve perdere de vista sempre più tutte le creature e tutte le immagini di esse, e deve sprofondarsi sempre più nella cognizione del suo vero, orribile nulla . . . procurare di morir sempre più a se stessa ed a tutto il creato, e poi mettere questo suo niente in quel tutto che è Dio, ed ivi perdersi ed abissarsi di maniera tale, che scordata di se stessa e di tutte le creature non abbia altro pensiero che di quest'oggetto d'infinita perfezione" (L 1:256, Aug. 4, 1740, to Agnes Grazi).

[69] Increasing familiarity with Surius-Tauler gave Paul, who was by then at the age of full "maturity" and an experienced director of conscience, an opportunity to stress proper interiorization even more than before. In the saint's way of thinking, correct interiorization results in a greater degree of differentiation, and he describes this detachment from created things mostly by the phrase *morte mistica* (see the next subsection, "Mystical death–divine nativity [*morte mistica–divina natività*]").

[70] Brovetto, *Introduzione alla Spiritualità*.

thought" in Chapter II), this section looks primarily at the meaning given to "divine nativity" and "mystical death" in the letters of St. Paul of the Cross.[71]

Indubitably, the notional pair "mystical death–divine nativity" did not originate with Paul of the Cross. Its premises are found in New Testament writings and in spiritual-theological Tradition.[72] Still, this principle, indicative of a polar-dialectical way of thinking, serves quite well in elucidating some essential features of the saint's spiritual doctrine.

Development of this principle. A complete and clear enunciation of the basic notional principle of *morte mistica–divina natività* made its appearance relatively late (probably 1748 or thereafter) in Paul's writing. This time period would have corresponded with Paul's incorporation of Taulerian ideas into his own teaching. The principle itself, however, may be identified in analogous forms earlier in his life. For example, several entries in his diary contain parallel formulations and "forerunners" of this principle. In a spiritual diary entry of November 25, 1720, Paul wrote, " . . . I seemed to have a heart that was buried, without any feeling of prayer. Still I do not recall that I desired relief from it, and in my mind I am content to have experienced them [temptations]."[73] In the entry of December 10–13, we read, " . . . the soul that God wants to draw into deepest union with him by means of holy prayer, must pass through this way of suffering [i.e., deprivation of sensible consolation] during prayer".[74] On December 31, Paul stated, "I was dry, distracted, but did enjoy interior peace . . . "[75] It may be said such and other similar

---

[71] In the Introduction of his study, Brovetto writes, "Ma confidiamo di non aver fatta una inutile fatica, affiancando al loro anche il nostro piccolo contributo, avviato piuttosto a indiduare ed illustrare teologicamente quella che potremmo chiamare la 'forma mentis,' l'idea centrale del Santo riguardo alla vita interiore: il concetto chiave insomma, che domina e modifica sotto la sua luce gli innumerevoli aspetti del cammino verso la perfezione, riducendoli ad originale ed interna unità." / "We are confident of not having made a useless effort, [in] putting at your disposal our small contribution, written especially to delineate and illustrate theologically what we could call *forma mentis,* the saint's central idea in regard to the spiritual life: in brief, the key concept that dominates and modifies in its light the innumerable aspects of the way of perfection, reducing it to an original and internal unity" (Brovetto, xii).

[72] See Basilio de San Pablo, *La Espiritualidad de la Pasión en el Magisterio de San Pablo de la Cruz,* 200–203.

[73] " . . . insomma mi pareva che avessi il cuore sepolto, senza alcun sentimento di orazione. Eppure non mi sovvenne di desiderarne il sollievo, e mentalmente sono contento di averle" (*Diario Spirituale,* 54f.; *Tagebuch* 59; Rouse, 29).

[74] "Pertanto so che Dio vuole tirare all'alta unione con Lui per mezzo della santa orazione, bisogna che passi per questa strada di patire nell'orazione anche, e dico patire senza alcun conforto sensibile . . . " / "That is why I know that God enables me to understand that the soul whom he wants to draw to deepest union with him by means of holy prayer, must pass through this way of suffering during prayer and must suffer without any sensible consolation . . . " (*Diario Spirituale,* 70; *Tagebuch,* 84f.; Rouse, 33).

[75] "Sono stato arido, distratto, ma con interna pace . . . " (*Diario Spirituale,* 85; *Tagebuch,* 109; Rouse, 37).

formulations have in their background a "to die–to live" dualism, which Paul uses in trying to describe a "purgative process" in his diary entries.

In the Introduction to the original Rule written in 1720, we also come upon a phrase often used in the saint's later life in connection with the notion of *morte mistica,* namely, "total detachment from all created things" (*il totale staccamento da tutto il creato*).[76] Indeed, this phrase demonstrates the strong emphasis Paul placed on solid spirituality even in the early period of his life.

An examination of the letters written by the saint during this earlier period (1730 or before) with regard to the principle of *morte mistica–divina natività* reveals the presence of ideas that anticipate this principle and that serve as indicators of development in spiritual and theological thinking. In making such an examination, one also finds that the biblical and christological basis of his doctrine becomes more and more clear cut.[77]

In an Easter letter of 1726 written while still living as a hermit in the vicinity of Gaeta, the founder spoke of the necessary precondition of being allowed to sing "Alleluia" with the heavenly assembly. He stated,

> . . . to sing it properly, it is necessary to be stripped of the old self and to put on the new that is Jesus Christ. I mean adorned with the holy virtues, the way by which they are acquired having been made accessible for us by our victorious captain, Jesus Christ . . . [78]

Undoubtedly this biblical image of the "old" and the "new" has its foundation in the biblical "to die–to live" polarity (see Col 3:9–10), a polarity that resonates in the words chosen by the saint. The more extended sense in which this metaphor is used both in the Letter to the Colossians and in Paul's letter has a moral aim, namely, the imitation of Christ's virtues.

This death-life antithesis is also found in another letter belonging to the early period of the saint's life. Toward the end of November 1730, the Passionist founder informed his former confessor Don E. Tuccinardi of ani-

---

[76] After having described the "history of his call" to establish a Congregation, the saint began to speak of the Congregation's aim in the following words: "Sappiasi che l'intenzione che Dio mi dà di questa Congregazione non consiste in altro che in primo luogo d'osservare con perfezione la legge del nostro caro Iddio con l'osservanza perfetta de'suoi ss. consigli evangelici, e singolarmente il totale staccamento da tutto il creato . . . " / "Let it be known that the intention God gave me with regard to this Congregation was none other than this: in the first place, to observe God's law perfectly together with the perfect observance of his evangelical counsels, especially through total detachment from all created things . . . " (L 4:220).

[77] The several citations, presented in support of this statement, are an eloquent proof of its validity.

[78] " . . . per cantarlo come si deve, bisogna essere spogliati dell'uomo vecchio ed essere vestiti dell'uomo nuovo, che è Gesù Cristo, voglio dire essere adornati con le virtù sante, all'acquisto delle quali ci ha facilitata la via il nostro e vittorioso Capitano Gesù Cristo . . . " (L 1:63, Apr. 21, 1726, to N. Percorini Martinez).

mosities present in his new Congregation. Bearing them, however, did not make Paul despondent but proved and strengthened his confidence in God. He wrote,

> God's works are always attacked in order that God's magnificence may be displayed. Namely, when things seem to be mostly fallen to the ground, then it turns out that they are raised to an unexpected height: *"Dominus mortificat et vivificat, deducit ad inferos et reducit"* [1 Sam 2:6—The Lord kills and makes live; he brings down to hell and brings back again].[79]

Introducing this quotation from Samuel clearly demonstrates that our saint did not consider life and death to be pure biological facts. Rather, he held *God*, almighty Creator and Preserver of the universe, to be the only being having power over life and death. We will have further reference to this divine causality when Paul speaks, especially in his latter years, of "mystical death" and "divine rebirth".

It can be generally said that while the death-life antithesis held no prominent place in the early years of Paul's spiritual teaching, the concept was used by him in urging others on in the practice of virtue and in helping those whom he directed to cope with suffering and adversity through trust in God.

Even prior to the full conceptual development of the notional pair of "mystical death–divine nativity", Paul wrote in terms of a "death–new life" polarity. In a letter to Agnes Grazi in the year 1734, he stated,

> Oh, my daughter! fortunate that soul detached from its own joy, its own feeling, its own understanding! This is a most sublime lesson. God will teach it to you if you place your contentment in the cross of Jesus Christ, in dying on the Savior's cross to all that is not God.[80]

At this time, Paul had already noted a twofold dimension of death: first, the death of aspiration and inclinations that have the ego as their end point; and, secondly, the death of interest in exterior things that cannot bring man closer to God. Only from Christ and his cross, the instrument of our redemption, did he expect plenitude, life, and joy.

As demonstrated above, a "death-life" polarity was active in the spiritual and theological thought of the saint even *before* his coming into contact with Taulerian ideas. This fundamental principle, however, was more thematically developed and more frequently discussed by the saint in his spiritual letters *after* he read the works of the Rhineland mystic (about 1748).

---

[79] "Le opere di Dio sono state sempre combattute, acciò risplenda la Divina Magnificenza. Quando le cose paiono più a terra, è quando più si vedono sorgere in alto: 'Dominus mortificat et vivificat, deducit ad inferos et reducit' " (L 1:86, Nov. 29, 1730, to Fr. Erasmo Tuccinardi).

[80] "Oh! mia figlia! fortunata quell'anima, che si stacca dal suo proprio godere, dal proprio sentire, e dal proprio intendere. Altissima lezione è questa; Dio glie la farà imparare, se lei metterà il suo contento nella Croce di Gesù Cristo, nel morire a tutto quello, che non è Dio, su la Croce del Salvatore" (L 1:107, Mar. 17, 1734).

It is undisputed that the "birth of God in the soul" was one of Tauler's central themes, perhaps even the main theme of his spiritual doctrine. Although he seldom spoke of "mystical death", he did say things conceptually close to it. Neither did Paul of the Cross coin the phrase *mystical death;* rather, he encountered it in his spiritual-theological reading.[81] We may suppose, however, that the Taulerian metaphor of "divine nativity" inspired the founder to speak more emphatically of "mystical death". Thus, Paul's teaching of *morte mistica* appears to be the fruit of an encounter in thought with Tauler's spiritual doctrine. It also needs to be recalled that Paul, as previously mentioned,[82] did not simply incorporate into his own teaching the topos of "divine rebirth in the ground of the soul" but modified it according to his own basic theological convictions.

It may be noted that in letters written after 1748 the founder spoke relatively frequently of "mystical death" and "rebirth of the soul in the incarnate Word". The content presented below focuses on this "late period"—by which time Paul had already achieved great personal and human maturity and had acquired a wealth of personal spiritual-religious experience. Briefly stated, the following material examines *"morte mistica—divina natività"* symbolism from the point of view of an experienced spiritual director.

To die with Christ. Of the numerous letters in which the saint wrote of the fundamental principle of mystical death and divine nativity, let us first select one written to a fellow religious, Fr. Thomas (formerly Thomas Fossi)[83] during the late period in Paul's life. Fittingly, this letter presents us with a thematically elucidated interpretation of this principle written from the perspective of a man of seventy-five years, and it assumes even greater importance when one considers the concrete occasion that evoked its writing. It was written as a letter of personal congratulations sent by the saint shortly before Christmas of 1768 to the newly ordained, fifty-seven-year-old Fr. Thomas, a fellow Passionist and friend whom Paul had known for thirty-five years, including the years during which Fossi was a married layman "in the world".

Let us look at the text of the letter. After a first part in which the saint expressed his joy upon Thomas' ordination and celebration of his first Holy Mass, Paul wrote, "The life of true servants and friends of God consists in dying every day: *'Quotidie morimur—mortui enim estis et vita vestra abscondita est cum Christo in Deo'* [To die daily—for you are dead and your life is hidden

---

[81] It is impossible today to say with exactitude the founder's source of the metaphor "mystical death". Suffice it to say it was in widespread use during the era of quietism. See Guibert, *Documenta,* 285f., 298f.

[82] Refer to text above, pp. 135–46.

[83] Refer to what was said of Fossi in text above, pp. 158–59.

with Christ in God]" (see I Cor 15:31 and Col. 3:3).[84] The reference to "God's friends" in the first sentence is, without a doubt, a Taulerian reminiscence, as the founder often read about "God's true friends" in Surius-Tauler.[85] The mixed citation from I Corinthians 15:31 and Colossians 3:3 illustrates the biblical, theological, and christological orientation of the mystical teaching of the saint. Finally, the matter under discussion is a question of both "dying with Christ" and "living with Christ". Let us permit the founder himself to continue:

> ... and as I have a firm belief that you will be reborn in Jesus Christ to a new deific life through the celebration of the divine sacred mysteries, I very much desire that you die mystically in Christ more and more each day; and, considering all those butterflies flying about in your mind as nothing, let them disappear in the abyss of divinity: *et vita tua abscondita sit cum Christo in Deo* [Col 3:3].[86]

The reference to participation in the celebration of Holy Eucharist makes apparent the manner in which Paul existentially lived the sacramental mysteries and how strongly they influenced his thought. It also indicates that the notion "mystical" in the phrase *morte mistica* is used in the same sense as it is used in the sacramental mysteries,[87] and that the word *mysticism* in the thinking of the saint referred more to an intense and existential form of faith than to phenomenal and extraordinary events of religious life.

The importance of interiorization. When Paul used the metaphor of butterflies' flying about trying to move the spirit in another direction, he introduced a dimension that, more often than not, is in complete accord with the phrase *mystical death,* namely, correct interiorization. At the same time, his use of phrases such as *detachment from all created things* (*staccamento da tutto il creato*) and the need *to die to everything that is not God* (*morire a tutto quello, che non è Dio*) are not to be thought of as statements of frustration, excuses for making an embittered withdrawal from the world, or indicators of a rigorous asceticism. Rather, the aim and meaning of such a "death" were, for Paul, legitimate and

---

[84] "La vita dei veri servi ed amici di Dio è di morir ogni giorno: 'Quotidie morimur: mortui enim estis et vita vestra abscondita est cum Christo in Deo.'—Or questa è quella morte mistica che io desidero in lei" (L 1:787, Dec. 29, 1768).

[85] See Surius-Tauler, 154, 502f., 626f., et passim.

[86] " ... e siccome nella celebrazione dei Divini Sacrosanti Misteri, ho tutta la fiducia che sarà rinato in Gesù Cristo ad una nuova vita deifica, così bramo che muoia in Cristo misticamente ogni giorno più e lasci sparire tante farfalle che le svolazzano per la mente, di cose da nulla, nell'abisso della Divinità, 'et vita tua abscondita sit cum Christo in Deo'" (L 1:788).

[87] The strong connection between the notions of "mysticism" and "mystery" in the spiritual-theological tradition has been convincingly demonstrated several times. See L. Bouyer, " 'Mystisch'—Zur Geschichte eines Wortes", 57–75, esp. 64–73. Also see H. de Lubac, "Christliche Mystik in Begegnung mit den Weltreligionen", 77–110, esp. 87–93.

fruitful only if grounded in a death "in" and "with" Christ. Greater union with Christ and a more intense intimacy with God—these were the end points of "mystical death" as intended by the saint.

The word *death* alludes to an important facet in the life of every person: its end. The seriousness of the unavoidable reality expressed in this notion effects in many who do not understand their being and existence from a deeply religious viewpoint a certain aversion to using the term, especially when it is a matter of speaking of the end of one's own life.

One might think that when St. Paul of the Cross spoke of mystical death that this notion was devoid of its existential seriousness and that it served merely as an ascetical-technical term. That the founder understood this notion with all its existential profundity, however, is indicated by the following quotation from one of his letters:

> Many a year ago, I spoke once with a poor, ill man from the region of Naples, and he told me, "Listen, my father. I think of nothing but one thing." "And", I asked him, "of what do you think?" And he, "I always think of my death." "This is good", I replied; and I gave him other, well-intended advice.[88]

The fact that the founder, at the time of writing this letter, had already on several occasions "settled" his earthly affairs and had looked at death "in the face" (in the true sense of the word)[89] allows us to gauge the depth with which he spoke of mystical death. Once we realize how serious he was, it may then amaze us—or we may be inclined to think of his words as indiscreet or harsh—when we read that he wrote of mystical death to those near physical death and of his desire for them "to die mystically in pure love".[90]

---

[88] "Molti anni sono parlavo con un poverello infermo napoletano, e mi diceva: Senti Padre mio: io penso in coppa ad una cosa sola. E che pensi? gli risposi io. Ed egli: Penso in coppa alla morte. Fai bene, replicai, e gli diedi altri salutari avvisi ecc" (L 1:788).

[89] See Bialas, *Im Zeichen des Kreuzes,* 54–62.

[90] On Oct. 7, 1755, Paul writes the following to Sr. Colomba Gertrude Gandolfi: "Aspettavo la nuova dal P. Confessore della vostra morte e sepoltura, per celebrare la santa messa in suffragio dell'anima vostra, ma siccome non ho avuto altra notizia, stante la mia assenza, così suppongo che siate ancora viva e ristabilita in mediocre salute, sebbene vorrei sentirvi morta e morta misticamente nel puro amore. Loderò la divina misericordia in sentire qualche notizia del vostro spirito e godrò che mi diate nuova della vostra preziosa morte mistica e se l'amore purissimo dello Sposo Celeste vi abbia ancor crocifissa e sepolta nell'abisso della sua divina carità." / "I was waiting for news of your death and burial from your father confessor in order to celebrate Holy Mass for your soul, but, as I had not received any news in my absence, I supposed you are still living and have recovered your mediocre health. Know well I would like that you were dead and mystically dead in a pure love. I will laud the divine mercy when I receive any news about your soul, and I will be glad to hear of your precious mystical death, and let me know if the purest love of the heavenly Spouse keeps you still crucified and buried in the abyss

Let us return to the letter of 1768 in which he writes to his fellow religious and friend Thomas Fossi:

> My dear Thomas, think always of mystical death. Whoever is mystically dead thinks of nothing except living a Godlike life; he wants no other object save the great and good God and leaves aside all other thoughts, even though they be good, to have one alone: God, the supreme Good.[91]

Perhaps this statement sounds exaggerated, overly exalted. These words, however, are not to be understood from a psychological point of view. Were they meant to be carried out literally they would have, at the very least, condemned the person to complete inactivity. If the meaning is not to be found in a psychological-cognitive plane, then it must be derived from a dialogical-personal one. This is exemplified in the following example: persons, linked one to the other by a bond of deep, unselfish love, preserve the thought of the beloved always in mind, no matter what kind of outer influences or impressions try to distract their thought in another direction. This thought of the beloved accompanies the lover constantly. In the long run, there is not even a concrete thought but a kind of fundamental state, which becomes a part of the self-consciousness of each. For true, selfless love is a power which afflicts the very core of the human person with wounds of sorrow and joy and shapes every life situation.

This personal relationship with God and the desire to be so entirely filled with God that one does God's will alone—the energy for such action lies in the power of personal love—essentially defines what Paul of the Cross meant by his expression *mystical death*. One who possesses such an intense relationship of love with God has a strong desire to do his will alone and to let the Beloved work in him or her. Of this, the saint wrote,

> ... and wait without worry for that which God wants to do, cutting off all that is from the outside [*tutto ciò che è di fuori*] so that nothing will be an impediment for the divine action which takes place in the innermost chamber [*dentro nel gabinetto intimo*], where no creature can enter, neither angelic nor human, but [where] God alone dwells in the intimate space [*in quell'intimo*] or maybe essence, mind, or sanctuary of the soul.[92]

---

of divine charity" (L 2:482f.; in a similar vein, see L 3:73, Nov. 11, 1750, to Canon Gigli).

[91] "P. Tommaso mio, pensa in coppa alla morte mistica. Chi è misticamente morto, non pensa più ad altro, che a vivere una vita deiforme; non vuole altro oggetto, che Dio Massimo, Ottimo, tronca tutti gli altri pensieri, abbenchè siano le cose buone, per averne un solo, che è Dio ottimo" (L 1:788).

[92] "... ed aspetta senza sollecitudine ciò che Dio dispone di esso, troncando tutto ciò che è di fuori, affinchè non gli sia impedimento al lavoro divino che si fa dentro nel gabinetto intimo, ove non si puol accostare creatura veruna, nè angelica nè umana, ma solo Dio abita in quell'intimo o sia essenza, mente e santuario dell'anima ... " (L 1:788).

With this assertion, we have penetrated to the center of the saint's mysticism of interiority. Again and again, the founder emphasized in his letters that the "innermost" part of the person, the center of his being, the deepest level of the person is not accessible to any creature. He described this innermost part by using a multitude of terms.[93] Certainly Paul's "localizing" of divine causality in the human person places him within the grand tradition of Christian mysticism. It would be too much to suppose that he is a solitary following his own way. As we have already noted, he was deeply influenced—especially in terms of his insistent call to interiorization—by John Tauler. Undoubtedly, too, Paul's use of similes such as *gabinetto intimo* and *sanctuario dell'anima* corresponds with Tauler's metaphor of the "ground of the soul".

This mystical death, this self-interiorization and relativizing of all that is created, is not an aim or goal in itself but a basis for "divine nativity". Let us now read how the saint himself described this nativity in the letter to Thomas Fossi:

> There [in the sanctuary of the soul] human powers wait attentively for the divine action and for this divine nativity celebrated each moment in those having the good fortune of being mystically dead.[94]

As soon as the person, with the help of God's grace, achieves greater interiority and enters into the innermost part of self (*gabinetto intimo*), then he or she attains to a state of inner tranquility. At this point, the powers of memory, intellect, and will are neither active nor productive but remain in a sort of open "passivity", "attentive expectation", or "waiting", as the saint himself expressed it. Even though mystical death concerns itself with the powers of memory, intellect, and will, however, it is basically not a psychological state because the aim and effect of this death is divine nativity, an action (or outcome) of God's grace in us.

"To die with Christ" is another way of expressing the mystical death that serves as a prelude to divine nativity.[95] This death does not allude to or

[93] Additional examples include regno interiore, tempio, cella interiore, gabinetto più intimo dello spirito, ritiro, romitorio, tabernaculo interno, solitudine profonda, deserto interiore, grano che Dio semina nel campo della chiesa, etc. (interior kingdom, temple, interior cell, most intimate chamber of the soul, retreat, hermitage, inner tabernacle, profound solitude, interior desert, grain that God sows in the field of the Church, etc.).

[94] " . . . ove le stesse potenze stanno attente al divin lavoro ed a quella divina natività che si celebra ogni momento in chi ha la sorte d'essere morto misticamente" (L 1:788).

[95] The above-quoted letter represents one of the few places in which Paul of the Cross speaks, for all intents and purposes, of the "divine nativity". As already noted, in the majority of cases, he speaks of "rebirth in the Divine Word Jesus Christ" (rinascere nel Divin Verbo Gesù Cristo). See L 1:526, Dec. 15, 1761, to Sr. M. Cherubina Bresciani; L 1:603, June, 1751, and L 1:783, Sept. 15, 1768, to Thomas Fossi; L 2:522 (no date given), to Sr. C. G. Gandolfi; and L 3:482f., Nov. 5 (year unknown), to Sr. M. Innocenza of the Most Holy Mother of Sorrows.

represent a total isolation of the person. Rather, it is something that leads to greater attachment to God. Accordingly, it is something worth striving for and a cause of happiness for the person who undergoes it.

Paul was quite conscious of the difficulty involved in explaining this concept in writing. He spoke of it in terms of being difficult to explain and easy to misunderstand. He even ended his letter with the following caution:

> This is a letter that delves deeply into mysticism and, therefore, is not intended for those who affect piety but for the mature, etc., and so one must speak of this *cum grano salis* [with a grain of salt], for in this matter one can make a great mistake.[96]

It may be St. Paul of the Cross had before his eyes, at this point, quietistic errors in which mystical death played a role.[97]

Although an examination of this one letter written by the founder to his friend and fellow religious Thomas Fossi has been useful in achieving some degree of clarity with regard to the symbolic language[98] of mystical death and divine nativity, the same two points are also covered in numerous other letters. These will be examined also in order to illustrate further interrelated topics in the saint's spiritual doctrine.

Interiorization and the practice of virtue. An essential effect of *morte mistica* and *rinascita del Divin Verbo incarnato* (rebirth of the divine incarnate Word) consists of imitation—in a perfect manner—of the holy virtues of the Lord. With this emphasis on the practice of virtue, the saint's doctrine is obviously different from the quietistic teaching on mystical death.[99] Altogether it may be said that St. Paul of the Cross' spiritual doctrine is characterized by a surprising balance: interiorization, contemplation, and entering into one's own inner solitude, on the one hand, as well as the practice of virtues and "faith with good deeds" (James 2:14–17), on the other hand, and all equally emphasized.

This balance may be seen in just a few brief sentences taken from the first part of a letter written by Paul to Sr. Maria Cherubina Bresciani. In it, the saint discussed the interconnectedness of mystical death, life in Christ, and the imitation of his virtues. He stated,

---

[96] " ... questo è un biglietto troppo mistico e non è da bizzocche, ma da gente maschia ecc. e se ne deve parlare 'cum grano salis' perchè si può sbagliare molto ... " (L 1:788)

[97] See n. 81 above.

[98] Symbolic language is proper to mystics. Their preference is the use of symbols in speaking. In *Das Mysterium und die Mystik* (97), H. de Lubac makes a basic point: "Any mystical thought must be expressed in symbols." Characteristic words of mystical literature were investigated by the linguist J. Seyppel and reported in the same text in an article entitled "Mystik als Grenzphänomen und Existenzial" (111–53).

[99] See Brovetto: *Introduzione alla Spiritualità*, 36–40.

May the mercy of God grant you still more time in life so that you can become completely crucified with the Divine Spouse by means of mystical death, death to everything that is not God, with a continual detachment from all created things, wholly concealed in the divine bosom of the celestial Father in true inner solitude. Do not live any longer in yourself, but let Jesus Christ live in you in such a way that the virtue of this Divine Savior may be resplendent in all your actions, in order that all may see in you a true portrait of the Crucified and sense the sweetest fragrance of the holy virtues of the Lord, in interior and exterior modesty, in patience, in gentleness, suffering, charity, humility, and in all others that follow.[100]

As can be seen from the above, Paul stressed above all else the acquisition of the "passive virtues", and truly these are the virtues that characterize a Christian's basic mode of behavior—a mode which attained its perfect expression in the life of Jesus, especially in his passion. As evident in the first few lines, the founder had the suffering Christ most in mind, with mystical death being the means by which one is crucified with him. Furthermore, when Paul wrote to his correspondent that after dying mystically it is no longer she who lives in herself but Christ who lives in her, it is clear he was thinking of the Apostle Paul's statement: "With Christ I am nailed to the cross. It is no longer I that lives, but Christ who lives in me" (Gal 2:19–20).

We find this affirmation of Pauline thought, which is the core clause of Paulacrucian Christ mysticism, in other letters in which the founder speaks of mystical death. Thus he explained to Lucy Burlini that "to be dead mystically" means "to be dead to everything that is not God", and it was this same principle that formed the basis underlying his statement "to be detached from all created things".[101]

Later, Paul paraphrased the above-mentioned citation from Galatians in a personal and friendly section of the same letter. He wrote, "Lucy must not live in herself any longer, but in God—Jesus lives in Lucy and

[100] "Ma la misericordia di Dio che la concede più tempo di vita, acciò tutta crocefissa collo Sposo Divino per mezzo d'una morte mistica, a tutto ciò che non è Dio, con la continua astrazione da ogni cosa creata e tutta nascosta nel seno divino del Celeste Padre in vera solitudine interiore, non viva più in se stessa, ma in Gesù Cristo; anzi Gesù Cristo viva in lei, ed in tal forma risplenda la virtù di questo Divino Salvatore in tutte le sue operazioni, acciò tutti vedano in lei un vero ritratto del Crocefisso, e sentano la fragranza soavissima delle sante virtù del Signore, nella modestia interna ed esterna, nella pazienza, mansuetudine, sofferenza, carità, umiltà, con tutto il seguito di ogni altra ... (L 1:508, Sept. 1, 1752).

[101] In a letter of May 25, 1751, Paul wrote, "Se la vostra orazione è frutuosa, massime questa d'adesso, deve tenervi in una morte mistica a tutto ciò che non è Diò, con un'altissima astrazione da tutto il creato, che è lo stesso." / "If your prayer is fruitful, [then] most important for the present is that you must remain in a mystical death to everything but God, with the greatest detachment from all created things, which means the same thing" (L 2:722).

Lucy in Jesus. Tell me, please. Is it so? If it is so, then it is good!"[102]

No doubt this statement from Galatians is to be considered within the framework of the whole Pauline theology of baptism and law.[103] While the Apostle Paul talked of the "natural man" being delivered over to the desires of the "flesh" and as having been "sold into the power of sin" (see Rom 7:14), Paul of the Cross—in a similar manner—spoke of the human "strivings of nature" as being self-centered and as always being "in search of personal gain".[104] Indeed, for Paul, one of the benefits of mystical death was precisely this happy release from a relentless search for personal gain. He described this "holy, mystical death" as being "more precious than life". He went on to say that it consists of a "dying of disordered inclinations and passions". And why? So as not to impede that "most sweet of all quiet of holy contemplation", so that nothing at all may stand in the way of the soul living a "deified life in God: *Vivo ego iam non ego, vivit vero in me Christus*' [Gal 2:20, I live now not with my own life but with the life of Christ who lives in me]. So spoke the loving Apostle Paul, whose name I bear unworthy though I be."[105]

Although St. Paul of the Cross did place this quotation from Galatians within the framework of a Paulacrucian mysticism of interiority, he did not use it to enter into a discussion of its greater link with the Pauline theology of baptism and law. Nevertheless, this Pauline sentence has, for the religious-existential domain, an uncommon depth and force of expression. It is this depth that induced the founder to attempt an explanation of what he understood by mystical death. For both the Apostle Paul and for Paul of the Cross the ultimate goal was an intensely lived union with Christ in faith. It was Paul of the Cross' desire that mystical death lead the person to this goal.

Mystical death and the passion of Jesus. It is not astonishing that the founder of a religious Congregation that has the suffering Lord as the center of its

---

[102] "Lucia non deve più viver in sè, ma in Dio: Gesù vive in Lucia e Lucia in Gesù. Ditemi: va così? Se va così, va bene!" (L 2:722).

[103] See F. Mußner, "Der Galaterbrief", 179–83.

[104] " . . . i moti della natura, che cerca sempre il proprio comodo . . . " / " . . . the movements of nature, that always seek their own comfort . . . " (L 3:756, Dec. 28, 1768, to Marianna Girelli).

[105] In the same letter of Dec. 28, 1768, the saint writes, " . . . e se le inclinazioni naturali ed i moti delle passioni non muiono del tutto, restano però talmente mortificati, che non sono d'impedimento alla quiete sopra dolcissima della santa contemplazione e si cominciano a provare gli effetti di quella santa morte mistica, che è più preziosa della vita, poichè l'anima vive in Dio vita deifica: 'Vivo ego iam non ego, vivit vero in me Christus', diceva il grand'amante Apostolo, di cui io porto tanto indegnamente il nome." / " . . . even though the natural inclination and movements of the passions are not completely dead, they must remain so mortified that they no longer impede the most sweet quiet of holy contemplation [so that you] begin to experience the effects of that holy mystical death, which is more precious than life, since the soul lives a deiform life in God. 'I live, not I, but Christ lives in me', said the great loving Apostle, whose name I so unworthily bear" (L 3:756).

spirituality kept the death of Jesus on the cross before his eyes in a special manner when he spoke of mystical death. In a letter written in 1750, Paul encouraged his correspondent to consider suffering as the "holy cross of Christ"[106] and brought to mind that Jesus, in his suffering on the cross, cried, "My God, my God, why have you forsaken me?" (Mk 15:34). Herein lies the basis of Paul's concept of "naked suffering without comfort" (il suo nudo patire senza conforto).[107] He wrote further,

> Oh, fortunate that soul who, in such abandonment to the divine will without comfort either within [intus] or without [foris], bows the head and says, "Pater, in manus tuas commendo spiritum meum" [Father, into your hands I commend my spirit (Lk 23:46)], and mystically dies to all that is not God, so as to live the divine life in God in the same bosom of the heavenly Father.[108]

By his death on the cross, Jesus descended into the darkness and abyss of death. Yet he did not remain in these dark depths; through the resurrection, his heavenly Father raised him up again to his former power and glory. In the same way, mystical death did not represent for St. Paul of the Cross the terminus of a road walked by the person in his journey to God. Rather, mystical death was a passing over, a passage into divine life, and this "life in the bosom of the heavenly Father" rendered the person immensely glad and happy.

The last section of this letter shows how separate ideas in the saint's spiritual doctrine completed one another. Here, for instance, Paul referred to abandonment to the will of God as a mystical death. Such radical turning to the divine will gives the soul an inner openness to the Divine Thou and facilitates closer communication and unity with him. In order to attain to the fulfillment of this inner potentiality of readiness and unity, it is necessary to restrain the egocentric will of the "carnal" or natural person, however. This does not happen without a battle. Jesus himself on the Mount of Olives underwent an inner struggle in accepting the will of the Father (Mt 26:36–46). Paul spoke of this *fiat* of Jesus in one of his letters.[109] In its very inception, Paul encouraged his correspondent to pronounce together with Jesus the words *"fiat voluntas tua"* (Mt 26:42) in a "pure spirit of faith and love" and, too, to pray with Jesus

[106] In language full of symbols, the saint writes, " . . . che viene a visitarlo in spiritu su la Santa Croce del dolce Gesù, in cui lei gusta i frutti di quest'albero sacrosanto di vita . . . " / " . . . may the holy cross of the sweet Jesus visit you in spirit, the cross in which you can taste the fruit of the sacred tree of life . . . " (L 3:17, Apr. 2, 1750, to D. Panizza).

[107] The phrase *nudo patire* has an important role in the founder's spiritual teaching.

[108] "Oh, fortunata quell'anima che in tale abbandono d'ogni contento 'intus et foris', cibandosi della divina volontà, china il capo e dice con Gesù: 'Pater in manus tuas commendo spiritum meum', e muore misticamente a tutto ciò che non è Dio, per vivere in Dio vita divina nel seno stesso del celeste Padre . . . " (L 3:17).

[109] See L 3:819f., Dec. 31, 1768, to Anna Calcagnini.

his words from the cross, *"In manus tuas, Domine, commendo spiritum meum"* (Lk 23:46).[110] Paul continued,

> Then, in a pure way, die that mystical death which is more precious and more desirable than life. Therefore, abandon your spirit into the hands of God and see then the wonders of love which his divine majesty will work in your soul.[111]

In the Pauline theology of baptism, "to die with Christ" is interpreted as "being dead to sin" (Rom 6:2–11). A more exact consideration of St. Paul of the Cross' fundamental principle of mystical death and rebirth in Christ reveals that the founder's conceptualization of mystical death referred to sin also. In a letter written in 1751 to Lucy Burlini in which he clarified, in a special way, this basic principle of his doctrine, Paul called mystical death an "annihilation" (*annichilarsi*).[112] As previously noted, this *annichilarsi* (to become nothing) was for the founder a manner of speech signifying one's stance before God in one's own nothingness and horrible nothingness, that is, in one's own human fallibility and sinfulness.[113] However, God, who is "All", has liberated the person from the darkness and "horrible nothingness of sin". If, therefore, annihilation or becoming nothing corresponds to mystical death, then whoever is mystically dead is also dead to sin, and, as the saint mentioned in his letter, "the soul is [then] reborn each moment to a new life of love in the Divine Word . . . "[114]

Also, this identification of the expressions *nothingness* and *mystical death* clearly shows how the thought categories in the spiritual doctrine of the founder touch upon one another and sometimes even cross over into one another. It is difficult to limit concepts a mystic uses to convey his experience to concise and definitive formulations. Even though difficult, it would be inappropriate, unjust, and superficial to doubt—on the basis of this reason—

---

[110] In this letter, Paul writes, "Il dolce Gesù dunque stette nella sua divina orazione in agonia e vi sudò sin sangue, e non gli uscì di bocca lamento veruno; solo disse più d'una volta, *'Pater mi, fiat voluntas tua.'* Oh, altissima e dolcissima orazione! poichè in queste divine parole è compendiata tutta la santità. Così fate voi, figliuola benedetta. In mezzo alla più grande desolazione ed agonia di spirito, dite al sovrano divin Padre, ma ditelo nell'intimo centro dell'anima, in puro spirito di fede ed amore. Padre mio, *'Pater mi, fiat voluntas tua.'* E poi dite, *'In manus tuas, Domine, commendo spiritum meum'* " (L 3:819f.).

[111] "E poi morite pure di quella morte mistica che è più preziosa e più desiderabile della vita. Abbandonate dunque il vostro spirito nelle mani di Dio e vedrete poi le meraviglie di amore che S.D.M. (i.e., Sua Divina Maestà) opererà in esso" (L 3:820).

[112] See L 2:724–26, Aug. 17, 1756.

[113] See above, pp. 163–67.

[114] " . . . l'anima rinasce ogni momento a nuova vita di carità nel Divin Verbo . . . " (L 2:724, Aug. 17, 1751, to Lucy Burlini).

the validity of mystical communication.[115] In mysticism, as J. Seyppel expresses it, there is no question of "systematic thought" but rather of "existential thought,"[116] with its characteristic limitations in grammar, logic, and literary expression.[117] If, in the broader context, someone were to ask in what context St. Paul of the Cross spoke most often of mystical death and rebirth in the Divine Word, the answer would be that he primarily used this symbolic pair when the point in question was that of self-withdrawal, interiorization, and correct interior prayer. The founder never tired of encouraging recollection and interior withdrawal to those who placed themselves under his spiritual direction. He asked them to enter into "the interior solitude" (*solitudine interiore*), devoid of all images, and to "plunge into God" in pure faith and holy love.[118] This "introversion into God" (*introversioni in Dio*),[119] as the saint expressed it, permits the soul "to be reborn always to a new life of love in the Divine Word, Jesus Christ".[120]

It is obvious from the above that mystical death and rebirth in the Divine Word, Jesus Christ, were fundamental principles in the spirituality of Paul of the Cross. This observation stands whether or not Paul himself was the author of the treatise on mystical death.[121] We would, however, like only to draw attention to what the founder wrote to the religious to whom he gave the treatise. First of all, he asked her to read often the "directive on mystical death".[122] He then spoke of two things characteristic not only of his own teaching on mystical death but of his entire spiritual doctrine. On the one hand, he encouraged her to practice interior recollection and self-withdrawal,

[115] J. Seyppel writes of the way in which language is used in mystical literature in his article "Mystik als Grenzphänomen und Existenzial", 111–53. See also nn. 87 and 98 above.

[116] In making this distinction, Seyppel is referring to the Kierkegaard vs. Hegel polemic. See Seyppel, 113 and 145, n. 4.

[117] See Seyppel, Secs. V and VI, 121–28.

[118] Paul writes to a Sister of Spoleto, "La sua orazione deve essere continua, cioè di starsene in solitudine interiore . . . spogliata d'immagini, ma in pura fede e santo amore . . . faccia della introversioni di Dio . . . " / "Your prayer must be continual, that means to remain in interior solitude . . . devoid of images, but in pure faith and holy love . . . made through introversions [acts of turning inward] to God" (L 3:337, June 21, 1755, to Sr. M. Maddalena Anselmi).

[119] Paul many times speaks of "introversioni in Dio", in, for example, the letters of Dec. 13, 1764, to Sr. Colomba Gertrude Gandolfi (L 2:515) and of Aug. 17, 1751, to Lucy Burlini (L 2:725).

[120] "In tal forma ogni volta che ciò farà . . . rinascerà sempre a nuova vita d'amore nel Divin Verbo Cristo Gesù." / "In such a way, wherever you will do it . . . you will always be reborn to a new life of love in the Divine Word Christ Jesus" (L 3:337).

[121] See n. 3 to the Preface of this book and pp. 246–58.

[122] The statement reads, "Vorrei che lei leggesse spesso quella direzione della morte mistica, che io le mandai in quel libricciolo manoscritto, che so che molto le gioverà." / "I would like you to read often that directive about mystical death that I have sent you in the little manuscript, which I know you will enjoy a lot" (L 3:610, Sept. 10, 1762, to Sr. A. M. Maddelena of the Seven Sorrows).

recommending to her that "holy solitude and sacred interior desert in which the soul completely alone rests in the bosom of the Divine Father in the sacred silence of faith and love". On the other hand, he asked her to remain true to the practice of virtue, especially "humility of heart, silent patience, gentleness, and charity".[123] Then he introduced the topic of mystical death: "[You must be] dead and buried in everybody's eyes so that God [may transform] you into a great saint, but in the secret holiness of the cross."[124]

In this last citation, the main principles of St. Paul of the Cross' spiritual teaching are once again repeated and clearly explained, namely, self-withdrawal and interiorization along with the practice of virtue. Taken together, they lead men to greater holiness and greater union with God. Certainly, all spiritual masters have had the same final goal, i.e., greater union with God; however, the paths leading to this goal are quite different. The path followed by the Passionist founder and the one which he presented to others received its unambiguous direction from a unique fact in salvation history: the cross and passion of Jesus Christ. We shall speak of this aspect in the following section.

CONTEMPLATION OF THE PASSION OF OUR LORD JESUS CHRIST IN THE SAINT'S LIFE AS A FOCUS AND FUNDAMENTAL SOURCE OF HIS SPIRITUAL—THEOLOGICAL THOUGHT

An examination of St. Paul of the Cross' letters (that source which most reliably provides an authentic picture of the saint's being and thinking) in terms of their totality and content reveals the outstanding place occupied by the passion of Christ. Furthermore, the founder's passioncentrism was no empty theory or teaching derived, in one way or another, from astute reflection.[125]

[123] Following immediately upon the part in which he writes of the "handwritten booklet", Paul further states, "Sopra tutto le raccomando sempre più il raccoglimento, quella santa solitudine e sacro deserto interiore, in cui l'anima sua se ne deve stare sola sola nel seno del divin Padre in sacro silenzio di fede e di santo amore.—Sia fedele nell'esercizio delle sante virtù, massime dell'umiltà di cuore, pazienza silente, mansuetudine e carità ... " / "Above all I always recommend more recollection, that holy solitude and sacred interior desert in which your heart alone can rest, alone in the bosom of the divine Father, in the sacred silence of faith and love.—Be faithful in the practice of the holy virtues, especially humility of heart, silence, patience, gentleness, and charity" (L 3:610).

[124] "Morta sepolta agli occhi di tutti, affinchè Dio vi faccia santa grande, ma della santità segreta della Croce" (L 3:610).

[125] This is not to say, by way of generalization, that reflection and systematic thinking are irrelevant for faith and its works. Nevertheless, there are persons who, by reason of a special gift granted them by God and also through their own decisive collaboration with the grace of God, arrive at some insights of faith otherwise unattainable by objective theological reflection. (With regard to the polarization of religious experience–theological learning, see explanatory words given by J. Sudbrack in "Die Geist-Einheit von Heilsgeheimnis und Heilserfahrung", 9–55.)

If the founder of the Passionists spoke so convincingly and solicitously of *Christus crucifixus*, it was because of his God-given charism. It is very difficult, if not impossible, to find any other objective explanation for this ability.[126]

Characteristic of charismatic individuals is that their *being and acting, life and thought* stand out as a harmonious whole.[127] A charism not only impresses itself upon the thinking of a person but also directly affects the concrete development of that person's life.[128] In the following material, we primarily present some ways in which Paul's passioncentrism was "incarnated" in his life. Lastly, we examine his charism as it may be grasped from a study of his spiritual doctrine.

1. Contemplation of the Passion of Our Lord Jesus Christ in the Saint's Life

In liturgy and throughout the Church year. During the beatification and sanctification processes, more than a hundred persons who had personally known Paul of the Cross unanimously reported the predominant place the Lord's suffering had in the founder's life. A lay brother who had lived in the same cloister with the saint for some years reported that Paul took every opportunity to draw others more deeply into the mystery of Christ's passion. The founder did this so often and so ardently that it was as if he had "always present in his memory" the Lord in his passion.[129] The same fellow religious could still remember well

[126] It is certainly conceivable that some facts in the life of the saint may be interpreted as "possible explanatory causes" of this charism, e.g., his mother's intense worship of Jesus Christ in his passion. (See what has been said of this in Chap. I, n. 13.) Another possible "cause" may be attributed to the physical and spiritual suffering that the founder so often had to endure. These facts alone, however, do not succeed in explaining his charism, but they must be taken into account, as "existential premises leading" to this charism and, at the same time, as its inner component as well.

With regard to the importance of a charismatic to the Church, Karl Rahner states, "Thus, the charismatic is as much a necessary and stable part of the essence of the Church as the holy office and the sacraments". See *Lexikon.*

The question of how Jesus' call is considered a charism for his followers (Mt 8:21–22) may be pursued in the exegetical work of M. Hengel, *Nachfolge und Charisma* (Berlin, 1968), 41–93.

[127] Thus, for instance, St. Francis of Assisi lived radical poverty and conveyed this charism to the Order established by him.

[128] This unity of thinking and acting, however, is not at all just a matter of course in the life of a person.

[129] In the informative process of Vetralla, the following declaration was made by Bro. Barnabas of the Sorrows of the Virgin Mary: "Riguardo poi al voto di promuovere la divozione alla Passione Santissima di Gesù Cristo, se ne mostrò così osservante e premuroso, che oltre di averla inculcata e promossa con gran tenerezza, divozione e lagrime e gran frutto spirituale dell'anime, com'è cosa publica e notoria, era talmente divoto

the self-composure and great unction with which Paul officiated at Holy Week liturgies. On one occasion, the "saint of the cross" himself reported that the liturgy of Good Friday so moved him interiorly that, at the unveiling of the holy cross, he was hardly able to sing the prescribed acclamation Ecce lignum crucis (behold the wood of the cross).[130] Another witness bore testimony that the Passionist founder, while meditating with others upon the way of the cross, was so filled with interior compassion that it was obvious he was deeply moved when making introductory meditations at each station.[131]

It has been handed down to us that, even as a young man still living with his family, the founder celebrated Friday as a special day. In the informative process of Alessandria his sister Teresa Danei related that he performed special penitential exercises on Fridays.[132] Because Friday was the day our Lord offered his life on a cross for humankind, it was of real import to Paul that he commemorate it in a special manner.[133]

Although we have not learned from others the way in which he celebrated Friday as the "day of the passion of Christ", Paul himself often spoke of it. In the Epilogue of the original edition of the Rule of the Order, we find the request that members of the new Congregation practice special exercises of penance on Friday and take upon themselves voluntary sacrifices. Paul wrote,

---

della medesima, che spesso parlava de' di lei misteri; onde sembrava che la portasse sempre scolpita nella memoria." / "Regarding then the vow of promoting devotion to the most holy passion of Jesus Christ, he showed himself to be so observant and so eager, that—besides the fact that he inculcated it and promoted it with great tenderness, [with] piety [to the point of] tears and with great spiritual fruit for the soul, as everyone very well knows—his devotion was so great that he often spoke of its mysteries as if he had them preserved, carved in his memory" (POV, 1275r., Processi 1:577).

[130] The exact text reads, "Le sagre funzioni della settimana santa le celebrava con i medesimi sentimenti di dolore e con lagrime; e fra l'altre mi ricordo che nella funzione del venerdì santo, allo scoprire del crocifisso e nel proferire quelle parole: 'Ecce lignum crucis,' prorompeva in un dirotto pianto." / "The sacred offices of Holy Week were said by him with the same feelings of sorrow and with tears, and, among other things, I remember that, during the showing of the cross on Good Friday, when the crucifix was unveiled, and when he said the words 'Ecce lignum crucis', he burst into tears openly" (ibid.).

[131] The following is written in the acts of the process: "Diede dunque principio il Servo di Dio ed ad ogni stazione faceva una piccola, ma fervorosissima riflessione, con tanto affetto, sentimento e lagrime di tenerezza, che a tutti eccitava non solo la divozione, ma ancora le lagrime." / "Therefore, the servant of God began [the Way of the Cross] and at every station he made a small but very fervent meditation and with so much affection, sentiment, and tears of love that [it] excited not only devotion but tears also" (POV, 577v.–578r., Processi 1:258, testimony of Br. Paschal of Mary Most Holy).

[132] See POV, 119v.–120r. (Processi 1:26), and POV, 128v. (Processi 1:29).

[133] See Pompilio, 7–13; and Storia Critica 2:1174–77, 1428–30.

Oh, dearly beloved, one who really loves [is one who] whenever Friday is brought to mind has cause to die. To say "Friday" is to say the day when my God-Made-Man suffered so much for me that he gave his life by dying on the hard wood of the cross.[134]

In the diary entry of Dec. 20, 1720, Paul called Friday "a sad and sorrowful day", the remembrance of which "could make one collapse with sorrow".[135] Some sixteen years later, St. Paul of the Cross again wrote of the meaning of Friday in a letter to Agnes Grazi. He emphasized that Friday was a day to commemorate the sufferings of the Sorrowful Mother[136] and the passion of our Lord Jesus Christ. Furthermore, the Passionist founder desired that the sorrows of the Mother of God and those of Jesus' passion be engraved upon the hearts of all "so that the world be kindled by holy love".[137] Herein, it is obvious that the founder's real aim of contemplating the suffering Lord was not to sorrow and mourn but to attain a deeper union of love with God.

The saint's depth of participation in the liturgical celebration of the sacred triduum (*triduum sacrum*) is apparent in the following statement written on the eve of Holy Thursday:

Now is not a proper time to write but to lament: Jesus has died to give us life. Every creature is in mourning, the sun is growing obscure, the earth is

---

[134] "Oh carissimi . . . in farsi venire in memoria venerdì, sono cose da morire, chi amasse daddovero; perchè il dire è un giorno quando il mio Umanato Dio tanto patì per me che poi ha lasciata la sua SS. Vita, morendo su un duro tronco di Croce" (L 4:220, Dec. 1720, to Bishop Gattinara).

[135] In this entry, he writes, "Mi sovviene che la sera antecedente del Giovedì dicevo che il ricordarmi del giorno funebre e doloroso del Venerdì sono cose da spasimare." / "I recall that on the previous Thursday night I was saying that the remembrance of the sad and sorrowful day of Friday was something to cause great suffering and to make one collapse with sorrow" (*Diario Spirituale,* 72; *Tagebuch,* 88; Rouse, 34).

[136] When the founder speaks of the passion of Christ, he also often mentions the sorrows and sufferings of Mary. Generally speaking, we can say a marked Mariology is manifest in his spiritual doctrine. See "Basilio de San Pablo: La Mariologia en el marianismo de San Pablo de la Cruz" (*Ephemerides Mariologicae* 8 [1958]: 125–38).

[137] In a letter dated Mar. 15, 1736, the saint writes, "Venerdì è il giorno della Passione della mia Santissima Madre Addolorata, ma le raccomandi assai, acció mi restino impressi nel cuore i suoi dolori e la Passione del mio Gesù, che tanto e poi tanto lo desidero, e vorrei imprimerla nel cuori di tutti, che cosi brucerebbe il mondo di Santo Amore." / "Friday is the day of the passion of my most holy Mother of Sorrows. I prayed to her so much that I preserved engraved on my heart her sorrows and the passion of my Jesus, whom I desire much, so much that I would like to impress him upon everyone's heart, so that the world would thus be enkindled by holy love" (L 1:134).

quaking, the rocks are rending, and the curtain of the temple is tearing in two . . . [138]

Undoubtedly, the *drama* of Golgotha was deeply impressed upon Paul's soul at the time he wrote these lines.

Another event mentioned by the founder clearly shows the depth of his interior union with *Christus patiens* (the suffering Christ). After having overcome many great obstacles and after having confronted inexpressible difficulties, the first monastery and a small church of the new Congregation were built on Mount Argentario.[139] The feast chosen (and not just a chance occurrence) for the dedication was that of the Exaltation of the Cross. In a letter, the saint reported the following:

> After no few troubles, the apostolic brief was delivered, and on the fourteenth of September, the Feast of the Exaltation of the Cross, the main feast for our small but growing Congregation, the festive procession and holy dedication of the church and cloister took place. I had the happiness to enter first with the exalted cross and with a rope about my neck. Eight fellow religious came after me . . . [140]

Certainly, the accoutrements of this dramatic procession such as the rope may have been conditioned by the time, since such were common in baroque penitential processions.[141] St. Paul of the Cross, however, was not merely acting so as to conform to the conventional. Rather, his external behavior was an expression of what he thought and was interiorly: a fervent adorer of Christ's passion, one who always had *Christus crucifixus* before his eyes.

How much the saint thought of the mystery of the cross, how he lived it, and how alive and present to himself he made the historical occurrence of Jesus' passion and death are indicated in the following admonition to a Sister who had neglected her duty in the sacristy. Paul told her how her "holy duty" could lead to "constant prayer". He also gave her a "mystical interpretation"

[138] "Ora non è tempo di scrivere, bensì di piangere. Gesù è morto per darci vita; tutte le creature sono in duolo: il sole s'oscura, la terra trema, le pietre si spezzano e il velo del Tempio si squarcia . . . " / "Now is not the time to write but to weep. Jesus died to give us life; all creatures are in mourning: the sun is growing obscure, the earth is quaking, the rocks are being rent, and the curtain of the temple is tearing in two . . . " (L 1:350, Apr. 3, year unknown, to Agnes Grazi). In another letter dated Mar. 26, 1753, Paul writes the following to Sr. Colomba Gertrude Gandolfi: " . . . we are to observe this holy day in which the burial of the heavenly bridegroom is celebrated with an interior emotion of sorrowing love and of loving sorrow" (L 2:450).

[139] See Bialas, *Im Zeichen des Kreuzes,* 38–41.

[140] "Dopo non pochi travagli, uscì un Breve Apostolico, ed ai 14 settembre, giorno dell'Esaltazione di Santa Croce, festa principale della nostra minima nascente Congregazione, si fece il solenne ingresso, e Santa Benedizione della Chiesa e Ritiro. Io ebbi la sorte andare avanti con la Croce inalberata, con fune al collo, e mi seguitarono otto compagni . . . " (L 1:455, Nov. 20, 1737, to Sr. M. Cherubina Bresciani).

[141] See above, pp. 87–91 and pp. 94–96.

for the liturgical objects and vestments needed for the celebration of Holy Eucharist. The saint's elaboration upon the theme is striking in that it reveals how exclusively he kept the Gospel history of the passion before his eyes.[142] His interpretation indicates that the eucharistic feast was, for Paul, the *memoria Passionis Iesu Christi* (memory of the passion of Jesus Christ). This direct reference to the historical suffering of Jesus is not so pronounced when the founder speaks *in general* about the celebration of the Mass or about the Blessed Sacrament.[143] In his spirituality and personal piety, however, worship of the eucharistic Lord occupied a predominant place.

In numerous letters Paul of the Cross wrote of the mystery of the Blessed Sacrament.[144] He referred to it as "sacramental love" (*Amore Sacramentato*)[145] and as sacramental spouse (*Sposo Sacramentato*).[146] Even when the saint, in describing the greatness and inestimable value of this sacrament, did not explicitly refer to Christ, this relationship was for him always operative, because Christ's passion and the Blessed Sacrament were, for him, one—the revelation of God's love for us. Accordingly, he wrote in a letter;

> First and foremost, I take delight in God that you are often plunged and immersed in the most holy passion of the sweet Jesus and in the great

[142] The saint writes the following in detail: "Ha V. R. avuto l'ufficio di sacrestana, ha dunque un impiego santo, un ufficio con cui lei può continuamente fare orazione, mentre l'amitto significa quello straccio con cui bendarano a Gesù Cristo gli occhi nella sua Passione, il camice quella veste bianca con cui lo fece vestire Erode, come se la Sapienza Divina fosse pazza, il cingolo, le funi con cui fu legato dai Guidei, il manipolo e stola altre funi e catene ... la pianeta finalmente significa quello straccio di porpora, con cui dopo la flagellazione fu ricoperto e mostrato a popolo. Queste ed altre cose significa no i paramenti sacri. Il calice significa quel calice che gli presento l'Angelo nell'orto ... La pisside puo figuare sia il Santo Sepolcro in cui fu collocato dopo essere deposto dalla Croce ... " / "You have the position of sacristan, [and] have, therefore, a holy employment, a position in which you can pray continuously, because the amice represents that cloth with which they bound the eyes of Jesus Christ during his passion, the surplice represents that white garment with which he was clad by Herod, as if Divine Wisdom could be made a fool, the cincture the ropes with which he was bound by the Jews, the maniple and stole other ropes and chains ... the chasuble, finally, signifies that scarlet cloak with which he was clad and shown to the people after his scourging. The sacred vestments represent these and other things. The chalice signifies that chalice offered him by the angel in the garden ... the pyx or ciborium may represent the holy sepulchre in which Jesus was laid after having been taken down from the cross ... " (L 4:148, May 20, 1774, to Sr. Mary Magdalen of the Cross). He speaks similarly in another letter written in 1749 (L 1:504, June 18, 1749, to Sr. M. Cherubina Bresciani).

[143] This emphasis may be surprising since relatively seldom has such a strong relationship between the sacrament of the altar and the passion of Christ been expressed (*expressis verbis*).

[144] See Pompilio, 13–17; also see *Storia Critica* 2:1465–1503.

[145] Among others, L 1:194, Aug. 28, 1737; and L 1:213, July 16, 1738, to Agnes Grazi.

[146] See the entries of Dec. 5 and 7, 1720, and that of Jan. 1, 1721, in the spiritual diary. Also see L 3:342, July 14, 1755, to Maria Colomba di Gesù e Maria.

furnace of this *Summo Bene Sacramento,* since there you can drink the fiery rivers of holy love and the treasures of divine grace and the holy virtues.[147]

The frequent use of similes and metaphors in these formulations indicates how greatly the saint was striving to communicate, albeit inadequately, his inner "intuition" of things that moved him deeply and interiorly.

As has been mentioned previously, Paul of the Cross was in favor of frequent, even daily Communion.[148] This practice—exceptional in his day— can be seen as a consequence of his ardent devotion to the passion of Christ, a devotion which was made concrete in the celebration of the liturgy and in the reception of the sacrament.

In his apostolate. St. Paul of the Cross was not a person interested solely in his own welfare and salvation; he knew he was bound to his neighbor and to others and felt himself to be in solidarity with them.[149] Consequently, he was filled with an ardent desire to do his best for them. As one whose life was shaped by a vibrant faith in God and by a deep interior union with Christ, he was aware that these eighty or ninety years of earthly life do not represent all there is. God has made us for eternity and for a life without end. Ultimate happiness or unhappiness (salvation or damnation) depends on the manner in which a person lives his "time of probation" here, on this earth. The person, however, is not forsaken or left to himself, compelled to work out salvation alone. God himself has sent his Son into these earthly "confines", with redemption having been acquired by this same Son's passion and death on a cross. God's will is, therefore, that each reach salvation through the Person of Jesus Christ.

Given this background rooted in basic Christian anthropology, it is understandable that St. Paul of the Cross, desiring the best, devoted himself to people's eternal salvation, above all other considerations. Their salvation was for him a fundamental concern. Even in the earliest available records, this apostolic care of and responsibility for his neighbor was strongly emphasized. How seriously the founder considered this apostolic call is evident in the spiritual diary entry of December 4, 1720, in which—in a rather drastic formulation—he wrote, "I desired to be torn to pieces for the salvation of one soul."[150]

---

[147] "Sopra tutto godo nel Signore che spesso vi troviate immersa ed abissata nella SSma. Passione del dolce Gesù e nella gran fornace del Sommo Bene Sacramentato, perchè ivi beverete a fiumi di fuoco di santo amore i tesori della divina grazia e sante virtù" (L 4:96, July 14, 1768, to Sr. M. Crucified of Jesus).

[148] See above, pp. 71–79.

[149] In his book *Jesus der Christus,* W. Kasper makes an interesting attempt to interpret the salvific activity of Jesus Christ as "solidarity in redemption" (see 254–70).

[150] " . . . e gli dicevo che mi desidererei scarnificato per un anima . . . " (*Diario Spirituale,* 63; *Tagebuch,* 73; Rouse, 31).

An entry on the same day expresses—with all desirable clarity—the inner relationship between the apostolate and the contemplation of the passion of Christ, a relationship that was decisive for Paul's entire life. He wrote, "Alas, I felt that I would die at seeing the loss of so many souls, who do not experience the fruit of the passion of my Jesus."[151] In other words, for Paul of the Cross, the proclamation and contemplation of Christ Crucified was the effective means of leading people to the attainment of their final goal—eternal joy and blessedness in heaven. We find in an earlier Paul, the great apostle to the nations, a no less pronounced emphasis on Christ Crucified when he resolved to know nothing but "Jesus and him crucified" (1 Cor 2:2).

In the previously cited Epilogue of the first edition of the Rule, written in December of 1720, Paul included another obvious allusion to a passioncentric apostolate. The saint was primarily preoccupied that future members of the new Congregation always have the passion and death of our Lord Jesus Christ as a living remembrance in their hearts, and he was concerned that they communicate their passion-centeredness to others. He stated, "And so, let each of the Poor of Jesus take care to instill in others meditation on the suffering of our Jesus."[152]

The above words from his spiritual diary and from the Epilogue of the Rule and belonging to that time period in which Paul was at the very beginning of his call as founder of the Passionist Congregation demonstrate that, even in his early life, contemplation of the passion of Jesus was the preferred content and final goal of his apostolate.[153]

Even in those years when the founder and his brother John Baptist were living more or less the life of anchorites in hermitages in northern and middle Italy, Paul took advantage of opportunities to give pastoral care. Several have testified that he held catechism classes in neighboring parishes on Sundays.[154]

---

[151] "Ahimè! mi pareva languire, vedendo la perdita di tante anime che non sentono il frutto della Passione del mio Gesù" (Diario Spirituale, 63; Tagebuch, 73; Rouse, 31).

[152] "E pertanto ognuno de' poveri di Gesù procuri d'insinuare a chi potrà la pia meditazione de'tormenti del nostro dolcissimo Gesù . . . " (L 4:221, Dec. 1720, to Bishop Gattinara).

[153] What a central place the passion of Jesus had in the saint's apostolate was described by N. Demeck in his work The Master Idea and the Fount of the Apostolate of Saint Paul of the Cross.

[154] At the informative process of Alessandria, Count Cesare Nicola Canefri bore the following testimony: " . . . viddi più volte il padre Paolo andar in giro nelle domeniche per la terra, colla croce portata da lui stesso, a raccogliere non solo i fanciulli, ma gli adulti, e condurli alla dottrina cristiana, gridando ad alta voce: 'Padri e madri, mandate i vostri figli alla dottrina cristiana, altrimenti ne darete strettissimo conto a Dio?' La qual cosa credo si vada continuando in detta terra." / " . . . many times I saw Fr. Paul walking around the country on Sundays, bearing a cross, to gather together not only the children but also the adults to direct them in Christian doctrine and crying out in a loud voice: 'Fathers and mothers, send your sons and daughters to learn Christian doctrine lest you have to give a very serious account to God.' Such a thing, I believe, was continuously happening in the

In a letter written to his spiritual director Bishop Gattinara, about four weeks after the saint's forty days of preparatory exercises in January of 1721, he himself spoke of this apostolate:

> On Sunday, that is, yesterday, I began to go around with bell and cross inviting people to praise God and attend Christian doctrine. By God's mercy, everything went well in an orderly way. For the first time, quite a number of people turned up, and I was very fervent in speaking the word of God. When I went through the streets and on turning around saw the children trooping after me, such was the joy of my heart that I could scarcely hold back my tears.[155]

Although at the time neither priest nor brother, Paul often preached sermons in several churches on Sundays at the special request of the respective priests and with the approval of the responsible bishop.[156] At the beatification processes, some witnesses testified that he was even asked to conduct triduums and lay missions.[157] One witness reported that the bishop of Gaeta, Msgr. Pignatelli, gave the zealous hermit the task of conducting spiritual exercises for seminarians.[158]

---

stated land." See POA, 153r. (*Processi* 2:38); also see POV, 134r. (*Processi* 1:34), testimony of Fr. John Mary; and POA, 186r. (*Processi* 2:47), testimony of his brother Joseph Danei.

[155] "Domenica, cioè ieri, principiai andare attorno con la croce ed il campanello ad invitare le creature a lodar Dio alla Dottrina Cristiana, e per misericordia del Somma Bene, tutto riesce con buon ordine, e per la prima volta, ci è venuto numero particolare di popolo, ed io ancora gran fervore nel dirgli la s. parola di Dio. Quando andavo per la strade, che voltandomi indietro mi vedevo squadra di figlioli appresso, mi giubilava tanto il cuore, che trattenevo con forza le lagrime" (L 1:19f., Jan. 27, 1720, to Bishop Gattinara).

[156] See POA, 135v.–136r. (*Processi* 2:32), testimony of his sister Teresa Danei.

[157] The following was reported in the informative process of Alessandria: "... come in effetto ha celebrato in San Stefano, un triduo con gran concorso del popolo, predicando lui in que' giorni alla mattina e alla sera distintamente, ora agli uomini ed ora alle donne; e si è finito colla communione generale del popolo, e con una processione di penitenza." / "... how in effect he celebrated with the aid of the people a triduum in San Stefano, preaching distinct [sermons] in the morning and in the evening, now to men, now to women; that triduum ended with a general communion by the populace and a procession of repentance as well." See POA, 134r. (*Processi* 2:32), testimony of Teresa Danei. In a letter to Bishop Gattinara, the saint himself speaks of a triduum he is to conduct: "... circa poi al proseguir il triduo o sia ottavario, prenderò quel tempo, che meglio piacerà a V.S. Illma." / "... then, about the triduum to be held, or maybe an octave, I shall choose the time that Your Most Illustrious Reverence considers best" (L 1:27, Apr. 12, 1721). Also see POV, 135r.–136v. (*Processi* 1:44f.), testimony of Fr. John Mary; and POA, 299r. (*Processi* 2:79), testimony of Filippo Damele.

[158] The priest Stefano Mancini, who was professor of moral theology at the time of the informative process of Gaeta, gave the following details: "... e prima, per ordine del detto Mons. Pignatelli, furono fatti gl'esercizj spirituali da tutti li promovendi agl'ordini, e questi esercizj spirituali ci furono dati dal padre Paolo della Croce, benchè allora non fosse neppure ordinato, ma semplice eremita, che dimorava nel romitorio della Madonna della Catena ..." / "... and firstly, by order of the said Msgr. Pignatelli, spiritual exercises were to be

Contemplation of the passion of Jesus was an important part of Paul's preaching even during the saint's initial experiences in "God's vineyard". For example, Canon Sardi, a friend from Paul's youth, testified to this when he spoke of the founder's activity as preacher in Castellazzo:

> He held many hours of prayer: in the morning and afternoon for women, and in the evening for men. He especially directed them in the contemplation of the passion of our Lord Jesus Christ. I myself many times took part in these meditations.[159]

Were one to inquire about the importance attached to contemplation of Jesus' passion in the life and work of St. Paul of the Cross, the answer would have to include consideration of the principal work of the saint, that is, the establishment of the Passionist Congregation. Although in the 1720 Rule, its first edition, Paul named the Order "the Poor of Jesus" (*I poveri di Gesù*),[160] he called his Congregation by another name in the Rule of 1736: "Congregation of the Holy Cross and Passion of Jesus Christ".[161] This name highlighted the characteristic nature and specificity of the Order.

The Rule's first chapter, which dealt with the aim of the Congregation,[162] stated that the goal of the Order consisted not only of leading its members to

---

conducted for all who were to be ordained, and these spiritual exercises were held by Fr. Paul of the Cross, who then was not ordained but a simple hermit, dwelling in the hermitage of Madonna della Catena . . . " See POG, 429v.–430r. (*Processi* 2:145f.).

[159] " . . . ha fatti molti oratorj, cioè alla mattina o al dopo pranzo, per le donne; ed alla sera per gli uomini, esercitandoli specialmente nella meditazione della Passione di Gesù Cristo, alle quali funzioni sono intervenuto anch'io molte volte . . . " See POA, 241r. (*Processi* 2:64).

[160] The Introduction to the Rule of the Congregation states, " . . . e con la permissione di santa madre Chiesa fondare una Congregazione intitolata, 'I poveri di Gesù' . . . " / " . . . and with the permission of holy Mother Church to establish a Congregation entitled 'The Poor of Jesus' . . . " (L 4:220, Dec. 1720, to Bishop Gattinara).

[161] The exact title runs *"Congregazione dei Minimi Chierici Scalzi sotto l'invocazione della Santa Croce di Gesù Cristo, e della Sua Passione"* / "The Least Discalced Clerics of the Holy Cross of Jesus Christ and of His Passion" (*Regulae et Constitutiones*, 2).

[162] In the Italian manuscripts of 1736 and 1741, the chapter is entitled "Del fine dell'Istituto" (On the end of the institute) and in the Latin texts of 1746, 1769, and 1775, "De fine Congregationis" (On the end of the congregation). See *Regulae et Constitutiones*, 2. During the 250 years since the first composition of the Rule in 1720, the text has been repeatedly modified and improved, above all from a linguistic-stylistic point of view, with a few changes in content being made (as of today, there have been nine editions of the Rule, the first six having been made during the lifetime of the founder). In all editions, however, the first chapter represents an essential one for the Congregation. This statement remains true of the redactions both before and after 1959. Until then, the division of chapters and the formulations developed by the founder himself had generally remained the same. At the 1970 General Chapter (the thirty-ninth in the Congregation's history), these old divisions and formulations were changed. Even in the new text, however, the six articles of the first chapter deal with the essence and aim of the Order. See "Fasciculum Speciale: Documentum Capitulare" (*Acta Congregationis* 25 [1970]: 149–51).

union with God through prayer but also of "directing our neighbors to the same goal".[163] Methods to be followed in this apostolate were stipulated at the end of the same chapter. The brethren were to guide people through missions and other pious exercises in meditation upon the mysteries of the most holy passion and death of Jesus Christ.[164] Ordinarily, this was to be done during the preaching of missions, in the sacrament of penance, in conferences, and on other occasions because "this is the most efficacious means of fighting evil and of directing souls, in a short time, to greater holiness".[165]

Such was the concern of the saint to preach *Christus crucifixus* that he required each Passionist to take a fourth vow, binding the person to "further among believers veneration of the passion and death of Jesus".[166] This "fourth vow" will be discussed thematically in another chapter on the Rule of the

---

[163] The exact formulation in the 1741 text of the Rule reads as follows: "E siccome uno dei fini più principali di questa minima Congregazione si è non solamente d'esser indefessi nella santa orazione per noi stessi affine d'attendere alla santa unione con Dio, ma ancora d'incamminarvi i nostri prossimi, instruendoli nel migliore e più facil modo che si potrà in questo santo esercizio." / "One of the principal ends of this least Congregation is not only to apply themselves untiringly to holy prayer so as to devote themselves to holy union with God but also to lead others to do the same, teaching them this holy exercise in the best and easiest manner possible" (*Regulae et Constitutiones, 2*, col. 2).

[164] The original 1741 edition states, "Pertanto i Fratelli di questa minima Congregazione, che saranno conosciuti abili, dovranno (tanto nelle Missioni, quanto in altri divoti esercizi) dare a viva voce ai popoli la meditazione sopra li Misteri della Santissima Passione, e Morte di Gesù nostro vero Bene." / "The members of this least Congregation who are recognized as capable should, therefore, both during missions and in other religious exercises, teach the people by word of mouth how to meditate on the mysteries of the most holy passion and death of Jesus, our true Good" (*Regulae et Constitutiones, 2*, col. 2).

[165] The last part of the first chapter reads as follows: "E questo dovrà farsi ordinariamente dopo la predica della Missione e come si stimerà meglio; dovranno anco promuoverla dai confessionali, nelle conferenze e in altre occasioni, che se gli appresenterano, per essere mezzo efficacissimo a distruggere l'iniquità ed incamminare le anime in poco tempo a gran santità." / "Ordinarily, this should be done after the mission sermon or at some other time that may be judged more opportune. Such meditation should also be promoted in the confessional, during conferences, and on other occasions that may present themselves, since it is a most efficacious means of destroying evil and of leading souls to great holiness in a short time" (*Regulae et Constitutiones, 2,* and *4*, col. 2).

[166] The Congregation's Rule calls this vow "Voto di promovere nei fedeli la divozione alla Passione e Morte di Gesù Signor nostro" / "Vow of promoting in the faithful devotion to the passion and death of our Lord Jesus Christ". It would be a false interpretation of this vow, however, to have it considered only as a special form of "devotion". This superficial interpretation is supported by J. G. Gerhartz in his work " 'Insuper promitto', Die feierliche Sondergelübde katholischer Orden, 203f. The fourth vow deals not simply with the further-ance of a certain "devotion"—even though the term *divozione* is used in the Rule—but rather with the essential charism of St. Paul of the Cross, above all to preach *Christus crucifixus* (see I Cor 2:2). It is possible to look upon this special vow as an "institutionalization" of this charism (see A. M. Artola, "La memoria de la Pasión y el voto especial de los pasionistas", 559–80.

Order.[167] It is not surprising that the founder himself strictly observed this vow, containing as it does the basis of the charism with which he had been so richly endowed.

The great enthusiasm and power of conviction with which he spoke of the passion and death of Jesus during lay missions and spiritual exercises were stressed by numerous witnesses in the beatification and canonization processes. For example, his fellow religious and confessor of many years Fr. John Mary bore witness at the informative process of Vetralla to the following:

> After the sermon, he used to do a brief meditation on the mystery of the sorrowful passion of Jesus Christ with such unction and fervor of spirit that one could see how the audience would melt into tears of compassionate love for the suffering Christ, an admirable attestation of the gift granted him by the Lord to make the Crucified Love known to the world.[168]

Several other witnesses reported that Paul of the Cross himself, whenever he led meditations on the passion of Jesus, was so interiorly moved that he would begin to weep and his voice would flag. As a result, many could hardly keep back their tears. In keeping with this line of thought is the testimony of Don Giovanni A. Lucattini. At the process in Corneto/Tarquinia, he declared,

> Who could not at least grasp if not explain the pious affection with which he spoke of this? When preaching, copious tears could very often be seen in his eyes . . . so that all in the audience, very greatly grieved and moved to compassion by the suffering Divine Good, began to sob and weep.[169]

For northern and middle Europeans, more bent to soberness and impassivity, this may understandably appear to be "emotional exaltation", and one may be prone to label such as "sentimentalism". They need be cautioned, however,

---

[167] Besides what has been said regarding passioncentrism in the Passionist apostolate in the first chapter, we will be explaining in this chapter how each of the brethren not directly involved in the apostolate, especially lay brothers and clerical students, was to fulfill the "special vow". Besides certain prayers of "remembrance of the bitter passion and death of Jesus" to be prayed daily, each member of the Congregation was to "keep daily half an hour of contemplation on the passion of our Lord Jesus Christ" (*Regulae et Constitutiones*, 58).

[168] "Doppo la predica soleva fare al popolo una breve meditazione sopra un mistero della dolorosa Passione di Gesù Cristo con tale unzione, e fervore di spirito, che si osservava l'udienza disfarsi in lagrime di amor compassivo verso Gesù appassionato, atteso l'ammirabile dono ricevuto dal Signore di far conoscere al mondo il Crocifisso Amore" (POV, 168r.–168v. [*Processi* 1:61]).

[169] "E chi può intendere, non che spiegare, con qual pio affetto ne discorreva? Nel discorrere bene spesso vedevasi tramandar dagli occhi copiose lagrime . . . che l'uditorio, grandemente compunto e commosso alla compassione dell'appasionato divin Bene, si scioglieva tutto in dirottissimo pianto" (POC, 412r. [*Processi* 2:542]. Also see POC, 459v. [*Processi* 2:567], testimony of M. A. Lucattini; POO, 190r.–190v. [*Processi* 2:203f.], testimony of Fr. Louis of the Heart of Jesus; POV, 995r.–996v. [*Processi* 1:452], testimony of Sr. M. C. Serafina).

that those from the southern regions feel quite differently. Furthermore, the baroque era was a "time of exaltation".

All these testimonies indicate that the founder, when speaking of the passion of our Lord Jesus Christ, was not preaching distantly "about something"; rather, he put his entire being into his words. This was felt by the audience and gave his meditations their originality and power of conviction. Lucy Costantini, who together with her spouse ceded all their property to the Passionist nuns in Corneto/Tarquinia for the building of their first monastery, summed up her thoughts on the saint's preaching in her declaration that "in this [form of] meditation, the Servant of God[170] was quite singular".[171]

The most important effects of his passion meditations, however, were in the domain not of the emotional but of the existential-religious. Here, we could cite numerous and often extraordinary conversions that occurred and were mentioned in the processes.[172] For example, one witness included in his deposition his own experience of conversion,[173] which occurred during a meditation on the passion given by the saint during one of his lay missions. St. Paul of the Cross himself thought that several conversions prompted by his sermons and meditations, and which did not remain concealed from him, were an obvious "fruit of the passion of Christ". In a letter of 1750, he stated, "Rich were the fruits, excessively rich the conversions—all, however, being the effects of Jesus Christ's grace through the infinite merits of his most holy passion."[174]

In reading the acts of the beatification and canonization processes, one is amazed at the frequency with which witnesses attest to the stirring nature of the saint's meditations and at the high degree of agreement that exists on this point among the depositions. Even taking into account the partialities and exaggerations present in some of the testimonies, the fact remains that his extraordinary charism (to preach Christ Crucified to the world) remains well documented historically. One can affirm with Vincent Strambi, the founder's first biographer, that "somebody would have to have [Paul's] heart and his

[170] Servant of God (*Servus Dei*) is a title attributed to every person whose cause for beatification is being investigated (CIC, cc. 1999–2135, prior to the revision).

[171] "In questa meditazione era assai singolare il Servo di Dio" (POC, 595v. [*Processi* 2:631]).

[172] Examples of astonishing conversions may be found in *Storia Critica* 3:1135–72 and 1200–1206, among others.

[173] See POV, 832r.–833v. (*Processi* 1:376), testimony of Fr. Valentine of St. Mary Magdalen.

[174] "Grande è stato il frutto, sopragrandi sono state le conversioni: tutti effetti della grazia di Gesù Cristo per i meriti infiniti della SSma. sua Passione" (L 3:72, Oct. 2, 1750, to the priest Cesare Macali).

tongue to be able to express well the affection with which he meditated upon the Lord's passion and the fruit he obtained".[175]

In concluding this subsection, however, let us allow the saint to speak for himself. In a letter clothed in symbolic and mystical language and written to the bishop of Viterbo, Paul describes his fundamental conception of the apostolate and its central focus. He states,

> I shall guard the souls of the inhabitants of Viterbo with the same eye with which the merciful Lord has always made me look at people wherever I have been, that is, in the most holy wounds of our gentlest Redeemer — wounds torn and bleeding more because of his infinite charity than because of the hard nails so that [from that delightful stream] they may be given to drink of the saving waters of his grace from these fountains of eternal life [Ps 36:9–10].[176]

2. *The Passion of Jesus Viewed as the "Miracle of Miracles" of Divine Love* (miracolo dei miracoli del divino amore)

As has been pointed out, St. Paul of the Cross lived in deep interior union with the suffering Christ (*Christus patiens*) and took as his own the responsibility to preach *Christus crucifixus*. Because of this, it is not surprising that the paschal mystery, especially the passion and death of Jesus, was the mystery of faith that, more than any other, had a lasting influence upon his thought and spiritual doctrine. What central credence he gave to the *passio Domini* when imparting advice and helping people along in their "path to God" we shall try to examine by an investigation of available records.

The passion of Jesus impressed Paul deeply and lastingly when, at an early age, he set aside forty days of solitude, recollection and prayer to prepare himself for the establishment of his Congregation. During this time he remained in an intimate union of prayer with the suffering and crucified Lord. A sentence in an entry of November 27, 1720 (the fifth day of his preparatory exercises), marked the course or direction of the saint's spirituality: "I said to my beloved Jesus, 'Your afflictions, dear God, are the pledges of your love.' "[177] These words (these existential-experiential terms) contain that faith mystery

---

[175] "Bisognerebbe avere il suo cuore e la sua lingua, per poter bene esprimere l'affetto con cui meditava la Passione del Signore ed il frutto che ne otteneva" (Strambi, *Lo Spirito*, 202).

[176] " . . . e guarderò l'anime dei cittadini di Viterbo con l'istesso occhio, con cui il misericordioso Signore me l'ha fatte sempre mirare ovunque sono stato, cioè nelle Piaghe Sacratissime dell'Amabilissimo nostro Redentore, squarciate ed aperte più dall'infinita sua carità, che dai duri chiodi, affinchè bevessimo *in gaudio,* le acque salutari della grazia in queste fonti di vita eterna" (L 2:339, Sept. 9, 1742, to Bishop Alessandro Abbati).

[177] " . . . le tue pene, caro Dio, sono i pegni del tuo amore" (*Diario Spirituale,* 57; *Tagebuch,* 63; Rouse, 30).

that completely stamped the saint's personality, namely, the passion of Jesus as proof of God's love for humankind.

Paul's "colloquies" (*colloqui*), which he had with the crucified Lord, illustrate the existential depth with which the founder's attachment was anchored to the suffering Lord. In the entry of November 26, 1720, he noted,

> I know that I also had some colloquies on the sorrowful passion of my beloved Jesus. When I speak to him about his suffering, I say, for example: "O my good God, when you were scourged, what did you feel in your most sacred Heart? My beloved Spouse, how much did the vision of my great sins and my ingratitude afflict you? O my Love, why do I not die for you? Why am I not overcome with sorrow?"[178]

Paul also taught those whom he directed this kind of prayer dialogue. In a letter written in 1736, he advised;

> If you are unable to meditate on the passion of Jesus, at least speak to his divine majesty in a loving colloquy: "O my Love! How did your Heart stand it in the garden? Oh, what pain! Oh, how much blood! Oh, what a bitter agony! And all for me!"[179]

These colloquies with the suffering Lord, which pertained to situations in the historical reality of the passion of Jesus, represented a form of prayer practiced with devotion by the saint in his later life, too. They were also an important component of the passion meditations given by him in lay missions. To make concrete and to illustrate the passion in this way, which depended heavily upon fantasy, was meant to prepare an inner predisposition on the part of his listeners or correspondents so as to deepen their insight into the faith mystery of God's love.

On the whole, however, Paul of the Cross recommended this discursive contemplation of Jesus' historical passion relatively seldom in his letters of spiritual direction, and then only when it was a question of persons still being in the initial states of the spiritual life. This does not mean, however, that contemplation of Christ's passion was meant only for "beginners" or that it was meant to be depended upon exclusively, in completely the same way,

---

[178] "So che feci anche dei colloqui sopra la dolorosissima Passione del mio caro Gesù; quando gli parlo dei suoi tormenti v. g. gli dico: Ah mio Bene! quando foste flagellato come stava il vostro Santissimo Cuore? Caro mio Sposo, quanto vi affliggeva la vista dei miei gran peccati e delle mie ingratitudini! Ah, mio Amore! perchè non muoio per Voi? perchè non vengo tutto spasimi?" (*Diario Spirituale,* 56; *Tagebuch,* 61; Rouse, 29; see a similar citation in the entry of Dec. 28).

[179] "Se non puole meditare la Passione di Gesù, ne parli con S.D.M. [Sua Divina Maestà] con qualche colloquio amoroso: Oh, amor mio! Come stava il vostro cuore in quell'orto! Oh, che pene! Oh, quanto sangue! Oh, che amara agonia! e tutto per me!" (L 1:401, June 26, 1736, to F. A. Appiani; also see L 1:108, Mar. 17, 1734, to Agnes Grazi).

regardless of the stage of prayer which the person being directed had attained. In his letters the saint emphasized, as we shall later see, that the individual must never lose sight of the passion. Nevertheless, when the person, by the help of divine grace, has reached a higher level of interiority and has begun to have a presentiment of the mystery of God's love manifested in Christ's passion, then meditation on the passion of our Lord Jesus Christ becomes increasingly "spiritualized". Discursive thought and laborious reasoning give way to interior intuition and existential experience.

There is nothing astonishing, therefore, when we encounter in the Passionist founder's letters references to the passion expressed in a highly spiritualized language replete with symbols. It is not surprising because the favored object of his thought and prayerful reflection throughout his life had been *Christus crucifixus*. While a symbolic way of speaking is certainly neither as concise nor as precise as a conceptual-abstract manner of expression, it does possess greater flexibility and is able to suggest a depth that is expressible conceptually only with difficulty. Symbolic thinking also facilitates the expression of that which is alive, dynamic, and existential. It is understandable, therefore, that symbolic thought is predominant among mystics, since so much of their thinking is rooted in their own existential experience.

This holds true for the Passionist founder also. For example, he often used the symbol "sea". God was for him, above all else, a "sea of infinite charity" (*mare d'infinita carità*).[180] Furthermore, from this sea another proceeds: "The sea of the most holy passion of Jesus Christ, and these two are but one."[181] In this symbolic treatment of the "two seas that are but one", the extent to which the saint found the preexistence of the incarnate Word of God in the passion of Christ becomes clear. For—to stay with the image—when two seas are linked one with the other, to the point of being one, then both seas are filled with the same water. This signifies that the true essence of God is love, and it is this same love that is manifest in the self-sacrifice of Jesus.

When the saint tried to explain the importance the passion of Christ had for the "soul on its path to God", he would speak with predilection of "the sea". He often talked of the need to fish in this sea (*pescare in questo mare*). In a letter to the Carmelite Sister Rosa Maria Teresa of Vetralla, he explained the meaning of this fishing. Even his explanation is useful to us because it presents some aspects of his specific "way", that is, of his own inner mysticism of the passion. The saint writes,

Besides, I want you to go fishing sometimes. How? I will tell you. The most holy passion of Jesus is a sea of sorrows but, at the same time, a sea of love.

[180] See L 1:280 and 283, Apr. 23 and May 26, 1742, to Agnes Grazi. Also see L 1:455, Nov. 20, 1737, to Sr. Maria Cherubina Bresciani, among others.
[181] "...da cui ne procede questo mare della Passione Santissima di Gesù Cristo, che sono due mari in uno..." (L 2:717, July 4, 1748, to Lucy Burlini).

Pray to God that he teach you to fish in this sea; then dive into [its depths]. No matter how deep you go, you will never reach bottom. Allow yourself to be penetrated completely by sorrow and love. In this way, you will thoroughly appropriate the passion of Christ and make his sufferings your own. Fish for the pearls of the virtues of Jesus. This divine fishing is done without words; faith and love will teach you this.[182]

Sorrowful love and loving sorrow (amore doloroso e dolore amoroso). It is significant that St. Paul of the Cross called the passion of Jesus not only a "sea of love" but also a "sea of sorrow". This polarization of sorrow and love, used by the founder when speaking of the significance of contemplating the *passio Domini,* is a fundamental principle characterizing his mysticism of the passion. Even at the time he wrote his spiritual diary, he explicitly mentioned this "double effect" of passion meditation.

In the notes of December 27, 1720, he tells us he experienced a certain spiritual repose.[183] This repose, he writes, is

mingled with the sufferings of my Redeemer, in which the soul takes its delight. Love and sorrow were blended. On this point I do not know how to make myself understood because I cannot explain it.[184]

On the following day, when meditating upon the suffering and sorrow of Mary, the Mother of God, and interiorly reflecting upon it, he wrote, "In my own poor soul, there was a mingling of sorrow and love, with many tears and much delight."[185] Previously, on December 8, he spoke of a colloquy he had with the suffering Jesus. At that time, he wrote that the soul, seeing the suffering of Jesus, remains in a "loving and sorrowful contemplation". For Paul, these were the experiences that constituted "loving sorrow".[186]

---

[182] "Vorrei ancora che qualche volta andaste a pescare. E come? Eccolo. La Passione SSma. di Gesù è un mare di dolori, ma è altresì un mare di amore. Dite al Signore che v'insegni a pescare in questo mare; immergetevi in esso e più v'immergerete, mai troverete fondo. Lasciatevi penetrare tutta dall'amore e dal dolore. In questa forma vi farete tutte vostre le pene del dolce Gesù; Pescate le perle delle virtù di Gesù; questa divina pesca si fa senza parole, la fede e l'amore la insegnano" (L 3:516, Apr. 8, 1758, to Sr. Rosa Maria Teresa).

[183] He writes there, " . . . sentendo con infusa intelligenza, e con l'altissime consolazioni dello spirito un certo riposo dell'anima . . . " / " . . . Through infused understanding and the deepest consolation of the Spirit I experienced a certain spiritual repose . . . " (*Diario Spirituale,* 81; *Tagebuch,* 102; Rouse, 36).

[184] " . . . un certo riposo dell'anima frammischiato con le pene del Redentore, nelle quali l'anima si compiace; si frammischia amore e dolore. Di questo non so farmi intendere, perchè non si può spiegare" (ibid.).

[185] "Si frammischiava nella poverissima anima mia il dolore, e amore con gran lacrime, e soavità" (*Diario Spirituale,* 82; *Tagebuch,* 104; Rouse, 37).

[186] The entry states, "Sappia che nel raccontare le pene al mio Gesù . . . l'anima non può più parlare e sente a liquefarsi; sta così languendo con altissima soavità mista con lagrime . . . e se ne sta così in Dio con quella vista amorosa e dolorosa." / "Know that in talking to my Jesus

Because the passion of Jesus is the "greatest and most stupendous work of divine love" (*la più grande e stupenda opera del divino amore*),[187] Paul referred to it as an "infinite sea of love". At the same time, the *passio Domini* is also a "sea of sorrows". In other words, the immersion of self in this passion effects a twofold suffering in the person: the pain of compassion and another pain derived from the awareness of the strong connection that exists between the passion of Jesus and sin. The saint insisted greatly upon this and explained that, during contemplation of *Christus crucifixus*, the soul does not receive love and sorrow as two independent effects. Rather love is permeated with sorrow and, vice versa, sorrow with love. He says, therefore, that love and sorrow are "blended" or "mingled"[188] with each other. In his letters, Paul accordingly played upon the words *sorrowing love* and *loving sorrow* (*amore doloroso* and *dolore amoroso*). Because sorrow and love are so intimately linked with each other, the saint—in a somewhat prosaic formulation—would speak of it as a "mixture". In a letter to a Capuchin Sister, he wrote, "Just as the passion of Jesus is a sea of love and of sorrow, allow yourself, when you are entirely penetrated with love, to become a mixture of sorrowing love and loving sorrow."[189]

In another letter written by the founder to Sr. Colomba Gertrude Gandolfi in the year 1743, Paul clearly explained that, in the long run, love is the true power which changes a person thoroughly immersed in the passion of Jesus. The following letter illustrates the unsoundable depths reached by the saint's thought and the intensity and vitality of his own personal experience:

Love is a unifying virtue that makes its own the pain of its beloved Good. If you feel yourself penetrated from within and without by the pain of the Spouse, then celebrate this as a feast. But I can tell you this feast is celebrated in the furnace of divine love, because the fire that penetrates through to the marrow of the bones transforms the lover into the beloved, and by mingling, in a great way, love with sorrow and sorrow with love, a loving and sorrowful blend occurs, but so united that one cannot distinguish love from

about his own sufferings, sometimes as soon as I have repeated one or two of them, I have to stop there because the soul can say no more and feels that it is melting away. It remains thus, languishing with deep delight mingled with tears . . . and remains thus in God with that loving and sorrowful contemplation" (*Diario Spirituale*, 67f.; *Tagebuch*, 79f.; Rouse, 32).

[187] L 2:499, Aug. 21, 1756, to Sr. Colomba Gertrude Gandolfi.

[188] For instance, on Dec. 27, 1720, he wrote, " . . . si frammischia amore e dolore . . . " / " . . . love and sorrow were blended . . . " (*Diario Spirituale*, 81; *Tagebuch*, 102; Rouse, 36). On Dec. 28, he wrote, " . . . si frammischiava nella poverissima anima mia il dolore e amore . . . " / " . . . In my own poor soul there was an intermingling of love and sorrow . . . " (*Diario Spirituale*, 82; *Tagebuch*, 104; Rouse, 37).

[189] "E siccome la Passione di Gesù è un mare d'amore e di dolore, così penetrata tutta dall'amore dello Sposo, lasciate che si faccia un misto d'amore doloroso e di dolore amoroso" (L 3:465, Mar. 21, 1757, to Sr. M. Chiara of St. Philip).

sorrow or sorrow from love as long as the loving soul takes delight in its sorrow and celebrates a feast in its sorrowing love.[190]

It is amazing to see with what insistence and with what certainty the saint stressed the union between sorrow and love. Here a question may be raised. In general, is personal and genuine love—and, for St. Paul of the Cross, love is a linkage between God and the human person and the human person and God—*always* a union of pain and love? In fact, love means that the person must force open his interior, opening the boundaries that surround the innermost layer of the self, allowing the "you" to enter and letting this entered "you" to become lost in the other. This process of liberation from one's own limitations, this "exodus" toward the "you" is linked—one may say—necessarily with suffering as long as we are here on earth, *in statu viatoris* (in the way of the pilgrim). This is because a person must go out of self, forget self, if he truly wants to find and take seriously the "you" of another. When, in this profound dimension, love is achieved, there is always a moment of sorrow, of suffering. To put this another way: Whenever a person no longer desires to remain merely at the stage of independence, of being only for himself, but rather desires to transcend to the being of another, then self-injury occurs; he "suffers" from love. Surely, the loving person continuously experiences a kind of joy, too, when he abandons self to the beloved, when he is lost in another. Nevertheless, this love is necessarily painful even if it is experienced as a joyful pain.

"Infused pain" (pene infuse) *or the "impression of the passion"* (impressione della Passione). According to St. Paul of the Cross, one essential effect of this contemplative immersion of the self in the passion of Jesus consists of the fact that the soul, in being "penetrated" by love and pain, "thoroughly makes the passion of Jesus its own".[191] This participation in the love and the pain of the passion of Jesus, however, may not be acquired through a person's own effort. Neither does it depend upon a certain technique of meditation, nor is it a necessary consequence of contemplation. Rather, it is a pure gift of God, what is called in spiritual-mystical theology *gratia gratis data.* It is for this reason the saint, when speaking of the effects of meditating upon the passion, spoke of

---

[190] "L'amore è virtù unitiva e fa proprie le pene dell'Amato Bene. Se vi sentite tutta penetrata di dentro e di fuori dalle pene dello Sposo, fate festa; ma vi posso dire che questa festa si fa nella fornace del Divino Amore, perchè il fuoco che penetra sin nelle midolla delle ossa trasforma l'amator nell'amato, e mischiandosi con alto modo l'amor col dolore, il dolore coll'amore, si fa un misto amoroso e dolorosa, ma tanto unito che non si distingue nè l'amore dal dolore nè il dolore dall'amore, tanto che l'anima amante gioisce nel suo dolore e fa festa nel suo doloroso amore" (L 2:440, July 10, 1743, to Sr. Colomba Gertrude Gandolfi).

[191] The quotation, already introduced, states, "Since the passion of Jesus is a sea of love and sorrow, let yourself, when completely penetrated by the love of [your] Spouse, become a blend of sorrowing love and loving sorrow" (see n. 189 above).

"infused pain or infused torments" (*pene infuse, tormenti infusi*) or about the "impression" (*impressione*) of the passion of Jesus in the soul. This conceptual framework and its express content seem to indicate the Passionist founder contributed a note of originality to spiritual-mystical literature, since a similar observation may scarcely be found in any other source.

This *participation* in the love and pain of the passion played an important part in the saint's passion mysticism and was evident even in the early period of his call. In the entry of the fourth day of his forty-day retreat, Paul wrote briefly of his colloquy with the suffering Jesus. He stated, "Then I feel that sometimes my soul can no longer speak, and it remains thus in God with his sufferings infused into the soul, and sometimes it seems that my heart would break."[192] In another entry in his diary, he tried to explain participation in the passion of Jesus more clearly. Finding it to be an ineffable experience reaching down into the innermost part of the human soul, he tried to express this experience in the following way:

> [The soul] remains thus, languishing with a deep delight mingled with tears and with the sufferings of the Spouse infused into her; or indeed, to explain myself better, the soul is plunged into the Heart and into the holy sorrow of her beloved Spouse, Jesus . . . and remains thus in God with that loving and sorrowful contemplation [*con quella vista amorosa e dolorosa*]. This is very difficult to explain, and it seems to me to be always something new.[193]

Paul also often wrote of "infused suffering" in letters of spiritual direction. For example, in a letter to Sr. Colomba Gertrude Gandolfi, he spoke of the "frequent impression" of the most holy passion upon the soul and called this "one of the great graces granted by God".[194]

As the founder always maintained, it is necessary to make the will of God the ruling principle of life, to place hope and trust solely in God, who is the highest Good, who is "All". Furthermore, it is necessary to admit and to recognize the human person's own creatureliness because his littleness and nothingness are manifest "before God". Finally, it is necessary to let this

---

[192] The entry of Nov. 26, 1720, states, "E poi sento che alle volte lo spirito non può più parlare, e se ne sta così in Dio con i suoi tormenti infusi nell'anima; ed alle volte pare che si disfacci il cuore" (*Diario Spirituale*, 56; *Tagebuch*, 61; Rouse, 29).

[193] "Sta così languendo con altissima soavità mista con lagrime, con le pene del suo Sposo infuse in se, o pure, per più spiegarmi, immersa nel cuore e dolore santissimo del suo Sposo dolcissimo Gesù . . . e se ne sta così in Dio con quella vista amorosa e dolorosa; ciò è difficilissimo a spiegarsi; parmi sempre cosa nuova" (*Diario spirituale*, 67f.; *Tagebuch*, 79f.; Rouse, 32).

[194] In a letter of Aug. 13, 1757, Paul wrote, "Una delle grandi grazie che le fa Dio si è quella frequente impressione che fa nell'anima sua della SSma. sua Passione in nuda fede." / "One of the great graces given you by God is the frequent impression of his most sacred passion imprinted upon your soul in naked faith" (L 2:503).

"nothing" be filled by God's "All."[195] When, as the founder explained in a letter written in 1757, a person remains "in the holy desert of one's interior", contemplating the passion of Jesus, then God will give him a share in his Son's passion, that is, a share in love and sorrow. In language replete with symbols, the saint continued,

> [If, while] contemplating the pain and sorrow of the most sacred side of Jesus . . . the sovereign divine Artisan, with his chisel and hammer of love, penetrates you and makes you taste, by impression, some drops of his pain and suffering, do not complain but love and suffer in silence. Even more, lose yourself completely in the sea of the sufferings of your Spouse.[196]

As these words indicate, the effect of this impression of the passion upon the soul is that the person receives a share in the love and sorrow of Jesus. He thus becomes more capable of loving God and neighbor unselfishly and, at the same time, receives power and might to bear suffering. This strengthening in love and increase in ability to suffer may not be acquired by the power of the person but is graciously given to him by God. The person, on his own part, must be interiorly opened to God and, "in pure faith", wholly immersed in the sea of Jesus' passion.

The fact that these *tormenti infusi* are produced by God and experienced only "in pure faith" is discussed by the founder in another letter in which he himself tries to explain better this graced participation in the passion of our Lord Jesus Christ. Let us allow the saint to speak for himself:

> The point Your Reverence does not understand, of making the most holy sufferings of the sweet Jesus your own through love, will be explained to you by his divine Majesty when he so desires. This is entirely a divine labor. When completely immersed in pure love, without images, in a most pure and naked faith and (when it pleases the highest Good), the soul in an instant finds itself wholly immersed in the sea of suffering of our Savior. Then, with the eyes of faith, without knowing how, the soul understands all its suffering, because the passion of Jesus is a work of love; and, when totally lost in God, who is charity, who is all love, the soul becomes a blend of love and sorrow, since it remains completely penetrated by and wholly immersed

---

[195] The saint very often presents complete resignation to the Divine Will (*rassegnazione alla Divina Volontà*) and remaining in one's nothingness (*stare nel suo nichilo*) as prior conditions for receiving the grace of the *tormenti infuse* (see, for example, L 1:488f. and 3:149 and 515f., among others).

[196] " . . . contemplando nel Costato SSmo. di Gesù le sue pene, i suoi dolori, e nel tempo stesso il sovrano divino artefice collo scalpello e il martello dell'amore la penetra col farle gustare per impressione qualche goccia de' suoi dolori e pene, non abbia ardire die lamentarsi, ma ami e peni in silenzio, anzi si perda tutta nel mare delle pene dello Sposo" (L 3:465, Mar. 21, 1757, to Sr. M. Chiara of St. Philip).

in sorrowing love and in loving sorrow: *Opus Dei* [the work of God] . . . [197]

In reading these lines, one can see how difficult it was for the saint to describe adequately the manner in which a person received these *tormenti infusi* within the dimension of faith. Clearly explained, however, is the fact that this "impression of suffering" is a graced event, which takes place in faith—in a radical openness to God. The consequences of these "infused sufferings" consist primarily of the fact that the person, in a freely graced and mystical way, obtains a real share in the passion of the Son of God—or, better said, participates in the love and sufferings of *Christus crucifixus*.[198]

Participation in the virtues of the suffering Jesus: "To fish in the sea of the passion of Jesus". The previously quoted letter to the Carmelite Sister Rosa Maria Teresa contained two characteristics of the passion mysticism under study here. The saint asked his correspondent "to fish" and immediately explained what he understood by this expression.[199] Completely imbued with love and suffering, she was to fish for "the pearls of the virtues of Jesus in the sea of the passion of our Lord Jesus Christ."[200]

The balance we find in the spiritual doctrine of St. Paul of the Cross is astonishing. On the one hand, he indefatigably encouraged meditation, recollection, and deeper immersion in the spiritual-mystical realm. On the other hand, he required of those he directed an ever stronger and more decisive practice of virtues, as has already been mentioned to some extent in connection with Paul's application of the spirituality of Tauler.[201] This polarity between spirituality and the practice of virtue was also found in Paul's passion mysticism. One may even say that an essential effect of the *impressione della passione*, of the *pene infuse*, consists therein, that is, that the person so

---

[197] "Il punto che V. R. non capisce, di farsi sue per opera d'amore le Pene SSme. del dolce Gesù, glielo farà capire S.D.M. quando le piacerà. Questo è un lavoro tutto divino; e l'anima tutta immersa nell'amore puro, senza immagini in purissima e nuda fede (quando piace al sommo Bene) in un momento si trova pure immersa nel mare delle pene del Salvatore, ed in un'occhiata di fede l'intende tutte, senza intendere, poichè la Passione di Gesù e opera tutta d'amore, e stando l'anima tutta perduta in Dio ch'è carità, ch'è tutt'amore, si fa un misto d'amore e dolore, perchè lo spirito ne resta penetrato tutto e sta tutto immerso in un amore doloroso ed in un dolore amoroso: *Opus Dei* . . . " (L 3:149, July 14, 1756, to Fr. John Mary of St. Ignatius).

[198] Similar interpretations of "infused sufferings" are found in L 1:512, July 18, 1753, to Sr. M. C. Bresciani; and L 2:440, July 10, 1743, to Sr. Colomba Gertrude Gandolfi.

[199] See n. 182 above.

[200] The founder states, "Lasciatevi penetrare tutta dall'amore e dal dolore. In questa forma vi farete tutte vostre le pene del dolce Gesù. Pescate le perle delle virtù de Gesù . . . " / "Allow yourself to be penetrated completely by love and sorrow. In this way you will make all the sufferings of Jesus your own. Dive for the pearls of the virtues of Jesus . . . " (L 3:516, Apr. 8, 1758, to Sr. Rosa Maria Teresa).

[201] See above, pp. 135–46.

graced practices virtue in ever greater measure—primarily, those virtues so visible in the passion of Our Lord Jesus Christ.

For St. Paul of the Cross—and not merely for him—love of God and neighbor, always the ultimate issue for the saint, was not a noncommittal feeling of well-being or goodwill but a power decisively shaping one's thoughts and actions as expressed in relationship to another at the level of a personal "you". When one lives by this primary power of love, which embraces the whole person, he will necessarily arrive at that behavior which we designate as virtue. Love and the practice of virtue (where virtue is thought of in the Christian sense) are closely linked to each other. Love lends virtue a "transcendental power", and the practice of virtue becomes "of necessity, a sharing of the action of love".

According to St. Paul of the Cross, an essential effect of "being penetrated by the passion of Jesus" consisted of an increasingly strong desire to imitate the virtues of the crucified Lord. In his vivacious, symbolic language, Paul explained this in the following way:

> When God takes pleasure in granting you such a grace [the impression of his passion], then you can do nothing but immerse yourself completely in the sea of his most holy passion . . . and therein fish intently for pearls and all other precious stones, since they are the virtues of the divine crucified Bridegroom, in order to adorn yourself well for the purpose of being always a victim sacrificed in the holocaust of the fire of holy love.[202]

For the saint, spirituality and the practice of virtue represent not two opposing paths but parallel ones on the *only* road of perfection. In a letter to Lucy Burlini, Paul urged her to be "humble, patient, gentle, and full of love for everybody", and he immediately adds another exhortation: "Not to neglect interior recollection and self-withdrawal".[203] After having explained the fruitfulness of being immersed in the sea of the passion of Jesus, he continued,

[202] " . . . quando piace a Dio di concederle tal grazia, non può a meno, replico, di non immergersi tutta nel mare della SS. Passione . . . ed ivi fa gran pesca di perle e di tutte le gioie che sono le virtù dello Sposo divino appassionato, per adornarsi bene, affine di essere sempre vittima sacrificata in olocausto nel fuoco del Santo Amore" (L 3:336f., June 21, 1775, to Sr. M. M. Anselmi).

[203] Simultaneously, in one breath, he exhorts us to the practice of virtue and to the practice of interiority. He writes, "Oh, quanto dovete essere umile, caritativa con tutti, mansueta, paziente, aver buon concetto di tutti; fuorchè di voi stessa! Oh, quanto dovete essere amica del silenzio, dello star ritirata, di fuggir l'ozio, ma lavorar e tacere e dentro star con Dio, come ho detto di sopra." / "Oh, how much you must be humble, charitable with everybody, meek, patient, having a good opinion of all but yourself! Oh, how much you must be a friend of silence, of remaining secluded, of fleeing idleness, of working and being silent in order to remain interiorly united with God as I have said above" (L 2:725, Aug. 17, 1751, to Lucy Burlini).

In this vast sea of the most holy passion, fish for the pearls of all the virtues of Jesus Christ. This divine fishing trip in the vast sea of the sorrows of the Son of God is made, however, without leaving solitude or interior silence. Jesus will teach you everything, if you remain humble and dead to all.[204]

In the long run, love—which God imparts through the "impression of his passion" to everyone who has immersed himself in the "sea of the passion of Jesus"—is that virtue which motivates the person and gives him the power to imitate the virtues of the crucified Jesus.[205] A true, genuine love is necessarily actualized in "acts of charity". Love is, therefore, the energy spurring a man or woman on to the practice of virtue. This relationship between love and virtue is described by the founder in a letter written to a religious in the following way:

> Remain in the awareness of your own nothingness and be faithful to the practice of the most holy virtues, especially in imitation of the sweet, patient Jesus, because this [imitation] is the great thrust of pure love.[206]

Paul's above reference to "remaining in your own nothingness" indicates how the components of the founder's spiritual doctrine fuse one into the other and reach their culmination in the mysticism of the passion. In this case, the starting point is the principle of the nothingness of the human person in comparison with the all that is God.[207] In the same letter, Paul referred to the cross of Jesus as being the complete surrender to the will of God or, better said, of "total transformation in the divine good pleasure".[208]

In another letter, this interweaving of characteristic themes of the saint and the emphasis in his thought on the *passio Domini* is brought out even more clearly. First he wrote of the necessary humility one must have before God

---

[204] "In questo gran mare della SSma. Passione, pescherete le perle di tutte le virtù di Gesù Cristo. Questa divina pesca nel gran mare delle pene del Figliuolo di Dio si fa senza partirsi della solitudine e dal silenzio interiore. Gesù v'insegnerà tutto, se sarete ben umile e morta a tutto ecc" (ibid.).

[205] In a letter to Sr. M. C. Bresciani, Paul makes the basic assertion, "L'amore è virtù unitiva, e fa sue le pene dell'Amato Bene." / "Love is a unifying force and makes its own the sufferings of the Beloved Good." He then discusses the effects of *tormenti infusi:* "Restandosene in quel sacro silenzio, in quel sacro stupore, che più innamora di Dio." / "Remain then in the sacred silence, in that sacred languor, that all the more inflames the love of God" (L 1:489, Jan. 2, 1743). Consequently, the more radically and more resolutely a person practices the virtues of the crucified Jesus, the greater is the resultant union with God in love.

[206] "State nella cognizione del vostro nulla e siate fedele nell'esercizio delle ss. virtù e massime in imitare il dolce Gesù paziente, perchè questo è il gran colpo del puro amore" (L 2:440, July 10, 1743, to Sr. Colomba Gertrude Gandolfi).

[207] See content regarding the principle of the human person as "nothing" and God as "All" (*Niente-Tutto*) above, pp. 162–69.

[208] " . . . la totale trasformazione nel Divin Beneplacito" (L 2:440, July 10, 1743, to Sr. Colomba Gertrude Gandolfi).

and of entering into one's own nothingness, a nothingness that must then become lost in the "all" of God, who is love. Then he explained in detail that the soul must suffer mystical death so as to be "born again in the Divine Word, our Lord Jesus Christ". Later, he described this "rebirth of the soul" as follows:

> And if, in such solitude, you are reborn to a new deiform life, that is, to a holy life, the Divine Spouse will lead you to fish in the sea of his most holy passion; fish there, my daughter, allowing yourself to be wholly penetrated by love and sorrow and make your own the pains of Jesus.[209]

The student of the spiritual and theological thought of St. Paul of the Cross will not always find, in express language (*expressis verbis*), references to the passion and death of our Lord Jesus Christ in each of Paul's letters. As demonstrated in the previous section, it is certainly possible to find and to consider other themes and principles characteristic of his doctrine. In terms of importance, the passioncentrism of his thinking, however, is not merely *one* feature of his thinking in line with or *approaching* other principles. Rather, this passioncentrism is the basic source and final goal of his "religious-mystical development". To put it plainly, the suffering and crucified Lord occupies such a preeminent place in the life and thought of the Passionist founder that passion mysticism must be presented as the first and foremost characteristic of his "religious way",[210] a way traveled throughout his long life and one presented to others by him as the best way, more than that, as the *only* way to salvation.

The "insuperable" meditation on the passion. We come upon statements showing us the great stress the saint placed upon habitual contemplation of Christ's passion even in letters that date back to his early period. For example, in a letter written in 1722, he asked his sister to confess frequently so as to receive Eucharist. Then he added,

---

[209] "E se in tal solitudine, è rinata a nuova vita deifica, che vuol dire vita santa, lo Sposo Divino vi porta a pescare nel mare della SSma. sua Passione; pescate pure, figliuola, lasciatevi penetrare tutta dall'amore e dal dolore, e fatevi vostre le pene di Gesù" (L 2:725, Aug. 17, 1751, to Lucy Burlini). The founder speaks in a similar way of the "practice of the Lord's virtues" as a fruit of "mystical death" in a letter to Sr. M. C. Bresciani (L 1:508, Sept. 1, 1752).

[210] C. Brovetto, in *Introduzione alla Spiritualità*, considers the sole principle of *morte mistica–divina natività* as the central idea or *forma mentis* (xii) of the founder's spiritual-theological thought. This interpretation, however, is conditional. The archetypal topos "humiliation-exaltation" must be considered as a basic principle of thought in the foundation of the saint's religious doctrine. Within this field, the principle "mystical death–divine rebirth" represents the clearest expression; and, starting from this point, one can say that this latter principle is the explicit, fundamental axiom of the founder's thought. Yet, from the point of view of content, one ought not consider it to be a "superior" principle. This is so because, before all other reasons, there is the fact that this principle comes to the fore only after 1748, and even then it was often included along with passioncentric statements of the founder.

Let no day pass without praying mentally for half an hour or, at least, for a quarter of an hour upon the sorrowful passion of our Redeemer; and, if you can, pray longer, but at least the time mentioned above should be used for this.[211]

Above all else, the saint considered two things as indispensable in the religious-spiritual life: encounter with the word of God and prayerful contemplation of the passion of our Lord Jesus Christ. The unique importance he ascribed to contemplation on the passion is shown in the following quotation:

> I say to you the best and holiest thing is to think of the most holy passion of our Lord and to pray over it, because this is the way to arrive at union with God . . . in this holy school the person learns true wisdom. Here is where the saints have gained their knowledge.[212]

In the same letter of 1729, the saint explained to his correspondent, the Marchioness of Pozzo, that she is to meditate upon the passion no longer as in the beginning but "in conformity with the inspiration of the Holy Spirit" and yet not to leave behind but to continue to contemplate upon the "most holy life, passion, and death of our Redeemer".[213]

The passion and death of Jesus—and God's love revealed therein—are always to remain a mystery of faith in which the person, inspired by the Holy Spirit, must always plunge himself in prayer and meditation. In this, it is indifferent if the individual is still in the first phases of meditative prayer and is able to bring the crucified Lord to his mind only by means of concrete images, or if he has already attained a stage of prayer called the "prayer of simplicity",

[211] "Non passi giorno che non facciate una mezz'ora, o almeno un quarto d'ora di orazione mentale sopra la dolorosa Passione del Redentore: e se potete, fatene di più, ma almeno questo tempo non si lasci mai" (L 1:54, Feb. 21, 1722). This astonishingly long letter (Paul of the Cross had to have spent several hours in writing this letter—the text fills five printed pages) exclusively contains pieces of advice and recommendations for a true spiritual-religious life. The principles that would form the later spiritual-theological thought of the founder were already present in the letter. Furthermore, we scarcely find in the letter any subsequently abandoned, essential ideas about the spiritual-religious life. Later comparisons show rather a development and a maturation, which clearly must be taken into account.

[212] "Le dico che è cosa ottima e ssma. il pensare alla SSma. Passione del Signore, il far l'orazione sopra l'istessa, e questo è il modo di arrivare alla s. unione con Dio . . . in questa ssma. scuola s'impara la vera sapienza: qui è dove hanno imparato i Santi ecc." (L 1:43, Jan. 3, 1729, to the Marchioness del Pozzo).

[213] In the letter, he further writes, "ma deve avvertire che non sempre l'anima puole fare in quel modo che faceva al principio, e però bisogna secondare gl'impulsi dello Spirito Santo e lasciarsi guidare come vuole S.D.M. Mi dice che non sa fare alcuna orazione che sopra la SS. Vita, Passione e Morte del Salvatore. Sequiti pure questa con la ss. benedizione del Signore . . . " / "But you should realize that the soul cannot always do as in the beginning, and that you must submit to the impulses of the Holy Spirit and let yourself be guided as his divine Majesty wills. You tell me you do not know how to make prayer except on the life, passion, and death of our Savior. Continue this with the benediction of the Lord . . . " (ibid.).

in which interior intuition and an existential encounter take over, or—and according to Paul of the Cross this only happens for a few—one receives from God the gift of "pure infused prayer":[214] the preferred content of prayer always being Christ in his sufferings.

What fundamental and "insuperable" significance Paul ascribed to the contemplation of the passion of Christ may be seen in another letter written to a friend and confidant, Thomas Fossi:

> It's true that the memory of the most holy passion of Jesus Christ with the imitation of his holy virtues is never to be left aside, even if you have a great degree of recollection and the highest gift of prayer, since it is the door through which the soul enters and is led to intimate union with God, to interior recollection, and to the most sublime contemplation.[215]

The words clearly and distinctly emphasize what an important role the saint attributed to meditation upon the passion and to imitation of the virtues of the crucified Lord.[216]

There is, however, another motive that impelled the experienced director of conscience to recommend so continually meditation upon *Christus crucifixus:* self-immersion in the Lord's passion represents a "sure way ... without peril of being misled".[217] To underscore the importance of contemplating the

---

[214] The saint is of the opinion that infused contemplation (*contemplatio infusa*) is the portion of only a few. He writes to Thomas Fossi, "L'orazione altissima infusa le dà S.D.M. alle anime ben purgate e staccate, dopo lunghe prove, e non a tutte, ma a poche, secondo piace alla Divina Sua Provvidenza." / "The highest degree of infused prayer is given by his divine Majesty only to souls well purged and detached, after a long series of proofs, and not to all but only to a few, according to the pleasure of his divine providence." In the same letter, Paul adds that one is not to try to obtain this gift forcibly. He gives the following advice: "Adunque gli insegni a meditare la Passione di Gesù Cristo, i Novissimi ecc., che così faranno gran profitto." / "Therefore, please teach them [Thomas Fossi's children] to meditate upon the passion of our Lord Jesus Christ, upon the last judgment, etc., and thus they will profit greatly" (L 1:625, June 2, 1753).

[215] "Vero è che tal memoria della Passione SSma. di Gesù Cristo con l'imitazione delle sue sante virtù non si deve lasciare, abbenchè vi fosse il più profondo raccoglimento ed alto dono d'orazione, anzi questa è la porta che conduce l'anima all'intima unione con Dio, all'interiore raccoglimento ed alla più sublime contemplazione" (L 1:582, July 5, 1749).

[216] In a similar manner, St. Teresa of Avila considers the meditation upon the childhood of Jesus—but, before all else, meditation on his passion and death—as the gate through which a person enters the mystery of the "Almighty Majesty". In her *Autobiography,* she writes, "I have seen clearly that it is by this door that we must enter if we wish his Sovereign Majesty to show us great secrets" (*Sämtliche Schriften der hl. Theresia von Jesu* 1:208; in English, see Peers, *Autobiography,* 213; also see *Die Seelenburg* 6:166).

[217] In a letter to Thomas Fossi, Paul writes, " ... continui la sua orazione e sempre la fondi sopra i Divini Misteri della Santissima Vita e Passione di Gesù nostra vita, chè questa è la via sicura ... senza pericolo d'inganno." / " ... continue your prayer and always ground it in the divine mysteries of the most holy life and passion of Jesus, our life, since that is the sure way ... without peril of being misled" (L 1:615, May 30, 1752).

passion, the saint at one point, citing the Gospel of St. John, wrote, "Never must one lose sight of this divine example of Jesus crucified." Then, quoting John (14:6), Paul continued, " *'Ego sum via, veritas et vita, nemo venit ad Patrem, nisi per me'* [I am the way, and the truth, and the life. No one comes to the Father, but through me], says the Divine Master."[218]

As it has been shown, the call to interiority occupied a central place in the spiritual and theological doctrine of our saint.[219] Emphatically and steadfastly, Paul urged the person seeking union with God to remain in the "interior chamber", to enter into "that vast solitude . . . , in the ground or center of the soul", and there "to lose one's self completely in that Infinite Good".[220] This entry into the "interior", this "introversion", as the founder often called it, is to occur in a specific manner. In the same letter, he wrote, "Enter there, but enter entirely clothed in the sufferings of the most holy Divine Spouse."[221] These words illustrate how Paul's mysticism of interiority was stamped with passioncentrism.

Because Paul of the Cross was convinced that the continual contemplation of *Christus crucifixus* is the best and surest way to a more intensive encounter and union with God, it is understandable that, over and over again in his letters, he asked those whom he directed to make habitual, and even more than that, daily meditation on the passion. This prayerful contemplation of the passion of Jesus was recommended equally to priests[222] and religious, to

---

[218] "Mai si deve lasciare di vista questo Divino Esemplare di Gesù appassionato. *'Ego sum via, veritas et vita, nemo venit ad Patrem, nisi per me'*, dice lo stesso Maestro Divino" (ibid.).

[219] Refer to what has been said above of Tauler's influence on St. Paul of the Cross, pp. 122–46.

[220] Paul explains to Sr. Rosa Maria Teresa, "State nel gabinetto interiore ed adorate l'Altissimo in spirito e verità. Entrate in quella vastissima solitudine (dico nel fondo e centro dell'anima), ed ivi perdetevi tutta in quell'Infinito Bene." / "Remain in the interior chamber [of your soul] and adore the Most High in spirit and truth. Enter into that most vast solitude (I speak of the ground or center of your soul) and there lose yourself entirely in that Infinite Good" (L 3:515, Apr. 8, 1758).

[221] "Entrate qui, ma entrate tutta vestita delle pene ssme. dello Sposo Divino" (ibid.). When the Passionist founder speaks of "being vested", he has certainly taken this metaphor from Scripture, as in Rom 13:14, "Rather, put on the Lord Jesus Christ . . . ", and Gal 3:27, "All of you who have been baptized into Christ have clothed yourselves with him."

[222] The saint insistently recommends to the vicar general of Alessandria that he take time to meditate upon the Crucified Lord, despite all the work necessitated by his position. In a letter, Paul writes, " . . . anche in mezzo alle occupazioni della faticosa carica addossatale dall'amorosa provvidenza dell'Altissimo, in cui più che mai è necessario confortare e fortificare lo spirito ai piedi dell'Amor Crocefisso nella santa meditazione delle santissime sue pene, dove l'anima, come ape ingegnosa, succhia l'ineffabile dolcezza del santo amore." / " . . . even in the midst of all the work of your difficult office entrusted to you by the loving providence of the Most High, it is, more often than not, necessary to comfort and to fortify your spirit by holy meditation on the most holy sufferings of crucified love, from which the soul, like the ingenious bee, is sucking the ineffable sweetness of holy love" (L 2:364, July 5, 1742).

mothers and fathers,[223] to children[224] and adults, to rich and poor, since contemplation of the passion, according to Paul of the Cross, was the best and surest way to attain greater union with God and the "door through which the soul enters and is led to intimate union with God".[225]

The trinitarian dimension: "in the bosom of the heavenly Father" (nel seno del Padre celeste). The human person has been created by God in such a manner and with such a capability that he can recognize and love the Creator. As formulated in an older theology, the human person is *capax infiniti* (capable of the infinite). This fundamental striving toward God has been expressed by St. Augustine in his *Confessions* in the famed words: "You arouse us to take joy in praising you,

---

To Canon Don Joseph Rotondi, Paul writes, "Non lasci però mai la santa orazione e meditazione, massimamente sulla Passione di Gesù Cristo di cui i sacerdoti devono essere devotissimi, e così il suo interno si conserverà raccolto e sarà più desposto ad accostarsi al Sommo Bene Sacramentato." / "Never omit prayer and meditation, especially on the passion of Jesus Christ, to which priests must be the most devoted. In this way, your interior will remain recollected and you will be more disposed to draw near to the Supreme Sacramental Good" (L 3:422, Apr. 13, 1756).

[223] To a friend and married benefactor who had many children, Paul writes in the following way: "Non si scordi mai di parlare in casa ai figli della Passione di Gesù e dei dolori di Maria SSma; gliela faccia meditare come fa lei, e s'accerti che la di lei benedetta famiglia sarà arricchiata da Dio con grazie inestimabili di generazione in generazione." / "Never forget to speak to your family and to your sons of the passion of Jesus and the sorrows of his most holy Mother; teach them to meditate as you do and be certain that your blessed family will be enriched by God with inestimable graces from generation to generation" (L 2:377, Sept. 28, 1749, to John Francis Sancez).

In a letter to Mr. Sancez's daughter, who was married and the mother of several children, Paul urges her to contemplate the passion of Jesus. Among other things, the saint writes, " . . . e bramo che le resti impressa nel cuore la divozione alla SSma. Passione di Gesù Cristo, acciò possa istillarla ancora nel cuore e nello spirito dei suoi benedetti figli." / " . . . I am longing for the devotion to the most holy passion of Jesus to remain impressed in your heart, so that you can instill it into the heart and spirit of your blessed sons" (L 3:666, Nov. 11, 1763, to Maria Teresa Sancez Zelli).

Also see L 3:196, Oct. 12, 1753, to Dr. Giovanni Benci; L 3:687f., Dec. 22, 1763, to Antonio Frattini; L 2:613, Aug. 27, 1757, to Girolama Ercolani; and L 4:135, Mar. 25, 1770, to Agata Frattini.

[224] Paul recommends to his friend of many years and future fellow Passionist Thomas Fossi that he instruct his children in contemplation of the passion of Jesus. At the same time, the saint adds that the children must not be overloaded, but rather their child psyches must be taken into consideration. Then Paul gives some concrete advice: "Gl'insegni a meditare la Passione SSma. di Gesù con modi facili, semplici, e cominci da un quarto d'ora la mattina e l'altro la sera, acciò non gli venga tedio, ed a poco a poco imparino questo divino esercizio e s'innamorino di Gesù Cristo, e da questo impareranno la modestia, l'obbedienza, l'umiltà e mortificazione ecc." / "Teach them to meditate upon the most holy passion of Jesus in an easy, simple way, beginning with a quarter of an hour in the morning and another in the evening—so that it does not become tedious for them. Thus, little by little, they will learn this divine exercise and will love Jesus Christ more and more and from him learn modesty, obedience, humility, mortification, etc." (L 1:566, June 8, 1748).

[225] See n. 215 above.

for you have made us for yourself, and our heart is restless until it rests in you."[226]

For St. Paul of the Cross, too, the praise of God was the final goal he pursued in life. For him, the infinite God was the sole content of his longing and striving; only in him did Paul's heart find rest. The ultimate goals of his passioncentric, spiritual doctrine were "rest in the bosom of the heavenly Father" (*riposare nel seno del Padre celeste*), "immersion in the infinite ocean of Divinity" (*immergersi nell'infinito oceano della Divinità*), "union with God" (*l'unione con Dio*), as he himself would express it. Certainly, these formulations are images, metaphors, symbols, all weighed down by anthropomorphic insufficiency, all simple descriptions trying to express, through language, the vital experience of encountering God.

There is a basic principle in the spiritual and theological thought of the founder that has never been abandoned: The human person can arrive at union with God *only* by meditating upon the *humanity* of Jesus. This fundamental principle, already clearly formulated, may be found in the entries of his spiritual diary. Among other points, the saint noted the following on January 1, 1721:

> I also knew that my soul was being united in a bond of love to the most sacred humanity, and at the same time liquified and raised to a very deep and experiential knowledge of the Divinity. Since Jesus is both God and man, the soul cannot be united to the most sacred humanity without being at the same time liquified and raised to a very deep and experiential knowledge of the Divinity. This stupendous and most sublime marvel cannot be procured by oneself, nor can it be explained even by one who experienced it.[227]

The principle affirmed here is put forth with such simple formulations that it may be considered banal or trivial if passed over with haste. This principle, however, is undoubtedly the basis of every genuine Christian spirituality, the beginning and the final goal of every specifically Christian mysticism. About twenty years later, we come across this principle again, this time enunciated in a letter sent to Agnes Grazi:

[226] "Tu excitas, ut laudare te delectet, quia fecisti nos ad te et inquietum est cor nostrum, donec requiescat in te" (J. Bernhart, *Augustinus, Confessiones,* 13f; in English, see translation by John K. Ryan, *The Confessions of St. Augustine,* 43).

[227] "Avevo anche cognizione dell'anima in vincolo d'amore unita alla SS. Umanità, ed assieme liquefatta ed elevata alla cognizione alta e sensibile della Divinità, perchè, essendo Gesù Dio ed Uomo non suol l'anima essere unita con amore SS.alla SS. Umanità ed assieme liquefatta ed elevata alla cognizione altissima e sensibile della Divinità. Questa stupenda ed altissima maraviglia non puole nè dirsi, nè spiegarsi nè meno da chi prova..." (*Diario Spirituale,* 85–87; *Tagebuch,* 110–12; Rouse, 38).

... for you cannot pass to the contemplation of the infinite and immense Divinity without entering through the door of the divine humanity of the Savior, by imitating faithfully his highest virtues and principally the deepest humility and annihilation which he so divinely taught in all his actions [see Phil 2:6–11].[228]

After the historical fact of God's self-revelation in the Person of Jesus, there is for us—who have been informed of this liberating entrance of God into history— no other way to life's final goal than the way of faith in our Savior, Jesus Christ, who said of himself, "I am the way, and the truth, and the life" (Jn 14:6). This basic truth of Christianity decisively influenced the spiritual-theological thought of St. Paul of the Cross. To Sr. Colomba Gertrude Gandolfi, he wrote,

... I pray that the Lord leads back your spirit to his divine sheepfold, which is the bosom of the heavenly Father, where one does not enter but through Jesus Christ the Lord, our true God and Savior.[229]

For our saint, therefore, there is one way of bringing the person to greater closeness to God, leading him to "union" with God. This way is the Person of Jesus Christ. When someone considers the spiritual doctrine of the founder, taken as a whole, and especially his mysticism of interiority, then he may observe the presence of a strongly marked Christocentrism. The specific difference (*differentia specifica*) of his spiritual and theological thought, however, resides undoubtedly in his passioncentrism.

Since, according to our author, the *passio Christi* is first and foremost a work of God's love, it is possible for the individual, by immersing himself in the "sea of the passion of Jesus", to enter into the field of attraction of this love and to be drawn closer to the Father. Consequently, the person who wills to undertake this "flight to the heights" in God can best accomplish it through meditation and contemplation upon *Christus crucifixus*. Through the use of symbolic language, the founder described this "ascent" of the soul to God:

I also want to know whether the soul made her flight into God with wings of faith and the fire of love, and also whether that flight was made through the door that is Christ, our Lord, by the immersion of the soul in the sea of

---

[228] " ... non si puole passare alla contemplazione della Divinità Infinitissima ed Immensissima, senza entrare per la porta dell'Umanità Divinissima del Salvatore, con imitare fedelmente le sue altissime virtù e principalmente quella profondissima umiltà ed annichilamento che in tutte le sue santissime azioni ci ha tanto divinamente insegnato" (L 1:256, Aug. 4, 1740).

[229] " ... prego il Signore a ricondurre il suo spirito nel suo divino ovile, che è il seno del Padre celeste, in cui non si entra se non per Gesù Cristo Signor nostro e vero nostro Dio e Salvatore" (L 2:518, Nov. 4, 1766, to Sr. Colomba Gertrude Gandolfi).

his most holy passion, which is the greatest and most astounding work of divine love.[230]

This quotation, filled with imagery, brings out clearly the "fundamental trinitarian structure" of the saint's spiritual doctrine; and the ultimate goal of all striving for perfection consists therein, that is, in the attainment of the greatest degree of union with God or to be "in God", as the founder writes. The means by which the soul can climb or ascend to God are: faith and love. There is, however, *only one* way, *only one* door, through which the soul can attain "to God". This way is Jesus Christ, or better said, *Christus patiens* and *crucifixus.*

The person, however, cannot undertake this "soaring flight into God" with his own energy; he cannot fly unless the Father "draws" him (Jn 6:44). That force by which the soul is lifted up is the Holy Spirit. St. Paul of the Cross writes about this work of the Holy Spirit in a letter to Agnes Grazi in which he again uses his favorite metaphor of the sea. The saint explains,

> Stay alone in your solitude, despoiled of all created things [let] your nothingness be cast by the gentle breeze of the Holy Spirit into the immense sea of the most holy life, passion, and death of our Jesus.[231]

When the founder begins to speak of these deep, interior relationships, which may scarcely be described in words, he stresses again and again that the happenings occur in "pure faith" and "without images" (*senza immagini*). In the same letter, he writes, "All this is done with a single glance in pure faith." To clarify further his thought and to add emphasis, he continues,

> All this is practiced in the most holy Heart of Jesus, because, being entirely united to the most holy humanity of Jesus Christ, the true God, the soul cannot help but abase itself entirely in the infinite ocean of the Divinity.[232]

---

[230] "Bramerei ancora sapere se l'anima faccia il suo alto volo in Dio, con ali di fede e di fuoco d'amore e se questo volo si faccia passando per la porta che è Cristo S.N. abissandosi nel mare della SSma. sua Passione, che è la più grande e stupenda opera del divino amore" (L 2:499, Aug. 21, 1756, to Sr. Colomba Gertrude Gandolfi).

[231] In this letter is written, "Stia nella solita solitudine, spogliata di tutto il creato . . . che è lo stesso suo nulla, sia abissata dall'aura amorosa dello Spirito Santo nel mare immenso dell'infinita carità di Dio, da cui esce quel gran mare della Vita Santissima, Passione e Morte del nostro Gesù." / "Remain in your usual solitude, stripped of all created things [in your own] nothingness, cast by the loving breeze of the Holy Spirit into the immense sea of the infinite love of God, from which proceeds that great sea of the most holy life, passion, and death of our Jesus" (L 1:283, May 26, 1742).

[232] "Tutto ciò si fa con una sola occhiata in pura fede. Tutto ciò si practica nel Cuore SS. di Gesù, perchè stando tutta unita a quell'Umanità SSma. di Gesù Cristo vero Dio, non può a meno l'anima di non abissarsi tutta nell'infinito oceano della Divinità" (L 1:283, May 26, 1742).

To recapitulate, we may say the following about the mysticism of St. Paul of the Cross: The chief goal of the search for perfection is to meet God fully, to come so close to him, in fact, as "to become one" with him. There is *only one* way to reach the Divinity of God, and this way is Jesus Christ, the Son of God and Redeemer of the world. As the passion of Jesus represents the clearest expression and the "most astounding" work of God's love, the *best* way to arrive at greater union with God is meditative self-immersion in the "sea of the passion of our Lord Jesus Christ".

As an epilogue to this section, we would like to also present the Marian aspect of the passion mysticism of the Passionist founder. In one of his letters, Paul spoke of " . . . the great sea of the pains of Jesus and of the sorrows of the most holy Mary",[233] and he urged his correspondent "to throw herself into the arms of the most holy Mary, our Lady of Sorrows, and to run back to her as Mother of Mercy".[234] The saint presented Mary as the greatest model of "childlike simplicity" and "true humility"[235] and praised her, calling her blessed, since she was chosen by God to participate so deeply in the passion of Jesus.[236]

[233] " . . . gran mare delle pene di Gesù e dei dolori di Maria Santissima" (L 1:280, Apr. 23, 1742, to Agnes Grazi).

[234] Writing to Lucrezia Bastiani Paladini some months before his death, the saint stated, "Si getti nelle braccia di Maria SSma. Addolorata, ricorra a lei come a Madre di Misericordia . . . " (L 3:594, Aug. 12, 1775).

[235] In another letter written to Agnes Grazi on the Feast of the Nativity of the Blessed Virgin Mary, the saint speaks of Mary's childlike simplicity (*semplicità fanciullesca*) and true humility (*vera umiltà*), which ought to be imitated. See L 1:321, Aug. 31, year unknown.

[236] In another letter to Agnes written for the Feast of the Assumption of Mary, Paul emphasizes how Mary interiorly participated throughout her life in the passion of her Divine Son (L 1:348–50). See Basilio de San Pablo, "La Mariología en el marianismo de San Pablo de la Cruz", 125–38, *Ephemerides Mariologicae.* Also see N. García Garcés, "Vivencia del misterio de María en San Pablo de la Cruz", 441–73.

EXCURSUS: PAUL OF THE CROSS AND THEOLOGY

Preliminary remarks

If, in this excursus, we attempt to make some suggestions with regard to the essence and task of theology, we do so not with the intent of making a systematic analysis well thought through down to the very last consequence. Rather, we do so only to formulate some ideas that have recurred again and again in this present theological investigation and evaluation of the personality and thought of St. Paul of the Cross. Although we could accommodatingly make the observation that the formulation of the problem presented here has received a great deal of consideration in several theological debates, we must go beyond these bounds if we are to deal properly with the data related to this particular theme.

In presenting the following, our purpose has been, first and foremost, to link together more strongly theological reflection and the exercise of faith and, at the same time, to submit some ideas useful in narrowing the gap between scientific theology and concrete religious life.[1] We do not pretend to give an exhaustive definition of the task of theology. Yet, it seems right and proper to locate this task between the two poles of conceptual and existential thought.

I. The bipolar structure of theology

Etymologically, *theology* means the study of God. Defined as such, theology's first premise is that the human spirit's primordial question regarding the existence of God may be answered affirmatively.[2] The cognitive act leading to this fundamental option is structured in a bipolar manner.[3] One element

---

[1] We are thinking especially of the great theologians of the past who have contributed to our long theological tradition, e.g., Augustine, Thomas Aquinas, Bonaventure, and Anselm of Canterbury, to name but a few. These theological "giants" (it is possible and even advisable to add even more names to this list) are exemplary by the fact that they related and blended theological reflection and religious life into a harmonious whole. See W. Beinert, "Die Erfahrbarkeit der Glaubenswirklichkeit", 132–45.

[2] See Bialas, "Human Suffering", 98f. In Italian see Bialas, "Il dolore umano", 2:53–67, esp. 53–55.

in this structure consists of the argumentative-syllogistical act of human reason. Because this type of cognition is executed on a purely abstract and theoretical plane, the human subject is actively busy. The second structural element is of another kind. It lies in the domain of the personal. Therefore, the human subject, after having stretched his intellect, assumes a passive-receptive attitude of openness and lets himself be impressed by the inner power and dynamism springing from the "Object" of study.[4] This *Getroffensein* calls the human person to do something and requires an answer on the subject's part.[5] We call this answer *faith*. Faith is, however, possible only when the subject is open to God and God himself "communicates" to the individual person the fundamental capability of being a "listener of the word".

This two-part act of knowing God is of great importance for self-understanding and for the task of theology, because every theological reflection is built upon this "fundamental act". Theology must, therefore, always keep in mind this reference to the theoretical-abstract and to the personal-existential poles. Only then will it be able to act powerfully in history and in the transformation of the human person.[6]

Theology should be a help for us (at least implicitly) in the ongoing process of coming to know God ever more fully since, in the view of the passive-receptive aspect that summons us to decision and to active response, the process is never completed once and for all but must be repeated and confirmed. In other words, theology must be answerable to faith; ultimately it is the servant of faith.[7]

---

[3] The valuable suggestions developed and presented to us by J. Ratzinger in his article "Ich glaube an Gott, den allmächtigen Vater", 10–18, played an important role in the following observations.

[4] J. Ratzinger comments in this regard, "What is being spoken of here is direct experience: the knowledge of God and the avowal of God represent an active-passive occurrence, be it either of a theoretical kind or of a practical one; this is an act of *Betroffenseins* [this concept cannot be translated adequately]. Thought and action may respond to it, or it may be freely refused" (ibid.).

[5] The Apostle Paul describes the response in terms of glorifying God and giving him thanks (Rom 1:21). This act of *Betroffensein* plays a great role in the "existential interpretation" of the New Testament, as R. Bultmann has explained in his theology. Undoubtedly Bultmann here touches upon an important concept, although the overemphasis of this element and the conclusions drawn from it do not correspond to the intent of the New Testament.

[6] In terms of its power to transform the person, the power of theology does not primarily reside in the acuteness of its reasoning or in its conclusions. Rather, its efficiency depends essentially upon the measure in which it succeeds in bringing the process of theological reflection into touch with the personal state of "involvement", which is increased by the contemplation of the respective "Object".

[7] Not every theological problem or question is directly or immediately related to faith

A fundamental kerygmatic-mystagogic characteristic belongs to the essence of Christian theology. To create a basic division, such as theology "as a reflection in pure objectivity" and theology "as a practical doctrine of life", does not correspond to the essence of a Christian theology; more than that, such a division goes against the theological spirit. God's revelation of himself in the Person of Jesus Christ, as we encounter him in the New Testament books, is something personal. It takes the form of a personal dialogue inviting us to a free and responsible decision.

God has revealed himself in the Person of Jesus Christ—not primarily but before all else—to impel the human person to progress in knowledge and, even more, to offer a suitable way of establishing a dialogical-personal relationship with him. This fundamental message is manifest in all the writings of the New Testament. In spite of all the diversity present in the efficacious theologies of the New Testament, we find in all the writings and in the groups of writings a consensus with regard to the message, namely, to lead the reader to a deeper belief, that is, to a more enlightened decision for God and to a closer personal relationship with him through the Person of Jesus Christ.

One could raise an objection that a personal-dialogical factor that evokes a decision on the part of the person belongs not within the framework of a solidly scientific theology but has its place in preaching, in spirituality, and in mysticism. The following reply may be given, however. Certainly, on the one hand, there is some content in theology in which use of reflection does not lead to a situation requiring decision but rather touches the personal-dialogical plane only in terms of conclusions drawn and their usage. On the other hand, there are areas in theology which deal thematically with the transmission and exercise of faith. But theology must not limit itself exclusively to the theoretical, to the abstract, to objectivity apart from relationship. If we were to introduce these limitations, we would be outside the realm of Christian theology, which is based on the data of written revelation, and theology would be watered down to nothing more than an arbitrary philosophy and history of religion. What Christian theology must and must not be is not determined by arbitrary shifts in emphasis which proceed from the current status of human

---

in the same way. But will not science's "freedom from bias" be called into doubt by the requirement that theological reflection be based on faith? In answer, it may be said that today absolute freedom from bias has proven to be an illusion. Every science has its "special interests", already presupposed in the reflection process. Thus, for example, natural sciences in their intellectual endeavors always consider feasibility and practicability as "special interests". So also with theology, relatedness to faith is already a legitimate part of the process.

reflection.[8] The essence and task of Christian theology are to be traced to the content and intent of the writings of revelation. Surely, nobody earnestly desires to dispute that the God of the Bible is not primarily the "God of the philosophers" but the "God of Abraham, Isaac, Jacob, and, above all, God and Father of Jesus Christ".[9]

Taking into consideration the bipolar structure of the act of knowing God results not just in a plane of knowledge that is theoretical and abstract or logical and argumentative but also in a theology that has as its task the act of preparing space for a dialogical-personal faith. Hence, theology should be characterized by an immanent, polar tension. To take into consideration both poles in earnest means to avoid ascending, in the extreme, to an academic theory alien to the person or to descend into a skewed, pragmatic doctrine of life.

2. Theology and experience

On the basis of what has been said above and its consequences, it is wise for the practice of theology, viewed as an all-embracing theology, not just to stress the importance of furnishing the "Object" for consideration—reflected upon from a distance and analyzed by the use of argumentative-logical tools—but also to stress the importance of the experience of every person as relevant and of interest to theology, especially every person whose life and thought distinguish themselves so that theology may have the opportunity to focus its attention entirely upon the re-flection, which he employed and which resulted in the commitment of his entire being to this "Object".

This is especially true of saints. Of course, there were saints who tried in their lives to reach the "Object" of theology by "conceptual work" and who thereby entered history as renowned specialists in theology. In addition to these were men and women completely filled with the realization of God, who did not try to ponder this "God" by sophisticated trains of thought but restrained themselves to reporting, in simple words, their "experiences" of their

---

[8] It is certainly the task of theology to attain its respective goal in agreement with the other spiritual disciplines. But this effort should not give the impression that theology may abandon its proper stamp as it draws from the content of Scripture.

[9] It is precisely the relationship of Jesus to his Father that is the starting point from which the humanity and divinity of Jesus can be expressed conceptually. Jesus being "in" the Father is especially prominent in the theological works of J. Ratzinger, insofar as he defines the Person of Jesus as "praying being". Another theology, that of the Evangelical systematist W. Pannenberg, tries (while desiring to overcome the one-sidedness of a "Christology from below" and a "Christology from above") to define the significance of the Person of Christ as the self-realization of God in Jesus (see Pannenberg, "Christologie und Theologie", 159–75).

own personal and existential relationship with God—and, should the occasion arise, to share these experiences with others interested in receiving advice regarding their own relationship to God. Such sharers of their God experience are generally called charismatics, mystics, and teachers of spiritual doctrine.[10] To them belongs our author, St. Paul of the Cross.[11]

St. Paul of the Cross' many letters, of which the greatest part have been preserved in their original form, give us the opportunity of directly and immediately encountering his personality in his expressed thoughts, feelings, intentions, and experiences. These letters (the letters of spiritual direction), written with a strong, personal, and sometimes intimate tone, are not precisely limited to the objective-abstract plane of thought, in which case the content could be called pertinent and informative; but they are written on the personal-dialogical plane.[12] The writer and the correspondent are in an active-receptive position of openness; better said, they meet each other through the exchange of written words. In this way, Paul's personal letters make it possible to draw forth content from the personal-dialogical realm and to make this available to others.

It is significant that intellectual *argumentation* is not a strong component in the letters of St. Paul of the Cross. Rather, he frequently tries to *describe* and *interpret* some facts.[13] Our author does not like to lead a person to deeper knowledge of God or to a greater "understanding" of God by logical conclusions and the stringency of intellectually contrived theses and convictions but by the material content of a theology catalyzed by his own personal experience.[14] Thus, his personal "experience" of faith represents the fundamental source that furnishes the power of conviction that underlies statements in his letters.

Undoubtedly, one who is bound to a unilateral, scientifically objective

---

[10] Such personalities are not automatically written off as of no interest to "scientific" theology, since their radicalness of faith and the logical conclusions they draw from it can be for theology an effective appeal to accept truly its role in laying the groundwork of faith. For the rest, the various charisms with which the saints are often gifted can act as a stimulus for reflecting on individual questions and problems, thereby assuring theological fruitfulness.

[11] St. Paul of the Cross did not write any comprehensive monograph or treatise dealing thematically with the spiritual life. However, the numerous records that have been handed down to us (his letters must be mentioned here, above all) contain enough material to reconstruct his "spiritual doctrine" and explain his "implicit theology".

[12] This has both advantages and disadvantages for the theological interpretation of the material in his letters. Advantages are that, through his letters, we come into contact with St. Paul of the Cross' main theological convictions, their directness, and their "existential setting", and we obtain a better measure of their originality and authenticity. However, the implicit theology, although present and adhering to its own inner logic, is nonetheless difficult to establish.

[13] This is especially true for his letters of spiritual direction.

[14] Naturally, such an existential acceptance presumes a rational assent to the truths of faith. This act of the intellect is only a first step in a total personal encounter.

222 THE MYSTICISM OF THE PASSION

terminology will raise doubts and reservations about someone who would like to introduce the factor of mystical experience into the process of theologizing, because the experience does not allow for deductions or for a meticulous, in-depth scrutiny. Nevertheless, personal experience plays an important role in faith, according to what has been suggested above, and in theology. Take, for example, the various theologies with which we meet in New Testament writings. Essentially, each was influenced by means of the experiences lived first by one and then by another author with the historical and resurrected Lord Jesus.[15]

Current theological discussion examines the role of personal experience on the part of the compilers of the New Testament texts. Here I am thinking, above all, of those theological commentaries that have led to the coining of the phrase *narrative theology*. They begin with the observation that the literary species of narration plays a great role in the New Testament. Certainly, we need to state that these new approaches, not yet sufficiently developed and matured, do not constitute a new kind of theology that will replace or call in question all past theological endeavors. We also need to specify that we do not intend to discuss all the problems raised by narrative theology in what follows.[16] We restrict ourselves merely to drafting some considerations motivated by the spiritual-theological thought of St. Paul of the Cross.

A basic intent of narrative theology consists of its attempt to draw attention to the fact that theology ought not to restrict itself to just the logical plane of thought but that it ought to evaluate better the essence of human communication, which has the capability of speaking to the depths of the human person.

[15] Pauline theology can be presented as a classic and instructive example. It is especially characterized by an intense encounter with Christ, which for St. Paul began on the road to Damascus and continued throughout his apostolic vocation as an essential dimension of his thought. The personal Christ-centered mysticism that comes to light in his letters is evidence of this.

[16] See H. Weinrich, "Narrative Theologie", 329–34. The renowned linguist notes, in bold relief, that the species of narration occupies a prominent place in the corpus of biblical writings. His consideration of the inherent laws proper to narration as a literary species motivates him to propose a "historical science", since "it is especially difficult to understand why theologians together with historians are staring fixedly at a point when it is a question of the truth of a story" (Weinrich, 333).

Weinrich's requirement in general for a greater relativization or even cancelation of the significance of historical facts in theology (a requirement that seems to indicate the entire thrust of this work) raises strong doubts. Here we could reply with something analogous to what has been said before regarding Bultmann's "existential interpretation" and his implicit relativization of historical facts, but we cannot go into greater detail.

Nevertheless, the claim for a theology that cannot be described exclusively as "scientific" and does not consider its only mission to be "discussion and reasoning, *ergo*-tizing and theoretizing" (Weinrich, 331) has its place and is justified.

The importance of the "narrative" in theology and its possible consequences are studied by J. B. Metz in his article "Kleine Apologie des Erzählens", 334–41.

The literary genus "narration" is the type of communication used in narrative theology. By means of several narrative texts found in the writings of revelation,[17] not only is the reader as thinker informed, but also the reader as listener is "required to become an actor in the narration and to follow the narrated action".[18] J. B. Metz, in his contribution *Kleine Apologie des Erzählens,* remarks that among other things theology should "not theoretically consider the category of narration as an uncritical form of expression",[19] because only narration is in the position of articulating through the vehicle of language the original experiences of faith.

Beyond all doubt, experience is an important factor in narrative.[20] A few considerations will make this clear.[21] An important part in answering the question of whether or not the narration is "true" is determined by the personal experiences lived by the narrator and the listener. For instance, when someone is narrating the story of his life and speaks of personal experiences which happen to have been lived in a similar way by a listener, the latter spontaneously expresses such words of approval as "Yes, it is true!" The reason for this approval, for this recognition of truth in the narrator's story, is derived not from logical conclusions drawn but from similarity in the lived experience.[22]

[17] H. Weinrich notes, "For a great part of the canonical text of the Christian Scriptures, both that which is written and that which was once oral consist of narrative" (Weinrich, 330).

[18] Ibid.

[19] Metz, 335.

[20] Metz demonstrates that a theology that disqualifies the category of narration as uncritical and unscientific is scarcely able to articulate the experience of faith, and therefore such a theology has lost its power and capability of mediating the "experience" (Metz, 334f.). In his work, the author tries to present what a broad and new dimension would be available to theology if it more attentively considered the structure of narration. He also warns against the current but all too simplistic distinction "prophecy narrates, theology argues" (ibid., 337). In his opinion, theology has a "narrative structure at its base" (ibid.).

[21] At the end of his study, Metz puts forth a number of questions that lead to an appreciation of when the narrative element in theology possesses great importance. One of the questions reads, "What does it mean to say a story is 'true', and in what sense can one speak about the narrative disclosure of truth?" (ibid., 341). This question provided the underlying motive in our attempt to put forward here some far-reaching questions and to try out some possible answers.

[22] This fact is of importance because the initial impulse in the process of verification is not a theoretical, logical one but an existential, personal one. This does not mean the laws of logical-abstract thinking are not to be applied, but just that they are not the only ones—and, above all, they are not the primary criteria for finding the truth. Certainly, such "existential truth" experienced by an actual subject may be transferred from the sphere of pure subjectivity into the realm of objective argument. Nevertheless, the course of argumentation, by reason of the diversity of different subjects, will not be followed uniformly. The amazing thing is that the ability to identify subjectively with the experience, which is where the whole process begins, is quite powerful; this leaves a certain freedom in the subsequent process of analyzing, though it is still done within fixed limits.

The greater the likeness of the experience, the greater the intensity of approval.

Certainly in this case, much depends upon the personality of the narrator, too. This factor can exert upon the listener such a power of conviction that the narrated story, although not directly identifiable with the listener's own experience, reflects so much evidence of truth that it is rated as personal experience.[23] In this case, identification with the narrator becomes the criterion of identification with the story[24] and not, as in the first case, the result of comparing one's own personal experience with that of the narrated alien experience.

With this attempt at concretizing—which should not be taken as something hard and fast but rather as a clarification of boundaries—it may become clear that for many areas of human life abstract argumentation alone cannot accomplish very much unless it is completed by the personal element. If theology is based on faith, and faith belongs to the domain of the personal, then it must be a fundamental principle that theology must proceed not in a purely abstract way but must also deliberately accept as input that which belongs to the personal domain. To put it concretely: Theology must to a great extent respond to information given by persons who have had intense faith "experiences".

Serious problems, however, are found in this approach. How can an experience enclosed by an almost impenetrable web of subjective reality be relevant to theology? Furthermore, how can theology, which is a discourse about God and which must think of God as someone "entirely other", resort to human experience? To these, one might answer: The basic avowal of biblical writing does not consist in the affirmation that God is, but rather in that he, the Living One, is acting in history,[25] and, furthermore, that this God assumed a human nature and became man (Phil 2:6–11). Furthermore, it has been attested that this God and man, Jesus Christ, lived and suffered, was crucified and died, but "rose again on the third day" (I Cor 15:3) and sent his Spirit as permanent assurance of his active presence. From this, the following may be concluded:

---

[23] Certainly personal experiences cannot be fully communicated to others just by recounting them. Yet the telling—when the listener is receptive by reason of similar experiences of his own—may lead to a further experience. This further experience can have all the power of conviction and evidence of truth as the personal experience itself. See A. Jolles, *Einfache Formen, Legende, Sage, Mythe, Rätsel, Spruch, Kasus, Memorabile, Märchen, Witz.*

[24] This principle is of importance for the faith out of which the compilers of the New Testament saw the Person of Jesus. This faith did not appear (and, above all, was not primarily drawn) from the encounter of the disciples with the resurrected Lord or from the sending of the Holy Spirit (although such events had as a result the development and strengthening of their belief), but it basically was and already had been established through their personal acquaintance with the historical Jesus before the Passover.

[25] Christian theology, therefore, ought to be understood first and foremost as "the narration of God's deeds in the world" (using as model the writings of the Old and New Testaments).

On the one hand, God has given himself in Jesus Christ to all humankind, and Jesus gives himself by means of what we call grace. On the other hand, the human person (through the justifying sacrifice of Jesus) has received the fundamental capability of receiving this self-giving of God, and this is the experience of faith in those whose lives are entirely "open to grace". These faith experiences are not devoid of meaning for theology.

3. The saint's experience of faith

Of special interest are those whose lives have been officially and critically investigated by the Church and proved blameless and who have then been declared "saints" by the same Church.[26] These saints are, therefore, an obvious sign of God's presence and activity in the world.[27] Their thought and deeds represent an existential example of Christianity fulfilled, and the rich experience of their faith sets before theological reflection the task of making intelligible the principles underlying their implicit or explicit theology. The effort put forth in examining their thoughts and deeds from a theological point of view is advantageous for theology itself, since many saints were endowed with a special charism which, by being explicated in a systematic form, can greatly enrich theological discussion.

Deep faith experiences of saints certainly contain a mark of subjectivity, too. That the question in point is a matter of a "genuine" faith experience[28] ought to be presupposed, with the proof having been established in the lengthy and complicated processes preceding canonization. Subjectivity, proper to every experience, ought not to lead from the start to a condemnation in general of such faith experiences as irrelevant and uninteresting. This is especially true when one considers the symbolic character of canonization and when sanctity—as extraordinarily manifested in the saints—is recognized as the action of the Spirit of God.[29]

---

[26] See H. Vorgrimmler, "Heiligenverehrung" in *Lexikon* 5, col. 105f.

[27] The importance of saints in Christian faith is evident by the fact that the article of faith "communion of saints" (*communio sanctorum*) from the Apostles' Creed (where the word *saints* did not originally mean "canonized saints") has been preserved.

[28] We cannot detail here the manifold differences present within the large realm of the "experience of faith".

[29] The subjective factor itself brings a quality of originality to thought and makes it more lively and convincing. Certainly the structural elements of theology in the following exposition can be enriched by the affective-intuitive factor. This distinction would show that in the mystical theology of St. Paul of the Cross, besides his experience, there is a creative-constructive fantasy also operating. Several images and metaphors that he uses are proof in favor of this supposition. It would be interesting and rewarding to analyze, in a separate study, his typical images and symbols and try to find out their "place" in the life of the saint.

Here two objections might be raised. First, is the introduction of a subjective experience of faith compatible with the objectivity required of theology? Second, does a theology fulfill its "scientific" obligation when it has as its first and foremost object a concretely lived and experienced faith mysticism? To the first question, this should be said: If it is a question of expressing the personal being and meaning of the human person, pure objectivity is an illusion.[30] Inevitably, the experience repertoire of the subject[31] and consequent biases— or, more positively, the "interests"—are part of his baggage, even though they be involuntary and unconscious. Certainly, there are various degrees of objectivity, which depend on powers of abstraction and reflection. Yet the subjective element of theology should not primarily be considered as a disadvantage and an obstruction to the progress of knowledge; it has often happened in the history of theology that the intense experiences and insights of a theologian have led to trail-blazing developments in theological thought, and this has led to the development of various theological approaches and schools.[32]

With regard to the second question, one could answer that surely a mysticism of faith such as that found in the life of St. Paul of the Cross does not proceed in itself along the path of a scientifically based theology. Yet it is quite possible that subsequent theological reflection, which takes as its object mystical contemplation, may examine such by using an exact method in a reliable and scientific manner. Given what has been said about the bipolar aspect of theology at the beginning of this discussion,[33] then it appears even favorable and advantageous to include the existential factor in the material for reflection. In such cases, theological debate does not limit itself to the field of argumentation but accepts the plane of personal experience to preserve the basic relationship between theology and faith.

Now let us return to our author, St. Paul of the Cross. If one studies his life and thought in detail, he will soon clearly ascertain that the cross and passion of our Lord Jesus Christ occupied a predominant place. This strong focus on the *passio Christi,* which may be noted in his spiritual teaching and apostolic

---

Regarding the significance of fantasy, see the two-volume work *Die anthropologische Bedeutung der Phantasie* by H. Kunz.

[30] Subjective impulse is more strongly operant in the background of those scientific disciplines that limit themselves to the description of given realities and their phenomena and that use as methods observation and experimentation.

[31] *Experience* is understood here in a comprehensive sense, i.e., it consists not only of the sum of lived experiences but also of intellectual formation and education.

[32] Personal experiences have often led to new insights. In other cases there have been basic realizations that did not remain in the realm of abstract reflection but touched the person in the entirety of his personal dimension. Thus, realization became experience. This "realization-experience" becomes then the basis for further thought.

[33] See n. 1 above.

activity as well,[34] represents something special and remarkable, a charism graciously given him, a gift received by him and transformed by him into a lifelong task. The saint not only saw his own mission therein, that is, to place the crucified Christ before the eyes of all the people of *his* own time (Gal 3:1) but also wanted to preach the "word of the cross" to all peoples of all times, even after his death. That is why he established a religious community in which members commit themselves by vow "to keep alive the memory of the passion and death of Jesus Christ".[35]

Beyond a doubt Jesus' passion and death on a cross belong at the center of Christian faith; and, therefore, *Christus crucifixus* must remain within the range of subject matter available to theologies of all ages, if they are to be truly Christian. Even in today's theology, we can find theologians who focus their entire attention on the mystery of the crucified God. J. Moltmann summarizes the importance of this theological focus upon the cross of Christ in the following words:

> It is important today that the Church and theology reflect on the crucified Christ, in order to show the world its freedom, if they want to become what they claim to be, namely, the Church of Christ and Christian theology.[36]

Another great theologican affirms,

> We can be sure the theme of the cross will determine the theological agenda not just for us and for the immediate future, for if we have to express faith in a way that speaks to the world of today, we cannot speak of faith in God without mentioning the world's suffering.[37]

Without exaggerating, it may be said that in current studies the theology of the cross belongs to those themes stressed especially and discussed meticulously. This explains contemporary interest in the personality and charism of Paul of the Cross. It is certainly of interest and import for theology to find out the thought and theological principles underlying the doctrine of a saint and the founder of the Passionist Order, an engaging lay missionary and mystic.

---

[34] See Demeck.

[35] This vow is written in the following way in the 1736 edition of the Rule: "Dell'osservanza del voto di dover promovere nei fedeli la divozione della SS.ma Passione e Morte di Gesù Cristo." / "On the observance of the vow of promoting in the faithful devotion to the most holy passion and death of Jesus Christ" (*Regulae et Constitutiones,* 56, col. 1).

[36] J. Moltmann, *Der gekreuzigte Gott,* 7.

[37] H. Schürmann, *Jesu ureigener Tod,* 7.

4. The charism of St. Paul of the cross and ecumenism

To conclude these considerations, the import of reflection upon the passion and cross of Christ as a focus of Christian faith and its relationship to the *ecumenical movement* of the Church must be presented. In doing so, one finds that present theological discussion centering on the theology of the cross is not limited to the domain of a *single* confession but is encountered in various Christian theologies. For this reason, a contemporary theologian affirms,

> In any case, this is an astonishing phenomenon, scarcely expected a few years ago, that quite recently the theological work of both confessions[38] after far-wandering excursions into the almost boundless social, corporate, and political domain even to consideration of revolutionary problems has increasingly focused its attention upon its old, proper theme, the discourse about God in the light of the passion and death of our Lord Jesus Christ.[39]

The ecumenist J. Moltmann speaks thematically about the importance of the cross. In the lecture "Ecumenism beneath the Cross", given in Rome at the "International Congress on the Wisdom of the Cross Today",[40] he called the mystery of the cross the central and fundamental source of ecumenical unity.[41] At the very opening of his talk he stressed that the unity so desired by Christians of today will be attained not so much by efforts and actions of a few, such as specialists engaged in theological discussion or those attending high-ranking ecclesiastical meetings, but rather by the efforts of all Christians who stay *beneath* the Cross in order to experience the salvific and unifying "power of God" (1 Cor 1:18–24). He states,

> ... the renewal, liberation, and unification of the Church of Christ upon

---

[38] The question here is one of Catholic and Protestant theology.

[39] H. G. Link, "Gegenwärtige Probleme einer Kreuzestheologie", 337. This refers to a report of a meeting of the publishers of this journal held Oct. 12–14, 1972, in Grafrath. Among participants at this meeting dedicated to the theme "Theology of the Cross" were Catholic theologians W. Kasper and J. B. Metz. The July–Aug. 1973 (no. 4) issue is entitled "Toward a Theology of the Cross". A 1973 meeting of the editorial staff also dealt with the same theme. See the article "Kreuzestheologie im Neuen Testament" (*Evangelische Theologie* 34, no. 2 [Mar.–Apr.]: 113–218).

[40] The Congress "La Sapienza della Croce Oggi" of Oct. 13–18, 1975, was the occasion of the 200th anniversary of the death of St. Paul of the Cross. It was organized by the Congregation of the Passion in collaboration with the *Pontificio Ateneo Antonianum* and the international association of Stauros, an organization established through the initiative of the Passionists in Belgium in Oct. 1973. The aim of this international association, as written in the statutes of its foundation, is "to promote research regarding the message of the cross and of Christ's passion".

[41] See J. Moltmann, "Ecumenismo sotto la croce", 526–37. In English, see Moltmann, "Ecumenism beneath the Cross", 16–35.

earth will result, not primarily from theological strategy and ecclesiastical tactics of drawing together, but rather from the very root and wellspring of the Church, namely, from the power of Christ's own passion; since in his outpoured blood and in his opened Heart the Church is already renewed, liberated, and one. The core of the ecumenical movement toward unity consists in a movement coming from the cross of the one Lord.[42]

The path to be followed was concisely sketched by Moltmann in two programmatic theses: "From ecumenical dialogue about the cross to ecumenism beneath the cross"[43] and "the nearer we draw to the cross of Christ, the nearer we draw to each other".[44] The path indicated here, which Christians have to follow if they are to attain the unity for which Christ prayed (Jn 17:21), is certainly of central import since it begins from the "center of Christianity". It is, however, not enough to speak about the cross without participating in it. Moltmann continues,

> But this *fruitful dialogue about the cross of Christ* would remain abstract and merely theoretical if it did not at the same time lead to a *dialogue beneath the cross* — for the cross is not just one object among others, about which we may objectively speak.[45]

When theology wants to make an important contribution to ecumenism (and who would not agree that it could do so!)[46] in addressing itself to *Christus*

---

[42] Since the Acts of the Congress were published in Italian, we present the Italian text here: "Infatti il rinnovamento, la liberazione e l'unificazione della Chiesa di Cristo sulla terra non sono realizzate con strategie teologiche e tattiche ecclesiastiche della ricucitura. Esse sgorgano dall'intima radice della Chiesa, cioè della forza delle sofferenze di Cristo stesso, perché nel suo sangue sparso, nel suo cuore aperto la Chiesa è già rinnovata, già liberata è già tutta unita. Il nocciolo del movimento ecumenico verso l'unità della Chiesa sta nel muoversi dalla Croce di un unico Signore" (Moltmann, "Ecumenismo", 526; in English, Moltmann, "Ecumenism", 16).

[43] "Nessun dialogo sulla croce senza lo star insieme sotto la croce" (Moltmann, "Ecumenismo", 527; "Ecumenism", 18).

[44] "Più ci avviciniamo alla croce, più ci avviciniamo tra di noi" (ibid.).

[45] "Ma questo fruttuoso dialogo sulla croce di Cristo resterebbe astratto e solo teorico se non portasse contemporaneamente a un dialogo sotto la croce di Cristo. Perché la croce non è un oggetto tra gli altri su cui si possa obiettivamente parlare" (ibid.).

[46] To fulfill the growing desire for unity among Christians the way "from within" — living the Faith communally — is the most important. We call attention to two "movements" that have already started down this road (today perhaps still just a path!). They are the *communauté de Taizé* and the "charismatic movement". The former wants to serve the "striving for unity of all Christians" through life partnership, meditation, and celebration of liturgy and Eucharist as a "feast with no end" (see R. Schutz, "Cluny, Taizé", in *Lexikon* 2, col. 1241). This community has already developed into an ecumenical center that radiates its influence afar in the world. The latter is the "charismatic movement", which has sprung up in recent years among Christians of different confessions and has placed at its center the Holy Spirit as its binding and unifying force.

crucifixus, then it too must stand beneath the cross of Christ and not just describe the sacrifice from a rational and impartial distance. Only by standing beneath the cross can theologians develop a wholly enlightened theology, a theology that does not aim solely at argumentation and ratiocination but keeps its attention fixed upon the existential practice of faith, a theology that does not create faith but prepares its way.[47]

When, at the above-mentioned conference, Moltmann spoke of united endurance and shared suffering as the basis of true and lasting ecumenical unity,[48] it was a unity in Christ of which he spoke, a unity which Christians encounter in the difficult situations they face. It is this unity that represents "ecumenism at its core".

Christians of different confessions who intensely live this unity in Christ may, with the Apostle Paul, proclaim, "I have been crucified with Christ, and the life I live now is not my own; Christ is living in me" (Gal 2:19–20). Above all, these are the saints and "mystics",[49] who, delving into the depths of their own personal selves, radically live in rich relationship with Christ. Certainly, one is entitled to claim that their lives and thoughts, so completely shaped by their intense relationship with Christ, offer precious motivation and assistance to *all* Christians who long for communion in Christ and with Christ. If Moltmann's basic thesis is correct, i.e., *the nearer we come to Christ, the nearer we come together,* then, indeed, the saints and mystics of the different confessions[50] must have realized a high degree of the unity proceeding from their proximity to the mystery of Christ.

Arguing against this supposition, one may claim that traditional Christian mysticism has strong individualistic features and has as its goal, above all, union of the individual with God.[51] Furthermore, one can object that several saints and mystics had relationships that were limited to their own religious confession and, therefore, could scarcely be said to have acted effectively in an ecumenical manner. Nevertheless, we can reply that often saints and mystics have had a real impact upon ecumenism. Despite personality differences,

---

[47] See what has been said in n. 1 above.

[48] See Moltmann, "Ecumenismo", 531. In English, see Moltmann, "Ecumenism", 25.

[49] The notions *mystic* and *mysticism* sometimes have negative undertones in German and in English. When we use these words in this study, therefore, we—before all else—mean the intensity of the faith relationship to Christ, apart from certain extraordinary, occult phenomena, which are also found among "mystics" of other religions. Therefore, when we use the term *mysticism* in this study we always mean the Christian mysticism of faith.

[50] From our point of view, the decisive point is not whether or not these persons were canonized (a process of the Catholic Church alone) but rather if they sought and found, in their own lives, the "hidden treasure" and "the pearl of great price" who is Christ (Mt 13:44–46).

[51] But this does not mean that the relationship between Christ and these individuals is not of exemplary value for Christians of all confessions.

each — and this is the most important point — possesses *equality* and *unity*. Intensely united to Christ and with faith in that union, they have shaped their lives in a resolute and radical manner. As a result, there is much that is equal and similar in their lives and in their thoughts, especially with regard to the existential practice of their faith. Should theology accept the task of studying and transmitting the unity inherent in their lived Christianity, an important contribution to an ecumenical drawing nearer to each other among confessions will have been made. In so doing, a *never lost unity* might be discovered.

Although we cannot go into more detail at this point, a concrete example will be used to support the above statements. In the life of Nikolas von Zinzendorf (1700–1760), an Evangelical author of religious song and "someone representative of a characteristic type of German pietism",[52] we find a strong focusing of thought upon the crucified Christ. His "Litany of the Wounds" and thirty-four sermons, which serve to interpret his thought, show us the interior and mystical depth achieved by him in understanding Christ's passion and death.[53] One can say, therefore, that in his case we touch upon a mysticism in which Christ's passion and death were strongly impressed.[54] Just as for Zinzendorf, the "cross and figure of the Tortured One with his stigmata . . . represent the revelation of God's love",[55] our author, St. Paul of the Cross, sees in Christ's passion "the greatest and most astounding work of divine love"[56] and "the miracle of miracles of God's love".[57] Thus, for these two men, *Christus crucifixus* was, in the same manner, the focus upon whom their thought was concentrated. The contemplation of the crucified Lord added a true dimension of depth to their lives. If one of them (Zinzendorf) intervened actively in his life on behalf of Christian Church unity,[58] a sorrow

[52] P. Meinhold, "N. v. Zinzendorf", in *Lexikon* 10, cols. 1376–78; and E. Beyreuther, "Zinzendorf", in *Die Religion in Geschichte und Gegenwart* (3d ed.) 6, cols. 1913–16.

[53] See Nikolas Ludwig von Zinzendorf, *Hauptschriften* (E. Beyreuther and G. Meyer, eds.) vol. 3. (Hildesheim, 1962–66), 1–399.

[54] Zinzendorf is against a mysticism viewed, in his understanding, as "an attempt to [effect] an immediacy of a relationship with God". At the same time, he considers a Christocentric faith-mysticism as necessary: " . . . a personal relationship with the Savior is a necessity" (see O. Uttendörfer, *Zinzendorfs religiöse Grundgedanken,* esp. Chap. 10, 161; also see S. Eberhard, *Kreuzes-Theologie. Das reformatorische Anliegen in Zinzendorfs Verkündigung).*

[55] Meinhold, col. 1377.

[56] " . . . la più grande e stupenda opera del divino amore" (L 2:499, Aug. 21, 1756, to Sr. Colomba Gertrude Gandolfi).

[57] " . . . il miracolo de' miracoli dell'amor di Dio" (L 2:726, July 17, 1751, to Lucy Burlini).

[58] Even in his childhood and youth, Zinzendorf confronted the ecumenical situation. He was raised in the pedagogy of Halle (*hallische Pädagogium*) and remained there from 1710 to 1716, during which time he was influenced decisively by virtue of the missionary and ecumenical associations of Halle (Beyreuther, col. 1913). After having studied law and

preyed upon the other (St. Paul of the Cross) by reason of the conflicts among Christians,[59] because "whoever takes the cross seriously begins to feel pain at the divisions of the Church".[60]

theology in Wittenberg from 1716–19, he made an educational tour of the Netherlands, Belgium, and France, a tour "conducted from an ecumenical point of view" (Meinhold, col. 1376). In France, he made acquaintance with the cardinal bishop of Noailles, with whom he retained a friendly relationship over the years. "Zinzendorf tried to encourage a common love for Christ by the introduction of evangelical [Lutheran] songs and devotions into Catholicism" (Beyreuther, col. 1913).

[59] Although St. Paul of the Cross had no clear contact with other confessions during his lifetime, he did suffer because of the division within Christianity. This is evident even in his spiritual diary. How deep his sorrow was may be seen from the fact that, when he was twenty-seven years old, he desired to "die as a martyr" to "convert the infidels of England and neighboring countries", so that the "Most Blessed Sacrament of the Altar" be honored there also (see the entries of Dec. 26 and 29 in *Tagebuch,* 100 and 107; and in Rouse, 36 and 37).

Of course, we are not considering Paul's words here in terms of standards of ecumenical behavior as acted out in the Christian world of today. St. Paul of the Cross was a child of his time and influenced by the feelings and thoughts current in his own environment. Nevertheless, he possessed a pious and deep desire that Christ be loved by *all.* Why England, among all non-Catholic countries, aroused the saint's interest is a mystery, for which there is still no satisfactory explanation.

[60] "Chi prende seriamente la croce, comincia a soffrire delle divisioni della Chiesa" (J. Moltmann, "Ecumenismo", 530; in English, see Moltmann, "Ecumenism", 24).

CHAPTER IV

Participation in the Passion of Our Lord Jesus Christ

After these more or less basic and general considerations, let us return to the spiritual and theological thought of the saint. As already mentioned in the section on infused sufferings (*pene infuse*) (which play such an important role in the mysticism of the Passionist founder), the person to whom this grace is given receives, interiorly and mystically, a share in the sorrow and pain of the crucified Lord. Furthermore, the saint explains that such a person, having been meditatively and contemplatively immersed in the "sea of the passion of Jesus", is enabled to imitate the virtues of the crucified Jesus. We understand this to be primarily the passive virtues of humility, gentleness, and submission.[1] An examination of the main principles of the saint's spiritual teaching, as already delineated, reveals in them a main thrust moving the person to embrace a demeanor of openness and readiness for "passivity" (in the face of suffering).[2]

These factors, which belong to the specific features characteristic of the theological-spiritual thought of St. Paul of the Cross, point to a fundamental principle strongly imprinted in his spirituality and in his religious instruction that may be considered the grounding principle and end point of his thought: "participation in the passion of our Lord Jesus Christ". Infused suffering, practice of the virtues of the crucified Lord, and a basic readiness for suffering may be designated as the interior portion of participating in the passion of Jesus or, in other words, the preconditions for recognizing and accepting the cross of Christ in the concrete suffering one must bear.

---

[1] See above, pp. 202–8.

[2] This demeanor of "passivity" must in no way be labeled inactivity. The virtue of "being able to suffer" requires a high degree of victory over one's self on the part of the person, and a high degree of concentration in the use of one's willpower. That the submissive spirit's "ability for passivity" does not diminish a person's creative force, but even increases it, may be seen from the saint's life. During his lifetime he held more than 180 lay missions, gave spiritual exercises eighty times, and established twelve monasteries. A similar observation may be seen in the life of St. Teresa of Avila.

HUMAN SUFFERING VIEWED AS THE "CROSS OF CHRIST"

In his spiritual diary and in his letters of spiritual direction, Paul of the Cross explains over and over again that the correct attitude toward actual suffering— indifference, if it is a matter of unavoidable bodily pain or physical affliction— opens the person to the possibility of receiving a share in the "cross of Christ".

1. *"To be crucified with Jesus"* (crocifisso con Gesù).

In the saint's spiritual diary, the oldest preserved document available, and in its very first entry, we find an affirmation illustrative of the central significance that union with *Christus crucifixus* had for Paul. The last sentence of this entry reads, "Through the mercy of our good God, I know that I do not desire to know anything else or to taste any consolation. I desire only to be crucified with Jesus."[3] This formulation, "to be crucified with Christ", was the saint's program in life. It may be designated as the programmatic guideline or as the "hermeneutical key" by which one is able to unlock and explain the life and thought of the Passionist founder.[4]

We find a similar assertion in the writings of the Apostle Paul. The epistle to the Galatians states, "I have been crucified with Christ, and the life I live now is not my own; Christ is living in me" (Gal 2:19–20). Undoubtedly, these words belong to the sum and substance of the Pauline mysticism of Christ and the cross. That St. Paul of the Cross took these renowned words of the apostle as a model is very obvious from the above-quoted "programmatic dictum". A previous section elaborates upon the topic of the founder's predilection for Pauline writings.[5]

Participation in the passion of Jesus and imitation of *Christus crucifixus* belong to the main themes of his spiritual diary. In the entry of December 21, 1720, the founder reports interior and exterior sufferings that had to be borne that day. He then speaks of the positive function of suffering: it shows the person "the way toward perfection". However, for the founder, the strongest motive underlying a willingness to suffer physical and mental pain is to be

---

[3] "Io so che per misericordia del nostro caro Dio non desidero saper altro, nè gustare alcuna consolazione, solo che desidero d'esser crocifisso con Gesù" (*Diario Spirituale*, 53; *Tagebuch*, 57; Rouse, 29).

[4] In the previously cited work *La Mystique de la Passion*, Stanislas Breton sees in this "participation à la Passion" the unifying-creating principle of St. Paul of the Cross' passion mysticism. It is seen as a principle linking the affective spirituality of the Franciscan school with the Rhenish-Flemish mysticism of introversion—these two traditions having had the most influence upon the founder (see Breton, *La Mystique*, esp. 27–48 and 237–51; also see von Balthasar, "Mysterium Paschale", 156, n. 6).

[5] See above, pp. 101–4.

conformed to the crucified Lord. Paul writes, "[the soul] wants to be crucified with him, because that is more conformable to the beloved God who, during all his holy life, did nothing else but suffer".[6] Paul's longing for suffering is so strong that he admits to a "hidden fear" that his pain would cease.[7] In the long run, however, it is not the pain itself that links the soul to God but the love which bears the pain. A genuine, unselfish love is proved by the bearing of suffering. In other words, "suffering represents the deepest and most convincing kind of love".[8] The saint often picks up this theme in various entries in his diary, above all when he describes the good effects of contemplation of the passion of Christ. In these descriptions, he strongly emphasizes the deep relationship between love and suffering.[9]

For St. Paul of the Cross, therefore, physical or mental pain is neither an evil nor a calamity. On the contrary, he sees suffering primarily as a possibility of expressing love for the crucified Lord, of becoming one with Jesus. The saint considers suffering as being, above all, the "cross of Christ", and, because it is the cross of his Lord, he accepts and bears it gratefully—more than that, joyfully.[10] In the entry of November 26, he first speaks of the depression and melancholy of that day. Then he ends by saying, "I know that I tell my Jesus that his crosses are the joys of my heart."[11] In this statement we see how much St. Paul saw the cross and passion of Jesus Christ, whom the saint desired to follow most of all, "in the sadness, fears, and temptations of one devoted to God alone" (as J. Ratzinger characterized the interior suffering of Paul of the Cross).[12]

---

[6] " . . . volendo piuttosto essere crocifissa con lui, perchè ciò è più conforme all' amato suo Dio, il quale in tutta la sua ss. vita non ha fatto altro che patire" (*Diario Spirituale*, 75; *Tagebuch*, 94; Rouse, 35). That the entire life of Jesus consisted only of suffering may at first appear to be a skewed and exaggerated statement. Notwithstanding, we need to remember that for St. Paul of the Cross, "suffering" and "loving" are always closely connected (see above pp. 200–2 concerning *amore doloroso e dolore amoroso*). For Paul, therefore, the term *suffering* in the above statement could be replaced by the term *love*. The statement would then read, in effect, that "Jesus' entire life was love".

[7] In the entry of Dec. 21, 1720, we read, "La paura sopra detta viene dal desiderio, che l'anima ha di seguire Gesù nei patimenti" (*Diario Spirituale*, 74; *Tagebuch*, 92; Rouse, 35).

[8] Quoted from *Cursillo (Für eine Kirche in Bewegung)* 13 (1976): 100 (no author given).

[9] See entries of Dec. 8, 27, and 28.

[10] The saint's mysticism of the cross is, therefore, to be seen in the light of his general Christ-mysticism.

[11] "So che dico al mio Gesù che le sue croci sono le gioie del mio cuore" (*Diario Spirituale*, 57; *Tagebuch*, 62; Rouse, 29).

[12] In the Introduction to the German edition of St. Paul of the Cross' *Diario Spirituale*, J. Ratzinger observes that "the sadness, the fears, and the temptations" will appear to the reader as "the product of an excessive piety and the result of silence and solitude. But when one reads on," says Ratzinger (who appeals to the religious depths of the diary entries), "one notices how much Paul has to put up with weakness, passing restless nights, [etc.] to achieve real victory over human frailty. This plumbs the depth of

There are also several places in his diary where the founder ascribes a *purifying* function to suffering, especially interior, and to spiritual pain such as melancholy and desolation.[13] In the entry of December 23, 1720, in which he speaks of struggling against attacks of the devil during prayer, the saint uses imagery to try to explain the purifying effect of the suffering caused by the struggle. Suffering "purifies like billows purify rocks, which come through a storm not destroyed but cleansed".[14] The saint states in another entry that, by means of suffering prayer, God wants to make the soul "into an ermine of purity, a rock amidst suffering".[15] This purifying effect of suffering is that of which the saint speaks in the following entry of December 21, 1720:

> I would like to be able to say that everyone would experience this great grace which God in his mercy grants when he sends suffering to us, and especially when the suffering is devoid of consolation. Then the soul is purified like gold in the furnace and becomes beautiful and agile so as to take flight to the good God. . . . The soul carries her cross with Jesus and does not know it . . . she wants to be crucified with him.[16]

---

the abyss from which we are always fleeing" (*Tagebuch*, 6).

See the entry of Dec. 21 (*Diario Spirituale*, 74; *Tagebuch*, 92; Rouse, 35).

[13] In another place, St. Paul of the Cross considers suffering as a chastisement and as a satisfaction for past sins. On Dec. 26, he wrote, "I also had a special understanding of the infinite mercy of God as our Sovereign Good enabled me to perceive how great is the infinite love with which he punishes here on earth, so that we might be spared an eternity of torments. And because his infinite Majesty knows the place that his infinite justice has prepared for the just and well-deserved punishments of sin, his infinite mercy is moved by compassion to inflict loving chastisements. With these, he urges his sinful creatures to correct themselves so that they may avoid that eternal punishment and serve him in the first place" (*Tagebuch*, 101; Rouse, 36).

[14] See J. Ratzinger's Introduction to the *Tagebuch*, p. 6. For example, the founder of the Order describes the purifying effect of suffering with the following words: " . . . quando l'acqua del mare è in burrasche, la quale gonfiata da venti fa le onde grosse, le quali quando sono vicine a scogli, gli dànno colpi, che pare li vogliano fracassare e disfare; ma non è così, li dànno sì, ma non li penetrano nè li disfanno, puo esser che li disgranino qualche poco, ma poi per la durezza dello scoglio non vi e pericolo, che l'onde per grosse che siano, li rompano." / "[these thoughts come as] when the waters of the sea are very stormy, with great waves being raised by the tossing wind. When the waves approach the rocks, they strike them as if to smash them to pieces. But this does not happen. They strike them, but they do not penetrate them nor smash them to pieces. They knock off a small piece, but because the rocks are so hard there is no danger that the big waves will break them" (*Diario Spirituale*, 76f.; *Tagebuch*, 96; Rouse, 35).

[15] The entry of Dec. 10–13, 1720, reads as follows: "So che ho inteso, che questa sorte di orazione di patire è un grande regalo, che Dio fa all'anima per farla un armellino di purità, uno scoglio ne' patimenti . . . " / "I know that I have understood that this kind of suffering-prayer is a great gift, which God grants a soul to make it an ermine of purity, a rock amidst sufferings . . . " (*Diario Spirituale*, 70; *Tagebuch*, 84; Rouse, 33).

[16] "Vorrei poter dire che tutto il mondo sentisse la grande grazia di Dio che per sua pietà fa, quando manda da patire, e massime quando il patire è senza conforto, chè allora l'anima

The desire "to be crucified with Jesus", which Paul especially expresses when he meditates upon the passion of Jesus and when God grants him the grace of *tormenti infusi* (infused suffering),[17] is the strongest and deepest motive for embracing spiritual and bodily pain. This desire to be identified with *Christus crucifixus* is so strong that Paul asks God never to take his suffering from him.[18] He has, furthermore, an interior "longing for suffering",[19] a longing that impels him to say with St. Teresa, "To suffer or to die".[20]

These entries written by Paul of the Cross when he was nearing twenty-seven years of age obviously prove how deeply impressed was the charism granted him, even though it was a charism consisting of a desire to receive a share in the passion of Jesus and to become conformed to *Christus cruxifixus*. In the manner in which St. Francis of Assisi imitated Jesus in his poverty and St. Ignatius of Loyola showed to the world the obedience of the Son of God, so St. Paul of the Cross saw in the suffering and crucified Lord the "original image" of the Christian and invited all to imitate this *Christus patiens*.

2. *Through the cross to light* (per crucem ad lucem)

In the hundreds of preserved letters written by the founder for the purpose of spiritual direction in the interval between 1721 and 1775, we find a multitude of statements in which he expressed his opinion and evaluation of human suffering. Just four weeks after the close of his forty-day retreat, he wrote a letter to his former confessor and spiritual director Bishop Gattinara. In it, Paul revealed his interior religious life. He spoke of his extraordinary mental

---

resta purificata come l'oro nel fuoco, e viene bella e leggera per volarsene al suo Bene . . . porta la Croce con Gesù e non lo sa . . . volendo piuttosto essere crocifissa con lui" (*Diario Spirituale*, 75; *Tagebuch*, 94; Rouse, 35).

[17] This desire is expressed clearly by Paul in his diary entry of Dec. 6, 1720: "Ebbi molta intelligenza infusa degli spasimi del mio Gesù, e aveva tanta brama dell'essere con perfezione unito con Lui, che desideravo sentire attualmente i suoi spasimi, ed essere in Croce con Lui." / "I received a deep infused understanding of the sufferings of my Jesus, and I had such a desire for ardent union with him that I actually longed to feel his sufferings and to be on the cross with him" (*Diario Spirituale*, 65; *Tagebuch*, 76; Rouse, 32).

[18] The entry of Dec. 10–13 reads, " . . . anzi dicevo al mio Dio, che non mi levi mai i patimenti" / " . . . then I asked my God never to take my sufferings from me" (*Diario Spirituale*, 70; *Tagebuch*, 84; Rouse, 33; the entry of Dec. 21 contains a similar statement).

[19] "Nel segreto del cuore vi sta un certo segreto e quasi insensibile desiderio di sempre essere in patimenti, siano questi, siano altri." / "In the depth of one's heart there is a certain hidden and almost unfelt desire to be always immersed in suffering of one kind or another" (*Diario Spirituale*, 73; *Tagebuch*, 91; Rouse, 34).

[20] The Dec. 3 entry ends with the words " . . . mi viene da dire con santa Teresa, 'O patire, o morire' " / "I feel like saying with St. Teresa, 'To suffer or to die' " (*Diario Spirituale*, 63; *Tagebuch*, 72; Rouse, 31).

and corporal sufferings. Then he stated, "I said to myself, 'You have all eternity in which to be happy.' "[21]

In 1721, Paul answered a letter to a religious who had told him of her sufferings. The letter clearly indicates the inner conviction with which he speaks and the hymnlike and celebratory words he uses when writing of suffering as "participation in the cross of Jesus". At the opening of the letter, he proclaims,

> O sweet troubles, treasured tokens of the Sacred Heart of our spouse, Jesus Christ! Whoever loves Jesus seeks nothing else but suffering. I am consoled to know that you are one of those very happy souls who walk the path to Calvary following our Redeemer. Happy are you if you follow this precious path, for one day in the company of other lovers of the cross you will sing, "Your crosses, dear God, are the joys of my heart."[22]

It is certainly difficult to identify with such statements. But Paul of the Cross was so fully united with the suffering Lord that the power of God's love prepared him and enabled him to take upon himself what was otherwise distasteful. Love integrated the suffering (sorrowing love and loving sorrow) and made him forget his own suffering, because he saw therein the cross of Jesus.

In the citation quoted above, Paul writes, "Whoever loves Jesus seeks nothing else but suffering." In his diary, he had previously made his own the words of St. Teresa: "To suffer or to die".[23] In later writings, however, we find that when he speaks of participation in *passio Domini,* he speaks concretely of bearing pain. He no longer talks in an apodictic manner but points more clearly to the goal to be attained by the person when he becomes conformed to *Christus patiens.* This is apparent in a letter written in 1743 in which he starts off with St. Teresa's words but continues in a way proper to himself. To Sr. Colomba Gandolfi, he writes,

[21] The saint wrote the following to his confessor on Jan. 27, 1721: "Una mattina ero in qualche particolar patimento, più del solito, corporale, ed ero arido ed afflitto, e mi sentii dire: V'è del tempo tutta l'eternità da godere: e me ne stetti così in pace con Dio, desiderando sempre più patire." / "One morning I experienced some special pain in my body, more so than usual. I was dry and downcast and I said to myself, 'You have all eternity in which to be happy.' Then wishing to suffer still more, I remained thus in peace with God" (L 1:20).

[22] "O dolcissimi travagli, pegni diletti del Cuore Santissimo del nostro caro Sposo Cristo Gesù! Chi potrà spiegare la magnificenza di questi preziosi tesori dei quali il nostro Sommo Bene si serve per coronare le sue dilette Spose? Chi ama Gesù altra non cerca che patire. Mi consolo con lei sia una di quelle fortunatissime anime, che vanno per la strada del Calvario, seguendo il nostro caro Redentore. Felice lei se seguirà questa si preziosa strada, mentre un giorno canterà in compagnia degli altri innamorati della S. Croce: 'Le tue croci, caro Dio, sono le gioie del mio cuore.' Che bel patire con Gesù" (L 1:24, Feb. 6, 1721, to Sr. Teresa Costanza Pontas).

[23] " ... mi viene con S. Teresa: 'o patire, o morire'" (*Diario Spirituale,* 63; *Tagebuch,* 72; Rouse, 31; also see L 1:29, Dec. 29, 1721, to the Marchioness Marianna della Scala del Pozzo).

I believe the cross of our sweet Jesus has planted its roots more profoundly in your heart, and now you can sing, *"pati et non mori"* [to suffer and not die], or *"aut pati aut mori"* [to suffer or die], or, better still, *"nec pati, nec mori"* [to neither suffer nor die] but only total transformation in the divine good pleasure.[24]

How beautifully these words show that bearing of suffering in participation with the *passio Domini*, in intense union with *Christus crucifixus*, represents neither the final nor the ultimate goal of the spirituality of the Passionist founder. Just as Christ himself through his passion and cross entered into union with and into the glory of his Father, so too each of us through the "cross of Christ", when it has planted its roots more profoundly in our hearts (to use the saint's own words), may aspire to greater union with God and, more than that, to transformation in the "divine good pleasure".

3. *Naked suffering* (il nudo patire)

In the above-quoted letter of 1721, we find the versified sentence: "Your crosses, dear God, are the joys of my heart."[25] Mentioned in his diary, however, is another form of participation in the passion of Christ that is not mediated by any perceptible "joy". It is called "naked suffering" because it leaves the person stripped of any sensible comfort (*senza conforto*) and divested of all perceptible consolation and interior joy.[26] We find this phrase *bare or naked suffering* (*nudo patire*) especially quoted in the later period of his life.

[24] "Credo che la Croce del nostro dolce Gesù avrà poste più profonde radici nel vostro cuore e che canterete: 'Pati e non mori', o pure, 'aut pati aut mori', o pure ancor meglio, 'nec pati, nec mori', ma solamente la totale trasformazione nel Divin Beneplacito" (L 2:440, July 10, 1743).

[25] In his critical edition of Paul's *Diario Spirituale*, E. Zoffoli observes that there are similar rhythmic-sounding sentences in the entries of Nov. 26 and 27. He refers to this observation as "*Strofetta di versi quaternari, assai probabilmente dello stesso Santo*" (A little stanza of verses, each being a quatrain of four syllables, most likely [composed] by the same saint): "Le tue croce / caro Dio / son le gioie / del mio cuore" (Your crosses / dear God / are the joys / of my heart). See *Diario Spirituale*, 57f., n. 1.

[26] For instance, on Dec. 21, Paul wrote, "Vorrei poter dire che tutto il mondo sentisse la grande grazia che Dio per sua pietà fà, quando manda da patire, e massime quando il patire è senza conforto." / "I would like to be able to say that everyone would experience this great grace, which God, in his mercy, grants when he sends suffering to us, and especially when the suffering is devoid of consolation" (*Diario Spirituale*, 75; *Tagebuch*, 94; Rouse, 35). In the entry from Dec. 10–13, the saint wrote, " . . . bisogna che passi per questa strada di patire nell'orazione anche, e dico patire senza alcun conforto sensibile . . . " / "[the soul] must pass through this way of suffering during prayer—and must suffer, I say, without any sensible consolation" (*Diario Spirituale*, 70; *Tagebuch*, 85; Rouse, 33).

Explaining this naked suffering in a letter written in the year 1750, Paul recalls the crucified Christ, who in total interior desolation cried, "My God, my God, why have you forsaken me?" (Mk 16:34).[27] Undoubtedly, this naked suffering is experienced existentially as more difficult and painful than suffering accompanied by consolation. Precisely because of this, *nudo patire* permits the person to have a more intimate and deeper share in the Lord's passion.[28] Certainly, God does not give suffering amid desolation to *every* person. Those to whom he does give it, however, the all-good and all-merciful God prepares and strengthens to endure it.

The above observations show the existence of different degrees of participation in the passion of Christ according to the spiritual-theological thought of St. Paul of the Cross. In fact, one can distinguish (as does S. Breton in his valuable study on the passion mysticism of St. Paul of the Cross) three levels of participation. Breton, who views participation in the passion as the fundamental principle of the saint's mysticism, uses imagery expressive of interpersonal relationships to describe the intensity of participation.[29] Thus, according to Breton, intensity of participation may be classified in the following way: as that of a *good servant,* or as a *friend,* or as a *son.*[30] The faithful *servant* accepts and "joins" his will to that of the Lord's.[31] A *friend* evinces a great amount of

[27] The letter is addressed to Dominic Panizza. In its opening, Paul writes, "Amatissimo signor D. Domenico. Ecco il povero Paolo giunto in Roma due ore fa che viene a visitarlo in spirito su la Santa Croce del dolce Gesù, in cui lei gusta i frutti di quest'albero sacrosanto di vita. E se lei non gusta i frutti con sensibilità, anzi per cio lei e più felice ed avventurato, poichè in tal forma sa assomiglia più al nostro divino Salvatore che su la Croce esclamò al Padre: 'Deus, Deus meus, ut quid dereliquisti me?' esprimendo il suo nudo patire senza conforto. Oh, beata quell'anima che sta crocefissa con Gesù Cristo senza saperlo e senza vederlo, perchè priva d'ogni conforto sensibile!" / "Most Beloved Signor D. Domenico. Behold poor Paul having just arrived in Rome two hours ago, and coming to visit him in spirit is sweet Jesus' holy cross, in which Paul tastes the fruit of this holy tree of life. And, if he happens not to taste the fruit with sensible consolation, he is the more blessed and fortunate, since, in this manner, he is more like unto our Divine Savior, who cried out to his Father from the cross: Deus, Deus, ut quid dereliquisti me? [My God, my God, why have you abandoned me?] expressing thus his naked suffering without consolation. Oh, blessed is the soul nailed together with Jesus Christ without experiencing or seeing him, because [in that way] he is deprived of any perceptible consolation" (L 3:17, Apr. 2, 1750).

[28] See E. Henau, "The Naked Suffering (Nudo-Patire) in the Mystical Experience of Paul of the Cross", 210–21.

[29] Undoubtedly, some metaphors from the personal domain of thought are appropriated in a special way to provide a better explanation of St. Paul of the Cross' passion mysticism.

[30] See Breton, *La Mystique,* 226–29.

[31] With regard to this step, Breton remarks, "Le serviteur qui se résigne à la divine volanté est un serviteur fidèle, un tâcheron appliqué de la divine gloire. . . . Mais cette acceptation, si elle est copie conforme, est encore extérieure au vouloir." / "The servant who resigns his own self to the divine will is a faithful servant, a worker striving for divine glory. . . . But this acceptance, if it is a conformed copy, is still exterior to the will" (ibid., 226).

confidence, reciprocal intimacy, and a predominant "familiarity".[32] To participate as *son*, by which is meant the son-Father relationship, is above all else participation through the power of love.[33] This highest level of participation is described by the founder as *nudo patire* (naked suffering). In this most intense form of participation in the *passio Christi*, the person shares in the desolation of Jesus on the cross and surrenders himself full of confidence into the hands of the Father.[34]

These differing degrees of participation in the passion of Jesus are found throughout the writings of the founder, from his earliest days down to the last years of his life. In his diary entry of December 21, 1720, Paul wrote of the great grace of suffering sent by God, especially that suffering "which is devoid of consolation".[35] In his later years, he will call this kind of suffering naked (*nudo patire*). Whenever in his letters the saint recommends participation in *passio Christi* through bearing some concrete suffering, he is not making such a recommendation in a stereotypical manner. Rather, he takes into consideration the individual condition of the correspondent and the intensity of that person's faith, hope, and love. That is why one can find different stages of participation right next to one another in Paul's writings, which span a period of more than fifty years.

---

[32] "Au niveau de l'amitié, la résignation se détend dans un sourire. . . . On se meut dans l'atmosphère de familiarité." / "At the level of friendship, resignation relaxes itself with a smile. . . . One plunges into the atmosphere of familiarity" (ibid., 227).

[33] Because Christ is the Son of God, our union with Christ brings us into a filial relationship with the Father that takes the place of that of servant and friend. "C'est en union avec le Christ en croix que l'âme dépouillée de toute consolation accomplit d'une manière éminente cette divine volonté. . . . Ce nu-pâtir qui nous unit ainsi au bon plaisir du Père rejoint l'amour—nu ou le pur amour. A ce niveau, le négatif du nu-pâtir et le positif du saint abandon se répondent comme la déréliction et l' 'In manus tuas' du Golgotha." / "Only in this union with the crucified Christ, [with] the soul devoid of all consolation, does it fulfill the divine will in an eminent manner. . . . This naked suffering, which in this way unites us to the good pleasure of the Father, rejoins love—naked or pure love. At this level, the negative [field] of naked suffering and the positive of the saint's abandonment correspond to each other as do the dereliction and the 'In manus tuas' of Golgotha" (ibid., 228f.).

[34] For the sake of clarification, the following must be said: Since Jesus' suffering of "absolute desolation" on the cross, the human person is no longer situated in this "total solitude" of suffering because, from now on, he bears desolation in communion and in participation with *Christus crucifixus*. In his work *Der gekreuzigte Gott*, J. Moltmann deals in detail with the suffering of desolation by Jesus on the cross and the "liberating" effect of this suffering for people. On p. 265, we read, "If God became man in Jesus of Nazareth, then he entered not only into our finite nature, but also into the situation of desolation through death on the cross . . . Jesus emptied himself and embraced the eternal death of the wicked and forsaken, so that they could each experience communion with him."

[35] " . . . massime quando il patire è senza conforto" / " . . . especially when the suffering is devoid of consolation" (*Diario Spirituale*, 75; *Tagebuch*, 94; Rouse, 35).

4. *Long Live the Holy Cross* (Viva la Santa Croce)

Two small pieces of poetry composed by the saint need to be introduced during this discussion of the "mysticism of participation" in the passion of Jesus.[36] In them the founder explains the great importance suffering has for the person who yearns for greater union with God. The first poem consists of three stanzas only and is part of a letter written by the saint to Agnes Grazi in 1741.[37] Recognizable in these three stanzas are the three stages of participation discussed above. The first stanza speaks of the purifying power of suffering. By it the soul is purged, just as gold is purified in a crucible.[38] The second stanza considers the cross as something desirable, bringing with it a joy akin to drinking new wine.[39] In the last stanza, he speaks of the cross as friend. It reads, "Yes! the cross is a great friend / For one who loves the Sun Divine / And studies as much as she can / How to suffer without a sound."[40] In these few stanzas the founder of the Congregation tries to express the meaning of *nudo patire*.

The second piece of poetry, a kind of "hymn of the cross", consists of seven stanzas and was composed by the founder two years later. It, too, was included in a letter written to Agnes Grazi, who at that time was seriously ill and would die about eight months later at the age of forty-one years.[41] Because it bears the title *"Viva la Santa Croce"*, one would expect it to be a poem in praise of the salvific importance of Jesus' death on the cross.[42] How—

[36] Besides these two smaller pieces of poetry, the founder also composed a poem of twenty-nine stanzas in which his whole spiritual teaching is expressed (see above, pp. 116–23).

[37] See L 1:269, May 2, 1741.

[38] The first stanza runs thus: "Nelle pene si raffina / L'alma amante come l'oro / Che si purga nel crogiolo / Con quell'arte alta e divine" (In suffering is the loving soul refined / as gold is refined in the crucible / by an art exalted and divine) (L 1:269, May 2, 1741).

[39] "Se tu vuoi che te lo dica / È un segreto assai nascosto / L'ubriacarsi di quel mosto / E portar la Croce amica" (If you wish me to tell you / it is a secret very hidden / to drink this new wine / and to carry the dear cross) (ibid.).

[40] "Sì! è amica assai la Croce / Di chi ama il Divin Sole / E si studia quanto puole / Di patir senza dar voce." (Yes! The cross is a good friend / for whomever loves the Sun Divine / and studies as much as he can / to suffer without crying out) (ibid.).

[41] The letter and hymn were composed on Aug. 31, 1743, and Agnes Grazi died in June of 1744.

[42] This piece of poetry was published twice in Italian and in German. In German, it was included as a translation in prose in Martin Bialas' article "Leiden als Gnade in der Passionsmystik des Paul vom Kreuz", 439f. Its second publication was a translation in verse (by Seniormaster Franz Wanderer, Regensburg). See 116f. In English, a literal translation is presented in Fr. Roger Mercurio's and Fr. Fredrick Sucher's translation of the letters. Furthermore, the poem was put into poetic form by Mother Mary Agnes, C.P. (1896–1974), and included in the appendices of Brovetto, *Introduction to the Spirituality of St. Paul of the Cross*, and Bialas, *In*

ever, the first stanza indicates it is a poem in praise of participation in the passion of Jesus by bearing personal suffering. In this hymn, too, the varying degrees of participation are noted. The first stanza reads, "Through the cross, holy love / Perfects the loving soul / When fervent and constant / She consecrates to it her whole heart."[43]

In these lines, the matter of "perfection" corresponds to the purification the person "ought to endure" more or less actively.[44] The third and fourth stanzas describe participation as a friend in the cross of Jesus with joy, happiness, and security being the basic states of well-being in which the person is situated.[45] The fifth stanza presents "naked suffering", the highest form of participation in the cross. It runs, "Even more fortunate is the one / Who in naked suffering / Without a shade of joy / Is in Christ transformed."[46] This pure and naked suffering is further explained in the sixth stanza in the following way: "Oh, happy she who suffers / Without attachment to her pain, / But only wills to die to self / To love the more him who wounds."[47] The ultimate goal of participation in the passion and cross of Christ is, therefore, greater love of God so as to be "transformed" in Christ and "one" with God in love.

No wonder then that this saint, so strongly influenced by a mysticism of participation in the passion of Christ, over and over again encouraged women

---

This Sign, the Spirituality of St. Paul of the Cross, 138–39. The poem was also put into English poetic form by the late Brother Richard McCall, C.P. Unpublished copies are available (Holy Cross Province).

[43] "Nella Croce il Sant'Amore / Perfeziona l'alma amante / Quando fervida e costante / Gli consacra tutt'il cuore" (L 1:301, Aug. 31, 1743).

[44] This "devotion" corresponds to the behavior of the "true servant".

[45] The original text of these two stanzas reads, "Ma perchè è un grand' arcano / All'amante sol scoperto / Io che non sono esperto / Sol l'ammiro da lontano.—Fortunato è quel cuore / Che sta in croce abbandonato / Nelle braccia dell'amato / Brucia sul di Sant'Amore." ("But because it is a great secret / to the loving only discovered, / I, who have not experienced it, / only admire it from a distance.—Fortunate is that heart / which is on the cross abandoned / in the embrace of the Beloved / burnt up with Holy Love) (L 1:301, Aug. 31, 1743).

[46] "Ancor più è avventurato / Chi nel suo nudo patire / Senza ombra di gioire / Sta in Cristo trasformato" (ibid.).

[47] "Oh felice chi patisce / Senza attacco al suo patire / Ma sol vuol a sè morire / Per più amar chi lo ferisce!" (ibid.). As these two stanzas show, Paul of the Cross refers to that state in which one experiences neither comfort nor joy as "naked suffering". Therefore, it would be more accurate if Breton were to use the term *naked suffering* only for participation "in the manner of the Son". It must be noted that Breton also distinguishes in naked suffering three levels of abandonment: "Dès lors, comme nous avons distingué dans le nu-pâtir trois niveaux de 'déréliction', il faut s'attendre à ce que ce troisième ciel du saint abandon ait lui aussi ses 'demeures' et sa hiérarchie secrète." / "Then, just as we have distinguished three levels of 'dereliction' in naked suffering, we may also expect this third heaven of holy abandonment to have its 'dwellings' and its secret hierarchy" (Breton, *La Mystique,* 230).

and men to whom he wrote to accept actual suffering (when it cannot be avoided) as the "cross of Christ" and to endure it patiently.[48] Although this point could be supported with many illustrations from the letters of Paul, our explanation will be limited here to those exhortations to participate in the *passio Domini* by means of a specific kind of suffering only. The overall issue, however, is elaborated upon in other places.[49]

Paul frequently wrote to persons who were ill, encouraging them with words to the following effect: " . . . if you remain on your bed of pain, as if on sweet Jesus' cross, you will be his good companion by loving him with all your heart".[50] Hence unavoidable bodily suffering provides the sufferer with the opportunity of becoming more one with *Christus patiens*. Pain and suffering are given a meaning; more than that, they become a grace. This may be noted in the following excerpt from a letter in which Paul writes, "Long illnesses represent one of the greatest graces granted by God to those souls whom he most loves."[51] Certainly, these words contain a quality reminiscent of the verse from Proverbs: "For whom the Lord loves he reproves, and he chastises the son he favors" (Prov 3:12). At the same time, however, it is also evident that Paul of the Cross does not absolutize the value of suffering. In the same letter, he told the Sister he would pray

---

[48] What may be said about the value attributed to suffering by St. Paul of the Cross? When is suffering to be endured as the cross of Christ? It may not be affirmed that Paul of the Cross absolutized or even glorified suffering. When it was a question of curable illness, he recommended that every conceivable and possible thing be done to obtain a healing. A convincing proof of this is found in the Congregation's Rule written in his own hand. In the beginning of a special chapter devoted to the "Cure of Ill Brethren" (Chap. 39, *De cura fratrum aegrotantium*), Paul writes, "Valentibus praecipue curae sint Fratres aegroti. His exacta diligentia, et christiana charitate inserviant, nullumque corporale, aut spirituale remedium praetermittant, ut afflictis pro indigentia auxilientur, et prosint." / "Those in particular who are well should have concern for the brothers who are ill. They should take care of them with meticulous attentiveness and Christian charity, and they should not neglect any corporal or spiritual remedy so as to help and benefit the afflicted ones according to their need" (*Regulae et Constituiones*, 138, col. 3).

[49] See Bialas, "Leiden als Gnade", 427–41. Also see *Tagebuch*, 40–48. In Italian, see Bialas, "Il dolore umano", 53–67. In English, see Bialas, "Human Suffering", 98–121.

[50] In a letter to Thomas Fossi, the saint wrote, "Se ne stia sul letto della sua malattia, come su la Croce del dolce Gesù, e gli faccia buona compagnia con amarlo con tutto il cuore . . . " / "If you remain on your bed of illness, as on the cross of the sweet Jesus, you will be a good companion to him by loving him with all your heart . . . " (L 1:767, Mar. 18, 1763). Similar statements are found in other letters: L 1:239, Aug. 17, 1739, to Agnes Grazi; L 2:736, Dec. 18, 1765, to Sr. Marianna of Jesus; L 3:285, Dec. 12, 1754, to Nicola Coppelli, etc.).

[51] "Le malattie lunghe sono una delle più grandi grazie che Dio faccia alle anime sue più care" (L 3:606, May 8, 1762, to Sr. Angela Maddalena). See also L 1:685, Aug. 13, 1757, to Thomas Fossi; L 3:366, June 8, 1758, to Teresa Palozzi (later Sr. Angela Teresa); and L 3:629, Oct. 5, 1762, to Sr. M. Luisa of the Passion.

for her recovery even as he encouraged her to rest peacefully in silence "on the cross of Jesus".[52]

5. Suffering—Perfection—Glory

Still, the passion was not Christ's end point. His ultimate goal was his resurrection and glorification, the best proof of his mission. Similarly, for believers, there is the assurance that they will participate not only in Christ's passion but also in his glory.[53] Accordingly, the saint in a letter to his mother writes, "Those who suffer for the love of God", that is, who accept suffering as a participation in the passion of our Lord Jesus Christ, "help Jesus Christ carry his cross, and thus they will have a share in his glory in heaven . . ."[54]

For St. Paul of the Cross, a person's sharing in the cross of Jesus by enduring mental or physical pain represented a sign of election, a sign of incipient discipleship,[55] a sign of having been gifted with the "best way of perfection",[56] and, more than that, a sign of "God's love".[57] It is easy to see, therefore, why the saint refers to union with Christus patiens through suffering

[52] "Io pregherò il Signore che le conceda la sanità, ma non voglio che lei ne sia ansiosa, ma pacificamente ed in silenzio riposi su la Croce di Gesù." / "I will pray to the Lord to give you health, but I do not want you to be anxious but peaceful and to rest silently on Jesus' cross" (L 3:606, May 8, 1762).

[53] The first Epistle of Peter states, "Rejoice instead, in the measure that you share Christ's sufferings. When his glory is revealed, you will rejoice exultantly." Also see Rom 8:17–18; 2 Tim 2:11; Rev 2:10.

[54] "Quei che patiscono per amor di Dio, aiutano a portar la Croce a Gesù Cristo, e così saranno partecipi della sua gloria in Cielo . . ." (L 1:94, Dec. 15, 1734).

[55] In a letter of Sept. 5, 1743, Paul assured his friend Thomas Fossi, "Mi creda di certo, che mai è andata tanto bene come adesso: 'Nunc incipis esse Discipulus Christi!'" (L 1:553; also see Ignatius of Antioch's Epistle to the Romans, 4:3). A similar statement is found in L 4:25, Jan. 10, 1768, to Antonio Coccia: " . . . che ora veramente cominciate ad essere vero discepolo di Gesù Cristo, e lo arguisco dai travagli che vi permette la Divina Misericordia." / " . . . that you now truly begin to be a true disciple of Jesus Christ, and I infer this from the trials allowed you by permission of the divine mercy." Also see L 2:370, July 12, 1742, to the sisters Vallerani and his letter of Dec. 15, 1746, to his religious brethren of Mount Argentario Monastery, a letter published in Bollettino 7 (1926): 209.

[56] To Marianna Girelli, Paul wrote, " . . . godendo al sommo di sentirla crocefissa con Cristo, che è il mezzo più efficace per giungere alla perfezione del santo puro e netto amore, quale le desidero vivamente . . ." / " . . . I rejoice at hearing you are crucified with Christ, because it is the most efficacious means of attaining the perfection of holy, pure, and spotless love, which I so intensely desire . . ." (L 3:758, Apr. 25, 1769). He writes in a similar manner in L 1:110, Apr. 17, 1734, to Agnes Grazi; and L 1:476, Oct. 19, 1740, to Sr. Maria Cherubina Bresciani.

[57] "Sempre più conosco che S.D.M. l'ama teneramente come figlia, perchè la favorisce del continuo di nuove croci." / "I more and more know that his Divine Majesty tenderly loves you as a daughter, because he continually favors you with new crosses" (L 4:10, Mar. 29, 1768, to Agnes Segnéri). Also see L 4:125, Dec. 28, 1769, to a woman whose name is unknown; and L 3:629, Oct. 5, 1762, to Sr. M. Luisa of the Passion.

by such appelatives as "God's gift",[58] "treasure",[59] and "grace".[60] Suffering, however, is not an ultimate goal in itself but only a way, a means of arriving at greater union with God, a means of being changed thoroughly into the "divine good pleasure", as the saint himself says.[61]

This positive insight, this meaning attributed to human suffering as presented in the spiritual doctrine of St. Paul of the Cross, could and should be judged to possess lasting, indeed timeless validity. However great humankind's progress may be in the future, men and women will always have to confront, overcome and eliminate what is toilsome and difficult in order to achieve that progress; and, for this reason, suffering will remain a factor in the experience of the human person, who must endure it as "inevitable", in whatever manner he is disposed. For the one who believes in Christ, Paul's "mysticism of participation" is a help in that it gives to personal suffering (and this may sometimes reach a degree not thought endurable) a reason to master it and make it fruitful.

WHO IS THE AUTHOR OF THE TREATISE ON MYSTICAL DEATH?

Because many link Paul's mysticism of participation in the passion with the treatise "Mystical Death or Holocaust of Pure Spirit of a Religious Soul" (pp. 258–70), this chapter on participation in the passion would seem to be an appropriate place to bring forward my doubts about the authorship of the treatise. Therefore this section presents a slightly edited version of a paper delivered by me at a Congress on "Mystical Death" held in Zaragoza, Spain, from September 10 to 12, 1980. It needs to be noted that the thesis of this paper differs from that of the work of Fr. Antonio María Artola, C.P., author of the 1980 and 1986 texts *La Muerte Mística según San Pablo de la Cruz*. For the sake of scientific discussion, however, I thought it important that this paper be included in the English translation of this book on St. Paul of the Cross for three reasons:

1. Although the position presented here is an outgrowth of my original work published in Germany in 1978, it is sufficiently different that I

---

[58] "I patimenti sono i più preziosi regali che il nostro buon Dio soglia compartire alle anime sue dilette." / "Sufferings are the most precious gifts that our good God desires to share with his beloved souls" (L 2:30, June 20, 1760, to Maria Venturi Grazi).

[59] "Ringrazio Dio, che le fa parte del gran tesoro della Santa Croce, dei disprezzi ecc." / "I thank God that he has given you part of the great treasure of the holy cross, of contempt, etc." (L 1:118, Oct. 28, 1734, to Agnes Grazi). " . . . voi m'intendete di che tesoro parlo, che è il prezioso patire." / " . . . you understand the treasure of which I speak, that is, precious suffering" (L 2:443, Sept. 18, 1743, to Sr. Colomba Gertrude Gandolfi).

[60] "Fate gran conto del patire in silenzio, che è una delle grandi grazie che Dio le fa." / "Greatly esteem suffering in silence, which is one of the greatest graces granted by God" (L 3:366, June 8, 1758, to Teresa Palozzi).

[61] See n. 24 above.

cannot in good conscience merely republish a translation of the 1978 work, nor can I simply omit the section on mystical death as if it never existed.

2. The readership needs to be aware that a controversy surrounds the authorship of the treatise.

3. Presentation of the difficulties I encounter with the treatise on mystical death may stimulate further research.

The text of my 1980 paper, therefore, follows.

Preliminary Words

In the first place, I want to apologize and ask pardon because my presentation is not going to treat of the theme announced in the program, "Doctrine of Mystical Death in John Tauler and the School of Mystical Rebirth". The reason is the following: I began to treat of the subject matter in this sense, but as I delved deeper into the study of mystical death many more questions arose in my mind regarding the content and authenticity of the document. I am very interested in these questions, having already devoted four years to an intense study of its theme. In my doctoral thesis, "The Passion of Christ in St. Paul of the Cross", I dedicated ample space to an analysis of the treatise and published therein the complete text in Italian and in German.[62]

Well, then, in the study of the treatise "Mystical Death", numerous questions occurred to me, such as: Would Paul of the Cross talk in this way on the theme? Is it possible to integrate seamlessly the content of the treatise, as it is, within the general lines (or limits) of the saint's spiritual doctrine, as he revealed it to us in numerous letters? Do the diction and style allow us to affirm that St. Paul of the Cross is its author? Is the theological-spiritual basis here the same as that in his letters?

These and other questions occurred to me the deeper I went into my work. At last, an interior impulse carried me away. I decided to look for an answer to these interesting questions. I believe that other conference participants will have to confront them also. It is advantageous that we now examine the same questions from different angles and with complete independence of one from the other.

I know the answers I offer have the character of hypotheses only, but I have tried to support each with valid arguments. This Congress gives us a good opportunity to talk over and discuss these arguments, now that specialists who know the background of the treatise and who have studied the spirituality of St. Paul of the Cross are participating. The problem of authorship is of great

---

[62] M. Bialas, *Das Leiden Christi beim hl. Paul vom Kreuz (1694–1775): Eine Untersuchungn über die Passionszentrik der geistlichen Lehre des Gründers der Passionisten,* with Introduction by Prof. J. Moltmann (Aschaffenberg: Pattloch Verlag, 1978), 380–433.

importance. If this Congress succeeds in offering greater clarity in the solution of this problem, it will have made a great step forward. In the following notes and considerations, Fr. Antonio María Artola's study *La Morte Mistica di S. Paolo della Croce* has been a great stimulus to me. The degree of precision and the meticulous analysis of the work that occupies us is extraordinary and worthy of note.[63]

1. *Verifiable Facts*

Certainly, the June 26, 1976, discovery of the treatise on mystical death, considered to have been written by St. Paul of the Cross and sought for such a long time, was a decisive and joyous moment. In the convent of the Passionist nuns of Bilbao, a religious had discovered some time previously a notebook of forty manuscript pages; the first eighteen were a copy of the lost treatise on mystical death. I understand the surprise and joy of my fellow religious, who, after looking at and examining the text, arrived at the conclusion that they were, in effect, holding a copy of the lost treatise.

Some time later another, apparently older, copy was discovered in Mamers, France. When both manuscripts were compared, linguistic properties of style and orthography marked the Mamers copy as being an earlier Italian.[64] These two manuscripts allow us to conclude that we, in truth, have found the manuscript on mystical death of which our founder spoke in several letters. It is not necessary to go into detail about the witnesses at St. Paul of the Cross' beatification and canonization processes or about their depositions. The manuscripts found are copies of the treatise on mystical death that was attributed to St. Paul of the Cross.

A study of the treatise makes it easy to show there are in it themes that play a central role in the spiritual doctrine of St. Paul of the Cross. Among these is that of the concept of mystical death, a concept that pertains to the essence of the founder's doctrine and that appears constantly in his letters after his "discovery" of Tauler, i.e., after the year 1748. Fathers Brovetto and Artola have put together and have classified all the places in Paul's letters in which this concept appears.[65] In fact, the polarity mystical death–divine nativity is fundamental to his theological-spiritual doctrine, and, it is certainly within the realm of possibility to think the saint would have wanted to treat thematically of this polarity in a special manuscript. (We have to point out that the

---

[63] Antonio María Artola, *La Morte Mistica di S. Paolo della Croce.* Vol. I, *Commento ai Paragrafi I–X.*

[64] Artola, 105–9.

[65] Brovetto, *Introduzione alla spiritualità.* Brovetto identifies forty places. Also see Artola, 17–18 — thirty-one letters of the founder cited.

expression *mystical death* also had import in terms of quietism. This concept appears in many of the condemned phrases.) I will develop more fully the matter of the conceptual content of the term *mystical death* later in this paper.

Another basic principle characteristic of the treatise on mystical death is surrender to the will of God. Specialists in the letters and spirituality of St. Paul of the Cross have already spoken of this same construction, considering it as a principle amounting to a characteristic feature of the theological-spiritual thought of the saint.[66]

Also in need of mentioning is the central place held by the *passio Domini*. The treatise frequently reverts to the theme of the passion and death of Jesus. More than that, participation in the sufferings and in the cross of Christ is the predominant theme actuating the entire treatise. Passioncentrism is a characteristic that unmistakably marks the life and thought of St. Paul of the Cross.

In many of the saint's letters written to those whom he directed we also encounter the polarity between nothing and all (*niente-tutto*). Therefore, it is just, indeed necessary, to consider this polarity as something basic to the thought of the founder.[67] As frequently as we encounter the characteristic concepts of *niente* and *nulla* in the treatise on mystical death we encounter the concepts of self-humiliation and self-annihilation.[68]

This above-noted thematic congruence between the treatise on mystical death and the spiritual doctrine of St. Paul of the Cross is of the nature of a sample only. Many more examples may be given, as I have already treated elsewhere.[69] I now, however, prefer to propose my thesis: *Paul of the Cross is not the author of the treatise on mystical death.*

2. *Paul of the Cross Is Not the Author of "Mystical Death"*

Given similar principles and even thematic congruence, it is easy to understand how the treatise on mystical death could have been attributed to St. Paul of the Cross and, even more so, how Tradition would keep on attributing it to him. I myself was also of the same opinion at an earlier time.

But whoever knows well the authentic founts of the religious-spiritual thought of our founder, i.e., his numerous letters, will have compared the great diversity in style, terminology, lines of thought, and theological and spiritual presuppositions that exist between the letters and the treatise on mystical death.

[66] Viller, "La volonté", 132–34.
[67] Bialas, *Das Leiden Christi*, 266–274.
[68] "Mystical Death", art. I and XVII.
[69] Bialas, *Das Leiden Christi*, 380–408.

So, then, I will now formulate, in a more precise and complete manner, my thesis, which naturally contains much of a hypothesis also. It reads,

> The treatise on mystical death is not the work of St. Paul of the Cross. He neither wrote nor dictated it to another. The author is another person. The treatise appealed to St. Paul of the Cross, and for this reason he had it sent to the Carmelite Sister Angela M. Magdalen of the Seven Sorrows.

Because there are many fine St. Paul of the Cross specialists here now at this Congress, I would like to propose my thesis for discussion. It is a hypothesis that tries to examine by means of some arguments and—in keeping with my opinion—solves better than any other the questions and problems that arise in relation to the authenticity of the manuscript, in keeping with the actual state of affairs.

3. *Authentic Testimony Regarding the Manuscript: Two Letters of St. Paul of the Cross*

The most valid testimony regarding the treatise is that of the founder himself written in letters to Sr. Angela Magdalen of the Seven Sorrows and to the master of novices Peter of St. John, C.P. The following may be said of these letters:

1. Paul of the Cross talked objectively about the work "Mystical Death" or of "that directive on mystical death". There is not one indication that he claimed to be its author. Nevertheless, it would have been natural for him to have done so, i.e., to have mentioned himself as its author, had he been its author. I do not see any reason for him to have hidden or denied the authorship of the writing.

2. Both letters included a certain caution and warning with regard to the application of the content. St. Paul of the Cross liked the treatise and sent it on, but he counseled caution and prudence. I believe there are many things he could have told his correspondents in this regard.

One may ask: Why then did he send the manuscript to others, if he himself showed a certain reserve about its content? To this I would respond: the content was to a great extent in accord with the fundamental principles of his spiritual thinking; the concept and content of the document on mystical death are something that he had very much at heart. He liked the manuscript and therefore sent it to the Carmelite religious.

We also have to take note and be equally critical of those who witnessed to the authenticity of the treatise on mystical death at the processes. For example, Sr. Mary Celeste Seraphim testified, "Someone told me—I can't remember who—that the work had been written by the servant of God, Fr. Paul of the

Cross, and that he sent it to our religous Sr. Angela M. Magdalen of the Seven Sorrows."[70]

Therefore, certain rumor, certain fame: *"dicitur", "fertur..."* In no manner was the affirmation of Paul of the Cross as the author of the treatise on mystical death given or presented as precise information during the processes.

Another important witness was Sr. Maria Louise, sibling of the religious to whom St. Paul of the Cross sent the manuscript and who had "direct and personal knowledge of the manuscript", as noted by Fr. Artola. For this reason, her testimony has special value. With regard to the manuscript, she stated, among other things, the following: *"... se fosse composizione del Servo di Dio, no so accertarlo, il carattere no era suo..."* ("...I do not know if it was written by the servant of God; the handwriting was not his).[71] Although this statement does no more than make a reference to the penmanship of the saint, it insinuates that the Sister questions the document's authenticity. It is noteworthy that the religious does not attribute authorship of the manuscript to St. Paul of the Cross. That she declared herself in the processes in such a manner seems to me to be a valid argument for doubting Paul of the Cross' authorship. Neither do we know if there were other reasons for her to have made this statement. The context of the declaration permits such suspicions. Perhaps her own sister, who had received the treatise from St. Paul of the Cross himself, questioned its authorship or even knew it to have been composed by another.

4. Differences in Style and Terminology

One need not be a specialist to compare what we find in the treatise on mystical death with the distinct style in the epistolary of the saint. One could object that the mystical death treatise is not a letter but a systematic treatise, therefore requiring a distinct style and terminology. To this one may respond that it is not a scientific and abstract work but a manuscript on a concrete ascetic theme that has a very personal character to it, like that of a letter. In addition, its theme deals only with the concrete spiritual life. The greater part of the letters of St. Paul of the Cross are those of spiritual direction, and they have the same end point.

Knowing the style and terminology of the letters, it seems to me very unlikely, almost impossible, that St. Paul of the Cross either dictated or wrote "Mystical Death", constructed as it is in so distinct a manner. In the letters, Paul again and again used similar formulations to describe and express succinctly the same or similar spiritual realities. For this reason, it is possible to speak of *typical* expressions of his that we find in hundreds of letters.

I am going to present such expressions here, in the form of examples just

[70] Brovetto, *Introduzione alla spiritualità*, 26, n. 8.
[71] Artola, 66.

being tossed out: "interior chamber", "sacred desert", "interior desert", "to feed one's self on the will of God", "to be in your nothingness", "God is All", "to abandon one's self to the immense Divinity", "immense sea of charity", "naked suffering", "die to all that is not God", "in pure and naked faith", "clothed in Christ Jesus", "reborn in the divine incarnate Word", "detached from all created things", "in the bosom of the heavenly Father", "infused sufferings", "impression of the passion", "to fish in the sea of the passion", etc.

It is difficult to imagine that our founder would have written or talked about a purely spiritual theme without using expressions similar to or identical with those so commonly used in his letters. For this reason, I do not believe St. Paul of the Cross dictated this treatise to any other person since, as has already been said, more verbal and stylistic correspondence would be apparent.

These language differences are obvious. Subsequent to a critical analysis of the text, therefore, Fr. Artola — using an interesting design — divided the treatise into two parts, with the authorship of one part being attributed to St. Paul of the Cross and the other to an unknown redactor (thought to be Fr. John Mary). This solution does not seem convincing to me in that in the part assigned to Paul of the Cross, the same differences in style and expression remain. There is, of course, the possibility that we are dealing with a text on mystical death written by two authors, neither of whom is Paul of the Cross. However, were the text to be critically divided according to other points of view, e.g., along lines of correspondence of its content with terminology from his letters, then another totally distinct division would be made. For me, however, the critical division of the text is very hypothetical. Even though I am not an exegete, I cannot help but question not the soundness of the technique but its use here, for reasons given above.[72] It is, nevertheless, interesting that the authorship of the manuscript has proved to be of sufficient difficulty that such an artificial division of the text had to be made.

Neither am I convinced by the theory that the substance of the manuscript distances itself from the "personal plane" of the founder because he had consigned its writing to another. The difficulties pointed out remain, and, in addition, it is not likely Paul would have passed on to another the responsibility of responding to matters of such an intimate nature. He frequently counseled others not to pass on his letters to another person. This concern that privacy not be invaded was voiced strongly, even to the point of asking his correspondents to burn his letters so that they would not fall into the hands of others.

While speaking of style and literary form, it is natural to refer to the form and expression of his thought and to see how it appears in the treatise. I call attention, as did Fr. Artola,[73] to the stamp of consequential thought and

[72] Artola, 74–92.
[73] Artola, 72.

logic that hallmarks the text. However, Paul's writings and letters contain more impulsivity, spontaneity. Paul's reasonings are not put forward in the form of syllogisms but are rather explanations in spiral form, in that some circles embrace others. This observation brings to light yet another marked difference that argues against Paul of the Cross' being the author of the treatise on mystical death.

5. Differences in Content

Polarity of mystical death—divine nativity. It is certainly surprising to find in the treatise on mystical death numerous themes that play an important role in the spiritual doctrine of St. Paul of the Cross. But it has to be said here that the founder spoke of these in a manner distinct from that expressed in his letters. In this conference, I cannot go into all the details—that would involve too great an analysis of his letters and of the treatise. For this reason, I will limit myself only to differences in content that are most important and will explain these briefly.

If we study in detail the places in the letters in which mystical death or to die mystically is discussed, we will find that this reference is with great frequency—almost always—followed by the concept of divine rebirth or to be reborn in the Divine Word Jesus Christ. The imagery of mystical death is not a principle complete in itself but is the first member of a bipolar team. This polar thought is well noted in the spiritual doctrine of Paul of the Cross. Where it can be seen most clearly is in the polarity death-life, and with more precision in mystical death—divine rebirth. This will be better understood with a few examples.

In a letter, Paul describes the effects of the interior life in these words:

> Be it as it may, die mystically to all that is not God, with greatest detachment from all created things, enter alone into the depths of that sacred interior solitude, in that sacred desert.... And in this manner, the soul is constantly reborn to a new life of love in the Divine Word to whom it always listens, loves, etc. Oh, how many more things I would like to say.[74]

The sole objective of mystical death is "new life, new and divine life in the Divine Word Jesus Christ". In a letter to Anna Maria Calcagnini, Paul writes,

> Once you have died this mystical death, you will live a new life; better said, you will be reborn to a new, deified life in the Divine Word Jesus Christ, and oh, what a life that will be! You will be so great and full of heavenly

[74] L 2:724, Aug. 17, 1751, to L. Burlini.

intelligence that you will not even be able to talk to me, who serves your soul as a poor father.[75]

Mystical death and divine nativity are the same reality, two aspects of the graced movement of God in the most intimate part of the soul. In such a way does Paul express himself in a letter to Thomas Fossi:

> Think of mystical death. He who is mystically dead does not think of anything other than to live a deified life . . . and to await without anxiety all that God arranges for him, cutting off all that is of the outside, so as not to impede the divine work that is realized within the intimate chamber . . . , where the same powers are attentive to the divine work and to that divine nativity that is celebrated at every moment in him who has the fortune to be dead mystically.[76]

In these two examples, taken from Paul's letters and which we would be able to multiply with ease, the saint's point of view on mystical death and its relationship to new divine life can be clearly seen. It is because of this depth of religious-spiritual thought in the writings of St. Paul of the Cross that it becomes problematic to attribute to him the authorship of the treatise on mystical death. The concepts "rebirth", "divine nativity", "new, deified life", used in the letters in speaking of mystical death, do not appear in the treatise. Also far from actually being seen in the treatise are Paul's clear-cut polarizations, especially that of death-life.

Fr. Artola also talks at length of this problem, i.e., that the second member of the polar team (divine rebirth) does not appear in the treatise on mystical death. One could put forward the objection that article XVII refers to the resurrection in the words: " . . . to rise again with Christ who is triumphant in heaven". But this is not a reference to divine rebirth but to the eschatological event of resurrection. Divine rebirth is something that, by the grace of God, is realized here in this life. This can be seen clearly in the letters and has also been well demonstrated by Fr. Artola, who agrees that article XVII does not apply to mystical death. ("... che esclude intenzionalmente i rapporti tra Morte Mistica e Divina Natività".)[77]

To resolve this difficulty, Fr. Artola states that the reference to the resurrection in article XVII is not written by St. Paul of the Cross. The question has to be asked, however, whether Paul would have approved an explanation of the spiritual effects of mystical death that did not put into play the notion of divine rebirth, the second member of the polar team. I consider it very unlikely in that even in his letters both before and after the manuscript was sent to the Carmelite nun this polarity continually appears. I believe it highly unlikely that this experienced director of souls would take and write,

[75] L 3:826, Jul. 9, 1769.
[76] L 1:788, Dec. 29, 1768.
[77] Artola, 91.

above all his other rich religious-spiritual experiences, seventeen manuscript points on mystical death without, at the same time, making one reference to the reality of a new and mystical life in Christ Jesus, a life that, in the final analysis, for Paul takes first place, as can be seen in his letters.

Fr. Artola also acknowledges a similar problem when he writes the following in his study of the treatise on mystical death:

> It could be said that the actual treatise opens out like an arch that breaks precisely at its culminating point, when it should initiate the continuation of the theme of divine nativity. The treatise lacks that part which, in the typology of the death of Jesus, would correspond to the resurrection and which, in the epistolary, is precisely the new life: divine nativity of the soul in God.[78]

After having said what has been said about the differences in style and content between the treatise on mystical death and the letters, I should be able to rest the case, having shown that the founder did not personally write the treatise. But, in my opinion, I am also unable to admit that he would have dictated it, since in such a case there should appear, with regard to content, even more verbal correspondence between his thought and the text. There still remains the possibility that the saint could have entrusted another religious of the Congregation with its writing. This would be a possibility, and it should be considered but not assumed as fact. All we know is that St. Paul of the Cross sent a manuscript with the title "Mystical Death" to Sr. Angela M. Magdalen. Who its author was St. Paul of the Cross did not say. In the hypothesis that the founder might have entrusted its writing to another, the treatise itself would not be attributable to St. Paul of the Cross, but the author could have expressed in it the basic principles of the spiritual doctrine of the founder. The differences between the founder's and the author's approach, however, are more than sufficiently great. Coincidental presence of some themes is not sufficient evidence to attribute the authorship of the manuscript to St. Paul of the Cross.

Theological-spiritual foundation. In reading the treatise on mystical death it can be clearly seen that many phrases present themselves with an imperativeness that we could call "voluntative". The manuscript breathes a strong voluntarism. This also seems to explain the use of the first person. The auxiliary verb as in "I will . . . " underscores this voluntarism. In the letters of St. Paul of the Cross, however, we encounter another basic manner of comportment. In these, he animates the personal strength of the correspondent in the attainment of perfection and sanctity, but he always insists that the ultimate source is the grace of God. One is not able to attain sanctification alone on the basis of personal strength: that would be Pelagianism.

---

[78] Artola, 92.

While "Mystical Death" frequently talks of grace, this line of writing in the text is characterized by an imperative, categorical stamp or mark. In fact, its voluntarism at times degenerates into rigorism, but it needs a great gift of discernment of spirits to recognize it. This is not my personal judgment alone: St. Paul of the Cross also adverts to this. To the master of novices, Fr. Peter, to whom Paul also sent a copy of the treatise, he indicates that novices are not to receive the text until the end of the novitiate. He bases this advice on the following:

> Otherwise, if they were given this teaching at the beginning, there would be danger that they might consider the life of virtue too difficult. The important thing for them is to become accustomed to the regular holy observances, etc.[79]

The saint feared the manuscript would discourage them, making the path of virtue very difficult. Are such words not a criticism of the rigorism manifest in the treatise? I do not believe St. Paul of the Cross would have talked so about his own manuscript. And, even when in his letters he talks of concepts present in the treatise to persons not considered beginners but progressed in the spiritual life, he does not motivate them by means of voluntaristic rigorism. Rather, he leads them by way of mystical profundities none of which are easy to sift through and understand.[80]

The differences noted in relation to the presence or absence of voluntarism can be seen more clearly with some examples. Let us compare the manner in which Paul talks about mystical death in conjunction with the exercise of virtue—or, more precisely said, in conjunction with the *death* of one's own will and passions—with the way in which the same topic is covered in the treatise on mystical death. Indeed it is precisely this point of ascetic-moral vision, i.e., the *death* of one's will and passion, that appears so strongly in the treatise on mystical death. For the sake of comparison, Paul's letter to Sr. Marianna Girelli will be used.

First, let us look at the treatise. The rigorism mentioned above appears, most of all, in the second part of "Mystical Death", when in article X the metaphor of death, in clear and coherent imagery, is introduced to describe or explain the meaning of mystical death. In articles XI–XIII, this metaphor is used as an example for a life lived according to the evangelical counsels of poverty, chastity, and obedience. In articles XIV and XVI, it serves as the basis for silence in the former and for love of neighbor in the latter. Although the metaphor of death is not used in article XVII through to the end, expressions which seem rigoristic do recur, e.g., "rag of the monastery" (*straccio del monastero*) and the statement " . . . to destroy all my self-love, inclinations,

[79] L 3:442, May 17, 1765.
[80] L 1:788, Dec. 29, 1768, to Thomas Fossi.

passions, and desires". Perhaps these were the expressions that occasioned the caution advised by the founder: "...there would be danger that they might consider the life of virtue too difficult".[81]

Now, let us look at the letter to Marianna Girelli. In this letter, we find other ways of looking at natural inclinations and movements of the passions. Thus, Paul states, "[This even while] feeling still natural inclinations and movements of the passions that never die until we do."[82]

Some lines later, Paul accentuates this thinking even more by saying that although "the natural inclinations and movements of the passions will never die completely", they should be mortified so as to be no impediment. He then immediately goes on to describe the objective and manner by which mystical death works. This life in God is so intense that the person who experiences it is able to say with the Apostle, "...and the life I live now is not my own; Christ is living in me".

There is still another difference to which we will refer. The treatise on mystical death has the subtitle "Holocaust of the Pure Spirit of a Religious Soul". This expresses an upward movement of a person to God; but, in the letters of St. Paul of the Cross, mystical death is more frequently thought of as a pure grace of God. Certainly, the treatise talks about grace also; but the grace to which it especially refers is *gratia adjuvans,* i.e., that which is on the side of ascetical-moral effort, while Paul views mystical death as a pure and free action of God, that he communicates to a person. The following passage taken from a letter to Marianna Girelli exemplifies this assertion:

> ...it is necessary to die mystically to all things. [This even while] feeling still natural inclinations and movements of the passions that never die until we do, [because such] is not a thing of this life. It is necessary to wait until the visit of the sovereign Master.... In the meantime, therefore, vest the soul with the burning rays of his grace.[83]

In another letter, Paul qualifies mystical death as one of the greatest graces the mercy of God bestows on a soul.[84]

Anyone who knows the letters of our founder marvels, above all, at the spiritual and mystical depth of his piety. His personal experience of God is the primary fount from which this piety flows. Neither does our treatise lack a certain mystical aspect, but it does not reach the profound dimension that we see in Paul's letters. This also applies to the first part of the treatise on mystical death.

---

[81] L 3:442.
[82] L 3:756, Dec. 28, 1768, to A. M. Girelli.
[83] L 3:756.
[84] L 3:821, Jan. 31, 1769, to A. Calcagnini.

Final Notes

For adduced reasons, it is very difficult for me to acknowledge St. Paul of the Cross as the author of the treatise on mystical death. In keeping with the actual state of the science, therefore, I affirm that St. Paul of the Cross is not the author of "Mystical Death". I know not even one positive, authentic argument that effectively indicates he is.

With these considerations, I do not in any way want to create any kind of anxiety about the doctrine of the founder. On the contrary, I hope that what I have said will stimulate further the study of the authentic founts of the founder, above all, the numerous letters that bear a very profound mysticism, since it is in them where the authentic thought of St. Paul of the Cross appears most of all. From a greater study of the letters we will some day perhaps attain more light on this treatise on mystical death.

TEXT OF THE TREATISE "MYSTICAL DEATH OR HOLOCAUST OF THE PURE SPIRIT OF A RELIGIOUS SOUL"

"MORTE MISTICA OVERRO OLOCAUSTO DEL PURO SPIRITO DI UN'ANIMA RELIGIOSA"

I am writing these pages[85] lest through human weakness and my own negligence I lose those lights and holy inspirations which Jesus in his infinite mercy has deigned to give me. I am writing them so that, shaken out of the lethargy of my infidelity and laziness, I might rise to the light of divine grace and begin that way of perfection which will be more pleasing to my Lord. Therefore, in order to facilitate my journey and to walk with sureness, may the doctrine in these pages move me to go forward and to overcome my

Affinchè per umana fragilità e per mia negligenza avessi[86] a perdere quei lumi e sante ispirazioni, che Gesù per sua infinita misericordia si è degnato darmi perché scossa dal letargo della mia infedeltà e pigrizia, sorga al lume della divina grazia, ed intraprenda quella via di perfezione, che più piacerá al mio Signore: Quindi è che a fine di facilitarmene la strada e camminarvi con sicurezza, tutto quello che in questo foglio si contiene e che da me parmi richieda al presente Iddio, acciocchè approvatami dalla santa Ubbidienza, di cui

[85] In the original text, the first sentence consists of the entire first section divided into many subordinate clauses. This long sentence, therefore, was divided into several sentences in both the German and the English translations to increase the clarity of the content and to facilitate reading.

[86] Obviously, this is a corrupted text. To be logical and meaningful, the sentence ought

repugnance with generosity. God seems to be asking this of me now, with the approval of holy obedience, whose martyr[87] and faithful daughter I want to be right up to my last breath. May Jesus grant me the grace of a good beginning and holy perseverance.

God asks only one thing of me. But many other things are asked of me in order to achieve and attain it. Oh! God, what violence! My Jesus, I must *die and obey!* You ask too much of me in one thing, because you want me to die with you *on the cross.* A mystical death, a death however sweet, is too hard for me because I must undergo a thousand deaths before dying! Lord, human nature is frightened when it thinks of itself alone. It trembles and is dismayed at the very thought of it. But when you command, the spirit is indeed ready to accomplish it with the unfailing certainty that if you will it, your help in doing it will not be wanting. However, I must set aside such a thought so that I may run with complete indifference in blind faith, like a deer thirsting at the font of divine providence in total abandonment to you. I allow myself to

ne voglio essere martire e fedelissima figlia sino all'ultimo respiro di mia vita, mi serva di stimolo a proseguire e a vincere colle violenze le mie ripugnanze: Gesù dunque mi conceda la grazia di un buon principio, e santa perseveranza.

Una sola cosa richiede Dio da me, ma se ne richiedono moltissime per conseguirla e giungervi. Oh! Dio che violenza! Si deve *Morire ed Ubbidire* mio Gesù! in una cosa troppo mi chiedete perchè volete che io muoia con Voi *sulla Croce.* Morte mistica, morte per me troppo dura ma soave perché prima di morire a mille morti mi conviene sottopormi! Signore, al solo pensarvi l'umanità s'inorridisce trema e sgomenta, ma lo spirito quale Voi comandate, è già pronto per eseguirla sull'infallibile certezza che se voi la volete non mancherà il vostro soccorso per conseguirla; devo tuttavia lasciare un tale riflesso per potere in fede e alla cieca correre con tutta indifferenza, come cervo assetato al fonte delle divine disposizioni, con un totale abbandono in Voi, lasciandomi guidare come Voi volete, non cercando me stessa, ma solo che Dio com-

---

to contain the negative *non.* Most likely the author's original text contained the words *non venissi* instead of *avessi.* The following clue supports this supposition. In testimony given by a witness in the *processiculus diligentiarum* (CIC, c. 2061) of Vetralla (preserved in the *Regestum quorundam Actorum in causis Servorum Dei* of the Archives of the Congregation of Rites), the first line of the document "Mystical Death" is quoted as follows: "... è diviso in 17 §. Incomincia colle seguenti parole: 'Affinchè per umana fragilità e mia negligenze non venissi a perdere quei lumi' ecc. e termina colle seguenti: 'Gesù, l'ultimo respiro sia il vostro amore. Amen'" (as quoted in Brovetto, *Introduzione alla Spiritualità,* 26).

[87] This text is written like a formula for the consecration of a person in the religious state, and it was dedicated to a Carmelite nun. Throughout, the author composes the text as if it had been written by the Sister herself.

be guided as you will. I do not seek myself but only what is pleasing to God himself. I will annihilate myself by doing his will and marveling within myself how God wills to receive such meager pleasure from a miserable creature, full of so many faults and sins. To obtain this, I will always humble myself interiorly. I will consider myself as I am, and I will foster a very exalted idea of God as Master of all, immense Love, inexorable Judge, Goodness without end. O God!

I. I will in no way leave my own nothingness unless I am moved by God, my First Principle and Last End. I will not lift myself up more than what God wills, lest through presumption I cast myself down and fall. No, Lord!

II. I will be resigned and ready to do the divine will by *desiring nothing,* by *refusing nothing,* and I will be equally happy with his every will.

I will strip myself of everything by a complete abandonment of myself to God. I will leave the care of myself entirely to him. He knows what I need and I do not know. Therefore, I shall accept with equal resignation both light and darkness, consolation and calamities and crosses, suffering and joy. I will praise him in everything and for everything. Above all, I will bless that hand which scourges me, as I put my total trust in him.

And if sometimes he will grace me with his presence, either with just its effects or by the continual practice of it, I will never attach

piaccia se stesso, coll' adempimento della sua volontà mi annienterò in me stessa ammirando come Dio voglia ricevere tal minimo compiacimento, da una miserabile creatura ripiena di tanti difetti e peccati, e per tale effetto, mi umilierò sempre dentro me stessa stimandomi come sono, ed avrò un altissimo concetto di Dio, come padrone di tutto, amore immenso, giudice inesorabile, bontà senza fine. Oh Dio!

I. Non mi muoverò punto dal mio nulla se non venga mossa da Dio, primo principio ed ultimo fine, ed allora non mi alzerò più di quello che Dio vuole, affinchè per mia presunzione non venga a precipitarmi e cadere. No Signore!

II. Starò rassegnata e pronta al divino volere col *nulla bramare, niente ricusare,* ed *egualmente contenta* di *ogni suo volere.*

Mi spoglierò di tutto con un totale abbandono di me stessa in Dio, lasciando interamente la cura di me a Lui; Egli sà ed io non so, quello che mi conviene, e però riceverò con eguale rassegnazione si la luce che le tenebre, si le consolazioni che le calamità e le croci, si il patire che il godere; in tutto e di tutto lo benedirò, e più di tutto quella mano che mi flagella, fidandomi interamente di Lui.

E se talvolta mi vorrà aggraziare della sua presenza, o con soli effetti di essa, o con l'atto pratico e continuo, non mi attacherò mai al gusto

myself to the delights of the spirit.
Neither will I afflict myself through
fear of being deprived of it, but I
will be most ready for the pain of
his abandonment which I deserve. I
will always give him the gift of my
pure and naked *will*, by offering a
crucified and dead soul to Jesus, crucified and dead. I do this because it
pleases him that I return to darkness
and agony when he thus wills it,
with a happy and resigned spirit. I
ask him to let me say, *"After the
darkness I hope for light." My Jesus, I
adore you. I am dying by not dying. Oh,
what a holy death! What agony!*

III. If Jesus wants me to be desolate, dead and buried in darkness, I
will reflect that I ought to remain in
hell deservedly because of my enor-
mous sins. I should consider that it is
the goodness of my God which
has changed it into such sufferings
for me. I will unite myself very
firmly to the anchor of his most
powerful mercy so that, distrusting
myself, I will not offend his goodness, which is so great! *Oh, what
goodness of God!*

IV. I will try with all my strength
to follow the footsteps of my Jesus.
If I am *afflicted, abandoned, desolate, I
will keep him company in the Garden.*
If I am despised and injured, *I will*

dello spirito, né mi affliggerò per
timore di restarne priva, ma prontis-
sima alla pena meritata dei suoi abbandoni, gli farò sempre il dono della
pura e nuda mia *volontà* con *offrire
Lui a Lui*[88] *un anima Crocifissa e morta,
a Gesù Crocifisso e Morto*, poiché a Lui
così piace, contenta e rassegnata tornerò alle tenebre ed agonie, quando
così voglia pregandolo a permettermi
di poter dire: *Spero dopo le tenebre la
luce: Mio Gesù ti adoro e sto morendo
per non morire: Oh che santa Morte!
Perchè in agonia!*

III. Se Gesù mi vorrà desolata,
morta e sepolta nelle tenebre, riflet-
terò che dovendo per i miei enormi
peccati starmene meritevolmente nell'
inferno, essere bontà del mio Dio
avermelo mutato in tali pene, mi
attaccherò ben soda all'ancora della
potentissima sua misericordia, acciò
diffidando di essa non facessi torto
alla sua bontà tanto grande! *Oh che
bontà di Dio!*

IV. Procurerò a tutto mio potere
seguire del mio Gesù le pedate, se
afflitta, abbandonata, desolata, mi tro-
verò, *mi accompagnerò seco nell'Orto*.
Se disprezzata, ingiuriata, mi accom-

[88] The formulation *con offrire Lui a Lui* is not clear in this context. Since the personal
pronouns are capitalized, the following interpretation is possible: the accusative pronoun *Lui*
refers to Jesus, while the dative *Lui* refers to the Father. Notwithstanding, it is improbable
that the author would have used this short, grammatically austere form to speak of the First
and Second Persons of the Trinity. Besides, the preceding sentence talks of God and his will
and not of God the Father and God the Son. Therefore, we suppose we have here a mistake
made by the copyist. Perhaps the correct text was *offrirla a Lui,* in which the suffix *la* would
have referred to the will of God. This conjecture was avoided, however, in both the German
and English translations.

*keep him company in the Praetor-
ium.* If I am depressed and afflicted
in the agonies of suffering, I will
keep him company faithfully *on the
Mount,* and in a generous spirit I
will keep him company on the cross,
with the lance in my heart. *Oh, how
sweet it is to die!*

V. I will strip myself of every
interest of my own, looking *neither
to suffering nor to reward* but only to
the glory of God and his pure pleasure. I will strive to remain only
within these two terms: here to ago-
nize as long as God wills, and here
to die of his pure love. *Oh, how
blessed is the love of Jesus!*

VI. I will not seek nor will I
love anything other than God alone
because in him alone will I have the
joy of paradise, of peace, happiness,
and love. I will arm myself with a
holy and relentless hatred of everything which could turn me away
from him. *My Jesus, never let sin be in
my heart!*

VII. I shall banish every foolish
fear which can make me faint-hearted
in your holy service. This will be
my only rule: If I shall be strong
and faithful to God, he will always
be mine. I will fear him alone, and I
will always avoid what could bring
displeasure to him. I will always control myself. With all my strength I
will try not to displease him deliberately even in the least way, insofar
as it will be possible through his
divine grace. *Oh, what a beautiful
hope!*

VIII. If through weakness I should
fall into some fault, I will rise up

pagnerò *nel Pretorio.* Se depressa ed
angustiata nelle agonie del patire, con
fedeltà mi accompagnerò *al Monte,*
e con generosità alla Croce, colla
lancia nel cuore. *Oh che dolce morire!*

V. Mi spoglierò d'ogni mio proprio interesse con non riguardare *né
pena, né premio;* ma solo alla gloria di
Dio, ed al puro suo gusto, non cercando di stare che fra questi due
termini; Qui agonizare fino che Dio
vuole, e qui morire di puro suo
amore. *Oh che benedetto Amore di
Gesù!*

VI. Non cercherò né amerò altra
cosa che Dio solo, perché in questo
solo goderò il Paradiso, pace, contento, e amore; e mi armerò di un
odio santo ed implacabile contra
tutto quello che può da Lui distormi.
Gesù mio, mai peccato nel cuore!

VII. Sbandirò da me ogni pazzo
timore che render mi possa pusil-
lanime nel suo santo servizio; con
questa sola massima che, se sarò fedele
e forte a Dio, egli sempre sarà mio,
temerò Lui solo, e ciò che può apportargli disgusto fuggirò sempre, e per
ciò starò sempre sopra me stessa,
guardando a tutto mio potere non
apportargli volontariamente disgusto,
benchè minimo: per quanto colla
sua divina grazia mi sarà possibile.
Oh che bella speranza!

VIII. Se per mia debolezza cadessi
in qualche errore sorgerò subito col

immediately with repentance. I will
acknowledge my misery and what I
am and what I can do. With my
head bowed down and with tears in
my eyes and sighs in my heart, I will
beg God for pardon. I will ask for
the grace never to betray him again,
but to root myself more firmly in
him. Neither will I pause more than
is necessary in acknowledging my
misery, but I will turn to him saying,
*"My God, my Jesus, this is the fruit I
can give you. Do not trust me for I am
miserable!"*

IX. I will always set my heart on
God. With all my strength I will
detach myself completely from the
earth and from all that is not God. I
want to be the dwelling place of
Jesus.[89] I want to make that dwelling place a Calvary of suffering, as
the Blessed Clare of Montefalco[90] *did*.
I want to give the key only to him
so that he might be the absolute
Master to dwell there at his pleasure
and to put there what he pleases.[91]
My heart will no longer be mine,
because I am not my own anymore.
My heart will belong only to God:
He is my Love!

X. I will die completely to myself
and live for God alone. I will cer-

pentimento, riconoscendo la mia
miseria, e quello che sono, e quello
che posso, pregando il mio Dio col
capo a terra, colle lagrime su gli
occhi, e coi sospiri nel cuore per il
perdono e grazia di mai più tradirlo;
ma di stabilirmi più seco. Né qui mi
fermerò più di quello che mi conviene per riconoscere me stessa miserabile, ma tornerò a Lui dicendo:
Mio Dio, mio *Gesù, questo è il frutto
che posso rendervi: non vi fidate di me,
sono miserabile!*

IX. Stabilirò sempre il mio cuore
in Dio con distaccarlo a tutto mio
potere per forza dalla terra, e da tutto
quello che Egli non è. Voglio che sia
stanza di Gesù, e farmelo un Calvario
di pene, come *la B. Chiara di Montefalco*, dandone a Lui solo la chiave,
acciò ne sia assoluto padrone per
abitarvi a suo piacere, e riporvi ciò
che gli piace. Il mio cuore non sarà
più mio, perché neppure io sono
più mia, mio non sarà solo che Dio.
Ecco il mio amore!

X. Io morirò tutta a me stessa per
vivere solo a Dio, e a Dio certo

[89] This passage translates literally as a "room of Jesus".

[90] St. Clare of Montefalco, also surnamed Clare of the Cross, lived in Montefalco
(Umbria) from 1275 to 1308. "After eleven years of suffering, her extraordinary spirit of
prayer and repentance was rewarded by mystical gifts of grace, ecstasies, and the power of
working wonders." She was canonized by Leo XIII on Dec. 8, 1881 (see. W. Hümpfner, in
Lexikon 2, col. 1212f.).
Indeed, Paul of the Cross had a special devotion to St. Clare (at that time Blessed Clare).
Reasons for this may have been her special path of suffering along which she walked in her
life and her powerful mysticism of the passion (Oct. 30: Feast of the Impression of the
Crucifix in the Heart of St. Clare). Also see above, pp. 202–5.

[91] See Gal 2:20.

tainly die for God, because I cannot live without God. Oh, what a life! Oh, what a death! I will live, but like a dead person. With such a thought I shall spend my life by living a continual death. I want to resolve to die through obedience. *Blessed obedience!*

XI. I will ponder this strong maxim of the spirit of mystical death in the three religious vows of poverty, chastity, and obedience. I will imagine myself as dead in poverty. I will say to myself, a dead person has nothing but what is put on him, nor does he care whether it is good or bad. A dead person asks for nothing and wants nothing because he no longer belongs to this world and to this earth. I will be the poorest, like a dead person. Insofar as possible, I will not keep anything for myself. My sole thought will be that I must possess nothing, and that everything is superfluous as in the case of a dead person. Everything which is put on him is superfluous.

I will accept in charity whatever is given to me, without ever complaining. I will consider that it is always too much, because I deserve nothing. I shall not ask for anything except in extreme necessity, and I will accept this in pure charity. I will be slow in asking for it so as to experience and suffer the inconveniences of holy poverty. As for food and clothing, I will always seek the worst and die to every desire and pleasure of the senses. I shall not ask for or ever keep anything without the permission of my superiors. I

morirò, perché senza Dio vivere non posso: Oh che vita! Oh che morte! Viverò, ma come morta, e con tale riflesso passerò la mia vita con stabilirla in una continua morte. Mi voglio risolvere a morire per Ubbidienza. *Benedetta Ubbidienza!*

XI. Pondererò questa massima forte di spirito della Morte Mistica, nei tre Voti Religiosi, di Povertà, Castità, e Ubbidienza. Mi figurerò morta nella Povertà. Il morto, dirò a me stessa, non ha se non quello che gli si pone in dosso nè si cura che sia buono o cattivo; nulla chiede, e nulla vuole, perché non è più di questo mondo, ed ancora per non essere più di questa terra. Sarò poverissima come il morto, e per cuanto mi sarà possibile, non terrò cosa alcuna presso di me, con questo solo riflesso, che non devo aver niente, e ogni cosa è di più, come al morto, che è superfua ogni cosa che gli si pone in dosso.

Quello che mi verrà dato, lo riceverò per carità, senza mai lamentarmi, ma terrò sia sempre troppo, per non meritar niente. Non chiederò cosa alcuna, se non fosse per estrema necessità, e questa la riceverò per pura carità, e sarò tarda a richiederla, per provare e soffrire gl'incomodi della S. Povertà. Nel vitto e vestito procurerò sempre il peggio, morendo ad ogni desiderio e gusto del senso, non chiedendo e ritenendo mai niente senza licenza dei miei Superiori, e questi pregherò che mi siano sempre rigorosi, per soddisfarmi meno

will ask these superiors to be strict with me always and to satisfy me to the least extent possible, by entrusting me in everything to God.

Thus, I will seek to imitate *Jesus, who was poor in everything.* He, the Lord of heaven, was not ashamed to embrace this extreme poverty. He was not ashamed to live a very poor and lowly life in everything out of love for me and as an example for me.[92] I will despise myself and will take pleasure in being despised by others. I will take pleasure in being passed over by everyone. The real poor man of Jesus is the man who is dead to himself. He cares not about honors and contempt. Therefore, I shall show neither desire nor inclination for anything, so that I may not experience satisfaction. In a word, I shall try to be extremely poor, to be deprived of what I have, because it is not mine. I shall always try to become poorer so as to be conformed to the very poor Jesus. *May I die poor on the cross like you!*

XII. I will die through chastity by submitting my body to every kind of anguish and suffering out of love for my God. I will avoid every occasion of sin so that I may not rebel and tarnish such a beautiful lily. I will watch over my feelings with the utmost vigilance so that no evil may enter through them. A dead person has no feelings. Neither do I want to have any feeling which might offend my God.

I will also avoid every least occa-

che possono rimettendomi tutta a Dio.

Cercherò in questo d'imitare *Gesù povero in tutto:* essendo Egli Signore del Cielo e non si vergognò di abbracciare questa estrema Povertà, di fare una vita poverissima in tutto ed abbietta per mio amore ed esempio. Disprezzerò me stessa e goderò di essere disprezzata da gli altri, e posposta ad ognuno. Il morto è il vero povero di Gesù, non si cura de'gli onori e disprezzi, e però non dimostrerò neppure desiderio o inclinazione a cosa alcuna, affine di non esser compiaciuta, insomma studierò essere poverissima, di essere privata di ciò che ho, perché non mio, e di sempre più impoverirmi per rendermi simile a Gesù poverissimo. *Povera morire in Croce come Voi!*

XII. Morirò nella Castità col sottoporre il mio corpo ad ogni sorta di strazi e patimenti per amore del mio Dio, ed acciò non si ribelli per farmi offuscare un si bel giglio, fuggirò ogni occasione, e custodirò i miei sentimenti, con somma vigilanza, acciò per essi non entri cosa che sia cattiva. Il morto non ha sentimenti, così neppure io voglio avere alcun sentimento in offesa del mio Dio.

Fuggirò anche ogni minima occa-

---

[92] See Phil 2:6–11.

sion of attachment, because Jesus wants to be the sole Master of my heart. He wants my intentions to be pure. He wants me to live for the glory of God and the salvation of my soul. He wants my affections to be pure, with no love for creatures or anything else. He wants me to be free of desires and to seek only Jesus, who delights in the pure lilies. Thus I want to be dead to every pleasing of myself and to sacrifice myself continually on the most holy cross of my Spouse, Jesus. *Oh, the holy death of one who lives chastely for you, my Jesus!*

XIII. I will die through obedience. Oh, what a holy sacrifice! Oh, holy martyrdom of pure will, making me totally dead to myself. The object of this is to die by submitting one's will, overcoming it in everything and for everything, even to the point of death, without even giving forth a breath. By God's grace I will be untiring and ready to obey blindly and without objecting. If I am commanded to do something arduous and difficult and most repugnant, I will look at Jesus scourged at the pillar. I will look at him in the Garden of Gethsemane, in the agony of his prayer. I will look at him on the cross where he offered his last human breath to the Father through obedience. Keeping in mind the warnings he gives to me, I will say, *"Blessed obedience, holy obedience, make me die and I will become holy and finally a saint."* Thus, obedience will become

sione di attacco, perché Gesù del mio cuore vuole Egli solo esserne assoluto padrone: e pura d'intenzioni, gloria di Dio, salute dell'anima: pura di affetti, mai amore alle creature, né ad altro: pura di desiderii e non cercare altro che Gesù, che si pasce tra i gigli immacolati. Così mi voglio rendere morta ad ogni piacere di me stessa, sacrificandomi sempre alla Croce purissima del mio sposo Gesù. *Oh morte santa di chi vive casta per Voi, Gesù mio!*

XIII. Morirò nell'Ubbidienza. Oh che santo sacrificio! Oh santo martirio di volontà pura, dandomi totalmente morta in essa, qui si ha da finire di morire con sottoporre la volontà propria, ed in tutto e per tutto vincerla sino che sia morta affatto, senza dare neppure un sospiro. Sarò con la grazia del Signore pronta e indefessa nell' Ubbidienza, alla cieca, senza replica, e se mi fosse comandata cosa ardua e difficile, e di somma mia ripugnanza, un' occhiata a Gesù alla Colonna, un'altra all'Orto, nell'Agonia della sua orazione, un'altra sulla Croce in cui spirò per obbedienza all'Eterno Padre; nel primo ricordandomi[93] de' gli avvertimenti che mi dá dirò: *benedetta Ubbidienza, santa Ubbidienza mi fai morire, mi farò santa ed in fine beata:* così mi renderò dolce e soave l'Ubbidienza e l'eseguirò con contento. *Oh che beata morte di chi muore per*

---

[93] Instead of *ricordandomi,* it should read *ricordarmi.*

sweet and gentle for me, and I will be happy in doing it. *Oh, what a happy death for one who dies through obedience!* Like Jesus, the beloved Spouse of my soul, I will obey not only those I have to but also my equals and inferiors. I will try to be all things to all men so that everybody may freely give me orders. I will be indifferent in everything. I will not manifest displeasure or regret in anything so that they may feel a holy freedom to command me. I will always be careful not to give the slightest indication that I am dissatisfied with this or that, also for the purpose of being mortified. *I also want my self-love to weaken,* and in regard to this, to die completely. I shall be happy to do those repugnant things which are always commanded me against my desire and will. For I know through God's light that solid virtue consists in this strong point and that the obedience asked for is a true sacrifice of the spirit. I will always go contrary to myself and never trust myself. In this way I will crush[94] my evil inclinations, pride, and passions. I will always deprive myself of personal pleasure in both temporal and spiritual things. I will always be ready to leave God for God, with that holy freedom of spirit and purity of intention which a religious, who is dead to self even to the last breath, must have. *Oh, holy death which enables one to live in the true spirit of Jesus!*

ubbendienza! Come fece Gesù caro Sposo dell'anima mia. Non solo poi ubbidirò a chi devo ma anche alle eguali ed inferiori, procurerò essere tutta di tutti acciò tutti mi possano con libertà comandare; starò indifferente in tutto, non mostrando dispiacere o rincrescimento in cosa alcuna per dare una santa libertà di comandarmi. Starò sopra a me stessa sempre per non fare capire la minima inclinazione acciò non mi sia soddisfatta né a questo né a quello, anche sotto titolo di essere mortificata, volendo anche in questo *far languire l'amor proprio,* ed in tutto farlo morire; e piuttosto contenta a quelle ripugnanze acciò mi sia comandato sempre contro mia voglia e volontà conoscendo per lume di Dio consistere in questo forte punto la soda virtù, e l'ubbidienza che si[95] domanda vero sacrifizio dello spirito. Anderò così sempre contro me stessa, per non fidarmi mai di me, e calpestare così la mia inclinazione mala, superbia e passioni, privandomi sempre del proprio gusto si nel temporale che nello spirituale, ed in questo essere pronta a lasciare lo stesso Iddio per Dio, con quella santa libertà di spirito e depurata intenzione che deve avere una Religiosa morta a se stessa fino all'ultimo respiro. *Oh santa Morte che fa vivere di vero spirito di Gesù! Santa Ubbidienza! Santa Morte! Santo Amore!*

[94] The word used here is *calpestare,* which means "to trample on, to tread heavily upon, or to crush underfoot".

[95] In this context, the reflexive pronoun *si* is redundant.

Holy obedience! Holy death! Holy love!

XIV. I will avoid excessive talking. I will remain firm and consistent on this point, too, for Jesus rests in souls given to solitude. I will delight in speaking only to God, about God, and for God so that he may speak with me. I will not pour myself out in vain, superfluous, and useless words, lest excessive talking cause me to fail in charity and give way to idleness. In speech, too, I want to die completely. I want to be *considerate, brief, prudent, and holy* so that my tongue will be used only for good example and never for scandal. A dead person does not speak, and the religious who is dead to self must not speak to anyone except to God alone and for God. *Silence!*

XV. I will always remain in the background in religious matters, as if I were no good and of no account, never interfering and thus bearing my own nothingness. I will never give my own opinion but will leave everything to him who must do it, because in this way I must bear my own nothingness.[96] I will esteem myself as nothing. I will *know* and *understand* only this: *not to know and understand anything,* but only *to desire, to know, and to understand* the life of Jesus, humble, despised, and unknown. This is the way, the truth, and the life. Holy humility, I want *to die* in this way! *Oh, holy death!*

XVI. I will be charitable to all

XIV. Mi guarderò dal soverchio *parlare* stando anche in questo punto forte e costante, per riposarsi Gesù nelle anime Solitarie, gustando solo di parlare con Dio, di Dio, per Dio, acciò Egli parli con me. Non mi diffonderò in parole vane, superflue, ed inutili, acciò il soverchio parlare non mi faccia mancare alla carità e non mi ingombri nell'ozio; volendo morire anche del tutto nel parlare: e voglio che sia *considerato, poco, prudente e santo,* acciò la lingua mi serva solo per esempio, e non mai per scandalo. Il morto non parla, e la Religiosa morta a sè non deve parlare se non con Dio solo, e per Iddio. *Silenzio!*

XV. Starò sempre in dietro in tutte le cose della Religione, come cosa non buona, e da nulla, non ingerendomi in niente, così portando il mio niente; né darò mai il mio parere, lasciando tutto a chi deve farlo, perché così porta il mio niente. Stimarmi niente, e questo solo *sapere* ed *intendere:* di non *sapere ed intendere niente:* ma solo *bramare, sapere, ed intendere* la vita di Gesù, umile, disprezzata, e non conosciuta. Questa è la via, la verità, e la vita. Santa Umiltà, voglio *morire* con questa! *Oh Santa Morte!*

XVI. Userò carità con tutte ed in

---

[96] The words *perché così porta il mio niente* could be translated "since my nothingness requires this", if we take the verb *portare* to mean *comportare.* The use of simple verbs where compound ones were called for is a peculiarity of style common in the letters of St. Paul of the Cross, also.

and especially to those toward whom I may feel some antipathy. About those who have *shortcomings,* the *impatient,* and the *proud,* I will say, "Lord, *this is my reward."* This is my peace—to conquer myself by returning good for evil, love for hatred, humility for contempt, patience for impatience. A dead person does not feel resentment; this is what I want to do. The more charitable I am toward my neighbor, the more love Jesus will have for me; I am not mistaken in this. Charity conquers the heart for Jesus. In this way, I can become a great saint. *Yes, I want this: I want to die by dying to myself.*

XVII. I will have no compassion on myself. In this way I will become a penitent person who wants to gain heaven by means of violence. I will spend myself indefatigably for the glory of God and for our holy religion. In order to relieve the difficulties of others, I will offer myself to do what I can and give myself completely to my work. I will let my companion supervise while I will be there only to work, to serve, to humble myself, and to be commanded as if I were the lowliest in the monastery. In this I will imitate (I admit it with all my heart) the great Magdalen of Pazzi, that noble and delicate young woman but a great and humble penitent who used to say, *"I want to be the rag of the monastery."* My God, I will do this and more with the help of your grace. But if you withdraw from me, I will do more evil than the good I now resolve to do. In order

particolare con quelle colle quali avessi qualche controgenio. Colle *difettose, impazienti, superbe:* e dirò: Signore, *ecco il mio guadagno,* ecco la mia pace, vincere me stessa, con rendere bene per male, amore per odio, umiltà per disprezzo, e pazienza per impazienza. Chi è morto non si risente; così voglio far io. Più carità al prossimo e più Gesù l'avrà con me: qui non la sbaglio. La carità rubba il cuore a Gesù, con questa posso essere una gran santa. *Sì, lo voglio essere, sì voglio morire per morire a me stessa.*

XVII. Non avrò punto compassione a me stessa, portando così lo stato di una persona penitente, che voglia guadagnare il Cielo a forza di violenza. Mi affaticherò indefessa per la gloria di Dio, e per la Santa Religione, per sollevare dalle fatiche l'altre, mi offrirò a fare quanto posso, e comparire tutta nel mio uffizio, lascerò il sopraintendere alla mia compagna, standovi solo per operare, per servire, per umiliarmi, ed essere comandata come l'infima del Monastero, per essere come diceva (lo confesso di cuore) la gran Maddalena de'Pazzi, nobile e delicata giovane, ma gran penitente ed umilissima: *voglio essere lo straccio del Monastero.* Mio Dio, questo ed altro farò con la grazia vostra; ma se Voi punto vi discostate da me, farò più di male di quello che ora propongo di operare di bene; ed acciocchè questo per mia disgrazia non mi avvenga, di che molto temo, ma molto più confido

that this may not happen to my disgrace, which I fear very much, I will put all my trust in you. I will try to remain always united to you. I will fear being separated from you even for a moment because just one single moment apart from you may cause me to lose you. If I lose you, I lose everything.

In this way and with these holy sentiments, I want to enter into a *spiritual agony* so as to destroy all my *self-love, inclinations, passions, and desires.* I want to die on the cross with that holy death of Jesus which souls enamored of their Spouse experience on Calvary. They die by a more painful death than that of the body in order to rise again with *Jesus who is triumphant in heaven.*

Happy would I be if I would practice this holy death. I will praise it in my last moment to my great consolation.

May Jesus be always with me. Jesus, may my last word be your name. Jesus, may my last breath be your love. Amen.

The end.

Pray for me!!

in Voi. Procurerò di star sempre con Voi unita, e temerò non discostarmi un momento da Voi, perché un sol momento da Voi disgiunta posso perdervi, e perdendo Voi, perdo tutto.

Voglio così ridurmi con questi santi sentimenti ad un *agonia spirituale,* con cui voglio distruggere tutto il mio *amor proprio, inclinazioni, »passioni e volontà«.* Volendo così morire sulla Croce con quella santa Morte di Gesù, con cui muoiono sul Calvario collo Sposo delle Anime innamorate, e muoiono di una morte più dolorosa di quella del corpo, per poi risorgere con *Gesù trionfante nel Cielo.*

Beata me, se praticherò questa santa morte, la benedirò nell'ultimo mio punto con mia grande consolazione.

Gesù sia sempre meco: Gesù, la ultima mia parola sia il vostro Nome: Gesù, l'ultimo mio respiro sia il vostro Amore. Amen.

Fine.

Preghi per me!!

CHAPTER V

Participation in the "Power of the Resurrection"

An investigation that tries to present the passion of Christ in the spirituality of St. Paul of the Cross would be incomplete if it did not also try to point out the importance the *resurrection* of the Crucified had for the saint. This is so because, in theological reflection, Christ's death and resurrection are considered in unity, i.e., two aspects of the same one and fundamental mystery of faith: the paschal mystery (*mysterium paschale*). "The death and resurrection of Christ", stated Karl Rahner, "is a unique process, the two phases of which are essentially [interiorly] inseparable (see Lk 24:26–46; Rom 4:25 and 6:4ff.)."[1] In *Grundkurs des Glaubens, Einführung in den Begriff des Christentums,* the same theologian remarked, "The death of Jesus is unique in that it essentially moves toward the resurrection and dies there."[2]

How does St. Paul of the Cross conceive of this unity in the death and resurrection of Jesus? Undoubtedly, we find a strong passioncentrism in his spiritual-theological thought. Nevertheless, this strong emphasis upon the suffering and crucified Christ (*Christus patiens et crucifixus*) is neither one-sided nor exclusive. Certainly, in his writings, this "saint of the cross" shows a preference for the cross and passion of Jesus. He often speaks of the passion of the Lord (*passio Domini*), and he often places Christ crucified (*Christus crucifixus*) before our eyes while not, at the same time, referring to the risen Christ (*Christus resurrectus*). Nonetheless, we cannot conclude from this quantitative predominance of content on the suffering Christ that the spiritual teaching of the saint is characterized by a dismal dolorism. We can make this claim since suffering, pain, and death were neither the aim nor the end point for Christ, his followers, or, for that matter, Paul of the Cross. The passion of Christ and his death in utter abandonment reaches its fulfillment in the resurrrection;

---

[1] See *Lexikon* I, col. 1039 (keyword: *Auferstehung Christi: IV Zur Theologie der Auferstehung Christi,* cols. 1038–41).

[2] K. Rahner, *Grundkurs des Glaubens, Einführung in den Begriff des Christentums,* 262.

only as "the Risen One" does he draw close to the world.[3] And all those who believe in Christ not only receive a share in his passion but also participate in the "power of his resurrection" (see Phil 3:10). Those having died with Christ will be attracted by the field of force of *zoe*, the living principle of the "new creation" (see Rom 6:4f.; Eph 2:4–7).

Belief in the effectiveness of the Risen One's power is a fundamental principle for St. Paul of the Cross and the starting point from which he develops his spiritual-theological thought. This vivid faith in the resurrected Lord is, at the same time, the inner potential—ground of his intense mysticism of the passion.[4] Now we would like to show how strongly this positive, joyous resurrection faith pervades his theology and even his passion mysticism.

In the next section, we focus our attention upon those passages in which the founder expressly speaks (*expressis verbis*) about the resurrection. In the section after that we demonstrate how active are *each* of the poles (death-life) of the *mysterium paschale* in the teaching of the saint. The last section of this chapter clarifies the content of the formulation: to become reborn in the Divine Word Jesus Christ (*rinascere nel Divin Verbo Gesù Cristo*).

TO RISE WITH JESUS TRIUMPHANT IN HEAVEN (RISORGERE CON GESÙ TRIONFANTE NEL CIELO)

The actual human individual can experience the resurrection as the final "acceptance and salvation" only by attaining final fulfillment through death.[5] The founder developed this theme of a strongly "eschatological" view of the resurrection[6] in an Easter greeting of 1726 written to Nicolina Martinez. At its inception, the saint wrote—with solemn formulations—that God "has taken pleasure in arriving at the most solemn day of his most glorious

---

[3] K. Rahner, in *Lexikon* I, col. 1041.

[4] If we take into account the fundamental flow of Paul's spirituality, then we find the risen Christ (*Christus resurrectus*) implicit in it, even though Christ crucified (*Christus crucifixus*) is spoken of more frequently. This approach is similar to that of the apostle Paul, who desired to preach only Christ crucified (1 Cor 2:2), but who had before his eyes always the resurrected and glorified Lord (1 Cor 15:12–28).

[5] In regard to this, Karl Rahner states, "The resurrection of Jesus (as distinct from the resuscitations in the Old and New Testaments) involves the ultimate salvation of the individual human person by God and before God and the lasting value of each person's story, which is neither lost nor left to continue on into an empty void. This is why death, which alone brings finality, is an essential renunciation and fundamental abandonment before the imagined 'how' of this finality, whether it be that of the body or of the soul of a particular human person" (*Grundkurs*, 262).

[6] As opposed to the participation in the "power of the resurrection", which is granted believers even *in statu viatoris*.

resurrection".[7] Then the saint immediately considered its eschatological fulfillment in heaven. He wrote,

> In company with all the citizens of heaven, let us therefore sing *"Alleluia"*, which means: Praise the Lord! Oh, what a victorious word this is. It is that song of praise which the victorious citizens of heaven are singing in paradise. *"Alleluia"* is not a word to be found on earth: It is a hymn of paradise. To sing it properly, we must strip ourselves of the old person and put on the new, who is Jesus Christ [Col 3:9–10; Gal 3:27].[8]

Although the letter had been composed shortly before Easter, i.e., in Lent or even in Holy Week, it is worth noting that it does not mention the sufferings of the Lord but rather his resurrection. When one recalls that Paul participated in passiontide and in the sacred triduum with great existential devotion,[9] then the observation that he put the resurrection in the foreground in this letter has special significance. As the quotation indicates, the saint thought of human existence beyond the limits of time; that is, he thought in terms of a future life. Undoubtedly we cannot here, on earth, *in statu viatoris* (on our pilgrim way), give praise to God with full spontaneity, plenitude, and interior happiness; this is reserved for "the citizens of heaven". The human person while imprisoned in time still lives in the preliminary stage and must first pass through death's portal of transformation in order to arrive at fulfillment. Although it is true that the state of one's being is finally determined by the event of death, Christ has vanquished death by his resurrection (see 1 Cor 15:55–57), "has opened the gates of paradise", and has obtained for the human person acceptance by the Father and salvation.

Full participation in the life of the Risen One is reserved to the stage of fulfillment; only then, in the other future life, as St. Paul of the Cross puts it, will the person be able to sing *"Alleluia"*. At this point, a legitimate question arises: Why did the Apostle Paul, to whom the founder is so indebted in terms of his spiritual-theological thought, not speak about a "wisdom of the resurrection" but only about "a wisdom of the cross"? The answer could be

---

[7] The beginning of the letter runs thus: "Oh che sia sempre benedetto e lodato il nostro grande Iddio che si è compiaciuto di farci arrivare al solennissimo giorno della sua gloriosissima Risurrezione" / "May our good God be ever praised and glorified, for he has been pleased to let us reach this solemn day of his glorious resurrection" (L 1:63, Apr. 21, 1726).

[8] "Cantiamo dunque in compagnia dei Beati Cittadini 'Alleluia' che vuole dire 'laudate Dominum', lodate il Signore. Oh, che nome vittorioso è questo; egli è quel cantico di lode che cantano i vittoriosi Cittadini del Paradiso: 'Alleluia' non è voce che sia stata inventata in terra, egli è un inno di Paradiso, che per cantarlo come si deve bisogna essere spogliati dell'uomo vecchio ed essere vestiti dell'uomo nuovo, che è Gesù Cristo . . . " (L 1:63, Apr. 21, 1726).

[9] See above, pp. 185–90.

the same as that given by B. Ahern:[10] "Since St. Paul wrote his letters for people living in this world and not in the future one, to preach a 'wisdom of the resurrection' would lack the realism that his converts needed to face the actuality of life upon earth."[11]

This "wisdom of the cross", however, stands within the broad framework of the one and whole paschal mystery. Speaking with the Apostle Paul, we may say that we have not "been united with him not only in the likeness of his death" (Rom 6:5) but also "in the likeness of his resurrection" (Phil 3:10).

Through Jesus' death and resurrection, God redeemed humankind; God worked with his creative almightiness and created a "new creation" (Gal 6:15); and, in Christ, the human person became a "new being" (2 Cor 5:17). The believer now has the duty of making salvific in his own life "the power of Christ's resurrection". The founder speaks of this in the above-cited Easter letter. He stresses the necessity of "stripping the old self and putting on the new, who is Jesus Christ".[12] Surely the saint took these formulations from the theology of baptism and resurrection written by the apostle Paul.[13]

This oneness (one could even say intersection) of these two poles of the "Easter mystery", i.e., death and resurrection, is discussed clearly and in bold relief in the saint's letter written to Passionist Fr. Fulgentius in the year 1746. At the conclusion of the letter, Paul writes, "I greet all *et gloriemur in Cruce Domini Nostri Jesu Christi:* [an allusion to Gal 6:14] with a loving 'Alleluia'."[14] It is obvious from this short formulation that in the mind of St. Paul of the Cross, the "wisdom of the cross" is supported by a lively hope in resurrection.

[10] B. Ahern, a well-known exegete from the United States, is a member of the Passionist Congregation. Formerly, on the faculty of the Pontifical Gregorian University in Rome and a member of the International Theological Commission. In 1976, he delivered a noteworthy lecture on the theme "Christian Maturity and the Cross of Christ" at the International Congress devoted to the topic "The Wisdom of the Cross Today". The following quotation is also taken from Fr. Barnabas Ahern's talk.

[11] "Paolo scrisse le sue lettere per gente che viveva in questo mondo e non nel mondo futuro. Raccomandare loro la 'saggezza della risurrezione' avrebbe significato mancare del realismo di cui i suoi convertiti abbisognavano per affrontare le condizioni reali di vita sulla terra." / "Paul wrote his Epistles for people who lived in this world and not in the world to come. To commend to them 'the wisdom of the resurrection' would lack the realism that his converts needed to face the actuality of life upon earth" (in Italian, see *La sapienza della Croce Oggi* 2:16; in English, see *The Passionist,* no. 3 [1976]: 62).

[12] "... bisogna essere spogliati dell'uomo vecchio ed essere vestiti dell'uomo nuovo, che è Gesu Cristo" (L 1:63, Apr. 21, 1726, to Nicolina Pecorini Martinez).

[13] Col 3:9–10: "Stop lying to one another. What you have done is put aside your old self with its past deeds and put on a new man, one who grows in knowledge as he is formed anew in the image of the Creator." In Gal 3:27 we read, "All of you who have been baptized into Christ have clothed yourselves with him."

[14] "Mi saluti tutti 'et gloriemur in Cruce Domini Nostri Iesu Christi' con un dolce 'alleluia' " (L 2:103, Sept. 10, 1746).

When we think that the founder speaks of "alleluia" in an eschatological context (as is evident in the above), we may conclude that his "realistic" mysticism of the passion possessed a living faith in the resurrection, its fundamental premise. This faith, which in its existential practice develops into a confident and joyful hope, obviously appears in the above-cited letter to Fr. Fulgentius when, at its end, the saint speaks of the "holy trisagion", which everyone must sing when the cross and suffering are to be endured.[15]

Participation in the passion of Jesus and the joy of the glorious resurrection of the Lord are topics of another letter written by the saint on Easter Tuesday of 1742 and addressed to Msgr. Count Garagni, a convinced and resolute patron and protector of the Congregation. In this letter, the founder emphasizes first of all the importance of meditation on the passion, encouraging his correspondent to immerse himself through contemplation "in the sea of the bitterest suffering of Jesus" and to swim in "the sea of God's infinite love".[16] Later, he describes the object and end point of the meditative immersion in the sufferings of Jesus: " . . . so that having been totally transformed by love in Jesus Christ, Your Excellency may enjoy the plenitude of the ineffable sweetness of his glorious resurrection".[17]

As already demonstrated, the "infinite love of God" represented for St. Paul of the Cross the deepest and most convincing explanatory principle underlying Christ's passion and death. This love of God was "incarnated" in the person of Jesus and thus entered into the "limitation" of history. The death of Jesus on the cross in abandonment was the climax of this divine love, and the fact of the resurrection represented the sealing and the manifestation of this love. K. Rahner states, "It is only as the Risen One that Christ really draws close to the world." As a result, the human

---

[15] In this same letter, Paul further writes, "Un Paraninfo celeste diede un avviso mentre una persona parlava 'de Regno Dei', e del Cantico degli Angeli '*Sanctus*', e disse il Celeste Spirito: Cantate il sacro trisagio '*Sanctus*', quando avete croce ecc." / "Once, when someone was speaking about the kingdom of God and the canticle of angels, the 'holy, holy, holy', a heavenly paranymph appeared and said, 'Whenever you have crosses to bear, sing the sacred trisagion, sing, "Holy, holy, holy . . . " ' "

[16] At the beginning of the letter, Paul writes, " . . . non posso a meno di non desiderare al suo piissimo cuore in questi santi giorni le più penitranti e delicate impressioni di quell'infinito amore che fece immergere per nostra salute il dolcissimo Figliuolo di Dio in un mare d'amarissime pene, acciò nuotando con la santa contemplazione in questo gran mare d'infinita carità resti vieppiù arricchito di quegli altissimi tesori . . . " / " . . . at least, during these holy days, I cannot help but desire for you, my most pious friend, the most penetrating and delicate impressions of that infinite love that did immerse the sweetest Son of God in a sea of bitterest pain for our redemption, so that, swimming in holy contemplation in this immense sea of infinite charity, you may become more and more enriched by these highest of all treasures . . . " (L 2:224, Mar. 21, 1742).

[17] " . . . affinchè tutto trasformato per amore in Gesù Cristo, goda V. S. Illma. e Rma. la pienezza dell'ineffabile dolcezza della gloriosissima sua risurrezione" (ibid.).

person can participate in the "power of his resurrection" even here on earth.[18]

This sharing in the power of the resurrection is often described by the founder as "becoming transformed in Jesus Christ". This "transformation" may be accomplished in the believer here on earth, while still "on his pilgrim journey" (in statu viatoris). Yet, it is also true that the person will not experience the "fullness" of the resurrection in this earthly existence; but he already possesses, to some degree, by virtue of hope and by a delightful prejoy, an "anticipatory share" in this eschatological reality. It was of this threefold dimension of the *mysterium paschale* (communion in suffering, sharing in the power of the resurrection, and fullness of the resurrection) that the Apostle Paul wrote in his Epistle to the Philippians. Starting from the plane of the existential experience of faith, he declared, "I wish to know the power flowing from his resurrection, likewise to know how to share in his sufferings by being formed into the pattern of his death. Thus do I hope that I may arrive at resurrection from the dead" (Phil 3:10–11).

Certainly, in his spiritual teaching, the Passionist founder places his own distinctive emphasis on communion with the suffering and crucified Christ (*Christus patiens et crucifixus*). Yet, over and over again, we find a positive, eschatological view of the resurrection and of the future life of joy and beatitude. In one of three preserved letters of the saint to his mother, Paul wrote, "Blest are they who are suffering travail, infirmity, persecutions, ridicule, contempt[19] on account of their love for God; [they are] helping to bear the cross of Jesus Christ, and therefore they will be partakers of his glory in heaven . . . "[20] These are they who are happier than the rich of this world, happier too than they who share in earthly joys. Just as Jesus, through his passion and death, entered his Father's glory (Lk 24:26), similarly each disciple must also take up his own suffering and cross in order to share in Christ's splendor and glory.

To be like Christ means to live in true imitation of Jesus and to fashion one's life on him beginning with the rudiments of Christian Faith. The core of one's

---

[18] See n. 3 above.

[19] When the founder speaks here of "ridicule and contempt", he has a point of reference in mind. On Dec. 9 (six days prior to the composition of this letter), he had been summoned to appear before the ecclesiastical court of Inquisition. The point in question was a matter of purposeful calumny; the accuser was a priest whose name is unknown. The Inquisition rejected the accusation as "pure calumny". See *Storia Critica* 2:662, annotation 20. Also see G. A. De Sanctis, *L'avventura carismatica di S. Paolo della Croce,* 137f.

[20] "Beati quelli che patiscono travagli, infermità, persecuzioni, burle, disprezzi per amor di Dio . . . Quei che patiscono per amor di Dio, aiutano a portar la Croce a Gesù Cristo, e così saranno partecipi della sua gloria in Cielo . . . " (L 1:94, Dec. 15, 1734, to Anna Massari, the founder's mother).

faith in Jesus Christ is most deeply expressed by the bipolar content of the paschal mystery (*mysterium paschale*): the redemptive passion of Jesus on the cross and his resurrection and glorification by his Father. The existential appropriation of the content of this mystery of the Christian Faith is described by the Apostle Peter in the assertion, "Rejoice instead, in the measure that you share Christ's sufferings. When his glory is revealed, you will rejoice exultantly" (1 Pet 4:13). In a similar vein, the Apostle to the Gentiles explains to the Roman community the essence of Christian existence: "But if we are children, we are heirs as well: heirs of God, heirs with Christ, if only we suffer with him so as to be glorified with him" (Rom 8:17). To give additional stress to this last sentence, the apostle adds his own personal faith conviction: "I consider the sufferings of the present to be as nothing compared with the glory to be revealed in us" (Rom 8:18).

As the New Testament writings bear witness, the death and resurrection of Jesus have fundamentally changed the condition of humankind. The human person has become a "child of God" and "brother or sister to Christ". He is a "new creation" and lives in a "new age". As a recipient of eschatological and salvific goods in this earthly existence, he even now shares in the "power of Jesus' resurrection". With the cosmic event of the Incarnation of God in Jesus Christ, the last age has begun for humankind. This age, however, is character- ized by both "now" and "not yet"; that is, it is alive with the power of the Crucified and Resurrected One but must await the fullness of the redemption still to come. Nevertheless, Christ has risen, with his resurrection being the "firstfruits of those who have fallen asleep" (1 Cor 15:20), and he has gone to his Father "to prepare a place" for us (Jn 14:2–3). Because we are still looking forward to our final place with the Father, we can say that salvation in its definitiveness, the resurrection in its plenitude, and the true eschaton are to be enjoyed only after our "passage" through death and our arrival at our final validity.

The primary purpose of this section has been to present the "eschatological" aspect of St. Paul of the Cross' theology of resurrection. In each quotation from the writings of Paul presented herein, Paul used either the word *risorgere* (to resurrect) or the word *risurrezione* (resurrection). In later sections, we will show that when Paul speaks of the theology of resurrection he also uses other notions with predilection. But, in closing, it can be said that he uses the genuine term *risorgere* only when he implicitly or explicitly means the "eschatological" resurrection.

THE RESURRECTION AS AN IMPLICIT AND FUNDAMENTAL PRINCIPLE OF THE SPIRITUAL DOCTRINE OF ST. PAUL OF THE CROSS

If someone were to ask what fundamental and predominant mood is expressed in Paulacrucian spiritual doctrine as explained in this investigation, the answer would be that the teaching is life uplifting and hope and joy filled. Although the spiritual-theological thought of the saint is characterized by a continuous contemplation on the suffering and crucified Christ (*Christus patiens et crucifixus*), his spiritual-ascetical instructions are far from anything that might give the impression of a dismal dolorism. When this experienced director of conscience speaks of and emphasizes pain, suffering, and death, he has only one point in mind: to direct the person to a more intensive encounter and union with God. This more intense union with God and greater sharing in the life with Christ in faith effect inner contentment, liberty, and joy and, more than that, happiness. This basic and positive state of soul, when experienced in the profoundly deep, religious stratum of one's being, becomes an inexhaustible fountain of power and of a hope-filled joy in living.

If one were to ask about the *nucleus,* which infused life and dynamism into the thinking of St. Paul of the Cross, he would have to look for it in the founder's fundamental conviction that the passion of Christ represents the actualization of the greatest mystery of God's love. For him, the passion of Christ is the fullest expression of God's self-communicating love. Therein lies his charism, and this reality does not necessitate any justification or defense. Notwithstanding, a true charism is never skewed, overemphasizing a truth of faith to the "detriment" of others. A true charism is integrated within the whole system of truth, even though it occupies a predominant position.

As already noted at the beginning of this chapter, the death and resurrection of Jesus form a unit. Indeed, Christ's resurrection had not always occupied the same important position in theological reflection as it does today; and this is important to remember in the case of St. Paul of the Cross, who obtained his fundamental convictions in theology, above all, by reading the classics in the field of spiritual-theological doctrine. Nevertheless, theological findings based on elements of a resurrection theology present in the spiritual theology of the founder would remain incomplete were they limited to statements in which the concepts "to resurrect" and "resurrection" were expressly used. Even though these concepts are used relatively seldom in Paul's terminology, his spiritual-ascetical instructions reveal several reference points, which may be considered elements of a resurrection theology. Indeed, his passioncentrism is supported by a living faith in the risen Christ (*Christus resurrectus*), a faith

inviting all to participate in the passion of Jesus. Indeed, the saint is convinced of the invigorating efficiency of the "power of the resurrection". This faith in the risen Lord, viewed from an existential point of view, represents the true reason why the passion mysticism of the saint does not remain limited to a negativism of suffering and pain but rather leads the believer to a greater confidence in and greater love of God. This in turn effects inner contentment and great joy. In what follows we want to discuss these fundamental traits of the spiritual doctrine of the founder, which are after all elements of an implicit resurrection theology.

I. God's Love as the Most Profoundly Explicable Reason of the Paschal Mystery

In his book *Einführung in das Christentum*, J. Ratzinger gives a profound interpretation of this article of faith taken from the Creed: "He arose from the dead." Ratzinger starts with the text from the Song of Songs, "For love is as strong as death" (Song 8:6). After all, the resurrection means "that love is stronger than death".[21] Commenting on the two phrases referring to the Lord's resurrection found in the New Testament, "Jesus is risen" and "God (the Father) has raised Jesus", Ratzinger observes,

> Both formulations meet each other in the fact that the total love for all which led Jesus to the cross was fulfilled in a complete passage to his Father and thus became stronger than death, because it represents at the same time total dependence on him.[22]

If resurrection means that God "has drawn near to the world"[23] in a definitive way and forever, and if faith in the resurrection represents, first and foremost, "the knowledge of that love that has conquered death",[24] then it must be stated that the saint's spiritual teaching taken altogether, even in the depths of his passion mysticism, is penetrated by a resurrection spirit. That Paul's spiritual teaching is a unique confession of the love of God, a love revealed in Jesus Christ and brought near to humankind, indicates that elements of a resurrection theology are present in his spiritual-theological thought.

According to St. Paul of the Cross' conception, love is essentially linked to suffering.[25] In the entries of his spiritual diary, he speaks of a deep union of love and suffering. He feels a "grateful joy because of the pains of Jesus",

---

[21] J. Ratzinger, *Einführung in das Christentum*, 249.
[22] Ibid., p. 252.
[23] See K. Rahner, "Auferstehung Christi", in *Lexikon* I, 1041.
[24] Ratzinger, *Einführung*, 257.
[25] See above, pp. 200–202.

where "love and sorrow were blended".[26] He stresses in several letters that the pains of Jesus are "a sea of love and suffering". They who immerse themselves in this sea by means of contemplation will be graciously made by God partakers in suffering and in love.[27] Suffering and love, however, are so intimately connected that anyone having a share in this grace will not be able to distinguish suffering from love, or love from suffering, since it is a question of "a loving and sorrowful mixture".[28] Love represents that "unifying virtue" that makes one's own the pain of Jesus and more closely unites the person to God.[29]

As previously mentioned, the *mysterium paschale* contains two poles: death and resurrection. Here too we may speak of the inner unity of these two facts in the economy of salvation. The principle providing us with access into this mystery is knowledge of the love of God for humankind. In Jesus' crucifixion, this love is made manifest in a real and historical way; in the resurrection it is sealed and linked with humankind forever. Paul of the Cross sees the power of God's love preeminently embodied in the suffering and death of Jesus; in this saving event his love for us becomes visible—a love that is alive and effective even today, because it is "risen" and endures forever in the glorified Christ.

For the Passionist founder, *Christus patiens et crucifixus* represents the personification of God's salvific action. Paul's spiritual-ascetical instructions, however, remain very close to real life and avoid falling into an unreal euphoria. Neither does he fall into a dismal dolorism, since he sees in the passion of Jesus not suffering primarily but rather God's revealed love. Indeed, his spiritual teaching breathes the spirit of a realism fond of life; his passion mysticism is, after

[26] We read the following in the entry of Dec. 27, 1720: "...sentendo con infusa intelligenza, e con l'altissime consolazioni dello spirito un certo riposo dell'anima frammischiato con le pene del Redentore, nelle quali l'anima si compiace; si frammischia amore e dolore." / "Through infused understanding and the deepest consolation of the Spirit, I experienced a certain spiritual repose, mingled with the sufferings of my Redeemer, in which the soul takes its delight. Love and sorrow were blended" (*Diario Spirituale*, 81; *Tagebuch*, 102; Rouse, 36). See similar citations in entries of Dec. 8 and 28.

[27] The saint writes the following to the Passionist Fr. John Mary: "...poichè la Passione di Gesù è opera tutta d'amore, e stando l'anima tutta perduta in Dio ch'è carità, ch'è tutt'amore, si fa un misto d'amore e dolore, perchè lo spirito ne resta penetrato tutto e sta tutto immerso in un amore doloroso ed in un dolore amoroso: *Opus Dei* ... " / "...because the passion of Jesus is altogether the work of love, and while the spirit remains entirely lost in God, who is charity, who is all love, it is made a mixture of love and sorrow, because the spirit remains completely penetrated by it and stands immersed in sorrowing love and in loving sorrow: *Opus Dei* ... " (L 3:149, July 14, 1756).

[28] The founder writes of this to Sr. Colomba Gertrude Gandolfi: "...si fa un misto amoroso e doloroso, ma tanto unito che non si distingue nè l'amore dal dolore nè il dolore dall'amore ... " / "...it makes a loving and sorrowful mixture, so closely united that one can distinguish neither love from sorrow, nor sorrow from love ... " (L 2:440, July 10, 1743).

[29] "L'amore è virtù unitiva e fa sue proprie le pene dell'Amato Bene" / "Love is a unifying virtue that takes upon itself the torments of its beloved Lord" (see Chap. II, n. 213).

all, a "mysticism of God's love". This priority given to love is obvious in a letter written in 1743 to a religious sister:

> Love is a unifying virtue which takes upon itself the torments of its beloved Lord. It is a fire reaching through to the inmost soul. It transforms the lover into the one loved. More deeply, love intermingles with grief, and grief with love, and a certain blending of love and grief occurs. They become so united that we can no longer distinguish love from grief or grief from love. Thus the loving heart rejoices in its sorrow and exults in its grieving love.[30]

How well these words show that the desired goal is not suffering but a greater degree of love! Indeed, pain and love are deeply and interiorly fused one with the other. But wherever love is experienced (albeit a question of sorrowing love), there too is a sense of joy and happiness. As the last part of the above quotation indicates, joy even represents the dominant condition of the soul that experiences this fusion of love and sorrow, a fusion or intermingling that calls for rejoicing and celebration as for a feast.

It is true that the Passionist founder speaks only of the pain and passion of Jesus without mentioning expressly his resurrection. Yet, when the resurrection of Jesus is primarily considered as confirmation of the love of God for humankind, then the experience of this love (about which St. Paul of the Cross speaks with such interiorly responsive and profound words) is nothing else than a share in the *dynamics of resurrection*. One could cite many passages wherein he speaks of participation in the love of God in the context of the *passio Domini*. For this reason, we can conclude that Paul's passion mysticism, which is largely a glorification of God's love for the human person, is placed on the solid foundation of a resurrection theology, the principles of which—even though not reflected upon by the saint—are implicitly present and powerfully active.

2. God's Will as "Food", Means of Union with the Glorified Lord

The ultimate purpose of the spiritual-ascetical instructions of the Passionist founder consists of supporting a person so that he attains greater "union with God" in "faith, hope, and charity". In turn, greater union with God imparts greater personal joy and inner happiness and ultimately a "higher quality of life", a deeply rooted and incontestable security in God.

The true origin of the "positivism" found in his spiritual teaching, a

[30] "L'amore è virtù unitiva e fa proprie le pene dell'Amato Bene ... trasforma l'amator nell'amato, e mischiandosi con alto modo l'amore col dolore, il dolore coll'amore, si fa un misto amoroso e doloroso, ma tanto unito che non si distingue nè l'amore dal dolore nè il dolore dall'amore, tanto che l'anima amante gioisce nel suo dolore e fa festa nel suo doloroso amore" (L 2:440, July 10, 1743, to Sr. C. G. Gandolfi).

teaching that conveyed confidence, trust, and joy, was grounded in the saint's idea of God.[31] For St. Paul of the Cross, God is, first and foremost, the Good, the Merciful, the Loving One. In the notes of his diary, Paul praises God as "the sweet Giver of every good".[32] Then, full of interior ardor, the saint speaks of "God's infinite love".[33] Full of gratitude, he proclaims God's "infinite mercies".[34]

Because words alone are unable to express the "breadth and length, and height and depth" (Eph 3:18) of God's love, then Paul appeals, as mystics do with pleasure, to images. In his letters we often come across passages in which the saint calls God an "immense sea of love" (*mare immenso d'amore*).[35] God in his love, however, is not "closed in upon" himself. Rather, he bends forward toward the human person, takes an interest in and extends to him goodwill and provident care. Theologians have tried to describe this view or image of God as "absolute 'relativity', as in 'relatio subsistens'".[36] Using a form of expression which relies more on the saint's own existential experience of faith than upon abstraction, St. Paul of the Cross concretely expresses this loving relationship of God with the human person in the following way: "God is Father, and a most loving Father, who would sooner let sky and earth perish than a person who trusts in him."[37] Paul's positive idea of God is the true motivation underlying his incontestable faith in divine providence. In the same manner, the following ideas are also in conformity with the saint's convictions about God: God, after all, always means well for the human person and always desires the best for him, even though he may not recognize or understand it in a correct way.

As already demonstrated, the fundamental principle of "submission to the

---

[31] See *Tagebuch*, 31–34.

[32] The entry of Dec. 2, 1720, concludes with these words: " . . . in tutto sia benedetto il Dator dolcissimo d'ogni bene" / " . . . blessed be the sweet Giver of every good" (*Diario Spirituale*, 62; *Tagebuch*, 72; Rouse, 31).

[33] See the entries of Dec. 4 and 7, 1720.

[34] In the middle of the entry of Dec. 7, we read, "Oh, infinita misericordia del nostro Sommo Bene" / "Oh, the infinite mercy of our Sovereign Good." The last sentence of this entry runs, " . . . gli dico che con farmi tante grazie, es sì innumerabili favori risplenderanno più le sue infinite misericordie, perchè fa al più gran peccatore; in tutto sia lodato il suo SS. Nome." / "I tell him that in giving me so many graces and such innumerable favors, he only manifests his infinite mercies all the more because he gives them to the greatest of sinners. May his most holy Name be praised in all things" (*Diario Spirituale*, 66f.; *Tagebuch*, 77f.; Rouse, 32).

[35] For example, see L 1:280, Apr. 23, 1742, to Agnes Grazi; L 1:349, Aug. 21 (year unknown), to Agnes Grazi; and, finally, L 2:717, Aug. 4, 1748, to Lucy Burlini.

[36] See Ratzinger, *Einführung*, 253.

[37] " . . . è Padre e Padre amorosissimo che lascia perire piuttosto il cielo e la terra che chi confida in lui" (L 3:75, Sept. 7, 1751, to Giovanni Battista Pettirossi).

divine will" belongs to those basic convictions which manifest themselves most distinctly in the saint's spiritual-theological thought.[38] Furthermore, the founder distinguishes between varying degrees of "life lived according to God's will". In a letter written in 1743, he discusses these different degrees. He writes,

> This is a very important point: Great perfection is found in resigning yourself in all things to the divine will; an even greater perfection is to live abandoned, with complete indifference to the divine good pleasure; still the pinnacle of perfection is to nourish yourself on the divine will in a spirit of pure faith and love. . . . Remember this loving Savior said to his beloved disciples that his food was to do the will of his eternal Father: *"Meus cibus est ut faciam voluntatem eius, qui misit me, et ut perficiam opus eius"* [Jn 4:34].[39]

Paul's strong Christocentric teaching is obvious in his saying that "the greatest perfection" is "to nourish yourself on the divine will" as Jesus Christ, the Redeemer, has done. But the divine will of the Father consisted of sacrificing "his Son, out of pure love and provident care, for the salvation of the human person". The evangelist John describes this mystery of Christian life in these confidence-inspiring and basic terms: "For God so loved the world that he gave his only begotten Son, that those who believe in him may not perish but may have life everlasting" (Jn 3:16).

From the outset, the earliest Christian tradition saw Jesus' death out of love on the cross as the fulfillment of his heavenly Father's will, the will to save, about which "the writings and the prophets" had spoken. In St. Luke's Gospel even the Risen One explains this truth to his disciples on the road to Emmaus: "Was it not necessary that the Messiah should suffer these things to enter into his glory?" (Lk 24:26); and in the hymn in the Epistle to the Philippians was it not affirmed that Jesus "became obedient unto death, even to death on a cross" (see Phil 2:6–11)?

Now if the believer recognizes the will of God in the inevitable events of his life and accepts this will in union with the crucified and risen Lord (since Jesus considered his Father's will as "his food"), and if the person also recognizes that in the fulfillment of the Almighty's will lies the "food of eternal life", or

---

[38] See above, pp. 152–62.

[39] "Gran punto è questo: è gran perfezione il rassegnarsi in tutto al divino volere, maggior perfezione è il vivere abbandonata, con grande indifferenza, nel Divin Beneplacito, massima, altissima perfezione è il cibarsi in puro spirito di fede e d'amore della Divina Volontà . . . Si ricordi che quest'amabil Salvatore disse ai suoi diletti Discepoli che il suo cibo era di far la volontà dell'Eterno suo Padre. '*Meus cibus est ut faciam volutatem eius qui misit me et ut perficiam opus eius*'" (L 1:491, Dec 18, 1743, to Sr. M. C. Bresciani).

the "divine food" (as Paul later writes in the letter quoted above),[40] then this faith obedience is a form of "being in Christ" and a participation "in the power of Christ's resurrection". The Christocentric and eschatological orientation of this fundamental principle of "submission to God's will" may be viewed as an interior element of an implicit resurrection theology in the thinking of Paul of the Cross.

The founder considers submission to the will of God as an actualization of the "highest perfection": namely, when people accept that will in union with Christ and when they, like him, allow it to become "like unto food".[41] Obedience to his Father's will led the Divine Savior to his passion and ultimately to death in abandonment on the cross; but his Divine Father, "because of this, highly exalted him" (Phil 2:6–11). Something of this kind happens to Christ's disciples. The eternal Father's will permits believers, as explained by the founder, to suffer "inner and outer fears, desolation, aridity, forlornness of spirit, and bodily pain". However, he allows them, in and with Christ, "to have, in all these tribulations, God's will as food".[42] Furthermore, the saint assures his correspondent by saying, " . . . please, continue in this way so as to rest in the bosom of the heavenly Father" (see Jn 1:18).[43] In the last sentence of the quotation, it is clear that neither the conquest of one's will nor the endurance of desolation, forlornness, and bodily pain is the ultimate goal of submission to the divine will but rather "rest in the bosom of the heavenly Father". Therefore, the founder does not remain at the level of negation or negativism but opens his eyes and directs his gaze toward the positive, that is, to where the risen and glorified Lord is enthroned and reigns with his Father.

This positive gaze upon the crucified, raised, and glorified Christ is contained in another letter written in symbolic language and, at the same time, from an oracular-visionary angle. First, the founder encourages Sr. Colomba, who was very seriously ill, to accept her pain as God's will, in order to

[40] In the same letter the founder writes, "Si ricordi che questo cibo d'eterna vita che è il Cibo Sovrano di far la volontà dell'Altissimo . . . " / "If you keep in mind that this food of eternal life, which is the sovereign food, means the will of the Highest . . . " (ibid.).

[41] The founder writes the following to Maria Calcagnini: "Ora le dirò solamente una gran massima di fede, che abbraccia tutta la più alta perfezione. — Gesù Cristo disse un giorno ai suoi Apostoli che il suo cibo era il far la volontà del suo Eterno Padre . . . " / "Now I will merely say a great maxim of faith, which completely embraces the highest perfection. One day, Jesus Christ said to his apostles that his food was to do the will of his eternal Father . . . " (L 3:833, Dec. 1770 [date unknown]).

[42] In the same letter, Paul writes, "Oh, gran punto è questo! Dunque lei, in tutti gli eventi, in tutte le angustie interne ed esterne, desolazioni, aridità, abbandoni di spirito, pene di corpo ecc., in tutti questi incontri si cibi della Divina Volontà . . . " / "Oh, a great point is this! Therefore, you must have as food the divine will, in all these events, in all these inner and outer fears, desolations, aridities, abandonments of your spirit, bodily pains, etc., in all these tribulations . . . " (ibid.).

[43] "E prosiegua in tal forma a riposar nel seno del Padre Celeste" (ibid.).

become a living "image of the crucified Jesus, entirely sweet, meek, patient".[44] Then, he writes these promising words:

> Now, therefore, please remain wholly concealed in the crucified Jesus, with no other desire but to be completely changed by love into his good pleasure. You will see, at the opportune time, the opening of a great scene, and a great star will rise which will be the harbinger of a very clear day, a day with a brilliant sun that will not make any shadow and with its vital warmth will cause the vanishing of mountains of snow. I write you this enigma; you will understand it at the proper time.[45]

Evidently, the founder is alluding to the person's *eschaton* in this visionary description: death and then the future life in an eternal beatitude in union with the glorified *Kyrios*. It will be a life in which we will live an endless day, a day with a shining sun that never sets and where no shadow exists. A precondition for achieving this future life of untroubled and eternal joy consists therein: "To be concealed in the crucified Jesus" and "to be changed by love into the divine good pleasure".

3. To Let One's Own "Nothingness" Be Absorbed in God's "All" and Thus "to Be Changed in Jesus Christ"

As we have already noted, the fundamental principle of a person's "nothingness" and God's "all" occupies an important place in the spiritual teaching of St. Paul of the Cross.[46] After all, this antithetical discourse about nothingness and all is rooted in an existential experience of creatureliness, of what it means to be a creature. God created people in "his image and likeness" (Gen 1:27), and therein lies the grandeur of the human person, the "crown of creation". God has conferred on humankind the mission of "subduing the earth" and "of having dominion" over all other creatures (Gen 1:28). Nevertheless, the value

[44] The founder explains in this letter, " . . . godo in Dio . . . che la Sovrana Infinita Bontà vi abbia tirato allo stato in cui siete, cioè d'un nudo patire . . . ponga il suo contento in unirsi al beneplacito del gran Padre Celeste . . . che portate l'immagine di Gesù Crocefisso, tutto dolce, mansueto paziente ecc." / " . . . take delight in God . . . since the sovereign infinite Goodness has put you in the present state, that is that of naked suffering . . . place all your contentment in being united to the good pleasure of the great, heavenly Father . . . so that you bear the image of Jesus Crucified, entirely sweet, meek, patient, etc." (L 2:442, Dec. 18, 1743, to Sr. Colomba Gertrude Gandolfi).

[45] "Or via statevene così tutta nascosta in Gesù Crocefisso, senza desiderare altro che d'essere tutta trasformata per amore nel Divin suo Beneplacito in tutto. Voi vedrete che a suo tempo s'aprirà una gran scena, apparirà una grande stella che sarà foriera d'un giorno chiarissimo, in cui risplenderà un sole che non farà ombra, ed il suo vitale calore farà dileguare montagne di neve. Io scrivo quest'enigma, lo capirete a suo tempo" (ibid.).

[46] See above, pp. 162–69.

and distinction of this human person are truly rooted in his dependence upon God. The creature does not exist by self alone but rather owes his existence exclusively to the Creator.

This experience of one's own creatureliness and total dependence upon God is strongly underlined in the thought of the Passionist founder. Again and again in his letters, he emphatically shows men and women their own incapability, their complete ignorance and impotence, and recommends that they recognize their "nothingness". When the person begins to widen his spiritual horizon in self-recollection so as to have an "intuitive vision" of the infinite and almighty Being, then that person becomes aware of his smallness before God. The saint expresses with predilection this fundamental and religious experience in the phrase *to annihilate* one's self before God.

This annihilation (*annichilamento*), however, represents only the first element of the existential experience of creatureliness. The self-knowledge of one's own smallness in comparison with God of necessity keeps the human person from making the daring attempt to attain salvation by himself alone. It also prevents "self-glorification"—a matter of great importance in Pauline theology. The second element, which is the end point of this discussion on the nothingness of the human person, consists in this: The human person needs to cast his nothingness into the all that is God, completely immersing and sinking himself in this all.

Let us, however, allow Paul of the Cross to speak for himself. In a letter written in 1743, he writes,

> Besides, I would like you to practice this well: Namely, perfect knowledge of your own nothingness, and then I would like you to allow your own nothingness to be immersed in that immense all, who is our good God.[47]

Certainly, it is a question here of a daring formulation, of imagery used as an incentive by the saint. Although the founder had no philosophical-theological instruction, he considers it necessary to explain clearly that this immersion of one's own nothingness in the divine all must in no way be understood as the result of one's own ability to become one with divine nature. Paul speaks unequivocally of this in another letter,[48] but even so he feels his words might

---

[47] "Pertanto io vorrei che lei si esercitasse molto nella perfetta cognizione del suo nulla, e poi vorrei che abissasse questo suo nulla in quell'Immenso Tutto, che è il nostro buon Dio" (L I:488, Jan. 2, 1743, to Sr. M. C. Bresciani).

[48] In a letter to Sr. Colomba Gertrude Gandolfi, Paul writes, "In risposta della sua lettera ricevuta ier sera devo dirle che sempre più mi pare che la sua condotta interiore sia secondo Dio, e ve ne sono tutti i buoni segni. Questo sì, che Lei non si è spiegata bene, anzi ha sbagliato molto in dire, che in quel trasformativo divino abbraccio, l'anima perde il suo essere e vive con un essere divino, e pare che communichi la sua divina natura all'anima.—Tutto ciò è errore, perchè mai l'anima perde il suo essere. Bensì Sua Divina Maestà in quel divino

still be misunderstood. That is why he, in a spurt of enthusiasm, adds, "Oh, happiest loss, by which the soul who loses all in God will truly find its own self."[49]

If we take into consideration the fact that, for St. Paul of the Cross, God is above all else the "sea of infinite love" (*il mare dell'infinito amore*), then it follows that the immersion of one's own self in God's all leads to the "a complete sinking of the soul in the infinite love of the highest good".[50] That is why the founder calls this losing of self a "happy loss", because through it the soul is more intensely united with God. In contemporary language, we can express this in the following way: The human person attains, through his encounter with God, a deep self-discovery and a higher "quality of life".

If we consider more carefully this basic principle of the nothingness of the human person and the all who is God, then it strikes us that the founder is using as a model the example of Jesus, who "emptied himself" (Phil. 2:7).[51] This thinking is supported in a letter in which the saint describes the importance of the contemplation of the humanity of Jesus. Paul intimates that the person can arrive at contemplation of the divinity of the Redeemer only "by a faithful imitation of his highest virtues, especially that of deep

---

abbraccio la unisce talmente a sè per amore, che pare uno spirito seco: '*Qui autem adhaeret Domino, unus spiritus est*' (1 Cor 6:17), così dice S. Paolo, che altamente le provava." / "As an answer for your letter received last night, I must tell you that more and more it seems to me your interior behavior is in conformity with God, and all the signs are propitious. But it is true you have not explained yourself well; nay, you have erred a lot in your saying that in that transformative embrace the soul loses its own being and lives by means of a divine being that seems to communicate the divine nature to the soul.—All this is error, since the soul never loses its own being. Believe, rather, that his divine Majesty, in that divine embrace, is uniting the soul to himself, by his love, and in such a manner that it seems only one spirit with himself: '*Qui autem adhaeret Domino, unus spiritus est*' ['but whoever is joined to the Lord becomes one spirit with him', as in 1 Cor 6:17]. In such a way did St. Paul express himself and prove it in such a lofty way" (*Bollettino* 9 [1928]: 147–48, quoting a letter of Sept. 30, 1758). We can feel the saint's displeasure in these lines written after having discovered the false opinion of the religious Sister Colomba. This unequivocal statement shows us that St. Paul of the Cross' spiritual doctrine was very remote from what is commonly called "the mysticism of identity".

[49] "Oh, perdita felicissima, per cui l'anima perdendosi tutta in Dio resta ben trovata" (L 1:488, Jan. 2, 1743, to Sr. M. C. Bresciani).

[50] "... resta l'anima tutta immersa nell'Amore Infinito del Sommo Bene" / "... the soul remains wholly immersed in the infinite love of the highest good" (ibid.).

[51] Even in a letter written as early as 1726, Paul writes, "Ah quando imiteremo perfettamente questo caro Salvatore, che '*exinanivit se*', quando saremo sì umili ... " / "Ah, when shall we imitate perfectly this dear Savior who '*exinanivit se*' [emptied himself], when shall we be so humble ... " (L 1:68, Aug. 29, 1726, to Fr. E. Tuccinardi).

humility and annihilation [*annichilamento*], which he has taught us in so divine a manner by his holiest deeds".[52]

Jesus Christ "emptied himself" and lived in humility and in "nothingness". Whenever the human person so imitates this self-emptying of Jesus, he attains to a greater union of love with the Divine Redeemer. Therefore, the ultimate goal of this annihilation consists therein: a more intense union with Christ, nay, "to be changed" into him. The separate steps on this road to God, beginning with one's own "nothingness", are clearly presented in a letter written by the saint to a religious:

> What a noble exercise this is, therefore, to annihilate one's self before God in pure faith without images and then to cast our nothingness into that true all who is God, and there to lose one's self in that immense sea of infinite love in which the loving soul swims and is penetrated from both within and without. Thus, the soul is entirely united and changed into Jesus Christ through love and makes its own the sufferings and passion of the Well Beloved.[53]

The union between the soul and God occurs as a result of becoming one with Jesus Christ. Hence, we can also say that by annihilation before God, that is, by the existential practice of being a creature, the human person opens himself to God's love, which God desires to impart. The historical-salvific imparting of this love has been carried out in the Person of Jesus Christ, better said, in the suffering and crucified Christ (*Christus patiens et crucifixus*). This christological aspect comes to light even more clearly in another letter in which the founder speaks in great detail of the immersion and disappearance of one's own nothingness in the all of God. Paul writes,

> After you have been well annihilated, despised, and cast into nothingness, ask Jesus for permission to enter his Divine Heart, and you will obtain it immediately. Then fly in spirit into that beautiful Heart and there offer yourself as a victim upon that divine altar, in which the fire of holy love is

---

[52] To Agnes Grazi, Paul wrote, "... poichè non si puole passare alla contemplazione della Divinità Infinitissima ed Immensissima, senza entrare per la porta dell'Umanità Divinissima del Salvatore, con imitare fedelmente le sue altissime virtù e principalmente quella profondissima umiltà ed annichilamento che in tutte le sue santissime azioni ci ha tanto divinamente insegnato." / " ... for you cannot pass to the contemplation of the infinite and immense Divinity without entering through the door of the divine humanity of the Savior, by imitating faithfully his highest virtues and principally the deepest humility and annihilation that he so divinely taught in all of his actions" (L 1:256, Aug. 4, 1740).

[53] "Oh, che nobile esercizio è mai questo di annichilarsi avanti a Dio in pura fede senza immagini, e poi buttare questo nostro niente in quel vero Tutto che è Dio, ed ivi perdersi in quell'immenso mare d'infinita carità, in cui nuotando l'anima amante resta penetrata di dentro e di fuori da questo amore infinito, e tutta unita e trasformata in Gesù Cristo per amore, si fa sue le pene, la Passione dell'amato Bene" (L 1:484, June 26, 1742, to Sr. M. C. Bresciani).

always burning, and let yourself be penetrated through to the marrow of your bones by those sacred flames.[54]

This passage, full of symbols and images, shows how St. Paul of the Cross' religious experiences culminate in an intense friendship with Christ. When the matter in point is that of the "Divine Heart of Jesus", it is the human and divine nature that is intended. To acknowledge one's own smallness and nothingness before God, therefore, means neither resignation nor frustration for the human person—precisely because of God's greatness. Rather, this becoming nothing is an essential step for each person, a step to be made in and through Jesus Christ so as to be penetrated by the flames of God's love. The love of God is incarnated in Jesus Christ, God and man. This love is strikingly visible in Jesus' passion and death; and, through his resurrection, he has drawn near to and remains definitively close to the world. In his symbolic language, the founder speaks of the "Heart which is always burning in the fire of holy love". Finally, the fact of being penetrated by the flames of love, about which the saint speaks, represents a share in the power and might of the Risen One.

This christological foundation and orientation of the antithetical discussion of the nothingness of the human person and the allness of God is likewise obvious in another letter written in 1726 (during the saint's early years). To Fr. Erasmus Tuccinardi, Paul writes,

Oh, when shall we perfectly imitate this dear Savior who "emptied himself" [Phil 2:7] . . . ah, when are we going to become like little babes clinging to the breast of the charity of Jesus, our Spouse and Helper? When shall we become so simple and childlike so as to consider it great happiness to be the least of all, cast into nothingness?[55]

Many things may be said of the nothingness of the human person and the all of God. Beyond a doubt this principle is an eloquent proof of the radical way in which St. Paul of the Cross regards human "existence as totally dependent on God". This existential experience of being a creature leads Paul to a strong and unconditional trust in God. It is interesting to note how, for the saint, the practice of his faith as a creature passes into an experience of Christ's mystery:

[54] "Dopo che vi sarete ben annichilata, sprezzata ed abbissata nel niente, dimandate licenza a Gesù d'entrare nel suo Cuore Divino e subito l'otterrete. Poi volate in spirito in quel bel Cuore ed ivi mettetevi come una vittima sopra quell' Altare Divino, nel quale arde sempre il fuoco del S. Amore, e lasciatevi penetrare sino la midolla delle ossa da quelle sacre fiamme . . . " (L 1:473, Aug. 9, 1740, to Sr. M. C. Bresciani).

[55] "Ah, quando imiteremo perfettamente questo caro Salvatore, che 'exinanivit se', . . . quando saremo diventati così piccoli bambini attaccati alle mammelle della SSma. Carità di Gesù nostro caro Sposo, Padre e Tutore, e che saremo tanto semplici e piccoli che avremo per gran fortuna l'essere fatti gli ultimi di tutti, buttati nel niente . . . " (L 1:68, Aug. 29, 1726).

when the human person, in faith, allows his nothingness to disappear into God's all, when the soul becomes lost in the endless sea of love, then the soul is changed by love into Jesus Christ.

The christological aspect is already evident in the principle of submission to God's will, and—we should emphasize—the principle that we are nothing and God is everything has a very positive thrust. By living in conformity with the experience of the human condition of creatureliness, the person ought to arrive at a greater trust in God and a more intense union of love with God and in the long run be "changed by love into Jesus Christ". Therefore, the principle of the nothingness of the human person does not represent the predominant aspect. Rather, the *kerygma* (message) proper to this basic assertion is praise of God's love. This is so because the love of God was the original cause of creation, and this love has been revealed to us in the passion and death of Jesus. Finally, this love for the world has been confirmed by God definitively in the resurrection and glorification of Christ.

If St. Paul of the Cross sees the ultimate purpose and the true fruit of this immersion of one's own nothingness in God's all as being that of a soul "changed by love in Jesus Christ", then this signifies—in the language of existential experience—nothing else than being attracted by and received into God's *zoe* (life) through an intense participation in the "power of the resurrection".

4. The Incarnation and Holy Eucharist as Explanations or Unfoldings of Divine Love

Before attempting to present the elements of a resurrection theology extracted from the saint's fundamental principle of "mystical death and rebirth in the Divine Word", we want to draw the reader's attention first to other facets of Paul of the Cross' spiritual teaching. These demonstrate that his spiritual-theological thought has at its base *both* poles of the paschal mystery: death and resurrection, humiliation and exaltation. Of course, all this means is that his thought is fundamentally oriented in a positive direction. Before all else, the death of Jesus upon the cross is, for Paul, "the greatest and most astounding work of divine love" (*la più grande e stupenda opera del divino amore*);[56] and the *kerygma* of the resurrection may be described in the words of J. Ratzinger as "... the love that has permitted our breakthrough and has thus fundamentally changed our entire situation".[57] Undoubtedly, God's love for humankind represents the greatest and deepest thought content of the "Easter mystery", and this "self-communicating love" is, after all, the original cause of all salvific action of God toward all people.

[56] See L 2:499, Aug. 21, 1756, to Sr. Colomba Gertrude Gandolfi.
[57] Ratzinger, *Einführung*, 257.

The Incarnation as the "divine wedding of the Eternal Word with human nature" (Divino Sposalizio del Verbo Eterno con la natura umana). When we take into consideration the spiritual-theological thought of the founder, not partially but altogether, and therein seek the kernel or the starting point from which all his concepts spring and upon which all are focused, then we affirm unequivocally: The kernel of his thought is the mystery of the love of God for the human person. This starting point, which is not primarily the result of rational deliberation but has as its source an intense religious "experience", is the ground and guarantor of the thoroughly constructive and positive character of his thought. Because he sees God's love actualized most manifestly in the passion and cross of Jesus, Paul focuses upon *Christus patiens et crucifixus.*

The saint, however, sees other manifestations of the salvific economy within the framework of "God's self-communication in love". Of special significance for him is the mystery of the *Incarnation.* This causes no wonder since the "Easter mystery" composed of the death and resurrection of the God-man, Jesus Christ, has as a premise the mystery of "God's Incarnation". The theology of the cross and the theology of the Incarnation complement each other. St. Paul of the Cross sees hidden in the cosmic event of Bethlehem and in the sacrificial event of Calvary the same unfathomable mystery: the infinite love of God.

In a letter written by the founder to his fellow Passionist Fr. Hyacinth for the Christmas feast of 1768, Paul summarizes this homogeneous way of conceiving the central mysteries of Christian Faith. After inviting Fr. Hyacinth to prepare himself for this feast, Paul continues,

> One of the greatest graces consists therein, namely, to contemplate the excess of infinite love revealed to us by the eternal God and Father when he gave us his only begotten Son and the love of that same Son, who took on human flesh and submitted himself to such great pain and suffering to liberate us, the vilest creatures, from the servitude of the devil and to open to us the gates of paradise, which had been locked—not only to sinners but to the just as well—for so many centuries.[58]

As these words show, the Incarnation is oriented toward the cross, and the passion and cross have occasioned the deliverance of humankind and opened the gate of heaven, the gate of eternal bliss and happiness. The founder does not view the deliverance effected by the redemption as something that happens only in the future, as something given in the coming world only. Even

---

[58] " . . . una delle maggiori (grazie) si è in considerare l'eccesso d'infinita carità che ci ha dimostrato l'Eterno Divin Padre, in darci l'Unigenito suo Figlio e l'amor dell'istesso Figlio in prendere carne umana e soggettarsi a tanti disastri e patimenti per liberar noi vilissime creature dalla schiavitù del demonio ed aprirci le porte al santo paradiso che per tanti secoli erano state chiuse non solo ai peccatori, ma anche ai giusti" (L 4:105f., Dec. 20, 1768, to Fr. Paul Hyacinth).

here on earth, the human person *in statu viatoris* experiences the wonderful, redeeming power of redemption. In the above-quoted letter, the saint goes on to state,

> Therefore, strive during these holy days to [take time to consider] such a great mystery because, in this manner, you will be the more set afire with love for God and reborn to a life completely holy and deified, as I so heartily desire for you.[59]

St. Paul of the Cross considers the separate mysteries of the redemption (the birth of Jesus and his life, passion, death, and resurrection) as the actualization and revelation of a fundamental mystery: the endless love of God for man. Thus, in letters written by the founder on the occasion of Christmas, we frequently find allusions to the passion and death of Jesus. In another letter written for the occasion of Christmas 1761, he writes,

> I would like you to celebrate the holy feast of Christmas in the poor stable of your own heart, where the dear Jesus will be born in a spiritual way. Offer this poor stable to the holy Mary, Mother of God, and to the holy Joseph, so as to adorn it with virtue so that the Divine Babe will feel well there. Many years ago I had a beautiful card from Germany picturing a beautiful Babe sleeping peacefully upon a cross. Oh, how much I liked that symbol!... Therefore you, too, during this Christmas, when you have the holy Babe in your heart, completely transformed in him by love, rest with him upon the cradle of the cross. . . . [60]

For Paul, the crib and cross are, we could say, manifestations or concrete expressions of the unfathomable mystery of God's love. The life and death of Jesus Christ are the clearest revelation of this love. The human person has the task of being open to this love, striving for the fulfillment of the divine will, even in the face of sorrow and the cross. In another letter written on Christmas Eve of 1754, the saint wrote,

> The better and more perfect manner of celebrating Christmas consists therein, to strip away any joy of the senses, in order to take all your pleasure in the accomplishment of the divine good pleasure. The entire and most

[59] "Sicchè procurino in questi santi giorni d'andar facendo qualche considerazione su d'un tal mistero perchè in cotal guisa s'accenderanno vieppiù nel santo amor di Dio e rinasceranno ad una vita tutta santa e deifica, conforme vivamente desidero" (L 4:106).

[60] "Vorrei che V. R. celebrasse il S. Natale nella povera stalla del suo cuore ove nascerà spiritualmente il dolce Gesù. Presenti questa povera stalla a Maria SSma. ed a S. Giuseppe, acciò l'adornino di virtù affinchè il dolce Bambino vi stia bene. Molti anni sono io avevo un bel Bambino dipinto sopra una carta di Germania che se ne dormiva placidamente sopra una croce. Oh, quanto mi piaceva quel simbolo!... Dunque lei nel S. Natale, che avrà il Bambino nel suo cuore, tutta trasformata in esso per amore, dorma con lui nella culla della Croce . . ." (L 3:604, Dec. 18, 1761, to Maria Angela Cencelli).

holy life of Jesus was all cross . . . you have enough reason to be still more joyful than before, because now you are more hidden in Jesus Christ upon the cross. . . . Therefore, feed yourself upon the divine will in the greatest poverty of spirit and in naked solitude, and be sure that, in this way, you will—in your interior—provide a living retreat for the heavenly Bridegroom.[61]

It may at first sound like an exaggeration when the saint states that "the whole life of Jesus was a cross". When, however, one takes into consideration that Paul saw love and sorrow so closely united[62] that, for him, the passion of Jesus was a manifestation of the love of God, then this assertion in terms of its content is very close to another one of Paul's statements: "The entire life of Jesus was love." The experienced director of souls then exhorted his correspondent, a religious Sister, "to strip off any joy of the senses". Nonetheless, this renunciation was not a goal in itself but only a means of helping her experience a greater, purer, and deeper joy—that inner joy a person experiences when completely fulfilling God's will. In this way one becomes totally "hidden in Jesus Christ upon the cross", a "living retreat" provided for the "heavenly Bridegroom" in one's own interior. This means the risen and glorified Christ gives the person, even here on earth, a "foretaste" of heavenly bliss. Hence, it may be affirmed that the true concern of the Passionist founder was to lead the person to a complete, perfect joy and to a life of bliss. This is the ultimate purpose of Paul's spiritual instructions. To be Christian means to imitate Jesus. In so doing, the disciple of Christ faces temptations similar to those of his Lord and has nothing to do other than resist them in the company of the Master. The end point and ultimate purpose of this imitation is to be a partaker in the joy and glory of the risen Christ. In another letter written on the twenty-fourth of December, 1774, the last Christmas Eve of his life, Paul, writing in the positive tenor so characteristic of his life, again brings the following to light:

Live quietly and trust in your Spouse. Jesus wants you now to be his companion in the garden, in the manger, on Calvary. Be constant. Then he will liberate you, and after the tempest is past and your spirit has become

[61] "Il migliore e più perfetto modo di celebrare le sante feste natalizie è lo spogliamento d'ogni contento sensibile, acciò tutto il contento sia nell'adempimento del divin beneplacito. Tutta la vita ssma. di Gesù fu tutta Croce . . . Sicchè lei ha motivo di star più lieta di prima, perchè più nascosta in Gesù Cristo su la Croce . . . Si cibi dunque della divina volontà in alta povertà di spirito ed in nuda solitudine, e s'assicuri che in tal forma diverrà un vivo ritratto nel suo interiore dello Sposo Celeste" (L 2:468, Dec. 24, 1754, to Sr. Colomba Gertrude Gandolfi).

[62] See above, pp. 200–202.

tranquil, Jesus will grant you many graces. I do not cease to pray for you, and our Lord will grant you double bliss . . . [63]

The saint describes the Incarnation as the "divine wedding contracted by the eternal Word with human nature". Thus, the sense and the goal of "human" nature is to "be immersed in the sea of God's love" through this "spiritual wedding with Jesus Christ". In a letter to Agnes Grazi written on the occasion of an approaching Advent, Paul speaks of this profound dimension of human destiny in symbolically rich words:

> The holy time of Advent is drawing near when holy Mother Church celebrates the memory of the divine espousals which the eternal Word contracted with human nature in his holy Incarnation. My child, contemplate this exalted mystery of infinite love and allow your soul full freedom to plunge into and immerse itself in that infinite ocean of all good. Pray earnestly that there will soon be that great espousal of love between Jesus and your soul and pray also for me, a poor unworthy sinner.[64]

Paul's words stand in the mainstream of spiritual-mystical literature when he writes of "the wedding of love between Jesus and the soul" as a goal. Yet, it must be stressed that the Passionist founder, even when he arrives at the description of the summit of the religious and Christian experience, always keeps Christ conspicuously at the center. The symbol of the "bridal relationship" and of the "wedding" of the soul with God may be characterized, according to Henri de Lubac, as the "characteristic Christian" symbol of mysticism. Here it is a question of "a union of the soul with God, and not an assimilation or a becoming one or identical with God. It is a question of mutual love."[65] How often Paul's thought revolves about the central mystery of God's love is shown by the way in which he understands the Eucharist, about which we speak in the next subsection.

The sacrament of Eucharist as "the living source of life and love" (fonte viva della vita e dell'amore). God's infinite love for humankind determined that the eternal Word become flesh. The same love of God determined that the Son die in order to liberate all from "sin, death, and the devil". By his resurrection Jesus

---

[63] "Viva quieta e si fidi del suo Sposo. Gesù ora vuole che lei gli tenga compagnia all'Orto, al Presepio, al Calvario; ma sia costante; chè poi la liberarà e dopo la tempesta si quieterà il suo spirito e Gesù le farà molte grazie. Non manco di pregare per lei, ed il Signore le conceda raddoppiate felicità . . . " (L 4:150, Dec. 24, 1774, to Sr. Mary Magdalen of the Cross).

[64] "S'avvicina il tempo del Sacro Avvento, in cui la Santa Madre Chiesa celebra le memorie di quel Divino Sposalizio, che il Verbo Eterno ha fatto con la natura umana nella sua Sacratissima Incarnazione. Contempli, figlia mia, questo altissimo Mistero d'infinita carità, e lasci che l'anima sua abbia tutta la libertà d'ingolfarsi ed immergersi in quel Mare infinito d'ogni bene; desideri e preghi che presto si faccia il grande Sposalizio d'amore tra Gesù e l'anima sua, ed anche per me poverello indegnissimo" (L 1:160, Nov. 29, 1736).

[65] De Lubac, "Christliche Mystik", 97.

Christ, the God-Man, drew near to the world. God wanted to leave the world a permanent sign of his love, and therefore he gave to us the sacrament of love, Holy Eucharist. In this visible sign, which is after all a mystery that is not completely penetrable, the human person is, by faith, able to encounter Jesus Christ, the God-man. These terms more or less express in words the fundamental conviction of St. Paul of the Cross.

We find a strongly emphasized eucharistic devotion in the spiritual-religious thought of the founder. Beyond doubt, the Blessed Sacrament represents the *sacramentum proprium* (permanent sacrament) of the Easter mystery. It is the memorial celebration or, said in another way, the "sacramental actualization" of Christ's death and resurrection. By participation in the eucharistic feast, the believer shares in the Lord's death and resurrection. This "existential participation" is presented clearly in another of the saint's letters from the year 1768. In his existential-experiential language, in which the characteristic facets of his thought come clearly to light, the saint writes,

> The lot of the true servants and friends of God is [that one] dies day by day, *"Quotidie morimur: mortui enim estis et vita vestra abscondita est cum Christo in Deo"* [see 1 Cor 15:31 and Col 3:3]. This is the mystical death I desire for you. Therefore, I am fully confident that, at the celebration of the divine sacred mystery, you will be reborn in Jesus to a new deiform life, and thus I would like that you die more and more mystically in Christ every day . . . [66]

There are many places in the spiritual writings of St. Paul of the Cross in which he speaks of the "sacramental Jesus" (*Gesù Sacramentato*). In analyzing these, it becomes obvious that when the saint speaks of the Lord's presence in the sacrament of the altar, he brings to light general convictions which we could define as constitutive elements of an implicit resurrection theology. For example, he frequently speaks of the eucharistic Christ in terms of joy, life, and love. It is, therefore, appropriate to consider the eucharistic devotion of the Passionist founder as an expression of his faith in the risen and glorified Lord, as S. Pompilio does in his book on St. Paul of the Cross.[67]

Even in the entries in his spiritual diary, it is evident that the sacramental presence of Christ occupied a constitutive position in the founder's experience of faith. Perhaps we can best designate his existential relationship with the eucharistic Lord by the personal categories of friendship and confidence. He writes of this confidence in the entry of December 7, 1720, after having

[66] "La vita dei veri servi ed amici di Dio è di morir ogni giorna: *'Quotidie morimur: mortui enim estis et vita vestra abscondita est cum Christo in Deo'. —*Or questa è quella morte mistica che io desidero in lei; e siccome nelle celebrazione dei Divini Sacrosanti Misteri, ho tutta la fiducia che sarà rinato in Gesù Cristo ad una nuova vita deifica, così bramo che muoia in Cristo misticamente ogni giorno più . . . " (L 1:787, Dec. 29, 1768, to Thomas Fossi).
[67] See Pompilio, esp. 96–110.

referred to himself as "worse than a demon" and "a dirty cesspool". The entry reads,

> But I never lost my very great and tender confidence in my sacramental Spouse. I tell him that in giving me so many graces and such innumerable favors, he only manifests his infinite mercies all the more . . . [68]

Even in this early phase of life, the founder indicates that his eucharistic devotion has as its basis, first and foremost, an existential belief in the risen and glorified Christ. Thus, he reports, in one entry in his diary, that the reception of Holy Communion gave him a joyful and hope-filled "outlook" of his own proper *"eschaton"*. Paul writes, "My beloved God gave me an infused understanding of the joy which the soul will have when we shall see him face to face and shall be united with him in holy love."[69] Other entries also manifest clearly Paul's great confidence and unshakable belief in the eucharistic Lord, the sacramental Spouse (*Sacramentato Sposo*).[70] Not without good reason does the founder end his last entry in his spiritual diary with the words: "All this was accompanied by many tears along with great delight, especially upon seeing my Spouse, Jesus, present in the Blessed Sacrament."[71]

Interior joy and an intense experience of faith are frequently the effects lived by the founder in his faith encounters with the sacramental Spouse. Sometimes this interior experience of happiness is so strong that he believes he has had a foretaste of the "bliss of paradise". In a letter composed only a short time after the completion of his diary, we come upon this joyful exclamation: "Oh what beautiful conversations take place in the company of the angels before our sacramental Spouse! They are pure embraces of paradise."[72]

This "love having become sacrament" represents, for the saint, an inexhaustible fountain from which he draws joy and happiness, time and time

---

[68] " . . . ma non mi si parte giammai la grandissima e tenerissima confidenza con il mio Sacramentato Sposo; gli dico che con farmi tante grazie, e si innumerabili favori risplenderanno più le sue infinite misericordie" (*Diario Spirituale*, 66–67; *Tagebuch*, 78; Rouse, 32).

[69] Paul writes the following in the entry of Dec. 4, 1720: "Nella santissima Comunione fui molto in soavità; il mio caro Dio mi dava intelligenza infusa nel gaudio che avrà l'anima quando lo vedremo a faccia a faccia, che sarà unita con lui in santo amore." / "During Holy Communion I experienced much delight. My beloved God gave me an infused understanding of the joy that the soul will have when we shall see him face to face and shall be united with him in holy love" (*Diario Spirituale*, 63; *Tagebuch*, 73; Rouse, 31).

[70] See the entries of Dec. 5, 7, 14, and 27.

[71] " . . . e sempre con gran lagrime, miste con gran soavità, massime nel vedere il mio Sacramentato Sposo Gesù." / "All this was accompanied with many tears along with great delight, especially on seeing my spouse Jesus present in the Blessed Sacrament" (*Diario Spirituale*, 87; *Tagebuch*, 113; Rouse, 38).

[72] "Oh! che bella conversazione l'andarsene a stare in compagnia degli Angeli avanti al nostro Sacramentato Sposo! sono pure amplessi di Paradiso" (L 1:26, [date unknown] 1721, to Sr. Teresa C. Pontas).

again. He strove to present this "fountain of joy" to those whom he directed
and advised spiritually. This inclination is described in an expressive manner
in a letter written to Agnes Grazi for the feast of Corpus Christi in the year
1740. This letter bears, before the salutation, the significant motto *Viva il
Sommo Bene Sacramentato* (hail our all good, sacramental God). In this letter,
he bade his "spiritual daughter" to undertake her "grand flights to the Supreme
Good . . . acting like the butterfly which circles about the flame and then
burns itself up entirely in it".[73]

Continuing in his enraptured and enrapturing manner, the saint adds,

> . . . [The butterfly] circles the flame and then burns itself up entirely in it,
> and especially in this great sweet octave of sacramental love. Ah, my
> daughter, eat and drink and inebriate yourself. Fly, sing, jubilate, exult, keep
> a feast with your Divine Spouse.[74]

One can see by these exuberant passages how much the Passionist founder
feeds his own interior religious life on the reality of the Eucharist. For Paul,
Jesus in the Holy Eucharist represents that fountain through which flows such
a great share in the life and power of the risen and glorified Christ. Thus, the
saint concludes the above-quoted letter written for the feast of Corpus Christi
with the following petition:

> May Jesus enflame you with love and make you die in your spirit by his
> most divine Spirit, so that you may live, breathe, and do everything with
> the life and in the life of Jesus in the Blessed Sacrament.[75]

The life and power of the crucified and risen Lord are imparted to the
"followers of Jesus" by God's self-communication of love. The sacramental
reality of the eucharistic bread is fully charged with this divine love. St. Paul
of the Cross does not try to fathom this "absolute mystery" by his intellect but
rather again and again expresses his wonder and gratitude. More often than

---

[73] Paul writes the following in this letter: " . . . bisogna annichilarsi sempre più . . . lasciando
l'anima in santa libertà di far gran voli al Somme Bene, come Dio la porta, e far come la
farfalletta che gira intorno al lume, e poi si brucia in esso." / " . . . you must annihilate
yourself more and more and despise yourself more and more and throw yourself under the
feet of all, leaving your soul in holy freedom to make grand flights to the Supreme Good, as
God carries it, to act like the butterfly that circles around the flame and then burns itself up
entirely in it . . . " (L 1:251, June 15, 1740). St. Francis de Sales uses this same simile of the
butterfly in his treatise *On the Love of God*. The simile, however, appears in a different
context. See Reisinger 3:225.

[74] " . . . così l'anima giri pure intorno, anzi dentro a quel lume divino, e tutta s'incenerisca
in esso, e massime in questa grande e dolcissima ottava dell'amor sacramentato. Ah, figlia mia!
Mangiate, bevete e ubbriacatevi, volate, cantate, giubilate, esultate, fate festa allo sposo
divino" (L 1:251, June 15, 1740).

[75] "Gesù la bruci d'amore, e la faccia morire nel suo spirito e del suo spirito divinissimo,
acciò viva, respiri e faccia tutto colla vita e nella vita di Gesù Sacramentato" (L 1:252).

not, he terms this mystery the "fountain of love". Thus, in a letter in which he speaks about the great value of meditation on the passion, he says the following about the Blessed Sacrament:

> Oh, what a great treasure! It is the "fountain" of love and of holiness. Jesus says, "If anyone thirst, let him come after me and drink" [Jn 7:37]. Have you a thirst for becoming holy, of being completely inflamed with holy love? Why then do you not fly to embrace the sweet Bridegroom in the Blessed Sacrament?[76]

The spiritual counseling and instruction, which we find in his letters of spiritual direction, are unmistakably grounded, first and foremost, in Paul's own experience, in his encounter with God. Nevertheless, he seldom speaks directly of his own experience. There is, however, one letter in which the saint notes a personal religious experience. It was written to Agnes Grazi, who was directed by Paul until her death and with whom there existed a close friendship. In this letter, the interior weaving of Paul's deep passion mysticism with his keen eucharistic devotion becomes very obvious.

Since his description gives us an insight into the religious depths of the saint's life and simultaneously reveals to us the "positivity" of his passion mysticism, we are quoting here the entire part of the letter that deals with this point.

> You recall, my child, that yesterday in our devout conferences I confided to you that when it happened to me to pass through some great storm, and when I first put myself before my sacramental love, my soul flew in spirit to embrace [clasp to itself] this infinite charity exposed on the altar for the adoration of the people. I [then] heard this sweetest saying spoken to me by the Savior: "Son, whoever embraces me, embraces thorns." Do you believe, my daughter, that my soul does not understand that, but God makes it understand with this saying: *"Chi s'abbraccia a me s'abbraccia alle spine"* [Whoever embraces me, embraces thorns], that just as our dear Jesus wished that his most holy life here on earth should be always in the midst of the thorns, pains, labors, fatigues, toils, anguish, contempt, calumnies, sorrows, scourges, nails, thorns, and the most bitter death of the cross, so he made me understand that by embracing him, I ought to lead my life in the midst of pains. And, ah, with what jubilation my poor soul embraced all kinds of suffering![77]

[76] "Oh, che gran tesoro! Questo è il fonte dell'amore, della santità. Chi ha sete, dice il dolce Gesù, venga da me e beva. Ha sete lei di farsi santa, di ardere tutta di santo amore? e che fa dunque, che non se ne vola ad abbracciarsi al dolce Sposo Sacramentato?" (L 3:342, July 14, 1755, to Sr. Maria Colomba of Jesus and Mary).

[77] "Si ricorda, figlia mia, che ieri nella nostra divota conferenza le confidai, che quando m'è occorso di passar qualche grossa tempesta se mi sono prima trovato avanti al mio Amore Sacramentato, l'anima mia è volata in spirito ad abbracciarsi a quell'infinita carità, esposta su l'Altare all'adorazione de' popoli, e mi sono sentito fare dal Salvatore questa dolcissima

Some paragraphs later, the saint expresses something of a "forejoy" of the future life of glory in the following words:

> What will it be when we shall sing without ceasing that eternal trisagion *"Sanctus, Sanctus, Sanctus"*, when together with the saints we shall sing that sweetest "Alleluia"! . . . When, when will death come to break the walls of this prison! Ah, for that will be the day of our espousals, of our wedding, in which our soul in the highest manner will espouse herself to the dear Jesus and shall sit forever at the heavenly banquet.[78]

Of course, it is not at all surprising, as is apparent in this fragment of the letter, that the Passionist founder did obtain power and strength from the eucharistic Lord to accept and bear concrete pain and labor as "the cross of Christ". It is, however, the mystery of God's love that he contemplates and worships in this sacrament. He, therefore, does not speak objectively and "factually" about *the* sacrament. Rather, he always keeps in mind that Jesus Christ is present as the God-Man in this eucharistic mystery and that the believer, in a real and personal way, can encounter therein the crucified and risen Lord. He expresses this faith in another letter in the following way: "And look at him with a lively faith, love him and throw yourself into his divine arms and rest there, aflame in his holy love."[79]

Since the love of the God-Man, Jesus Christ, is present in such an extraordinary manner under the sign of the eucharistic bread and since, according to St. Paul of the Cross, the highest and the ultimate, definitive purpose of human life consists in reaching the closest possible union with God through love, the saint again and again urges believers to receive the eucharistic Lord in Holy Communion as often as possible.[80] Certainly, it is not exaggerated to

---

parlata: 'Figlio, chi s'abbraccia a me, s'abbraccia alle spine!' Che si crede, figlia mia, che l'anima mia non intendesse che il nostro Gesù è un mare d'infinite dolcezze? certo che l'intendeva, ma Dio le faceva altresì capire, con quelle parole: 'Chi s'abbraccia a me s'abbraccia alle spine', che siccome il caro Gesù ha voluto che la sua Santissima Vita qui in terra sia stata sempre in mezzo alle spine di pene, travagli, fatiche, stenti, angoscie, disprezzi, calunnie, dolori, sferzate, chiodi, spine e morte amarissima di Croce, così mi faceva intendere che abbracciandomi a lui dovevo menare la mia vita in mezzo alle pene! Ed oh, con quanto giubilo la povera anima mia abbracciava ogni sorta di penare!" (L 1:194, Aug. 29, 1737).

[78] "Che sarà quando cantaremo senza cessare quell'Eterno Trisagio: '*Sanctus, Sanctus, Sanctus*', quando insieme de' Santi cantaremo quel dolcissimo 'Alleluia!' . . . Quando, quando verrà la morte a rompere le mura di questa prigione! Ah, che quello sarà il giorno del nostro sposalizio, delle nostre nozze, in cui l'anima nostra con modo altissimo si sposerà al caro Gesù, e sederà in eterno a quel celesto banchetto" (L 1:195).

[79] " . . . e con viva fede lo rimiri, lo ami e si slanci tutta nelle divine sue braccia, ivi si riposi, bruciando del suo santo amore . . . " (L 3:598, June 14, 1760, to Sr. M. Magdalen of the Seven Sorrows).

[80] Refer to what has been said above about Jansenism, pp. 71–79.

maintain that the Passionist founder may be called an advocate of frequent, even daily reception of the Eucharist.

With the thought of daily Communion in mind, Paul sent Agnes Grazi a book which treated of the frequent and daily reception of Holy Communion to be given to a certain Fr. Francis to read.[81] (It is likely that, in his pastoral practice, this Fr. Francis did not agree with the idea of frequent Communion.) Paul also told Agnes to relay the following message to the priest:

> Please tell him, that the most unworthy and poorest [the founder is here speaking of himself] has the desire that souls may come to know God and to burn in his love and, in order to obtain this, there is no other way than to give them the sacrament most holy, which is the living fount of holy love.[32]

In 1768, Paul wrote to Anna Maria Calcagnini,

> As concerns Holy Communion, I would like you to receive every morning, without fail . . . there you will drink from the fount of holiness the living waters of eternal life [see Jn 4:14].[83]

Paul also speaks of the daily reception of Holy Communion in a letter to a religious, the abbess of the Capuchin convent of St. Fiora. He writes,

> I take delight in the Lord upon hearing that you have introduced daily reception of Holy Communion, and I assure you I have desired this since I was there. For this, I bless the Lord and give him thanks forever![84]

How much Paul's mysticism of interiority and his eucharistic devotion blend harmoniously one with the other is evident some lines further on in the same letter. Paul continues,

> I very much recommend to you inner solitude, standing continuously in that sacred, interior desert, resting in the bosom of the heavenly Spouse in the sacred silence of faith and holy love; and this will be

[81] In a letter of July 16, 1738, the saint wrote, "Le mando questo prezioso libro, che tratta della frequenza della SS. Comunione, ed anche quotidiana; lo consegni colle sue proprie mani al P. Francesco, e gli dica che ne legga un capitolo ogni giorno . . . " / "I send you this precious book, which treats of the frequency of the most Holy Communion. Consign it with your own hands to Fr. Francis and tell him to read a chapter every day . . . " (L 1:213).

[82] " . . . gli dica che il poverello indegnissimo ha intenzione che le anime conoscano Dio e brucino del suo amore, e che per questo non sa altra strada, che il dargli spesso il Sommo Bene Sacramentato, che è la fonte viva del S. Amore" (L 1:213f.).

[83] "In quanto alla santa comunione vorrei la faceste ogni mattina, senza lasciarli mai . . . ed ivi bevete nel fonte della santità le acque vive dell'eterna vita" (L 3:809).

[84] "Godo nel Signore di sentire che abbiano introdotto la SSma. Comunione quotidiana, e le accerto che io lo desiderai fin da quando fui costì. Ne sia benedetto e ringraziato il Signore in eterno" (Bollettino 8 [1927]: 178f., letter of Mar. 5, 1770).

a fruit of the daily reception of Holy Communion—and one must then never quit.[85]

The final end of every spiritual-ascetical effort consists in achieving, in faith, a more intense union with God. For the founder, the reception of Holy Communion is a superior, even the best, "means" by which a woman or man receives a share in "God's love". In a letter of 1760, Paul stated that the daily reception of communion represents that "exercise of devotion" which "most unites the soul to God".[86] In a manner difficult to explain and yet real, the person—by receiving the Body of Christ—is introduced into the trinitarian mystery by "becoming Christ". The founder describes this actualization of faith as follows:

> Jesus, who is the way and the truth and life [Jn 14:6] will teach you everything, especially when you have him in you sacramentally; but, as you have him as food, let him have you as food, too, and change you into himself by love.[87]

As these reflections point out, St. Paul of the Cross looked with predilection upon God's love for the human person—a love "incarnated in the God-Man, Jesus Christ"—in the eucharistic mystery. Whenever the person eats the eucharistic bread, he—in an intense and unparalleled manner—is attracted to and enters into the stream of God's self-communicating love and obtains through this a rich share in the power and might of the crucified and risen Lord. Thus, through the eucharistic feast and reception of Holy Communion, he is virtually attracted to and enters into the "mystery of God" and "changed into Jesus Christ" through the love of God. The transforming force of this divine love is so strong that the communicant can declare together with the Apostle Paul, "It is no longer I who live, but Christ who lives in me" (Gal 2:20). Indeed, these words of the Apostle Paul are frequently cited by St. Paul of the Cross

---

[85] "Loro raccomando molto la solitudine interna, standosene di continuo nel sacro deserto interiore, riposando nel seno dello Sposo celeste in sacro silenzio di fede e di santo amore; e questo sarà un gran frutto della SSma. Comunione quotidiana; e poi mai devono lasciarla" (*Bollettino* 8 [1927]: 179).

[86] The letter contains the following passage: "Molto ho gradito di sentire che in questa ottava del SSmo. Sacramento le sia stata concessa la SSma. Comunione ogni mattina, ed io vorrei che proseguisse, mentre non vi è esercizio di pietà che più unisca con Dio di questo." / "I am very happy upon hearing they have conceded to give you Holy Communion every morning of this octave, and I would like you to continue this [practice] since there is no other exercise of piety that unites you more closely to God than this" (L 3:375, June 13, 1760, to Teresa Palozzi).

[87] "Gesù che è la nostra via, verità e vita v'insegnerà tutto, massime quando l'avrete dentro di voi Sacramentato; ma lasciate che siccome voi vi cibate di lui, così esso si cibi di voi e vi trasformi in sè per amore" (L 2:464, July 30, 1754, to Sr. Colomba Gertrude Gandolfi).

in his letters to express the transforming power and might of the Risen One.[88]

"TO BE BORN AGAIN IN THE DIVINE WORD JESUS CHRIST" AS A PARTICIPATION IN THE "POWER OF HIS RESURRECTION" (RINASCERE NEL DIVIN VERBO GESÙ CRISTO).

Whoever delves deeply into the spiritual-theological thinking of the founder of the Passionists will soon notice the focus of his thought is on *Cristus patiens et crucifixus*. Further investigation will reveal that, at the same time, there lies concealed within the dynamics a hopeful and joyful "positivity" rooted in Paul's faith in the resurrection, existentially conceived. This observation has been previously made by E. Henau, who studied the saint's passion mysticism in detail. He concluded his study *De Passiemystiek van Paulus van het Kruis* with the inference that faith in the resurrection—in the saint's spiritual teaching—is embodied above all in Paul's fundamental principle of "divine rebirth".[89]

Analysis of the several places in which St. Paul of the Cross speaks either of "becoming born again" or of "mystical death" indicates clearly that elements of an *implicit* resurrection theology are present in these formulations. Because the Passionist founder does not reflect the content of faith in a theoretical-abstract manner in his letters of spiritual direction but rather speaks and instructs from his own personal experience of faith, we do not find any *explicitly* developed resurrection theology in them. Given this background, it may be said in the manner of a heuristic hypothesis that St. Paul of the Cross' existential faith in the resurrected and glorified *Kyrios* is first and foremost expressed by the formula: to be born again in the Divine Word Jesus Christ (*rinascere nel Divin Verbo Gesù Cristo*).[90]

---

[88] L 2:322 (date unknown), to Mother Mary Crucified Costantini; L 2:722, May 25, 1751, to Lucy Burlini; and L 3:756, Dec. 28, 1768, to Marianna Girelli.

[89] On the last page of his unpublished dissertation, Henau writes, "Wij kunnen toch besluiten met hieromtrent een vermoeden uit te spreken: naar ons gevoelen is een verrijzen-isgeloof helemaal niet afwezig. Het gaat hem hier eenvoudig om een terminologisch probleem. Wij geven onmiddellijk toe dat woorden als 'verrijzenis', 'opstanding' en 'verheerlijking' ontbreken, maar wij menen dat de werkelijkheid die met deze woorden wordt bedoeld in het vocabularium van Paulus van het Kruis te vinden is in het begrip 'geboorte' " (Henau, 273).

[90] There are more than sixty places in the letters where Paul speaks of "being born again". He almost always uses the same formulation; therefore it is appropriate to call it a "formula". At the end of his book, C. Brovetto includes a table noting all the letters in which the concept *rinascere natività* (to be born again) occurs. See Brovetto, *Introduzione alla Spiritualità*, 207f.

Before focusing our attention upon concrete statements in his different letters, we first want to draw the reader's attention to a few other points in order to explain better the scope of meaning contained in this hypothesis. To begin with, we want to point to a linguistic affinity worth mentioning. The Italian verb *rinascere* (to be born again) possesses an affinity of content with the word *risorgere* (to rise or to resurrect). Thus the verb *rinascere* used in the formula *rinascere a nuova vita* also contains the meaning *to rise, to resurrect*.[91] Paul uses this formula almost exclusively with the noun *life* (*vita*).

As previously mentioned, the Passionist founder developed the above formula after reading Surius-Tauler.[92] We have also previously shown the change in the wording of the formula from "God's birth in the ground of the soul" to "being reborn in the Divine Word Jesus Christ", and we have discussed the substance of this change.[93] The concept *rinascere* is found in Paul's letters only *after* 1748. This fact does not at all mean that *before* 1748 his faith in the resurrection was any less emphasized in his spiritual-theological thinking. In fact, the elements of an "implicit theology of resurrection" have already been explained in the introduction to this chapter, and they have been noted in letters from the saint's early period and even included in entries from the saint's spiritual diary. The distinction is that *after* 1748 the saint spoke of participation in the "power of the resurrection". In contrast, in some letters written *before* 1748, he uses expressions such as "vested solely with Jesus Christ",[94] "transformed by love into Jesus Christ",[95] or "to be hidden in the great Heart of Jesus".[96] While all these formulations speak of a share in the power of the Risen One, later formulations, especially "to be reborn to a new and deified

---

[91] Refer to Palazzi, 998. Also see, Langenscheidts, *Handwörterbuch Italienisch,* vol. 1 (3d ed.) (Berlin, 1970), 343.

[92] See above, pp. 135–46.

[93] Ibid.

[94] In a letter from 1738, Paul wrote the following: "... prego Suo Divina Maestà la spogli di tutto il creato, acciò sia vestita solamente di Gesù Cristo ... morta a tutto e viva a Dio." / "... I beseech his Divine Majesty that he strip you of all created things so as to be vested only in Christ ... dead to all and alive to God" (L 1:387, Dec. 10, 1738, to Francesca Lucci; similarly, see L 1:141, June 29, 1736, to Agnes Grazi).

[95] On Holy Thursday the saint wrote, "... affinchè tutto trasformato per amore in Gesù Cristo, gode V. S. Illma. e Rma. la pienezza dell'ineffabile dolcezza della gloriosissima sua risurrezione." / "... so that being completely transformed by love into Jesus Christ, you enjoy the fullness of the ineffable sweetness of his most glorious resurrection" (L 2:224, Mar. 21, 1742, to Msgr. Count Garagni). See n. 17 above. Also see L 1:63, Apr. 21, 1726, to Nicolina Martinez.

[96] This formulation may be found in a letter of Aug. 4, 1740. Among other things, it states, "Oh, quanto è fortunata l'anima, che si nasconde come un puro nulla in quel gran Cuore di Gesù ..." / "Oh, what a fortunate soul is she who conceals herself as a pure nothing in that great Heart of Jesus ..." (L 1:256). Also see the section entitled "Nel Cuore Sacratissimo de Gesù" in *Storia Critica* 2:1449–64.

life in the Divine Word Jesus Christ" (*rinascere nel Divin Verbo Gesù Cristo ad una vita nuova e deifica*), express more strongly the element of *new life* in a way that reflects Taulerian as well as Paulacrucian thought.

We must also draw the reader's attention to another point: If we investigate in detail the saint's use of language in his letters, then it is striking that by his use of the terms *risorgere* and *risurrezione* Paul means, or is at least thinking of, the "eschatological resurrection".[97] In contrast, when the verb *rinascere* is used, the saint refers to the "power of the Risen One" as it is effective in the "earthly existence" of the human person.

When we take into consideration the thought of St. Paul of the Cross in its totality and we look therein for its fundamental intent, then we should mention two elements that moved him so strongly and continuously: first, his constant concern for a strong interiorization; and, second, his emphasis upon *Christus patiens et crucifixus*. Therefore, in the following, when the subject matter is "rebirth in the Divine Word Jesus Christ", the reader ought to keep in mind Paul's starting point, i.e., his mysticism of interiority and his passioncentrism.

1. Interiorization as a Preliminary Condition for Being Born in or Coming to Life in the Word of God

Faith in the resurrection of Jesus is a "unique fact", as underscored by K. Rahner in his work *Grundkurs des Glaubens*.[98] This faith is attested to in the Gospels' descriptions of the encounters with the resurrected Lord. In spite of the variations in Gospel reports and their sometimes dramatic styles of presentation, the apostolic witness is essentially one of their experience that Jesus lives.[99] Reports of the encounters of witnesses to the risen Lord are strong reasons for our faith. From a theological point of view, the resurrection of Jesus is not seen primarily as something that happened to him alone. Rather, the resurrection is the pledge and beginning of the world's restoration.[100]

St. Paul of the Cross was a mystic, that is, a person who understood his own existence, in a radical and exclusive way, as a function of God's creating power and salvific action, a person who considered the sense or purpose of his life solely as a drawing near—in the existential experience of religion—to "the mystery of God", and a person who tried to direct others to the same

[97] See what has been said above, pp. 272–77.
[98] Karl Rahner introduces the chapter "Zum Verständnis der Auferstehung Jesu" in the following way: "Faith in the resurrection of Jesus exists. That is a unique fact. This in itself is worth pondering. This uniqueness consists therein that he is alive, although there are many, e.g., the murdered prophets, of whom it is said that they live." See Rahner, *Grundkurs*, 269.
[99] Ibid., 271f.
[100] Karl Rahner, in *Lexikon* I, col. 1041 (keyword: *Auferstehung Christi*).

experience. For him, there was only one road leading a person to the fathomless mystery of God: the Person of the God-Man, Christ, who said, "I am the way, and the truth, and the life; no one comes to the Father but by me" (Jn 14:6).

The underlying principle at the basis of the entire mysticism professed by the Passionist founder is that of seeking by means of an existential faith experience the reality that Jesus lives. Naturally, the apostolic experience of resurrection was that of a completely different kind, which may be labeled as "strict *sui generis*",[101] and which, therefore, could be in no way compared with the religious experience of the mystic. Furthermore, it should be stated that Paul's faith in the Risen One represents solely the origin and the start of his Christ mysticism.

The resurrection of Jesus is the "beginning of the restoration of creation". The risen and glorified *Kyrios* is the definitive pledge of God's nearness to his people.[102] Certainly, St. Paul of the Cross did not think explicitly upon these fundamental principles of resurrection theology, yet they were implicitly contained in his existential faith in the efficacy of the "power of the risen Christ".

But now let us focus our attention upon separate affirmations present in his letters. More often than not, the saint encourages his correspondent to strive after a deeper interiorization, to acquire "interior solitude" so as to be opened in this way to the unfathomable mystery of God. The purpose of such "introversion", as the saint himself calls it, is to gain a share in the "new life in Jesus Christ". This interiorization ought to prepare the person to open and to become receptive to the action of God.

In June 1755 he wrote the following to a religious Sister:

> Your prayer must be continuous, that is, remain in interior solitude, clothed in Jesus Christ . . . further make introversions in God, that is, sweet renewals of faith, wordlessly casting yourself all the more into the abyss of God. In this way, whenever you truly annihilate yourself in God, you will be reborn always to a new life of love in the Divine Word Christ Jesus.[103]

These words demonstrate that the ultimate goal of this *introire in seipsum* (to enter into one's self) is the attainment of a share in a "new life of love", in the life that the Divine Word-Made-Flesh brought with him for humankind. By the death and resurrection of Jesus, man has become a "new

---

[101] Rahner, *Grundkurs*, 272.

[102] K. Rahner, in *Lexikon* I, col. 1039ff.

[103] "La sua orazione deve essere continua, cioè di starsene in solitudine interiore, vestita di Gesù Cristo . . . faccia delle introversioni in Dio, cioè dolci ravvivamenti di fede, anche senza parole e più s'abissi in Dio. In tal forma ogni volta che ciò farà con vero annichilamento di se stessa in Dio, rinascerà sempre a nuova vita d'amore nel Divin Verbo Cristo Gesù" (L 3:337, June 21, 1755, to Sr. Maria Maddalena Anselmi).

creature" (see 2 Cor 5:17), in whom love predominates. This is so because the resurrection of Christ revealed that love "is stronger than death".[104]

"Interiority of confidence" as prerequisite and *"removal of sin"* as consequence of *"being reborn in the Divine Word"*. For the Passionist founder, interiority and recollection are not formal concepts applied as if they were components of a "technique" of meditation so as to obtain a greater capability of concentration. Rather, interiority and recollection have for Paul a directional goal in substance, and one can define them as ways of achieving the "activation and intensification of the basic Christian attitude". Such a basic attitude, which we find strongly emphasized in the founder's mysticism of interiority, is a childlike, carefree trust in God, the loving and good Father. This "interiority of confidence" represents at the same time the preliminary condition of "becoming born again in the Divine Word", of being able to receive the "power of his resurrection". Paul writes in a letter,

> May Jesus make you as holy as I desire, and may he more and more increase in you the holy interior recollection that I have always recommended to you, in order that your spirit, resting always like a little girl in the divine bosom of the heavenly Father, will be able to be born again each moment in the Divine Word Jesus Christ.[105]

As this quotation indicates, a person cannot arrive at this "interiority of confidence" by his own power but stands in need of Christ's help and grace; Jesus is he who leads the soul into "the bosom of the Father" to find rest there, in that "bosom" from which the Word proceeds (see Jn 1:18). Thus, when the founder speaks of "being reborn in the Divine Word Jesus Christ", he implicitly attests to the preexistence of the Son of God and, by this attestation, to the trinitarian dimension of God's activity. The Divine Word proceeds from the Father and took "the form of a slave" (Phil 2:7). As God-Man and as the "ultimate Redeemer",[106] Christ shows us the way to the "bosom of the Father"

---

[104] See Ratzinger, *Einführung*, 249–57. Also see what has been said on this subject above, pp. 279–81.

[105] "Gesù la faccia tanto santa quanto desidero, e le accresca sempre più quel santo raccoglimento interiore che tanto le ho raccomandato sempre, affinchè il suo spirito, riposando sempre come bambina nel seno divino del Celeste Padre, possa rinascere ogni momento più nel Divin Verbo Cristo Gesù" (L 2:46, Dec. 18, 1768, to M. G. Venturi Grazi; similarly, L 1:602f., June 1751 [date unknown], to Thomas Fossi).

[106] The concept of *"absoluten Heilbringers"* (absolute bearers of salvation) belongs to Karl Rahner. It is a key concept in "Neuansätzen einer orthodoxen Christologie" (see K. Rahner and W. Thüsing, "Christologie—systematisch und exegetisch" [*Quaestiones Disputatae* 55, (1972)]: 59–69; and Rahner, *Grundkurs*, 287–95). Rahner would like with his "transcendental Christology", culminating in his concept of the "absolute bearer of salvation", to introduce the principle of an orthodox "Ascendence-Christology", which is meant to be an equivalent for a "later" Christology of the Son and Logos from the New Testament. Some remarks about this: In terms of St. John's Logos-Christology, this principle may be an equivalent; but,

by giving himself to us in love. Entrance of the human person into this "self-communication of God" is described by the saint as "rebirth in the Divine Word Jesus Christ".

The God-Man, Jesus Christ, has *redeemed* humankind. His death on a cross was a death for our sins (Proto-Evangelium, 1 Cor 15:3). God "has delivered us from the power of darkness and brought us to the kingdom of his beloved Son, in whom we have redemption, the forgiveness of our sins" (Col 1:13–14). By Christ's resurrection from the dead, God has given humankind the gift of redemption in a definitive and permanent way—a gift which is, first and foremost, a liberation from sin[107] according to the accounts of the New Testament. This death and resurrection have resulted above all in humankind's liberation from the "devil's circle of

---

for the New Testament Son-Christology, which the first Councils of the Church have further clarified, no. This is because the Son-Christology moves more on an existential level and is more experience oriented. Rahner's "transcendental Christology", in contrast, remains more on the abstract-philosophical plane, even though factors related to experience are present in it. See the section "Appelle an die 'suchende Christologie' " in Rahner, *Grundkurs,* 288–91. The question still remains whether "transcendental Christology" is able to achieve for the existential practice of faith what the New Testament (even if "later") and the ecclesiastical Son-Christology offers us. In *Grundkurs,* Rahner himself stresses the necessity of an "existential Christology" (298f.).

[107] A significant "weakness" of Rahner's "new Christology" consists in the fact that in it the original religious concept of "sin" is scarcely found. Rahner reproaches "classical" Christology for an "insufficient emphasis upon the soteriological meaning of the Christ event" (*Grundkurs,* 286). One must certainly accept, as J. Ratzinger affirms, that "Christology and soteriology have become separated in the course of the historical development of the Christian Faith" (*Einführung,* 186). Of course, this has affected the all-embracing vista of the "Christ event" in a detrimental way. Yet, it remains to be investigated if Rahner's "transcendental Christology" can express in general the religious depth of what the New Testament calls "redemption", when it fails to see an explicit hamartiology or theology of sin. Furthermore, one is entitled to ask if the contemporary person really is no longer able to accept the New Testament's interpretation of the death of Jesus as "sacrificing" love for the atonement of "our sins" (see Rahner, *Grundkurs,* 267f.). Beyond a doubt, the concepts of "sacrifice" and "sin" are primarily and characteristically religious concepts, and the "religious" man or woman of today still has a sense of these and of the meaning of these notions. To discard the content of these concepts (we cannot explain these concepts here in great detail) would eliminate an important religious dimension of Christian faith, a dimension that has been handed down to us in the New Testament. It seems that this plane of Christian-religious reality could also be satisfactorily clarified starting from Rahner's "transcendental initiative". In brief, Rahner's *three* "appeals" for a "searching Christology"—an absolute love for our neighbor, preparedness for death, hope in the future (*Grundkurs,* 288–91)—should be made complete by a *fourth* appeal, i.e., the consciousness of one's sins and the need for redemption. Although it is true that Rahner speaks in another source (*Dritter Gang: Der Mensch als das Wesen der radikalen Schuldbedrohtheit,* 97–121) of sin and the necessity of salvation, it must be considered a "shortcoming" when a new, even a "searching", Christology does not explicitly present and place in bold relief this fundamental datum of Christian faith.

sin"[108] and the "transfer, through love, into the Son's kingdom". Whenever the person declares a "radical" engagement of faith in Jesus Christ, then "redemption" acts efficiently upon him, and he "is risen to a new life of love", as St. Paul of the Cross explains it.

Paul, speaking in a letter of the Crucified and Risen One's power over sin, starts with the "interiority of confidence" and continues,

> ... I would like you to refocus yourself in the interior part of your soul, and there with living faith rest in the bosom of God, like a little child, in the sacred silence of faith and holy love. Whenever you are completely recollected in God, in the interior temple of your spirit, the soul is reborn to a new life of love in the Divine Word Jesus Christ.... In this recollection, in the fire of holy love, all the rust of sin is destroyed, and the soul is renewed in God.[109]

In almost all places in which St. Paul of the Cross speaks of being "reborn in the Divine Word Jesus Christ" (*rinascere nel Divin Verbo Cristo Gesù*), we find a declaration explaining that this "rebirth" means a "rising" to a *new life*. In other words, the matter in point is that of a "new, deiform life", which tells us unequivocally that we are dealing with elements of a resurrection theology. In the revelatory writings of the New Testament the concept life (*zoe*) plays an important part. Therefore, together with F. Mußner, we may affirm the following with regard to the concept of *zoe* in the writings of the apostle Paul:

> In Pauline theology, the believer's life is entirely understood as a share, by grace, in the Risen One's life, in the life of the eschatological Adam, as a consequence of the justification and of the new creation.[110]

This statement, as a whole, could be used to indicate the theological background that lies at the base of Paul of the Cross' formula: "To be born again in the Divine Word Jesus Christ". This affinity to Pauline theology will be better specified later in the course of our presentation.[111]

As we have already observed, the Passionist founder in his use of the phrase "being reborn" was inspired by Tauler's phrase "divine nativity in the ground

---

[108] Many valuable suggestions concerning the capability of the human person to interpret redemption "in a modern manner" may be found in Moltmann, *Gott,* 268–92.

[109] " ... vorrei che lei spesso si riconcentrasse nel suo interno, ed ivi con viva fede si riposasse nel seno di Dio come una bambina, con sacro silenzio di fede e di santo amore; ogni volta che l'anima si raccoglie tutta in Dio, nel tempio interno del suo spirito, rinasce a nuova vita d'amore nel Divin Verbo Cristo Gesù ... In questo raccoglimento, nel fuoco del santo amore, si distrugge tutta la ruggine del peccato e si rinnovella l'anima in Dio" (L 1:525f., Dec. 15, 1761, to Sr. Maria Cherubina Bresciani).

[110] F. Mußner, in *Lexikon* 6, col. 855 (keyword: Leben).

[111] In the text beginning on p. 316, we will examine especially the death-life polarity.

of the soul". Paul's background, however, differs from that of Tauler. Johannes Tauler was indebted to neo-Platonic teaching on emanation; Paul of the Cross, in contrast, used biblical categories as his starting point.[112] Certainly, the founder always kept in mind the verses from the Gospel of John in which "being born again" is the subject matter in a conversation with Nicodemus (see Jn 3:1–14). The translation from John 3:3, "Truly I say to you, unless one is born from above, he cannot see the kingdom of God", was imposed at a later date.[113] The founder's formulation was also influenced by the statement from 1 Peter 1:23.[114] There is another place in the First Letter of Peter that speaks of being reborn in light of the resurrection of Jesus, too. In the introductory part of the Epistle, we read, "Blest be the God and Father of our Lord Jesus Christ! By his great mercy we have been born anew to a living hope through the resurrection of Jesus Christ from the dead" (1 Pet 1:3). Thus, we can affirm that the formula of "being born again", which we frequently find in Paul's letters written for the purpose of spiritual direction, represents before all else a declaration of his belief in the Risen One, better said, a declaration of his belief in the "power of the Risen One", who confers upon his believers his *zoe,* his divine life.

To allow one's own nothingness to sink into the all of God viewed as divine nativity. Now after these general considerations, let us return to the saint's own proper sayings. Among his religious and basic faith experiences most obviously discernible in his spiritual writings belong those of being a creature (creatureliness) and of being saved (salvation). He best expresses the existential practice of his own creatureliness in his antithetical discourse on the nothingness of the human person and the allness of God,[115] while he describes his existential sense of being saved by use of the formulation "being born again". Take, for example, the following passage from a letter written by the saint on Palm Sunday of the year 1755:

> Whenever your spirit is centered on God, let your horrible nothingness disappear in the infinite all that is God himself. It is certain then that your soul is reborn to a new life full of love and grace in the Divine Word, but no one should be curious and try to find out how this divine nativity is accomplished by the Supreme Good in the ground of the soul. These are sublime mysteries . . . [116]

---

[112] See above, pp. 135–46.

[113] The Vulgate translates this section as *nisi quis renatus fuerit denuo* (Jn 3:3). The Passionist founder read the Vulgate translation of the Bible and quoted from it in Latin.

[114] This verse is as follows: "You have been born anew, not of perishable seed but of imperishable, through the living and abiding word of God."

[115] See above, pp. 162–69.

[116] "Ogni volta che il suo spirito si riconcentra in Dio, lasciando sparire l'orribil suo nulla in quell'infinito tutto che è Dio medesimo, è certo che allora l'anima rinasce nel Divin Verbo

This unconditional and trusting abandonment of self into the all of the infinite God prepares the soul to enter into the "new life" of the crucified and risen Lord, of the divine *Logos,* Jesus Christ. This is a life in which Jesus' love and grace fill the soul so much that (as the founder affirms later in the same letter) the soul "is sacrificed as a victim of love in the flame of divine charity" and "expresses continuous gratitude for these gifts of the Lord"[117] in inner joy. In these formulations, it is worth noting how the saint, through use of his interior religious sense, elucidates something of God's unfathomable mystery so well that it seems to be his own lived experience. Yet he does not feel himself able to describe these "sublime experiences" by adequate or even approximate concepts, images, or symbols. Certainly, the human person can reach, through religious experience, the highest degree of self-knowledge (in an analogical, restrained way one could even speak of "experiencing God"). This capability of experiencing the religious, of having a "presentiment of God"—even though God's mystery is unfathomable to us—is a most fundamental characteristic of human existence; that is, it is "proper" to human existence. St. Paul of the Cross was a "mystic", a man who lived and understood his life and being according to his own radical encounter with faith: a strong faith in the "Divine Word Jesus Christ" as the God-Man, who has brought to humankind the knowledge of the trinitarian mystery and of salvation for every person.

The Passionist founder, however, did not want to keep for himself this grace of faith, this "presentiment" and "lived experience", but he tried to lead others, too, who like himself were directing their lives toward a more intensive encounter with God. This inherent task formed the background in all his letters written for the purpose of spiritual direction. In a letter written in July 1757 (and therefore not in Christmastide),[118] Paul, using images and symbols, wrote of the communication between God and the soul and how the soul, gifted by grace, may experience a "touch" of God. He wrote,

> Still more will I show you a shorter way. It consists in contemplating, with the eye of faith, your own horrible nothingness;[119] and then, hor-

---

a nuova vita d'amore e di grazia, ma tal divina natività non bisogna esser curiosa come si faccia dal Sommo Bene nel più intimo dell'essenza dell'anima. Questi sono arcani eccelsi . . . " (L 2:475, Mar. 22, 1755, to Sr. Colomba Gertrude Gandolfi).

[117] The following is written in this letter: " . . . e dare a Dio tutta la gloria con esser vittima di amore, sacrificato in olocausto nelle fiamme della divina carità in continuo ringraziamento dei doni del Signore." / " . . . and to give God all the glory by being a victim of love, sacrificed in holocaust in flames of divine charity in continual gratitude for the gifts of the Lord" (ibid.).

[118] Letters written during the Christmas season are still to be discussed.

[119] The saint explains again that the person draws near to God only "in faith". The

rified by the sight, take refuge at once in the "inner desert" [*ad interiora deserti*] [see Ex 3:1],[120] in the abyss of the Divinity. There let your own nothingness disappear and receive "without your own doing" [*passivo modo*] divine impressions [*impressioni*], so that abandoning yourself completely to him, you allow him to work in that most intimate recess of your spirit, where the divine nativity takes place [*fit Divina Nativitas*].[121] Here we ought to speak of great paradoxes, but it is better to keep silent about these.[122]

Of course, these statements are based on deep religious experiences and subtle insights into the relationship between God and the soul. The Passionist founder never tries (as is done in the speculative mysticism of being) to transform these experiences and insights "into concepts" and thus to build up a closed "system". Here it is worth observing how S. Breton, a French philosopher who has intensively studied the ideas of St. Paul of the Cross,[123] taking as a starting point the saint's discussion of the nothingness of the human person, has developed a "nonontology" (or an "ontology of nonbeing"), which presents a number of subtle, philosophical trains of thought. In a much appreciated lecture on the theme of "the cross of nonbeing" (*La croce del non-essere*) presented by Breton at the congress in Rome on the "Wisdom of the Cross Today",[124] he discussed points of contact between the "nonbeing"

---

founder's mysticism is, even to the most minute detail, a "mysticism of faith".

[120] The founder has in mind here the passage from Ex 3:1: "Moyses autem pascebat oves Iethro soceri sui sacerdotis Madian: cumque minasset gregem ad interiora deserti, venit ad montem Dei Horeb. Apparuitque ei Dominus in flamma ignis de medio rubi ... " / "Now Moses was keeping the flock of his father-in-law, Jethro, the priest of Midian; and he led his flock to the west side of the wilderness, and came to Horeb, the mountain of God ... " In another letter also written to Passionist Fr. John Mary, Paul gives an allegorical meaning to the same phrase, *ad interiora deserti*. See the letter of June 30, 1757, in *Bollettino* 7 (1926): 246f. Also see p. 132, n. 324, above.

[121] These two formulations, *fit Divina Nativitas* and *passivo modo*, were taken from Surius-Tauler. Tauler's influence is evident in this passage. Also see above, pp. 130–35.

[122] The original Italian text reads as follows: "Anzi le dirò una via più corta ed è di rimirare con occhio di fede il proprio orribil nulla e come spaventato di tal vista, fuggirsene subito *ad interiora deserti* nell'abisso della Divinità, lasciando ivi sparire l'orribile proprio nulla, ricevendo, *passivo modo*, le divine impressioni e con alto abbandonamento in Dio lasciare che S.D.M. faccia il divino suo lavoro nel più intimo dello spirito, in cui *fit Divina Nativitas*. Qui vi sarebbero dei gran paradossi da dire, ma tacciamoli" (L 3:160, July 25, 1757, to Fr. John Mary of St. Ignatius).

[123] Breton belongs to the Passionist Congregation. He is the author of the previously mentioned study *La Mystique de la Passion*. Another work of Breton's, *La Passion du Christ et les Philosophies*, is also worth quoting.

[124] This lecture was published in the acts of the Passionist Congregation, *La Sapienza della Croce Oggi* 3, "La Sapienza della Croce nella Cultura e nella Pastorale", 21–35.

of the soul (which is the basic topos of speculative mysticism) and the "nonbeing" of the crucified Christ, which is considered to be a *Nihil per excellentiam.*[125] Beyond doubt this contribution may be considered as a successful attempt to transfer the founder's purely existential mysticism of experience into the realm of a philosophical-speculative one.

But let us go back to our theme: The resurrection of Jesus did not mean a return to earthly life. Yet, through his resurrection the God-Man, Jesus Christ has drawn definitively and lastingly near to the world and to each individual person as a present and eschatological intercessor "between God and man" (1 Tim 2:5). Consequently, we may affirm: Through the resurrection, the person and the work of the incarnate *Logos* have been liberated from the limitation of time. The believer, in confessing his faith in the crucified and risen Lord, can encounter him in the "immediacy" of faith. The temporal distance from the historical event of Jesus Christ's life to this "absolutely unique cosmic event" has, thereby, no role to play.

The "Christmas-paschal" character of "becoming born again." As we have already shown, the mystery of resurrection is preeminent in the saint's spiritual-

---

[125] In this regard, Breton has said, "Visto in questa prospettiva, l'antico problema *vexata quaestio* per eccellenza, della relazione ontologica fra fede e ragione, s'illumina un po' alla luce di una comune *meontologia.* Egualmente, il *nulla per eccesso* o il *Nihil per excellentiam* non si identifica, senz'altro, al Dio della croce che non è niente di ciò che è, nemmeno l' 'Io sono colui che sono', di una certa metafisica tomista dell'Esodo. Ma se noi ci rifiutiamo ad ogni assimilazione sommaria che confonderebbe i piani, siamo tanto più liberi di segnare i punti di tangenza tra ciò che può restare, nella sua rude apparenza, un'austera astrazione, e la drammatizzazione incomparabile che ci offrono, tra cielo e terra, il segno, il simbolo e il mistero della croce. Infine, per concludere questo parallelismo, si osserverà che, da una parte e dall'altra, il nulla dell'anima e il nulla di Dio si conguingono in un *germen nihili* in un 'germe del non-essere', da dove procedono, con lo stesso impeto, l'anima che si fa ciò che è e il mondo che essa si dà. (L'espressione *germen nihili* è neo-platonica. Proclo parla effettivamente di 'sperma mè ontos', lo chiama spesso 'uno dell'anima', di cui è la scintilla generatrice.)" / "Viewed in this perspective, the ancient problem, the *quaestio vexata* par excellence, of the ontological relationship between faith and reason is clarified somewhat in the light of a common "nonbeing". Nevertheless, the "nothingness by excess" or the *nothingness par excellence* is not immediately identified with the God of the cross, who is nothing of what is, not even the "I am who am" of a certain Thomist metaphysics of the Exodus. But if we refuse to accept every arbitrary likeness that would confuse the two levels, we are so much freer then to indicate the contact points between what could be roughly a barren abstraction and the incomparable dramatization that the sign, the symbol, and the "mystery" of the cross offers us between heaven and earth. Finally, to conclude this parallelism, it should be observed that on either side, the nothingness of the soul and the nothingness of God meet again in a *germen nihili,* in a seed of nonbeing whence with the same impetus proceed the soul, which becomes what it is, and the world, to which the soul dedicates herself. (The expression *germen nihili* is neo-Platonic. Proclus actually speaks of the *sperma me ontos* and often calls it "the first act of the soul" and which is its generating spark.)" Ibid., 28.

theological thought.[126] Since the founder wrote numerous letters during the Christmas season, it is not surprising that in several we find references to "being born again in Jesus Christ". This is thoroughly understandable since Christmas is a feast of the "birth of Jesus". Justifiably, the founder may have been inspired at such a time to speak of "being born anew in the Divine Word". We must add, however, that the passages that have been introduced until this point more often than not are taken from letters not written at Christmas time. The fact that the saint speaks of "being born again" in letters other than his Christmas ones indicates that this formulation is not rooted primarily in the Incarnation; but, given its "terminological affinity" for Christmas, it is understandable that the founder did use the phrase at this time. For example, he wrote the following during the Christmas season of 1770:

> I do and shall include you always in my poor and very cold prayers, especially during these holy days and particularly on the solemnity of Christmas, so that his Divine Majesty may bring about in you the rebirth of the divine incarnate Word, [a rebirth] to a Godlike, deiform life, so that no longer you but Jesus Christ will live in you.[127]

Indeed, in his formulation, the verb *rinascere* has the meaning *to rise, to resurrect,* since it is directly related to *life.* The effect and the goal of this "being born again in the Divine Word" consists in receiving a share in the life and power of the crucified and resurrected Lord so that finally what will be obtained is a kind of symbiosis. Certainly the founder was influenced in the last part of the above formulation by the Pauline statement "and the life I live now is not my own" (Gal 2:20).

To participate in the "power of the resurrection" by sharing in the divine life of Jesus is not an isolated happening for St. Paul of the Cross, a happening offered to the person only once or at some special times, for instance, at Christmas. As soon as a believer reaches the "interiority of confidence", exactly at that moment he is risen to this new life in Christ. This "rebirth" or "being risen" is, therefore, not so much an occurrence of an act but a state that endures. This is made very clear in a Christmas Eve letter in which the founder states the following:

> I ask you to try to celebrate the sweetest solemnity of Christmas every day, even every moment in the interior temple of your spirit, remaining there

---

[126] See above, pp. 291–94. "The Incarnation as the 'divine wedding of the Eternal Word with human nature' (Divino Sposalizio del Verbo Eterno con la natura umana)."

[127] "Io non manco nè mancherò di farle parte delle povere freddissime mie orazioni, massime in questi santi giorni e specialmente nella Solennità Natalizia, acciò S.D.M. la faccia rinascere nel Divin Verbo Umanato a vita deifica deiforme, acciò non viva più lei, ma viva in lei Gesù Cristo" (L 2:322, to Mother Mary Crucified Costantini; this letter is undated but, according to one of the depositions, it was written before Christmas of 1770).

like a baby in the bosom of the heavenly Father, in order to be reborn each moment in the Divine Word Jesus Christ.[128]

Of course, for the founder, Christmas represents, above all, a memorial feast of the historic fact of the God-Man's birth. However, he does not consider the mystery of the Incarnation for itself alone but rather in the *wholeness* of the mystery: the birth of Jesus and his life, death, resurrection, and enthronement at the right hand of the Father. The salvific action of God in Jesus Christ is not, for the saint, something belonging to the past, something to which we no longer have access due to the temporal gap, but rather a continual manifestation of God to us in Jesus Christ. Through the resurrection, the Person and work of Jesus have gone beyond temporal limitations; by faith, the Savior, Jesus Christ, is near to every person of every time and place. Of course, we do not encounter such theological reflections on the resurrection of Jesus in the writings of St. Paul of the Cross, but he acts as though they are evident, since only thus can he speak of a "continual rebirth in the incarnate Word of God".

Through God's self-communicating love we are made into the likeness of the Divine Savior and bear his image. According to St. Paul of the Cross, people have the duty to be ready, by means of interiorization and of trust, for the efficient action of this divine nativity. This sequence of thought is evident in the following excerpt from a letter of January 1, 1770:

> . . . I desire that you be born anew, each day, in the divine incarnate Word to a completely holy life and, in this way, to become a living retreat of Jesus Christ. All this will happen if you are faithful and remain in your own interior hermitage, resting your spirit in the divine bosom of the heavenly Father, where this divine nativity is celebrated each moment. In this manner, you will always be celebrating Christmas in the little stable of your spirit.[129]

From these short passages it is again apparent that the Passionist founder sees in *introire in seipsum* (entering into one's self) and in unlimited faith in God two important effects: The soul will be born again "in the Divine Word Jesus Christ" and this "divine nativity" will be celebrated in the "interior temple of the soul". Certainly the saint had a special predilection for the concepts *rinascere* and *rinascità* (to be born again and rebirth). This is especially true

---

[128] "Prego però che la dolcissima Solennità Natalizia, procuri di celebrarla ogni giorno, anzi ogni momento nel tempio interiore del suo spirito, standosene come bambina nel seno divino del Padre Celeste, affine di rinascere ogni momento nel Divin Verbo Cristo Gesù" (L 2:28, Dec. 24, 1759, to M. G. Venturi Grazi).

[129] " . . . desidero che rinasciate ogni giorno nel Divin Verbo umanato a vita tutta santa e siate un vivo ritratto di Gesù Cristo; e tutto ciò sarà, se sarete fedele a starvene solitario interno, riposando lo spirito nel seno divino del celeste Padre, in cui si celebra ogni momento questa divina Natività; e sarà in tal forma sempre Natale nella stalletta interiore del vostro spirito" (L 3:297, Jan. 1, 1770, to Bro. Bartholomew of St. Louis).

after his discovery of Tauler in 1748. Surely, when St. Paul of the Cross uses these words, the mystery of the Incarnation remains the immediate point of reference. To speak metaphorically, however, his "Christmas discourse" is absolutely a "paschal" one. In the long run, the founder has the intention of demonstrating how the person is able, through correct interiorization and unconditional trust, to obtain a share in the "new life" of Jesus Christ, the incarnate *Logos,* in a life that makes the person "similar to God", since this new life yields an ability to love. The ultimate aim of this "rebirth in the Divine Word" is, therefore, the presence of the human person in the all-inclusive movement of the love of God, a love that "became man", a love revealed most obviously in the cross of Jesus, a love that defeated death in his resurrection and glorification, and consequently a love that has drawn near to humankind forever.

When it is a matter of this "new life of love" having been brought to humankind by the God-Man, Jesus, the founder especially makes use of a "Christmas-paschal" formula. A letter has been preserved which, as the saint himself remarks, was written on Holy Saturday immediately before the celebration of the resurrection and in which he goes into detail regarding "becoming born anew in the Divine Word". Let us allow the saint to speak for himself:

> Use all your diligence to remain in solitude in that sacred interior desert, barring the door to every created thing. In this desert let your spirit rest on the divine bosom of the heavenly Father in the sacred silence of faith and holy love. There you will be born again in the Divine Word Jesus Christ to a new life of love, to a deified life, a holy life. All this is accomplished in pure and naked faith, without any images of your own fancy. God is worshipped in spirit and in truth [see Jn 4:24]. There one loves in a sublime manner and learns the science of the saints. This is the gratitude that everyone should give to our blessed God.[130]

It is obvious the founder correctly sees in this "interiority of confidence" a precondition for rebirth of the soul in the Divine Word. The circumstances surrounding this letter, i.e., that the saint is looking forward to Easter and the fact that he speaks of a "rising to a new life of love", demonstrate that his faith in the risen and glorified Lord has found its expression first and foremost in the phrase "born anew in the Divine Word Jesus Christ".

[130] "Tutta la di lei diligenza sia in star solitaria in quel sacro deserto interiore, chiudendo la porta a tutto il creato, ed in questo deserto lasci riposare il suo spirito nel seno Divino del Padre Celeste in sacro silenzio di fede e di santo amore. Ivi rinascerete nel Divin Verbo Cristo Gesù a nuova vita di amore, vita deifica, vita santa. Tutto ciò si fa in pura e nuda fede senza immagini della fantasia, ma si adora Iddio in spirito e verità, ivi si ama alla grande e s'impara la scienza de' Santi. Questa è la gratitudine che deve avere a Dio benedetto" (L 4:4, Apr. 18, 1767 [Holy Saturday], to Agnes Segnéri).

2. The "Power of His Resurrection and the Sharing in His Sufferings" (Phil 3:10)

As we have already pointed out,[131] Jesus' death and resurrection are to be considered as two poles of *one* paschal mystery. The death of Jesus on the cross and his Father's raising him from the dead must be viewed in their interrelated, reciprocal connectedness: Jesus' death occurred "on the eve of Easter", and his resurrection is understandable only through the "drama of Golgotha". This unifying view of the paschal mystery, where abasement and glorification of Jesus are two aspects of the *one* salvation history, are expressed in St. John's concept of "being lifted up" (Jn 12:32). One can say with J. Blank, "The lifting up of the Son of Man is already the lifting up to reign, the solemn enthronement (lifting up!) as a new cosmic Lord and Giver of Life."[132]

That the risen and glorified Lord is indeed the Risen One is emphasized in the Gospel accounts of the resurrection by the fact that the resurrected body of the *Kyrios* was marked by the stigmata (see Lk 24:39; Jn 20:20–27). Through the resurrection, the historical cross achieved its eternal definitiveness, and in the risen and crucified Jesus Christ, God has drawn near to us forever. St. John's concept of "being lifted up" reveals to us that the one "lifted up" is the Crucified and "no one can succeed in being lifted up by avoiding the cross but only by being upon the cross".[133]

A similar unifying view of the cross and resurrection may also be found in Pauline theology: Everyone who believes in Christ and who is granted, by *his* grace, salvation, deliverance, and justification is "united with him in his death and will certainly be united with him in his resurrection" (see Rom 6:5). According to the Apostle Paul, one cannot achieve justification by the exertion of one's own power or "by the works of the law", but only "through faith in Jesus Christ". The disciple of Jesus expected his one and only redemption to come from the crucified and risen Christ. The existential completion of this faith is expressed in the following programmatic statement from the Letter to the Philippians: "That I may know him and the power of his resurrection and may share in his sufferings, becoming like him in his death" (Phil 3:10).

Even in the spiritual doctrine of Paul of the Cross we find faith in the power of Jesus' resurrection combined with participation in sufferings. One can conclude: The Pauline theology of the cross and resurrection and St. John's topos about "being lifted up" build the theological framework in which the

---

[131] See the first section of this chap.

[132] J. Blank, *Krisis, Untersuchungen zur Johanneischen Cristologie und Eschatologie,* 286f. Also see the basic work by W. Thüsing, *Die Erhöhung und die Verherrlichung Jesu im Johannesevangelium* (Neutestamentliche Abhandlungen 21, 1–2, Münster, 1960).

[133] Blank, 287.

founder's spiritual-religious thought develops, since for him and St. John, the passion and death of Jesus are principal manifestations of God's infinite love for us, a love that in the resurrection is revealed to be a timeless and definitive event. Furthermore, for Paul of the Cross, this participation in the Risen One's "new life" means that Christ's disciple must also enter into a sharing in the passion of the Lord, just as the apostle Paul always stresses.

The importance of "participation in the passion of Jesus" has already been demonstrated.[134] In this last section of this investigation, we will analyze the manner in which the human person, through sharing in the suffering of the Lord, achieves a share in the "power of the resurrection", and, too, how he may (using the words of the founder), "through the cross, be born again to a new life in the Divine Word Jesus Christ".

To die mystically by means of interior and exterior suffering in order "to be born again to a new life in Jesus Christ". Neither suffering nor death represents an end point for the Passionist founder. Rather, he directs others to inner joy, to life, to a "new and deiform life in Christ". This fundamental desire appears over and over again in his spiritual instruction. It is made very clear in a letter written in 1769 to Anna Maria Calcagnini, a single woman, whom the saint had known for a long period of time and who would later bear testimony at the informative process at Gaeta (1777).[135] Judging from the content of the letter, Anna Maria was ill and confined to bed. The founder begins his letter by calling to mind the example of Jesus Christ, who, by his suffering on the cross, "offered himself as a sacrifice" to the Father and through this "completed the work of redemption".[136] The saint continues,

> Now you are in an agony on that treasured bed of the cross; what could you better do than to breathe forth your spirit into the bosom of the heavenly Father, saying, "My sweetest Father, into your hands I commend my spirit"? And, having said this, to die full of happiness by means

---

[134] See Chap. IV of this text.

[135] See *Processi* 2:125-33.

[136] In this letter, he writes, "... perchè ora vi assomigliate più allo Sposo Divino, abbandonato da ogni conforte mentre stava moribondo in Croce; ma in tal abbandono fece il gran sacrificio e lo perfezionò con l'ultime divine parole che disse; e furono: Padre, nelle vostre mani raccomando il mio spirito, e ciò detto spirò l'anima sua ssma. nelle mani dell'Eterno Padre e compì l'opera della umana Redenzione. Così fate voi, figliuola benedetta." / "... since now you are more like unto the divine spouse, lacking every consolation while dying on the cross; but in such abandonment he performed a great sacrifice and perfected it by his last pronounced words, which were: 'Father, into your hands I commend my spirit.' And having said this he breathed out his holiest Spirit into the hands of the eternal Father and thus completed the work of humankind's redemption. Just so do you, my blessed daughter" (L 3:825f., July 9, 1769).

of that precious mystical death of which I have spoken to you at other times.[137]

The founder is thereby encouraging his correspondent to accept her illness as the cross of Christ by pointing to Jesus, who breathed his last with the words, "Father, into your hands I commend my spirit" (Lk 23:46). Paul then links Jesus' death with her own mystical death. However, when the saint speaks of that "precious mystical death", by which one dies happily (*felicemente*), he indicates that this death is not the "absolute end", nor is it accomplished in "total isolation". Rather, it is a kind of death accompanied by a faithful and joyful trust. It is a death that passes in the long run to an unexpected "plenitude of life".

In the same letter, the saint described the effect of this mystical death and its proper goal. With solemn, emphatic, and hymnlike formulations, he continues,

> After having died this mystical death, you will live a new life; more than that, you will be born again to a new deiform life in the Divine Word Jesus Christ; and oh, what wonderful life that will be! It will be so splendid and full of heavenly knowledge that you will not be able to tell me anything of it.... [138]

These affirmations make abundantly clear that the founder is primarily interested in *life,* in a "plenitude of life", in a "deiform life" in Jesus Christ. Finally, the thought of this "new life" represents the essential motive, the basis by which the saint can affirm that mystical death is "precious," nay, that everybody dying this "death" is "happy" and blessed.

If we look at the whole letter more attentively, we find striking the observation that the founder, in giving the example of Jesus, stresses only his death upon the cross before saying, "And thus he completed the work of redemption." Although there is no mention of Jesus' resurrection, the following explanation of mystical death shows beyond a doubt that the resurrection is implicit even though it is not expressly mentioned in words. The thinking of St. Paul of the Cross contains a natural premise that Jesus remained neither in the "agony of dying" nor in the "darkness of death" but has been resurrected in the glory and light of eternal life. After all, how could a Crucified and Dead One give life? The answer is found in the words of St. Paul of the Cross: "To be born again to a new and deiform life in Jesus Christ" is possible only if Jesus Christ himself lives, if he has passed from death to life, better said, to "life in glory".

---

[137] "Ora siete in agonia sul letto ricchissimo della Croce; che vi resta dunque da fare se non spirare l'anima nel seno del Padre Celeste dicendo: 'Padre dolcissimo, nelle vostre mani raccomando il mio spirito?' E ciò detto, morite pure felicemente di quella preziosa morte mistica di cui v'ho parlato altre volte" (L 3:826).

[138] L 3:826. On the theme of the divine nativity, see K. Rahner, "Die Gottesgeburt. Die Lehre der Kirchenväter von der Geburt Christi im Herzen des Gläubigen", 333–418.

This assertion is no pure supposition or logical conclusion imposed upon the saint's thinking. Take, for example, a subsequent letter to the same Anna Maria Calcagnini written some months later in December of 1769. Speaking in reference to interior and exterior suffering, the saint explains that it is necessary to pass through naked suffering (*nudo penare*) to arrive at "rest in the heavenly bosom" of God, who is love, first and foremost.[139] Then, using the same formulations included in the previous letter of July 1769, Paul elaborates upon the meaning of mystical death, yet with a difference: He now speaks explicitly of resurrection. He writes,

> "Father, into your hands I commend my spirit." After having said this, breathe out your life with Jesus Christ and in Christ die that mystical death of holy and pure love, so that you may rise with Christ to a new, deified life and there live a life full of holy love, in the purest love of the great king of our hearts. . . . [140]

These two passages convincingly demonstrate how the saint's faith in the Risen One is the fundamental reason underlying his thought on and use of the term *being born again.*

In his spiritual instructions, the founder continually emphasizes the necessity of sharing in the suffering of Christ Crucified so as to obtain a share in the dynamics and life of the risen Christ. This participation in his passion and share in the "power of resurrection" are not to be considered as two successive actions, since the acceptance of the interior and exterior sufferings of the cross of Christ already presupposes the power of faith in the Crucified and in the *pneuma* (spirit) of the Risen One. Still, in our earthly existence, we always experience "being in Christ" as a sharing in the passion. This is a fundamental conviction and part of the basic principles of the spiritual-theological thought of the Passionist founder.

The same fundamental principle is also strongly emphasized in Pauline theology (see Rom 6:4; 8:10f.; Gal 2:19f.; Phil 3:10). This participation in the dynamics of the resurrection is always experienced *in statu viatoris* (in the pilgrim way) as being crucified with Jesus. This idea is present and clearly

---

[139] In the letter of Dec. 12, 1769, the founder wrote, " . . . sento lo stato presente in cui si trova d'aridità, abbandoni, pene interne ed esterne . . . è necessario che passiate per la trafila d'un nudo penare . . . e si riposi nel seno celeste del santo e puro amore che è Dio Sommo Bene e tutt'amore e carità." / " . . . I sense the present state in which you are—aridity, abandonment, interior and exterior suffering . . . it is necessary to pass through the agony of naked suffering . . . and then you will repose in the heavenly bosom of the holy and pure love who is God, the Supreme Good and total love and charity" (L 3:827).

[140] "Padre, nelle vostre mani raccomando il mio spirito; e ciò detto con Gesù Cristo spirare e morire in Cristo della morte mistica del santo e puro amore, per poi risorgere con Cristo a nuova vita deifica, ed ivi vivere una vita tutta di santo amore, nell'amore purissimo del gran re dei cuori . . . " (L 3:827).

emphasized in Philippians 3:10: "I wish to know Christ and the power flowing from his resurrection, likewise to know how to share in his sufferings by being formed into the pattern of his death."[141] Together with J. Gnilka, we can summarize the content of this verse in the following way: "For earthly existence, the destiny of death represents the moment of uniformity."[142]

The saint paraphrases this sharing in the passion and death of Jesus through use of the concepts *nudo patire* and *morte mistica*. In a letter written in June of 1765, the saint speaks of *nudo patire* as "suffering without any consolation whatsoever".[143] This description culminates in the following exhortation:

> Often offer yourself to the Divine Majesty, as a victim of sacrifice on the altar of the cross, and there end by dying that mystical death in Christ, which brings with it a new life of love, a deified life, since it is united to the Supreme Good by charity.[144]

These sentences are interiorly connected to what the evangelist John desires to express by the use of his topos of Christ's being "lifted up" on the cross.[145] On the one hand, the cross is the deepest point of abasement of and contempt for Jesus (St. John speaks of this in his narrative of the passion). On the other hand, the "lifting up upon the cross" is the beginning of Jesus' glorification, because the "loving commitment of God for humankind" becomes visible in an extraordinary way in the death of Jesus on the cross.[146] Since, for Paul of the Cross, the passion and death of Jesus manifest above all God's love for the human person, then by "dying mystically in Christ" the person comes to share "in the new divine life of love".

Participation in the "holy cross of Jesus" and participation in a "deiform life in Jesus Christ" are two themes present in another letter written by the Passionist founder on April 2, 1750. Because it was composed on Holy Thursday, and because the saint wrote it—one could say—first and foremost

[141] This verse runs thus: "That I may know him and the power of his resurrection and may share his suffering, becoming like him in his death."

[142] In Herder, *Theologischer Kommentar zum Neuen Testament* 10, 3 (Der Philipperbrief, Freiburg, 1968), 196.

[143] The letter is addressed to Mother Mary Crucified Costantini. It contains the following lines: "Spero che V. R. stia volentieri crocefissa con Gesù Cristo, senza conforto, giacchè ne porta il nome. Oh, che gran tesoro racchiude il nudo patire senza conforto, nè dal Cielo nè dalla terra! Ne faccia grande stima, ne sia grata a Dio . . . " / "I hope that Your Reverence is willingly crucified with Jesus Christ, without comfort, since you bear that name. Oh, what a great treasure naked suffering contains, a suffering without comfort either from heaven or from earth. Esteem it highly, and be grateful to God for it . . . " (L 2:306, June 15, 1765).

[144] " . . . si offerisca spesso vittima di olocausto a S.M.D. sull'altare della Croce, ed ivi finisca di morire di quella morte mistica in Cristo, che porta seco una nuova vita d'amore, vita deifica, perchè unita per carità al Sommo Bene" (L 2:306).

[145] See R. Schnackenburg, "Erhöhung und Verherrlichung Jesu", in Herder, 498–512.

[146] See Schnackenburg, 512.

from a "paschal point of view", this letter possesses special significance in terms of the questions raised in this chapter through which we try to determine elements of an implicit theology of the resurrection.

Instead of a personal salutation, the letter bears the title *Viva la Santa Croce ricca d'ogni bene!* (Long live the Holy Cross, rich in every good!). These words already express the paschal significance of the cross. In the first sentence the saint speaks of the suffering of Fr. Dominic Panizza, the correspondent to whom the letter is addressed. The manner of expression makes clear that the saint had a close relationship with this priest. Paul writes,

> My dearest Signor D. Domenico! Behold the poor Paul, having arrived in Rome two hours ago, made a visit in spirit to the holy cross of the sweet Jesus, in which are tasted the fruits of the most sacred tree of life. And, if you do not taste these fruits, you are more happy and fortunate for this reason.... [147]

When the founder calls the cross the "tree of life" and speaks of its "fruit", he places himself by the use of these symbolic phrases in a long line of traditional, spiritual-mystical literature,[148] a tradition having its origin and point of reference in biblical writings.[149] Nevertheless, it is worth noting that he expressly affirms that the "fruits of the cross" lead us to greater happiness and to a more intense joy in life. Certainly, this positive orientation can be explained only if the cross is seen from the viewpoint of the resurrection.

For the saint, "happiness and joy" are the result and the purpose of inevitable suffering, if it is accepted and borne as "the cross of Jesus". Then, focusing his eyes upon the Lord's final agony on the cross, Paul states,

> ... since in such a manner a person becomes more like unto our Divine Savior, who upon the cross exclaimed, *"Deus, Deus meus, ut quid dereliquisti me?"* [Mt 15:34], thus expressing his naked suffering without consolation.[150]

These words once more express the saint's strong Christocentric passion mysticism. "Naked suffering" in abandonment upon the cross was not for Jesus the end point, because this was followed by the resurrection through

[147] "Amatissimo signor D. Domenico. Ecco il povero Paolo giunto in Roma due ore fa che viene a visitarlo in spirito su la Santa Croce del dolce Gesù, in cui lei gusta i frutti di quest'albero sacrosanto di vita. E se lei non gusta questi frutti con sensibilità, anzi per ciò lei è più felice ed avventurato ... " (L 3:17, Apr. 2, 1750).

[148] See A. Legner, in *Lexikon* 6, col. 864f. (keyword: Lebensbaum). Also see W. Baier, "Flores et fructus arboris vitae Iesu Christi des Kartäusers Ludolf von Sachsen († 1378)" and "Ein Horologium des Lebens Jesu für alle Horen an den sieben Tagen der Woche", 321–41.

[149] See E. Lohmeyer, *Urchristliche Mystik, Neutestamentliche Studien,* esp. Von Baum und Frucht, "Eine exegetische Studie Zu Matth. 3, 10", 33–56.

[150] " ... poichè in tal forma si assomiglia più al nostro divino Salvatore che su la Croce esclamò al Padre: 'Deus, Deus meus, ut quid dereliquisti me?' esprimendo il suo nudo patire senza conforto" (L 3:17).

which he entered into the divine life of glorification. Consequently, everyone who accepts "suffering without consolation" as the "cross of Christ" receives a share in the "power of the resurrection" and will enter into the "divine life" of the risen and glorified Jesus. Yet, the soul must first "die mystically" so as to be capable of living "in God".

To what degree the saint has a life of joy and happiness, the *divine* life, before his eyes when he speaks of suffering and death is evident in the following letter, in which he writes,

> Oh, blest is this soul that stands crucified with Jesus, without knowing or seeing him, since [such a soul] is deprived of any sensible consolation! Oh, fortunate the one who . . . bows his head and says with Jesus, *"Pater, in manus tuas commendo spiritum meum"* [Lk 23:46], and thus dies mystically to everything that is not God, in order to live in God a divine life in the same bosom of the heavenly Father.[151]

There is no doubt whatsoever that his enthusiastic words regarding the joy and happiness in which those who have "died mystically" share in the "life in God" represent a clear-cut way of expressing a "resurrection theology". It is, therefore, of little importance that the saint does not explicitly use the concept of "resurrection". In this context, he might just as well have spoken of "being born anew" or of "having risen", formulations which the founder used in synonymous ways, as has been shown in an earlier part of this section.[152] Divine life, life in God, and life in the bosom of the heavenly Father are surely formulations that have as their basis the saint's living faith in the risen and glorified Lord.

Here we refer, once more, to a characteristic approach included in this Holy Thursday letter. After having spoken of life in God, of "life in the bosom of the heavenly Father", Paul continues to characterize more appropriately this "divine life" in the following way:

> . . . completely vested in Jesus Christ Crucified, that is, the soul is entirely united with his sufferings, nay, the loving soul makes his pain its own through the union of love with the Supreme Good.[153]

---

[151] "Oh, beata quell'anima che sta crocefissa con Gesù Cristo senza saperlo e senza vederlo, perchè priva d'ogni conforto sensibile! Oh, fortunato quell'anima che . . . china il capo e dice con Gesù: 'Pater, in manus tuas commendo spiritum meum' e muore misticamente a tutto ciò che non è Dio, per vivere in Dio vita divina nel seno stesso del celeste Padre . . . " (L 3:17).

[152] See nn. 138 and 140 above.

[153] " . . . tutta vestita di Gesù Cristo Crocifisso, cioè tutta unita alle sue pene le quali l'anima amante se le fa sue, mediante l'unione di carità col Sommo Bene" (L 3:17). In another writing, quoted in connection with Tauler (see Chap. 2, n. 350), Paul clarifies the "new life in the Divine Word Jesus Christ" with similar words when he writes, " . . . ivi rinascete ogni momento a nuova vita deifica nel Divin Verbo Cristo Gesù, e l'amore vi faccia vostre le sue

With these assertions, we are again introduced into the inner, even into the kernel of this "passion mysticism" characteristic of the "saint of the cross", in the topos *pene infuse* or *impressione della passione*.[154] Consequently, one might conclude that St. Paul of the Cross fails to depart from his passion mysticism and reproachfully add that the saint is unable to raise himself to a "pure mysticism of resurrection". In fact, the Passionist founder would accept this reproach. We would indeed seek vainly for a "pure mysticism of resurrection" based on a "pure theology of resurrection" in his spirituality. Furthermore, we ourselves might very well ask in turn: Does a "pure" theology of resurrection even exist?

As we have already discussed in the introduction to this chapter, the death and resurrection of Jesus must be considered as a *unit* both in theological reflection and in the existential fullness of faith. According to Karl Rahner, the death of Jesus upon the cross and his resurrection from the dead, through the Father, are "only one event, and its two phases are interiorly and indissolubly conjoined".[155] Theology and spirituality (the latter may be considered as an "applied theology") must always express *both poles* of the Easter mystery.

Taking into account all that has been said until now about elements of an implicit theology of resurrection, so evident in the spiritual teaching of the Passionist founder, we can affirm that St. Paul of the Cross' spirituality, the spirituality of this "charismatic of the cross", well contains the necessary cross-resurrection polarity presented in this unit. We can also add that the "spiritual vision" of the Passionist founder, although more strongly focused upon *Christus crucifixus,* is not done so in an exclusive way, as if his visual field were limited or hemiopic, incapable of expressing the unity and wholeness of the paschal mystery.

When St. Paul of the Cross describes "life in God" as being "vested with the crucified Christ", then both poles of the Easter mystery, i.e., death and resurrection, are included in this assertion. The same meaning, albeit in another formulation, lies at the basis of the previously quoted verse from Philippians 3:10: For every believer in Christ, the way to salvation consists of sharing in the "power of the resurrection" and in a communion of "suffering with him".

"It is now no longer I who live but Christ lives in me" (Gal 2:20). In New Testament writings, we find some statements which seem to contain unfathom-

---

pene, per impressione sacra di santo amore, in nuda fede, senza immagini." / " . . . there you will be reborn, each moment, to a new deified life in the Divine Word Jesus Christ. Let this love impart to you its pains, which are to become your own, through the sacred impression of holy love, in naked faith, and without images" (L 3:191, Aug. 16 [year unknown], to Fr. John of St. Raphael).

[154] See above, pp. 202–5.

[155] See n. 1 above.

able depth, and in this group belongs the Apostle Paul's affirmation, "I have been crucified with Christ; it is no longer I who live but Christ who lives in me" (Gal 2:20). In these words, cross and resurrection are indissolubly linked. This is the "core" of Pauline mysticism of the cross, and it is understandable only if we take into account his belief in the resurrection (see 1 Cor 15:14–20).

Paul of the Cross was influenced by the expressive power of this assertion. Explicitly mentioning the Apostle Paul, the Passionist founder made these words his own in a letter written when he was about seventy-nine years of age. He first encouraged his correspondent, Marianna Girelli, to persevere patiently in her interior sufferings. The saint called these pains an "agony" through which men and women must pass so as to await holy, mystical death in a patient and gentle mood.[156]

By these words, Paul meant that mystical death is nothing to be afraid of but a good which as soon as it is achieved gives an abundance of joy. The reason for this positive characterization of mystical death consists therein, that the soul, while dying this death, is opening itself all the more to receive "divine life", which yields joy and bliss. Therefore, whenever the founder speaks of mystical death, he has "life in God" before his eyes and above all else. This allows him to designate this kind of death as something "worthier than life".

But let us allow the saint speak for himself. He writes,

> ... as one begins to experience the effects of that holy mystical death, [one notes it is] more precious than life, because the soul now lives a deified life in God: *"Vivo ego, iam non ego, vivit vero in me Christus"* [Gal 2:20]; so said the great loving apostle whose name I so undeservedly bear.[157]

Even if the founder does not use the concepts of "rising" or "being born anew", he speaks emphatically of life, since the meaning and ultimate aim of every belief in resurrection is life, "life in God".

In the same letter this joyful expectation of life is once more expressed in the following way: " ... patiently and gently await holy mystical death, and then you will exult in a new life in God, our true life".[158]

In a letter written after 1748, there are also several statements that have

---

[156] In this letter, he writes, "Lei li patisce, lo so, ma tal patimento è l'agonia che deve soffrire, aspettando pazientemente e dolcemente la santa morte mistica ... " / "You are suffering, I know it, but such a suffering represents the agony you must suffer, patiently and in sweet anticipation of holy mystical death ... " (L 3:756f., Dec. 28, 1768).

[157] " ... si comminciano a provare gli effetti di quella santa morte mistica che è più preziosa della vita, poichè l'anima vive in Dio vita deifica: *'Vivo ego, iam non ego, vivit vero in me Christus';* diceva il grand'amante Apostolo, di cui io porto tanto indegnamente il nome" (L 3:756f.).

[158] " ... aspettando pazientemente e dolcemente la santa morte mistica, ed allora esulterà in una nuova vita in Dio, nostra vera vita" (L 3:757).

"being born anew in the Divine Word Jesus Christ" as their subject matter. Sometimes the saint speaks of the purgative function of suffering.[159] At other times, he speaks of the fact of "being born again" in connection with the practice of virtue.[160] Nevertheless, time and time again, the effect or target object of *rinascere* is "new *life*", a new "deiform" and "Godlike" *life*.

In another letter to Lucy Burlini, Paul writes about the "new life of love in Jesus Christ" in the following way:

... [Enter] into the most intimate part of your soul to be born again in the Divine Word to a new life of love. God is resting in you; God is penetrating you completely, and you are transformed entirely into God and in his love, etc. Ah, here I lose my thoughts, and I lack concepts![161]

Still, he tries once more to describe in more concrete and picturesque language this ineffable mystery. In words expressive of his warm goodness of heart and his friendship, he writes, "Lucy must live in herself no longer, but in God. Jesus lives in Lucy and Lucy in Jesus. Tell me, please: Is it so? If it is so, then all goes well!"[162]

This hopeful and joyful belief in the resurrection is strongly expressed by St. Paul of the Cross even *before* the year 1748 using different images, similes, and metaphors by which he described the "power of the resurrection" and the joy of entering into the "coming life in plenitude". Take, for example, a letter written in the year 1739 to Agnes Grazi, who was suffering a serious illness at

[159] In a letter to Passionist Father Fulgentius of Jesus, Paul writes, "Oh, quanto bramo che i nostri s'avvezzino uomini interni che sappiano essere costanti in patire le pressure, prove e travagli interiori, tanto necessari per purificare lo spirito, acciò ogni momento si rinuovi quel divino rinascimento in Cristo Gesù in purissima fede e santo amore! Ma il punto sta in saper soffrire tali pressure *in silentio et in spe* ecc." / "Oh, how much I would like us to accustom ourselves to being men of the interior [life], constant in enduring trials, ordeals, and interior pain, so necessary for the purification of the soul, so that, at any moment, it may be renewed in that divine rebirth in Jesus Christ, in purest faith and holy love! But the point is to know how to suffer these trials *in silentio et in spe* [in silence and in hope], etc." (L 2:150, July 31, 1748). Also see L 2:724, Aug. 17, 1751, to Lucy Burlini; and L 3:482f., Nov. 5 (year unknown), to Sr. Maria Innocence.

[160] On Christmas Eve in 1763, Paul wrote the following to Teresa Palozzi: "Se lei vuole che Dio la faccia rinascere in Gesù Cristo a nuova vita d'amore e santa, procuri di esercitare le virtù insegnate e praticate dal dolce Gesù, massime l'umiltà di cuore, la mansuetudine, la pazienza, il silenzio ecc." / "If you desire that God effect your rebirth in Jesus Christ to a new and holy life of love, try to exercise the virtues taught and practiced by our sweet Jesus, especially, humility of heart, meekness, patience, silence, etc." (L 3:386). As a supplementary letter, see L 3:624, Dec. 1760 (date unknown), to a Passionist superior.

[161] "... nell'intimo dell'anima vostra rinasciate nel Divin Verbo a nuova vita d'amore. Dio si riposa in voi: Dio tutta vi penetra e voi tutta in Dio e voi tutta trasformata nel suo amore ecc. Ah, che si perde la mia mente e mancano i concetti!" (L 2:721, May 25, 1751).

[162] "Lucia non deve più viver in sè, ma in Dio: Gesù vive in Lucia e Lucia in Gesù. Ditemi: va così? Se va così, va bene!" (L 2:722).

the time. With this long quotation, we let the saint himself speak, and his words are meant to be the closing words of this study. He writes the following:

> ... leave your heart entirely free to aspire to that glory which is awaiting you because of the infinite merits of Jesus. Oh, here certainly it is necessary to leave the way entirely clear for you, so you can more and more desire that beautiful paradise where we shall always be at an eternal feast, praising our Supreme Good without ceasing, without danger of losing him again. If then you must remain in bed, take your sleep in God, and let yourself be lost entirely in that immense sea of charity. At the same time, rest on your bed as upon the cross of your Divine Spouse. I already see that the walls are wearing thin, and the poor prisoner wishes to fly out to her homeland, which her dear Jesus has purchased for her with his precious Blood; but you must note that in escaping your prison you are clothed in an ashen garment on which is written, "I am a pure nothing, I am only an abyss of evils. You alone, O my God, are he who is, and from you I expect all my good through the merits of the Blood of my Jesus." As you go forth from the prison with this poor garment of ashes with its inscription of nothingness, God, who is all, will ordain that you be divested of this dress of ashes and your soul be clothed in the robe of a queen, dyed in the Blood of the immaculate Lamb and enriched with his divine virtues, and, so gloriously clothed, you will come, being placed in his kingdom, to sit eternally at his divine table to sing forever, "Holy, holy, holy, you alone are holy, you alone are most high, O Jesus Christ!" With this truth, that I am writing you, you may allow your heart to rejoice, and I give you complete freedom to long after that glory. . . . [163]

[163] L 1:239, Aug. 17, 1739, to Agnes Grazi.

AFTERWORD

We have tried in this investigation to present the spiritual-theological thought of a man whose life and doctrine were oriented, in an extraordinary manner, to the mystery of *Christus crucifixus*. Without a doubt, the passion and cross of Jesus belong to the core of Christian Faith. Everyone can note that these subjects are frequently the topics of even present-day theological discussion. A renowned theologian observed, "If I am not totally wrong, the theme of the cross will dominate theological discourse in neither a secondary manner nor for a short period of time."[1] This strong interest in the passion and death of Jesus is not limited to only one Christian confession but is noted in different "confessional theologies".[2]

This study of passioncentrism in the spiritual teaching of St. Paul of the Cross is meant to present how a concrete personality interpreted the mystery of faith concerning the passion and death of Jesus and made it the focus of his existential fullness of faith. This exposition may also be considered as a contribution to the deepening of the mystery of Christ's cross and passion in the future.

Certainly, the passion mysticism of this charismatic of the cross is *only one* among many ways of attaining to a greater union with God. It is a "way" that is not at all easy, and it is recommended only for Christians profoundly rooted in faith. Nevertheless, we find in his spiritual-religious thought many things of permanent validity, independent of time. Here Paul's "mysticism of participation" needs to be emphasized especially, since every person will be confronted with suffering in his own life. Even when one does all that is possible to avoid pain, there still remains an amount of suffering to be endured in this earthly existence. The life and thinking of St. Paul of the Cross provide

[1] Schürmann, 7.

[2] The Evangelical theologian H. G. Link observes, "It is a question of a phenomenon which is astonishing and which was unimaginable several years ago, the fact that the theological work in the two confessions (Catholic and Evangelical), after ample research in the almost unlimited domain of the social, cultural, political, and going even into revolutionary questions, has recently changed its field of research and is now focusing its attention upon its very own theme, namely, the discourse concerning God from the point of view of the passion and death of Jesus Christ."

brilliant and convincing examples of the manner in which one can endure and overcome an inevitable and even undeserved sorrow by the power of a fulfilled Christian faith. The saint sees in unavoidable pain, which the believer must endure, first and foremost a possibility for sharing in the cross of Christ. This participation in the cross allows the individual to experience "the power of the resurrection" and to "be born again to a deiform life", since the ultimate aim of this way is "life in God", which always means peace and joy.

Even when the founder does not speak expressly of the resurrection, about "being born anew", or about a "new life in Christ", his passion mysticism is stamped in a uniquely positive way. His unshakable faith in God's love and goodness tells him that God always desires the best even when he sends a sorrow that must be endured. Paul's profound consciousness of faith urging him, in such a sorrow, to become like unto the "crucified Christ" gives him courage, power, even joy to accept and endure the pain. By means of this gaze of faith at *Christus patiens et crucifixus,* suffering becomes deprived of the taint of brutal fact (*factum brutum*) and devoid of the accusation "meaningless". Consequently, it may be said that St. Paul of the Cross' passion mysticism conceals in itself a liberating force, since the endurance of sorrows is faith-motivated, and the problem is "managed" in a Christian way.

It must be underscored that such a positive view and understanding of suffering ought not to be misinterpreted in order to justify human shortcomings, injustices, or other transgressions. It is true that St. Paul of the Cross does not speak explicitly about this problem because he wants, above all, to help men endure concrete, unavoidable, and undeserved suffering by accepting it as the "cross of Christ". At the same time, by stigmatizing sin as the principal evil that must be avoided in all circumstances, he condemns human injustice and sin, from which pain springs. Hence, we can conclude as an interiorly logical consequence of the saint's spiritual-theological thought that an abuse of his passion mysticism (with a view to justifying injustice and sin) would be like a "sin against the Holy Spirit".

When one takes into account the entire spiritual teaching of this "specialist in the interior life" and inquires about other fundamental characteristics of his thought, then the following two must be put in bold relief: a harmonious balance between longing for interiority and the practice of virtue, and an emphasis placed on faith and on a Christ mysticism. These characteristics correspond to the following factors found in his life: a balance between contemplation and action and an ardent zeal to announce *Christus crucifixus* to all.[3]

[3] Pope Paul VI spoke of these characteristic features in the life and thought of St. Paul of the Cross. In a special greeting addressed by him to the members of the fortieth General Chapter of the Passionist Congregation at a general audience on Oct. 13, 1976, he said, "Here it is enough to recommend to you, time and again, the example and testimony of your

The saint's charism consists therein: to be a herald of the "word of the cross" to all men. The Congregation of the Passion founded by Paul[4] has the duty, at all times, "in season and out of season" (2 Tim 4:2), to draw the attention of the Church and the world to the central mystery of *Christus patiens et crucifixus*. As already pointed out in the exposition on his spiritual doctrine, Paul's passioncentrism is not exclusively one-sided but rather is situated in the complete purview of the paschal mystery. Despite his emphasis on the passion and death of Jesus, his spiritual-theological thought is far remote from that doctrine which may be designated as a dismal dolorism (*tristen dolorismus*). On the contrary, it is characterized by a "healthy positivity" in which the "power of the resurrection" shines brilliantly. In this manner, the "liberating power" of the cross of Jesus becomes visible, a power that communicates to human-kind the life of God, a life of hope, trust, even joy.

To understand the *kerygma* of the cross of Christ in its depth, one should not speak of it in an "objective" way only but should be willing to stand "beneath the cross",[5] as J. Moltmann expresses it, and contemplate this mystery in the light of faith. In the spiritual doctrine of the Passionist founder, we have an eloquent example of this faith-filled reflection on the passion and death of Jesus.

The spiritual-religious doctrine of St. Paul of the Cross could have a twofold impact upon theological works. First, it could provide a stimulus to theological research on the significance of innocent and unavoidable suffering. Before all else, the saint sees such as an opportunity "to participate in the passion of Jesus". This response cannot be investigated in "a rational manner" but may be existentially understood through faith. This, however, does not mean that it cannot be theologically grounded.[6]

Second, the spiritual-theological doctrine of the Passionist founder provides another stimulus to theology insofar as he calls for an "all-embracing theology". This means a theology which is not limited to reflecting upon the content of faith, distantly and in a detached, abstract, conceptual way, but rather one that tries to introduce into the content a dimension of depth grounded in existen-tial faith. Indeed, the original type of Christian theology, which we encounter above all in the revealed writings of the New Testament, is marked by bipolar tension. One of the poles consists of the "exertion of notion", abstract and objective. The other pole, dealing with the practice, fruition, and avowal of

---

founder, [an example] to be kept continually before your eyes. He was a true contemplative man and an indefatigable missionary, a man [who] understood [how] to make the cross of Christ the inspiring motive of his spiritual experiences and of his apostolic activity" (as quoted in the German edition of *L'osservatore Romano*, Nov. 19, 1976: 3).

[4] The official abbreviation of the Passionist Congregation is C.P. (Congregatio Passionis).

[5] See above, pp. 228–32.

[6] In the course of this work, we have often tried to present such theological bases.

faith, belongs to the existential, personal domain. In other words, it is clear that a theology delimited by ratiocination and syllogizing (since theology is meant to be an objective-scientific discipline) is incapable of sounding the depth dimension of the content of faith.

However, an "all-embracing or complete theology", which introduces the existential practice of and the fullness of faith as a legitimate "interest" in theological reflection, is able to penetrate into the "core" of the truths of faith and to act in both preparing for and strengthening faith. In this study, we have tried to present to the reader the spiritual teaching of St. Paul of the Cross, the Passionist founder, with its strong orientation to the suffering Christ. It remains as an expectation and desire of ours that the spiritual-theological thought of this remarkable saint will find a welcome audience in the English-speaking world.

In closing, we would also like to mention other themes which might provide opportunity for theological elaboration, using as a starting point the doctrine of this "charismatic of the cross". For example, one could investigate thematically ways indicated by the saint to overcome unavoidable pain and, at the same time, to compare these ways with the methods of contemporary psychology or those envisaged by depth psychology.[7] Or one could study the question: What is the relationship between sin and the passion of Jesus?[8] Finally, although St. Paul of the Cross was not himself confronted with the question of ecumenism, it would be rewarding and fruitful to draw a comparison between his passioncentric spiritual doctrine and the passion mysticism of a spiritual writer belonging to another Christian confession.[9] It is likely that such an investigation would lead to a high, possibly amazingly high, degree of similarity between the two. A never-lost element of the existential fullness of faith may be found.

[7] Here one ought to think, above all, of the logotherapy of V. E. Frankl. See V. E. Frankl, "Annotazioni sul significato della sofferenza", 36–44.

[8] This question is touched upon in this study but only in an occasional way. However, it is worth a proper thematic investigation.

[9] For example, the passion mysticism of Nicholas von Zinzendorf, a very good spiritual writer, could be taken into consideration here. See above, pp. 15–16 and 231–32.

BIBLIOGRAPHY

PRIMARY SOURCES

Amedeo of the Mother of the Good Shepherd, Fr., ed. *Lettere di San Paolo della Croce.* 4 vols. Rome, 1924.

Burke, E., R. Mercurio, and S. Rouse, trans. and ed. *Words from the Heart, A Selection from the Personal Letters of Saint Paul of the Cross.* Dublin, 1976.

Gaetano dell'Addolorata, Fr., ed. *Edition.* Vol. 1, *Testimonianze del processo informativo di Vetralla.* Rome, 1969. Vol. 2, *Testimonianze dei processi informativi di Alessandria, Gaeta, Orbetello, e Corneto.* Rome, 1973.

Giorgini, F., ed. *Regulae et Constitutiones Congr. SS.mae Crucis et Passionis D.N.I.C.* (Editio Critica Textuum). Rome, 1958.

P. Giovanni Maria di S. Ignazio (Fr. Gaetano dell'Addolorata, ed.). *Annali della Congregazione della SS.ma Croce e Passione di N.S.G.C.* Rome, 1967.

I Processi di Beatificazione e Canonizzazione di S. Paolo della Croce. Ms., 22 vols. In Archivium Generale Congregationis Passionis, Rome, SS. John and Paul.

Mercurio, R., and F. Sucher, trans. *Letters of St. Paul of the Cross.* Louisville, Ky., 1953.

St. Paul of the Cross (P. A. Blanco, ed., C. Lizzaraga, Spanish trans.). "Morte Mistica ovvero olocausto del puro spirito di un'anima religiosa". Bilbao, 1976. English translation and annotation, S. Rouse. Owensboro, Ky., 1976.

Rouse, S., trans. and annotator. *Letters to Mother Mary Crucified.* Rome, 1983.

Zoffoli, E., ed. *Diario Spirituale di S. Paolo della Croce, Testo Critico, Introduzione e Note.* Rome, 1964. German translation, M. Bialas, ed. (with Introduction by J. Ratzinger), *Das geistliche Tagebuch des heiligen Paul vom Kreuz.* Aschaffenburg, 1976. English translation, S. Rouse (with Preface by S. Breton), "The Spiritual Diary of St. Paul of the Cross, Translation, Introduction and Notes". In J. Mead, *St. Paul of the Cross, A Source/Workbook for Paulacrucian Studies.* New Rochelle, N.Y., 1983, pp. 21–52.

331

LITERATURE ON ST. PAUL OF THE CROSS

Almeras, C. *St. Paul de la Croix, le fondateur des Passionistes*. Desclée, 1957. English translation, *St. Paul of the Cross: Founder of the Passionists*. New York, 1960.

Amedeo of the Mother of the Good Shepherd, Fr. Un confessore della Fede, Brevi Cenni sul Beato Vincenzo M. Strambi. Rome, 1925.

———. *Il fondatore dei Passionisti, S. Paolo della Croce*. Turin, 1948.

Anselmi, M. " 'L'anthropologia crucis' nelle lettere di San Paolo della Croce". In B. Rinaldi, ed., *La sapienza della croce oggi*. vol. 2. Turin, 1976, pp. 104–26.

Artola, A. M. "La memoria de la Pasión y el voto especial de los pasionistas". *Teología Espiritual* 19 (1975): 559–80.

———. *La Morte Mistica di S. Paolo della Croce*. Vol. I, *Commento ai Paragrafi I–X*. CISP–ROMA, academic year 1979–80 (first semester), Rome, 1979.

———. *La Muerte Mística según San Pablo de la Cruz, Introducción Crítica, con edición Facsímil del Manuscrito de Bilbao; transcripción del Manuscrito de Mamers; más las traducciones de la M. Soledad Solaun, C.P. y el anónimo de Deusto*. Deusto-Bilbao, 1980.

———. *La Muerte Mística según San Pablo de la Cruz, Texto Crítico y Síntesis Doctrinal*. Bilbao, 1986.

Basilio de San Pablo, Fr. "La contemplación reparadora en San Pablo de la Cruz". *Revista de Espiritualidad* 16 (1957): 449–65.

———. "La suave y dulce dirección de San Pablo de la Cruz". *Vida Sobrenatural* 58 (1957): 347–57.

———. "La contemplación de la Pasión de Cristo como puerta para la contemplación de la divinidad, en el magisterio de San Pablo de la Cruz". *Teología Espiritual* 2 (1958): 81–99.

———. "La Mariología en el marianismo de San Pablo de la Cruz". *Ephemerides Mariologicae* 8 (1958): 125–38.

———. *La Espiritualidad de la Pasión en el Magisterio de San Pablo de la Cruz*. Madrid, 1961.

———. "La espirtualidad pasionista". *Manresa* 23 (1961): 99–118.

———. *Espiritualidad de la Pasión y espiritualidad de los pasionistas, Sus fundamentos doctrinales en el magisterio de San Pablo de la Cruz*. Madrid, 1967.

——. "Pasiocentrismo en la vida mística y apostolado de San Pablo de la Cruz". *Teología Espiritual* 11 (1967): 431–54.

——. "Cómo quiso San Pablo de la Cruz a los pasionistas". *Teología Espiritual* 19 (1975): 609–18.

Bernardino dell'Addolorata, Fr. *Quarant'anni d'apostolato di S. Paolo della Croce, Episodi e fatti prodigiosi.* Rome, 1929.

Bernardo M. di Gesù, Fr. *Cenni Biografici di alcuni religiosi Passionisti, che professarono l'Istituto nel suo primo periodo di cinquant'anni.* Rome, 1886.

——. *Memorie dei primi compagni di S. Paolo della Croce.* Viterbo, 1884 (2d ed., Rome, 1932).

Bialas, Martin. "Paul vom Kreuz, ein Künder Christi, des Gekreuzigten". In *Passioni Domini Devoti* (written in honor of 50th anniversary of establishment of Southern German–Austrian Province of the Passionists), ed. by Passionist Provincialate, Schwarzenfeld (with collaboration of Michael Schmaus and Franz Mußner). 1973, pp. 17–30.

——. *Im Zeichen des Kreuzes, Leben und Werk des heiligen Paul vom Kreuz, des Gründers des Passionisten.* Leutesdorf, 1974. In Portuguese, Pedro Becker, trans., *São Paulo da Cruz, Vida e Espiritualidade.* Bosquejo, São Paulo, 1975.

——. "Leiden als Gnade in der Passionsmystik des Paul vom Kreuz". In H. Roßman and J. Ratzinger, eds., *Mysterium der Gnade, Festschrift für J. Auer.* Regensburg, 1975, pp. 427–41.

——. "The Passion of Christ and Our Holy Founder's Spirituality". *The Passionist* no. 2 (1975): 95–112.

——. *Das geistliche Tagebuch des heiligen Paul vom Kreuz* (with Introductory Word by J. Ratzinger). Aschaffenburg, 1976.

——. "Il dolore umano come grazia in san Paolo della Croce". In B. Rinaldi, ed., *La sapienza della croce oggi.* vol. 2. Turin, 1976, pp. 53–67. In English, "Human Suffering as Grace in the Thought of St. Paul of the Cross". *The Passionist* 2, no. 3 (1976): 98–121.

——. "Quién es el autor de la 'Muerte Mistica' ". *Boletín Informativo del Centenario de la llegada de los pasionistas a España–N.º 10, Conferencia Interprovincial Iberica.* Zaragoza, 1980. In English, see above, pp. 247–58.

——. *In This Sign, the Spirituality of St. Paul of the Cross.* Dublin, 1984.

Biddle, W. "Paul Daneo—A Heart Open to All". *The Passionist* 1, no. 2 (1975): 82–94.

Breton, S. *La Mystique de la Passion, Étude sur la Doctrine spirituelle de Saint Paul de la Croix.* Tournai, 1962.

――. "La croce del non-essere". In B. Rinaldi, ed., *La sapienza della croce oggi.* Vol. 3. Turin, 1976, pp. 21–35.

Brice, R. *In Spirit and in Truth: The Spiritual Doctrine of St. Paul of the Cross.* New York and Cincinnati, 1948.

Brovetto, C. *Introduzione alla Spiritualità di S. Paolo della Croce, Morte Mistica e Divina Natività.* San Gabriele dell'Addolorata, Teramo, 1955. In English, S. Wood and S. Rouse, trans. *Introduction to the Spirituality of St. Paul of the Cross, Mystical Death and Divine Nativity.* Owensboro, Ky., 1976.

――. "Il Cantico della Croce". *Fonti Vive* 1 (1955): 84–108, 200–213, 415–28; 2 (1956): 255–66; 3 (1957): 228–38, 383–98.

――. "La vita contemplativa secondo S. Paolo della Croce". In R. Spiazzi and S. Gabriele dell'Addolorata, eds., *La vita contemplativa nella Congregazione della Passione.* Teramo, 1958, pp. 57–122.

――. "San Paolo della Croce 'un san Paolo apostolo dei nostri tempi' ". In B. Rinaldi, ed., *La sapienza della croce oggi.* Vol. 2. Turin, 1976, pp. 18–36.

Burke, E., R. Mercurio and S. Rousse, eds., *Words from the Heart: A Selection from the Personal Letters of St. Paul of the Cross,* Dublin, 1976.

Casetti, A. *S. Paolo della Croce, Dall'Epistolario.* Milan, 1925.

Chiari, C. *Le tre Lampade di S. Paolo della Croce.* Verona, 1968.

――. *Come visse S. Paolo della Croce.* Verona, 1969 (3d ed. of *Il Gigante della Croce*).

――. *Magistero Spirituale di S. Paolo della Croce, S. Zenone degli Ezzelini.* Treviso, 1973.

――. "Il mistero della croce nella direzione spirituale di san Paolo della Croce". In B. Rinaldi, ed., *La sapienza della croce oggi.* Vol. 2. Turin, 1976, pp. 127–34.

――. *Spiritualità della Croce, Antologia di figure e testi spirituali dal 1900 ad oggi.* Vol. 1 (1903–26). Editrice ECO―S. Gabriele, Teramo, 1976.

――, ed. Paolo della Croce, Scritti Spirituali. Vol. 1, *Diario Spirituale―Lettere a familiari e laici.* Rome, 1974. Vol. 2, *Lettere a laici ed ecclesiastici.* Rome, 1974. Vol. 3, *Lettere a religiosi.* Rome, 1975.

Cristoforo dell'Addolorata, Fr. (Chiari). *Il Gigante della Croce, S. Paolo della Croce secondo i documenti originali.* Alba, 1952 (2d ed., Caravate, Varese, 1959).

——. *Il Cavaliere della Croce, Piccolo storia di San Paolo della Croce, Fondatore dei Missionari Passionisti.* Verona and Sezano, 1956.

Coccalotto, R. "L'influsso di Taulero nella vita e nella dottrina di S. Paolo della Croce". *Vita Cristiana* 20 (1951): 136–45, 287–309.

Colosio, I. "A proposito di una recente opera sul B. Enrico Suso". *Rassegna di Ascetica e Mistica* 14 (1972): 167–83.

Congregation of the Oratory of St. Philip Neri. *Life of Blessed Paul of the Cross.* English trans. of biography by V. M. Strambi. Vols. 1 and 3. London, 1853.

Das Leben des Hl. Paul vom Kreuze, Stifters der Congregation der unbeschuhten Cleriker des heiligsten Kreuzes und des Leidens Jesu Christi oder der Passionisten, aus dem Italienischen von einem Mitgliede der Congregation der Passionisten. Baltimore, 1873 (German translation of biography written by V. Strambi).

De Lugo, A. "La contemplación y el apostolado en la vida mixta de los pasionistas, según su fundador San Pablo de la Cruz". *Teología Espiritual* 19 (1975): 539–57.

Demeck, N. *The Master Idea and the Fount of the Apostolate of St. Paul of the Cross.* Unpublished dissertation. Rome, 1956.

De Sanctis, G. A. *L'avventura carismatica di S. Paolo della Croce.* Rome, 1976.

Díez, Merino L. "La Biblia en el magisterio de San Pablo de la Cruz". *Teología Espiritual* 19 (1975): 475–503.

Disma, Fr., ed. St. Vincent Mary Strambi, *Lo spirito di S. Paolo della Croce.* Alba, 1951.

Dominguez, O. "Espiritualidad pasiocéntrica de San Pablo de la Cruz". *Teología Espiritual* 19 (1975): 353–77.

Edmund, Fr. *Hunter of Souls: St. Paul of the Cross.* Dublin, 1946.

Filippo della Concezione, Fr. *Vita del Ven. Servo di Dio P. Paolo della Croce.* Rome, 1821.

Filippo della S. Famiglia, Fr. *S. Paolo della Croce e la provincia di Maria SS.ma Addolorata nella Congregazione dei Passionisti.* Tip. dell'Abbazia di Casamari, 1967.

Frasconi, P. M. *L'Ultimo dei Crociati. S. Paolo della Croce, Fondatore dei Passionisti.* Turin, 1948.

Gaetano of the Holy Name of Mary, Fr. "S. Paul de la Croix, directeur des âmes. Magnanimité, confiance et dilatation de coeur au service de Dieu". *RAM* 9 (1928): 25–54.

——. *Oraison et Ascension Mystique de Saint Paul de la Croix.* Museum Lessianum, Section Ascétique et Mystique, no. 29, Louvain, 1930.

——. *Doctrine de Saint Paul de la Croix sur l'Oraison et la Mystique.* Museum Lessianum, Section Ascétique et Mystique, no. 35, Louvain, 1932.

——. *S. Paul de la Croix, Apôtre et Missionaire.* Tirlemont, 1933.

——. *S. Paul de la Croix et l'institut des passionistes.* Tienen, 1933.

——. *Recrutement, formation et gouvernement des religieux—Méthode et exemples de S. Paul de la Croix.* Tienen, 1934.

——. *S. Paul de la Croix et la Fondation des Religieuses Passionistes.* Tirlemont, 1936.

——. *S. Paul de la Croix et la formation des religieuses passionistes.* Tienen, 1937.

——. *Esprit et Vertus de S. Paul de la Croix, Ouvrage posthume recueilli et revu par le P. Thomas.* Tirlemont, 1951. In English, Cajetan Reynders, C.P. *Saint Paul of the Cross, His Spirit and Virtues.* New York, 1960.

——. *Saint Paul de la Croix et la Fondation des Passionistes, Ouvrage posthume recueilli et revu par le P. Thomas.* Tournai, 1956.

——. *Vie de Saint Paul de la Croix, Oeuvre posthume recueillie et publiée par le P. Thomas.* 2 vols., hectographed. Ere, 1958.

Gaetano dell'Addolorata, Fr. "S. Paolo della Croce e la soppressione della Compagnia di Gesù". *Rivista di Storia della Chiesa in Italia* 13 (1959): 102–12.

——. *I Processi di Beatificazione e Canonizzazione di S. Paolo della Croce, Fondatore dei Passionisti e delle Claustrali Passioniste.* Vol. 1. Rome, 1969. Vol. 2. Rome, 1973.

——, ed. *Annáli della Congregazione, P. Giovanni Maria di S. Ignazio.* Rome, 1967.

García Garcés, N. "Vivencia del misterio de María en San Pablo de la Cruz". *Teología Espiritual* 19 (1975): 451–73.

Garrido Bonaño, M. "La oración personal y la litúrgica en San Pablo de la Cruz". *Teología Espiritual* 19 (1975): 505–38.

Garrigou-Lagrange, R. "Nuit de l'esprit réparatrice en S. Paul de la Croix". *Études Carmélitaines* 23 (1938): 287–93.

Gedda, L. *San Paolo della Croce è tra noi, Discorso commemorativo del I Centenario della Canonizzazione di San Paolo della Croce* ... Tipografia Poliglotta Vaticana, 1968.

Giorgini, F. C. *Fontes Historicae Congregationis Passionis.* Vol. 2, *Consuetudines Congr. SS.mae Crucis et Passionis D.N.I.C.* Editio Critica Textuum P.P. Dominici, Seraphini, Bernardi, Rome, 1958.

——. *Fontes Historicae Congregationis Passionis.* Vol. I, *Regulae et Constitutiones Congr. SS.mae Crucis et Passionis D.N.I.C.* Editio Critica Textuum, Rome, 1958.

——. *Fontes Historicae Congregationis Passionis.* Vol 3, *Decreti e Raccomandazioni dei Capitoli Generali della Congregazione della SS. Croce e Passione di N.S.G.C.* Rome, 1960.

——. *La Maremma Toscana nel Settecento: Aspetti sociali e religiosi.* Edizioni ECO—S. Gabriele dell'Addolorata, Teramo, 1968.

Guibert, de J. "Le Journal de Retraite de Saint Paul de la Croix". *RAM* 6 (1925): 26–48.

Henau, E. *De Passiemystiek van Paulus van het Kruis, Structuuranalyse van een christelijke ervaring.* Unpublished dissertation. Löwen, 1966.

——. "El Diario Espiritual de San Pablo de la Cruz". *Revista de Espiritualidad* 26 (1967): 424–32.

——. "The Naked Suffering (Nudo-Patire) in the Mystical Experience of Paul of the Cross". *Ephemerides Theologicae Lovanienses* 43 (1967): 210–21.

——. "Riflessioni sulla predicazione di S. Paolo della Croce". *Rivista di Ascetica e Mistica* 6 (1968): 508–16.

——. *Paulus van het Kruis (1694–1775), Stichter van de Passionisten.* Stauros, Leuven, 1975.

Huerga, A. "San Pablo de la Cruz, un místico insigne de la época de la Illustración". *Teología Espiritual* 19 (1975): 331–51.

Laer, van H. *Saint Paul de la Croix et le Saint-Siège (1721–1768).* San Gabriele dell'Addolorata, Teramo, 1957.

Langenberg, P. *Passionsblumen aus dem Garten des heiligen Paul vom Kreuz, Zum zweihundertjährigen Gedächtnistage der Gründung der Passionsgenossenschaft.* Buenos Aires, 1920.

Lebreton, J. "L'union au Christ souffrant". In *Tu solus sanctus. Jésus Christ vivant dans les Saints. Etudes de théologie mystique.* Paris, 1948, pp. 216–36.

Lehnerd, V. *Der große Volksmissionär der Neuzeit, Der hl. Paul vom Kreuz.* Innsbruck, 1926.

Liphold, F. *Der heilige Paul vom Kreuz, Stifter des Passionistenordens.* Dülmen i. W., 1930.

Llamas, P. E. "San Pablo de la Cruz y San Juan de la Cruz: En busca de las fuentes de su doctrina mística". *Teología Espiritual* 19 (1975): 581–607.

Louis-Thérèse de Jésus Agonisant, Fr. *Histoire de S. Paul de la Croix.* Bordeaux, 1866. In Italian, *S. Paolo della Croce, Fondatore dei Passionisti.* Alba, 1952 (4th ed.).

Luca di S. Giuseppe, Fr. *Un Grande Apostolo del Crocifisso nel secolo decimottavo o S. Paolo della Croce, Fondatore della Congregazione dei Passionisti.* Florence, 1908.

Madden, P. M. "The Spirit of St. Paul of the Cross". *The Passionist* 1, no. 2 (1975): 75–81.

Mauro dell'Immacolata, Fr. *Sulle Orme di S. Paolo della Croce, Fondatore dei Passionisti, Vita e Opere (1694–1775).* Rome, 1959.

Mead, J. *Priestly Spirituality According to the Doctrine of St. Paul of the Cross.* Rome, 1975.

——. "San Paolo della Croce e la spiritualità sacerdotale". In B. Rinaldi, ed., *La sapienza della croce oggi.* Vol. 2. Turin, 1976, pp. 68–75.

——, ed. *St. Paul of the Cross, A Source/Workbook for Paulacrucian Studies.* New Rochelle, N.Y., 1983.

Mercurio, R. "Paulacrucian Sources". *The Passionist* 2, no. 4 (1976): 4–12.

Mitterrutzner, L. *Leben des seligen Paul vom Kreuz.* Innsbruck, 1860.

Monsegú, B. *Cartas y diario espiritual de San Pablo de la Cruz.* Madrid, 1968.

——. "Semblanza del fundador de los pasionistas y de su Instituto". *Teología Espiritual* 19 (1975): 295–329.

Naselli, A. "Paolo della Croce, predicatore del Crocefisso". *Fonti Vive* 2 (1956): 496–518.

——. *La devozione di S. Paolo della Croce alla Chiesa e al Papa.* Editrice ECO, San Gabriele dell'Addolorata, Teramo, 1958.

——. "L'orazione nei primi Compagni e Discepoli dei S. Paolo della Croce". In R. Spiazzi and S. Gabriele dell'Addolorata, eds., *La vita contemplativa nella Congregazione della Passione.* Teramo, 1958, pp. 125–91.

——. *Spiritualità della Croce, Antologia di profili e testi spirituali dal 1900 ad oggi.* Vol. 2, 1928–46. Editrice ECO, S. Gabriele dell'Addolorata, Teramo, 1976.

Nesti, P. "Principi biblico-teologici della spiritualità passionista". In B.

Rinaldi, ed., *La sapienza della croce oggi.* Vol. 2. Turin, 1976, pp. 76–103.

Oischinger, J. N. *Das Leben des ehrwürdigen Dieners Gottes, P. Paul vom Kreuz.* Regensburg, 1846.

Oswald, P. "La personalité de S. Paul de la Croix". *Études Carmélitaines* 23 (1938): 282–86.

———. *De mystieke weg van de H. Paulus van het Kruis (1694–1775).* Mook, 1954.

Pacho, E. "La croce nella mistica di san Giovanni della Croce e di San Paolo della Croce". In B. Rinaldi, ed., *La sapienza della croce oggi.* Vol. 2. Turin, 1976, pp. 181–96.

Paolo della Croce (P. A. Blanco and C. Lizarraga, eds.). "Morte Mistica ovvero olocausto del puro spirito di un'anima Religiosa". Bilbao, 1976.

Paolo Giuseppe dell'Immacolata Concezione, Fr. *Vita di San Paolo della Croce.* Rome, 1867.

Patrizio di N. Signora del S. Cuore di Gesù, Fr. *Lo Spirito del Passionista.* Rome, 1930.

Pellegrino del Cuor di Gesù, Fr. *Compendio della Vita del Beato Paolo della Croce.* Monza, 1853; Rome, 1855.

Piélagos, F. *Testigo de la Pasión, S. Pablo de la Cruz.* Biblioteca de Autores Cristianos — Popular, Madrid, 1977.

Pio del Nome di Maria, Fr. *Vita del Beato Paolo della Croce.* Rome, 1853.

———. *Vita di S. Paolo della Croce.* Isola del Liri, 1928 (5th ed.).

Pomes, F. *Paolo della Croce, Apostolo per vocazione.* Manduria, Taranto, 1975.

Pompilio, S. *L'esperienza mistica della Passione in San Paolo della Croce.* Rome, 1973.

Pourrat, P. "S. Paul de la Croix". *La spiritualité chrétienne* 4 (1947): 496–504.

Ravasi, L. *La Congregazione dei Passionisti verso la Metà del Secolo XIX.* Rome, 1963.

———. *Due Secoli di S. Paolo della Croce sul Celio.* Edizioni "Fonti Vive", Rome, 1973.

Rice, F. "Passionistic Spirituality". *Review for Religious* 10 (1951): 241–46.

Rinaldi, B., ed. *La sapienza della croce oggi, Atti del Congresso internazionale, Rome, 13–18 ottobre 1975.* Vols. 1–3. Turin, 1976.

Rouse, S. "St. Paul of the Cross—Spiritual Guide". *The Passionist,* no. 4 (1976): 79–109.

Sierra, F. *La virtud de la humildad en S. Pablo de la Cruz.* unpublished dissertation. Rome, 1953.

Spagnolo, M. *S. Paolo della Croce, Fondatore dei Passionisti.* Manduria, 1969.

Spiazzi, R., ed. *La vita contemplativa nella Congregazione della Passione.* Edizioni ECO, S. Gabriele dell'Addolorata, Teramo, 1958.

Stanisiao dell'Addolorata, Fr. *Il fondatore dei Passionisti.* Rome, 1917.

——. *Diario di S. Paolo della Croce, con introduzione e commenti.* Turin and Rome, 1926 and 1929 (2d ed.).

——. *Il più bel fiore di Ovado.* Varese, 1930.

Strambi, V. M. *Vita del Ven. Servo di Dio, P. Paolo della Croce.* Rome, 1786. In English, Congregation of the Oratory of St. Philip Neri, trans., *Life of the Blessed Paul of the Cross.* Vols. 1 and 3. London, 1853.

——. *Part 2: Lo spirito di S. Paolo della Croce.* P. Disma, ed. Alba, 1951. Abbreviated German translation, *Das Leben des hl. Paul vom Kreuz.* Baltimore, 1873.

Tito di S. Paolo della Croce, Fr. *Vox Patris, Massime Spirituali di S. Paolo della Croce.* Turin, 1949.

Viller, M. "La mystique de la Passion chez Saint Paul de la Croix". *RSR* 40 (1951): 426–45.

——. "La volonté de Dieu dans les lettres de S. Paul de la Croix". *RAM* 27 (1951): 132–74.

Walz, A. "Influencia Tauleriana en S. Pablo de la Cruz". *Teología Espiritual* 5 (1961): 397–408.

——. "Tauler im italienischen Sprachraum". In E. Filthaut, ed., *Johannes Tauler, ein deutscher Mystiker.* Essen, 1961, pp. 371–95, esp. 382–87.

Ward, F. *The Passionists.* New York, 1923.

Wilson, A. *The Life of St. Paul of the Cross, Founder of the Passionists.* N.p., n.d.

Wood, S. "The Liturgical Spirit of St. Paul of the Cross". *Orate Fratres* 23 (1949): 448–54.

Yuhaus, C. J. "Paul of the Cross, A Historical Reflection". *The Passionist* 2, no. 4 (1976): 13–34.

Zoffoli, E. *I Passionisti, Spiritualità e apostolato.* Rome, 1955.

——. *La povera Gemma, Saggi critici storio-teologici.* Rome, 1957.

——. *S. Paolo della Croce, Storia Critica.* 3 vols. Rome, 1963, 1965, 1968.

——. *Diario Spirituale de S. Paolo della Croce, testo Critico, Introduzione e Note.* Rome, 1964.

——. *S. Paolo della Croce, Profilo.* Rome, 1967 and 1975 (2d ed.).

——. *S. Paolo della Croce.* Manduria, Taranto, 1975.

GENERAL LITERATURE

Note: This list represents works important to this study or quoted frequently. Articles from various lexicons and other theological reference books are not included but have been referenced exactly in the notes.

Adinolfi, M. "Cristo crocifisso . . . stoltezza per i pagani". In B. Rinaldi, ed., *La sapienza della croce oggi.* Vol. 1. Turin, 1976, pp. 21–32.

Ahern, B. *New Horizons, Studies in Biblical Theology.* Notre Dame, Ind., 1963.

——. "La maturità cristiana e la croce". In B. Rinaldi, ed., *La sapienza della croce oggi.* Vol. 2. Turin, 1976, pp. 9–17. In English, "Christian Maturity and the Cross of Christ". *The Passionist*, no. 3 (1976): 52–64.

Alkofer, A. *Sämtiliche Schriften der hl. Theresia von Jesu.* Vols. 1–6. Munich, 1931–41.

Aloysius ab Immac. Conceptione, Fr., and Ambrosius a S. Theresia, Fr., ed. *Des Heiligen Johannes vom Kreuz: Sämtliche Werke.* Vols. 1–5. Munich, 1956–58.

Auclair, Marcelle. *Teresa of Avila.* Wakefield, Mass., 1953.

Auer, A. *Leidenstheologie des Mittelalters.* Salzburg, 1947.

Auer, J. "Kleine Theologie des Kreuzes". In H. Schlier et al., eds., *Strukturen christlicher Existenz, Festgabe für F. Wulf.* Würzburg, 1968, pp. 161–74.

——. *Kleine Katholische Dogmatik.* J. Auer and J. Ratzinger, eds. Vol. 5, *Das Evangelium der Gnade.* Regensburg, 1970. Vol. 6, *Allgemeine Sakramentenlehre und das Mysterium der Eucharistie.* Regensburg, 1971. Vol. 7, *Die Sakramente der Kirche.* Regensburg, 1972. Vol. 8, *Die Welt—Gottes Schöpfung.* Regensburg, 1975.

——. "Auferstehung des Fleisches. Was kann mit dieser Aussage heute gemeint sein? Ein Versuch". MThZ 26 (1975): 17–37.

Baier, W. "Flores et fructus arboris Vitae Iesu Christi des Kartäusers Ludolf von Sachsen († 1378).—Ein Horologium des Lebens Jesu für alle Horen an den

sieben Tagen der Woche". In H. Roßmann and J. Ratzinger, eds., *Mysterium der Gnade*. Regensburg, 1975, pp. 321–41.

Balthasar, H. U. von. *Herrlichkeit—Eine theologische Ästhetik.* Vol. 2, *Fächer der Stile.* Part 1, *Klerikale Stile.* Einsiedeln, 1969 (2d ed.); Part 2, *Laikale Stile.* Einsiedeln, 1969 (2d ed.).

——. "Mysterium Paschale". *Mysterium Salutis* 3, no. 2 (1969): 133–326.

——. *Verbum Caro, Skizzen zur Theologie.* Vol. 1. Einsiedeln, 1969 (2d ed.).

——. *Schwestern im Geist, Therese von Lisieux und Elisabeth von Dijon.* Einsiedeln, 1973.

Barcia y Zambrana, J. de. *Sermonarium, Christ-eyfriger Seelen-Wecker oder lehrreiche Predigten.* Trans. from Spanish by M. Fridl. 6 vols. Augsburg and Dillingen, 1715–20.

——. *Svegliarino cristiano di discorsi dottrinali sopra particolari assunti.* Translated from Spanish by G. A. Panceri. 3 vols. Milan, 1719 (2d ed.).

Basilio de San Pablo, Fr. *La meditación en la Pasión de Cristo.* Madrid, 1967.

——. *Reflexiones sobre la Pasión de Cristo.* Madrid, 1968.

Beinert, W. "Die Erfahrbarkeit der Glaubenswirklichkeit". In v. H. Roßmann and J. Ratzinger, eds., *Mysterium der Gnade, Festschrift für J. Auer.* Regensburg, 1975, pp. 132–45.

Benedictines of Stanbrook. *The Letters of St. Theresa.* 2d impression with additional notes by Benedict Zimmerman, O.C.D. Vols. 1 and 4. London, 1924 and 1926.

Bernhardt, J. *Augustinus, Confessiones—Bekenntnisse.* Munich, 1966 (3d ed.).

Beyreuther, E., and G. Meyer, ed. *Nikolaus Ludwig von Zinzendorf, Hauptschriften.* Vols. 1–6. Hildesheim, 1962–66.

Bihlmeyer, K., and H. Tüchle. *Kirchengeschichte.* Vol. 3. Paderborn, 1961 (17th ed.).

Blank, J. *Krisis, Untersuchungen zur Johanneischen Christologie und Eschatologie.* Freiburg, 1964.

Bouyer, L. " 'Mystisch'—Zur Geschichte eines Wortes". In J. Sudbrack, ed., *Das Mysterium und die Mystik, Beiträge zu einer Theologie der christlichen Gotteserfahrung.* Würzburg, 1974, pp. 57–75.

Bowker, J. *Problems of Suffering in Religions of the World.* Cambridge, 1975 (2d ed.).

Breton, S. *La Passion du Christ et les Philosophies.* Vol. 2. Edizioni "ECO", S. Gabriele dell'Addolorata, Teramo, 1954.

——. "La Passion du Christ et la Réflexion philosophique". *Sciences Ecclésiastiques* 18, 1966, 47–63.

Büchi, H. "Ein Menschenalter Reformen der Toten Hand in Toskana (1751 bis 1790)". In *Historische Studien,* no. 99. Berlin, 1912 (reprinted, Vaduz, 1965).

——. "Finanzen und Finanzpolitik Toskanas im Zeitalter der Aufklärung". In E. Eberling, ed., *Historische Studien,* no. 124. Berlin, 1915 (reprinted, Vaduz, 1965).

Colledge, E., and Sr. M. Jane, O.P. *Spiritual Conferences by John Tauler.* St. Louis, 1961.

Cordara, G. C. "Autobiographie: Teildruck". In J. Döllinger, ed., *Beiträge zur politischen, kirchlichen und Cultur-Geschichte.* Vol. 3. Regensburg, 1882.

Cursillo. *Für eine Kirche in Bewegung* 13, nos. 8–9 (1976).

Delling, G. *Der Kreuzestod Jesu in der urchristlichen Verkündigung.* Göttingen, 1972.

Denifle, H. S. *Die deutschen Mystiker des 14. Jahrhunderts.* Posthumous ed. published by O. Spiess, Freiburg, Switzerland, 1951.

Dinkler, E. *Signum Crucis.* Tübingen, 1968.

Duquoc, C. "Attualità teologica della croce". In B. Rinaldi, ed., *La sapienza della croce oggi.* Vol. 1. Turin, 1976, pp. 11–17. In English, "The Theological Relevance of the Cross". *The Passionist,* no. 3 (1976): 5–15.

Eberhard, S. *Kreuzes-Theologie. Das reformatorische Anliegen in Zinzendorfs Verkündigung.* Munich, 1937.

Elliott, W. *The Sermons and Conferences of John Tauler.* Washington, D.C., 1910.

Endersbee, M., ed. *Taught by Pain.* London, 1972 (2d ed.).

Federico dell'Addolorata, Fr., ed. *Ven. Domenico della Madre di Dio, Traccia della divina misericordia per la Conversione di un Peccatore.* Brescia, 1959.

Ferguson, J. *The Place of Suffering.* Cambridge and London, 1972.

Frankl, V. E. "Annotazioni sul significato della sofferenza". In B. Rinaldi, ed., *La sapienza della croce oggi.* Vol. 3. Turin, 1976, pp. 36–44.

Gardropoli, G. "Il 'mysterium crucis' nella metodologia pastorale". In B. Rinaldi, ed., *La sapienza della croce oggi.* Vol. 3. Turin, 1976, pp. 432–48.

Gerhartz, J. G. "'Insuper Promitto', Feierliche Sondergelübde katholischer Orden". In *Analecta Gregoriana* 153 (Rome, 1966).

Giovanna della Croce. *Enrico Suso, La sua vita, la sua fortuna in Italia.* Milan, 1971.

Gollwitzer, H. *Krummes Holz—aufrechter Gang. Zur Frage nach dem Sinn des Lebens.* Munich, 1973 (6th ed.).

Guibert, J. de. *Documenta ecclesiastica christianae perfectionis.* Rome, 1931.

Hedinger, U. "Wider die Versöhnung Gottes mit dem Elend, Eine Kritik des christlichen Theismus und A–Theismus. In M. Geiger, ed., *Basler Studien zur historischen und systematischen Theologie.* Vol. 60. Zürich, 1972.

Heer, J. *Der Durchbohrte—Johanneische Parallele zur Herz-Jesu-Verehrung.* Rome, 1969.

Heppe, H. *Geschichte der quietistichen Mystik in der katholischen Kirche.* Berlin, 1875.

Herbstrith, W. *Teresa von Avila—Die erste Kirchenlehrerin.* Bergen and Enkheim, 1971.

Hildebrand, D. von. *Uber das Herz, Zur menschlichen und gottmenschlichen Affektivität* (German translation of *The Sacred Heart*). Regensburg, 1967.

Hofmann, G. *Johannes Tauler, Predigten.* Freiburg, 1961.

——. "Literaturgeschichtliche Grundlagen zur Tauler-Forschung". In E. Filthaut, ed., *Johannes Tauler, ein deutscher Mystiker.* Essen, 1961, pp. 436–82.

——. *Heinrich Seuse, Deutsche mystische Schriften.* Düsseldorf, 1966.

Horkheimer, M. *Die Sehnsucht nach dem ganz Anderen, Ein Interview mit Kommentar von H. Gumnior.* Hamburg, 1970.

Hülsbusch, W. *Elemente einer Kreuzestheologie in den Spätschriften Bonaventuras (Themen und Thesen der Theologie).* Düsseldorf, 1968.

Hutton, Arthur Wollaston. *The Inner Way, Thirty-Six Sermons for Festivals by John Tauler.* London, 1909.

Jedin, H., ed. *Handbuch der Kirchengeschichte.* Vol. 5, *Die Kirche im Zeitalter des Absolutismus und der Aufklärung.* Freiburg, 1970.

Jolles, A. *Einfache Formen. Legende, Sage, Mythe, Rätsel, Spruch, Memorabile, Märchen, Witz.* Tübingen, 1968 (4th ed.).

Kasper, W. *Jesus der Christus.* Mainz, 1975.

Kessler, H. *Die theologische Bedeutung des Todes Jesu, Eine traditionsgeschichtliche Untersuchung (Themen und Thesen der Theologie).* Düsseldorf, 1971 (2d ed.).

——. *Erlösung als Befreiung.* Düsseldorf, 1972.

Kitamori, K. *Theologie der Okumene.* Vol. II, *Theologie des Schmerzes Gottes.* Göttingen, 1972.

Klappert, B. *Die Auferweckung des Gekreuzigten, Der Ansatz der Christologie Karl Barths im Zusammenhang der Christologie der Gegenwart.* Neukirchen-Vluyn, 1971.

Knox, R. A. *Christliches Schwärmertum* (German translation of *Enthusiasm*). Cologne, 1957.

Kremer, J. *Das Ärgernis des Kreuzes, Eine Hinführung zum Verstehen der Leidensgeschichte nach Markus.* Stuttgart, 1969.

"Kreuzestheologie im Neuen Testament". *Evangelische Theologie* 34, no. 2 (Mar./Apr. 1974).

Küng, H. *Menschwerdung Gottes, Eine Einführung in Hegels theologisches Denken als Prolegomina zu einer künftigen Christologie (Ökumenische Forschungen).* H. Küng and J. Ratzinger, eds., Vol. I. Freiburg, 1970.

———. "Gott und das Leid". In H. Küng, ed., *Theologische Meditationen.* Vol. 18. Einsiedeln, 1971 (4th ed.).

Kunz, H. *Die anthropologische Bedeutung der Phantasie.* 2 Vols. Basel, 1946.

Lersch, P. *Aufbau der Person* (4th ed. of *Der Aufbau des Charakters*). Munich, 1951.

Link, H. G. "Gegenwärtige Probleme einer Kreuzestheologie". *Evangelische Theologie* 33 (1973): 337–45.

Loewenich, W. von. *Luthers Theologia Crucis.* Witten, 1967 (5th ed.).

Lohmeyer, E. *Urchristliche Mystik, Neutestamentliche Studien.* Darmstadt, 1958 (2d ed.).

Lubac, H. de. "Christliche Mystik in Begegnung mit den Weltreligionen". In J. Sudbrack, ed., *Das Mysterium und die Mystik.* Würzburg, 1974, pp. 77–110.

Mancini, I. "Venerdì Santo speculativo". In B. Rinaldi, ed., *La sapienza della croce oggi.* Vol. 3. Turin, 1976, pp. 9–20.

Martin, J. "Die Theologie des Franz von Sales. Rottenburg, 1934.

Metz, J. B. "Kleine Apologie des Erzählens". *Concilium* 9 (1973): 334–41.

Metz, J. B., and J. Moltmann. *"Leidensgeschichte". Zwei Meditationen zu Markus* 8:31–38. Freiburg, 1974.

Moltmann, J. *Der gekreuzigte Gott.* Munich, 1972.

——. "Ecumenismo sotto la croce", in *La sapienza della croce oggi*. B. Rinaldi, ed. Vol. I. Turin, 1976, pp. 526–37. In English, see "Ecumenism Beneath the Cross". *The Passionist*, no. 3 (1976): 16–35.

Mühlen, H. *Die Veränderlichkeit Gottes als Horizont einer zukünftigen Christologie. —Auf dem Wege zu einer Kreuzestheologie in Auseinandersetzung mit der altkirchlichen Christologie*. Münster, 1969.

Mußner, F. "Der Galaterbrief". In *Herders theologischer Kommentar zum Neuen Testament*. Vol. 9. Freiburg, 1974.

Novoa, L. *Religionsfreiheit in Spanien. Geschichte—Problematik—Zukunftsperspektiven.* Frankfurt, 1978.

Ortkemper, F. J. *"Das Kreuz in der Verkündigung des Apostels Paulus. Dargestellt an den Texten der paulinischen Hauptbrief"*. In *Stuttgarter Bibelstudien*, Vol. 24. Stuttgart, 1967.

Palazzi, F. *Novissimo Dizionario della Lingua Italiana*. Milan, 1970 (2d ed.).

Pannenberg, W. *Grundzüge der Christologie*. Gütersloh, 1964.

——. "Christologie und Theologie". *Kerygma und Dogma* 21 (1975): 159–75.

Pastor, Ludwig von. *Geschichte der Päpste seit dem Ausgang des Mittelalters*. Vol. 15, *Von der Wahl Klemens' XI. bis zum Tode Klemens' XII., (1700–1740)*. Freiburg, 1930.

——. Vol. 16, 1, *Von der Wahl Benedikts XIV. bis zum Tode Pius' VI. (1740 bis 1799), Erste Abteilung: Benedikt XIV. und Klemens XIII (1740–1769)*. Freiburg, 1931.

——. Vol. 16, 2, *Klemens XIV. (1769–1774)*. Freiburg, 1932.

——. Vol. 16, 3, *Pius VI. (1775–1799)*. Freiburg, 1933.

Peers, Allison E. *The Book of the Foundations*. In *The Complete Works of St. Teresa*. Vol. 3. London, 1946.

——. *The Complete Works of St. John of the Cross* (trans. from the critical edition of Fr. Silverio de Santa Teresa). 3 vols. Westminster, Md., 1946.

——. *The Interior Castle*. In *The Complete Works of St. Teresa of Jesus*. Vol. 2. London, 1946.

——. *The Autobiography of St. Teresa of Avila, The Life of Teresa of Jesus*. New York, 1960.

Petrocchi, M. *Il Quietismo Italiano del Seicento*. Edizioni di "Storia e Letteratura", Rome, 1948.

Pleuser, C. "Die Benennungen und der Begriff des Leides bei J. Tauler". In

W. Binder et al., eds., *Philologische Studien und Quellen*, no. 38. Berlin, 1967.

Pohlmann, C. *Kanzel und Ritiro: Der Volksmissionar Leonhard von Porto Maurizio.* Werl, 1955.

Poletti, U., Card. "Croce e esigenze sociali di una metropoli moderna". In B. Rinaldi, ed., *La sapienza della croce oggi.* Vol. 3. Turin, 1976, pp. 407–17.

Popkes, W. "Christus Traditus, Eine Untersuchung zum Begriff der Dahingabe in Neuen Testament". In *Abhandlungen zur Theologie des Alten und Neuen Testaments.* Vol. 49. Zürich and Stuttgart, 1967.

Potterie, I. de la. "La sete di Gesù morente e l'interpretazione giovannea della sua morte". In B. Rinaldi, ed., *La sapienza della croce oggi.* Vol. 1. Turin, 1976, pp. 33–49.

Rahner, H. "Die Gottesgeburt. Die Lehre der Kirchenväter von der Geburt Christi im Herzen des Gläubigen". *ZKTh* 59 (1935): 333–418.

——. *Symbole der Kirche.* Salzburg, 1964.

Rahner, K. *Zur Theologie des Todes.* In *Quaestiones Disputatae.* Vol. 2. Freiburg, 1958 (5th ed.).

——. *Sendung und Gnade, Beiträge zur Pastoraltheologie.* Innsbruck, 1959.

——. *Grundkurs des Glaubens, Einführung in den Begriff des Christentums.* Freiburg, 1976 (2d ed.).

——. "Morte di Gesù e definitività della rivelazione cristiana". In B. Rinaldi, ed., *La sapienza della croce oggi.* Vol. 1. Turin, 1976, pp. 50–58. In English, "The Death of Jesus and the Finality of Revelation". *The Passionist*, no. 3 (1976): 36–51.

Rahner, K, and H. Vorgrimmler, eds. *Kleines Konzilskompendium—Alle Konstitutionen, Dekrete und Erklärungen des Zweiten Vaticanums in der bischöflich beauftragten Ubersetzung.* Freiburg, 1966.

Ratzinger, J. *Einführung in das Christentum.* Munich, 1968 (4th ed.).

——. *Glaube und Zukunft.* Munich, 1971 (2d ed.).

——. *Vom Sinn des Christentums.* Munich, 1971 (3d ed.).

——. *Dogma und Verkündigung.* Munich and Freiburg, 1973.

——. "Ich glaube an Gott, den allmächtigen Vater". *Internationale Katholische Zeitschrift* 4 (1975): 10–18.

Raze, de. *Concordantiarum SS. Scripturae manuale.* Paris, 1929 (20th ed.).

Reisinger, F., ed. *Werke des hl. Franz von Sales.* Vols. 1–6. Eichstätt and Vienna, 1958–65.

Rinaldi, B. *La presenza della croce nelle principali lettere di S. Paolo.* Editrice "Fonti Vive", 1972.

———, ed. *La sapienza della croce oggi, Atti del Congresso Internazionale.* Vols. 1–3. Rome, Oct. 13–18, 1975; Turin, 1976.

Roßmann, H., and J. Ratzinger, eds. *Mysterium der Gnade, Festschrift für J. Auer.* Regensburg, 1975.

Rotter, F. *Das Seelenleben in der Gottesliebe nach dem "Theotimus" des hl. Franz von Sales.* Freiburg, 1935.

Ryan, John K. *The Confessions of St. Augustine* (trans., introduction, and notes). New York, 1960.

———. *On the Love of God.* Vols. 1 and 2. New York, 1963.

———. *Introduction to the Devout Life* (trans.). New York, 1972.

Sartori, L. "La croce principio di vera riforma ecclesiale e di dialogo ecumenico". In B. Rinaldi, ed., *La sapienza della croce oggi.* Vol. 1. Turin, 1976, pp. 485–507.

Scheeben, H. C. "Zur Biographie Johann Taulers". In E. Filthaut, ed., *Johannes Tauler, Ein deutscher Mystiker.* Essen, 1961, pp. 19–36.

Schillebeeckx, E. *Jesus, Die Geschichte von einem Lebenden.* Freiburg, 1976 (2d ed.).

Schlüter, D. M. "Philosophische Grundlagen der Lehren Johannes Taulers". In E. Filthaut, ed., *Johannes Tauler, Ein deutscher Mystiker.* Essen, 1961, pp. 122–61.

Schreiber, G. "Der Barock und das Tridentinum". In G. Schreiber, ed., *Das Weltkonzil von Trient.* Freiburg, 1951, pp. 381–425.

Schulze, H., ed. *Der leidende Mensch, Beiträge zu einem unbewältigten Thema.* Neukirchen and Vluyn, 1974.

Schürmann, H. *Jesu ureigener Tod.* Freiburg, 1975.

Schweizer, E. *Erniedrigung und Erhöhung bei Jesus und seinen Nachfolgern (Abhandlungen zur Theologie des Alten und Neuen Testaments).* Vol. 28. W. Eichrodt and O. Cullmann, eds. Zürich, 1962 (2d ed.).

Seyppel, J. "Mystik als Grenzphänomen und Existenzial". In J. Sudbrack, ed., *Das Mysterium und die Mystik.* Würzburg, 1974, pp. 111–53.

Silverio de Santa Teresa, Fr., ed. *Obras de San Juan de la Cruz.* Burgos, 1940 (2d ed.).

Sölle, D. *Leiden.* Stuttgart, 1973.

Stephenson, G., ed. *Der Religionswandel unserer Zeit im Spiegel der Religionswissenschaft.* Darmstadt, 1976.

Stockmeier, P. *Theologie und Kult des Kreuzes bei Johannes Chrysostomus, Ein Beitrag zum Verständnis des Kreuzes im 4. Jahrhundert.* In *Trierer theologische Studien,* Vol. 18. Trier, 1966.

Sudbrack, J. *Die geistliche Theologie des Johannes von Kastl.* Münster, 1966.

———. "Die Geist-Einheit von Heilsgeheimnis und Heilserfahrung". In J. Sudbrack, ed., *Das Mysterium und die Mystik, Beiträge zu einer Theologie der christlichen Gotteserfahrung.* Würzburg, 1974, pp. 9–55.

Tauler, Johannes (Surius-Tauler). *La Vita et Institutioni del sublime et illuminato Teologo Giovanni Taulero.* Tradotte nuovamente di Latina in lingua Toscana dal R. P. F. Serafino Razzi, Dell'Ordine de' Frati Predicatore in Fiorenza, 1590.

———. *D. Ioannis Thauleri, Clarissimi ac illuminati Theologi Sermones de Tempore et de Sanctis totius anni . . . Opera Omnia,* a R. F. Laurentio Surio Carthusiano in Latinum Sermonem translata . . . *Coloniae.* Apud Arnoldum Quentelium, 1595.

Taylor, V. *The Cross of Christ.* London, 1956.

Uttendörfer, O. *Zinzendorfs religiöse Grundgedanken.* Herrnhut, 1935.

Varga, P. "Schöpfung in Christus nach Johannes vom Kreuz". In *Wiener Beiträge zur Theologie.* Vol. 21. Vienna, 1968.

Vetter, F. *Die Predigten Taulers aus der Engelberger und der Freiburger Handschrift sowie aus Schmidts Abschriften der ehemaligen Straßburger Handschriften.* In *Deutsche Texte des Mittelalters.* Vol. 11. Der Deutschen Akademie der Wissenschaften, eds. Dublin and Zurich, 1968 (2d ed.).

Walz, A. "Tauler im italienischen Sprachraum". In E. Filthaut, ed., *Johannes Tauler, ein deutscher Mystiker, Gedenkschrift zum 600. Todestag.* Essen, 1961, pp. 371–95.

———. " 'Grund' and 'Gemüt' bei Tauler, Erwägungen zur geistlichen und predigerischen Ausdrucksweise eines Rufers zur Innerlichkeit". *Angelicum* 40 (1963): 328–69.

Wehr, G. *Wege zu religiöser Erfahrung, Analytische Psychologie im Dienste der Bibelauslegung.* In *Impulse der Forschung.* Vol. 13. Darmstadt, 1976.

Weilner, I. *Johannes Taulers Bekehrungsweg, Die Erfahrungsgrundlagen seiner Mystik.* Regensburg, 1961.

Weinrich, H. "Narrative Theologie". *Concilium* 9 (1973): 329–34.

Wulf, F., ed. *Ignatius von Loyola, Seine geistliche Gestalt und sein Vermächtnis (1556–1956)*. Würzburg, 1956.

Wyser, P. "Der 'Seelengrund' in Taulers Predigten". In Philosophischen Fakultät der Universität Freiburg/Switzerland, eds., *Lebendiges Mittelalter, Festgabe für W. Stammler*. Freiburg, 1958, pp. 203–311.

Zervos, G. "La santa croce nella Chiesa Ortodossa". In B. Rinaldi, ed., *La sapienza della croce oggi*. Vol. I. Turin, 1976, pp. 508–25.

Zoffoli, E. *La Passione mistero di salvezza*. Manduria, Taranto, 1970. In Spanish, *La Cruz misterio di salvación*. Zaragoza, 1971.

"Zur Kreuzestheologie". *Evangelische Theologie* 33, no. 4 (Jul./Aug. 1973).

ABBREVIATIONS

Acta Congregationis	*Acta Congregationis Passionis Iesu Christi.* Rome, SS John and Paul (before 1930, *Bollettino*).
AGCP	Archivium Generale Congregationis Passionis, Rome, SS. John and Paul.
Annali	*Annali della Congregazione,* by Fr. John Mary of St. Ignatius, ed. by Fr. Gaetano dell'Addolorata, Rome, 1967.
Bollettino	*Bollettino della Congregazione della SS. Croce e Passione di N.S.G.C.,* Rome, SS. John and Paul (1920–29).
Diario Spirituale	*Diario Spirituale di S. Paolo della Croce, Testo Critico, Introduzione e Note,* ed. by E. Zoffoli, Rome, 1964.
L	*Lettere di S. Paolo della Croce,* with numbering system as used by Fr. Amedeo della Madre del Buon Pastore, 4 vols., Rome, 1924.
"Morte Mistica"	San Paolo della Croce, "Morte Mistica ovvero olocausto del puro spirito di un'anima religiosa", ed. by P. A. Blanco, Bilbao, 1976.
MThZ	*Münchener Theologische Zeitschrift*
"Mystical Death"	St. Paul of the Cross, "Mystical Death, Holocaust of the Pure Spirit of a Religious Soul", trans. and annotated by S. Rouse, Owensboro, Kentucky.
PAC	Processo Apostolico di Corneto-Tarquinia (Apostolic Process of Corneto-Tarquinia), (manuscript of all the following processes are in AGCP).
PAR	Processo Apostolico di Roma.
PAV	Processo Apostolico di Viterbo.

POA	Processo Ordinario di Alessandria (Informative Process of Alessandria)
POC	Processo Ordinario di Corneto-Tarquinia.
POG	Processo Ordinario di Gaeta.
POO	Processo Ordinario di Orbetello.
POR	Processo Ordinario di Roma.
POV	Processo Ordinario di Vetralla.
Processi 1	*I Processi di Beatificazione e Canonizzazione di S. Paolo della Croce,* Vol. 1 (depositions of witnesses of the Informative Process of Vetralla), ed. by Fr. Gaetano dell'Addolorata, Rome, 1969.
Processi 2	*I Processi di Beatificazione e Canonizzazione di S. Paolo della Croce,* Vol. 2 (depositions of witness of the Informative Processes of Alessandria, Gaeta, Orbetello, and Corneto-Tarquinia), ed. by Fr. Gaetano dell'Addolorata, Rome, 1973.
RAM	*Revue d'ascetique et de mystique*
Regulae et Constitutiones	*Regulae et Constitutiones Congr. SSmae Crucis et Passionis D.N.I.C. (Editio Critica Textuum),* ed. by Fr. Fabiano Giorgini, Rome, 1958.
RSR	*Recherches de science religieuse*
Storia Critica	E. Zoffoli, *S. Paolo della Croce, Storia Critica,* 3 vols. Rome, 1963, 1965, 1968.
Strambi, *Vita*	V. M. Strambi, *Vita del Ven. Servo di Dio P. Paolo della Croce,* Rome, 1786.
Strambi, *Lo Spirito*	S. Vincenzio Maria Strambi, *Lo Spirito di S. Paolo della Croce,* ed. by Fr. Disma dell'Addolorata, Alba, 1951.
Tagebuch	*Das geistliche Tagebuch des heiligen Paul vom Kreuz,* German translation of the *Diario Spirituale,* ed. by Fr. Martin Bialas with Introductory Word by J. Ratzinger, Aschaffenburg, 1976.
ZKTh	*Zeitschrift für Katholische Theologie*
ZThK	*Zeitschrift für Theologie und Kirche*

INDEX OF PERSONS